The British Museum
Occasional Paper
Number 108

Catalogue of Stone Age Artefacts from Southern Africa in The British Museum

Peter Mitchell with contributions by
Alison Roberts, Alan Cohen and Karen Perkins

Publishers
The British Museum
Great Russell Street
London WC1B 3DG

Production Editor
Josephine Turquet

Distributors
The British Museum Press
46 Bloomsbury Street
London WC1B 3QQ

Occasional Paper No. 108
Catalogue of Stone Age Artefacts from Southern Africa in The British Museum

Peter Mitchell with contributions by
Alison Roberts, Alan Cohen and Karen Perkins

ISBN 0 86159 108 9
ISSN 0142 4815

Front cover: Acheulean handaxes and cleavers,
Pniel, Northern Cape Province, South Africa
(photograph, P. Mitchell)

For a complete catalogue giving information on the full range
of available Occasional Papers please consult:
www.thebritishmuseum.ac.uk/occasionalpapers
or write to:
The Marketing Assistant
The British Museum Press
46 Bloomsbury Street
London WC1B 3QQ

Printed and bound in the UK by Antony Rowe Limited

Acknowledgements v

1. Introduction and Geographical Background 1
The Scope of the Study 1
Physical Geography of Southern Africa 2
Physiography 2
Climate 4
Ecological zones 5
Historical Geography of Southern Africa 5

2. Southern African Archaeology and its Changing Relationship with Britain 9
Introduction 9
Colony and Metropole: The Antiquarian Era of Southern African Archaeology 9
The British Association for the Advancement of Science 11
Study and Research in the United Kingdom 12
British Archaeologists Working in Southern Africa 12
Based in Britain: Research Projects Conducted in Southern Africa 13
British Sources of Funding for Archaeological Research in Southern Africa 14

3. The History and Contemporary Significance of the Collections 17
Peter Mitchell and Alison Roberts
The History of the Collections 17
Where are the collections from? 17
When were they collected? 17
Who collected them? 21
The acquisition of Stone Age material from southern Africa by The British Museum 25
The Present Day Significance of the Collections 27

4. Terminology and Typology 31
Terminology 31
The historical development of Stone Age terminologies in southern Africa 31
Current terminologies for the southern African Early and Middle Stone Ages 34
Current terminology for the southern African Later Stone Age 35
Typology 39
Typological glossary 40
Raw materials 43

5. **Gazeteer of the Southern African Stone Age Collections in The British Museum** 47
Introduction: Organization of the Gazetteer 47
Concordance of Provenances of the Southern African Stone Age Collections of The British Museum 48
South Africa 55
Eastern Cape Province 55
Free State 69
Gauteng 81
KwaZulu-Natal 85
Mpumalanga 96
North West Province 98
Northern Cape Province 106
Northern Province 126
Western Cape Province 128
South Africa – no further provenance 143
Angola 145
Botswana 146
Lesotho 151
Mozambique 152
Namibia 155
Swaziland 157
Zimbabwe 158

Appendix 1. Southern African Stone Age Collections in the Department of Ethnography of The British Museum 179

Appendix 2. Other African Stone Age Archaeological Collections in The British Museum 183
Karen Perkins

Appendix 3. Stone Age Archaeological Collections from Southern Africa in other Museums in the United Kingdom 193
Alison Roberts

Appendix 4. Individual Collectors Represented in The British Museum Southern African Stone Age Archaeological Collections 209
Alan Cohen

Bibliography 221

Acknowledgements

Many people have helped to make this monograph possible and I should like to take this opportunity of thanking them all. In particular, I owe a tremendous debt to Alison Roberts, now of the Ashmolean Museum, Oxford, for the initial suggestion and for giving so much time and energy to facilitating access to The British Museum's collections and associated records, corresponding with other institutions and providing a sounding board for ideas. Both Alison and I should like to thank Jill Cook, Head of the Quaternary Section of The British Museum's Dept of Prehistory and Early Europe, who sponsored the project, organized access to the Department's collections and saw the Catalogue through to its publication with great enthusiasm and support. Both Jill Cook and Ray Inskeep deserve many thanks for reading, commenting on and significantly improving earlier drafts of the text. Of present and former staff of The British Museum's Quaternary Section we should like to thank Karen Perkins for preparing the collections for study and curation, Phil Dean for maps, Hazel Martingell for illustrations of stone artefacts from Alfred County Cave, Justin Morris and Mick Lindop. In addition, Stuart Airey and Alex Mackenzie both helped track down artefacts and references, while Dr Alan Cohen spared no effort in carrying out research on the lives of those responsible for accumulating The British Museum's southern African Stone Age collections; Appendix 4 represents only part of the effort that he put in and we have also drawn heavily on his researches in writing Chapter 3. Within the Department of Ethnography of The British Museum we should also like to thank Jim Hamill and Julie Hudson for providing the information used in construction of Appendix 1. Last, but by no means least, a heartfelt thank you to Josephine Turquet for her patience and perseverance in seeing the Catalogue through to publication.

Both Alison and I owe a further debt of gratitude to all those individuals at other Museums in the United Kingdom who took the time and trouble to reply to letters asking about southern African Stone Age collections in their care or biographical information on individual collectors. The comprehensiveness of Appendices 3 and 4 is owed to: Ms S. Beeby, Dr R. Boast, B. Chisholm, Ms B. Conradie, Ms B. Crozier, Ms S. Giles, Mrs W. Glover, Dr P. Hughes, Dr L. Keppie, Mr R. Langley, Mr K. Leahy, Fr T. McCoog, Capt. D. O'Reilly, Mr J. Parsons, Dr A. Prag, L. Rechterstchort, P. Sanders, Ms L. Stumpe, Mrs G. Turner, Dr L. Washington, Mrs V. Ward and Mr P. Watson. A particularly big thank you is due also to Zoë Henderson and Sven Ouzman, both of the National Museum, Bloemfontein, Gwilym Hughes of the Dyfed Archaeological Trust (formerly University of Birmingham), Mary Leslie of the South African Heritage Resources Agency, David Morris of the McGregor Museum, Kimberley, Prof. Desmond Clark of the University of California, Berkeley, and Dr Roger Summers for providing information on individual collectors and answering other queries. Prof. Jeff Guy of the University of Natal, Durban, kindly drew attention to the archaeological connections of Bishop Colenso and his family.

My own interest in southern African archaeology is the result of a personal connection with two British archaeologists whose names figure prominently in the development of the subject in the sub-continent. Fittingly, both Ray Inskeep and Pat Carter worked in museum departments at different times of their careers and I hope they will not feel it presumptuous if I offer this work to them. Finally, *voglio dire tante grazie a Gloria perchè mi ha fatto ricordare che c'è di piu nella vita di queste pietre.*

Note: the catalogue was completed in early 1998 and reflects the state of archaeological knowledge of southern Africa at that time. For a more recent assessment that includes references to key papers published in 1998-2001 readers should look to P. Mitchell (2002) *Archaeology of Southern Africa* (Cambridge: Cambridge University Press).

Contact addresses

Peter Mitchell
Lecturer in African Prehistory, St Hugh's College, Oxford OX2 6LE

Alison Roberts
Collections Manager, Department of Antiquities, Ashmolean Museum, Beaumont Street, Oxford OX1 2PH

Alan Cohen
42 Meadow Road, Pinner, Middlesex HA5 1ED

Karen Perkins
Department of Medieval and Modern Europe, The British Museum, Great Russell Street, London WC1B 3DG

1. Introduction and Geographical Background

1. The Scope of the Study

Museums are places in which artefacts and other objects are gathered together, studied and presented to the public. But they, their records and their collections are also, in a sense, living historical documents that can be used to trace and interpret the development of a discipline. The present work sets out to exemplify all of these matters by establishing a *catalogue raisonée* of the southern African Stone Age collections in the British Museum. The intention is to provide not only a gazetteer and catalogue of the British Museum holdings in this field, but also to present sufficient additional information to place them within their historical and contemporary archaeological context. It is hoped that the Catalogue will thus not only alert students, professional archaeologists and museums to the research potential of the collections, but also be of use to those involved in the management of such collections at other museums.

The British Museum, as the foremost archaeological and anthropological institution of its kind in the United Kingdom, was well-placed to accumulate such material in the 19th and earlier 20th centuries, not least because of the vast part of the southern African sub-continent that had passed under British rule by 1914. London and its museums were natural magnets for the accumulation of prehistoric and ethnographic artefacts, acquired by presentation from a range of travellers, surveyors, academics, missionaries and others, by exchange from developing museum institutions within the sub-continent, or by purchase from antiquities dealers. Coombes (1994) has explored the reasons for the development of ethnographic collections in 19th- century Britain and the rôle played by changing conceptions of 'Africa' and 'Empire' in this process. How far similar reasons were at work in the acquisition of prehistoric artefacts from southern Africa is difficult to say, but documentation of the universality of the broad developmental stages of palaeolithic archaeology first established by Anglo-French workers from the 1850s onward was certainly one factor (Trigger 1989). The close links apparent between many of those contributing to the British Museum southern African collections and leading archaeologists and anthropologists of the second half of the 19th-century, only some of which are touched on in Chapter 3, suggest that this is an area where much further work could profitably be undertaken.

Having introduced the scope of the present study in this Chapter, Chapter 2 considers the changing relationship between southern African archaeology and archaeological individuals and institutions in Britain. This offers a historical perspective on the southern African Stone Age collections within British museums and provides a starting point for the more detailed assessment of the history and contemporary significance of the collections of the British Museum itself (Chapter 3). Before proceeding to the Gazetteer itself, Chapter 4 then discusses the development of the cultural taxonomies used in the study of the southern African Stone Age and provides a guide to current terminological practice, as well as a typological glossary and background on the lithic raw materials available to prehistoric stone-knappers. Chapter 5, the Gazetteer, constitutes the main body of the work, presenting the British Museum Stone Age collections from southern Africa on a geographical basis. The choice of the mode of presentation is defended at the end of this Chapter and explained further in the introduction to the Gazetteer. In addition to providing an extensive bibliography to the material covered, the Catalogue concludes with four appendices. Appendix 1 gives brief descriptions of the southern African Stone Age holdings of the British Museum's Department of Ethnography. Appendix 2 lists the British Museum Stone Age holdings from other regions of Africa, with the exception of Egypt, an exception dictated by the size of its Egyptian collections and their historical placement within a separate Department of Ancient Egypt and Sudan Antiquities. Appendix 3 lists the southern African Stone Age collections of all other museums that could be contacted within the United Kingdom; though not exhaustive, it is comprehensive and collates this information for the first time. Finally, Appendix 4 provides biographical information on the individuals who contributed to the British Museum collections and, in many cases, to those of other institutions as well. The appendices are cross-referenced with the Gazetteer.

Before bringing these introductory remarks to a close it is necessary to make some comment on my use of the term 'Stone Age archaeological collections'. This is employed as a shorthand reference to the fact that the collections on which I have worked are those belonging to the Quaternary Section of the British Museum's Department of Prehistory and Early Europe. It is clear that, with virtually no exceptions, the southern African artefacts housed in this Department of the Museum are the material remains of those stone-using hunter-gatherer or pastoralists populations conventionally referred to by archaeologists as Later Stone Age or of their Pleistocene (Early and Middle Stone Age) predecessors. Stone artefacts, such as grindstones, large hammerstones used in mining operations, or figurines (as from Zimbabwe), associated with Iron Age agropastoralist sites belong to the British Museum's Department of Ethnography and are excluded from this Catalogue. The comparatively few stone artefacts of Later, Middle or Early Stone Age origin in the British Museum ethnographic collections and housed in the Department of Ethnography are, as indicated above, included in Appendix 1.

2. Physical Geography of Southern Africa

Southern Africa may be defined as that portion of the African continent south of the Cunene and Zambezi Rivers. This includes the entirety of the modern states of Botswana, Lesotho, Namibia, South Africa, Swaziland and Zimbabwe, though only the southern half of Mozambique. Since the British Museum has such little Stone Age material from the northern part of Mozambique or from Angola, these areas have also been included in the Gazetteer. As well as a high degree of correspondence with modern political boundaries, southern Africa also has an archaeological integrity of its own. This can be seen, for example, in the distribution of various Middle and Later Stone Age industrial traditions (Sampson 1974; J. Deacon 1984b). To some extent the discreteness of some of these entities may reflect varying intensities of research – Barham's (1995) recent work at Mumbwa Cave in Zambia, for example, raises the possibility there of a Middle Stone Age assemblage with segments and other backed microliths comparable to the better-known Howieson's Poort assemblages of South Africa, Lesotho and southwestern Zimbabwe (Volman 1984; Walker 1995). The suitability of the Zambezi as a boundary is also queried by the similarities that some have noted between Later Stone Age assemblages in Mashonaland on the one hand and the Nachikufan tradition of Zambia on the other, with the Matopo Hills sequence in southwestern Zimbabwe more strongly similar to industries otherwise represented south of the Limpopo.

On the other hand, there is a real sense in which, certainly for the last 100,000 years or so, the cultural trajectories of those parts of Africa lying to the north and south of the Zambezi have diverged, a divergence that some (H. J. Deacon & Thackeray 1984) have invoked as contributing to the evolution of a specifically Khoisan genotype and phenotype. This divergence is perhaps most elegantly shown by a study of the differential spatial distributions of scrapers and backed microliths, artefacts interpreted from ethnographic analogy, experiment and use wear studies, as skin-working tools and arrow armatures respectively (H. J. Deacon & J. Deacon 1980); but see also Wadley & Binneman (1994) on the microwear analysis of segments. Later Stone Age assemblages in which scrapers are the most common formally retouched tool type are common to the south of the Zambezi and again in much of East Africa. Between them, covering much of Zambia, Malawi and Tanzania, are assemblages in which backed microliths are dominant. It seems likely that differences in the materials used to make clothing (skins in southern and East Africa, bark-cloth in south-central Africa) are largely responsible for this patterning (H. J. Deacon & J. Deacon 1980). This is a conclusion that, quite subtly, points up the value of considering the physical geography of Africa as a backdrop for discussion of its archaeological record.

A second reason for discussing briefly the physical and historical geography of southern Africa is that topography and climate have, either directly, or through their influences on recent patterns of population distribution, urbanization and infrastructural development, led to some regions being comparatively favoured, or neglected, from the standpoint of archaeological research. Not until the 1980s, for example, did the western lowlands of Lesotho see their first professional archaeological excavation (Mitchell 1992), while much late 19th-century collecting, as this Catalogue indicates, concentrated around the Cape Town metropolitan area and along the diamantiferous gravels of the Vaal River (Chapter 3).

Physiography

Fundamental to an understanding of the physical geography of southern Africa (**Fig. 1**) is the recognition that this is a very old landscape. Over almost the whole sub-continent the most recent volcanic activity of any significance was the extrusion of the lavas of the Lesotho Formation some 170 million years ago (Moon & Dardis 1988). Since that time the pre-eminent processes that have moulded southern Africa into the shape in which we see it today have been processes of erosion. The consequence is that the sub-continent can basically be divided into three physiographic zones.

The first of these zones is the Great Escarpment that runs, in attenuated form, from the highlands of Namibia and thence south through the Cape Fold Mountain Belt up into the Drakensberg and Maluti Mountains of the northeastern Eastern Cape Province, Lesotho and the latter's border with KwaZulu-Natal. Continuing north the Drakensberg escarpment runs through western Swaziland and up through South Africa's Mpumalanga province parallel to Kruger National Park. Skipping the Limpopo Valley, it re-emerges as the Chimanimani Mountains and Inyanga Highlands that form the border between Zimbabwe and Mozambique.

The regions coastward of the Escarpment form the second of the zones that I define, but nowhere, except in Mozambique and KwaZulu-Natal, does this extend into a particularly large lowland area. Indeed, because of the comparative shallowness of the continental shelf around most of southern Africa, even at the maximum depression of global sea-level during the Pleistocene an extensive coastal plain developed only in the restricted area south of the present shoreline between the Cape of Good Hope and Cape St. Francis (Van Andel 1989).

Inland of the Great Escarpment southern Africa consists of an extensive plateau, dipping slightly towards the north and west. Because the uplift that created the Great Escarpment was greatest in the east, the Gariep/Vaal river system flows into the Atlantic, rather than the Indian Ocean. In the central part of the sub-continent's interior uplift was interrupted by downward movement, producing the Kalahari Basin, now blanketed in sands. The Okavango Delta, lying in the extreme north of this basin, is the only part of southern Africa to experience tectonic activity of any significance today with seismic events in this area being implicated in changes in regional drainage patterns (Moon

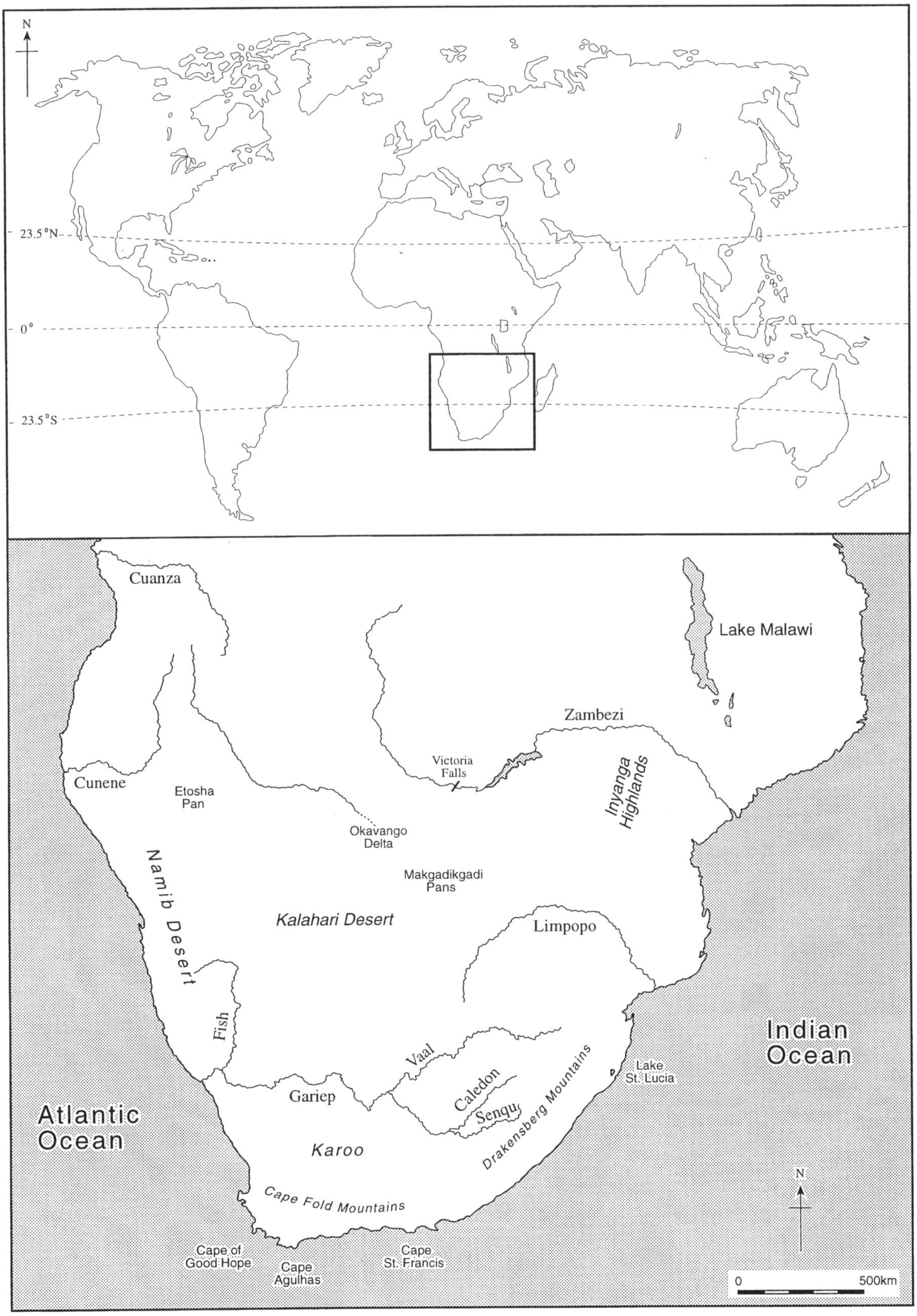

Fig. 1. Southern Africa: principal geographical features

& Dardis 1988: 129). One further topographical feature deserves mention: the numerous volcanic dykes of the Karoo and Free State regions of the interior plateau. Responsible for the formation of the *kopjes* or small, isolated hills or mesas, that dot the landscape here and often served as foci for prehistoric activity (Sampson 1985), these dykes were also an important source of hornfels for prehistoric stone-knappers.

The sub-continent is drained by three major river systems, four if one includes the Cunene River that defines the modern boundary between Angola and Namibia. East of this frontier and rising in the highlands of eastern Angola is the Zambezi, one of Africa's longest rivers, which flows into the Indian Ocean about halfway along the Mozambican coastline. Most of the Zambezi's water comes from rain falling into Angola and Zambia, but several of the rivers draining the Zimbabwean plateau also flow north into it. The Victoria Falls lie on the Zambezi, shortly after its entrance into Zimbabwe. They form a locality well represented in the British Museum Stone Age collections because of their location close to the Livingstone Museum in Zambia and the potential for relative dating afforded by the sequential upstream movement of the Falls themselves (Clark 1950, 1959).

Southern Africa is often divided into two, with greater South Africa (the modern states of South Africa, Lesotho and Swaziland) sometimes spoken of as Africa south of the Limpopo. This river, the headwaters of which derive from plateau watersheds well behind the Great Escarpment (Wellington 1955: 428), drains a substantial part of the extreme north of South Africa, as well as parts of Botswana and southern Zimbabwe, before entering Mozambique to enter the Indian Ocean at about 25° S of the Equator. Unlike the Zambezi, however, the Limpopo is not a substantial impediment to the movement of people: in drought years, such as 1993-94, it may cease to flow continuously above ground, forming numerous pools for much of its length.

The third of southern Africa's major river systems is that of the Gariep (formerly Orange) and Vaal Rivers. This river system differs from both the Zambezi and the Limpopo in that it flows west, reaching the Atlantic along the border between Namibia and South Africa. Of its two main branches, the Gariep has an origin in the highlands of Lesotho, where it is known locally as the Senqu, while the Vaal rises close to the border between KwaZulu-Natal and the Free State in a northward extension of the Drakensberg Escarpment. A smaller river, the Caledon, drains the western edges of the Lesotho highlands and adds significantly to the flow of the Gariep, which it joins some 85 km downstream of Aliwal North. The Gariep then flows in a northwesterly direction before reaching its confluence with the Vaal, after which it turns west towards the Atlantic. Although the Caledon may cease to flow in exceptionally dry winters, the Gariep and Vaal are both perennial rivers. Associations of stone artefacts with the gravel terraces of the Vaal River in localities such as Vereeniging and Christiana at one time played an important part in the construction of the chronostratigraphic framework of the southern African Stone Age (Clark 1959).

The area between the coast and the Great Escarpment is split into several, much smaller drainage basins throughout South Africa, Swaziland and Mozambique. Those of the Thukela River in KwaZulu-Natal, the Great Kei and Great Fish Rivers in the Eastern Cape Province and the Olifants and Berg Rivers in the Western Cape Province are among the most important. Free-standing surface water, however, in the form of lakes is a rare phenomenon in southern Africa. With the exception of coastal lakes or estuaries (known locally as *vleis*) and of seasonally filled depressions (*pans*), such bodies of water are missing, save in the Okavango Delta of northwestern Botswana. Furthermore, over much of the Kalahari, the western third of South Africa's interior (the Gariep River excepted) and all of Namibia there are no permanently flowing rivers at all. Although palaeoenvironmental data indicate that this situation ameliorated in the Interpleniglacial and after the Last Glacial Maximum (J. Deacon & Lancaster 1988), the availability of water must be considered to have been a significant factor in the adaptations of most past human inhabitants of the sub-continent.

Climate

Precipitation, rather than temperature, is thus the more important climatic factor across most of the sub-continent. Two patterns stand out. Firstly, some 90% of southern Africa experiences comparatively wet summers and dry winters. This summer rainfall pattern is produced mostly by oceanic air-streams entering the interior from areas of high pressure off the east coast (Wellington 1955: 247). Only the west coast of South Africa lies within a winter rainfall zone in which this seasonal pattern is reversed. Here the dominant factor in producing precipitation are eastward-moving cyclones from the South Atlantic. The area between these two belts, running from approximately Gans Baai to Port Alfred, and inland to the Escarpment, receives rainfall on a year round basis, with most of it falling on the coastal side of the Cape Fold Mountains. The second pattern derives from the fact that precipitation in the summer rainfall area declines markedly from east to west on moving away from the coast and the orographic potential of the Great Escarpment. Along the Namibian and Namaqualand coasts, which lie within the winter rainfall area, markedly arid conditions are produced by the cold water upwelling associated with the Benguela Current: the name 'Skeleton Coast', reflecting the numbers of shipwrecked sailors who died here from thirst, adequately describes the lack of water in this part of the Namib Desert. Rainfall reliability shows similar trends, with the Karoo, Namaqualand and the Kalahari/Namib areas as those most susceptible to drought (Wellington 1955: 262-269).

Temperatures across most of southern Africa can, in very general terms, be described as mild to warm. Mean annual temperatures are, for example, 16.7°C in Cape Town and 18.9°C in Bulawayo. Nevertheless, temperature does create problems of adaptation for human populations. High summer temperatures, particularly in the Karoo, the Kalahari and Namibia pose the danger of heatstroke, while winters, again in these arid areas, but also in the highlands of Lesotho, the Drakensberg Mountains and eastern Zimbabwe, can be bitterly cold at night: temperatures of -10°C are not uncommon, for example, along the Senqu (Orange) River Valley in Lesotho during July and August. In the winter rainfall area of the Western Cape cold conditions are made more miserable by the heavy rain that can persist, unrelentingly, for several days at a time.

Ecological zones

In combination climatic and topographic factors such as those just outlined provide a basis on which to divide southern Africa into a number of ecological zones. Such zones also take into account variation in the distribution of plant and animal communities across the sub-continent. A classification of southern African ecological zones that has enjoyed some favour among archaeologists interested in the structured links between human adaptations and environmental variables (e.g. H. J. Deacon & Thackeray 1984; Wadley 1993) is that of Devred, as presented by De Vos (1975). Six such ecological zones occur within the southern African sub-continent (**Fig. 2**), the following account being taken largely from Klein (1984a: 108-120):

1. The Zambezian Ecozone consists largely of wooded savanna in which trees such as *Brachystegia* in the north and *Colophospermum mopane* in the south are scattered throughout a more-or-less continuous grassland. Average precipitation is > 500 mm pa and surface water is available throughout the year. Because of its rich vegetation and varied opportunities for both grazers and browsers, this zone has the highest large mammal diversity in southern Africa with species such as elephant (*Loxodonta africana*), giraffe (*Camelopardis giraffa*), blue wildebeest (*Connochaetes taurinus*), kudu (*Tragelaphus strepsiceros*), buffalo (*Syncerus caffer*) and Burchell's zebra (*Equus burchelli*) prominent.

2. The Transvaalian Ecozone is a more semi-arid belt immediately south of the Zambezian Ecozone. Rainfall is lower and surface water less abundant. Vegetation varies, with shrubby acacia grassland prevalent in the west of the zone, but denser bush and forest in its east and along the coast. Large mammals are similar to those found in the Zambezian Ecozone, though Klein (1984a: 118-119) suggests that its animal biomass was probably lower.

3. The Kalaharian Ecozone corresponds broadly to the Kalahari region of Botswana and eastern Namibia, with rainfall decreasing from a mean of almost 500 mm pa in the northwest to one of 200 mm pa in the southwest. Porous, sandy soils mean that water is rapidly absorbed, producing a scarcity of surface water, especially in the central Kalahari. Vegetation varies from relatively rich acacia woodland in the north to sparser woodland in the drier south. Ungulates are generally similar to the previous two zones, but drought-adapted springbok (*Antidorcas marsupialis*) and gemsbok (*Oryx gazella*) are common.

4. The Basutolian Ecozone is formed by the Drakensberg Mountains and their adjacent plateau in the interior of South Africa, Lesotho and western Swaziland. Mean annual precipitation is quite high (620-750 mm), with marked diurnal and seasonal ranges of temperature. Except on the plateau east of the Great Escarpment where forest patches were more common, the indigenous vegetation is essentially pure grassland. As a result, this ecozone had the highest animal biomass of any in southern Africa. Dominant ungulates include black wildebeest (*Connochaetes gnou*), springbok, red hartebeest (*Alcelaphus buselaphus*), blesbok (*Damaliscus dorcas*) and quagga (a now extinct subspecies of Burchell's zebra).

5. The Karoo-Namaqualian Ecozone is made up of two distinct units. Forming a narrow band along the Namibian coast is the Namib Desert, in which mean annual rainfall is < 130 mm and often considerably less than this. Vegetation here is very sparse. In the western third of South Africa the Karoo region has a higher rainfall (130-400 mm pa) and richer, though still scrub-like, often succulent-dominated, plant communities with some grasses. Dominant ungulates are the same as those found in the Basutolian zone, but with drought-adapted gemsbok and springbok particularly well-represented.

6. The Cape Ecozone consists of the mountains of the Cape Fold Belt and the adjacent coastal forelands. As previously remarked, this zone differs in having winter or all-year round rainfall, the amount varying from 250 mm on its interior margins to 750 mm or more in favoured parts of the coast. Grassland is rare in this zone, with the dominant vegetation a sclerophyllous shrub and heathland similar to those of the Mediterranean and California. Dense, evergreen forests occur in some well-watered areas, particularly around Knysna. With grasses rare in the Cape ecozone, grazers are also uncommon and browsing species, such as Cape grysbok (*Raphicerus melanotis*) and steenbok (*R. campestris*), assume a greater importance than elsewhere.

3. Historical Geography of Southern Africa

Today southern Africa, as defined here, comprises eight independent states (**Fig. 3**). Several of these countries have undergone changes of name at either the national, regional or city level, particularly during the last two decades. Given this and given also that all the material reviewed here was first acquired during the colonial era when many of today's political divisions had not yet been formalized, it seems useful to review briefly some of the changes in the sub-continent's historical geography.

The modern country of South Africa, from which the bulk of the Museum's southern African material derives, was established in 1910 by the Union of four existing British colonies - the Cape of Good Hope, Natal, the Orange River Colony and the Transvaal - that formed the provinces of the new unitary state. The last two of these had, until 1902, been independent states, under the names of the Orange Free State and the South African Republic (Davenport 1978). Notwithstanding the creation within them of so-called 'national' states for various ethnic groups

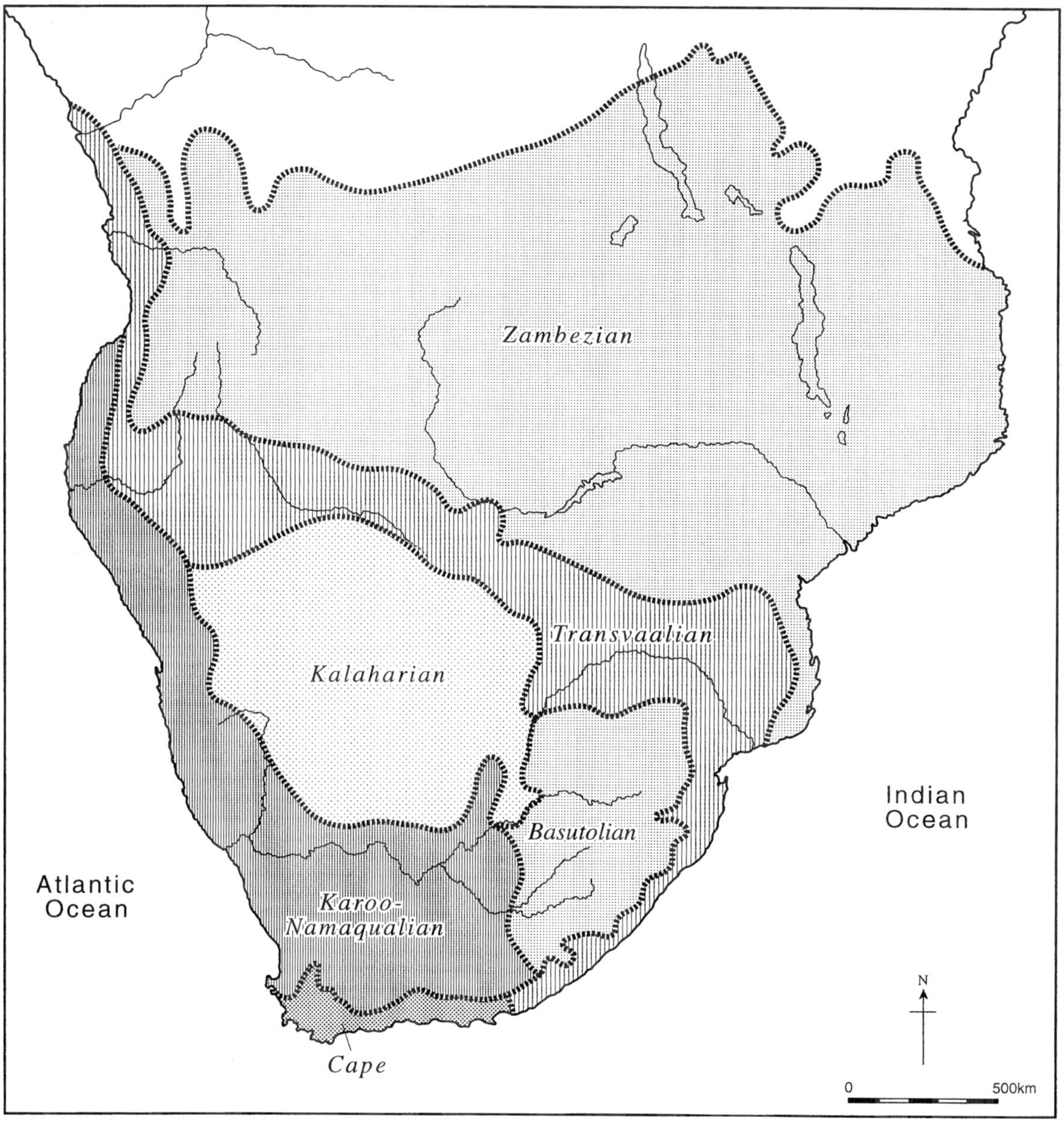

Fig. 2. Southern Africa: ecological zones after Devred (De Vos 1975)

during the apartheid period, all four of these provinces remained in existence until the adoption of the Interim Constitution of 1994 (Humphries *et al.* 1994). They have now been replaced by the nine new provinces shown in **Figure 4**.

During the 19th century the colonies of the Cape of Good Hope and Natal grew by the incorporation of areas along their borders that, for a time, often had a separate colonial administration (Davenport 1978). Three of these entities are reflected in the Gazetteer entries: Zululand (now part of the province of KwaZulu-Natal), British Kaffraria (now part of the Eastern Cape Province) and British Bechuanaland (now part of the Northern Cape Province), the source of some of the material provenanced simply as Bechuanaland.

The former Rhodesia, which as Southern Rhodesia was colonized by Cecil Rhodes' British South Africa Company in 1888-1890, became independent as Zimbabwe in 1980. It has since introduced several changes of name for cities, towns and geographical features to bring them into line with indigenous pronunciations or designations. Examples that affect material in the Gazetteer include the changing of Fort Victoria to Masvingo, Gwelo to Gweru and Salisbury to Harare.

Name changes affecting the remaining southern African countries have been comparatively minor. The former German colony and (after World War I) Mandated Territory of South West Africa became the independent republic of Namibia on the withdrawal of South African forces in 1990, while the former British protectorates of Bechuanaland and Basutoland both changed name on becoming independent in 1966: Bechuanaland, inhabited predominantly by speakers of the SeTswana language, became Botswana and Basutoland reverted to its indigenous name of Lesotho. Swaziland, which gained independence from Britain in 1968, has retained the name it had during the colonial period, while the small amount of material from Mozambique and Angola, both of which became independent of Portugal in 1975, comes from places whose names have also remained the same.

Fig. 3. Southern Africa: political divisions as of 1.1.1999

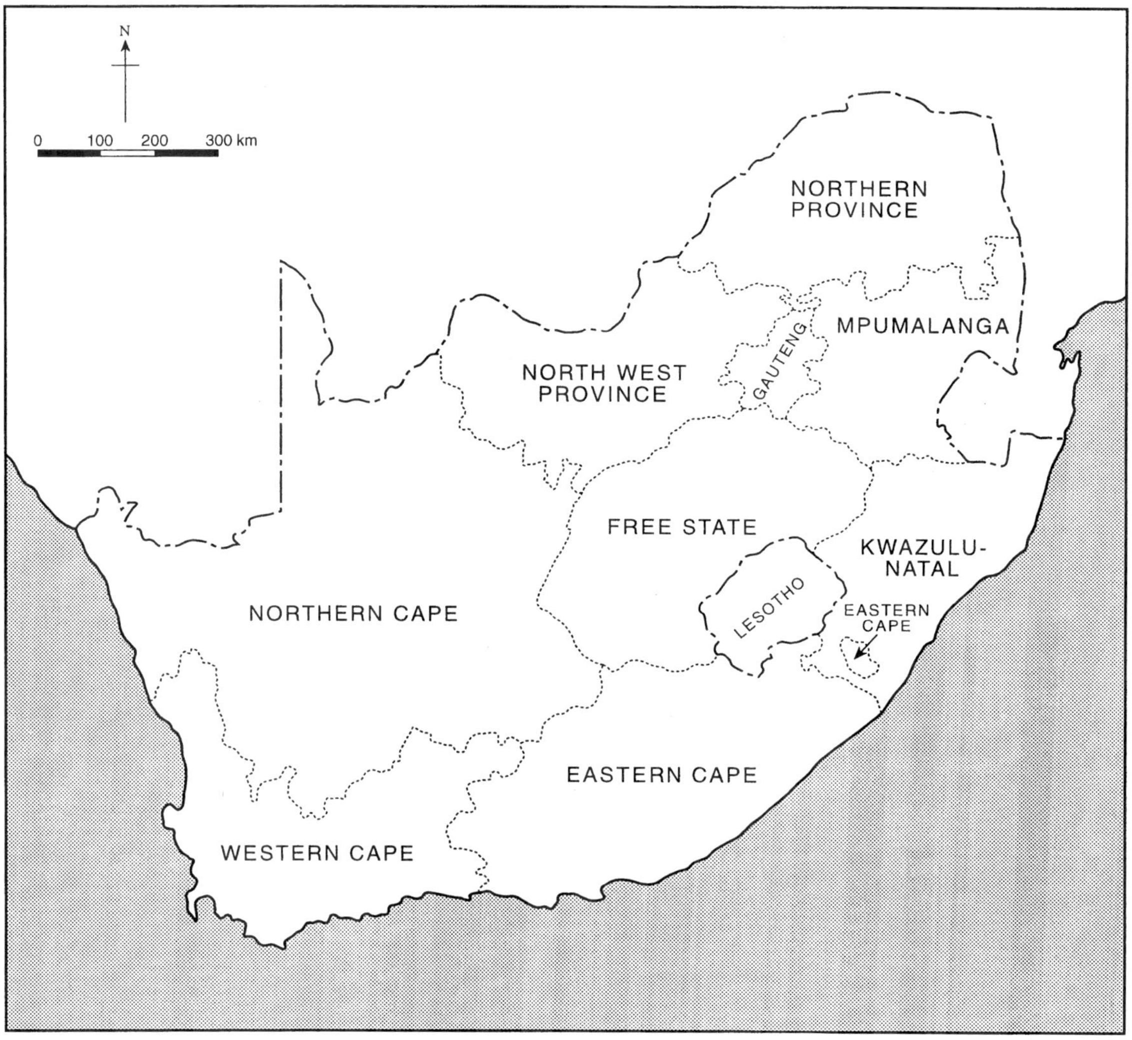

Fig. 4. South Africa: political divisions as of 1.1.1999

2. Southern African Archaeology and its Changing Relationship with Britain

1. Introduction

In recent years the history of Stone Age archaeological research in southern Africa has been the subject of an excellent synthesis by J. Deacon (1990a). Much fuller reviews of the period during which the great mass of the material held by the British Museum was acquired have also been conducted by Goodwin (1935, 1946a). For these reasons it seems inappropriate to recapitulate old ground and attempt to present here a full account of either the development of Stone Age archaeology in the sub-continent or the framework of ideas that guided that development (Parkington 1984). The interested reader is referred to these basic sources and to the extensive references that they contain. Instead, I propose to concentrate on changes in the relationship between southern African archaeological research and the United Kingdom, hoping that this may be more in keeping with the overall theme of this Catalogue of southern African material housed in the British Museum. I identify six areas of interest, which, to a certain extent, trace a chronological development of their own:

- the early development of southern African archaeology when an emphasis can be detected on locating and legitimizing developments within this 'colonial outpost' through links with London, the imperial metropole;
- connected to this, but arising only in the early part of the 20th century when a strong antiquarian presence had already developed in southern Africa, the impact on local archaeology of visits by the British Association for the Advancement of Science;
- visits to academic institutions in the United Kingdom by southern African archaeologists, whether for study or, especially in more recent times, for research;
- the impact of British expatriate archaeologists on the development of archaeology within southern Africa, a process that was particularly strongly marked in the 1960s and 1970s;
- research projects conducted in southern Africa by British archaeologists who remained based within the United Kingdom, although generally working in close collaboration with local specialists;
- financial support offered to archaeological projects in southern Africa by British-based funding agencies.

2. Colony and Metropole: The Antiquarian Era of Southern African Archaeology

Trigger (1984; 1989) has shown how the later 19th century development of archaeology in Europe's overseas colonies followed broadly similar patterns. J. Deacon (1990a: 40) has further characterized the dominant paradigm of this period in southern Africa, which ran from roughly the 1850s through until as late as the early 1920s, as one of work by largely amateur collectors whose 'overriding goal was simply to record the range of artefacts found and to compare them with those found in Europe'. As part of this process of comparison many of these early collectors were concerned to dispatch at least some of their finds to Britain, so drawing both them and themselves to the attention of a much wider scientific public through the presentation of the artefacts and papers about them at meetings of learned societies. Acceptance of the genuine nature of their finds by leading European scholars, such as Sir Charles Lyell, Sir John Lubbock and Sir John Evans, simultaneously validated the artefacts and assured their collectors of the significance of their role in a much broader academic community and development. Hillier (1898: 124) explicitly states this when commenting that:

> several of the implements taken from this gravel [at East London by George McKay, qv, Appendix 4] have been sent to the Jermyn Street and British Museums; and their genuiness has been recognised by Sir Roderick Murchison and Sir J. Lubbock.

This concern was, perhaps, particularly marked in the 1860s and 1870s when antiquarian collecting was beginning to take off in southern Africa. At precisely the same time European Palaeolithic archaeology, following what Daniel (1975) referred to as the annus mirabilis of 1859, was in a phase of rapid growth, spurred on by the publication of Darwin's *On The Origin of Species* and by the acceptance of the work of Boucher de Perthes in the Somme gravels and of Pengelly at Torquay. At the British Museum Sir Augustus Franks, Keeper of British and Medieval Antiquities from 1866 to 1896, played an important part in this process. A close friend of both Lubbock and Evans (Cook 1997), he was also a prominent member of the Society of Antiquaries (President, 1891-1897) and a Trustee of the Christy Collection. Well-connected and well-informed, he was in an excellent position to purchase material that he considered worthy or interesting for the British Museum and played an extremely significant rôle in building up its Stone Age collections (Cook 1997).

It is within this overall context that we can, for example, place the collections of T. H. Bowker, first made near East London in the Eastern Cape Province in 1858 (Hewitt 1955: 95). Bowker had by 1866 presented 41 stone artefacts to the Royal Artillery Museum, then housed in Woolwich, London (Feilden 1883); they were transferred to the Tower of London in 1924. His brother, J. H. Bowker shared his antiquarian interests and reported the discovery of stone artefacts at several localities, as well as the continued use in the mid-19th century of both stone and broken glass to make arrowpoints by surviving San groups

(Bowker 1872). Both contributed to the collections of the British Museum, J. H. Bowker presenting artefacts from Rorke's Drift in KwaZulu-Natal collected in the aftermath of the Anglo-Zulu War of 1879 and T. H. Bowker being the ultimate source of the artefacts donated by Sir George Grey (1869) from the family farm at Tharfield in the Eastern Cape Province.

Artefacts collected in the 1860s by C. J. Busk and the Rev. (later Sir) Langham Dale from sites on the Cape Flats were also sent to Britain and first published by the former's brother George Busk (1869), who exhibited them at the Third International Congress of Archaeology that took place in Norwich in 1868. These artefacts served, in Goodwin's (1935: 295) phrase, as 'ammunition' in the struggle between Sir John Lubbock and Thomas Huxley for dominance over the newly created society being formed at this time by the merger of the Ethnological and the Anthropological Societies of London. Lubbock (1869) published a brief account of the Busk/Dale collection and followed it up with a further paper comparing African stone artefacts with others from Europe and Syria (Lubbock 1870a); in a third paper he comments on Dale's subsequent collection of what would now be termed Middle Stone Age points, again from the Cape Flats (Lubbock 1870b), and in a fourth exhibited artefacts to the Society of Antiquaries (Lubbock 1871). Having established his credentials, as it were, as a leading authority on the Stone Age archaeology of several different parts of the world, Lubbock was, at the beginning of 1871, and on Huxley's suggestion, elected the first President of what became the Anthropological Institute of Great Britain and Ireland (Goodwin 1935: 296). Partly under his patronage, southern African artefacts continued to be exhibited and discussed at the Institute's meetings through the 19th and early 20th centuries, while others received a wider audience when displayed in such contexts as the Colonial Exhibition of 1886 (Hamy 1899).

Paralleling this interest, British museums, like their counterparts on the European mainland, actively sought to collect the skeletal remains of southern Africa's indigenous populations. As A. Morris (1987, 1992) shows, this was largely the work of travellers who acquired human remains, particularly crania, incidental to their visits to southern Africa. Additionally, some were collected as 'trophies' during military conflicts along the expanding frontier of the Cape Colony (A. Morris 1996). The majority of the Khoisan skeletal remains that survive from these 19th- and early 20th- century British collections belong to the Natural History Museum (A. Morris 1987). None appear to have been collected by any of the individuals responsible for the British Museum's archaeological collections from southern Africa.

As Lubbock's use of the Dale collection shows, there was considerable interest in southern African prehistory among mid-19th- century scientists and this actively contributed to the search for stone artefacts in southern Africa and, indeed, to wider social and political developments in the British colonies there. This is evident, for example, in the career of John Colenso, Anglican Bishop of Natal, who was moved to develop a sustained critique of traditional, fundamentalist beliefs in the veracity of the Old Testament partly because of the need to convey Christianity in a credible fashion to his Zulu converts, but partly because of his exposure to evolutionary theory, geology and palaeolithic archaeology (Guy 1983). Accused of heresy, he was supported by Sir Charles Lyell, Charles Darwin and Thomas Huxley among others when seeking reinstatement as Bishop, a case in which he was ultimately successful, but at the cost of permanently dividing the Anglican Church in South Africa. His wife, Frances Colenso, corresponded with Lyell's wife and sister-in-law for almost 30 years after the heresy trial and, in a letter of January 31st 1866, obviously in response to an enquiry from the Lyells, remarks that:

> I have not yet heard of any flint knives in this part of the world, and am almost afraid to enquire lest the natives shall think I want them to make them for me. (Rees 1958: 103).

Though there is no further mention in their published correspondence of Mrs Colenso seeking out stone artefacts, this letter points up the way in which the educated élite of the British colonies in southern Africa was part of a broader academic and intellectual community. Further evidence of such networking is provided by the fact that Thomas Bowker stayed with the Colensos in the lead-up to the Anglo-Zulu War of 1879 and by the friendship between Mrs Colenso and Lucy Lloyd, sister-in-law of and co-worker with Wilhelm Bleek, a Cape Town-based philologist who initiated the study of the language and belief systems of the /Xam Bushmen of the Northern Cape (Rees 1958). The massive archive that Lloyd and Bleek produced during the 1870s and 1880s not only forms the basis for current understanding of southern African rock art (Lewis-Williams & Dowson 1989), but also offers a unique insight into the ways in which South African hunter-gatherers resisted, but were ultimately dispossessed and assimilated by, European colonialism (J. Deacon 1996).

With southern Africa firmly established as an area from which stone artefacts comparable to those becoming known in Europe could be found, papers by Layard (1870), Dale (1871), J. Anderson (1878), Holub (1880), Frere (1881) and others began to appear regularly in the Anthropological Institute's *Journal* in the latter part of the 19th century. Though indigenous southern African journals began publishing at this time (the semi-popular *Cape Monthly Magazine* and, from 1878, the *Transactions of the South African Philosophical Society*), both British visitors to the sub-continent and locally based collectors directed many of their papers to British-based journals of arguably greater prestige and circulation. This is particularly the case, for example, when we consider that the first general syntheses of southern African prehistory were published in this way - Gooch's (1881) 'Stone Age of South Africa' in the *Journal of the Anthropological Institute* and Rickard's (1881a, 1881b) two papers in the *Proceedings of the Cambridgeshire Antiquarian Society*. The prominence of this trend, which continued until the development of the *South African Journal of Science*, the *Proceedings of the Rhodesian Scientific Association* and the *Annals of the South African Museum* in the early part of the 20th century, is evident in Table 1, taken from the comprehensive bibliography in Goodwin's (1935) review of the early history of Stone Age archaeological research in the sub-continent. Not until the establishment of the *South African Archaeological Bulletin* in 1945 was there a southern African journal devoted specifically to the publication of archaeological research.

3. The British Association for the Advancement of Science

Following on from the demonstration of human antiquity in southern Africa provided by collectors in the later 19th century, not least in British-based journals, the British Association for the Advancement of Science held two meetings in southern Africa in the first third of the 20th century. In both 1905 and 1929 these meetings had important consequences for the development of archaeology in the sub-continent, promoting new initiatives in the fields of classification and cultural systematics, heritage legislation and archaeological fieldwork.

Meeting in South Africa in 1905 the British Association for the Advancement of Science acted as an important stimulus for the development of southern African archaeology (Goodwin 1935: 313), in part through the publication of papers by Johnson (1905) and Péringuey (1905) summarizing recent discoveries of midden sites on the Cape Flats and of Early Stone Age artefacts near Vereeniging and elsewhere. Several of the Association's members subsequently visited the Victoria Falls and papers by Lamplugh (1905a; 1905b) and Feilden (1905) report on the occurrence of stone artefacts from above and below the Falls, in river gravels and in the ancient river channel. However, the most important archaeological consequence of the Association's visit was the address given by A. C. Haddon (1905) in his capacity as President of the Association's section H. Referring to Britain's own recent experience in the establishment of an Ancient Monuments Act, Haddon (1905) argued that 'all relics of the past...should be jealously preserved, and guarded from intentional and unwitting injury' (quoted in Goodwin 1935: 316). He saw these aims being achieved through both the scheduling of sites and their excavation and conservation by suitably appointed curators or inspectors. These remarks directly encouraged the passage of antiquities legislation by the government of Rhodesia (then including both Zambia and Zimbabwe), as well as the establishment of an Ancient Monuments Commission in South Africa following Union in 1910.

Drawing an analogy between archaeology and geology, Haddon also emphasized the virtues of developing a firm handle on the chronostratigraphic relationships of artefact finds, arguing, in particular, that:

> It would probably be to the interest of South African archaeology if the terms 'Eolithic', 'Palaeolithic' and 'Neolithic' were dropped, at all events for the present, or restricted solely to the type of technique; it might prove advantageous if provisional terms were employed, which could later either be ratified or abandoned, as the consensus of local archaeological opinion should decide (Haddon 1905, quoted in Goodwin 1935: 315).

Haddon's plea for the abandonment of the earlier Eurocentric terminology of Gooch (1881) and others achieved some initial success with Péringuey's (1911) recognition of three main 'types' in the South African Stone Age and later with Neville Jones' (1920, 1926) sequencing of finds from the Northern Cape Province and Zimbabwe, though both authors retained such classically European terms as 'Solutrean' or 'Mousterian'. But in the subsequent creation of a thoroughly indigenous classification of the southern African Stone Age by Goodwin and Van Riet Lowe (1929) Haddon's imprint can also be found: Goodwin had been a student of his at Cambridge (J. Deacon 1990: 42). Indeed Goodwin (1935: 334) explicitly acknowledged that, in establishing their new system (described in Chapter 4), they were acting on Haddon's advice to reject direct parallels, in nomenclature as much as in artefact description and analysis, with European assemblages and thus also the diffusionist view that Europe should be seen as the ultimate 'presumed source of all things' (Goodwin 1935: 334) in southern African prehistory.

Following the British Association's first meeting in South Africa in 1905, 24 years passed before it again met in the sub-continent. During that period the most important contributions to southern African archaeology by British-based scholars were the general account produced by Henry Balfour (1910) and the visit of Miles Burkitt in 1927. Balfour, then Curator of the Pitt Rivers Museum in Oxford, had visited southern Africa for the British Association's meeting in 1905 and echoed Haddon's (1905) address at that time in stressing the need for organized research and the enactment of rigorous antiquities laws, an argument that saw its first effects in 1911 and 1913 with the passage of the Bushman Relics Protection Acts. Burkitt (1928) repeated Balfour's call for an emphasis on the establishment of clear associations for excavated and collected material during his own visit in 1927. In addition, he quickly produced a general introduction to southern African prehistory that drew heavily on the rapid expansion of research by Goodwin, Van Riet Lowe, Hewitt, Jones and others earlier in the decade (Goodwin 1935: 329-339).

The British Association for the Advancement of Science met again in South Africa (in both Johannesburg and Cape Town) in 1929, bringing to the sub-continent a range of distinguished anthropologists and archaeologists from Europe, including Balfour and Haddon (for the second time), the Abbé Breuil (thus initiating a long association with the region), Louis Leakey and Hermann Braunholtz (already at the British Museum and at that time serving his first term as President of the Royal Anthropological Institute). The meetings provided the occasion for the presentation of preliminary reports on two recent excavations. At Fishhoek (Skildergat) Cave on the Cape Peninsula Peers (1929) had found Middle Stone Age assemblages in stratigraphic relation to each other for the first time. Further north, Armstrong and Jones had re-excavated Bambata Cave in the Matopo Hills of Zimbabwe specifically at the invitation of the Association, demonstrating a sequence there of successive Early, Middle and Later Stone Age occupations (Armstrong 1931). Their motivation for doing this was partly the relative lack of scientifically uncontrolled, 'indiscriminate digging' (Armstrong 1931: 239) that sites in Zimbabwe had then experienced, and partly the significance attached to that country's geographical position within a diffusionist model that saw all major developments in South African prehistory originating from much further north. Elsewhere in Zimbabwe the Association sponsored Caton-Thompson's (1931) excavations at the same time at Great Zimbabwe, which confirmed MacIver's (1906) earlier finding that the stone enclosures there date to the first half of the second millennium AD and are the work of ancestral Shona communities. In addition to promoting and visiting these important fieldwork campaigns, several members of the Association went on an extended archaeological tour organized by Van Riet Lowe (1930), one useful consequence of which was that Breuil (1930, 1931) was able to produce some of the first Francophone syntheses of southern African prehistory.

4. Study and Research in the United Kingdom

Archaeology began to be taught formally in southern Africa when Goodwin commenced lecturing at the University of Cape Town in 1923, lectures that were the first to be offered in the subject anywhere south of the Sahara (J. Deacon 1990a: 46). Not until the 1960s, however, did the University of Cape Town offer a full single honours degree in archaeology alone and several of its graduates therefore proceeded to Britain for postgraduate training or research. In coming, as the vast majority did, to Cambridge, they not only attended one of the foremost archaeology departments in the country, but also followed in Goodwin's own footsteps; he had read Archaeology and Anthropology there immediately after the First World War (J. Deacon 1990a: 42). Among those of his students to trace the same path were Glyn Isaac (1959-61) and Carmel Schrire (1961-63), both of whom ultimately went on to distinguished academic careers in the United States. Though Isaac did not return to southern Africa to carry out fieldwork of his own, concentrating instead on projects in Kenya and Tanzania (Isaac 1989), Schrire (1995) has been both a leading figure in the development of historical archaeology in South Africa and an important voice in recent debates about the relationships between pastoralists and foragers in the Cape.

Other South African archaeologists to have undertaken part of their postgraduate training or research in Britain include Hilary Deacon, who spent a year in the 1960s at the Institute of Archaeology in London, and Garth Sampson, who completed a doctorate at Oxford in 1969, having previously read Part II of the Archaeology and Anthropology Tripos at Cambridge. On his return to South Africa Deacon became the first archaeologist in a generation to be appointed at the Albany Museum in Grahamstown and subsequently founding professor of the Department of Archaeology at the University of Stellenbosch. In part through the meticulous excavation of three sites with excellent organic preservation (Melkhoutboom, Boomplaas and Klasies River Mouth), he was one of the first southern African archaeologists to develop explicitly ecological and systemic models of cultural change and has more recently contributed significantly to the debate surrounding the origins of modern humans (H. J. Deacon 1976, 1989, 1993). Sampson, on the other hand, has been based largely in the United States, from where he has carried out one of the most comprehensive survey projects ever undertaken in southern African archaeology (Sampson 1985), attempted to identify group territories from the analysis of decorative motifs and techniques on Smithfield pottery (Sampson 1988) and conducted extensive research on the effects of European contact and settlement on the indigenous Bushmen of the upper Karoo (e.g. Sampson 1994).

More recently, the high costs of postgraduate study in the United Kingdom for overseas students have tended to discourage southern African graduates from coming to Britain to carry out postgraduate research. On the more positive side, the development of university departments within South Africa has provided local opportunities for postgraduate work for South African students (J. Deacon 1990a: 50), while students from Zimbabwe and Mozambique in particular have benefited from the Uppsala-based Swedish initiative on the development of urbanism in eastern and southern Africa (Sinclair 1989). Nevertheless, during the period 1985-1996 at least seven archaeologists, four of them in professional employment in southern Africa at the time of writing, worked towards or completed postgraduate degrees at the Universities of Cambridge, Leicester, London and Oxford. One of these individuals was, until recently, the sole professional archaeologist in Namibia, a second is based at the National Museum, Bloemfontein, South Africa, and a third at the National Museum of Botswana, while a fourth is the first Botswanan archaeologist to obtain a doctorate and occupy a permanent teaching post in her own country.

It is to be hoped that the recent welcome growth in interest in African archaeology in Britain, exemplified by the creation of university lecturerships earmarked for Africanists, may afford further opportunities for future generations of African students to carry out research in British institutions. One aspect of this that has only recently begin to develop is the visit to Britain by southern African archaeologists to carry out research on collections housed in British museums. Examples include Janette Deacon's (1984a, 1984b) study of arrows made by 19th century /Xam Bushmen that form part of the collections of the Pitt Rivers Museum, Oxford and Tim Maggs' recent search for ethnographic material removed from KwaZulu-Natal in and after the Anglo-Zulu war of 1879. Archaeologists such as J. Deacon and Cedric Poggenpoel have also visited Britain to see how current British practices in heritage management and museum presentation may be of assistance in developing these fields in South Africa.

5. British Archaeologists Working in Southern Africa

Beginning in 1961 when Ray Inskeep was appointed to succeed Goodwin as Head of Archaeology at the University of Cape Town (UCT), a series of British nationals was recruited into museum and university based archaeological positions in South Africa. Inskeep himself worked at UCT until 1972 and in that time strengthened the teaching of the subject there and oversaw its expansion into a separate department. As well as directly teaching or supervising many of those who still hold professional appointments in South Africa, he also vigorously advanced the case for archaeology and museums in general to receive more generous state support. Partly as a result of his lobbying, a new professional body, the Southern African Association of Archaeologists, was set up in 1972; it continues to represent archaeologists within South Africa, as well as organizing a series of successful biennial conferences and field excursions and acting as a forum that, especially since the ending of apartheid, brings South African scholars together with archaeologists working in other southern African countries. It would be misleading, however, to suggest that Inskeep's impact on South African archaeology was only in the fields of teaching and infrastructural development. Editing the *South African Archaeological Bulletin* offered another powerful means of raising the discipline's profile and it was effectively under his editorship that the *Bulletin* evolved from a journal with a significant antiquarian/amateur element in its pages to a much more strongly academic publication. In addition to an extensive excavation programme of his own focussed on the late Holocene levels of Nelson Bay Cave on South Africa's southern coast (Inskeep 1987), Inskeep also facilitated the entry into southern African archaeology of Richard Klein, a leading faunal analyst, who excavated the early Holocene and late Pleistocene levels at Nelson Bay (Klein 1972), and of Ron Singer, who sponsored the first excavations at Klasies River Mouth (Singer & Wymer 1982).

Inskeep arrived in South Africa from Livingstone Museum, Zambia, having previously lectured at the University of Cambridge. This Cambridge connection was strengthened in 1967 when John Parkington joined the staff of the UCT Department. The past 35 years have seen Parkington develop a research unit of his own at UCT that has provided probably the most detailed archaeological study of a small scale area (centred on the Verlorenvlei River of the Western Cape) ever undertaken in the sub-continent (Parkington & Hall 1987). Numerous publications attest to the wealth of information obtained by Parkington and his students and co-workers on the prehistory and palaeoenvironmental record of the region which serves as a model study of, for example, the archaeology of the Pleistocene/Holocene transition (e.g. Parkington 1988, 1990) and of the integration of rock art, field survey and excavation into a single research project (e.g. Parkington 1989, Parkington *et al.* 1986).

The focus in much of Parkington's work on questions of subsistence, land-use and environmental change derives in part from the Higgs school of palaeoeconomy, influential at Cambridge through the 1960s. The work of Pat Carter in Lesotho and the southern Drakensberg discussed below falls more explicitly within this palaeoeconomy paradigm, while Peter Robertshaw, who held a position at the Albany Museum in Grahamstown in the late 1970s, undertook research into the origins of pastoralism that involved an examination of shellfish and fishing economies before conducting further fieldwork in the Eastern Cape Province (Robertshaw 1979, 1984). Other British (and ex-Cambridge) archaeologists who held positions in South Africa at this time include David Seddon (1967), who worked at UCT in the mid- 1960s, and Robin Derricourt (1977), who taught at the University of Fort Hare in the Eastern Cape Province in the 1970s. Also from a Cambridge background, Rona MacCalman was persuaded by Ray Inskeep (pers. comm.) to go to Namibia in the early 1960s and worked there at the State Museum in Windhoek for several years. She thus became the first woman to hold an archaeological position anywhere in the subcontinent and the first female British archaeologist to work in southern Africa since Caton-Thompson (1931) in 1929. In addition to undertaking several important surveys and excavations, mostly of Middle Stone Age sites (MacCalman 1962, 1963, 1965), she produced one of the very few firsthand studies of stone artefact production and use by southern African foragers (MacCalman & Grobbelaar 1965).

During the 1980s and 1990s the earlier pattern of British archaeologists taking up permanent academic positions in South Africa disappeared. In part this reflects the substantial numbers of South African nationals now graduating and seeking employment in archaeology, though the effects of relative international isolation in the dying years of the apartheid régime have also to be considered. British nationals have, however, played a significant rôle in the development of archaeology in two other countries within the sub-continent. In Zimbabwe Robert Soper has lectured at the University of Zimbabwe since 1985, while Charlotte Taggart and Gwilym Hughes held positions at, respectively, the Queen Victoria Museum and Great Zimbabwe National Monument for varying periods of time during the 1980s. In Botswana a local archaeological presence has been developed within the History Department of the University of Botswana, in part staffed by British nationals on short-term contracts; both Paul Lane and Andrew Reid conducted important survey and excavation programmes on aspects of local Iron Age archaeology (Lane 1996; Reid *et al.* 1997).

6. Based in Britain: Research Projects Conducted in Southern Africa

At the same time as British archaeologists have taken up teaching and research posts at southern African institutions and southern African archaeologists have come to Britain to study or to carry out research projects of their own, a third dimension of the relationship between the two has developed in recent decades. Beginning in the late 1960s British archaeologists operating from within United Kingdom universities have conducted sustained fieldwork programmes of their own in southern Africa.

One of the earliest of these projects was the investigation by Pat Carter, then of the University of Cambridge, of Middle and Later Stone Age land-use strategies in the Lesotho highlands and the southern Drakensberg. His research, which included the first systematic archaeological excavations to be undertaken in Lesotho, formed part of a more broadly conceived study of hunter-gatherers in this region as it was conducted in collaboration with Patricia Vinnicombe's (1976) recording and analysis of rock paintings in the same areas. Far from being a refuge area in which hunter-gatherer settlement had a time depth of no more than a few centuries as suggested by Davies (1951), their work demonstrated that people had lived in the Lesotho highlands since at least the end of the Early Stone Age, developed models of how they had used the region's landscapes and resources under both glacial and interglacial conditions and initiated the investigation of its palaeoenvironmental history (Carter 1970, 1978). Vinnicombe (1976) simultaneously collated much valuable information on the history of local hunter-gatherers during the 19th century and pioneered the use of Bushman-ethnography to understand southern African rock art.

British-based archaeologists have continued to maintain an interest in the archaeology of this southeastern part of southern Africa. Charles Cable (1984) carried out extensive field surveys in southern KwaZulu-Natal in 1979-80 and explored the evidence for Carter's (1970) seasonal mobility model in much greater detail for his doctorate at Cambridge. Peter Mitchell then analysed the artefact assemblages from Carter's excavation at Sehonghong rock-shelter in eastern Lesotho (Carter *et al.* 1988) as part of an Oxford-based doctoral project examining the late Pleistocene Later Stone Age of southern Africa (Mitchell 1988). He subsequently carried out the first excavation-based project in western Lesotho (Mitchell 1994a) and has more recently undertaken further excavations at Sehonghong itself. These have sought to refine our understanding of the cultural-stratigraphic sequence at one of the few southern African sites with occupation before, at and after the Last Glacial Maximum (Mitchell 1993), while further survey work in the surrounding area has confirmed Carter's original assessment of its importance for improving upon our knowledge of southern African prehistory (Mitchell 1996), most recently through excavation of a multi-phase open-air occupation site with evidence for intensive fish exploitation (Mitchell & Charles 1996).

Moving further north and east, David Price-Williams of the University of London has carried out a long-term programme into the Later Stone Age prehistory of Swaziland (Price-Williams 1981; Price-Williams & Watson 1982). Much of the analysis of the artefact assemblages recovered has been the work of Larry Barham (1990), working out of the University of Bristol, who has more recently excavated at Middle Stone Age sites in Zambia (Barham 1995). An important component of the Swaziland project was the investigation of late Quaternary palaeo-environmental change, a topic addressed in part through analysis of charcoals from archaeological sites (Prior & Price-Williams 1985) and in part through geo-morphological studies of calcretes and other landforms (Price-Williams & Watson 1982). On the opposite side of the sub-continent Myra Shackley (1985) of the University of Leicester carried out field surveys for Stone Age sites in Namibia about the same time. Finally, a team from the University of Liverpool led by Patrick Quinney, Tony Sinclair and John McNabb carried out investigations of the Middle Pleistocene archaeology and landscapes of the Makapansgat/Cave of Hearths area of the former Transvaal in the 1990s.

Zimbabwe has been the other main focus of work by British-based archaeologists. Gwilym Hughes (pers. comm.) has helped to direct a project that has excavated at Old Bulawayo, the later 19th century capital of King Lobengula of the Matabele. The site is being partially reconstructed to serve as a museum. Since 1993 the British Institute in Eastern Africa (which is based in Nairobi as an overseas school of the British Academy) has also conducted fieldwork in Zimbabwe. This project was focused on the history and function of agricultural terrace systems in the Inyanga Highlands and was undertaken in close collaboration with the University of Zimbabwe (Soper 1994). Having assisted in this project, one of the British Institute's former graduate scholars, Nick Hanson-James, undertook a Cambridge-based doctoral research project into the origins, dating and significance of Bambata Ware, a pottery style first identified from Armstrong's (1931) excavations at Bambata Cave (qv, Chapter 5); this pottery is associated with some of the earliest evidence for domestic livestock in southern Africa.

7. British Sources of Funding for Archaeological Research in Southern Africa

While British-based researchers have been able to call upon funds located in the United Kingdom for the support of archaeological research in southern Africa, it seems appropriate to round off this review of the relationship between southern African archaeology and Britain by examining briefly the support that some of those funds have given to southern African archaeologists.

Foremost among those funds is undoubtedly the Swan Fund, established under a bequest from James Swan, himself an important collector of stone artefacts principally from the Northern Cape and North West Provinces of South Africa (Appendix 4). The Swan Fund, which operates under the aegis of trustees holding professorial appointments in the University of Oxford, was set up in order to support archaeological and anthropological research on the Bushman peoples of Africa and their ancestors. Since its inception, it has sponsored numerous archaeological and anthropological research projects. While some of these have involved work in other parts of the African continent, the majority of grants have been given to research projects within southern Africa. In particular, one may note the support given to research projects on the Later Stone Age archaeology of the Western Cape undertaken by John Parkington's Spatial Archaeology Research Unit at the University of Cape Town (e.g. Manhire 1987; Parkington 1988; Jerardino & Yates 1996), research on Later Stone Age pastoralists carried out by Andrew Smith (e.g. Smith *et al.* 1991) of the same university, Aron Mazel's (1989) long-running investigation of the hunter-gatherer prehistory of the Thukela Basin of KwaZulu-Natal and studies by Anne Solomon (1995) of the rock art of the southeastern mountains.

The Boise Fund, also administered by trustees holding academic positions within the University of Oxford, has a comparable origin. Established under a bequest from Charles Boise, its purpose is to promote research on hominid evolution. Although a considerable amount of its income has been used to support research on early hominids in East Africa and on aspects of primatology, it has also provided funding for archaeological work in southern Africa, including recent excavation of the late Quaternary site of Sehonghong Shelter in the Lesotho highlands (Mitchell 1993).

The Swan and Boise Funds are, in a sense, open to all-comers, in that, though based in Oxford, membership of the University is by no means a prerequisite for application. Other funds with specific links to one or more British institution have, however, also supported archaeological research in southern Africa. The Sir Henry Strakosch Memorial Trust, which seeks to strengthen ties between Britain and South Africa, provided generous support for research by Cable (1984) in KwaZulu-Natal in 1979-80 and by Mitchell (1994a) at sites in the Caledon Valley in 1989. The Smuts Memorial Fund, located at Cambridge University, also supported Cable's (1984) research, while occasional valued support for projects in southern Africa has also come from the Prehistoric Society and the Society of Antiquaries of London. Further academic links between Britain and southern Africa in the field of archaeology have come through the work of the British Council, while links between the University of Oxford and the sub-continent have recently been strengthened by the establishment of the Oppenheimer Fund, which seeks to promote academic exchanges and visits between Oxford and universities in South Africa. Finally, we may note that the British Institute in Eastern Africa's field project in the Inyanga Highlands of Zimbabwe has received important support from the Trustees of Rhodes House (Soper 1994).

Through all of these bodies, as well as through the continued work of British or British-based archaeologists in southern Africa and of southern African researchers at British universities, the links forged in the 19th century at the outset of archaeological research in the sub-continent continue to grow. The British Museum continues to play an important rôle in this process. From the standpoint of the collections themselves, one recent example relates to Nick Walker's (1995) recent synthesis of the Stone Age prehistory of the Matopo Hills of southwestern Zimbabwe, which was partly informed by his examination of the original material excavated in the 1929 by Armstrong (1931) at Bambata Cave. Organizationally too the British Museum is actively contributing to African archaeology, hosting a conference in October 1995 that brought British and Belgian Africanist archaeologists together to present new research findings and discuss the future of African archaeology.

Table 1. Journals publishing archaeological papers relating to the southern African Stone Age 1858-1920 (after Goodwin 1935).

Decade	-1870	-1880	-1890	-1900	-1910	-1920	Total
Europe							
J(R)AI	4	6	4	7	2	3	25
L'Anthropologie	/	/	/	-	2	-	2
Man	/	/	/	/	8	5	13
Nature	-	-	-	-	5	1	6
Other	3	7	4	3	14	7	38
Sub-total	7	13	8	10	31	16	84
	58.3 %	52.0 %	88.9 %	55.6 %	36.9 %	51.6 %	47..2 %
Southern Africa							
AMR	/	/	/	/	2	1	3
ASAM	/	/	/	/	1	2	3
CMM/CIM	5	10	1	/	/	/	16
PRSA	/	/	/	-	15	2	17
SAJS	/	/	/	/	5	5	10
TGSSA	-	-	-	-	11	3	14
TRSSA	/	/	/	/	9	-	9
TSAPS	/	2	/	7	5	2	16
Other	-	-	-	1	5	-	6
Sub-total	5	12	1	8	53	15	94
	41.7 %	48.0 %	11.1 %	44.4 %	63.1 %	48.4 %	52.8 %
Total	12	25	9	18	84	31	178

Key

/	Denotes decades in which a journal had not yet been published or had ceased to be published
AMR	*Albany Museum Records*
ASAM	*Annals of the South African Museum*
CMM	*Cape Monthly Magazine (semi-popular journal)*
CIM	*Cape Illustrated Magazine (semi-popular journal)*
J(R)AI	*Journal of the (Royal) Anthropological Institute, including Journal of the Ethnological Society and Journal of the Anthropological Society*
PRSA	*Proceedings of the Rhodesian Scientific Association, including Proceedings of the Rhodesian Association for the Advancement of Science*
SAJS	*South African Journal of Science*
TGSSA	*Transactions of the Geological Society of South Africa*
TRSSA	*Transactions of the Royal Society of South Africa*
TSAPS	*Transactions of the South African Philosophical Society*

3. The History and Contemporary Significance of the Collections

Peter Mitchell and Alison Roberts

1. The History of the Collections

In discussing the historical origins of the British Museum's southern African Stone Age collections, three factors stand out as being of particular importance: their geographical origin, the date at which they were collected and/or acquired by the Museum and the professional background (in so far as this can be established) of the individuals who collected them. The motivation behind the original collection of the objects, and how and why they were subsequently acquired by the British Museum, are among the principal questions that this chapter seeks to address. All these factors are also connected to the political, social and economic history of southern Africa during the late 19th and 20th centuries. Their consideration also helps to determine the contemporary significance of the material, a subject which forms the final section of this Chapter.

Where are the collections from ?

Table 2 provides a breakdown of the geographical origins of the British Museum southern African Stone Age collections by country and, for South Africa, by province. Not surprisingly, given its longer colonial history and more developed industrial, academic and educational infrastructures, which have strong 19th-century roots, South Africa occupies by far the dominant position within the collections, whether these are assessed as number of provenances or number of separate collections from those provenances (74.4 % and 76.6 % respectively). Zimbabwe and Botswana account for the bulk of the remaining collections, with Angola, Lesotho, Mozambique, Namibia and Swaziland barely represented, and then by the activities of only one or two individuals at one or two localities in each case. The higher profile of Botswana and Zimbabwe reflects similar factors to those that account for the dominant position of South Africa, such as the activities of individuals involved in the gold-mining industry of Botswana and the early development of a professional infrastructure in Zimbabwe.

In addition, an examination of the breakdown of provenances and collections within South Africa shows a far from random situation (Table 2). Some provinces, especially Mpumalanga and the Northern Province, are scarcely represented at all; they account for only 1.0 % and 2.1 % of all provenances and 1.0 % and 1.4 % of all collections respectively. At the other end of the scale, the Western Cape and Northern Cape are represented by almost 40 % of the total number of provenances and by almost 50 % of the total number of collections. Of the remaining provinces, two groups can be identified, with Gauteng and KwaZulu-Natal each accounting for 5-10 % of the collections and provenances, and the Free State, Eastern Cape and North West each accounting for 10-15 % of the collections and provenances. The explanation of this patterning lies largely in the interconnectedness of the history of South African archaeology and the wider social, economic, political and military history of the country. It may suffice to flag here just a few of these broader historical processes, such as the concentration of 19th century collecting around the two educational and political hubs of the then Cape Colony - Cape Town (in the Western Cape) and Grahamstown (in the Eastern Cape). Both cities developed museums at a comparatively early date and archaeology and archaeologists (such as Layard, Péringuey and Hewitt) figured prominently in this process. Two further historical developments that need to be borne in mind are the discovery of diamonds in the Barkly West/Kimberley area in the 1860s and 1870s and the various military conflicts of the late 19th century, particularly the Anglo-Zulu War of 1879 and the Second South African War of 1899-1902. The first of these processes led to the rapid identification of prehistoric stone artefacts in the gravel terraces of the Vaal River (e.g. Stow & Jones 1874) and subsequently spawned much more sustained archaeological exploration (Beaumont & Morris 1990). The conflicts of 1879 and 1899-1902, on the other hand, are responsible for many of the British Museum collections from KwaZulu-Natal and the North West Province.

When were they collected?

Table 3 provides a decade-by-decade breakdown of the chronology of acquisition of the British Museum southern African Stone Age collections and **Fig. 5** summarizes this information in graphical form for South Africa. It is quite clear, even from a cursory inspection of these data, that the collections were not acquired at an even rate. This section discusses some of the reasons for this chronological patterning and, in so doing, refers back to some of the historical developments in the relations between southern African archaeology and Britain considered in Chapter 2.

For reasons discussed in the previous Chapter many of the earliest collectors of southern African stone artefacts ensured that parts of their collections were dispatched to Britain, often for exhibition at conferences (e.g. the Third International Congress of Prehistoric Archaeology held at Norwich in 1868) or at meetings of learned societies, such as the Anthropological Institute. Once displayed, the material was not normally shipped back to southern Africa. Instead, much of it found its way (directly or indirectly) into the British Museum. It was in this way that many of

Table 2. Geographical patterning in The British Museum's southern African Stone Age collections.

Country	Provenances		Collections	
	No	.%	No.	%
Angola	1	0.4	1	0.3
Botswana	21	8.1	24	6.4
Lesotho	1	0.4	2	0.5
Mozambique	2	0.8	2	0.5
Namibia	4	1.6	4	1.1
South Africa	192	74.4	288	76.6
Swaziland	1	0.4	1	0.3
Zimbabwe	36	14.0	54	14.4
Total	258	100.1	376	100.1

Province	Provenances		Collections	
	No.	%	No.	%
Eastern Cape	27	14.1	36	12.5
Free State	24	12.5	30	10.4
Gauteng	12	6.3	15	5.2
KwaZulu-Natal	14	7.3	18	6.3
Mpumalanga	2	1.0	3	1.0
Northern	4	2.1	4	1.4
Northern Cape	52	27.1	83	28.8
North West	27	14.1	29	10.1
Western Cape	23	12.0	58	20.1
Total	192	100.1	288	100.0

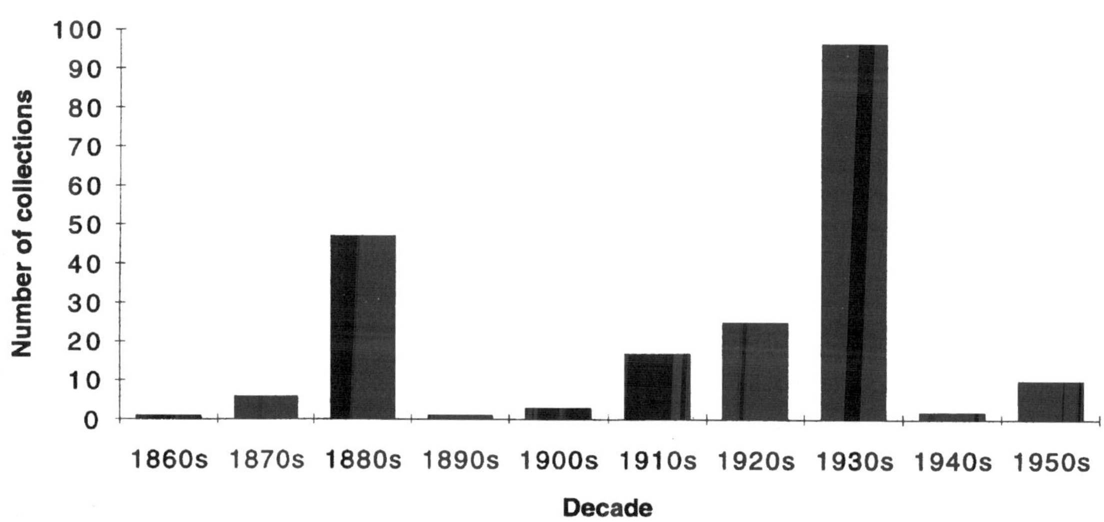

Fig. 5. Chronology of acquisition of British Museum's Stone Age Collections from South Africa.

Table 3. Chronological patterning in the acquisition of The British Museum southern African Stone Age collections, (excluding transfers from the Geological Museum, the Manchester Museum and the Passmore-Edwards Museum)

Decade Country	1860s	1870s	1880s	1890s	1900s	1910s	1920s	1930s	1940s	1950s
Angola	-	-	-	-	-	-	-	-	-	1
Botswana	-	-	11	-	-	-	-	12	-	1
Lesotho			-	-	-	-	-	-	-	-
Mozambique	-	-	-	-	-	1	-	-	-	-
Namibia	-	-	4	-	-	-	-	-	-	-
South Africa	1	-	47	1	3	17	24	94	2	10
Swaziland	-	-	-	1	-	-	-	-	-	-
Zimbabwe	-	-	3	-	1	1	16	16	1	11
Province of South Africa										
Eastern Cape	1	3	3	-	-	3	6	9	-	-
Free State	-	-	4	-	-	2	2	15	1	4
Gauteng	-	-	2	-	-	3	1	1	-	-
KwaZulu-Natal	-	-	6	1	-	1	2	2	-	2
Mpumalanga	-	-	-	-	-	-	2	1	-	-
North West	-	-	7	-	1	5	1	10	1	1
Northern Cape	-	-	24	-	-	3	7	38	-	3
Northern	-	-	-	-	-	-	1	3	-	-
Western Cape	-	1	1	-	2	-	2	15	-	-
No further provenance	-	2	-	-	-	-	1	2	-	1

the British Museum's first southern African Stone Age collections, among them those donated by Layard, Dale, Busk and Spence from the Cape Flats between 1865 and 1872, were obtained. Although in this earliest phase of the collections' history the emphasis was very much on the Western Cape Province of what is now South Africa, the Eastern Cape is also represented, initially by donations of artefacts from Grahamstown, Kleinemonde and Tharfield by Sir Charles Lyell and Sir George Grey. The middle years of the 1870s saw further additions to the Museum's holdings from both parts of the Cape Colony with the donation of the Thurburn collection from Port Beaufort in 1873 and of the collections made by Dr Atherstone, principally from the Eastern Cape, in 1876. Of other figures active in the early years of South African archaeology, Hillier (1898) gave to the Museum in 1887 some of the finds from his excavations near the mouth of the Buffalo River, while the donations of both Dale (in 1872) and Lubbock (in 1916) include artefacts found by George McKay in his excavations in the East London area (Binneman 1990).

The major increase in the size of the British Museum holdings from South Africa in the 1880s was, however, largely the result of the interests of just two men, whose activities reflect, in part, themes within the broader history of South Africa at this time: exploration and military conflict. Andrew Anderson, an explorer and surveyor, sold his extensive collections to the Museum on October 20th 1885. They were accessioned as part of the Christy Collection (see below) and cover 49 distinct provenances from not only four South African provinces (Northern Cape, North West, Gauteng and Free State), but also three other countries in the sub-continent (Botswana, Namibia and Zimbabwe). Many of his finds from the Northern Cape Province were made in the Kimberley area and derive from sites along the Vaal River; reflecting the explosive growth of diamond digging, and consequent discovery of stone artefacts, here after 1867 (Davenport 1978).

In part encouraged by the wealth being produced from the Cape Colony's diamond fields, British policy in southern Africa moved in the 1870s toward one of seeking the confederation of all the region's political units, including the Boer republics of the Orange Free State and the Transvaal, under British hegemony (Davenport 1978). In 1877, Britain annexed the Transvaal, and in 1879, invaded Zululand, events that led to the Anglo-Zulu War of 1879 and the First South African War of 1880-1881. These conflicts both brought to South Africa several individuals with wide-ranging intellectual interests, and provided new opportunities for those already living there to pursue their research. The British Museum collections reflect this political situation in part through material donated by Sir Bartle Frere (the British High Commissioner who had initiated the Zulu War) and Colonel J. H. Bowker (who visited Rorke's Drift in 1880). Much more important, however, are the collections of Colonel H. Feilden, who served at this time in both Natal (material collected at Buffalo River, Estcourt, Isandhlwana, Natal, Newcastle,

Pietermaritzburg and Zululand) and the Transvaal (material collected at Rustenburg). Fielden also made extensive collections on the Cape Flats during the Second South African War (1899-1902), presenting artefacts to Norwich Castle Museum (sold to Liverpool Museum in 1956) and Cambridge University's Museum of Archaeology and Anthropology.

Fielden was not the only army officer with antiquarian interests posted to the sub-continent during the Second South African War. While Major F. Smith was responsible for the donation of a single handaxe from Pienaarsrivier in Gauteng, Colonel E. Collins collected widely as trenches were dug in military operations across South Africa. The British Museum holds artefacts that he collected from sites in the North West Province, Gauteng, Free State and Eastern Cape, many of them described in a paper that he later co-authored with Reginald Smith of the British Museum (Collins & Smith 1919). As a postscript to the impact on the development of the British Museum collections of military conflicts in late 19th century southern Africa, we can note the acquisition from Major-General H. G. White of artefacts collected by him in Griqualand West and the 'Bechuana Province' during the Bechunanaland Expedition of 1884 (Shillington 1985).

Through the late 19th and early 20th centuries several amateur archaeologists continued the tradition of exhibiting their finds to the broader archaeological and anthropological fraternity in Britain, usually by presenting them at meetings of the Royal Anthropological Institute. Accounts of their work then appeared in the Institute's publications (the *Journal of the Royal Anthropological Institute* and *Man*). Examples include Fielden's (1883) collections discussed above, Leith's (1898) finds from the Pretoria gravels, R. Jones's (1898) presentation of artefacts from Swaziland and the results of excavations by Frames (1898) and Bazley (1905) in what is now KwaZulu-Natal. Many of these artefact collections were subsequently donated to the British Museum, not surprisingly perhaps given the close relationship between the Institute and the Keepers of the British Museum's Department of British and Medieval Antiquities and Ethnography. The period 1905-1930 saw the gradual disappearance of this acquisition route, a consequence of the growing professionalization of archaeology within southern Africa and the establishment of a variety of journals there interested in publishing archaeological finds. Jansen's donation (in 1918) of finds from Victoria West are probably the last example of this kind (Smith 1919; Jansen 1926).

Nevertheless, the Museum did acquire a considerable quantity of material from southern Africa during the 1920s, including donations from two museums, Bulawayo Museum in what is now Zimbabwe (in 1921) and the Albany Museum, Grahamstown (in 1922). This period also saw the first of several donations by James Swan, a long-term employee of De Beers, the Kimberley-based diamond producers, and an enthusiastic amateur archaeologist. Reflecting his geographical base, almost all of his collections were made in the Northern Cape and North West Provinces, though the bulk of them were donated to the McGregor Museum, Kimberley, and the then Archaeological Survey of South Africa, located in Johannesburg. Also arriving during this period were collections made by Neville Jones from Taung in the North West Province (in 1919) and several sites in the Free State and Northern Cape (in 1928), artefacts purchased from the Wilson brothers collected at Middledrift near King Williams Town, Eastern Cape Province (in 1926, 1931) and the extensive Ward collection from several sites near Carnarvondale, also in the Eastern Cape (in 1931).

Despite the importance, in some cases considerable, of these individual collections, it was the two successive meetings in southern Africa of the British Association for the Advancement of Science that had the greatest impact on the British Museum's acquisition of artefacts from the sub-continent during the 20th century. The importance of the 1905 meeting for initiating the study of Early Stone Age assemblages in the Victoria Falls area was mentioned in Chapter 2 (Lamplugh 1905a; Feilden 1905). It is reflected in the number of finds from the Zambian side of the Falls that the Museum now has, though from South Africa only nine bifaces from Simondium in the Western Cape Province came the British Museum's way. The 1929 meeting of the Association was, however, a different matter. Following the formal sessions of the conference, several of its participants, including the British Museum's own Hermann Braunholtz, went on an extensive tour of South Africa guided by Clarence Van Riet Lowe. It is abundantly evident from the British Museum South African collections that Braunholtz took advantage of this opportunity to acquire 'representative' artefacts from many of the 'type-sites' recently recognised by Goodwin & Van Riet Lowe (1929) in their synthesis of the region's Stone Age prehistory. Furthermore, the extensive collections donated in 1929, 1930 or 1931 by South African amateur archaeologists (De Villiers, Hardy, Van Alphen, Van Heerden) and professionals (Van Riet Lowe, Wilman) alike suggests that the connections Braunholtz made at this time were amply repaid. Key sites from which material was acquired include Avalon, Brakfontein, Canteen Kopje, Fauresmith, Lockshoek, Pniel, Sheppard Island, Skildegat, Stellenbosch and Ventershoek, all represented in Goodwin & Van Riet Lowe (1929) for reasons discussed in greater detail in the Gazetteer.

In addition to the fruits of Braunholtz's own activities, the British Museum acquired in 1930 or later collections made by several British archaeologists who were in southern Africa for the Association's meeting. Kathleen Kenyon's donation of a group of handaxes and grindstones from Paarl in the Western Cape is one example of this. On a larger scale we can point to the Favell collection from Taung Mission Spruit acquired on his death in 1936 and to the more extensive Armstrong collection from there and from sites such as Alexandersfontein, De Kiel Oost, Jacobsdal and Kimberley in the Free State and Northern Cape that he bequeathed on his death in 1959. In short, the 1929 British Association meeting and its immediate aftermath contributed material from over 40 distinct provenances within South Africa and represents the high watermark of the British Museum's acquisition not just from there, but from southern Africa as a whole.

At the 1905 meeting of the British Association in South Africa Haddon (1905) had made a plea for the establishment of an Ancient Monuments Protection Act and of an inspectorate that could enforce its provisions (Goodwin 1935: 316), but the two Bushman Relics Protection Acts of 1911 and 1913, passed in the aftermath of Union, had little impact. Having failed adequately to define what the terms 'Bushmen' or 'relic' meant, the sale and export of artefacts, particularly to overseas museums, continued unabated (Goodwin 1946a: 129). The establishment of a Historical Monuments Commission in 1923 did little to address the issue since the relevant act contained no provision for the declaration of National Monuments and failed to allocate funds to the Commission (Abrahams 1989). Three years later Gill (1926) expressed additional concerns about the absence of any system for licensing archaeological excavations or ensuring that they maintained minimal standards of excavation, recording or publication. Gill's paper and representations made by Goodwin, then lecturer in archaeology at the University of Cape Town, did, however, eventually bear fruit in 1934 with the enactment of the Natural and Historical Monuments, Relics and Antiques Act (J. Deacon 1990a). This repealed previous legislation, empowered the Historical Monuments Commission to proclaim specific monuments, relics and antiques and prohibited the destruction or alteration of such proclaimed monuments. Henceforth, archaeological excavations also required a permit issued by the Commission and the export of archaeological materials from South Africa was prohibited, except where the exchange of collections between South African museums and those of other countries might be authorized by the Commission (Goodwin 1946a). The consequences of the Act were felt almost immediately with a dramatic fall-off in the acquisition of South African prehistoric material by overseas institutions. Indeed, with the exception of some of the collections made by James Swan from sites in the Northern Cape and North West Provinces, individual artefacts from Mafikeng and Kimberley and small collections from Weenen and Modderpoort acquired between 1935 and 1940, it brought the collection of South African stone artefacts by the British Museum to a close.

For most of the other countries of southern Africa the British Museum has too little in its collections to make a discussion of chronological patterning in their acquisition worthwhile. We note, nevertheless, that the British Museum collections from Namibia all derive from the activities of Andrew Anderson, who was also an important collector within what is now Botswana; with one exception, the remainder of the British Museum Stone Age collections from Botswana were acquired from H. S. Gordon in 1930 and 1934. For Zimbabwe, however, further consideration is worthwhile. Patterning in the acquisition of this part of the British Museum Stone Age collections follows broadly the same trends as in the case of South Africa, though it is a little more compressed chronologically because of the later date at which archaeological research began. With the exception of the few artefacts from river gravels and surface contexts in Matabeleland found by A.A. Anderson (1887a) and purchased from him in 1885, all of the Zimbabwean part of the collections discussed were excavated or collected after 1900. The earliest phase of antiquarian research is represented by the White collection from the Matopo Hills, Khami and Plumtree (donated in 1922), while the 1905 visit of the British Association for the Advancement of Science contributed the Lamplugh collection from the Matetsi Valley. However, the bulk of the remaining collections firmly date to the 1920s and 1930s. At the beginning of this period a donation from the Bulawayo Museum in 1921 added material from several localities (Charter District, Gweru Kopje, Sawmills River, Shangani, Victoria Falls), much of it collected by W. H. Kenny, an early prospector. Five years later Father King sold finds acquired from Gardner's work at Driefontein and in 1928 and 1930 Neville Jones respectively sold and donated artefacts that he had collected from several sites in Matabeleland.

The following year's meeting of the British Association for the Advancement of Science in South Africa sponsored, as we have already seen, two major excavations in Zimbabwe, those of Caton-Thompson (1931) at Great Zimbabwe and of Armstrong (1931) and Jones at Bambata Cave and other sites in the Matopo Hills. The immediate consequence of this for the British Museum was Braunholtz's acquisition for the Museum (in 1930) of finds from a range of other sites in Matabeleland (Hope Fountain, Imbusini, Mauchini Brook, Powola Brook). The finds excavated by Armstrong, though exported from Zimbabwe at the end of the Rhodesian Archaeological Expedition's activities there, were only formally acquired by the British Museum some time later. The first phase of this is marked by the bequest made in 1936 by Dr R. Favell, who had participated in the expedition, of artefacts from Nswatugi Cave, along with others that he had either collected himself or been given by other archaeologists (Gweru Kopje, Gokomere Cave, Inyati, Sawmills). Most of the finds from Armstrong's excavations, however, were only acquired following their bequest at his death in 1959, along with further material from Gokomere Cave that he had been given by Gardner. By this time Armstrong had given parts of his collections to other museums, though as far as Zimbabwean sites are concerned the only consequence of this was that it was not until 1987 that the Manchester Museum transferred to the British Museum the outstanding part of the Armstrong Collection from Bambata Cave itself. Following South Africa's example, the then Southern Rhodesia banned the export of archaeological finds without a license from the National Monuments Commission in 1936. Though they were only acquired by the British Museum after 1936, the Favell and Armstrong Collections, as well as the much smaller Hobley Collection from Sawmills, had already been removed from Zimbabwe several years before this legislation came into force.

Who collected them?

Table 4 summarizes data on the occupations, where known, of the individuals responsible for the collection of the British Museum southern African Stone Age holdings. The emphasis is very much on the activities of individual collectors since only a small proportion of the total holdings from southern African Stone Age contexts derive from exchanges with, or donations from, museums in the sub-continent. Such museums are, with their provenances, the National Museum in Bloemfontein (South Africa, no further provenance), the Albany Museum in Grahamstown (Alicedale, Grahamstown, Kasouga River and Wilton Large Rock Shelter) and the Bulawayo Museum (Gweru Kopje, Nswatugi Cave, Powola Brook, Sawmills, Victoria Falls).

In compiling Table 4 a difficulty was posed by the fact that many of the indviduals who contributed to the British Museum collections were, in a very real sense, polymaths. This is evident in the brief biographical details of them provided in Appendix 4 and can be illustrated, for example, by Dr Hugh Exton, who was responsible for the Museum's three artefacts from Lesotho. Exton was born in England, studied there and in the Netherlands and eventually qualified in medicine in Germany. Moving to South Africa he prospected for gold in Zimbabwe, travelled through Botswana, moved to Bloemfontein and there became the city's mayor, a leading member of the committee that set up the National Museum in 1878 and its first Honorary Curator. Having published a paper on the auriferous rocks of the Witwatersrand, he went on to become the founding President of the South African Geological Society, as well as President of the South African Medical Society, a military surgeon during the Second South African War and an amateur ornithologist. How to classify such a man ? Despite his many accomplishments, Exton was first and foremost a doctor and is included as such in Table 4, but it is worth bearing in mind that there is an unavoidable element of arbitrariness in such a decision.

With this caveat in mind, what general conclusions can be drawn from an examination of Table 4? The largest single professional category represented is that of geologists and mining prospectors, who together account for just over one-fifth of all the individual collectors. Interestingly, however, given what we have already said about the boost to the British Museum collections provided by discoveries made during diamond digging operations on the Vaal River, few of these individuals had any specific connection with the diamond industry. The most notable exception to this generalization is James Swan, who collected extensively in the Northern Cape and North West Provinces, both during and after his employment by De Beers at their Kimberley headquarters. Swan was also responsible for the donation made to the Museum by S.H. Routley, an employee of the London-based Diamond Corporation Ltd. Otherwise, the strong representation of geologists in Table 4 seems rather to derive from their coming across stone artefacts in the course of their geological work or prospecting, a coincidence that in several cases (notably that of Edward Wayland) led to a substantial redirection of their work and research in a more strictly archaeological direction. Other examples of such individuals would include both Lamplugh (1905a, 1905b) and F. White (1900, 1905), respectively the first individuals to publish on the archaeology of the Victoria Falls and to excavate at rock-shelter sites in Zimbabwe.

Closely allied professionally to the geologist/miner group are those individuals classified in Table 4 as engineers and surveyors, several of whom (e.g. Frames, Frylinck and Trevor) worked for mining companies; Trevor (1930), indeed, combined his mining expertise and archaeological interests to publish one of the first papers on Iron Age mines in the former Transvaal province of South Africa. Andrew Anderson, who has already been mentioned, also fits perhaps within this general grouping, although he has been included as an explorer in Table 4. He was a qualified surveyor, had his map of southern Africa published by the Royal Geographical Society in 1885 and also found several of his Northern Cape archaeological specimens in diamond diggings, one of them, a Middle Stone Age point from Klip Drift (part of Christy Collection +7872), on his own claim.

Many of the individuals who contributed to the British Museum collections from southern Africa were employed in Government service, either as colonial administrators in the 19th century, as civil servants or in the military. Together, these categories include a further fifth of the individuals whose occupations are known, more if one bears in mind that several geologists, engineers and doctors were employed by Government. The apex of colonial society is represented by the donations made by Sir George Grey (Governor of the Cape Colony and High Commissioner of South Africa 1854-1861) and Sir Bartle Frere (who occupied the same positions between 1877 and 1880). District magistrates are represented by only three individuals (Jansen, Orpen and Van Alphen), a perhaps surprisingly small percentage. It would be of interest to know from an examination of museum collections in South Africa if the low representation of government officials is a general pattern in the 'antiquarian' phase of southern African archaeology and, if so, what other intellectual or scientific interests such individuals may have pursued. The example of Colonel J. H. Bowker, who, in addition to his career as a soldier and civil servant, collected stone artefacts, co-authored a work on South African entomology and was also a noted botanist, comes to mind.

Both the Anglo-Zulu War of 1879 and the Second South African War of 1899-1902 resulted, largely through the activities of Colonel Feilden and Major Collins, in significant additions to the British Museum collections, notably from KwaZulu-Natal and the North West Province. Other military men also contributed to the British Museum southern African holdings. In addition to J. H. Bowker just mentioned, these include his brother, Commandant T. H. Bowker (Rorke's Drift - in the aftermath of the Anglo-Zulu War), Colonel Goldsmid (South Africa, no further provenance - Second South African War), Major Smith (Pienaarsrivier, Second South African War) and Major-General White (Bechuana Province - Bechuanaland Expedition of 1884). Several other individuals, especially some of those included in Table 4 under the category of 'doctors', also had strong military connections, among them Colonel Hardy (Fish Hoek, Noordhoek), founder member and first President of the South African Archaeological Society, as well as an important collector of Middle and Later Stone Age artefacts from the Cape Peninsula (Goodwin 1926a; Malan 1939).

Table 4. Occupations of private individuals who contributed to The British Museum southern African Stone Age collections (sources given in Appendix 4).

	Number	Percentage	Percentage excluding unknowns
Archaeologist/Anthropologist	4	4.5	6.1
Civil servant	6	6.8	9.1
Collector	5	5.7	7.6
Doctor	7	8.0	10.6
Educationalist/Teacher	3	3.4	4.5
Engineer	7	8.0	10.6
Explorer	1	1.1	1.5
Geologist/Miner	12	13.6	18.2
Horticulturalist	1	1.1	1.5
Museum curator	5	5.7	7.6
Priest	6	6.8	9.1
Soldier	9	10.2	13.6
Unknown	22	25.0	-
Total	88	99.9	N = 66

Note. The data used to compile Table 4 have been taken from Appendix 4 with individuals classified by occupation as follows:

Anderson	Explorer	Fuller	Unknown	Rothwell	Unknown
Armstrong	Archaeologist	Gardner	Priest	Routley	Unknown
Atherstone	Doctor	Goldsmid	Soldier	Seton-Karr	Collector
Avebury	Collector	Gordon	Soldier	Smith	Soldier
Ayres	Unknown	Grey	Civil servant	Spence	Unknown
Bain	Geologist	Hall	Unknown	Spencer	Geologist
Bays	Doctor	Hardy	Doctor	Sturge	Collector
Bazley	Engineer	Heanley	Unknown	Swan	Geologist
Bird	Unknown	Hewitt	Museum curator	Thomasset	Engineer
Bowker, T. H.	Soldier	Hillier	Doctor	Thurburn	Soldier
Bowker, J. H.	Soldier	Hobley C.	Geologist	Trechmann	Geologist
Braunholtz	Anthropologist	Jansen	Civil servant	Trevor	Engineer
Brown	Unknown	Jones	Museum curator	Tribe	Priest
Busk C. J.	Unknown	Kenny	Miner	Van Alphen	Civil servant
Collins	Soldier	Kenyon	Archaeologist	Van Heerden	Doctor
Cookson	Unknown	Kettlewell	Priest	Van Riet Lowe	Archaeologist
Cranswick	Priest	King	Priest	Walsh	Unknown
Dale	Educationalist	Lamplugh	Geologist	Wansborough	Teacher
De Villiers	Unknown (child)	Layard	Civil servant	Ward	Unknown
Du Toit	Geologist	Leith	Teacher	Warren	Unknown
Dunn	Geologist	Leviseur	Engineer	Wayland	Geologist
Elliott	Horticulturalist	Liepner	Unknown	Whitaker	Geologist
Evans	Collector	Lyell	Geologist	White, F.	Engineer
Exton	Doctor	McKay	Unknown	White, H. G.	Soldier
Favell	Doctor	Matley	Geologist	White, R. L.	Priest
Feilden	Soldier	Newberry	Unknown	Wigram	Unknown
Fisher	Unknown	Orpen, F. H. S.	Civil servant	Wilman	Museum curator
Frames	Engineer	Péringuey	Museum curator	Wilson Brothers	Unknown
Frere	Civil servant	Read	Museum curator		
Frylinck	Engineer	Robertson	Unknown		

Note: The term 'collector' is used with reference to Avebury, Evans, Lyell, Seton-Karr and Sturge in recognition of the fact that all had originally acquired southern African material second-hand from actual collectors in the field.

Professional archaeologists, anthropologists and museum curators form a further component of Table 4, accounting for almost another fifth of all those individuals whose occupations are known. That this figure is not higher reflects the comparative lack of professionalization of archaeology in southern Africa, as elsewhere, well into the 20th century and the high profile of amateur antiquarians as a result. To count figures such as Sir John Evans and Sir John Lubbock as archaeologists only goes to confirm this, since the first was, in fact, the owner of a printing company and the second a bank-owner and politician. Nevertheless, the list also includes Kathleen Kenyon and Clarence Van Riet Lowe, while a further significant component of the British Museum southern African Stone Age holdings result from the collecting activities of individuals professionally employed in the museum world. Neville Jones, whose archaeological interests led him to abandon the missionary field to become Zimbabwe's first museum-based archaeologist, is one of the most important of these, although Layard and Péringuey (both curators of the South African Museum, Cape Town) and Hewitt (Director of the Albany Museum) contributed a small component of the British Museum collections, along with Maria Wilman (Director of the McGregor Museum, Kimberley), one of only five women to be represented in Table 4. The British Museum's own staff are represented by Sir Charles Read, Keeper of the Department of British and Medieval Antiquities and Ethnography from 1896 until 1921, and by Hermann Braunholtz, Keeper of the Department of Oriental Antiquities and Ethnography (1938-1945) and Keeper of the Department of Ethnography (1945-1953). Read's contribution from southern Africa is restricted to a few handaxes from Simondium (Western Cape) and the Shangani River (Zimbabwe), but Braunholtz's is much more substantial and spans five South African provinces, as well as Zimbabwe. The two visits to southern Africa of the British Association for the Advancement of Science already remarked on provide the context for their visits and their acquisitions, though it is also worth mentioning that it was via his connection with Read that William Bazley (1905) donated some of the finds from his excavation of the Alfred County Cave in KwaZulu-Natal.

A theme that has received relatively little mention in earlier discussions of the early history of southern African archaeology is that of the interconnectedness of many of the early collectors. As one example of the ties of friendship, and in some cases marriage, that linked together many of the intellectual leaders of South Africa in the latter half of the 19th century, we have already commented on the connections between Sir Charles Lyell and his family on the one hand and Mrs Frances Colenso on the other and noted the connections between her and Lucy Lloyd, co-recorder of the Bleek/Lloyd archive that is fundamental to any understanding of southern African rock art or the history of the /Xam Bushmen (Lewis-Williams & Dowson 1989; Skotnes 1996). As another, and more extensive example, of such a network we can take the two Eastern Cape figures of Drs Atherstone and Kannemeyer, the first a contributor to the British Museum collections principally from what is now the Eastern Cape Province (Bushman's River, East London, Keiskamma River), the latter author of an important early paper (Kannemeyer 1890) that is 'one of the few detailed descriptions of the use and making of stone tools ever published in Southern Africa' (J. Deacon 1990a: 41).

A true polymath who combined his medical profession with active interests in botany and geology, Atherstone was related by marriage to the Bowker brothers (Mitford-Barberton & Mitford-Barberton 1952) through two different connections: both his cousin, Frederick Barber, and his brother, John Atherstone, married two of the Bowkers' sisters, respectively Mary Elizabeth and Anna Maria. Atherstone's own interest in geology had been inspired through his friendship with Andrew Geddes Bain, generally regarded as the father of the subject in South Africa. Bain himself contributed stone artefacts from Kleinemonde on the Eastern Cape coast to the British Museum, while others originally collected by him there were donated via Sir Charles Lyell, the leading British geologist of the time. Atherstone too donated artefacts from Kleinemonde: Tharfield, the Bowker family farm, lies only a few kilometres away. Both Atherstone and J. H. Bowker were keen botanists and sent specimens of plants that they had collected to Sir Joseph Hooker, Director of Kew Gardens in London. Hooker himself was centrally located within the mid-19th-century British scientific elite, a colleague and friend of Sir Charles Lyell, as well as of Darwin and Huxley. It was to Hooker, apparently for want of direct access to Lyell, that J. H. Bowker sent the finds from his excavations in Lesotho (Royal Botanic Gardens, Kew, Director's Correspondence South Africa vol. 189, no. 388), although elsewhere he refers to sending artefacts directly to Lyell (Bowker 1884). Both sets of finds appear now to be lost, along with the artefacts from the mouth of the Great Fish River sent by his older brother, T. H. Bowker, to the Royal Artillery Museum in 1866; J. H. Bowker's subsequent collection of artefacts from Rorke's Drift in KwaZulu-Natal did, however, pass to the British Museum.

One of J. H. Bowker's other interests was butterflies, a passion that he shared with Dr Daniel Kannemeyer, who may also have served with him in the Cape Mounted Rifles' campaign against Chief Moorosi in Lesotho in 1879. Kannemeyer practised medicine at Burgersdorp in the Eastern Cape, using the opportunities this offered him of meeting surviving San individuals to accumulate information on the last forager communities of the surrounding area (Kannemeyer 1890). He worked closely with Alfred Brown, another Eastern Cape doctor and antiquarian, Brown concentrating on the collection of Middle Stone Age artefacts and Kannemeyer on those of Later Stone Age origin (Goodwin 1946a: 31); neither published extensively. Kannemeyer did, however, inspire George Leith to develop an interest in archaeology, introducing him to the subject by showing him rock paintings near Burgersdorp when Leith was teaching there in 1886 (Goodwin 1946a: 36; Leith 1964: 13). Leith (1898) went on to excavate at Cave St. Blaize near Mossel Bay at Kannemeyer's instigation in order to vindicate the views previously advanced by Atherstone (1871) that the shell midden deposits there were of human origin. Some of the material from his excavations, along with eoliths and Early Stone Age artefacts from several sites in Pretoria, form part of the British Museum collections, together with J. P. Rothwell's finds from Vogelstruisfontein, Gauteng, whom Leith also knew. As a codicil to this part of the Atherstone/Bowker network, we may note Kannemeyer's connections with Péringuey (Goodwin 1946a: 34) and with Dr Selmar Schönland, curator of the Albany Museum, Grahamstown, and a former associate of Henry Balfour (1910), the curator of Oxford's Pitt Rivers Museum, to which Schönland donated finds from the Eastern Cape.

Mary Barber, sister of the Bowker brothers, was herself a noted natural historian, author of a brief note on stone artefacts (Barber 1872) and a contributor of information to Edgar Layard, first curator of the South African Museum in Cape Town, for his book *The Birds of South Africa,* which was published in 1867. It was to Layard that her brother, T. H. Bowker, sent stone artefacts that he had excavated near the Fish River some time before 1858 (Hewitt 1955 pace Busk 1869). When this or a later consigment of artefacts found by Bowker was unpacked in Cape Town around 1860, Mrs Emma Dale was present and 'was inoculated with...enthusiasm' for archaeology (Hewitt 1955: 94, quoting Layard 1872). At the time, her husband, the Rev. Langham Dale, was Superintendant-General of Education in the Cape Colony and it seems likely to have been through this connection that Dale was, in Goodwin's (1935: 296) words, brought 'into the magic circle of archaeologists' and encouraged to begin collecting stone artefacts of his own from the Cape Flats, while also acquiring others from George McKay's excavations near East London. As well as publishing himself, Dale (1870a, 1870b, 1871) sent some of his finds to Britain, along with others collected by Charles Busk. The latter's brother, the palaeontologist George Busk, presented them at the Norwich Congress of Prehistoric Archaeology in 1868 and later published them (Busk 1869). Busk was one of the key scientists working on subjects connected to the debate concerning human antiquity in the mid-19th century and well-known to others, such as Joseph Prestwich, Hugh Falconer, John Evans and John Lubbock. It was presumably through this acquaintance that Lubbock first became aware of the South African artefacts to which he later referred in several papers (Lubbock 1869, 1870a, 1870b, 1871) that helped him in his campaign to become founding President of what later became the Anthropological Institute of Great Britain and Ireland (Goodwin 1935). Many, possibly all, of the artefacts sent to Britain at this time by Dale and Charles Busk, including those illustrated in the Proceedings of the Norwich Congress (Busk 1869), now form part of the British Museum collections.

Connections of friendship and intermarriage link all the individuals just discussed and some of these were formalized through the discussion circle established by Dr Richard Rubidge, a leading Eastern Cape surgeon between 1844 and 1869. Both Atherstone and Andrew Geddes Bain were members of this group, along with George William Stow, a geologist who compiled a major work on the prehistory of southern Africa (1905) and was one of the first people to begin the recording of the sub-continent's rock art (Stow & Bleek 1930).

A second series of interconnections reflected through the collections of the British Museum was founded on links made through the Church, particularly the Society of Jesus. One of the earliest pioneers of Zimbabwean archaeology was Father Thomas Gardner, a Jesuit missionary, based successively at missions such as Driefontein and Gokomere, both of which are represented in the British Museum collections. Gardner reached the then Southern Rhodesia in 1902 and commenced a long career publishing archaeological papers four years later with a report on finds made near Bulawayo (Gardner 1906). He was a close friend of a fellow Jesuit, Father Philip Stapleton, who taught at St. George's College in what is now Harare between 1929 and 1928 and had previously taught at St. Aidan's College, Grahamstown. While in the Eastern Cape, Stapleton had been closely associated with John Hewitt, the Director of the Albany Museum, an association that included the excavation of the Howieson's Poort type-site (Stapleton & Hewitt 1927) and a general review of South African archaeology in the mid-1920s (Hewitt & Stapleton 1925). Though Stapleton himself is not represented among the British Museum's donors, another Jesuit priest, Father Edward King, visited Rhodesia in 1931-32 and must have met both him and Gardner at that time; King sold to the Museum a further collection of artefacts from Driefontein acquired prior to this visit from Gardner. Stapleton's time in Grahamstown coincided with the presence there not only of John Hewitt, but also of an Anglican priest, Reverend Percy Kettlewell, Headmaster of St. Andrew's School between 1909 and 1933. It was Kettlewell who was responsible for the donation by the Trustees of the Albany Museum of artefacts from several Eastern Cape sites (Alicedale, Grahamstown (Sugar Loaf Hill), Kasouga River, Wilton Large Rock Shelter). As one point of connection between this clerical circle (also represented in the early years of Zimbabwean archaeology by Reverend Neville Jones and in the British Museum collections by both him and Reverend Rupert Cranswick) and the Atherstone-Bowkers-Kannemeyer circle we can isolate Dr Selmar Schönland, colleague of Kannemeyer, biographer of Mary Barber (née Bowker) and immediate predecessor of Hewitt as director of the Albany Museum.

The acquisition of Stone Age material from southern Africa by The British Museum.

In considering the history of the southern African collections now held by the Department of Prehistory and Early Europe (PEE), attention must also be paid to the curatorial history and departmental structure of the British Museum itself. This department was only founded in 1969 (as the Department of Prehistoric and Romano-British Antiquities) and thus acquired virtually none of its southern African collections while in its present form. Indeed, the only such acquisitions made since 1969 have been by transfer from other institutions: the Geological Museum (in 1989), the Passmore Edwards Museum (in 1996) and the Institute of Archaeology (1989). In each of these cases, southern African artefacts were included as part of larger transfers of Stone Age archaeological material which the transferring institutions felt it was no longer appropriate for them to curate under the terms of their present collecting policies. It should also be remembered that this Catalogue deals directly only with the material held by PEE, including that transferred to that department by the Department of Ethnography in the 1970s. Material still retained by the Department of Ethnography was not examined, but is listed in Appendix 1.

The bulk of the collections now held by PEE were acquired by the Victorian Department of British and Medieval Antiquities and Ethnography, which was founded in 1866 as an offshoot of the Department of the Oriental (Egyptian and Assyrian) Antiquities, and disbanded in 1921 to form the Department of British and Medieval Antiquities (parent of both PEE and the present Department of Medieval and Early Europe) and the Department of Ceramics, Oriental Antiquities and Ethnography (parent *inter alia* of the present Department of Ethnography). The collecting policies of the first Keeper of this Department, Augustus Woolaston Franks, were highly influential in building up the national collections in a wide variety of areas, including Stone Age material (Cook 1997). Franks began his career at the British Museum in 1851, when the issue of an extended antiquity for humankind was still the subject of fierce debate, took over the running of his own department the year after Lubbock (1865) coined the term 'Palaeolithic', and managed to build up one of the finest and most comprehensive Palaeolithic collections in the world while the subject itself was still in its infancy. Both his policies and methods were maintained by his protégé and successor, Sir Charles Hercules Read, the second and last Keeper of the Department.

In building up the Palaeolithic collections Franks was assisted by two main factors: firstly, the Christy Collection and Fund, and secondly his friendships with leading figures in the emerging subject of Palaeolithic archaeology. Both these factors are evident in the acquisition of Stone Age material from southern Africa. Following the death of the businessman Henry Christy in 1865, Franks was named one of four trustees of Christy's vast private collection of ethnographic objects and prehistoric archaeological material recovered from his excavations at caves in the Dordogne, carried out in collaboration with the French palaeontologist Edouard Lartet (Cook 1997). The trustees were instructed to present both the collection and a fund to maintain it to a permanent institution, or to set up a new museum. Franks was able to persuade both his fellow trustees and the Trustees of the British Museum that the latter should accept the bequest. Due to the size of the Christy collection, however, it had to be housed elsewhere until sufficient space was created for it in Bloomsbury in the 1880s, when the natural history collections were moved to their new home in South Kensington. Franks and his successors were able to use the financial resources and collection policies of the Christy Collection to acquire ethnographic and prehistoric material which might otherwise have been beyond the means of the British Museum. Separate registers were kept of this material well into the 20th century, including Stone Age finds from southern Africa. These registers, the 'Christy Slip Catalogue' to which reference is made in Chapter 5, include 'details of how, from whom and, if relevant, at what price an object had been obtained' along with a description, drawing and reference to any relevant publications (Cook 1997: 121).

Franks was also assisted in expanding his Department's collections by his extensive network of friends and colleagues. Men such as Sir John Lubbock and Sir John Evans were often able to provide advice and/or introduce him to people who might wish to donate or sell material to the British Museum, or the Christy Collection. It is obvious, for example, from correspondence preserved both at the British Museum and at Oxford's Ashmolean Museum that Sir John Evans was the intermediary in the Christy Collection's acquisition of material from Andrew Anderson (Appendix 4). British Museum archives also indicate that other colleagues occasionally alerted Franks to further possibilities. For example, Major-General Henry White's artefacts from the North West Province and the Northern Cape were acquired by Franks for the Christy Collection following an enquiry by White to the Natural History Museum. A letter in the British Museum's archives (MME Letters archive) shows that on 16th July 1885 Franks wrote to White referring to that enquiry and stated that '... we have a fairly large series of South African stone implements, which we should be glad to improve'.

Other examples of how and why southern African material was acquired by the British Museum have been discussed above and elsewhere in this volume, among them the influx of artefacts from Hermann Braunholtz's trip to the sub-continent in 1929 for the meeting there of the British Association for the Advancement of Science, and the presentation of material previously exhibited at the Royal Anthropological Institute. Both of these examples also emphasise the point that archaeological materials from southern Africa was often acquired in a manner similar to ethnographic materials well into the 20th century.

Not all Stone Age finds from southern Africa were donated directly to British institutions. A proportion found their way into the hands of private collectors, some of whom were, perhaps, more concerned with obtaining and/or exchanging 'specimens' than with the archaeological context or scientific value of the material. Some of these collections were indeed subsequently acquired by museums, but they often have little useful associated contextual information, even regarding the provenance from which the 'specimen' was derived. An example of such collecting is provided by the more than 600 artefacts provenanced only to 'South Africa' included in the vast bequest of stone tools left to the British Museum by Dr William Allen Sturge (R. Smith 1937). Other parts of that collection are better documented and a series of letters from the South African collector George Leith to Sturge dated 1898-1899 illustrates several points concerning such private collecting (Sturge Archive, PEE). The earliest of these letters (29th August 1898) refers to Leith having agreed to exhibit artefacts and read a paper at a British Association meeting to be held two weeks hence. Leith writes from Aberdeen to ask Sturge if he can borrow back an object previously given to him in order to display it at the meeting. Leith also mentions that he has 'selected a pretty complete series for you here which will be sent to you in due course'. The next letter is written from Bristol and Leith states that 'I have left a good few of the drift gravel implements for you in the schoolroom where the paper was read. Please send to get them lest they be 'jumped'.' By 17th December 1898 Leith is back in Pretoria and writes to Sturge explaining how 'before leaving Aberdeen for Bristol I sorted out a box of Coast flake implements into 4 lots and put a card with your name into the lot intended for you'. He also hints as to why he has sent material to Sturge and was now arranging to send more: 'I shall be very pleased indeed if you will pack the Danish implement securely and send it by Post together with any other of the finer specimens that you are sending me.' The full extent of this 'exchange' is revealed in the final letter, dated 30th June 1899. This letter also shows that the arrangement with Sturge was not an isolated occurrence on Leith's part:

> ...Shortly after I left here your exchange came to hand but it was only last night that I had the pleasure of unpacking them. They arrived I am glad to say in perfect order thanks to your careful packing. I am perfectly satisfied with the Danish spearheads you sent in exchange for my Mossel Bay celt.... I am particularly pleased to get the Italian implements and the bone needles from Switserland. I have a few French palaeoliths recd in exchange from Prof Boyd Dawkins, a fairly good collection of American implements from Prof Putnam and English palaeoliths from Col Underwood. I propose sending you some implements from the Stormberg Cave Shelter some from the Waterberg flats and one or two perforated digging stones and rubbers from various districts. In exchange I would like specimens from various European countries, from Egypt or India...

The Boyd Dawkins and Underwood material is now held by other British museums (Appendix 3) and it can be assumed that the material sent to Putnam is now somewhere in America. What became of the objects that Leith traded for his South African material is unknown. Fortunately, however, few of the collections held by the British Museum fall into this category of material acquired from secondary collectons. Other examples may include the five pieces from Trechmann (Coega, Zwartkops River, both in South Africa's Eastern Cape Province) and the single object donated by Horace Brown (Beyers Kloof Farm in South Africa's Western Cape Province), a man known in other contexts to have enhanced his own collection by exchanging antiquities with others.

Such exchanges of material were commonplace between collectors during the late 19th and early 20th centuries, and, indeed, museums also participated in such practices - often in the name of 'education' and/or to further their own acquisitions. A noteworthy example from among the British Museum's southern African Stone Age collections is the material donated from Alfred County Cave in KwaZulu-Natal by William Bazley. We discuss the significance of these finds in the following section, but consider here such evidence as survives in the British Museum's archives (MME Letters archive) relating to their acquisition. The earliest surviving correspondence dates to March 1904 and records that Sir Charles Read, then Keeper of the Department of British and Medieval Antiquities and Ethnography, sent a parcel of 17 British Palaeolithic and Neolithic artefacts and a copy of the British Museum's *Stone Age Guide* to a Mr Henry Higgs at Treasury Chambers for his 'South African correspondent'. A letter from Higgs to Read dated 20th July 1904 clarified that this was indeed William Bazley, whom he described as an 'eccentric old colonist'. Higgs then sent Bazley's material to Read with a note stating that 'The things he sends are for you, not for the museum.' Two copies of *Man* containing Read's report on Bazley's finds (Bazley 1905) were then sent to Bazley on 20th January 1905. Higgs, who was later to become Principal Clerk in H.M. Treasury, had presumably made Bazley's acquaintance while serving as Special Commissioner to Natal in 1902-1903, not long before this exchange of correspondence began. Why Read sent the European material to Natal is unknown, but it is possible that this may have been in response to an enquiry from Bazley about the prehistoric material that he had found

Judging by Reginald Smith's description in the 1926 third edition of the *Guide to Antiquities of the Stone Age in the Department of British and Medieval Antiquities*, a large part of the southern African Stone Age collections was then on display, or accessible to the public in glass-topped drawers below the table cases. The only major collection which seems to have been missing is that included in the Sturge bequest, which amounted to several tonnes of artefacts from around the world. This was stored elsewhere because of its magnitude and was only available upon request. Smith briefly discusses the African collections and attempts to structure his discussion by reference to the chronological sequence then known from western Europe. Although he was quite cautious about drawing direct comparisons, he described artefacts from Rustenburg in the former Transvaal and from Swaziland's Mbabane River as being 'somewhat in the St. Acheul style' (ibid. 179-180). Other objects from the Cape Flats were compared to material from the classic French Palaeolithic sites of Le Moustier and Solutré, although with the qualifying comment that 'these may simply be chance coincidences' (ibid. 180). Finally, material from the Wilton Large Rockshelter and Kimberley was described as similar to 'those of Maz d'Azil date in Europe (the pygmy period)' (ibid. 180). Smith did, however, commit himself so far as to say that 'A find in the Umhlatuzane river valley near Mariannhill, Natal, confirms the opinion that the handaxes of Africa and Europe belong equally to the Drift period', but again qualified his statement by adding that '...it remains to be proved whether the hand-axe remained the typical implement till comparatively recent times' (ibid. 179). The Smith display had to be disbanded during the Second World War and there has not been a significant proportion of the southern African collections on exhibition in the British Museum since that time. The collections have, however, continued to remain available for research.

2. The Present Day Significance of the Collections

Assessing the significance of cultural remains is increasingly a feature of modern archaeology, whether in determining what to conserve, display or repatriate, or in considerations of how best to mitigate the impact on the archaeological environment of a range of development projects and activities (*cf.* Schiffer & Gumerman 1977). In discussing the significance of the British Museum southern African Stone Age collections, three interrelated themes can briefly be addressed: the significance of the collections as historical documents, their significance for education and their potential for further research. We take each of them in turn.

As the preceding sections of this chapter have hopefully shown, the British Museum collections help document virtually the first hundred years of Stone Age archaeology in southern Africa. They do this by providing material evidence of the interests of many of those involved with the southern African past between *c.* 1860 and 1950, by suggesting what was of value to these archaeological pioneers and by showing which periods or issues in prehistory exercised the greatest attraction over them. This is readily illustrated with two examples that concern the work of a single collector, George Leith. Leith's (1898) paper on South African archaeology not only reported the results of his excavations at Cape St. Blaize Cave, Mossel Bay, which conclusively showed the human origin of its shell midden deposits, but also addressed the differentiation of naturally from humanly flaked pieces of stone in his consideration of finds from the Pretoria gravels. The first issue, previously debated by Barrow (1801), Lichtenstein (1928-30), Atherstone (1871), 'F' (1871) and others, exactly parallels slightly earlier debates on the origins of Denmark's *kjökkenmöddinger* (Daniel 1975: 87-88), while the second forms, as Leith (1898: 268-269) himself indicates, part of the then ongoing controversy over the authenticity of so-called 'Harrisonian eoliths' in Kent and elsewhere (Daniel 1975: 230-231).

Our discussion of the chronological and geographical patterning in the activities of those individuals who contributed to the British Museum holdings from southern Africa adds a further dimension to the historical significance of those collections. It is clear, for example, that important political and economic events and processes (such as the discovery of diamonds, the Anglo-Zulu War and the Second South African War) had an effect on the manner in which and the areas from which the Museum acquired its southern African collections. What is also evident is the importance of ties of friendship and of professional connections between many of the collectors which resulted in them forming parts of intellectual networks not only within southern Africa, but also extending to the scientific elite of contemporary Britain. Southern African prehistory, right from its earliest days in the 1860s, was never peripheral to developments in the wider fields of palaeolithic archaeology and hunter-gatherer research.

It is this historical dimension of the British Museum collections that is, perhaps, foremost in considerations of their contemporary significance. However, we ought not to forget the importance of the British Museum holdings as by far the largest and most diverse Stone Age archaeological collection from southern Africa at any British institution (*cf.* Chapter 5 with Appendix 3). This makes the British Museum, in particular, central to any consideration of the relations between the evolving discipline of archaeology within the sub-continent and Britain, but also offers to the British Museum an unparalleled opportunity, outside of southern Africa, for the public display and interpretation of southern African archaeology.

Yet museums exist to provide opportunities for research, as well as to conserve, to present and to educate. One aspect of the research potential of the British Museum collections forms the basis of and justification for the present chapter, i.e. their own history and what this can tell us about the motives and interests of those people who acquired them. Unfortunately, because so much of the British Museum southern African collections (e.g. many of the artefacts collected by Andrew Anderson) come from undateable surface contexts, have little or no stratigraphic provenance or represent highly selected and biased components of much larger assemblages, few of them have the potential to inform us about southern African prehistory, rather than the prehistory of the region's archaeology. But there are exceptions to this generalization and these are picked up and discussed in the Gazetteer. Notable among them are Bambata Cave, where the British Museum now has nearly the entirety of the artefact assemblages recovered by Armstrong and Jones in their excavation of 1929 (Armstrong 1931), along with tracings of the now sadly faded rock paintings that cover its walls. Walker (1995: 152) makes explicit reference to having examined the British Museum collection from Bambata when reassessing the site's stratigraphy and cultural sequence; part of the same collection has also been recently examined by Nick Hanson-James (pers. comm.), whose doctoral thesis addresses the significance and spatio-temporal parameters of the distinctive Bambata Ware ceramic tradition named after the site. Remaining within Zimbabwe, Walker's (1995) recent synthesis of the archaeology of the Matopo Hills mentions other excavations carried out there in the early decades of the 20th century, notably by White (1905) at a shelter near World's View and by Armstrong (1931) at Gumali Shelter. Walker (1995: 188) comments in the first case that 'most of the material has been lost' and in the second that 'the excavated material is no longer available'. However, in both cases some, albeit probably highly selected, artefacts survive in the British Museum. Not only do these confirm Armstrong's (1929) reference to the presence of both a Later and a Middle Stone Age component at Gumali (and further demonstrate that the former is of mid/late Holocene Age), but they also attest to the previously unremarked fact that White (1905) dug at two separate shelters near World's View; the artefacts in his collection from the Matopos are clearly provenanced to a shelter A and a shelter B.

Such instances may be few, but a final example illustrates their importance, and suggests that other surprises may still be found in early collections. As has already been remarked, near the beginning of the 20th century William Bazley, an engineer, excavated at a site in the then Alfred County of what is now southern KwaZulu-Natal. Bazley (1905) published only brief details of his excavation, which was carried out with few stratigraphic controls. As Goodwin (1935: 314) commented, had things been otherwise 'it should have yielded very valuable evidence from this part of the country', not least because the site appears to have had up to 5.6 m of deposit, contained well-preserved faunal remains and also three human skeletons (Bazley 1905). In his *Loom of Prehistory* Goodwin (1946a: 78-79) refers to Bazley having sent some of his finds to C. H. Read and urged 'the Natal authorities to locate his sites and collections'. Neither he, nor later reviewers of the prehistory of KwaZulu-Natal (e.g. Vinnicombe 1976; Cable 1984), were able to do this, yet over 200 of the artefacts from this site have remained in the British Museum's Christy Collection since being given to Read (the then Keeper of British and Medieval Antiquities and Ethnography) in 1905. Their analysis, as part of this project, confirms Goodwin's suspicion that a Middle Stone Age assemblage was present at the site, but also suggests the presence of a Later Stone Age occupation both across the Pleistocene/Holocene boundary and during the mid/late Holocene, as well as of a Howieson's Poort occurrence. Though small, the surviving Bazley collection is sufficient to confirm the importance of the site and to justify a further search to relocate it. No shelter with such a long, complex and potentially informative cultural sequence is known elsewhere along the 750 km of South Africa's eastern seaboard between Kaplan's (1990) excavations at Umhlatuzana near Pietermaritzburg and Klasies River Mouth, with its early anatomically modern humans of Last Interglacial Age (H. J. Deacon 1989, 1995).

4. Terminology and Typology

1. Terminology

The historical development of Stone Age terminologies in southern Africa

Although various attempts, often influenced by prior European studies, were made in the late 19th and early 20th centuries to classify Stone Age artefact assemblages from southern Africa, the terminology in use today has its roots in the work of Goodwin and Van Riet Lowe (1929). The origins of their system and the transformations that it has undergone since, as well as the factors, theoretical and logistical, that contributed to these developments have been well reviewed by several recent authors (e.g. Parkington 1984; J. Deacon 1990a) and require little comment here. This section is therefore restricted to a largely descriptive treatment that relates present day terms to those of the older literature.

Southern Africa's own 'Three Age System', as it might fairly be called, was developed by Goodwin when, invited to bring order to the collections of the South African Museum in Cape Town, he was seized by 'the absolute necessity for evolving an entirely new cultural terminology' (Goodwin 1958: 25). This he achieved by placing artefacts into typological groups, identifying recurrent assemblages believed to be of cultural significance from the repeated co-occurrence of particular artefact types and dating them by degree of patination and all too rare stratigraphic information (J. Deacon 1990a: 43). Basing himself on collaboration with other workers, particularly Van Riet Lowe, whose primary field of expertise lay in the Orange Free State and Transvaal, rather than the sites of the Cape Fold Mountain Belt and its coastal forelands, Goodwin was led to propose a division into Earlier (or Early) and Later Stone Ages. The Earlier Stone Age was represented by what was then known as the Stellenbosch Culture, regarded as equivalent to the Acheulean or Lower Palaeolithic of Europe. The Later Stone Age, in which two industries, the Wilton and the Smithfield, were identified, was thought similar to the Middle and Upper Palaeolithic and Mesolithic of Europe (J. Deacon 1990a: 44). This scheme won general acceptance at the 1926 meeting of the South African Association for the Advancement of Science (Goodwin 1926b), but received a much fuller exposition in *The Stone Age Cultures of South Africa*, which Goodwin and Van Riet Lowe (1929) co-authored three years later. In this monograph, the term Middle Stone Age (**Fig. 6**), the third of the 'Three Ages', was introduced to designate assemblages distinguished by having triangular flakes with convergent dorsal scars and faceted butts.

Sub-divisions of the Early, Middle and Later Stone Ages were initially few, but in the 1930s and 1940s a plethora of industries and their variants were identified, particularly in the case of the Later Stone Age (LSA). Parkington (1984) has reviewed these terms for the LSA and has shown how they in part reflect the problems of dealing with the influence of raw material on assemblage composition and appearance. Other factors considered at the time were the respective rôles of temporal variation within individual industries (notably Goodwin's (1938) analysis of the sequence at Oakhurst Shelter) and of differential activity performance (e.g. the specialization in wood-working thought by Van Riet Lowe (1936) to lie behind the large numbers of notched scrapers found in Smithfield assemblages in KwaZulu-Natal). None of the terms developed during this period, however, remain current today. The same is true of the various sub-divisions recognised previously for the Middle Stone Age (MSA), with the exception of the Howieson's Poort, a term extended by Goodwin (1929) from the type-site in the Eastern Cape Province to include material from several surface sites (and later also from rock-shelters) in the Western Cape (Sampson 1974: 232). Recognised through the presence of relatively high frequencies of backed pieces, including segments that resemble those of the Wilton, smaller flakes and flake-blades and finer-grained raw materials, the **Howieson's Poort** remains a widely recognised sub-division of the southern African MSA (**Fig. 7**).

With the expansion of archaeological research in the 1930s and again after the Second World War, it began to be recognised that Goodwin and Van Riet Lowe's (1929) threefold basic division of the southern African Stone Age could not readily accommodate cultures thought to be transitional between the 'Ages' that it identified. In response to this feeling, the Third Pan-African Congress on Prehistory, which met in Livingstone, Zambia, in 1955, created two intermediate periods - the First Intermediate connecting the Early and Middle Stone Ages, the Second Intermediate linking the Middle and Later Stone Ages. The First Intermediate included the **Fauresmith Industry**, named from a type site in the Free State from which the British Museum has material, which combines bifacially worked handaxes and cleavers with a range of scrapers, prepared cores and long blades. Fauresmith assemblages were recognised across most of South Africa and in Lesotho (Clark 1959: 147-149). The term Sangoan was employed to refer to a roughly contemporary industry, containing large numbers of picks and core-axes, north of the Limpopo River (Sampson 1974: 107), with the **Charaman** recognised as a late expression of this in Zimbabwe, e.g. at the base of the Bambata Cave sequence (Cooke 1966).

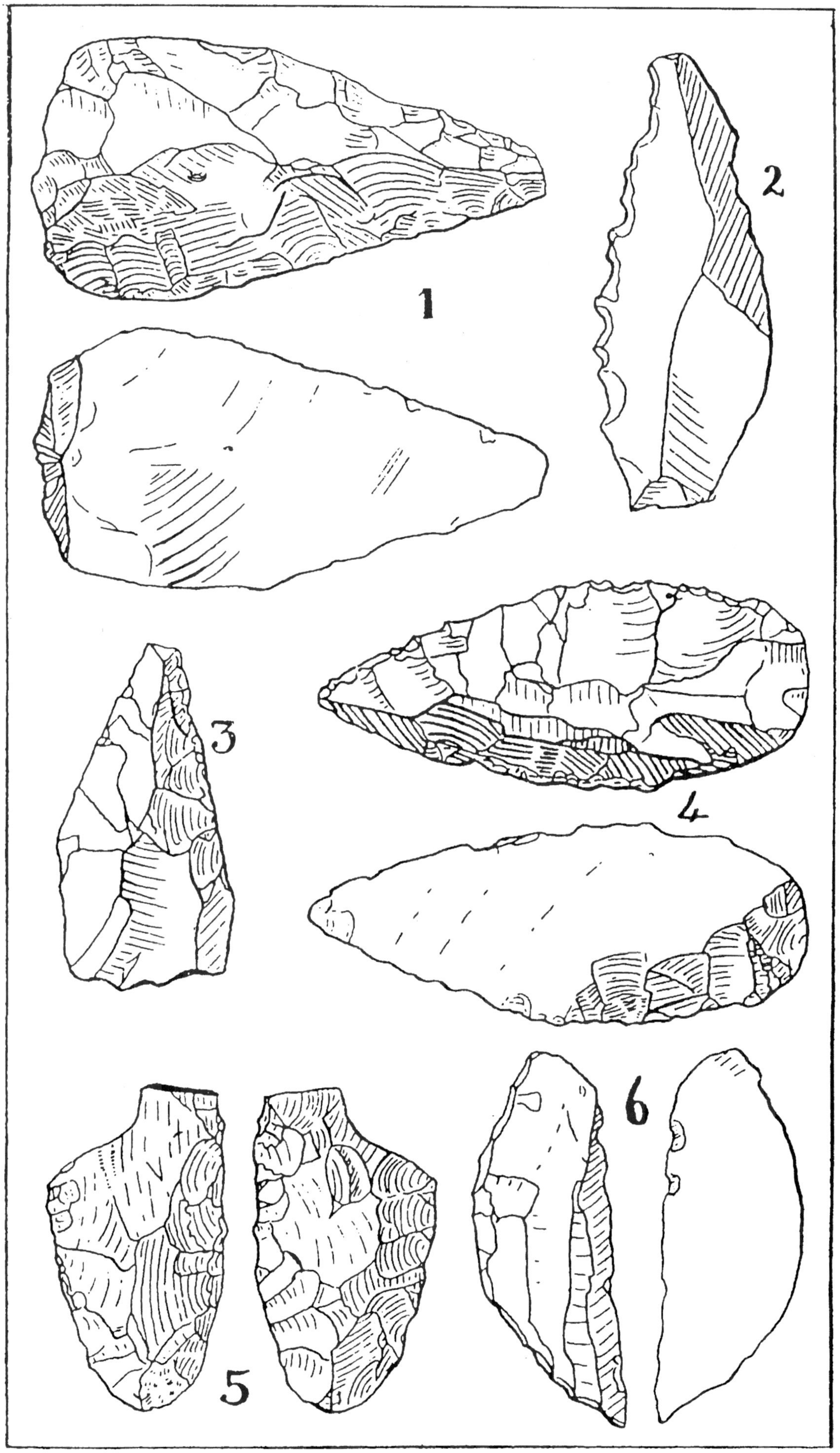

Fig. 6. Middle Stone Age unifacial points and flake-blades (after Goodwin & Van Riet Lowe 1929: 121-from Maitland, Stillbay and Fish Hoek).

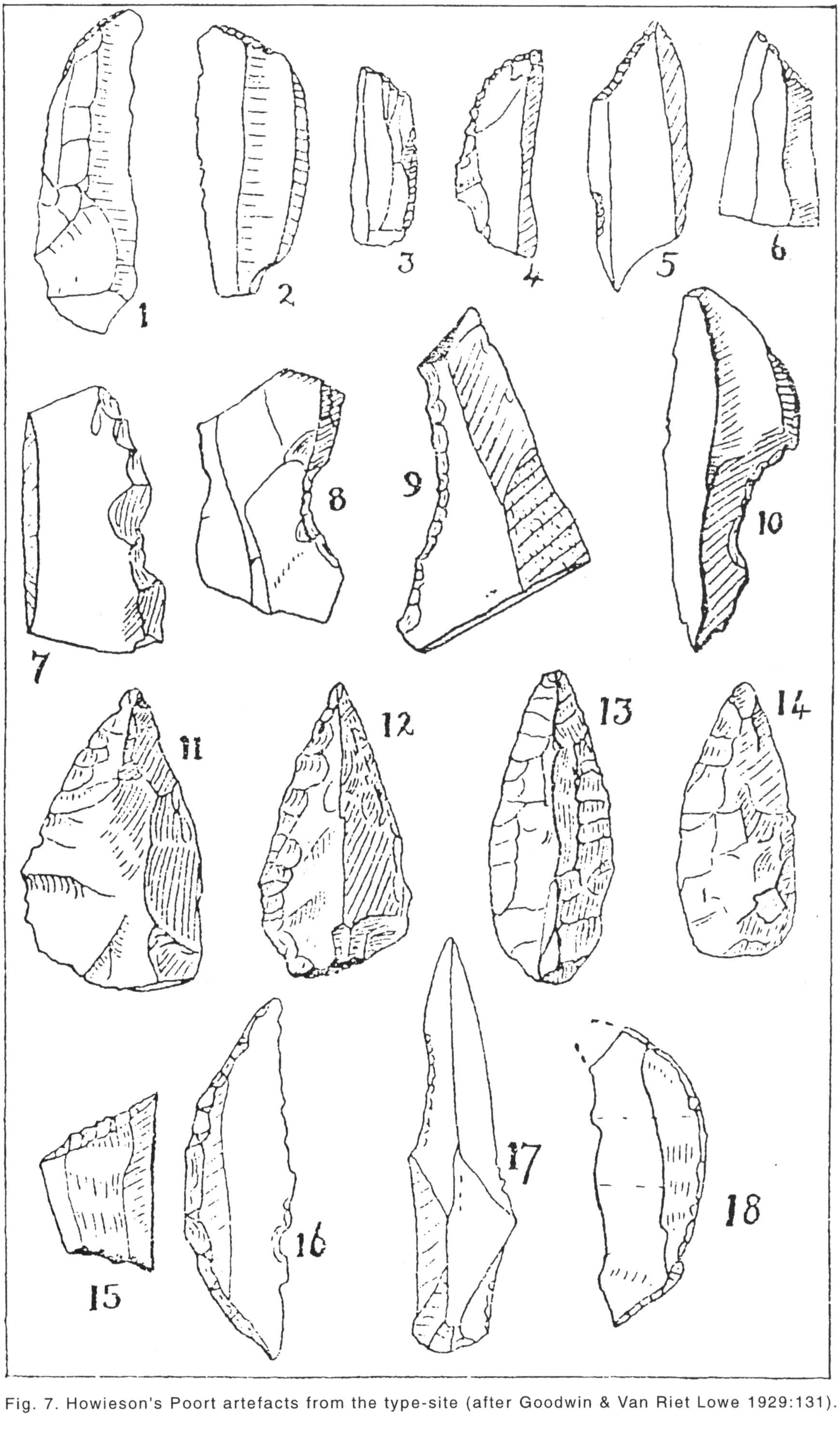

Fig. 7. Howieson's Poort artefacts from the type-site (after Goodwin & Van Riet Lowe 1929:131).

Although the terms Fauresmith (Beaumont & Morris 1990) and Sangoan (McBrearty 1988) remain in use to describe geographically quite widespread industrial traditions that do indeed appear to show features transitional between Early and Middle Stone Age lithic technologies, the Second Intermediate has completely fallen by the wayside. The term **Magosian,** widely used from the 1930s to the 1960s to describe assemblages of the Second Intermediate Period that combined prepared core techniques with small blades and backed tools, was jettisoned when it was realised that the type site and many other assemblages were mixed surface collections or came from stratigraphically disturbed contexts in rock shelter excavations (Sampson 1974: 236). Within southern Africa recent work by Walker (1980) in Zimbabwe has shown that the same is true of the so-called Tshangulan assemblages, which display a similar combination of MSA flaking technology and backed microliths. Further south, the supposedly Magosian sequence at Rose Cottage Cave in the eastern Free State has turned out to encompass several successive MSA occurrences, only one of which - described as Howieson's Poort - features large numbers of backed pieces (Wadley & Harper 1989). The Howieson's Poort alone survives as a useful term and, although Parkington (1991) has questioned whether everything described as Howieson's Poort really forms part of the same entity, it is clear from excavations at sites such as Klasies River Mouth (Singer & Wymer 1982; H. J. Deacon & Geleijnse 1988) and Border Cave (Beaumont *et al.* 1978) that Howieson's Poort assemblages occur sandwiched within the overall Upper Pleistocene Middle Stone Age sequence.

As one of the results of a conference of Africanist archaeologists held at Burg-Wartenstein in Austria in 1965, far-reaching suggestions were made to improve the cultural systematics of the African Stone Age (Bishop & Clark 1967), in part because of the wild abandon with which terms such as 'Wilton' had been applied as far from South Africa as Somalia and Kenya (Inskeep 1967). The Burg-Wartenstein Conference proposed that **archaeological occurrences** be grouped into **phases**, that might be either temporal or spatial in nature, and that these phases in turn should be grouped into **industries** and then **industrial complexes**. These proposals have been less than wholly successful, in part because the entities were not clearly enough defined, and in part because underlying assumptions remained unchallenged. In particular privileging stone tools at the expense of other datasets and expecting that all aspects of a cultural system will be equally represented at all sites have proven problematic.

Garth Sampson (1972) presented the results of his extensive excavation and survey work along the middle Gariep River Valley within the format laid down at Burg-Wartenstein, and subsequently produced a synthesis of southern African Stone Age archaeology along the same lines (Sampson 1974). With this one exception, however, the last three decades of archaeological research have tended to eschew the formal definition or proliferation of taxonomic schemes in favour of questioning the assumptions to which reference has just been made. Instead of emphasizing the details of lithic typology, H. J. Deacon (1972, 1976) developed a model of the southern Cape LSA in which patterning among assemblages, linked to distinctive patterns of food wastes in archaeological sites, was viewed as reflecting subsistence and settlement strategies, albeit that broad correlations with stone artefact sequences were also apparent (J. Deacon 1984a). Other studies, notably by Mazel & Parkington (1981), Carter (1978) and Cable (1984) have stressed the influence of seasonal mobility on assemblage composition, developing Van Riet Lowe's (1938) and Clark's (1958) earlier insights into the importance of spatial variability in the activities performed at different points on the landscape. More recently, and as part of an overall shift from an ecological paradigm that emphasized people-to-nature research questions toward one that is much more centrally concerned with people-to-people topics of social relations and ideology (J. Deacon 1990a), there has been renewed interest in attempts to isolate identity-conscious prehistoric communities from variation in the spatial patterning of material culture items (e.g. Sampson 1988; Mazel 1989; Binneman 1994a). Going still further, Lewis-Williams (1993) has powerfully urged the wholesale abandonment of lithocentric terminologies of any kind in favour of a periodization and organization of our data that stresses changing patterns of social relations. The implications of his critique have still to be fully taken on board by southern African archaeologists, but will doubtless be an important source of debate in future years.

Current terminologies for the southern African Early and Middle Stone Ages

As Volman remarks, it is possible to identify only broad, poorly distinguishable divisions within the timespan of the Early Stone Age, which covers more than a million years. Older developmental schemes suggesting progressive refinement in the production of handaxes and other artefacts can no longer be sustained (Sampson 1974), but the rarity of *in situ* assemblages and firm dating controls hinders any attempt to assess or understand assemblage variability on anything more than the grossest level. Volman (1984: 180), indeed, distinguishes only between a Lower and an Upper Acheulean for the period 1.6 to 0.2 million years ago, with older artefacts from excavations in Member 5 at Sterkfontein and Member 1 at Swartkrans comparable to the Oldowan/Developed Oldowan assemblages of East Africa. He notes, however, that no clearcut typological differences have been demonstrated between the Lower and Upper Acheulean and that a 'chronological boundary at about one million years ago may prove more satisfactory' (Volman 1984: 181). For this reason no sub-division of the Acheulean has been attempted in the present Catalogue. The term 'Fauresmith' has, nevertheless, been retained, following Beaumont & Morris (1990: 4-5) to refer to those very late Acheulean assemblages that include some use of parallel-sided and convergent flake-blades and Levallois prepared core technology; as they point out (*pace* Humphreys 1972b) such artefacts are found in a range of raw materials and are not merely the consequence of the exploitation of horfnels in order to make stone tools. Dating is extremely tentative, but somewhere within the range 250,000 - 190,000 years ago is likely (Beaumont & Morris 1990: 5).

Current practice in discussion of the southern African Middle Stone Age, as illustrated by Thackeray's (1991) recent survey, is to follow the terminology devised by Volman (1981), who has produced the most thorough reassessment. Volman identified four successive temporal subdivisions - MSA 1, MSA 2, Howieson's Poort and MSA 3 (Table 5) - based largely on the sequence from Klasies River Mouth, although he still found it necessary to describe his scheme as 'informal', given the variability that characterizes the MSA and the difficulties of dating, and thus correctly correlating, individual sequences and assemblages. Even in the case of the Howieson's Poort, it is by no means clear that all assemblages assigned to this group on the basis of enhanced frequencies of backed pieces, fine-grained raw material use or smaller artefacts, do genuinely belong together (Parkington 1991).

Volman (1984: 207) himself emphasized that the assemblages he grouped together as MSA 3 share little in common, other than their presumed or definite post-Howieson's Poort age. Indeed, the suspicion exists that during the period 25 - 60,000 BP quite different cultural trajectories may have been followed in different parts of the sub-continent. There are indications, for example, that in the Boomplaas sequence from the Cape Fold Mountain Belt large flake-blades and points of 'classic' MSA form continued in use until some time after 32,400 BP (H. J. Deacon 1995). In the Lesotho highlands, on the other hand, there appears to be a stronger case for a gradual shift in patterns of raw material usage and towards the production of more clearly microlithic assemblages (Parkington 1991), even though MSA formal tools continued to be produced as late as the beginning of Oxygen Isotope Stage 2 at some sites (Opperman & Heydenrych 1990; Mitchell 1994b). Despite these differences, problems of chronological control as the radiocarbon barrier is approached and the paucity of well-published, large assemblages for study have so far precluded the recognition of regional industries or industrial phases within the MSA 3. This is to be regretted as more tightly defined spatio-temporal patterning in lithic traditions seems, at least in some parts of the Old World, to be associated with the development during the timespan of the MSA 3 of more modern forms of cultural behaviour (Mellars & Stringer 1989; Mellars 1991).

Current terminology for the southern African Later Stone Age

The most recent general survey of the southern African Later Stone Age as a whole is that produced by J. Deacon in 1984, although Wadley (1993) has discussed the Pleistocene LSA south of the Limpopo and Mitchell (1997) discusses the Holocene LSA in the same region between 10,000 and 2000 BP; more regionally focused summaries are *de rigueur* in many doctoral theses (e.g. Mazel 1989; S. Hall 1990; Bousman 1991). J. Deacon (1984b) has divided the LSA into four broad units that have proved to be of general heuristic value as a means of organizing the various industries of the last 20 - 25,000 and more years: late Pleistocene early microlithic, terminal Pleistocene/early Holocene non-microlithic, Holocene microlithic and late Holocene with pottery. These divisions are followed here (Table 6).

Within J. Deacon's (1984b) category of Pleistocene early microlithic assemblages a primary distinction can be drawn between assemblages marked by a heavy investment in the specialized production of unretouched bladelets and those that lack even this degree of formality. The first of these groups is generally referred to as **Robberg** (in the Western and Eastern Cape) or **Robberg-like** (in the remainder of South Africa, Lesotho and Swaziland) and is associated with radiocarbon dates of between 19 000 and 12, 000 BP (J. Deacon 1984b; Mitchell 1995). The interaction network suggested by the strong bladelet emphasis common to all Robberg assemblages and such features as identically ornamented bone beads from sites as far apart as Mpumalanga and the Western Cape Province (Wadley 1993) does not seem to have extended significantly north of the Limpopo or Gariep Rivers. Contemporary assemblages in Namibia, Zimbabwe and Botswana are highly informal, indeed not even markedly microlithic in the case of those from sites such as Apollo 11 Cave and Pockenbank 1 (Wendt 1972; J. Deacon 1984b), though more bladelet-rich assemblages are reported from Mashonaland (Walker & Wadley 1984) and the Tsodilo Hills (Robbins *et al.* 1996).

Predating the Robberg at several sites in South Africa and Lesotho are informal microlithic assemblages that lack its characteristic bladelet cores and large numbers of unretouched bladelets. These assemblages do, however, clearly belong within the LSA as it is generally defined: witness, for example, the presence of bone points and ostrich eggshell beads in the LP and LPC layers at Boomplaas Cave (J. Deacon 1990b; H. J. Deacon 1995). The term **'Early Later Stone Age'**, often abbreviated to 'ELSA', has come into general use to describe such occurrences, following its invention by Beaumont and Vogel (1972). However, this has proven contentious, with the so-called ELSA assemblage from Rose Cottage Cave turning out to be a composite of several LSA occurences of different ages (Wadley 1991) and that from Border Cave, effectively the type-site for the concept, perhaps more appropriately considered to be transitional between MSA and LSA stone-working technologies (Mitchell 1988; Barham 1990). Though there certainly is a degree of unity between at least some bladelet-poor, early microlithic assemblages of pre-19,000 BP age, the extent to which it is still useful, rather than confusing, to refer to them as 'ELSA' is open to question (Wadley 1991). The cultural systematics of the earlier part of the Pleistocene LSA is consequently a continued topic for debate, a discussion tied up with explanations for the transition from MSA to microlithic stone-working traditions and for the appearance in the archaeological record of a whole range of new kinds of material evidence, such as art, personal ornament, bone tools etc. (J. Deacon 1990b; Mitchell 1994b).

Goodwin and Van Riet Lowe (1929) did not have the data to hand that might have suggested to them that the LSA extended back into the Pleistocene. However, the basic distinctions that they were able to draw within the material known to them have largely withstood the test of time and continue to form the basis for our structuring of post 12,000 BP LSA assemblages. Broadly speaking, three divisions are now recognised. The oldest of these, referred to either as late Pleistocene/early Holocene non-microlithic assemblages (J. Deacon 1984b) or, more commonly, as the **Oakhurst** Complex (after Sampson 1974), is broadly equivalent to Goodwin and Van Riet Lowe's (1929) Smithfield A assemblages. Important characteristics are a general preference for coarser-grained raw materials and/or those that occur as larger preforms, a tendency for both flakes and scrapers to be longer and broader than either before or afterward and an overall low frequency of formally retouched artefacts. Associated with many of these assemblages, which are largely bracketed between about 12,000 and 7/8,000 BP, are increased frequencies of items such as worked bone and ostrich eggshell beads. In some parts of the sub-continent regional industries are recognised within the Oakhurst Complex: the **Albany** in the coastal forelands of the Eastern and Western Cape, the **Lockshoek** in the Karoo and along the central portions of the Gariep River Valley, the **Pomongwan** in southwestern Zimbabwe (Sampson 1974) and the **Kuruman** in the Northern Cape (Humphreys & Thackeray 1983). Elsewhere (e.g. in the Magaliesberg Mountains - Wadley (1987)) the more general terms **Oakhurst** or **Oakhurst-like** are used. In areas such as Lesotho there is, from about the late tenth millennium BP, a marked increase in formal tool frequency associated with the appearance of highly distinctive end-retouched scrapers that also have adze-like retouch and/or less extensive trimming along their lateral margins (**Fig. 8**). To distinguish such assemblages from older Oakhurst occurrences that consistently lack these features, the term **'later Oakhurst'** has been informally used (Mitchell 1994a; 1996).

Of the two LSA industries recognised by Goodwin and Van Riet Lowe (1929) it is the **Wilton** that has survived least changed from its original formulation. Assemblages featuring large numbers of small, often thumbnail-shaped scrapers and backed segments (**Figs. 9 and 10**) are found throughout the sub-continent during the middle Holocene, though with a marked geographical cline in their first date of appearance. Janette Deacon (1984b: 249) suggests that this pattern shows that the new industrial tradition developed initially in Namibia and Zimbabwe, for reasons as yet unknown. Its gradual southward spread, appearing south of the Gariep after 7500 BP, is not inconsistent with some kind of diffusionary process, though the details of this remain obscure. Assemblages attributed to the Wilton Complex are found in the same areas as the Oakhurst, but, with the exception of Sampson's (1974) recognition of separate coastal and interior industries, no regional sub-divisions are in common use. More generally employed, is Sampson's (1974) term **'Post- classic Wilton'**, which has emerged as a useful summary term for assemblages that, while clearly forming part of the same tradition as the Classic segment-rich Wilton of the middle Holocene, see segments effectively replaced by other kinds of backed microliths, shifts in scraper morphology and increased use of adzes. Areas in which this term has seemed particularly useful include Gauteng (Wadley 1987), the eastern Free State (Wadley 1996) and Lesotho (Mitchell *et al.* 1994).

Pottery was added to most Stone Age traditions in southern Africa at one or other time during the last two millennia BP, with recent work in both southwestern and southeastern southern Africa raising the possibility that its adoption may have predated the local adoption or introduction of elements of food-production (Mazel 1992a; Sealy & Yates 1994; *cf.* Henshilwood 1996). As a consequence, microlithic assemblages from this period are often referred to as **Ceramic Wilton** (Sampson 1974) or **Post-classic Wilton with pottery** (e.g. Wadley 1991). Local variants of this phenomenon in the Northern Cape Province have been designated the **Swartkops** and **Doornfontein** Industries (Beaumont *et al.* 1995), the former with high frequencies of backed blades and coarse, undecorated, commonly grass-tempered ceramics, the latter with a high incidence of quartz, few formal tools and thin-walled, sometimes decorated pottery.

No longer in use for the Lockshoek Industry (the former Smithfield A) or the Post-classic Wilton assemblages of the Caledon Valley and KwaZulu-Natal (the former Smithfield C and N), the term **Smithfield** is used today only with specific reference to a series of late Holocene assemblages from South Africa's interior plateau. Best known from Sampson's (1972, 1985) work along the middle stretch of the Gariep River and in the Seacow Valley, these assemblages are characterised by endstruck scrapers larger than those found in earlier Wilton occurrences in the same area and by highly distinctive ceramics that emphasize the use of a variety of impressed decoration techniques and a grass-tempered fabric (Sampson 1988). Associated dates begin as early as *c.* 600 BP and Smithfield assemblages continued to be made into the 19th century by the last hunter-gatherer groups to inhabit the Karoo, with recent work increasingly showing the complex variability in material culture that marked this area over the last few hundred years (e.g. Sampson & Vogel 1995; Bollong & Sampson 1996).

In Zimbabwe Walker (1995) has recently revised previous terminologies for the Later Stone Age, drawing largely upon the results of his fieldwork in the Matopo Hills. He notes that in many cases the industries previously recognised by Cooke (1975) and by Cooke *et al.* (1966) were defined without critical examination of the material from their supposed type-sites and that these were, in any case, often unsealed surface scatters or excavations with poor stratigraphic controls. A serious lack of dating and a failure to consider the possibility of variability in assemblage composition between sites belonging to the same, contemporaneous cultural group are additional problems, most obviously in Cooke's (1979) study of the Later Stone Age of Mashonaland. Walker's re-excavation of sites such as Pomongwe Cave and reanalysis of older collections has shown that the so-called 'Tshangulan Industry' (Cooke 1963), once thought to be a late example of a basically Middle Stone Age technology that had taken on such LSA innovations as bored stones and worked bone, is the result of stratigraphic mixing. However, some degree of core preparation and production of prepared points may

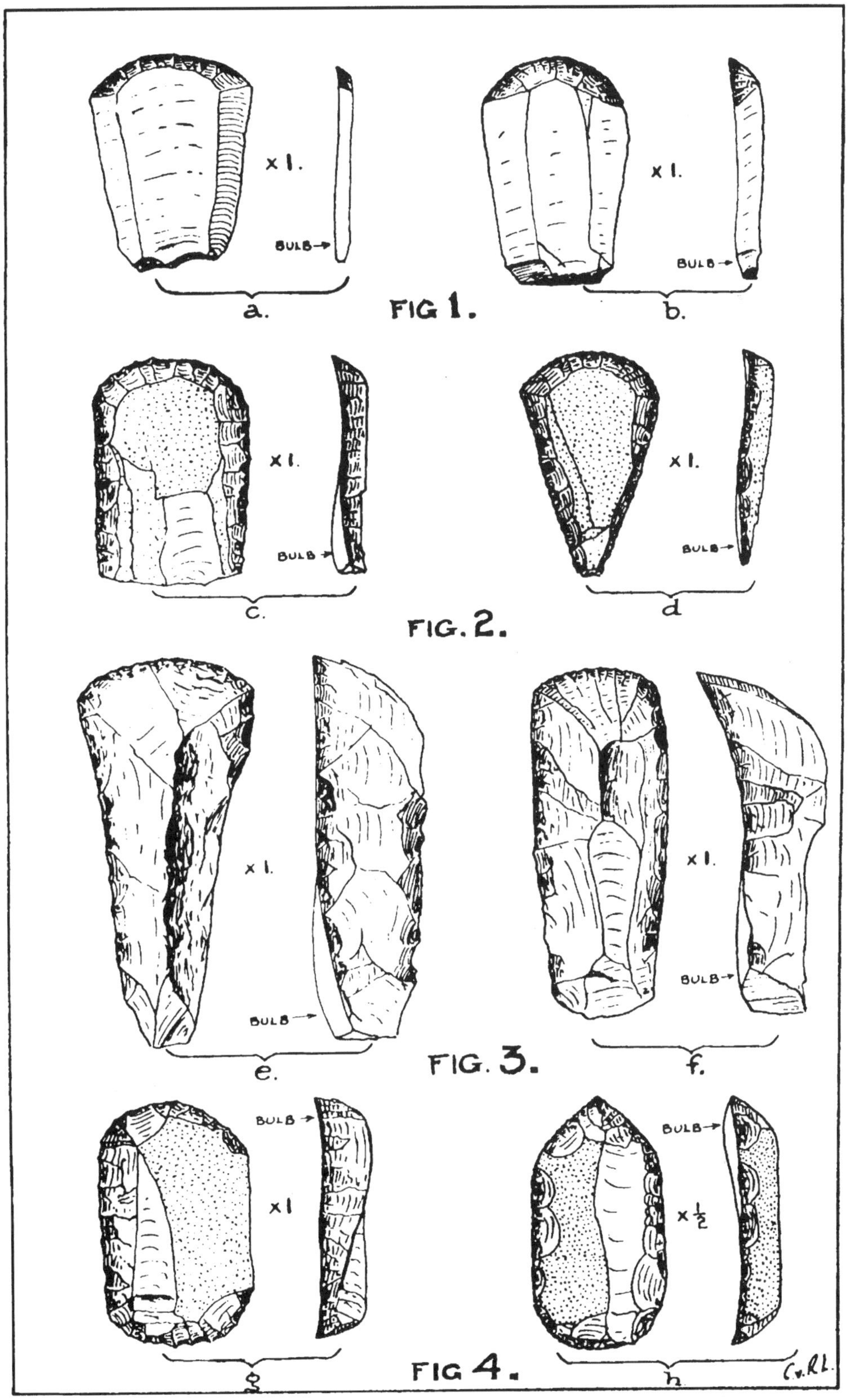

Fig. 8. Duckbill scrapers typical of the later stages of the Oakfield Complex (after Goodwin & Van Riet Lowe 1929:Plate XXV).

be genuinely associated with the late Pleistocene Maleme Industry of 12-13,000 BP at Cave of Bees and Pomongwe (Walker 1995: 204 cf. Walker 1995: 151).

The Holocene prehistory of the Matopos is characterized by four successive industries, now termed Pomongwe, Nswatugi, Amadzimba and Ceramic Matopan, though these stages 'are probably no more than artificial segments of a continuum' (Walker 1995: 99). The Pomongwe Industry has few backed tools and scrapers of larger average size relative to its successors and with dates ranging between 9400 and 11,000 BP crosscuts the Pleistocene-Holocene boundary (Walker 1995: 73); relative to earlier assemblages, a wide range of worked bone artefacts is found in Pomongwe assemblages. The Nswatugi

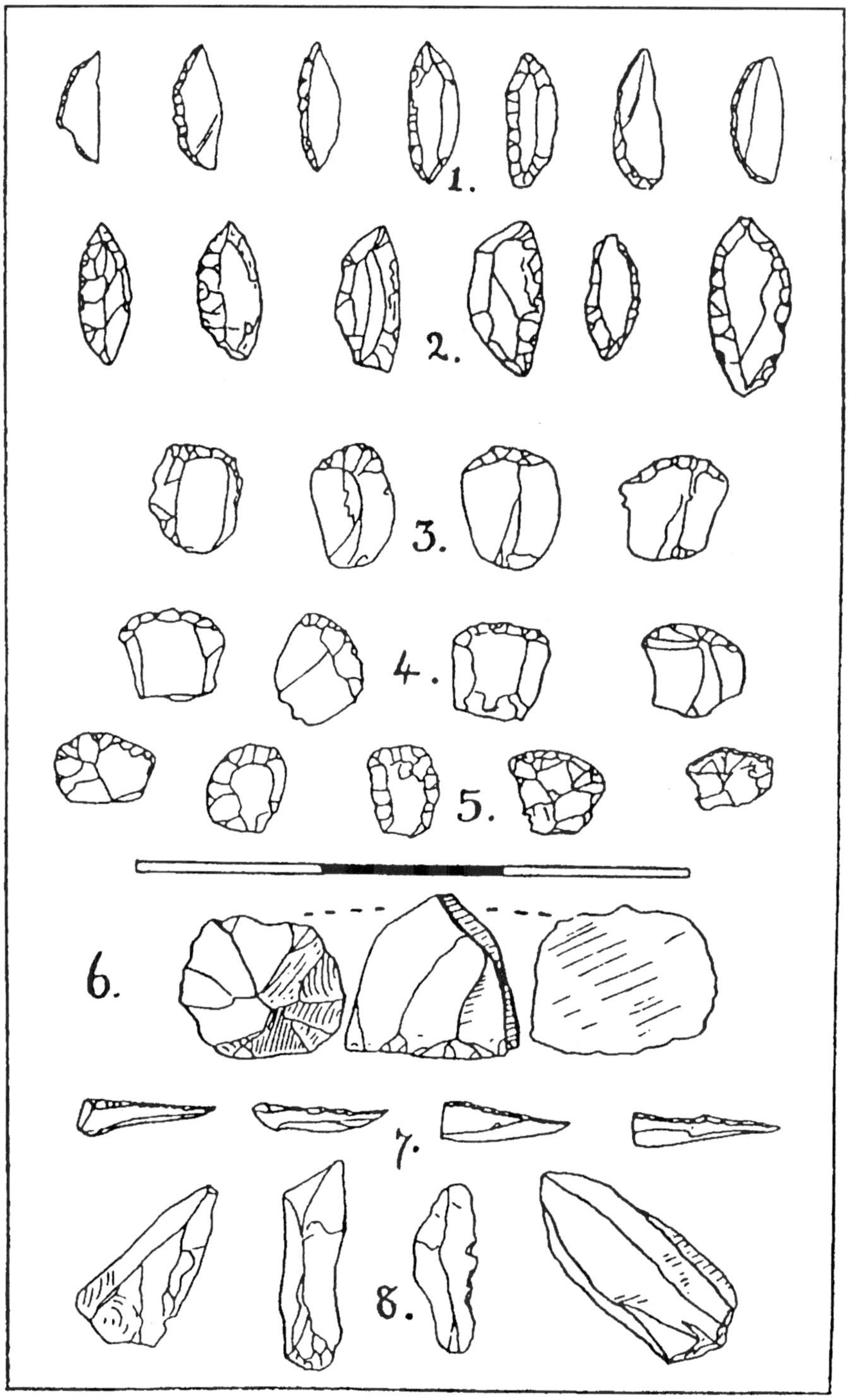

Fig. 9. Wilton Industry backed microliths,scrapers,cores,borers and unmodified flakes from the Cape Flats (after Goodwin & Van Riet Lowe 1929:Plate XLI).

Industry (formerly Khami, Matopan or Wilton) exhibits a marked increase in backed tool frequencies and a reduction in scraper size, with several subdivisions recognised between 6500 and 9500 BP. From about 4800 BP Walker identifies an Amadzimba Industry marked by changes in raw material usage, backed tool frequencies and the innovation or increased use of a wide range of bone and shell artefacts. The final phase of the Later Stone Age in the Matopo Hills is associated with the introduction of pottery after c. 2150 BP. Though these ceramics are generally referred to as Bambata ware after the first site at which they were discovered, Walker (1995: 205) has urged that this be replaced by the term Gwanda ware after the Zimbabwean district in which it is mostly found, with the associated industry as a whole termed 'Ceramic Matopan'. Though his point in doing this is to avoid terminological confusion with the Middle Stone Age Bambata Industry, it is as yet too early to know whether his suggestions will become widely used. Associated with the spread into southern Africa of domestic small stock, the Ceramic Matopan, and thus archaeological evidence for the presence of foragers in the Matopo Hills, appears to come

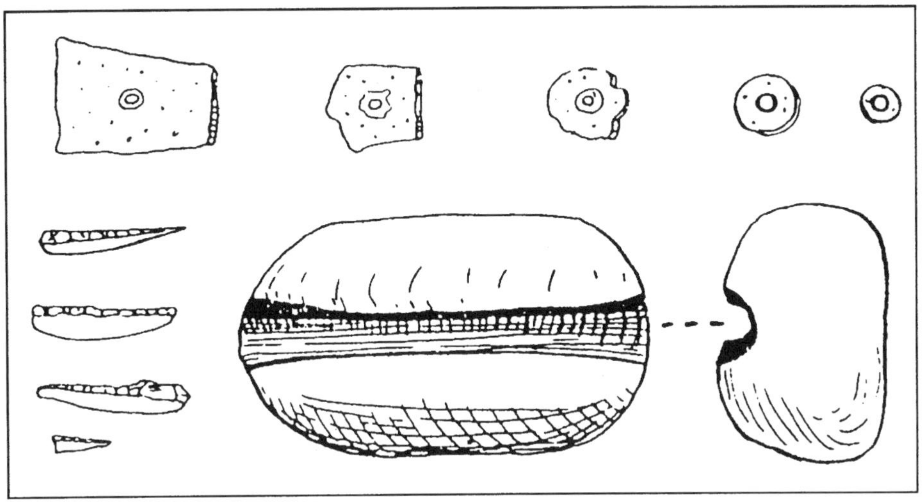

Fig. 10. Wilton Industry ostrich eggshell beads, borers and a grooved stone (after Goodwin & Van Riet Lowe 1929:269).

to an abrupt end *c.* 1500 BP, consequent upon the establishment of iron-using, agropastoralist communities in the region (Walker 1995: 205).

The relative lack of Stone Age archaeological research in other parts of Zimbabwe makes it difficult to know how far this Matopo Hills sequence is valid elsewhere, particularly given the abrupt breaks in occupation evident at Diana's Vow Shelter in Mashonaland (Cooke 1979) and in field survey results from the Zimbabwean lowveld (Walker in press a). The presence of a microlithic Pleistocene LSA assemblage at Duncombe Farm in Mashonaland (Walker & Wadley 1984) is one among several hints of inter-regional variability that remain to be explored. In general, however, the Matopos sequence, though also associated with parts of southern Africa lying to its north, has stronger similarities than they do with Africa south of the Limpopo (Walker 1995: 254). Thus, the Pomongwe can be considered a northerly expression of the Oakhurst Complex and the Nswatugi of the Wilton, while the Amadzimba and Ceramic Matopan parallel post-classic Wilton assemblages with and without pottery respectively.

In general, current practice among most southern African researchers is to employ specific names only for the highest order entities that they recognise among the Stone Age artefact assemblages of the sub-continent. Even for the Holocene, when the archaeological record is at its richest and dating controls at their most precise, most regional syntheses make reference to no more than three, perhaps four, designations (Oakhurst, Wilton, Post-classic Wilton, Smithfield). Indeed, some projects, such as those of Parkington and his co-workers in the Western Cape Province (Parkington & Hall 1987) or Mazel (1989) in the Thukela Basin of KwaZulu-Natal, have striven to avoid using industry or industrial complex names at all. On the one hand this has the effect of signalling a difference in priority from the traditional concerns of space-time systematics and a conscious shift to investigating issues of ecological, social and ideological change, a shift that is the defining feature of southern African archaeology over the last three decades. On the other, it indicates the rejection of a transformationalist, punctuated equilibrium view of societal change in favour of a model that views change as something much more continuous and accumulative (Parkington 1980).

Linked to these attempts to develop a more narrative approach to prehistory (Parkington 1993) has been a concern in some studies for the detailed investigation of spatial patterning in material culture. Identification of prehistoric alliance networks has, conversely, sometimes favoured the proliferation of regionally specific names for the phenomena under discussion, whether these are the **Ndaka**, **Toleni** and **Injasuthi** 'social regions' that Mazel (1989) identifies in the later Holocene of the Thukela Basin, or the **Kabeljous** and **Wilton** industries recognised by Binneman (1994b) along the western coastlands of the Eastern Cape Province. The tension between these two goals promises to produce further changes in Stone Age cultural systematics as southern African archaeologists increasingly grapple with both social issues and the effects on their data of varying levels of spatio-temporal resolution (Mitchell *et al.* 1996).

2. Typology

At the present time southern African researchers tend to analyse Early, Middle and Later Stone Age stone artefact assemblages using separate typologies as a reflection of what are perceived to be quite different ways of reducing and using stone (J. Deacon 1984a: 221). Although this practice is open to the criticism that it necessarily exacerbates differences between assemblages from each Age, thereby making it difficult, if not impossible, to identify and explain changes in the organizational properties of technological systems (Mitchell 1994b), it is followed here.

Early Stone Age artefacts have been described simply as either handaxes, cleavers or undifferentiated bifaces where they are not simply cores or flakes. Middle Stone Age artefacts have, in general, been described using a simplified version of the typology employed by Volman (1981), while the scheme developed by J. Deacon (1984a) has been used as the basis for the description of Later Stone Age artefacts. In each case these decisions reflect the most common contemporary usage. The accompanying glossary provides definitions of the terms employed here, grouping them according to the artefact classes recognised by J. Deacon (1984a): unmodified, utilised, formally retouched and ground.

Typological glossary of terms related to stone assemblages in Southern Africa

Adze: A flake, or sometimes a pebble, with one or more concave, sometimes straight, working edges shaped by one set of flake scars, as well as by secondary flaking that results from use. Mastic traces show that adzes were used hafted, probably in an end-mounted fashion (J. Deacon 1984a: 391). On some specimens retouch on opposing sides shows that they were sometimes reversed in their mount. Microwear analyses demonstrate that adzes were principally employed in wood-working activities (Binneman & Deacon 1984).

Backed bladelet: A bladelet that has at least one of its longitudinal edges modified by abrupt backing retouch. Sometimes both lateral edges may be backed. Where the tip of the bladelet is now missing it is not always clear if the artefact was originally a backed bladelet or a borer.

Backed flake: A flake of irregular size and shape that has one or more edges modified by backing retouch.

Backed microlith: In southern Africa the term 'microlith' is employed with reference to any small (generally less than 25 mm long) artefact, e.g. the large numbers of unmodified bladelets characteristic of the late Pleistocene Robberg Industry (Mitchell 1988). Hence, the term **'backed microlith'** is reserved for those flakes or bladelets less than 25 mm in size that have been backed on one or more edges, generally opposite to that which may display evidencc of utilisation. **Backing** refers to the blunting of an edge by abrupt vertical retouch, most commonly by pressing the edge against a hard anvil with either the ventral or the dorsal surface uppermost (J. Deacon 1984a: 388). It seems to have been employed to facilitate the holding of the microlith in a haft.

Backed point: A bladelet that has been backed along one lateral edge, leaving the other one sharp but unmodified, the two edges intersecting to form a point.

Backed scraper: A scraper that has been backed along one edge, generally that opposite to its retouched convex working edge.

Biface/bifacially worked implement: Often used as an imprecise or informal term for a handaxe, this term is employed here to refer to an artefact that resembles a handaxe or cleaver in overall morphology, but that is not clearly one or the other. Such artefacts may be roughouts that were abandoned before completion.

Bifacial point: Middle Stone Age points that have been retouched over a large part or the entirety of both the dorsal and the ventral surface. In at least some cases such retouch was accomplished by pressure-flaking. Further modifications, e.g. the presence of a tang, may have been designed to facilitate hafting, as in one example in the Christy (ex Dale) Collection from the Cape Flats.

Blade: A parallel-sided flake with one or more dorsal ridges and a length at least twice as great as its breadth. Blades are more than 25 mm long.

Blade core: A core with at least one platform from which blades have been struck.

Bladelet: A narrow parallel-sided flake with one or more dorsal ridges and a length at least twice as great as its breadth. Bladelets differ from blades in being no more than 25 mm long.

Bladelet core: A core with at least one platform from which bladelets have been struck.

Bored stone: A pecked and rounded cobble, variable in size, perforated from both sides to form an 'hour-glass' section. Bored stones were used ethnographically as weights for wooden digging sticks in some parts of southern Africa. They are found only in Later Stone Age contexts.

Borer: A bladelet with steep retouch along both lateral edges forming a point at the distal end suitable for boring holes in hide, ostrich eggshell and other materials. Microwear studies have so far only confirmed the first of these functions (Binneman 1982).

Chunk: A piece of stone considered to be the result of human intervention, but lacking the diagnostic features that would permit it to be classified as a core or a flake.

Cleaver: Similar to a handaxe, but with a broad axe-like cutting edge more-or-less at right angles to the long axis. Generally made on large, rectangular flakes, cleavers may be unifacially or bifacially worked.

Core: A piece of stone from which at least three flakes have been systematically removed from one or more clearly defined striking platforms. Several variants are separately defined: bladelet, disc, flat bladelet, irregular, Levallois, radial, Victoria West.

Core-reduced piece: Cores that have been worked so much that they can no longer be flaked. Usually quadrilateral in shape, they have one or more chisel-like striking platforms, often at opposed ends of the core. They differ from flat bladelet cores in that they do not have bladelet removal scars, and from *pièces esquillées* in that their platforms are not crushed. Core-reduced pieces show clear evidence of having been produced using a bipolar flaking technique and are thus most common where quartz or small-sized nodules of opaline were favoured as raw materials.

Core rejuvenation flake: A flake detached from one end of a core in order to remove an old, exhausted platform and simultaneously form a new one. Core-rejuvenation flakes may bear traces of the negative flake-scars struck from the old platform.

Core tablet: The flake produced as a result of rejuvenating an old platform by striking a blow at one end of the original platform to remove a wedge-shaped tablet and thus obtain a new striking platform immediately below the first.

Crested blade flake (*lame à crête*): An elongated blade or flake with a single dorsal ridge and triangular cross-section deriving from the initial stage of preparing the edge of a blade or bladelet core for the subsequent detachment of blades or bladelets. Crested blades often retain a small, bit-like piece of the core from which they were detached, are frequently curved and resemble burin-spalls. Flake scar remnants originate from the sinuous central ridge, rather than the edges of the artefact.

Disc core: A core in which flakes have been removed from around the perimeter of a piece of stone that has previously been prepared through repeated flaking of the perimeter to create a suitably acute platform angle.

Distal section: A broken fraction of a blade, bladelet or flake-blade that retains its tip, but has lost its butt.

Flake: Artefacts produced by percussion from a core with clear dorsal and ventral surfaces. The dorsal surface has negative flake scars from previous flaking events and/or retains cortex, while the ventral surface is flat and has a bulb of percussion marking the point of impact from the hammer. Unless broken, flakes also have a clear butt.

Flake-blade: A flake that is at least twice as long as it is wide and that has at least one dorsal ridge, but which does not necessarily have strictly parallel sides. The term is commonly employed in the analysis of Middle Stone Age assemblages and subsumes those artefacts that are, on the stricter definition given above, clearly blades.

Flat bladelet core: A specific kind of bladelet core, usually less than 20 mm long, that does not have a flat platform. Instead, the bladelets were removed from a chisel-like end, often employing a bipolar flaking technique. Flat-bladelet cores are thus found most commonly where quartz or small-sized nodules of opaline were favoured as raw materials.

Formal tool/formally retouched: Artefacts in which the working edge and/or other edges have been deliberately retouched to modify their shape to a predetermined and repeated pattern or to produce a desired working edge. Formal tools are more characteristic of Later than of Middle Stone Age assemblages since MSA retouched artefacts show comparatively little standardization of size or morphology.

Grindstone: Abrasive stones with signs of smoothing or pecking from being used as grinding surfaces, generally in the preparation of pigments and/or plant foods (Humphreys & Thackeray 1983: 301). **Lower grindstones** are flat slabs with one or more surfaces either ground smooth into a more-or-less marked hollow or a smoothed area that shows signs of pecking. **Upper grindstones** (or **mullers**) are cobbles with one or more smoothed facets that are the result of being used in the hand for grinding.

Grooved stone: A pebble or small cobble with one or more grooves pecked into its surface that have then been ground smooth. The grooves normally run the full length of the pebble, are seldom more than 10 mm wide and may be either U- or V-shaped in cross-section. Ethnographic data indicate that grooved stones were used for a variety of tasks, including straightening bone arrowpoints and reed or wooden arrowshafts after heat had been applied to the stone, applying poison to arrows and smoothing the edges of ostrich eggshell beads (Clark 1959: 225-226; 246).

Hammerstone: A cobble with pitting that results from its having been used in the hand as a hammer.

Handaxe: An elongated, often pear-shaped or triangular artefact terminating in a point that has a cutting edge on either side. The butt end, opposite to the point, may be left rounded and untrimmed. Handaxes are either made on large flakes or on cores and are generally worked on both faces. Handaxes were probably general purpose, hand-held tools, although experiments suggest that butchery seems likely to have been one important function (P. Jones 1980).

Irregular core: A core in which flakes have been removed from one or more platforms without giving the core any regular shape.

Knife: A particular class of Middle Stone Age retouched artefact, knives exhibit retouch along a straight edge. Two kinds can be distinguished: **unilateral**, where only one edge has been retouched, and **bilateral**, where two (generally opposing) edges have been retouched.

Levallois core: A roughly circular form of prepared core in which the core has first been trimmed so as to permit the detachment of a single flake of predetermined size and shape. One surface of the core is covered with preparation scars which have been truncated by the removal of the Levallois flake (Carter 1978: 142). Often at the point at which the detaching blow has been struck a series of very small flakes has been removed at right angles to the core to provide a **faceted striking platform**, part of which has then come away with the flake. Faceting is common in many Middle Stone Age assemblages and is an additional means of predetermining the size and shape of the flakes produced.

Mesial section: A broken fraction of a blade, bladelet or flake-blade that retains neither its butt nor its tip.

Milled-edge pebble: A small, round and relatively flat pebble the outer perimeter of which has been pitted through use as a hammerstone against a hard material. J. Deacon (1984a: 377) notes that they are generally made in quartzite.

Miscellaneous retouched piece: A term employed for artefacts which show sustained retouch, but cannot readily be accommodated within any of the formal tool classes distinguished by Middle or Later Stone Age typologies.

Naturally backed knife: A term devised by Parkington (1984: 127) to refer to large sidestruck flakes produced on a right-angled core edge such that they retain a natural cortex backing. They are retouched with overlapping step flaking to produced a gently convex edge opposite to the cortical backing. Naturally backed knives are most common in assemblages of terminal Pleistocene/early Holocene age and only rarely occur in materials other than hornfels.

Notched flake or blade: Artefacts showing a particular kind of utilisation in which damage to an edge has been sufficiently sustained for one or more clearly concave notches to form.

Pièce esquillée: *Pièces esquillées* are similar to core-reduced pieces except that their chisel-ended striking platforms exhibit definite signs of crushing. Furthermore, they are often larger than artefacts classified as core-reduced pieces. Although they too are probably exhausted bipolar cores, the crushing appears to be the result of their being used as a wedge to split wood, or perhaps bone, activities confirmed by microwear analysis of examples from Boomplaas Cave in the Western Cape Province (Binneman 1982: 318).

Point: A flake or flake-blade of Middle Stone Age origin that has been retouched on two converging edges to form a point. The term is restricted to retouched artefacts and is *not* used here for flakes or flake-blades which may be similar in overall shape, but remain unretouched. It seems likely that some, perhaps most, points, along with other Middle Stone Age formal tools and artefacts, were hafted in mastic as the cutting parts of composite tools (*cf.* Inskeep 1978: 57-58).

Proximal section: A broken fraction of a blade, bladelet or flake-blade that retains its butt.

Radial core: A core from which flakes have been removed from around the perimeter of a roundish piece of stone.

Scraper: Artefacts, commonly made on flakes or flake-fragments, though other blanks are sometimes used, characterised by a flat ventral surface and by a deliberately retouched convex edge. The convexity of the retouched edge distinguishes them from adzes, points and knives. Southern African archaeologists have differentiated between several different kinds of scraper on grounds of size (e.g. J. Deacon 1984a) and/or morphology (e.g. Sampson 1974). In a general work such as this such distinctions have not been pursued, except to note whether a scraper is also backed, whether it is of thumbnail type (i.e. < 20 mm in width and length and approximately quadrilateral in shape) and whether it does, or does not, have adze-like retouch along one or both lateral edges. Backed scrapers are distinctive of the southern Cape coastlands in the middle to late Holocene, thumbnail scrapers are characteristic of the Wilton Complex and scrapers with adze-like lateral retouch are most typical of the period 7000-9500 BP (J. Deacon 1984b). Microwear analyses demonstrate that scrapers were almost exclusively employed as hide-working tools (Binneman 1982).

Segment: A flake, or part of a bladelet, that has a straight, sharp edge opposite to a curved arc backed by abrupt retouch. In plan, segments are thus comparable to the segments of an orange. Segments, which are characteristic of the mid-Holocene Wilton Industry of the Later Stone Age have traditionally been interpreted as arrow armatures. Microwear analyses, however, demonstrate that they were also mounted (probably in series) as inserts in tools that were employed in the cutting, sawing and whittling of a variety of materials (Binneman 1982; Wadley & Binneman 1994).

Sinker: A small pebble with a groove around its middle to allow its suspension from a piece of string, used to help sink nets and found in coastal sites of mid-to-late Holocene age (J. Deacon 1984a: 400).

Spheroid: A battered and rounded spherical piece of stone, possibly used as a hammerstone.

Unifacial point: Middle Stone Age points that have been retouched over a large part or the entirety of the dorsal surface. In at least some cases such retouch was accomplished by pressure-flaking. Some unifacial points show further modifications, e.g. hollowing out of their base, that would have facilitated hafting (*cf.* Clark 1959: 175).

Unmodified: Artefacts that show no sign of macroscopically visible edge damage or retouch.

Utilised: An adjective used to refer to those artefacts with damage visible to the naked eye that is considered to be the result of the actions and activities in which the artefacts were employed. It must be remembered, however, that microwear studies have repeatedly shown that many artefacts which, from a typological standpoint, are classed as unmodified were clearly employed in a variety of tasks, though without leaving macroscopically visible evidence of this on their edges (Phillipson & Phillipson 1970; Binneman 1982). By convention, grindstones and hammerstones are also generally included within the utilised category.

Victoria West core: A core of proto-Levallois type in which a small boulder was roughed out to a plano-convex form. A striking platform was made by knocking off several flakes from one of the long sides at right angles to the boulder's prepared convex face. A large flake, suitable for making a cleaver or a handaxe, was then removed from the flat face (Clark 1959: 125-126). Such cores are sometimes also referred to as *hoenderbek* cores from the Afrikaans for 'hen's beak'.

3. Raw Materials

In contrast to the dominance of flint in most European Palaeolithic assemblages, southern African people made use of an extremely wide range of raw materials for making stone tools. Their distribution varies widely across southern Africa as a reflection of the sub-continent's complex and varied geology. Clark (1959: 5) still provides what is perhaps the clearest overview of the situation, although it is by no means exhaustive. Broadly speaking, it is possible to distinguish between the following raw material provinces (**Fig. 11**).

1. The Cape Fold Mountain Belt and its coastal forelands

An area where the geology belongs largely to the Cape System, which is of Palaeozoic age. Massive sandstones and quartzites form the basal (Table Mountain Sandstone) series and dominate the scenery since they form the mountains, including Table Mountain itself. The overlying Bokkeveld and Witteberg Series are made up of zones of sandstone and shale and of sandstone, quartzite and shale respectively (Wellington 1955: 21-22). The most common rocks used in manufacturing stone artefacts were **sandstone**, **quartzite** and **silcrete**.

2. The Karoo and most of the highveld outside the Drakensberg and Maluti Mountains.

The geology here, which forms part of the Karoo System, is essentially sedimentary in origin and dates to the late Carboniferous, Permian and Triassic periods. The rocks here consist largely of shales, siltstone-mudstones and sandstones cut through by extensive networks of dolerite dykes and sills (Wellington 1955: 22-5). **Dolerite** and **hornfels** are thus the most common raw materials, although finer-grained **opalines** and other rocks of volcanic origin are available in the *Gariep and Caledon Rivers* which drain the Lesotho highlands.

3. The Drakensberg and Maluti Mountains (including rivers draining from them)

The youngest of the major geological provinces of Africa south of the Limpopo, this area consists of sandstone capped by the Jurassic lavas of the Lesotho Formation, the most recent part of the Karoo System (Wellington 1955: 25). Although **hornfels** and **dolerite** occur where volcanic dykes have passed through older sandstones, the most common raw material, at least as far as Later Stone Age assemblages are concerned, is **opaline**, which derives from pipe amygdales in the Lesotho Formation lavas.

4. The Kalahari

This is an area now largely covered by sands of Tertiary and Quaternary age (Wellington 1955: 28-30) in which **opalines** and **silcrete** were the most commonly used raw materials.

5. The Northern Cape and North West Provinces (outside of areas covered hitherto)

Sandwiched geographically between the Karoo System and the Kalahari sands, this is an area of largely Pre-Cambrian geology in which a variety of rocks were used to make stone artefacts (Humphreys & Thackeray 1983: 17-19). **Chert**, **banded ironstone**, **quartzite**, **lavas**, **sandstone** and **opalines** were all employed.

6. KwaZulu-Natal

The Escarpment and foothills of the Drakensberg Mountains belong to the Karoo System, while older rocks of the Cape System and others of Archaean age are present in the south and midlands of the province; relatively recent Cretaceous, Tertiary and Quaternary rocks are present in much of Zululand and north to the Mozambique border (Burrows 1951: 32-35). Some of the materials used by Stone Age people (**opalines**, **hornfels**) derive from the Drakensberg volcanics, others (e.g. **quartz**, **quartzite** and **silicified limestone**) are native to lower-lying situations.

7. The former Transvaal (Gauteng, Mpumalanga, Northern Province) and Swaziland

Although some areas, such as northern Swaziland and the adjacent Barberton District of Mpumalanga, include ancient granites, gneisses, schistose rocks and others of igneous origin that are of Archaean age, the remainder of this region is largely made up of various Pre-Cambrian systems. Some of these (such as the Witwatersrand System and the Bushveld Igneous Complex) are responsible for much of South Africa's mineral wealth as they contain gold-bearing conglomerates and other economically important metals (Wellington 1955: 12-18). Archaeologically, their significance is that they offered, depending on locality, a wide variety of raw materials, of which **quartz**, **chert** and **lavas** were particularly important.

8. Zimbabwe

Largely consisting of Archaean granites and gneisses, the Zimbabwean Plateau is a region in which **quartz** and **quartzite** were among the most common materials employed by Stone Age people, although **opalines** were important in the *Matopo Hills* of Matabeleland.

9. Angola, Mozambique and Namibia

A glance at the map will show that these countries have quite complex geologies, but the extreme paucity of material from them in the British Museum collections means that detailed discussion of their geological history is unnecessary here.

In keeping with general practice among southern African archaeologists, a minimalist strategy has been followed in the recognition of different lithic raw materials among the artefacts examined in the British Museum collections. In other words, only a few basic categories have been employed and it is accepted that a finer sub-division, particularly of metamorphic and igneous rocks, would most likely result had the artefacts been subject to detailed petrological examination and analysis. Furthermore, the distinctions between different raw material classes are not always clearly evident. In the present study, for example, it was occasionally difficult to decide if a particular artefact was more appropriately classified as chert or as opaline, or, if from the Cape Fold Mountain Belt and its forelands, as a very fine-grained quartzite or (Table Mountain) sandstone. Specific raw material categories recognised are as follows:

Chert: Crypto-crystalline rocks similar to opalines, but differing in that they are somewhat less fine-grained and less translucent.

Dolerite: A medium-grained basic igneous rock occurring mainly in dolerite dykes or sills (Whitten & Brooks 1972: 131).

Granite: A coarse-grained igneous rock formed from a mass of interlocking crystals. The colour varies according to the rock's mineral makeup, but it always has a speckled appearance.

Hornfels: A generally quite fine-grained, greyish-black metamorphic rock produced by the metamorphosis of shale or mudstone and available either from specific point sources along dolerite dykes or eroded out in stream beds. Hornfels acquires a patina that varies from light grey to orange-red with age. Indurated shale and lydianite are synonyms that may be found in the older literature.

Ironstone/banded ironstone: A relatively coarse-grained sedimentary rock with a plate-like fracture pattern.

Opaline: Also known as crypto-crystalline silicas (CCS), a term that subsumes agate, chalcedony and jasper, opalines are fine-grained conchoidally fracturing rocks occurring as small nodules that derive from pipe amygdales in volcanic formations.

Quartz: A particular form of highly brittle crypto-crystalline silica often requiring the use of a bipolar technique for its flaking. Quartz does not have a well-developed conchoidal fracture pattern. Two varieties can be distinguished: crystal quartz is clear and glass-like, while vein quartz is milky white and variably opaque. Unworked quartz crystals are a feature of some assemblages and have sometimes been thought to have been used as shamanistic paraphernalia (Wadley 1987: 45-46).

Quartzite: Rocks that are visibly much coarser-grained than opalines or silcrete and formed almost entirely of fused quartz grains. Within the Cape Fold Mountain Belt and its coastal forelands quartzites grade into Table Mountain Sandstone.

Sandstone : A detrital sedimentary rock accumulated by either wind or water action in which the particles, mostly quartz grains, are < 2mm in size (Whitten & Brooks 1972: 30-31). Sometimes sandstone is found that has clearly been metamorphosed as a result of exposure to the heat from volcanic dykes. In these cases **baked sandstone** is the term used.

Silcrete: A fine-grained, very hard, brittle, intensely indurated and usually grey silicified sandstone (Cooke *et al.* 1993: 62) widely used for the manufacture of stone artefacts in both the Kalahari and the Western and Eastern Cape Provinces.

Silicified limestone: A distinctive, fine-grained variety of limestone that has undergone silicification (i.e. the introduction of silica into a non-siliceous rock) present only in the Bazley Collection from an unknown rock-shelter (Alfred County Cave) in southern KwaZulu-Natal.

Siltstone/mudstone: Relatively fine-grained sedimentary rocks, sometimes siltstones/mudstones are found that have clearly been metamorphosed as a result of exposure to the heat from volcanic dykes. In these cases the term **baked siltstone/mudstone** is employed.

Tuff: A rare category of raw material found only in the Lesotho highlands and in the rivers that drain them. Tuff is the consolidated ash and small, solid fragments of lava or country rock thrown out of a volcano (Whitten & Brooks 1972: 369-370).

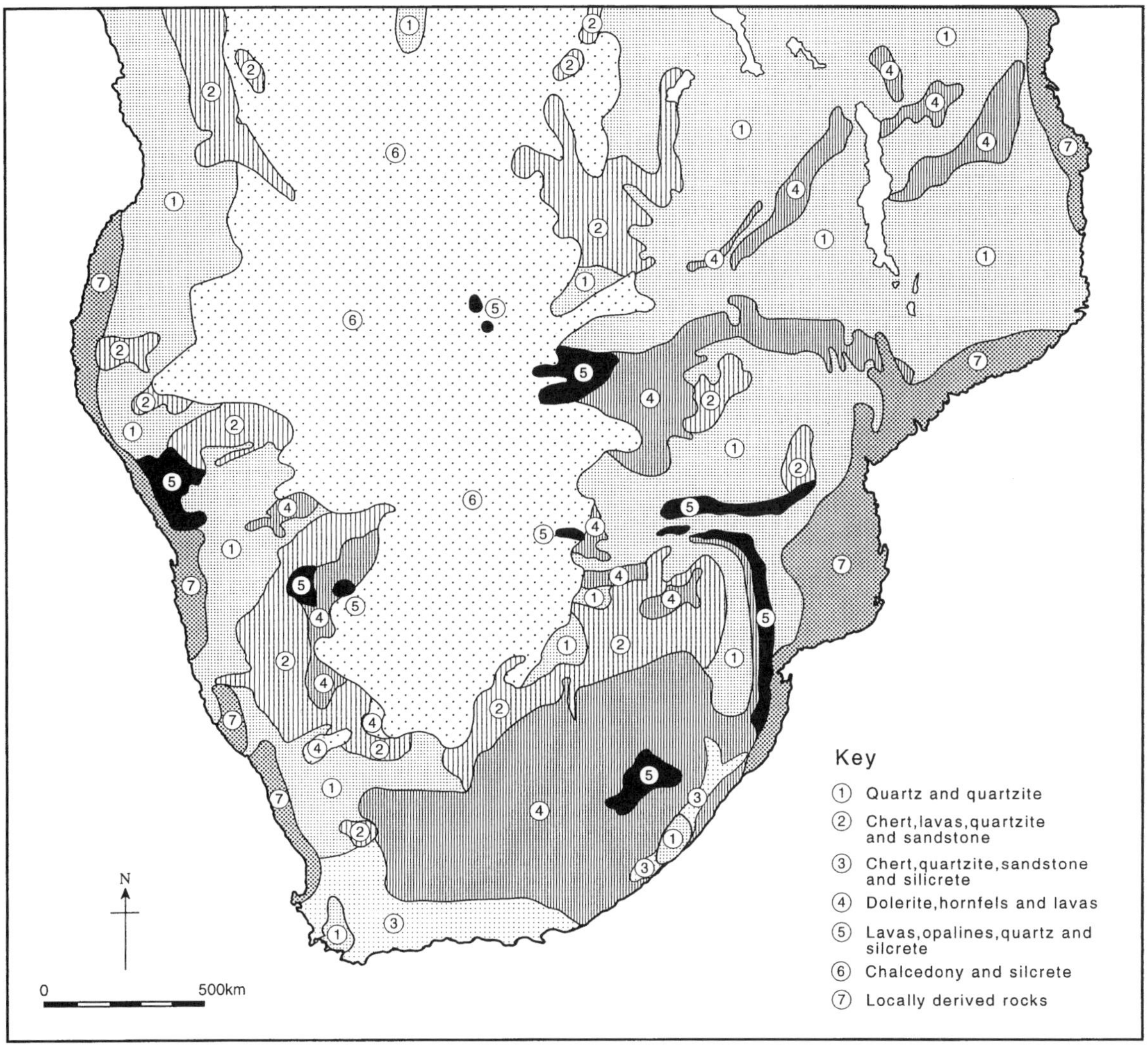

Fig. 11. Major lithic provinces of southern Africa. (after Clark 1959)

Table 5. Distinguishing features of successive subdivisions of the southern African Middle Stone Age (after Volman 1981, 1984; suggested ages after Volman 1984 and Thackeray 1991)

Sub-division and correlation with global $^{18}O/^{16}O$ curve	Cores	Flakes	Retouched artefacts
MSA 3 Stage 3		Highly varied, chief distinguishing feature is its post-Howieson's Poort age	Highly varied, but with fewer backed pieces than the Howieson's Poort
Howieson's Poort Stages 5a-4		Generally smaller, broader and with fewer faceted butts than either preceding or succeeding stages	Backed tools relatively common, including segments, most often in fine-grained rocks. Also scrapers, points
MSA 2 Stages 5e-5b	Prepared cores more common	Many flake-blades, decreasing in length with time	More common. Denticulates, points (unifacial and bifacial), scrapers. Backing rare
MSA 1 Stage 6	Many radial and disc cores	Small, broad, few have faceted butts	Rare. Points absent, scrapers few

Table 6. Sub-divisions of the southern African Later Stone Age

Smithfield 600BP	Either a late continuation of the Wilton tradition (Humphreys 1979) or a separate industry (Sampson 1974) found in the Free State and eastern Karoo, characterised by larger endstruck scrapers and a range of distinctive ceramics.
Ceramic Wilton/Post-classic Wilton with pottery 2000 BP	A continuation of the Wilton tradition, with the addition of ceramics and further changes in formal tool morphology and frequencies. In the Northern Cape regional industries are the Swartkops and Doornfontein and in the Matopo Hills occurrences are associated with Bambata Ware .
Post-classic Wilton c. 4500-2000 BP	A continuation of the Wilton, but with changes in formal tool frequencies and morphology, notably the gradual supercession of segments by other kinds of backed microliths. Known locally as Amadzimba in the Matopo Hills.
Wilton c. 4500-9500 BP	Microlithic assemblages characterised by a proliferation of small scrapers and backed microliths, as well as by enhanced use of fine-grained rocks. Known locally as Nswatugi in the Matopo Hills of Zimbabwe.
Oakhurst c. 8000-12 000 BP	Non-microlithic assemblages, often emphasizing coarse-grained rocks. Formal tools are few, except for large scrapers, though scrapers with adze-like lateral retouch are common after *c.* 9500 BP. Regional variants are Albany (southern and eastern Cape Fold Belt), Kuruman (Northern Cape), Lockshoek (Free State and Karoo) and Pomongwan (Matopo Hills).
Robberg c. 12 000-19 000 BP	Microlithic assemblages with few formal tools, but rich in unmodified bladelets and bladelet cores, preferentially made in fine-grained rocks.
Early Later Stone Age (ELSA) 21 000 BP	Some assemblages predating 21 000 BP that are microlithic, informal and quartz-dominated, e.g. Boomplaas, Members LP and LPC.

5. Gazetteer of the Southern African Stone Age Collections in The British Museum

1. Introduction: Organization of the Gazetteer

Various geographical divisions of the southern African sub-continent were considered in the initial stages of preparing the Gazetteer. One possibility would have been to employ a predominantly ecological framework, such as the ecological zones of Devred (De Vos 1975) discussed in Chapter 1, or the more recent definition of biomes produced by Rutherford & Westfall (1986). To do so would have been to follow the advice of Goodwin (1946a: 41) who argued for a framework in which 'areas or zones should be fundamentally selected to accommodate both man and his cultures, and should therefore fit environmental conditions, the types of raw material available and the techniques and variants that are normal to the zone'. Goodwin had, in fact, employed just such a framework in other discussions of the Early and Middle Stone Ages (Goodwin 1933; 1947), as had other writers before him (e.g. Gooch 1881; Van Riet Lowe 1938). Ecological subdivisions of this kind have, however, an inherent element of arbitrariness in them - what, after all, is significant about a particular vegetation type or climatic boundary ? - that suffers from two related disadvantages. Firstly, we know that southern African climates have changed extensively during the late Quaternary alone (J. Deacon & Lancaster 1988), let alone the much longer time span (extending possibly back into the Lower Pleistocene) represented by some of the material housed in the British Museum. Secondly, to retain or develop an environmental sub-division of southern Africa would be to privilege the very view of prehistory that Goodwin enunciated in his 1946 discussion of zoning. While ecological thinking in archaeology has been extremely productive in the explanation of the past of southern African hunter-gatherers, the last decade has seen a significant shift away from such models and towards a much greater use and development of 'people-to-people' models that also emphasize questions of social and ideological change (Mazel 1989; J. Deacon 1990b).

To these reasons another consideration needs to be added, that of the probable uses to which the Gazetteer will be put. It seems likely that users of it will first and foremost be interested in either establishing which collections have come from a particular geographical location or area, or in investigating the activities of a particular collector. Both purposes seemed best served by organizing the Gazetteer on the simplest possible basis, leaving it to future users to organize the information further according to their own research objectives. This has been achieved through a system that cross-references collectors with sites (Appendix 4) and through the presentation of the collections in terms of the contemporary political geography of southern Africa, divided up on a country by country basis and, within South Africa, by province.

Since South Africa alone accounts for almost three-quarters of the British Museum southern African Stone Age collections, it has been divided into its nine constitutent provinces and is treated first. The remaining countries of the sub-continent follow in alphabetical sequence. Provenances are listed alpabetically under their respective countries or South African provinces; a provincial or district affiliation is provided for the non-South African states. South African provenances which it has not been possible to locate within a specific provenance appear under South Africa, no further provenance. All provenances are spelt following modern spelling conventions, generally as given in the *Reader's Digest Illustrated Atlas of Southern Africa* (Reader's Digest 1994a). Older spellings appearing in the British Museum's accessions register or records are given in italics immediately thereafter. Where a provenance is clearly a specific locality within a larger area, for example in the cases of sub-divisions of Kimberley (South Africa, Northern Cape Province) or Carnarvondale Farm (South Africa, Eastern Cape Province) brackets are used to indicate this: thus, Kimberley (Belts), Kimberley (Bultfontein Mine), Kimberley (Du Toits Pan) etc. Where possible, each provenance is followed by its latitude and longitude.

Details of each collection's registration are as given in the British Museum register and follow the current practice of the Quaternary Section of the Department of Prehistory and Early Europe. Collections are named after the individual by whom they were donated, the term 'ex' referring to material originally collected by someone other than the donor. For example, the term 'Lyell Collection, ex Bain,' in describing artefacts from Kleinemonde in South Africa's Eastern Cape Province indicates that the material in question was donated to the British Museum by Sir Charles Lyell, but had originally been collected by Andrew Geddes Bain. Appendix 4 provides biographical detail on both these and other collectors. Collections are normally numbered showing the year and month in which they were accepted by the trustees. Thus, to use the same example, the details '1865 12-21 1-8' in the Lyell Collection, ex Bain from Kleinemonde indicate that it was donated in December 1865 and that it was the 21st collection accepted in that month. The numbers 1-8 indicate that the collection contains 8 individual objects. In 1968 individual departments of the Museum adopted their own registration prefix, 'P' in the case of the Department of Prehistory and Early Europe. Because the bulk of the Department's southern African collections had been obtained before that date, few bear this prefix other than those transferred from other institutions, such as The Geological Museum, e.g. The Geological Museum, ex Whitaker, Collection, P1989.3-1.96-100 which refers to five Middle Stone Age artefacts from the Cape of Good Hope. Material transferred within the British Museum from the Department of Ethnography to the Department of Prehistory and Early Europe retains the suffix (Ethno), as in the example of the Ward Collection (Ethno) 1934 10-18 22-41 from Carnarvondale (Woodbury site) in the Eastern Cape Province.

In the case of some late 19th and early 20th century bequests, the donors' terms require that the material retain, or be given, internal catalogue numbers, instead of being registered in the usual way. The most common example of this practice in the southern African collections of the British Museum is given by the artefacts in the extensive Christy Collection, which are all individually numbered with the number prefixed by '+'. They are also described in their own Christy Slip Catalogue, as in this further example from East London:

Christy Collection, ex McKay, +7721 - +7722.

Concordance of provenances of the southern African Stone Age collections of the British Museum

This concordance lists alphabetically all the provenances represented in the southern African Stone Age collections of the British Museum's Departments of Prehistory and Early Europe and Ethnography. Older spellings are given in italics with a note indicating the modern spelling under which they appear in the Gazetteer or Appendix 1. Where known the district (for Botswana), province (for Mozambique, South Africa and Zimbabwe) or region (for Angola) is also given. For provenances in South Africa the name of the relevant pre-1994 province is also given. To use the concordance and locate a particular provenance in the Gazetteer, look first for the country and then, for South Africa, the contemporary province in which the provenance is located.

Concordance of Provenances of the Southern African Stone Age Collections of The British Museum

Provenance	Country	Province, District or Region	Former Province (if in South Africa)
Alexandersfontein	South Africa	Northern Cape	Cape Province
Alfred County Cave	South Africa	KwaZulu-Natal	Natal
Alicedale	South Africa	Eastern Cape	Cape Province
Amantia[1]	South Africa	Unknown	-
Auob River	South Africa	Northern Cape	Cape Province
Avalon	South Africa	Free State	Orange Free State
Bamangwato	See Shoshong		
Bambata Cave	Zimbabwe	Matabeleland South	-
Barberton	South Africa	Mpumalanga	Transvaal
Barberton (Kaap Valley)[2]	South Africa	Mpumalanga	Transvaal
Barkly West	South Africa	Northern Cape	Cape Province
Bartlanarme	See Boatlaname		
Bechuana Province	South Africa	North West	Cape Province
Beyers Kloof Farm	South Africa	Western Cape	Cape Province
Blesbroekfontein	South Africa	North West	Transvaal
Blesmanspoort	South Africa	Northern Cape	Cape Province
Blickfontein	See Blikfontein		
Blikfontein	South Africa	Northern Cape	Cape Province
Bloemfontein	South Africa	Free State	Orange Free State
Bloemhof	South Africa	North West	Transvaal
Boatlaname	Botswana	Kweneng	-
Boetsap[2]	South Africa	Northern Cape	Cape Province
Boshof	South Africa	Free State	Orange Free State
Brakfontein	South Africa	Free State	Orange Free State
British Kaffraria	See East London (British Kaffraria)		
Bubi River	Zimbabwe	Matabeleland South	-
Buffalo River	South Africa	KwaZulu-Natal	Natal
Buffalo River Drift	South Africa	Eastern Cape	Cape Province
Buffalo (River) Shell Mound	South Africa	Eastern Cape	Cape Province
Buffelsjag	South Africa	Western Cape	Cape Province
Bulataga	Botswana	North-East	-
Burgersdorp	South Africa	Eastern Cape	Cape Province

Burgersdorp (Commonage)	South Africa	Eastern Cape	Cape Province
Burgersdorp Cave[2]	South Africa	Eastern Cape	Cape Province
Bushnanland	South Africa	Northern Cape	Cape Province
Bushman's River	South Africa	Eastern Cape	Cape Province
Bushman's River, near Weenen	South Africa	KwaZulu-Natal	Natal
Campbell	South Africa	Northern Cape	Cape Province
Canteen Kopje	South Africa	Northern Cape	Cape Province
Cape Flats	South Africa	Western Cape	Cape Province
Cape of Good Hope	South Africa	Western Cape (?)	Cape Province
Cape Padrone	South Africa	Eastern Cape	Cape Province
Cape Town[2]	South Africa	Western Cape	Cape Province
Carmarlo Drift	Zimbabwe	Matabeleland South	-
Carnarvondale Farm	South Africa	Eastern Cape	Cape Province
Carnarvondale (Bushy Park site)	South Africa	Eastern Cape	Cape Province
Carnarvondale (Hillary site)	South Africa	Eastern Cape	Cape Province
Carnarvondale (Van Riet Lowe's site)	South Africa	Eastern Cape	Cape Province
Carnarvondale (Wilman's site)	South Africa	Eastern Cape	Cape Province
Carnarvondale (Woodbury site)	South Africa	Eastern Cape	Cape Province
Charter District	Zimbabwe	Midlands	-
Christiana (Showlands Kopje)	South Africa	North West	Transvaal
Christiana (Soutpansdrift)	South Africa	North West	Transvaal
Chue Pan	South Africa	Northern Cape	Cape Province
Coega	South Africa	Eastern Cape	Cape Province
Commissie's Rust	South Africa	North West	Cape Province
Cubango River	Namibia	Unknown	-
Damaraland	Namibia	Unknown	-
De Kiel Oost	South Africa	Free State	Orange Free State
De Puts	South Africa	Free State	Orange Free State
Derré	Mozambique	Zambezia	-
Devondale Sidings	South Africa	North West	Cape Province
Doornlaagte	South Africa	North West	Transvaal
Douglas	South Africa	Northern Cape	Cape Province
Drakensberg Foothills[1]	South Africa	Mpumalanga or Northern Province	Transvaal
Driefontein	Zimbabwe	Masvingo	-
Dwarsberg	South Africa	North West	Transvaal
East London	South Africa	Eastern Cape	Cape Province
East London (British Kaffraria)	South Africa	Eastern Cape	Cape Province
Ematjeni River	Zimbabwe	Matabeleland South	-
Embusini	Zimbabwe	Matabeleland South	-
Estcourt	South Africa	KwaZulu-Natal	Natal
Fauresmith	South Africa	Free State	Orange Free State
Fish Hoek	South Africa	Western Cape	Cape Province
Fish River	Namibia	Unknown	-
Francistown Kopje	Botswana	North-East	-
Freevast	South Africa	Free State	Orange Free State
Garezi River[2]	Zimbabwe	Manicaland	-
Gariep River[1]	South Africa	Unknown	-
Gaseitisive's Country	Botswana	Southern ?	-
Gatooma Road Cave[2]	Zimbabwe	Mashonaland South	-
Gokomere Cave	Zimbabwe	Masvingo	-
Gonggong	See Gong-Gong		
Gong-Gong/Waldeck's Plant	South Africa	Northern Cape	Cape Province
Grahamstown	South Africa	Eastern Cape	Cape Province
Grahamstown (Sugar Loaf Hill)	South Africa	Eastern Cape	Cape Province
Great Fish River (mouth)[2]	South Africa	Eastern Cape	Cape Province

Great Salt Pan, Montshiva	South Africa	North West	Cape Province
Griqualand West	South Africa	North West	Cape Province
Griquatown	South Africa	Northern Cape	Cape Province
Gumali Cave	Zimbabwe	Matabeleland South	-
Gumani Cave	See Gumali Cave		
Gungwe Kopje	Botswana	North-East	-
Gwelo Kopje	See Gweru Kopje		
Gweru Kopje	Zimbabwe	Midlands	-
Hakskeenpan	South Africa	Northern Cape	Cape Province
Halseton	South Africa	Eastern Cape	Cape Province
Harare	Zimbabwe	Mashonaland South	-
Harrismith	South Africa	Free State	Orange Free State
Hartebeestfontein	South Africa	Northern Province	Transvaal
Harts River	South Africa	Northern Cape	Cape Province
Heilbron[2]	South Africa	Free State	Orange Free State
Hermanus	South Africa	Western Cape	Cape Province
Hogskin Vlei	See Hakskeenpan		
Hope Fountain	Zimbabwe	Matabeleland South	-
Hopetown Bridge	South Africa	Northern Cape	Cape Province
Hosluit	South Africa	Northern Cape	Cape Province
Hout Bay	South Africa	Western Cape	Cape Province
Ikomene Cave	See Gumali Cave		
Imbusini Brook	Zimbabwe	Matabeleland South	-
Impakwe River	See Mpakwe River		
Ingwe River Farm 203	Botswana	North-East	-
Inyanga	Zimbabwe	Manicaland	-
Inyati	Zimbabwe	Matabeleland North	-
Inyati (Huckle's Farm)	Zimbabwe	Matabeleland North	-
Isandhlwana	South Africa	KwaZulu-Natal	Natal
Isandulana	See Isandhlwana		
Jacobsdal	South Africa	Free State	Orange Free State
Kaffirland [*sic*]	South Africa	KwaZulu-Natal	Natal
Kalahari	South Africa	Northern Cape	Cape Province
Kalahara Desert	See Kalahari Desert		
Kalahari Desert	South Africa	Northern Cape	Cape Province
Karrieput	South Africa	Northern Cape	Cape Province
Kasouga River	South Africa	Eastern Cape	Cape Province
Keiskamma River Mouth	South Africa	Eastern Cape	Cape Province
Khama's Territory	Botswana	Central	-
Khami	Zimbabwe	Matabeleland South	-
Kheis	South Africa	Northern Cape	Cape Province
Kimberley	South Africa	Northern Cape	Cape Province
Kimberley (Belts)	South Africa	Northern Cape	Cape Province
Kimberley (Boskop Road)	South Africa	Northern Cape	Cape Province
Kimberley (Bultfontein Mine)	South Africa	Northern Cape	Cape Province
Kimberley (Du Toits Pan)	South Africa	Northern Cape	Cape Province
Kimberley (Golf Links)	South Africa	Northern Cape	Cape Province
Kimberley Sluits	South Africa	Northern Cape	Cape Province
King Williams Town	See Middledrift		
Kleinemonde	South Africa	Eastern Cape	Cape Province
Klerksdorp	South Africa	North West	Transvaal
Klip Drift	South Africa	Northern Cape	Cape Province
Koffiefontein[2]	South Africa	Free State	Orange Free State
Koffiefontein (Engravings Site)	South Africa	Free State	Orange Free State
Koffiefontein (Sekretaris Kop)	South Africa	Free State	Orange Free State
Koodoosberg Drift	South Africa	Northern Cape	Cape Province

Koranna Kolk[2]	South Africa	Northern Cape	Cape Province
Kuruman	South Africa	Northern Cape	Cape Province
Kuruman (Cotton End)	South Africa	Northern Cape	Cape Province
Lake Ngami	Botswana	Ngamiland	-
Langeberg	South Africa	Northern Cape	Cape Province
Last Hope	South Africa	Northern Cape	Cape Province
Leeuwfontein[1]	South Africa	Unknown	-
Limpopo River	South Africa	North West	Transvaal
Lockshoek	South Africa	Free State	Orange Free State
London	South Africa	North West	Transvaal
Loogkolk[2]	South Africa	Northern Cape	Cape Province
Mafeking	See Mafikeng		
Mafikeng	South Africa	North West	Cape Province
Makanikani Pans	See Makgadikgadi Pans		
Makgadikgadi Pans	Botswana	Central	-
Makumbi Mission[2]	Zimbabwe	Mashonaland South	-
Marandellas Rock Shelter[2]	See Marondera Rock Shelter		
Maritse River	See Ngwaritsi River		
Marondera Rock Shelter[2]	Zimbabwe	Manicaland	-
Massengana[2]	Mozambique	Manica	-
Matabeleland	Zimbabwe	Unknown	-
Matetsi Valley	Zimbabwe	Matabeleland North	-
Matopos Cave	Zimbabwe	Matabeleland South	-
Matopos Cave[2]	Zimbabwe	Matabeleland South	-
Matopos Cave[2]	Zimbabwe	Matabeleland South	-
Mauchini Brook	Zimbabwe	Matabeleland South	-
Mbabane River	Swaziland	Mbabane	-
Messina Copper Mine	South Africa	Northern Province	Transvaal
Meyerton	South Africa	Gauteng	Transvaal
Meyerton (Kookfontein)	South Africa	Gauteng	Transvaal
Middledrift	South Africa	Eastern Cape	Cape Province
Milnerton-Maitland	South Africa	Western Cape	Cape Province
Mitria (?) Cave[1]	South Africa	Mpumalanga or Northern Province	Transvaal
Modder River	South Africa	Northern Cape	Cape Province
Modderpoort	South Africa	Free State	Orange Free State
Molapo River	See Molopo River		
Molepolole	Botswana	Kweneng	-
Molopo River	South Africa	Northern Cape	Cape Province
Monapo River	Mozambique	Ilha	-
Monquato	See Shoshong		
Montsiva	See Great Salt Pan, Montshiwa		
Mossel Bay	South Africa	Western Cape	Cape Province
Mossel Bay Flats	South Africa	Western Cape	Cape Province
Mount Mavoio	Angola	Uige	-
Mpakwe River	Zimbabwe	Matabeleland South	-
Muden	South Africa	KwaZulu-Natal	Natal
Mutare[2]	Zimbabwe	Manicaland	-
Nata River	Botswana	Central	-
Natal	South Africa	KwaZulu-Natal	Natal
Newcastle	South Africa	KwaZulu-Natal	Natal
Newlands	South Africa	Northern Cape	Cape Province
Ngotwane River	South Africa	North West	Transvaal
Ngwaritsi River	South Africa	Northern Province	Transvaal
Nooitgedacht	South Africa	Northern Cape	Cape Province
Noordhoek	South Africa	Western Cape	Cape Province
Nordhoek	See Noordhoek		
Northern Transvaal[2]	South Africa	Northern Province	Transvaal

Nosop River	See Nossob River		
Nossob River	South Africa	Northern Cape	Cape Province
Notuane River	See Ngotwane River		
Nswatugi Cave	Zimbabwe	Matabeleland South	-
Oop River	See Auob River		
Orange River	See Gariep River		
Ovampoland	See Owambo		
Owambo	Namibia	Unknown	-
Paardeberg	South Africa	Free State	Orange Free State
Paarl	South Africa	Western Cape	Cape Province
Palmietpan	South Africa	Gauteng	Transvaal
Panfontein	South Africa	Gauteng	Transvaal
Petrus	South Africa	Free State	Orange Free State
Pienaarsrivier	South Africa	North West	Transvaal
Pietermaritzburg	South Africa	KwaZulu-Natal	Natal
Pietermaritzburg (New Park)[2]	South Africa	KwaZulu-Natal	Natal
Plumtree	Zimbabwe	Matabeleland South	-
Pniel	South Africa	Northern Cape	Cape Province
Pniel Mission Station	South Africa	Northern Cape	Cape Province
Pommeru	Zimbabwe	Unknown	-
Pommeru (Grave Site)	Zimbabwe	Unknown	-
Port Beaufort	South Africa	Western Cape	Cape Province
Potchefstroom	South Africa	North West	Transvaal
Powola Brook	Zimbabwe	Matabeleland South	-
Pretoria	South Africa	Gauteng	Transvaal
Pretoria (Arcadia)	South Africa	Gauteng	Transvaal
Pretoria (Camp Gravels)	South Africa	Gauteng	Transvaal
Pretoria (Meintjeskop)	South Africa	Gauteng	Transvaal
Pretoria (Muckleneuk)	South Africa	Gauteng	Transvaal
Pretoria (Wonderboom)	South Africa	Gauteng	Transvaal
Pretoria environs	South Africa	Gauteng	Transvaal
Prieska	South Africa	Northern Cape	Cape Province
Queenstown[2]	South Africa	Eastern Cape	Cape Province
Ramaquabana River	See Ramatlabama River		
Ramatlabama River	Botswana	North-East	-
Read's Drift	South Africa	Northern Cape	Cape Province
Riversdale Farm	South Africa	Free State	Orange Free State
Roedtan	South Africa	Northern Province	Transvaal
Rooipoort	South Africa	Northern Cape	Cape Province
Rorke's Drift	South Africa	KwaZulu-Natal	Natal
Rubie River	See Bubi River		
Rustenburg	South Africa	North West	Transvaal
Salisbury	See Harare		
Sawmills	Zimbabwe	Matabeleland North	-
Sawmills River	Zimbabwe	Matabeleland North	-
Schaapplaats Cave[2]	South Africa	Free State	Orange Free State
Schweizer-Reneke	South Africa	North West	Transvaal
Schwener-Reneke	See Schweizer-Reneke		
Sekonje River	Botswana	North-East	-
Senyowe Drift	Botswana	North-East	-
Sesfontein[2]	South Africa	Free State	Orange Free State
Shangani River	Zimbabwe	Matabeleland North and/or Midlands	
Sheppard Island	South Africa	North West	Transvaal
Shoshong	Botswana	Central	-
Siffonels	See Sivonel		

Silver Streams	South Africa	Northern Cape	Cape Province
Simondium (Vriedeslust Farm)	South Africa	Western Cape	Cape Province
Sivonel *(Siffonels)*	South Africa	Northern Cape	Cape Province
Skildegat Cave	South Africa	Western Cape	Cape Province
Smithfield[2]	South Africa	Free State	Orange Free State
Spitskop	South Africa	North West	Transvaal
Steenbokpan *(Steinbok Farm)*	South Africa	Free State	Orange Free State
Steenbokpan *(Steinbok Pan)*	South Africa	Free State	Orange Free State
Steinbok Farm	See Steenbokpan (*Steinbok Farm*)		
Steinbok Pan	See Steenbokpan (*Steinbok Pan*)		
Stellenbosch	South Africa	Western Cape	Cape Province
Stellenbosch (Bosman's Crossing)	South Africa	Western Cape	Cape Province
Stellenbosch (Lorraine Farm)	South Africa	Western Cape	Cape Province
Steynsdorp	South Africa	Mpumalanga	Transvaal
Still Bay	South Africa	Western Cape	Cape Province
Swartmodder	South Africa	Northern Cape	Cape Province
Swartmodder ?	South Africa	Northern Cape	Cape Province
Swartruggens[2]	South Africa	Eastern Cape	Cape Province
Swellendam[2]	South Africa	Western Cape	Cape Province
Sydney	South Africa	Northern Cape	Cape Province
Sydney Estate	South Africa	Northern Cape	Cape Province
Tati Goldfields	Botswana	North-East	-
Tati River	Botswana	North-East	-
Taung, Harts River Gravels	South Africa	North West	Cape Province
Taungs, Harts River Gravels	See Taung, Harts River Gravels		
Taung Mission Spruit	South Africa	North West	Cape Province
Taungs Mission Spruit	See Taung Mission Spruit		
Tharfield	South Africa	Eastern Cape	Cape Province
The Curragh	South Africa	KwaZulu-Natal	Natal
Tshesebe	Botswana	North-East	-
Tonga River	Botswana	Ngamiland	-
Tongaat[2]	South Africa	KwaZulu-Natal	Natal
Trelawney	Zimbabwe	Mashonaland North	-
Tsessebe	See Tshesebe		
Turk Mine	Zimbabwe	Matabeleland North	-
Umtali[2]	See Mutare		
Vaal River	South Africa	Northern Cape	Cape Province
Vegkop, Heilbron[2]	South Africa	Free State	Orange Free State
Ventershoek (Christol Cave)	South Africa	Free State	Orange Free State
Ventershoek (talus below Christol Cave)	South Africa	Free State	Orange Free State
Ventershoek (to west of Christol Cave)	South Africa	Free State	Orange Free State
Vereeniging	South Africa	Gauteng	Transvaal
Versonskraal, Wolmaranstad	South Africa	North West	Transvaal
Victoria Falls	Zimbabwe	Matabeleland North	-
Victoria West	South Africa	Northern Cape	Cape Province
Villiersdorp	South Africa	Western Cape	Cape Province
Vogelstruisfontein Farm	South Africa	Gauteng	Transvaal
Vukwe Drift	Botswana	North-East	-
Waldeck's Plant	See Gong-Gong/Waldeck's Plant		
Weenen (Townlands)	South Africa	KwaZulu-Natal	Natal
Westacre Farm	Zimbabwe	Matabeleland South	-
Wepener[2]	South Africa	Free State	Orange Free State
Wilton Large Rock Shelter	South Africa	Eastern Cape	Cape Province
Windsorton	South Africa	Northern Cape	Cape Province
Witsands Site I	South Africa	Northern Cape	Cape Province
Witsands Site II	South Africa	Northern Cape	Cape Province

Witsands Bay ?	South Africa	Western Cape	Cape Province
Witt Water	See Witwater		
Witwater	South Africa	Northern Cape	Cape Province
Wontimetia[1]	South Africa	Unknown	-
Worcester	South Africa	Western Cape	South Africa
Zululand	South Africa	KwaZulu-Natal	Natal
Zwartkops River	South Africa	Eastern Cape	South Africa
Zwartmodder[2]	See Swartmodder and Swartmodder ?		
Zwartruggens[2]	See Swartruggens		

Notes:

1. These South African provenances lack any detailed information as to their location and appear in the section 'South Africa, no further provenance'.
2. These provenances are only represented in the collections of The British Museum's Department of Ethnography and are thus listed in Appendix 1.

2.1 South Africa: Eastern Cape Province

Thomas Bowker's collection of stone artefacts on his family farm at Tharfield, south of Grahamstown, and from other localities in the Eastern Cape Province marks the beginning of archaeological research in South Africa (J. Deacon 1990a). Following his example, a variety of archaeological contexts, ranging from rock-shelters through shell middens to open air surface scatters, were investigated by other pioneers, such as Atherstone and McKay (Appendix 4). Working in the Aliwal North/Burgersdorp area of the Eastern Cape, Kannemeyer (1890) and Alfred Brown were also particularly important, though neither published widely (Goodwin 1946a: 30-1). More far-reaching and systematic in its effects was the appointment of John Hewitt (Appendix 4) as Director of the Albany Museum in 1910. Between 1920 and 1940, Hewitt excavated, or was involved in the excavation of, over 20 rock-shelters and published almost as many papers on the archaeology of the western half of the Eastern Cape (H. J. Deacon 1976: 2). Particularly noteworthy are his excavation of the typesites of the Wilton and Howieson's Poort Industries (Stapleton & Hewitt 1927), as well as of several other Holocene shelters with well-preserved organics, such as Uniondale and Melkhoutboom (Hewitt 1931).

Following Hewitt, relatively little archaeological work was undertaken in that part of the Eastern Cape centred on Grahamstown until Hilary Deacon initiated a major research programme there in 1963. This included the re-investigation of the Howieson's Poort name-site (J. Deacon 1995) and the excavation of an Acheulean site at Amanzi Springs (H. J. Deacon 1970). The main focus of Deacon's research, however, was the exploration of the subsistence ecology of Holocene Later Stone Age populations in the Eastern Cape. To this end he concentrated on the re-excavation of Melkhoutboom, while also extending archaeological observations further inland with the excavation of Highlands Shelter (H. J. Deacon 1976). Scott's Cave in the Gamtoos Valley (H. J. Deacon & J. Deacon 1963), Janette's Deacon clarification of the sequence at the Wilton type-site (J. Deacon 1972) and Mary Leslie's re-excavation of Uniondale Shelter (Leslie 1989) formed additional components of the overall project. H. J. Deacon's (1976) synthesis of its results was a landmark study in the development of South African archaeology, setting new standards of data recovery and interpretation and developing a model linking technology, subsistence ecology and human demography in a systemic perspective that transcended the limits of the discipline's previously narrow lithocentric terminology. Also in the 1960s, construction of the Gariep (formerly Verwoerd) Dam along the middle stretch of the Gariep River on the northern edge of what is now the Eastern Cape provided the impetus for a major archaeological research programme in and around the area to be flooded. Working from open air sites and excavations at several rock-shelters, Garth Sampson (1970, 1972) established a chrono-stratigraphic record for this previously largely neglected area and later used this as the basis for much of his synthesis of southern Africa's Stone Age prehistory (Sampson 1974).

Since the mid-1970s several further projects of importance have been undertaken in the western half of the Eastern Cape. Opperman (1987) has examined LSA settlement-subsistence patterns in the Maclear/Dordrecht/Sterkstroom areas, arguing for only small-scale seasonal movements above and below the Drakensberg Escarpment; more recently he has concentrated on excavation of shelters in the same area with high quality preservation of botanical and faunal remains associated with terminal Middle Stone Age assemblages (Opperman & Heydenrych 1990; Opperman 1996). Simon Hall's excavation of two rock-shelters in the Fish River Valley forms the centre piece of the most coherently argued case for middle and late Holocene social and economic intensification in southern Africa, simultaneously urging southern African archaeologists to consider a broader range of ethnographic comparisons beyond a purely Bushman set of analogies for the Later Stone Age (S. Hall 1990). Johan Binneman, who co-authored with Hall an important study of LSA burial practices in the region (S. Hall & Binneman 1987), has examined some of the same issues along the coast between the Tsitsikamma and Gamtoos Rivers (Binneman 1985; Henderson & Binneman 1997) and has recently carried out further excavations of organic-rich Holocene deposits further inland (Binneman 1994b, 1996, 1997).

Lying near the western edge of the Eastern Cape Province, the cave complex of Klasies River Mouth first attracted archaeological interest in the 1960s when excavations directed by John Wymer yielded the remains of several anatomically modern human individuals in Middle Stone Age deposits (Singer & Wymer 1982). Hilary Deacon's re-investigation of the site has emphasized micro-excavation in order to clarify its stratigraphy (H. J. Deacon & Geleijnse 1988) and thus obtain a much more refined picture of the palaeoenvironmental context in which the archaeological deposits were laid down (H. J. Deacon 1989, 1995). Associated projects have examined the stone artefact sequence (Thackeray 1989) and patterning in the organization of the use of space (Henderson 1992), but of greatest importance is confirmation of the age of the hominids found in the initial and recent excavations (H. J. Deacon 1993). Though accepted by the majority of palaeoanthropologists and archaeologists as among the earliest anatomically modern humans known and as strong support of the 'Out-of-Africa 2' hypothesis of modern human origins (Stringer & Gamble 1993), debate continues on whether this anatomical modernity necessarily implies sophisticated behaviour similar to that found among recent hunter-gatherers (*cf.* Binford 1984; H. J. Deacon 1989; Klein & Cruz-Uribe 1996).

Because of its large African population, those parts of the Eastern Cape lying to the east of the River Kei were separately administered for much of the 20th century, first as a 'native reserve' and later as the 'homeland' of Transkei. The consistent underfunding of this region is mirrored in the comparative lack of archaeological research to have been undertaken here. Chubb *et al.*'s (1934) excavation of Umgazana cave near Port St. John's demonstrated the presence of a complex series of Holocene deposits associated with human burials and a rich worked bone assemblage; Laidler (1933, 1937) carried out excavations at two inland shelters at roughly the same time. With these exceptions, Carter's (1978) excavation of Belleview Shelter on the Lesotho border and field survey and rock art recording by him and Patricia Vinnicombe (1976) in the Matatiele area, virtually no further work was undertaken in this part of the Eastern Cape until 1971. Derricourt (1977) provides a summary of the fieldwork that he carried out in the former Transkei, Ciskei and Border areas of the Eastern Cape between then and 1974, research that emphasized hunter-gatherer, pastoralist and Iron Age sites of the last 2-3000 years. Though Feely (1987) and Prins & Grainger (1993) have carried out much more extensive studies of early farming settlement in the region, Stone Age research has again been relatively neglected. Relations between the region's last Bushman inhabitants and their descendants and the production and use of rock paintings have, however, emerged as an active focus of investigation (e.g. P. Jolly 1986; Lewis-Williams 1986; Prins 1990; P. Jolly & Prins 1994).

The British Museum collections from the Eastern Cape (**Fig. 12**) include small numbers of artefacts from several important sites, among them the type-site of the Wilton Industry (Wilton Large Rock-Shelter), as well as others that are of historical significance for the development of archaeology in South Africa. Of importance here are the Avebury Collections from Buffalo River and East London and artefacts in the Christy Collection from East London, which represent finds made by George McKay, one of the pioneers of archaeological excavation in the Eastern Cape Province in the middle of the 19th century. Artefacts in the Christy and Sturge Collections from Grahamstown and in the Christy Collection from Tharfield are also of historical significance as they were among the first to have been collected by Colonel T. H. Bowker and sent overseas to Britain around 1860. The two largest collections from the Eastern Cape come from Middledrift and a series of sites near Carnavondale, which are also well represented in other museum collections in Britain.

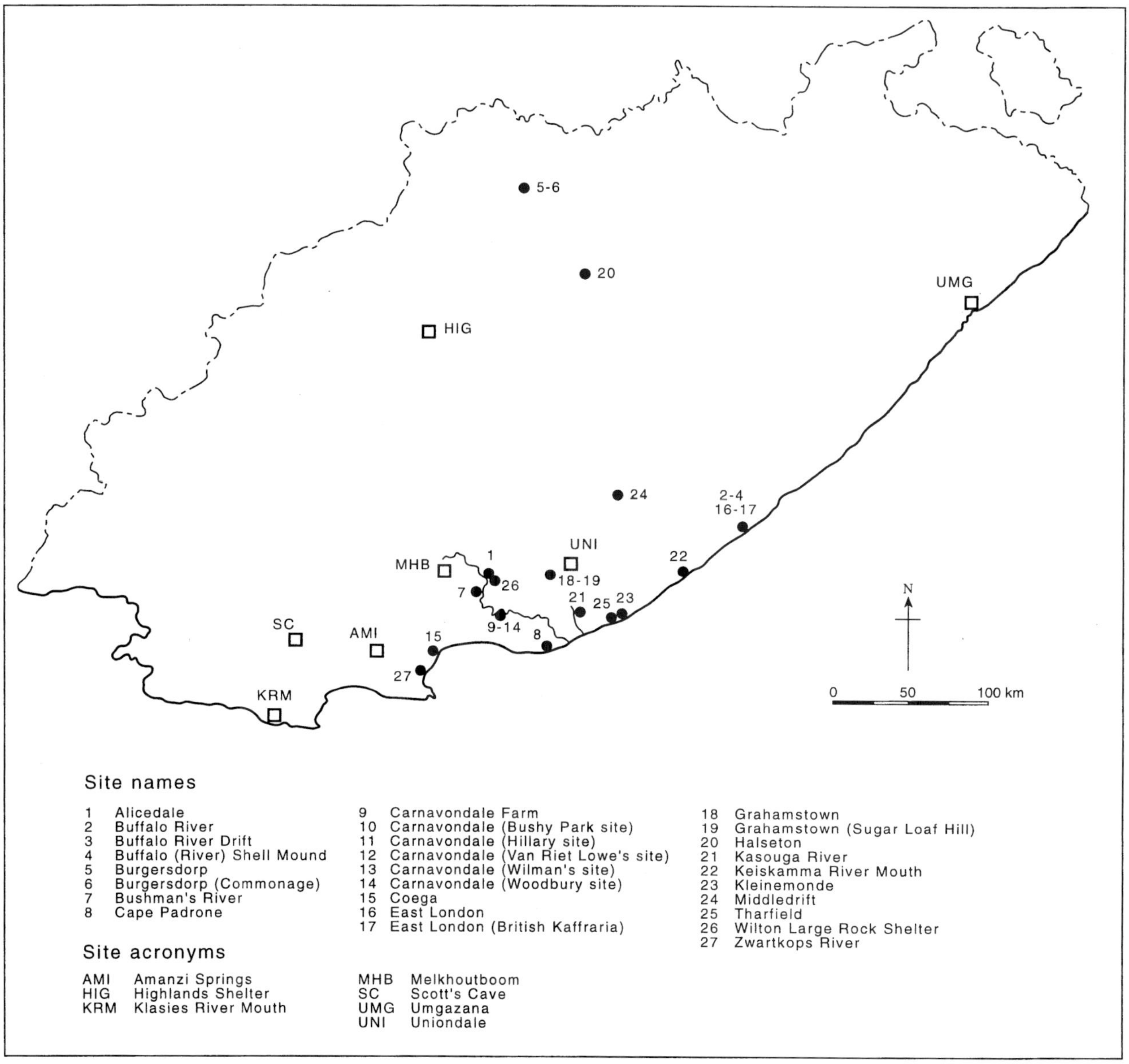

Fig. 12. Location of archaeological sites in the Eastern Cape Province and of Stone Age collections from there in the British Museum

ALICEDALE 33° 19'S, 26° 05'E

The small settlement of Alicedale lies only 5 km west of the typesite of the Wilton (qv) Industry, but the exact provenance of these artefacts is not clear. As well as Wilton itself, Hewitt, who was Director of the Albany Museum, Grahamstown, from 1910 until 1958, excavated at Spitzkop and Roodekrantz rock-shelters a little to the north of Alicedale and at Welcome Woods rock-shelter to its south (H. J. Deacon 1976: 3).

Albany Museum Collection, per Kettlewell, 1922.5-6.1-2, 6-7

A group of four Middle Stone Age quartzite artefacts.
2 irregular cores, 1 unmodified flake with a faceted platform, 1 scraper.

BUFFALO RIVER PROBABLY 33° 01'S, 27° 58'E

The Buffalo River enters the Indian Ocean at East London and these two artefacts are probably derived from excavations undertaken there either by McKay (1897) or by Hillier (1898).

Avebury Collection 1916.6-5.37-38

Two artefacts, of which the cleaver is probably of Early Stone Age origin and the flake-blade is either from a Middle Stone Age assemblage or belongs to an industry on the interface between Early and Middle Stone Age technologies.
1 large dolerite cleaver, 1 enormous (300 mm long), heavily patinated hornfels flake-blade with a faceted platform.

BUFFALO RIVER DRIFT 33° 01'S, 27° 58'E

Hillier Collection 1887.4-6.4-22

A group of 19 Middle Stone Age artefacts that clearly derive from a different site from the 'Buffalo Shell Mound' that Hillier also investigated along the Buffalo River.
1 irregular core (in hornfels), 10 unmodified flakes (1 in dolerite, 9 in sandstone), 3 unmodified flake-blades (1 in dolerite, 2 in sandstone), 5 flake-blade sections (1 proximal, 2 mesial, 2 distal, all in hornfels).

BUFFALO (RIVER) SHELL MOUND 33° 01'S, 27° 58'E

Open air middens containing pottery, stone artefacts and human burials are comparatively well known at the mouth of the Buffalo River and were investigated by Laidler (1935). As Derricourt (1977) indicates, some of these sites are of Early Iron Age origin, while others reflect the activities of forager groups, before and/or after the local onset of agricultural settlement. The two grindstones and one potsherd in the Hillier Collection from the 'Buffalo Shell Mound' are, unfortunately, not culturally diagnostic by themselves. Hillier (1898: 129-130) refers to the largest of the 'mounds' that he investigated being some 100 m long and 8 m high; in addition to briefly describing its stratigraphy he notes that it had produced a human skull. Whether this is the mound represented in the British Museum collections is unknown.

Hillier Collection 1887.4-6.28, 34-35

1 lower grindstone, 1 upper grindstone (both in dolerite), 1 grey/black undecorated rimsherd.
A block of sediment from this site includes a number of animal bones, among them a femoral shaft fragment and a right scapula; a lack of adequate comparative material precluded specific identification.

BURGERSDORP 31° 00'S, 26° 20'E

Although Collins collected mostly in Gauteng and the North West Province, he did publish a small number of artefacts from elsewhere in South Africa. This object was found 'in gravel 50 feet to 80 feet (15-25 m) above the stream that flows through Burgersdorp into the Orange River' (Collins & Smith 1919: 80).

Collins Collection 1919.2-10.20

One bifacially flaked large silcrete flake, one edge of which has scraper retouch and two others knife-like retouch. As one of the latter is on a truncation there is a superficial resemblance to an Acheulean cleaver (*cf.* Collins & Smith 1919: 80). However, in overall dimensions and retouch, it seems more likely that this object is of Middle Stone Age origin.

Additional material Department of Ethnography, British Museum (Appendix 1).Cambridge University Museum (Burgersdorp; Burgersdorp, Red House), Manchester Museum, Sheffield City Museum (Appendix 3).

BURGERSDORP (COMMONAGE) 31° 00'S, 26° 20'E

Passmore Edwards Collection, ex Fox, ex Robertson, P1995.4-1.225

1 heavily patinated and partly rolled hornfels handaxe found in 1910.

BUSHMAN'S RIVER PROBABLY CENTRED AROUND 33° 42'S, 34° 40'E

The Christy Collection Slip Catalogue states that these five Middle Stone Age artefacts derive from a 'kitchen midden east of Bushman's River'. Unfortunately, a more precise provenance is lacking.

Christy Collection, ex Atherstone, S. Afr. 13-17
2 unmodified flakes (in sandstone), 2 unmodified flake-blades (in sandstone), 1 point (in tuff). The point and one each of the flakes and flake-blades have faceted platforms.

Christy Collection, ex Atherstone, S. Afr. 31-32
4 pieces of pottery, 3 of which come from a locality to the west of Bushman's River (S. Afr. 31) and 1 from its east (S. Afr. 32). They are described in the Christy Slip Catalogue as follows:
S. Afr. 31 - 3 pieces of brown pottery, one side neatly finished, the other rough with quartz inclusions;
S. Afr. 32 - rough reddish-brown potsherd with a stone protruding from its inner surface, 84 mm.

Additional material Department of Ethnography, British Museum (Appendix 1).Cambridge University Museum (Appendix 3).

CAPE PADRONE 33° 47'S, 26° 28'E
Segments, such as these two artefacts from Cape Padrone, are typical of late Holocene assemblages from shell midden sites along the Eastern Cape coast from Klasies River Mouth in the west to the mouth of the Fish River in the east. They date to between approximately 5000 and 2000 BP and may be part of the material signature of coastal foragers with a mostly marine and littoral subsistence orientation (Binneman 1985).

Hewitt Collection, (Ethno) 1931.10-21.2-3
2 very large (55 and 80 mm long) quartzite segments, both showing clear utilisation along the edge opposite to the backing.

CARNAVONDALE FARM APPROXIMATELY 33° 26'S, 25° 56'E
Despite its prominence in the British Museum southern African collections, doubts remain about the exact location of some parts of the Carnarvondale complex of sites from the banks of the Bushman's River. However, five further sites, known respectively as the Bushy Park, Hillary, Van Riet Lowe, Wilman and Woodbury sites, are provenanced to 'Sandflats near Port Elizabeth', almost certainly a reference to the place Sandflats near Paterson on the upper reaches of the Bushman's River drainage basin; Woodbury itself is a farm just south of the river between Paterson and Alexandria. A document in the British Museum archives gives the names of the owners of Carnarvondale itself, as well as of Bushy Park, Woodbury and Hilary, implying that they are all probably farms.

Ward Collection, (Ethno) 1931.3-7.1-2, 4-7, 9-17, 21-31, 36-39
A group of 30 Middle Stone Age artefacts without any more specific provenance.

Table 7. Middle Stone Age artefacts in the Ward Collection from Carnarvondale Farm.

	Opaline	Hornfels	Silcrete	Quartz	Quartzite	Total
Irregular cores	4	-	1	-	-	5
Radial cores	-	-	-	-	1	1
Flakes	-	1	1	-	3	5
Flake-blades	-	-	-	-	2	2
Proximal sections (flake-blades)	-	-	-	-	1	1
Utilised flakes	1	-	-	-	-	1
Utilised flake-blades	-	1	-	-	-	1
Scrapers	1	2	6	1	1	11
Knives - unilateral	1	1	-	-	-	2
Points	-	-	1	-	-	1
Total	7	5	9	1	8	30

Ward Collection, (Ethno) 1934.10-18.210-213
A largely Later Stone Age group of 429 artefacts in which 4 Early Stone Age handaxes, 1 blade and 4 blade proximal sections (all Middle Stone Age ?) are the only disparate elements. Although the scrapers include two silcrete examples with adze-like lateral retouch (a possible early Holocene indicator, suggesting affinities to the Oakhurst Complex), the remainder are all clearly Wilton and/or post-classic Wilton.

In addition to the stone artefacts from this collection, a fragment of an unidentified mammal (possibly bovid) mandible is also present.

Table 8. Later Stone Age artefacts in the Ward Collection from Carnarvondale Farm.

	Opaline	Hornfels	Silcrete	Quartz	Quartzite	Total
Handaxes	-	-	-	-	4	4
Chunks	-	-	-	1	-	1
Irregular cores	6	-	1	1	-	8
Bladelet cores	1	-	2	-	-	3
Core-reduced pieces	2	-	3	-	-	5
Core tablets	4	-	2	-	-	6
Crested blades	5	-	-	-	-	5
Flakes	149	9	90	10	4	262
Blades	-	1	-	-	-	1
Bladelets	4	-	-	-	-	4
Proximal sections (blades)	-	1	-	-	3	4
Proximal sections (bladelets)	10	1	20	-	-	31
Mesial sections	4	-	25	-	-	29
Distal sections	4	-	8	-	1	13
Utilised flakes	1	-	-	-	-	1
Scrapers	21	1	26	-	-	48
Backed scrapers	2	-	1	-	-	3
Backed flakes	-	-	1	-	-	1
Total	213	13	179	12	12	429

Additional material Department of Ethnography, British Museum (Appendix 1).Pitt Rivers Museum (Appendix 3).

CARNARVONDALE (BUSHY PARK SITE) APPROXIMATELY 33° 26'S, 25° 56'E

Ward Collection, (Ethno) 1934.10-18.88-139

This is an entirely Middle Stone Age collection of 53 artefacts made in a variety of raw materials, with the hornfels specimens variably patinated. However, the presence of a crude bifacial implement (though one that could scarcely be considered a true handaxe) suggests that at least one Early Stone Age element may be present. 1 unworked piece of stone is also present.

Table 9. The Ward Collection from the Bushy Park site, Carnarvondale.

	Opaline	Hornfels	Silcrete	Quartzite	Dolerite	Sandstone	Total
Bifacial implement	-	1	-	-	-	-	1
Irregular cores	-	1	1	3	-	3	8
Blade cores	-	-	-	1	-	-	1
Bladelet cores	-	-	-	1	-	-	1
Crested blades	-	1	1	-	-	1	3
Flakes	1	9	2	13	-	-	25
Flake-blades	1	-	-	7	-	-	8
Proximal sections	-	-	-	-	1	-	1
Mesial sections	-	-	1	-	-	-	1
Utilised flakes	-	-	-	1	-	-	1
Scrapers	-	1	-	1	-	-	2
Points	-	-	-	1	-	-	1
Total	2	13	5	28	1	4	53

CANARVONDALE (HILLARY SITE) APPROXIMATELY 33° 26'S, 25° 56'E

Ward Collection, (Ethno) 1934.10-18.140-180

This collection appears to comprise two distinct components, one of Middle Stone Age origin and the other of Later Stone Age origin. The dominance of small, thumbnail type scrapers in the latter suggests an affiliation with the Wilton or post-classic Wilton Industries. The former group numbers 12 artefacts and the latter 28 artefacts. Two unworked pieces of stone are also present.

Middle Stone Age component: 2 irregular cores (1 in quartzite, 1 in hornfels), 7 unmodified flakes (4 in hornfels, 3 in quartzite), 2 points (in quartzite). Both the points, as well as one of the flakes, have faceted platforms.

Table 10. Later Stone Age artefacts in the Ward Collection from the Hillary site, Carnarvondale.

	Opaline	Hornfels	Silcrete	Quartz	Quartzite	Sandstone	Total
Irregular cores	2	-	-	-	-	1	3
Crested blades	-	-	-	-	1	-	1
Flakes	5	1	1	-	-	-	7
Scrapers	5	4	5	1	-	-	15
Segments	1	-	-	-	-	-	1
Retouched blades	-	1	-	-	-	-	1
Total	13	6	6	1	1	1	28

CARNARVONDALE (VAN RIET LOWE'S SITE)APPROXIMATELY 33° 26'S, 25° 56'E

Ward Collection, (Ethno) 1934.10-18.181-209

A group of 28 Later Stone Age artefacts, most likely to be of Wilton or post-classic Wilton affiliation given the morphology of the scrapers and the presence of two segments.

Table 11. The Ward Collection from Van Riet Lowe's site, Carnarvondale.

	Opaline	Hornfels	Silcrete	Tuff	Sandstone	Total
Irregular cores	3	-	-	-	-	3
Bladelet cores	2	-	2	-	-	4
Flakes	1	-	-	-	-	1
Blades	1	-	-	-	-	1
Scrapers	4	1	7	1	-	13
Adzes (backed)	-	-	1	-	-	1
Borers	-	-	1	-	-	1
Segments	-	-	1	-	1	2
Miscellaneous retouched pieces	2	-	-	-	-	2
Total	13	1	12	1	1	28

Additional material Pitt Rivers Museum (Appendix 3).

CARNARVONDALE (WILMAN'S SITE) APPROXIMATELY 33° 26'S, 25° 56'E

Ward Collection, (Ethno) 1934.10-18.42-87

Two components are present in this part of the Ward Collection from Carnavondale, a Middle Stone Age group of 5 artefacts and a Later Stone Age group of 41 artefacts, that consists mostly of a range of formal tools and, given the small thumbnail type of the majority of the scrapers, must be of Wilton/post-classic Wilton affiliation.

Middle Stone Age component: 5 unmodified flakes (4 in quartzite, 1 in silcrete, all with faceted platforms).

Table 12. Later Stone Age artefacts in the Ward Collection from Wilman's site, Carnarvondale

	Opaline	Silcrete	Quartzite	Total
Irregular cores	4	2	-	6
Flat bladelet cores	1	-	-	1
Flakes	3	5	1	9
Blades	-	-	1	1
Proximal sections	-	1	-	1
Distal sections	-	1	-	1
Scrapers	1	14	-	15

Table 12 cont. Later Stone Age artefacts in the Ward Collection from Wilman's site, Carnarvondale

	Opaline	Silcrete	Quartzite	Total
Adzes	1	-	-	1
Borers	1	-	-	1
Backed bladelets	2	2	-	4
Segments	-	1	-	1
Total	13	26	2	41

CARNARVONDALE (WOODBURY SITE) APPROXIMATELY 33° 32'S, 26° 11'E

Ward Collection, (Ethno) 1934.10-18.22-41

A small collection of mostly opaline and quartzite artefacts, at least some of which (to judge from the presence of a flake-blade, flake-blade sections and several flakes, all with faceted platforms) are of Middle Stone Age origin.

Table 13. The Ward Collection from the Woodbury site, Carnarvondale

	Opaline	Hornfels	Quartzite	Sandstone	Total
Irregular cores	-	1	1	-	2
Bladelet cores	1	-	-	-	1
Flakes	2	1	7	3	13
Flake-blades	-	-	1	-	1
Proximal sections	-	-	2	-	2
Utilised flakes	-	-	1	-	1
Miscellaneous retouched pieces	1	-	-	-	1
Total	4	2	12	3	21

Additional material Pitt Rivers Museum (Appendix 3).

COEGA 26° 45'S, 25° 40'E

Trechmann Collection, P1964.12-6.1501

1 quartzite handaxe.

EAST LONDON 33° 01'S, 27° 58'E

The East London area has been the focus of archaeological interest since the initial observation of stone artefacts prehistoric shell middens on the banks of the Quigney River by George McKay (1897) in 1857. He subsequently recovered artefacts from a number of locations within the general East London area, locating them on a map now held by the British Museum **(Fig. 13)** and referred to by Hillier (1898: 122). Subsequently, the work of these pioneers was followed up by Laidler (1934, 1935), Macfarlane (1935, 1936) and Hanisch (1958). Derricourt (1977: 33-34) indicates the presence of Early and, more commonly, Middle Stone Age artefacts in coastal clay deposits, and of numerous coastal shell middens around the mouth of the Buffalo River (qv) that have produced Later Stone Age material (Derricourt 1977: 113-114). Some of the latter, as well as Bat's Cave, which has a MSA deposit, were also investigated by Leith (1898: 264-265). However, the bulk of the British Museum holdings from East London reflect the collecting activities of Hillier (1898) and McKay (1897). The Avebury and Christy Collections probably derive ultimately from the latter's work.

Avebury Collection 1916.6-5.39-41

3 Middle Stone Age bifacial points (in silcrete).

Christy Collection, ex Atherstone, S. Afr. 11-12

2 Middle Stone Age unmodified flake-blades (1 in patinated hornfels, 1 in quartzite).

Christy Collection, ex Busk, ex Dale, ex McKay, +7698 - +7703

A group of five, almost certainly Later Stone Age artefacts from a 'kitchen midden' mentioned by Dale (1871: 348) in his paper to the Royal Anthropological Institute.

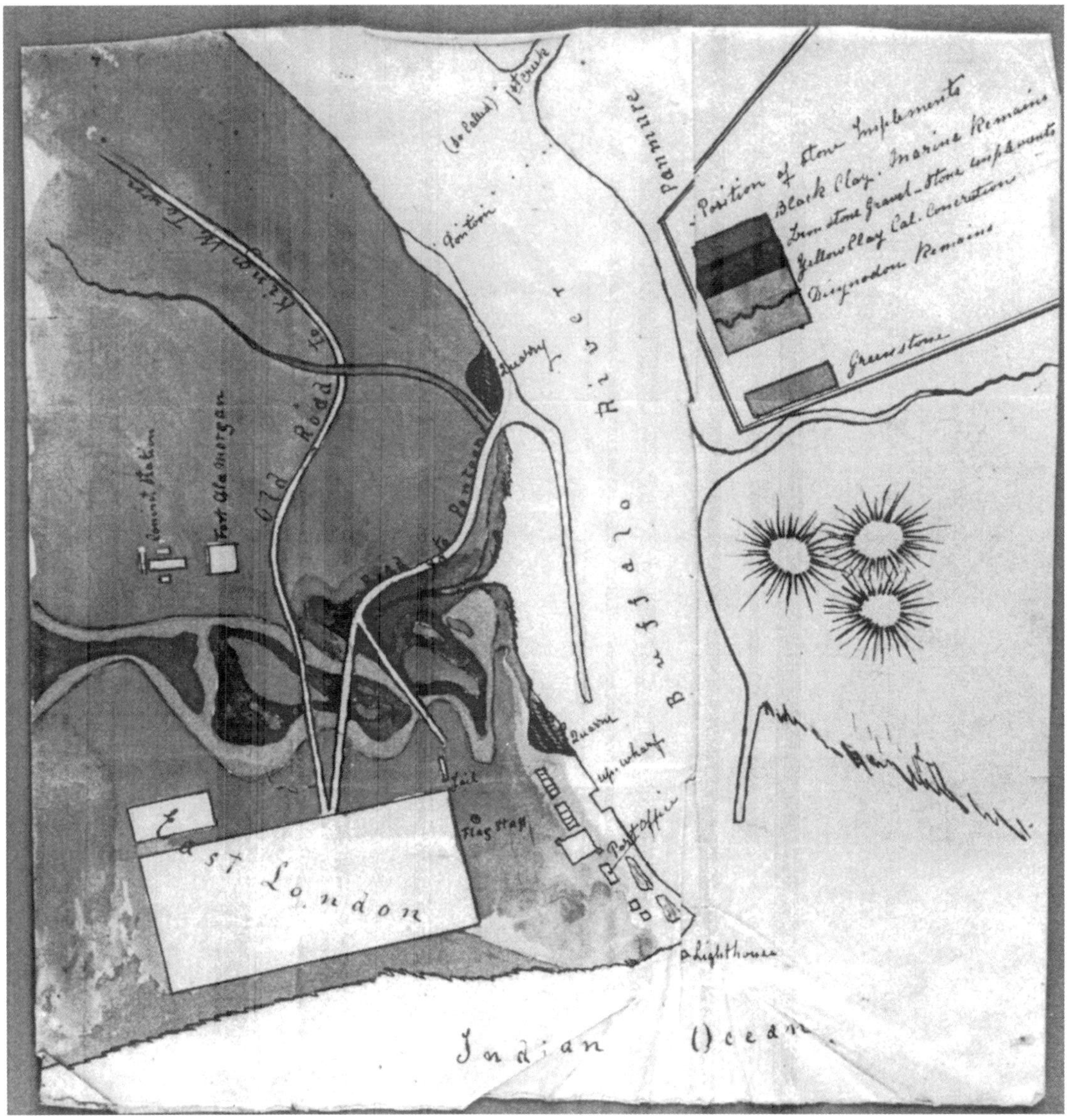

Fig.13. George McKay's map of his excavations in the East London area, Eastern Cape Province.

Artefact	Raw material	Figure no. in Dale (1871: 348)
Unmodified flake	Sandstone	19
Upper grindstone	Sandstone	22
Bored stone	Dolerite	51
Upper/lower grindstone	Sandstone	52
Upper/lower grindstone	Sandstone	53

Christy Collection, ex McKay, +7721 - +7722

2 Middle Stone Age unmodified flake-blades (in sandstone).

The Geological Museum Collection, ex H. W. Piers, P1989.3-1.101-109

Stated on the accompanying label to have come 'from gravel under 4 feet of clay', this group comprises nine, rolled and heavily patinated hornfels artefacts. Four have faceted platforms and all are likely to be of Middle Stone Age origin. A lump of non-artefactual ironstone is also present. These artefacts were almost certainly obtained from McKay's (1897) excavations as correspondence in the British Museum archives dated to 1867 show that Piers was instrumental in having some of McKay's finds sent to Britain.

9 unmodified flakes (in hornfels).

Hillier Collection, ex Atherstone, 1887.4-6.23-27
A group of 4 artefacts, a fifth piece being of natural origin. The two rolled flakes may be of Middle Stone Age origin, while the bored stone is of Later Stone Age origin.
3 unmodified flakes (all in hornfels; 2 in a heavily rolled condition are also patinated), 1 unfinished fragment of a bored stone (in dolerite).
In addition to these stone artefacts the Hillier Collection from East London also includes two longbone shaft fragments of a large-medium-sized bovid and a large concreted piece of shell midden deposit.

Additional material Cambridge University Museum (East London, west of Fort Glamorgan; East London, near Fort Grey), The Natural History Museum, Pitt Rivers Museum (Appendix 3).

EAST LONDON, *BRITISH KAFFRARIA* 33° 01'S, 27° 55'E AND 32° 59'S, 27° 56'E
McKay passed some of the artefacts that he collected in the East London area to the Rev. Langham Dale, who included them with material that he himself had collected on the Cape Flats in a consignment exihibited before the newly formed Anthropological Institute in London. Dale (1871: 347) reports that the artefacts in this collection from the Eastern Cape came from the mouth of the Buffalo River at East London and from the west bank of the Kahoon (*sic*, modern Nahoon) River, 1.5 miles (2.5 km) from the sea. Both localities now lie within the city of East London and the Christy Slip Catalogue only records more detailed provenances for some of the artefacts: +7704 from near the mouth of the Nahoon River and +7706 - +7711 from ? East London. For this reason a general provenance to East London has been given here.

Christy Collection, ex Busk, ex Dale, ex McKay, +7704 - +7718
A group of 16 partly rolled Middle Stone Age artefacts all made in dolerite. All retain their original labels.
10 unmodified flakes, 6 unmodified flake-blades (of which two have lost their tips and the largest - +7717 - has a faceted platform).

Additional material Department of Ethnography, British Museum (Appendix 1).Cambridge University Museum (East London, Nahoon River Mouth; Pitt Rivers Museum (Nahoon, Nahun River) (Appendix 3).

GRAHAMSTOWN 33° 20'S, 26° 38'E
Colonel T. H. Bowker, described by Goodwin (1946a: 18) as South Africa's 'first true antiquary', sent some of the artefacts that he collected from rock-shelters in Lesotho to Sir Charles Lyell (Bowker 1884). As early as 1855, Bowker was excavating stone artefacts near the Fish River just to the east of Grahamstown, some of which he also sent to Britain (Grey 1869; Feilden 1883). It is likely that all eight of these Middle Stone Age artefacts from Grahamstown form part of the material that Bowker excavated. They are probably the 'eight flakes or arrowheads of a siliceous sandstone found in the neighbourhood of Graham's Town' referred to in the 1867 issue of the *Proceedings of the Society of Antiquaries of London* (3: 235-236), an identification made more likely by the fact that at least those in the Christy Collection were presented to the British Museum in 1868.

Christy Collection, ex Lyell, +7752
A group of seven Middle Stone Age artefacts, all heavily rolled, patinated and made in hornfels.
6 unmodified flakes (3 with faceted platforms), 1 unmodified flake-blade of which the proximal section is missing.

Sturge Collection, ex Lyell,
1 unmodified flake-blade (in hornfels).

Additional material Ashmolean Museum, Cambridge University Museum (Grahamstown, Glencraig Farm), The Natural History Museum, Pitt Rivers Museum (Appendix 3).

GRAHAMSTOWN (SUGER LOAF HILL) 33° 20'S, 26° 38'E
Albany Museum Collection 1922.5-6.3-5
A group of three silcrete artefacts, not by themselves culturally diagnostic, found under 'several feet' of soil.
2 scrapers in rolled condition, 1 miscellaneous retouched piece.

HALSETON 31° 30'S, 26° 46'E
The precise location of the site from which this collection derives is unknown, other than that it was some '2 miles from the foot of the Stormberg Mountains' according to an accompanying label. Further to the northwest Kannemeyer (1890), Leith (1898) and Saw (Appendix 1) explored rock-shelters at the end of the 19th century, while immediately to the west Sampson (1970: 106-129) excavated a Holocene Later Stone Age sequence at Merino Walk Cave in the 1960s. Opperman (1987) found Grassridge rock-shelter near Sterkstroom, still further west, to have evidence of both mid-Holocene and Middle Stone Age occupation, but there is little published record of significantly older occupation in the area.

Bays Collection, (Ethno) 1923.4-14.1-37, 51-78

A collection of 64 mainly hornfels artefacts that mostly comprise unmodified flakes and flake-blades, although retouched pieces and a few bifaces are also present. Assuming that all the artefacts genuinely belong to the same assemblage, an attribution to the Fauresmith Industry is probable. One unworked piece of stone is also present.

Table 14. The Bays Collection from Halseton

	Hornfels	Quartzite	Dolerite	Sandstone	Total
Cleavers	-	-	2	-	2
Handaxes	2	-	1	-	3
Bifacial choppers	-	1	-	-	1
Irregular cores	4	3	2	-	9
Flakes	12	6	1	-	19
Flake-blades	10	-	-	1	11
Flake-blade proximal sections	2	-	-	-	2
Flake-blade mesial sections	5	-	-	-	5
Flake-blade distal sections	1	-	-	-	1
Utilised flakes	3	-	-	-	3
Utilised flake-blades	1	-	-	-	1
Scrapers	3	-	1	-	4
Retouched points	2	-	-	-	2
Unworked pebbles	1	-	-	-	1
Total	46	10	7	1	64

Additional material Department of Ethnography, British Museum (Appendix 1).Cambridge University Museum (Appendix 3).

KASOUGA RIVER 33° 40'S, 26° 44'E

The area around the Kasouga River is home to several Later Stone Age occurrences that feature distinctive artefacts known as Kasouga flakes. These artefacts, which exhibit scaled flaking down one or both sides of a long flake or blade, are one of several examples of an increasing regionalization of material culture that distinguishes the Cape Fold Mountain Belt and its coastal forelands in the Eastern Cape during the last 4-5000 years BP (S. Hall 1990).

Albany Museum Collection 1922.5-6.38-39

Two silcrete artefacts, both probably of Later Stone Age origin.
1 miscellaneous retouched piece, 1 invasively retouched mesial section of a bladelet (*cf.* Kasouga flake).

KEISKAMMA RIVER MOUTH 33° 17'S, 27° 29'E

Derricourt (1977: 111) records that several open air sites are known at the mouth of the Keiskamma River, some of them shell middens associated with pottery and ground stone artefacts, others of Middle Stone Age origin. Hollow-based Middle Stone Age points of the kind present in this collection from this locality are also recorded further to the west from Kleinemonde (qv; Clark 1959: 175) where Atherstone also collected.

Christy Collection, ex Atherstone, S. Afr. 18

1 hollow-based, but unretouched Middle Stone Age point (in hornfels).

KLEINEMONDE 33° 32'S, 27° 03'E

Atherstone collected several Middle Stone Age artefacts from Kleinemonde, some of which went to the collections of the Albany Museum, Grahamstown (Goodwin & Van Riet Lowe 1929: 115). A further 17 artefacts from sites in this area were presented to the British Museum. The locality itself lies only a few kilometres east of Tharfield (qv), family farm of the Bowker family and source of a further component of the British Museum southern African holdings. The Lyell Collection itself from Kleinemonde is, according to the Christy Catalogue, provenanced to a surface assemblage found under sand within a mile (1.5 km) of the sea.

Christy Collection, ex Atherstone, S. Afr. 1-9

A group of nine Middle Stone Age artefacts all with faceted platforms.
8 unmodified flakes (4 in hornfels, 1 in quartzite and 3 in silcrete), 1 unmodified flake-blade (in hornfels).

Lyell Collection, ex Bain, 1865.12-21.1-8

A group of eight unmodified Middle Stone Age flakes, all with faceted platforms.
8 unmodified flakes (5 in hornfels, 2 in quartzite, 1 in tuff).

MIDDLEDRIFT 32° 49'S, 27° 01'E

This site was visited by Miles Burkitt (1928: 45-46) during his tour of South Africa, at which time it was already well known as a source of Early and Middle Stone Age artefacts found in the alluvial deposits of the Keiskamma River or, more sporadically, on the surface; Goodwin & Van Riet Lowe (1929: 30) also mention it, commenting specifically on the work of the Wilson brothers here. Derricourt (1977: 31) adds that reports that some Middledrift artefacts had been sold to a foreign museum sparked 'a minor gold rush situation in pre-war years by amateur collectors'; other material from this site is widely distributed in museums at Fort Hare, Fort Beaufort, Grahamstown, King William's Town and Cape Town (Derricourt 1977: 32). He further cautions that because most finds from 'Middledrift', including those in the British Museum's own collections, lack any more detailed provenance, it is probably best to assume only a general location within this stretch of the Keiskamma River valley and no more; that this collection is clearly an amalgam of several different Early, Middle and Later Stone Age occurrences lends weight to this argument. Indeed, Derricourt (1977: 137-165) also reports the presence immediately south of Middledrift itself of a series of open air LSA scatters, as well as of ashy mounds that contain lithics, pottery, faunal remains and human burials; he associates these mounds with ceramic, stone-using pastoralists probably ancestral to the historic Gonaqua Khoi. All of the material from this locality was referred to by the original collectors as King Williams Town, the nearest large settlement.

Wilson Brothers Collection, (Ethno) 1931.18-45

A group of 28 artefacts, the vast majority of them clearly of Early Stone Age origin, though the upper grindstone is probably of much more recent (Later Stone Age) origin.
20 handaxes (17 in quartzite, 2 in dolerite, 1 in siltstone/mudstone), 3 cleavers (in quartzite), 1 bifacially worked implement (in quartzite), 2 irregular cores (in dolerite), 1 unmodified flake (in dolerite), 1 upper grindstone (in sandstone).

Wilson Brothers Collection, (Ethno) 1926.4-12.1-131 and 4-13.1-50

This extensive collection of 201 artefacts can be divided into separate Early/Middle, Middle and Later Stone Age components, respectively totalling 94, 16 and 101 artefacts.

Table 15. Early/Middle Stone Age artefacts in the Wilson Brothers Collection from Middledrift (Ethno) 1926.4-12.1-33 and 1926.4-13.1-50

	Hornfels	Silcrete	Quartzite	Sandstone	Total
Cleavers	-	-	13	-	13
Handaxes	-	-	37	-	37
Spheroids	-	-	4	-	4
Irregular cores	-	-	8	-	8
Blade cores	-	-	2	-	2
Crested blades	-	1	-	-	1
Flakes	-	-	5	-	5
Flake-blades	-	-	4	-	4
Hammerstones	-	-	1	-	1
Upper grindstones	-	-	-	3	3
Scrapers	-	-	6	-	6
Knives - unilateral	-	-	3	-	3
Knives - bilateral	-	-	3	-	3
Points	-	-	3	-	3
Unifacial points	1	-	-	-	1
Total	1	1	89	3	94

Table 16. Middle Stone Age artefacts in the Wilson Brothers Collection from Middledrift (Ethno) 1926.4-12.34-49

	Hornfels	Quartzite	Total
Irregular cores	-	1	1
Disc cores	1	1	2
Flake-blades	2	1	3
Mesial sections	-	1	1
Scrapers	2	2	4
Knives - unilateral	1	-	1
Knives - bilateral	1	1	2
Points	1	1	2
Total	8	8	16

Table 17. Later Stone Age artefacts in the Wilson Brothers Collection from Middledrift (Ethno) 1926.4-12.50-131 + unnumbered

	Opaline	Hornfels	Silcrete	Quartz	Quartzite	Baked sandstone	Total
Chunks	-	-	1	-	-	-	1
Irregular cores	-	-	3	-	-	-	3
Crested blades	-	2	1	-	-	-	3
Core rejuvenation flakes	-	-	2	-	-	-	2
Core-reduced pieces	2	-	-	-	-	-	2
Flakes	6	9	9	2	1	1	28
Bladelets	1	-	-	-	-	-	1
Proximal sections	-	1	1	-	-	-	2
Mesial sections	-	1	-	-	-	-	1
Scrapers	2	9	38	-	1	-	50
Backed scrapers	-	-	1	-	-	-	1
Borers	-	-	-	-	1	-	1
Backed bladelets	2	2	-	-	-	-	4
Backed fragments	1	-	-	-	-	-	1
Ventrally retouched bladelet mesial section	1	-	-	-	-	-	1
Total	15	24	56	2	3	1	101

The vast majority of the scrapers in this group are of the small thumbnail kind characteristic of Wilton Industry assemblages. This attribution, though not perhaps to the classic, segment-rich phase of the Wilton, is supported by the presence of several backed pieces. The possibility that an older Later Stone Age component is also present is suggested by the large size (> 30 mm) of six of the scrapers, two of which (both made in hornfels) have adze-like retouch along their lateral margins.

Additional material Department of Ethnography, British Museum (Appendix 1). Cambridge University Museum (Middledrift; Middledrift, Cildarra Road; Middledrift, Euphorbia Kloof; Middledrift, Fort Lex; Middledrift, Wilsons' Farm), Pitt Rivers Museum (Appendix 3).

THARFIELD 33° 32'S, 26° 59'

T. H. Bowker was collecting stone artefacts in the Eastern Cape at least as early as 1855 when Busk (1869) saw some of them in the collections of the South African Museum in Cape Town (Goodwin 1935: 295). Bowker (1884) himself recorded that he sent artefacts to the Royal Artillery Museum and to Sir Charles Lyell in Britain, but he clearly also passed others to Sir George Grey, Governor of the Cape Colony from 1854 to 1861. Tharfield was the Bowker family farm and adds a further locality to those from which T. H. Bowker and his brother were responsible for collecting material that became part of the British Museum collections. It lies only a few kilometres to the west of Kleinemonde (qv) from which the British Museum also has material.

Christy Collection, ex Grey,

With the exception of a single milled-edge quartzite pebble and a single Early Stone Age handaxe, this group is entirely

Middle Stone Age in origin (**Fig. 14**). A wide variety of materials is present, but faceted platformed unmodified flakes are numerically dominant. The Middle Stone Age artefacts total 39, the whole collection 41.

Table 18. The Christy Collection, ex Grey, from Tharfield

	Opaline	Hornfels	Silcrete	Quartzite	Siltstone/ mudstone	Baked silt- stone/mudstone	Sandstone	Total
Handaxe (ESA)	-	-	-	1	-	-	-	1
Disc cores	-	-	1	1	-	1	-	3
Flakes	1	8	2	2	1	6	4	24
Flake-blades	1	-	-	3	-	-	2	6
Milled-edge pebble (LSA)	-	-	-	1	-	-	-	1
Scrapers	-	1	-	-	-	-	-	1
Points	-	2	1	1	-	1	-	5
Total	2	11	4	9	1	8	6	41

The handaxe and the milled-edge pebble (along with another now not traceable) were exhibited at a meeting of the Ethnological Society in London in 1869. Grey's (1870) account of this meeting makes it clear that at least these two artefacts had originally been collected by T. H. Bowker (Appendix 4).

Additional material The Natural History Museum (Appendix 3).

WILTON LARGE ROCK SHEALTER 33° 20'S, 26° 09'E

Hewitt (1921) excavated two rock-shelters on the farm called Wilton near Alicedale (qv) and the material from these two sites subsequently formed the basis for the definition of the Wilton Industry, the principal mid-late Holocene Later Stone Age microlithic industry of southern Africa. One of these sites (the Large Rock Shelter) was re-excavated by J. Deacon (1972), who showed that it was occupied through most of the Holocene and that the high frequencies of segments thought at one stage to define the Wilton as a whole are, in fact, characteristic only of that part of the sequence dating to 4860 $\pm$ 115 BP (I-2565) and immediately thereafter (J. Deacon 1972: 36). The remainder of the Wilton typesite sequence includes both earlier and later phases of the same tradition (Early, Developed and Ceramic *sensu* Sampson 1974), as well as a basal assemblage that belongs to the Albany Industry and probably dates to around 10 000 BP.

The small collection from the Wilton Large Rock Shelter in the British Museum is obviously highly selected and numbers only 30 artefacts. However, for what it is worth the proportion of scrapers to segments is roughly the same as that in the Albany Museum's own collection from the site (J. Deacon 1972: 47).

Albany Museum Collection, per Kettlewell, 1922.5-6.8-37

Table 19. The Albany Museum Collection from Wilton Large Rock Shelter

	Opaline	Hornfels	Silcrete	Total
Crested blades	-	-	2	2
Flakes	-	-	2	2
Bladelets	1	-	5	6
Scrapers	1	1	17	19
Segments	-	-	1	1
Total	2	1	27	30

Additional material Cambridge University Museum, Pitt Rivers Museum (Appendix 3).

ZWARTKOPS RIVER 26° 50'S, 25° 34'E

This Early Stone Age artefact in rolled condition was found in gravels near Redhouse on the south bank of the river close to its mouth.

Trechmann Collection P1964.12-6.1502

1 handaxe (in quartzite).

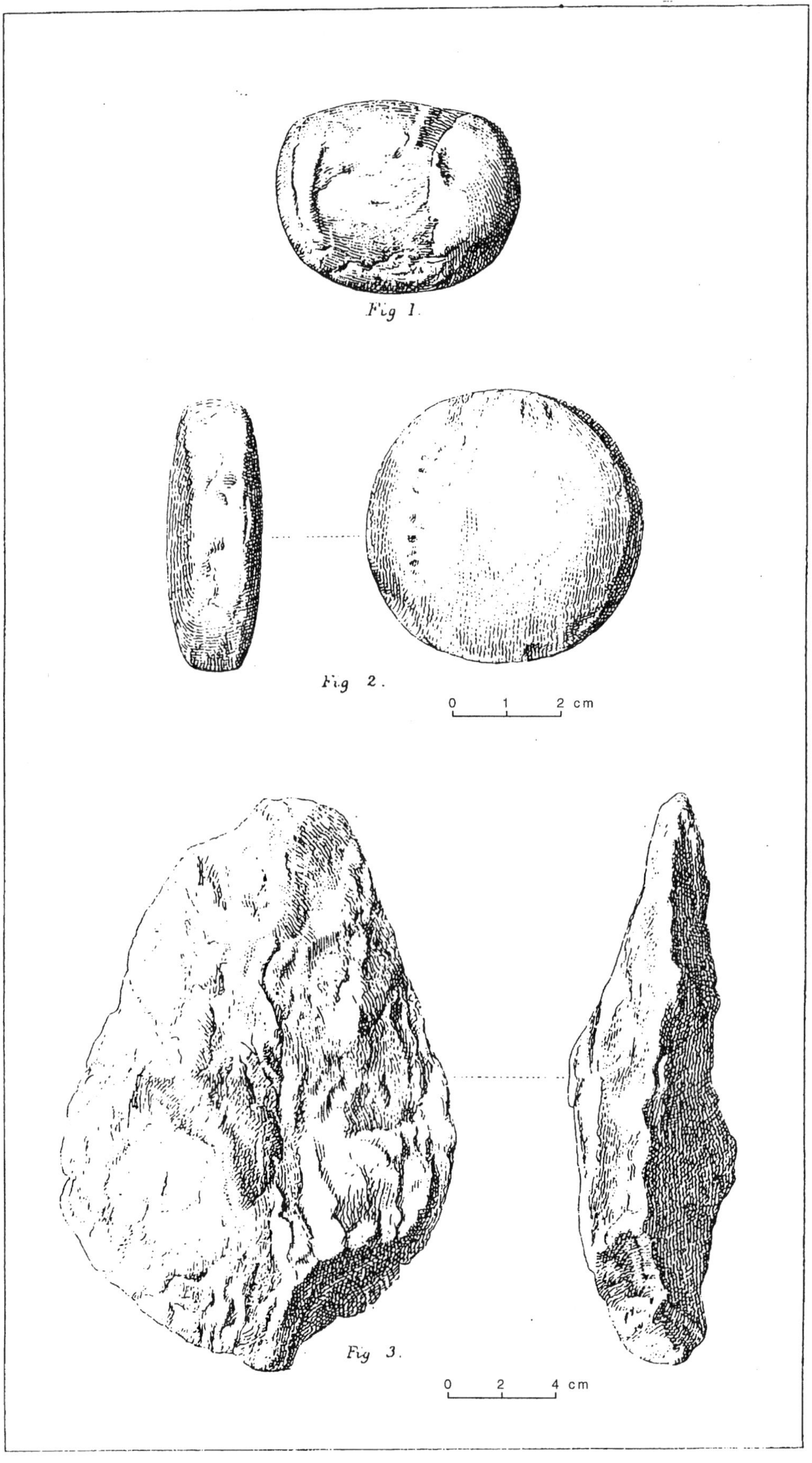

Fig. 14. Artefacts from the Christy ex Grey Collection from Tharfield, Eastern Cape Province (after Grey 1869:Plate 1). 1 milled-edge pebble (quartzite, not in the British Museums collections); 2 milled-edge pebble (Late Stone Age, quartzite); 3 handaxe (Early Stone Age, quartzite).

2.2 South Africa: Free State

The Free State was one of the great centres of archaeological research in the 1920s and 1930s, the decades when the subject was, for the first time, placed upon a systematic footing in South Africa. Credit for both of these developments goes, in large part, to Clarence Van Riet Lowe, who not only defined the Fauresmith Industry and three distinct phases of the Later Stone Age Smithfield Industry on the basis of surface collections from sites such as Fauresmith, Avalon, Lockshoek and Ventershoek (qqv; Goodwin & Van Riet Lowe 1929), but also carried out extensive surveys for painted and non-painted Stone Age sites in several parts of the province, not least the Little Caledon River Valley (Van Riet Lowe 1952a, 1956). Since then excavations at two Stone Age sites in the province - Florisbad and Rose Cottage Cave - stand out in terms of their stratigraphic complexity and overall significance for understanding hunter-gatherer behaviour. The archaeological potential of the several fossil spring eyes at Florisbad had been evident for almost 20 years before the discovery in 1932 of an archaic *Homo sapiens* cranium associated with a diverse faunal assemblage, including the bones of many extinct animals (Brink *et al.* 1996). On the basis of these and further excavations in 1952, the site was acquired by the National Museum in Bloemfontein in 1980. It has since been under continuous investigation. Re-study of existing faunal and artefact collections has greatly clarified their taphonomy (Kuman & Clarke 1986; Brink 1987) and provided new insights into the evolutionary ecology of various bovid taxa (e.g. Brink & Lee Thorp 1992). The expansion of the excavation has also provided more detailed palaeoecological evidence (e.g. Rubidge & Brink 1985), while exposing for study what is now recognised to be an *in situ* Middle Stone Age occupation horizon of Last Interglacial age (Z. Henderson, pers. comm.).

Lying in the Caledon River Valley, which marks the eastern edge of the Free State, Rose Cottage Cave has some 6 m of archaeological deposit and a long suite of Middle and Later Stone Age occupations initially investigated by B. Malan (1958) and then by Beaumont (1978). Since the late 1980s the site has been the focal point of a long-term research project into Free State prehistory directed by Lyn Wadley (1991, 1997). In addition to bringing much greater clarity into our understanding of the site's chrono-stratigraphic sequence, new excavations at Rose Cottage Cave have emphasized the recovery of a range of palaeoenvironmental data for what has, until now, been a comparatively unknown part of southern Africa (e.g. Plug & Engela 1992; Esterhuysen 1996; Smith 1997). They also continue to stress the analysis of the use of space within the site, including the recovery of spatial data relevant to the interpretation of gender-associated activities in the cave (Wadley 1997). Several further rock-shelters in the eastern Free State have been excavated as part of the overall Rose Cottage project (Wadley 1995). Though none have produced anything remotely comparable in terms of depth or complexity of deposit, collectively they promise to provide a much sounder basis for studying the history of forager communities in the area, including their relations to incoming farmers (Klatzow 1994; Thorp 1996) and European settlers (Wadley 1992).

Elsewhere in the Free State few sites have been excavated, among them rock-shelters in the Bethlehem/Clarens area (Harding 1951; Rautenbach 1967) and the lower Caledon Valley (Brooker 1980; Sampson 1970) and open-air sites at Voightspost in the more arid, western part of the province (Horowitz *et al.* 1978). The rich rock art record of the Free State has, however, been the subject of much recent research. Building on records developed over the last hundred years by numerous amateur archaeologists (from Stow (1905) to Woodhouse (1996)), rock art research is now also part of the National Museum's structure and aims at systematic recording of rock paintings throughout the province. This has provided a basis for considering the relations between hunter-gatherers and Iron Age agropastoralists (Loubser & Laurens 1994), as well as the integration of painted and excavated material culture (Ouzman 1997; Ouzman & Wadley 1997), including the study of wide-ranging LSA social networks (Ouzman 1995).

The Free State is, in terms of artefacts, the best represented of all South Africa's provinces in the British Museum Stone Age collections (**Fig. 15**). This is in large part to the activities of H. Braunholtz, who, as President of the Royal Anthropological Institute, played a major rôle in the 1929 meeting in southern Africa of the British Associaton for the Advancement of Science. The majority of the stone artefacts from the Free State in the British Museum are the result of collections he made during this visit to South Africa, at a time at which Goodwin and Van Riet Lowe (1929) were laying the foundations of their cultural taxonomy of the southern African Later Stone Age. As a consequence the British Museum has artefacts from several of the type-sites that they used in the definition of the A, B and C phases of the Smithfield Industry: Avalon, Lockshoek and Ventershoek respectively. Brakfontein, the type-site of the late Acheulean Fauresmith Industry, is also well represented in the Braunholtz Collection, along with further artefacts from two localities at Fauresmith itself. Smaller collections of interest include those from Modderpoort (Tribe Collection), an open air site in the eastern Free State at which B. Malan (1946) first identified the so-called Modderpoort variant of the Middle Stone Age.

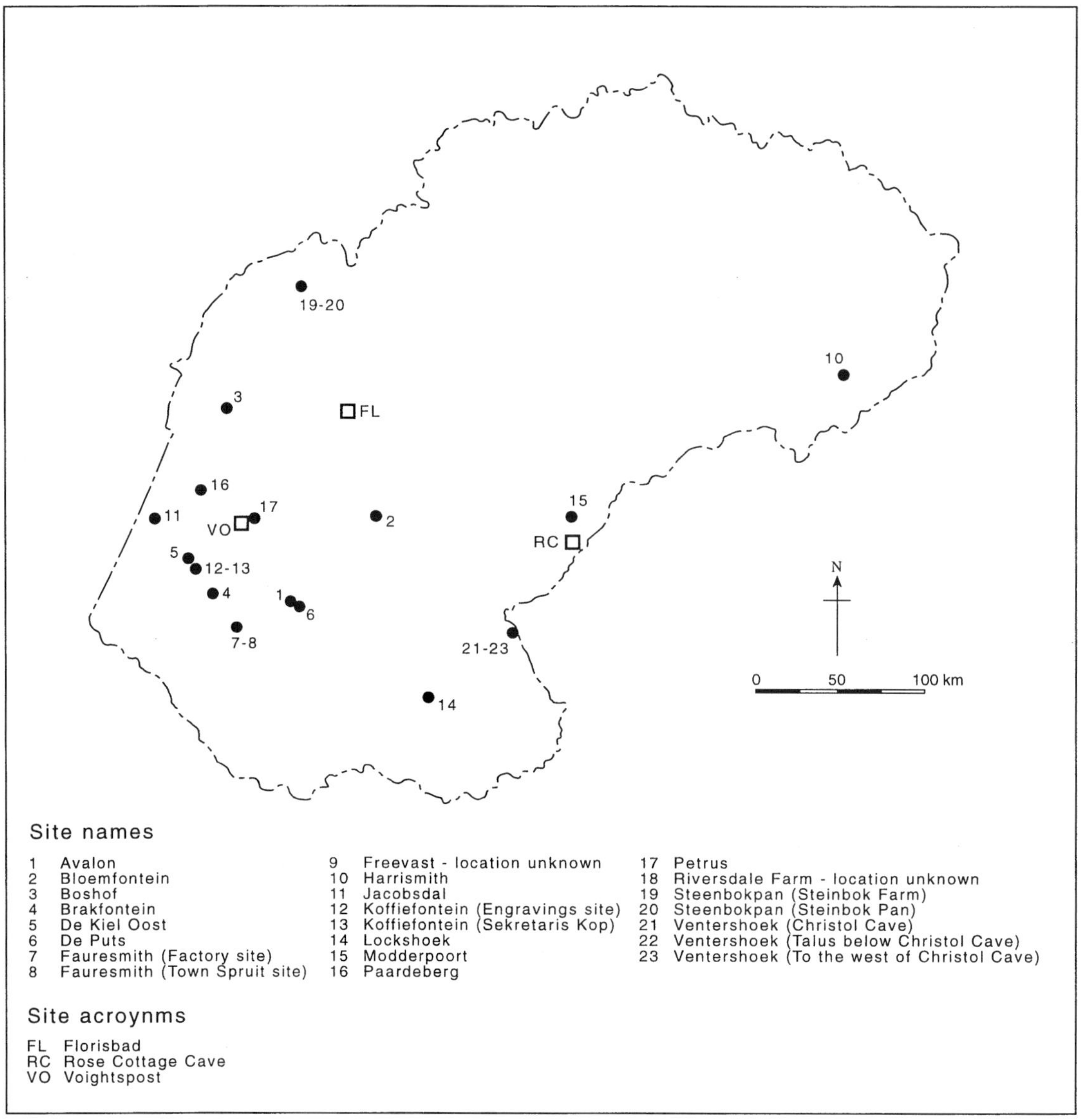

Fig. 15. Location of archaeological sites in the Free State and of Stone Age collections from there in the British Museum

AVALON 29 34'S, 25 40'E

Avalon was the type-site of the Smithfield B culture defined by Goodwin & Van Riet Lowe, no other site producing such 'a quantity of "finished" specimens' (Goodwin & Van Riet Lowe 1929: 179). The term 'Smithfield B' is, however, no longer current, having been rejected as based on poorly defined, selectively collected surface samples. The designation 'Smithfield' has, instead, come to be applied to terminal Later Stone Age occurrences from the Free State and upper Karoo made almost entirely in hornfels, virtually lacking in backed microliths and accompanied by pottery (Sampson 1985: 86-93).

Braunholtz Collection, (Ethno) 1930.1-24

The vast majority of the assemblage of 368 artefacts and eight unworked pieces of sandstone present in the British Museum collections is clearly a selected assemblage of Lockshoek Industry material. A few Middle Stone Age artefacts are also present, along with some scrapers that are probably of Wilton, or possibly Smithfield Industry, type. However, most of the scrapers are either large sidestruck examples or have typical Lockshoek adze-like lateral retouch. Although almost all artefacts are in hornfels, in varying degrees of patination from completely unpatinated to complete coverage with a orange-brown patina, a small number are made in opalines derived from the gravels of the Gariep and/or Caledon Rivers. Some of the artefacts have been made on reused MSA flakes or blades. This is the case for the single adze found (made on a reused MSA flake-blade section) and for possibly as many as five of the hornfels scrapers present. Such reuse of MSA artefacts is well attested in late Holocene contexts in the Western Cape, as well as at Rose Cottage Cave (Wadley 1992).

Table 20. The Braunholtz Collection from Avalon

	Opaline	Hornfels	Dolerite	Sandstone	Total
Handaxe	-	1	-	-	1
Chunks	2	-	-	-	2
Irregular cores	-	26	-	-	26
Bladelet cores	-	2	-	-	2
Crested blades	-	1	-	-	1
Flakes	2	80	-	-	82
Flake-blades	-	1	-	-	1
Blades	-	4	-	-	4
Bladelets	-	2	-	-	2
Utilised flakes	-	11	-	-	11
Grooved stone	-	-	-	1	1
Reamer	-	1	-	-	1
Scrapers	2	227	1	-	230
Adze	-	1	-	-	1
Miscellaneous retouched pieces	-	2	-	-	2
MSA point	-	1	-	-	1
Total	6	360	1	1	368

Additional material Department of Ethnography, British Museum (Appendix 1).Cambridge University Museum (Appendix 3).

BLOEMFONTEIN 29° 12'S, 26° 15'E

Van Heerden Collection, (Ethno) 1930.10-18.1-26

A group of 26 Later Stone Age artefacts. The hornfels artefacts are either unpatinated or lightly patinated, suggesting that they are not all of the same age. The probability that this is a mixed assemblage is enhanced by consideration of the scrapers; the nine large (> 30 mm) specimens and six specimens with adze-like lateral retouch most likely belong to the Lockshoek Industry, but four smaller convex scrapers are of 'thumbnail' Wilton type and one made on an endstruck flake may belong to the Smithfield Industry. All the artefacts are in hornfels unless otherwise stated.
2 irregular cores, 3 unmodified flakes (1 in siltstone), 21 scrapers (1 in opaline).

Additional material Birmingham Museum, Cambridge University Museum (Bloemfontein, Maselspoort; Bloemfontein, Samaria Road), Pitt Rivers Museum (Appendix 3).

BOSHOF 28° 32'S, 25° 14'E

Christy Collection, ex Anderson, +7913

Two lightly patinated Middle Stone Age flake-blades, both missing their butts, but having light trimming along their edges. Associated labels state that one was found in 1882, the other in 1883.
2 utilised flake-blades (in hornfels).

Additional material Cambridge University Museum, Pitt Rivers Museum (Appendix 3).

BRAKFONTEIN 29° 33'S, 25° 09'E

Braunholtz Collection, (Ethno) 1930.1-24

This material consists of two separate components, one Later Stone Age and the other Middle Stone Age. Information on attached cards indicates that these components come from two physically separate sites, respectively located to the north and to the south of the Riet River. However, the labels now present in the respective boxes are sometimes at odds with the contents, suggesting that material and/or labels have, at some time, moved between boxes and become mixed: for example, a group of 12 artefacts, including a naturally backed knife and five scrapers, as well as two MSA flakes, is now associated with a label stating them to be Fauresmith, while the label that clearly relates to this group of artefacts is now associated with a group of seven irregular hornfels cores. While this error is comparatively easy to make sense of, it is not possible to be certain that other boxes are wholly from the one location or the other. Based on artefact typology and associated labels, the most likely attribution is as follows:

Brakfontein Middle Stone Age Site

This site is stated, on an attached card, to be located south of the Riet River approximately 10 miles (15 km) before reaching Fauresmith. It is described briefly by Goodwin & Van Riet Lowe (1929: 86), who used it as the main type-site of the Fauresmith Industry. The 86 artefacts and two unworked pieces of stone from here are, except where indicated below, all made in hornfels which exhibits a variable grey/brown/red patina. Faceting of platforms is present on 29 % of the flakes and 69 % of the flake-blades and flake-blade butts. All this material is more-or-less heavily rolled, including a lightly patinated hornfels frontal scraper (*sensu* Sampson 1970), which is of Lockshoek type and the only Later Stone Age artefact present in the collection; a fresh-looking miscellaneously retouched piece made on a hornfels flake-blade section may also be more recent than the rest of the assemblage. Assuming that the remaining artefacts are all of the same age, the combination of flake-blade technology with small handaxes suggests that they should indeed be attributed to the Fauresmith Industry.
4 handaxes, 1 chunk, 6 irregular cores, 3 disc cores, 51 unmodified flakes, 9 unmodified flake-blades, 9 unmodified flake-blade sections (3 distal, 4 proximal, 2 mesial), 2 utilised flakes (1 in opaline), 1 scraper, 2 retouched flakes.

Brakfontein Later Stone Age Site

From a site located to the north of the Riet River, this collection of 77 hornfels artefacts and three unworked pieces of stone is described on an accompanying label as 'Factory site. Large scrapers, flakes and cores of indurated shale typical of 'Smithfield A' industry, Later Stone Age, including a concavo-convex and a discoidal scraper'. The artefacts are either unpatinated or only lightly patinated. The variation in scraper morphology suggests that, while most scrapers, including 11 with adze-like lateral retouch, belong to the Lockshoek Industry, some others may be more recent and perhaps have Smithfield Industry affiliations. If so, this might also account for some of the variability in patination. The presence of a clearly Middle Stone Age component indicated by the flake-blades and the faceting on four of the 14 flakes may be genuine, or may reflect errors in curation.
9 irregular cores, 1 crested blade, 14 unmodified flakes (4 with faceted platforms), 10 unmodified flake-blades (of which 1 has a faceted platform), 9 unmodified flake-blade sections (7 proximal, 2 distal), 33 scrapers, 1 naturally backed knife.

Van Heerden Collection, (Ethno) 1930.10-8.149

1 cast of a patinated hornfels flake that is culturally undiagnostic and marked 'B' for Brakfontein.

Additional material Cambridge University Museum, Institute of Archaeology (Appendix 3).

DE KIEL OOST 29° 19'S, 24° 51'E

The farm De Kiel Oost 101, 16 km north of Koffiefontein in the western Free State, gave Van Riet Lowe the first evidence for the presence in the previously undifferentiated Smithfield Industry of two distinct 'industrial groups' differentiated by patination and artefact types (Goodwin & Van Riet Lowe 1929: 153). Originally termed Lower and Upper Smithfield, these groups were redesignated Smithfield A and Smithfield B after discussion with Neville Jones, the leading archaeologist in Zimbabwe at this time, who emphasized the complete lack of stratigraphic evidence as to their relationship with one another. Subsequent research, notably by J. Deacon (1974) and Sampson (1974), has established that many of the occurrences assigned to these two phases cannot be relied upon as they are highly selective surface collections. However, in general terms the Smithfield A is an industry (now termed the Lockshoek Industry) of the Pleistocene-Holocene transition and the Smithfield B (now termed the Smithfield Industry) belongs to the terminal phases of the Later Stone Age during the second millennium AD.

Armstrong Collection, 1959.7-12

A group of 31 hornfels artefacts, the vast majority of them scrapers with variable degrees of patination. As in the other collections from this site, many of these scrapers are made on endstruck flakes or on blades, but they also include seven large side-retouched or circular examples. An attribution to the Lockshoek Industry of the Oakhurst Complex is possible on the basis of scraper size and morphology, but they may equally belong to the Smithfield Industry, or be a mixture of assemblages of different ages. The artefacts in this group are marked in the same handwriting as those in the Jones Collection from this site.
1 large irregular core, 30 scrapers.

Braunholtz Collection, (Ethno) 1930.10-9.1-24

This is by far the largest of the three collections from De Kiel Oost, as well as being one of the largest collections from a single southern African Stone Age site in the British Museum. A handwritten label in Braunholtz's own hand dated to August 27th, 1929 locates the site on the south side of the Kimberley (Jacobsdal-Jagersfontein) road and to the east of a bridge, 10 miles (16 km) from Koffiefontein.

Of the 479 artefacts, the vast majority (94.3 %) are made in hornfels, though a wide variety of other materials are also present. As with the Armstrong and Jones Collections from this site, while an attribution to the Later Stone Age is obvious, it is likely that both the Lockshoek and the Smithfield Industries are present in this assemblage. This is indicated by the considerable variability in the morphology of the scrapers present and in the degree to which the hornfels artefacts are patinated. The scrapers include not only thumbnail and endstruck examples, but also others made on sidestruck flakes and still others best described as frontal scrapers (Sampson 1974) and scrapers with adze-like lateral retouch. These last three types in particular are likely to belong to an earlier Lockshoek phase of activity at the site.

There is limited evidence for the re-use of Middle Stone Age artefacts at this site. In addition to the presence of single examples of a Middle Stone Age knife and flake-blade, one of the hornfels flakes has a faceted platform. More significantly, two hornfels scrapers have been made on what were originally Middle Stone Age flake-blades. This is attested at several other Later Stone Age sites (e.g. at Rose Cottage Cave in the eastern Free State, where Wadley (1992) links it to a reduction in range because of the presence in the local area of farming populations) and was commented upon in the original description of the site (Goodwin & Van Riet Lowe 1929: 154). Whether the same explanation might hold here is difficult to say, although the presence of a flake made from bottle glass does show that at least some of the De Kiel Oost artefacts were produced as late as the 19th century.

Table 21. The Braunholtz Collection from De Kiel Oost

	Opaline	Hornfels	Dolerite	Siltstone/ mudstone	Baked siltstone/ mudstone	Sandstone	Total
Handaxes	-	-	-	1	-	-	1
Chunks	-	6	-	-	-	-	6
Irregular cores	1	62	-	-	-	-	63
Blade cores	-	6	-	-	-	-	6
Core-reduced pieces	2	-	-	-	-	-	2
Core trimmers	-	5	-	-	-	-	5
Flakes	2	90	2	1	1	-	96
Blades	-	3	-	1	-	-	4
Bladelets	-	1	-	-	-	-	1
Flake-blades	-	1	-	-	-	-	1
Proximal sections	-	4	-	-	-	-	4
Utilised flakes	-	20	-	-	-	1	21
Utilised blades	-	1	-	-	-	-	1
Upper grindstones	-	-	2	2	-	-	4
Lower grindstones	-	-	-	-	-	1	1
Hammerstones	-	-	2	-	-	-	2
Grooved stones	-	-	1	-	-	-	1
Palettes	-	-	-	-	-	1	1
Ground sandstone	-	-	-	-	-	1	1
Scrapers	2	243	-	1	1	-	247
Adzes	7	-	-	-	1	-	8
Retouched flakes	-	1	-	-	-	-	1
Awls	-	1	-	-	-	-	1
MSA knives - bilateral	-	1	-	-	-	-	1
Total	14	445	7	6	3	4	479

Braunholtz Collection, (Ethno) 1930.10-9.1-13

A smaller group of just 13 variably patinated hornfels artefacts associated with a handwritten label referring to it as coming from 'Site Smithfield B, poss. Bushman or Hottentot', which may indicate that this material comes from a slightly different locality than the main body of the De Kiel Oost collection. While clearly of Later Stone Age origin, they may also be a mixture of material of different ages, as in the main part of the Braunholtz collection from this site.

3 irregular cores, 10 scrapers.

Jones Collection, (Ethno) 1928.10-15.17, 19-20, 22-23, 26, 28, 31-34, 36, 38-39

In addition to two grooved stones that were probably, on the basis of their U-shaped cross-sections, used for finishing ostrich eggshell beads, this collection consists of 14 hornfels scrapers. These are generally in fresh condition, although varying from unpatinated to being largely covered with a red-brown patina. This, along with the prevalence of endstruck examples, suggests they may belong to the Smithfield Industry, though it is not impossible that Lockshoek Industry material is also present in this collection. The artefacts in this group are marked in the same handwriting as those in the

Armstrong Collection from this site.
2 grooved stones (in sandstone), 14 scrapers (in hornfels).

Additional material Department of Ethnography, British Museum (Appendix 1). Cambridge University Museum, Pitt Rivers Museum (Appendix 3).

DEPUTS 29° 37'S, 25° 47'E

Leviseur Collection, 1919.12-9.1-84

The largest element in this collection is a group of 69 bifaces, of which both the handaxes and the cleavers exhibit considerable variability in size and detailed morphology. While this strong biface element suggests that the assemblage is largely Early Stone Age in origin, several of the flakes have faceted platforms and the three formal tools present are all of Middle Stone Age type. This suggests that either this collection consists of two different assemblages (though there is no documentary evidence or variation in patination to support this) or that it belongs to the Fauresmith Industry, a transitional industry between the Early Stone Age and later, more fully developed MSA industries (Beaumont & Morris 1990). All 84 artefacts are in hornfels and are covered with an orange-red patina; most are rolled.
30 cleavers, 39 handaxes, 10 unmodified flakes, 2 unmodified flake-blades, 2 scrapers, 1 point.

FAURESMITH (FACTORY SITE) 29° 45'S, 25° 19'E

Fauresmith is the type site for the industry of the same name, long considered to be transitional between Early and Middle Stone Age technologies. Artefacts were first found here by Leviseur (Appendix 4) and the site was subsequently investigated by Van Riet Lowe, who identified a Fauresmith Industry typified by small handaxes, flake-blades and some use of a prepared core technique (Goodwin & Van Riet Lowe 1929). This was seen as both chronologically and typologically 'intermediate' between Acheulean and Middle Stone Age technologies because of this combination of bifaces, flake-blades and the production of flakes with faceted platforms. Two (later three) stages of the industry were later recognised on the basis of observations made in the Vaal River gravels, both following on from a multi-phase Acheulean sequence (Van Riet Lowe 1937, 1952b). The term was formally abandoned at the 1965 Burg-Wartenstein Conference (Bishop & Clark 1967) and these complex developmental schemes have also been jettisoned (Sampson 1974; H. J. Deacon 1975). Assemblages previously recognised as 'Fauresmith' are included by Volman (1984: 180) within the Upper Acheulean and include some use of parallel-sided and convergent flake-blades and Levallois prepared core technology. While Humphreys (1972b) maintained the earlier view of Goodwin & Van Riet Lowe (1929) and Clark (1959) that these features were a consequence of the use of hornfels, Beaumont has shown in excavations in the Northern Cape that such assemblages are also made in quartzite and other materials. Arguing that terminology ought to stress the 'first regular appearance' of what is considered significant, he has proposed that the Fauresmith should be resurrected as a useful term and that it be recognised as part of the Middle Stone Age (Beaumont & Morris 1990: 4-5).

Braunholtz Collection, (Ethno) 1930.1-24

This is a collection of material belonging to the Fauresmith Industry stated on the old card that accompanied the artefacts to have been 'from surface c. 3 miles out of Fauresmith above river. Left side of road as one drives out of Fauresmith.' All 63 artefacts are partly rolled and in a heavily patinated hornfels, though a few pieces show signs of more recent retouch through the patina, perhaps implying a certain degree of re-use. The collection is dominated by bifaces and flakes and is tabulated below with the material from the Town Spruit site at Fauresmith.

FAURESMITH (TOWN SPRUIT SITE) 29° 45'S, 25° 19'E

Braunholtz Collection, (Ethno) 1930.1-24

Stated on the old card that previously accompanied these artefacts to have been collected from 'dry bed of Town Spruit (stream) 3 miles from Fauresmith nr bridge', this is also an assemblage belonging to the Fauresmith Industry. Though all 71 artefacts are again in hornfels, they have a much lighter, grey patina compared to the heavy brown colour of the artefacts from the Factory site. One unworked piece of stone is also present.

Table 22. The Braunholtz Collections from the Fauresmith Factory and Town Spruit sites

	Factory Site	Town Spruit Site
Cleavers	17	14
Handaxes	9	6
Irregular cores	8	6
Core trimming flakes	3	4
Flakes	22	24
Flake-blades	1	3
Proximal sections (flake-blades)	-	2

Table 22 cont. The Braunholtz Collections from the Fauresmith Factory and Town Spruit sites

	Factory Site	Town Spruit Site
Utilised flakes	-	3
Utilised flake-blades	3	6
Scrapers (clearly reused later than the original production of the blank)	-	1
Retouched points	-	2
Total	63	71

Additional material Department of Ethnography, British Museum (Appendix 1). Cambridge University Museum (Fauresmith; Fauresmith, just north of; Fauresmith, 25 miles north of; Fauresmith, 12 miles south of; Fauresmith, between Bethulie and Fauresmith; Fauresmith, Brakfontein Farm; Fauresmith, Prospect Farm) (Appendix 3).

FREEVAST PRECISE LOCATION UNKNOWN

Christy Collection, ex Anderson, +7913

This culturally undiagnostic artefact is labelled in ink as having been found 'on (a) stony hill by Freevast'. Unfortunately, it has not been possible to identify this locality and its provenance is therefore unknown, other than that the Christy Slip Catalogue records Freevast as lying within the Free State Province (at the time of Anderson's collection, the Orange Free State republic).

1 unmodified flake (in sandstone).

HARRISMITH 28° 46'S, 29° 07'E

Van Heerden Collection, (Ethno) 1930.10-8.120-143

A mixed collection of 24 Middle and Later Stone Age artefacts. Clear Middle Stone Age elements include two knife fragments, one in opaline, the other in tuff, and a tuff flake-blade, with the scrapers, core-reduced pieces and small size of the opaline débitage the probable Later Stone Age component; other artefacts are not easy to assign to either group.

Table 23. The Van Heerden Collection from Harrismith

	Opaline	Tuff	? Banded ironstone	Sandstone	Total
Irregular cores	-	2	-	-	2
Core-reduced pieces	3	-	1	-	4
Pièces esquillées	-	1	-	-	1
Crested blades	1	-	-	-	1
Flakes	6	1	-	1	8
Flake-blades	-	1	-	-	1
Blades	1	-	-	-	1
Proximal sections	1	-	-	-	1
Utilised flake (with faceted platform)	-	1	-	-	1
Scrapers	2	-	-	-	2
Knives - unilateral	1	1	-	-	2
Total	15	7	1	1	24

Additional material Cambridge University Museum (Appendix 3).

JACOBSDAL 29° 08'S, 24° 45'E

Armstrong Collection, 1959.7-12

Both these lightly patinated hornfels artefacts are of Later Stone Age affiliation, but it is difficult to be sure whether they belong to the Lockshoek or to a more recent industry. They are retouched along both their distal ends and one lateral edge. The handwriting on these artefacts is the same as that on the Jones Collection from this site.

2 scrapers (in hornfels).

Jones Collection, (Ethno) 1928.10-15.29

This lightly patinated artefact is also of Later Stone Age affiliation, though again it is not possible to be sure whether it belongs to the Lockshoek Industry or to a more recent industry. The handwriting on this artefact is the same as that on the Armstrong Collection from this site.

1 scraper (in hornfels, end-retouched with marginal lateral trimming).

KOFFIEFONTEIN (ENGRAVINGS SITE) 29° 25'S, 25° 00'E

Koffiefontein lies midway along the Riet River Valley, an area of intense archaeological fieldwork by Van Riet Lowe in the 1920s (Goodwin & Van Riet Lowe 1929: 153) that led to the identification of two phases within the then Smithfield Industry at the nearby site of De Kiel Oost (qv). The rock-engravings at Afvallingskop near Koffiefontein, which may be those meant here, are well-known, though not associated with this largely Middle Stone Age assemblage. Other engravings are present to the immediate east and west of the town of Koffiefontein itself (Goodwin & Van Riet Lowe 1929: pl. XXXVII).

Braunholtz Collection, (Ethno) 1930.1-24

A group of 105 artefacts, of which two opaline and two unpatinated hornfels flakes (all in fresh condition) seem out of place in comparison to the remainder, raising the possibility that an originally Middle Stone Age occurrence has been 'overprinted' by more recent activity at the same place. These 101 remaining artefacts are partly rolled and all made in a hornfels that is now covered with a thick, reddish-brown patina. Three unworked pieces of stone are also present.

Table 24. The Braunholtz Collection from the Engravings Site, Koffiefontein

	Opaline	Hornfels	Total
Irregular cores	-	18	18
Radial cores	-	1	1
Blade cores	-	1	1
Crested blades	-	2	2
Flakes	2	46	48
Flake-blades	-	12	12
Bladelets	-	1	1
Proximal sections (flake-blades)	-	2	2
Utilised flakes	-	6	6
Utilised flake-blades	-	1	1
Scrapers	-	5	5
Knives - unilateral	-	1	1
Knives - bilateral	-	5	5
Points	-	2	2
Total	2	103	105

One piece of reddish-yellow ochre is also present.

Additional material Department of Ethnography, British Museum (Appendix 1), specific provenance at Koffiefontein not given.Cambridge University Museum and Pitt Rivers Museum (Appendix 3), specific provenances at Koffiefontein not given.

KOFFIEFONTEIN (SEKRETARIS) 29° 25'S, 25° 00'E

This second assemblage from Koffiefontein comes from the surface close to a group of 'burials under stone mounds', in the words of an accompanying label, just to the east of Koffiefontein itself. Such graves, first described by Van Riet Lowe (1931), are characteristic of the Type R sites recognised by Humphreys & Maggs (1970) in the Riet River Valley. They involved placing the body at the bottom of a stone-packed circular shaft, which was then covered with a low mound of stones. Associated stone-walled enclosure sites are dated to between the 15th and early 19th centuries AD and appear, partly on the basis of early European accounts, to have been inhabited by settled pastoralists of 'Bushman' ancestry. It is not entirely clear, though perhaps likely, if these people were still using and making stone tools.

Braunholtz Collection, (Ethno) 1930.1-24

With the exception of a single opaline flake, all 139 artefacts from this site are in hornfels and only lightly patinated. The scrapers are mostly endscrapers and suggest that the bulk of the collection belongs to the Smithfield Industry. However, six scrapers with adze-like lateral retouch would fit more comfortably into the early or middle Holocene (e.g. the Lockhsoek Industry). Five round scrapers, notably larger than the others, and three flakes are also all covered by a rather greyer patina than any of the other artefacts, perhaps hinting that they are older in age than the rest of the artefacts. One unworked piece of stone is also present.

Table 25. The Braunholtz Collection from Sekretaris Kop, Koffiefontein

	Opaline	Hornfels	Total
Irregular cores	-	9	9
Flakes	1	65	66
Blades	-	1	1
Proximal sections	-	2	2
Distal sections	-	2	2
Utilised flakes	-	6	6
Scrapers	-	49	49
Adzes	-	3	3
Borers	-	1	1
Total	1	138	139

Additional material Department of Ethnography, British Museum (Appendix 1), specific provenance at Koffiefontein not given. Cambridge University Museum, Pitt Rivers Museum (Appendix 3), specific provenances at Koffiefontein not given.

LOCKSHOEK 30° 03'S, 26° 32'E

The type-site of the Smithfield A, as this was defined by Goodwin & Van Riet Lowe (1929: 171-172), the farm Lockshoek in the Fauresmith District of the Free State has given its name to the Lockshoek Industry, one of several regional variants of the terminal Pleistocene/early Holocene Oakhurst Complex since recognised by Sampson (1974).

Braunholtz Collection, (Ethno) 1930.1-24

A group of ten artefacts in a lightly brown-patinated hornfels. While clearly Later Stone Age in origin, they are difficult to attribute more precisely purely on the evidence of the tools themselves, though the provenance suggests they belong to the Lockshoek Industry.
6 unmodified flakes, 1 utilised flake, 3 scrapers.

MODDERPOORT 29° 06'S, 27° 26'E

The original monastic church established here by the Anglican Society of St. Augustine in 1869 was taken over by the Anglican Society of the Sacred Mission in 1902 and remained as a functioning mission until 1994. Immediately behind the mission itself is a rock art site featuring, unusually, paintings of several birds, though for the purposes of this Gazetteer Modderpoort's significance lies in the fact that it was on the basis of artefacts collected from an open air site here that B. Malan (1946) recognised the so-called Modderpoort variant of the Middle Stone Age later also identified in his excavations of the nearby site of Rose Cottage Cave (where he termed it Magosian). Both terms were later abandoned as being 'supported by only qualitative judgements on typology and presumed stratigraphic sequences' (Sampson 1974: 232). Re-analysis of Malan's excavated material from Rose Cottage Cave by Wadley & Harper (1988) has since shown that his 'Magosian' sequence includes assemblages from the MSA 2, Howiesons Poort and MSA 3 sub-divisions of the Middle Stone Age recognised by Volman (1984). The position of the Middle Stone Age occurrences from Modderpoort vis-à-vis the Rose Cottage sequence remains to be re-investigated. They come from what Tribe himself (*in litt.* 11.4.1940) referred to as a 'factory site' about 1.25 miles (2 km) due west of the Mission and on the plateau above it.

Tribe Collection, (Ethno) 1940.Af 5 1-41

A group of 41 Middle Stone Age artefacts previously assigned to the Magosian Industry. It may be noted that all of the baked sandstone flakes, and they alone, have faceted platforms.

PAARDEBERG 28° 58'S, 25° 09'E

Armstrong collection, 1959.7-12

Paardeberg was the scene of a major battle (fought on February 18th, 1900) that marked the first significant British victory in the South African War of 1899-1902 (Pakenham 1979). The two hornfels artefacts from this site were recovered from the battlefield. The first is probably of Middle Stone Age origin because it has a faceted platform, while the unpatinated condition and small size of the second suggests it belongs to one or other sub-division of the Later Stone Age.
1 unmodified flake (lightly patinated), 1 scraper (virtually unpatinated).

Additional material Cambridge University Museum (Appendix 3).

PETRUS 29° 07'S, 25° 25'E

Armstrong Collection, 1959.7-12

Five Later Stone Age scrapers all of which have the same light grey patina. Three have adze-like lateral retouch and one is a simple endscraper. All belong either to the Lockshoek Industry and/or the Smithfield/post-classic Wilton Industries of the Later Stone Age.
5 scrapers (in hornfels).

Jones Collection, (Ethno) 1928.10-15.30, 35

The first of these two Later Stone Age scrapers has adze-like lateral retouch and a similar patina to those in the Armstrong collection from this site, perhaps suggesting a common chronological and cultural origin. The second is an endscraper in less fresh condition and with a reddish patina, the cultural affiliations of which are less certain, though it too is likely to be Later Stone Age in origin.
2 scrapers (in hornfels).

Additional material Cambridge University Museum (Appendix 3).

RIVERSDALE FARM WITHIN THE GENERAL AREA OF 29° 48'S, 27° 05'E

Collins & Smith (1919: 80) describe this rolled Early Stone Age artefact as coming from the south-eastern corner of the Free State 'on the high watershed of the Orange and Caledon Rivers', suggesting that it must be located within the triangle formed by the Gariep and Caledon Rivers and the Lesotho/Free State border. A farm 'Riversdal 315' is located in the Zastron District of this part of the Free State (S. Ouzman, pers. comm.) and seems the most likely candidate, the spelling given by Collins & Smith (1919) perhaps reflecting an anglicization of the farm name. The single artefact described here was found on a ploughed surface along with 'neolithic' (presumably Later Stone Age) flakes and a broken bored stone (Collins & Smith 1919: 80).

Collins Collection, 1919.2-10.1

1 handaxe (in dolerite).

Additional material Cambridge University Museum (Appendix 3).

STEENBOKPAN (*STEINBOK FARM*) 27° 50'S, 25° 39'E

The locations of neither Steinbok Farm nor Steinbok Pan have been precisely identified and A.A. Anderson's (1887a) accounts of his travels almost entirely omit mention of the Free State, making them useless for this purpose. The farm registry list for the Free State has two farms by the name Steenbokpan (S. Ouzman, pers. comm.). The first, Steenbokpan 1958, is located in the Kroonstad District in the north-central part of the province, the second, Steenbokpan 41, in the Hoopstad District on the western border of the Free State, just south of the Vaal River. References to well-digging and waterworn gravels on the labels accompanying these artefacts, as well as to 'sand veldt' (*sic*) in the case of the single artefact from Steinbok Pan, are more in keeping with the drier conditions of the western Free State, rather than its north-central portion. This suggests that Steenbokpan 41 is the farm meant by Anderson's 'Steinbok Farm'.

Christy Collection, ex Anderson, +7870

A.A. Anderson (1887b: 165) refers elsewhere to his recovery 'in the Orange Free State, in well-digging, at 25 feet, four very good flint-scrapers' and it is possible that among these were the artefacts from Steinbok Farm now in the British Museum collections. They form a group of three Middle Stone Age artefacts, all individually labelled, the fullest details being that they were 'found 7 ft below the surface on digging a well at Steinbuck's farm on waterworn gravel on the slope of a ravine by Fk. Stones, Nov. 1882'.
1 unmodified flake-blade (in hornfels), 2 points (1 in hornfels, 1 in opaline).

STEENBOKPAN (*STEINBOK PAN*) NEAR 27° 50'S, 25° 39'E

While it seems likely that both Steinbok Farm (qv) and Steinbok Pan refer to localities at or close to the modern farm Steenbokpan in the Hoopstad District of the Free State, a more precise location for Christy +7912 is not possible as Anderson marked its provenance only to within 45 miles (72 km) of the pan.

Christy Collection, ex Anderson, +7912

A partly rolled artefact of Early Stone Age origin 'found on sand veldt 45 miles on road to Steinbok pan, Free State, 26 Feb. 1883'.
1 handaxe (in hornfels).

VENTERSHOEK (CHRISTOL CAVE) 29° 45'S, 27° 05'E

Ventershoek Shelter was first described by Goodwin & Van Riet Lowe (1929), who used it as the type-site of the so-called 'Smithfield C Industry', although most of the artefacts used to define it came from the talus below the shelter, rather than from an excavation within it (Sampson 1974: 130). Their definition emphasized such features as the generally microlithic character of the assemblages, the prevalence of small, thumbnail scrapers and the presence of bone points, pottery, adzes/spokeshaves, as well as a very strong association with painted rock-shelters. Though jettisoned for being inadequately defined on the basis of a selected sample, there is no doubt that, in recognising the 'Smithfield C', Goodwin & Van Riet Lowe (1929) were identifying a genuine aspect of the Later Stone Age of the Caledon River Valley, the material signature of its most recent Holocene hunter-gatherer occupants.

Two shelters are, in fact, present close to the Ventershoek stream; they lie within little more than 100 m of each other. Goodwin & Van Riet Lowe's (1929) type sample for their 'Smithfield C' came from one which has very limited deposit, but includes among its paintings a well-known, but badly damaged, scene showing a conflict over cattle between hunter-gatherers and Sotho warriors who are pursuing them. It is from this shelter and its talus that the first two collections described here derive. Sampson (1970: 130-159) excavated in the other shelter, which has a well-protected deposit and fewer paintings, some of which also feature cattle and Sotho warriors. His excavations produced a very late LSA assemblage with large numbers of thumbnail scrapers and adzes, some worked bone and pottery, that largely fits Goodwin & Van Riet Lowe's (1929) original characterization.

Additional material Department of Ethnography, British Museum (Appendix 1), specific provenance not given.

Braunholtz Collection, (Ethno) 1930.1-24

As expected of late Holocene Later Stone Age assemblages in the Caledon River Valley (*cf.* Mitchell *et al.* 1994; Wadley 1995), the majority of the 85 artefacts in this collection are in opaline and hornfels, with small scrapers and adzes the most common formal tool types. Interestingly, however, unmodified flakes comprise the largest artefact class present, which may indicate that the collection, however it was made, was not as selective (i.e. biased toward the recovery of the visually more impressive retouched pieces) as many of the other collections recorded here. The relatively high frequencies of hornfels artefacts recorded for this assemblage and the Braunholtz Collection from the talus below this site are at odds with both Sampson's (1970: 135) comments as to the poor quality of the local hornfels and the raw material composition of his own excavated assemblages nearby.

Table 26. The Braunholtz Collection from Ventershoek (Christol Cave)

	Opaline	Hornfels	Dolerite	Tuff	Baked sandstone	Total
Chunks	1	-	-	-	-	1
Irregular cores	4	4	-	-	1	9
Bladelet cores	1	1	-	-	-	2
Core rejuvenation flakes	3	1	-	-	-	4
Core-reduced pieces	3	-	-	-	-	3
Flakes	16	20	2	-	1	39
Bladelets	-	1	-	-	-	1
Proximal sections	-	1	-	-	-	1
Mesial sections	-	4	-	-	-	4
Utilised flakes	-	3	-	-	-	3
Hammerstones	-	-	1	-	-	1
Upper grindstones	-	-	6	-	-	6
Lower grindstones	-	-	1	-	-	1
Upper/lower grindstones	-	-	1	-	-	1
Bored stones (unfinished)	-	-	1	-	-	1
Ground and polished rings	-	-	-	-	1	1
Scrapers	1	3	-	-	-	4
Adzes	-	2	-	1	-	3
Total	29	40	12	1	3	85

Two potsherds are also present. One is an undecorated red body sherd, the other a grey-buff body sherd with two lines of comb-impressed decoration of the type associated with Smithfield Industry assemblages in the middle part of the Gariep River Valley (Sampson 1974) and the Seacow Valley (Sampson 1985). An iron knife, clearly of European origin, and three unworked pieces of stone complete this collection

VENTERSHOEK (TALUS BELOW CHRISTOL CAVE) 29° 45'S, 27° 05'E

Braunholtz Collection, (Ethno) 1930.1-24

Separately treated and curated is the following, obviously highly selected collection of 39 artefacts from the talus below this site, which differs in being overwhelmingly dominated by scrapers. Almost all of these scrapers are of the classic Wilton or Smithfield C thumbnail type. As is the case with the artefacts from within the type site itself, those made of hornfels are variably patinated, while some artefacts in all materials are partly rolled.

Table 27. The Braunholtz Collection from Ventershoek (talus below Christol Cave)

	Opaline	Hornfels	Tuff	Total
Core rejuvenation flakes	2	-	-	2
Flakes	5	3	1	9
Scrapers	7	21	-	28
Total	14	24	1	39

VENTERSHOEK (TO THE WEST OF CHRISTOL CAVE) 29° 45'S, 27° 05'E

Braunholtz Collection, (Ethno) 1930.1-24

The third element in the Braunholtz Collection from Ventershoek comprises a collection of 29 artefacts from a locality stated to have been '1/4 mile (400 m) west of Christol Cave on slope below rockshelter'. Presumably also a talus collection, it differs from the two preceding collections in being dominated by opalines. However, it is similar to the Christol Cave talus collection in being largely made up of scrapers, almost all of them of classic thumbnail type. All the artefacts are in opaline except where otherwise indicated.

1 core-rejuvenation flake (in hornfels), 3 unmodified flakes, 25 scrapers (including 6 in hornfels and 1 in tuff).

2.3 South Africa: Gauteng

Despite, or perhaps because of, its position as the largest metropolitan area in southern Africa and the focus, for over a century, of South Africa's gold-mining industry, Stone Age archaeological research within the modern province of Gauteng has been relatively limited in scale. This does not mean, however, that it has been limited in its consequences: far from it. Three main foci of excavation and survey can be identified, of which only the oldest, the exploration of the gravel terraces of the Vaal River in the general area of Vereeniging (qv), is represented in the collections of the British Museum. Observations made here, as further downstream in what are now the North West and Northern Cape Provinces, provided what Clark, as late as 1959, termed 'the yardstick by which much of the work to-day being done in South Africa is measured' (Clark 1959: 43): archaeological occurrences in successive gravel terraces were, until it was shown that many of the 'gravels' were derived and the samples themselves highly selective (Partridge & Brink 1967), placed in a developmental sequence; what is now recognised to be a spurious correlation with hypothetical pluvial and more arid climatic phases through the Pleistocene provided some guide to their absolute age.

More long-lasting and significant in its archaeological impact has been the excavation of eroding limestone caverns in the Sterkfontein Valley near modern Krugersdorp on the western side of the province. Commencing in the 1930s with the investigation of Sterkfontein itself by Robert Broom and extending in the 1940s to the nearby sites of Swartkrans and Kromdraai, this locality has yielded one of the highest densities of australopithecine fossils anywhere in Africa (Klein 1989: 113-117). A continuing programme of excavations is in place at both Swartkrans and Sterkfontein and further sites with Plio-Pleistocene faunal assemblages have recently begun to be investigated nearby. While Brain's (1981) study of the faunas from the Sterkfontein Valley sites and the more northerly site of Makapansgat simultaneously dismissed Dart's (1957) osteodontokeratic hypothesis and contributed powerfully to the development of the sub-discipline of faunal taphonomy, more recent work at Swartkrans has identified the use of bone splinters, possibly to extract geophyte bulbs from the soil, and also advanced strong arguments that by 1 million years ago hominids at the same site were able to make and use fire (Brain 1988). Stone artefact assemblages are known from both Sterkfontein and Swartkrans and may be comparable to the Oldowan and Developed Oldowan of East Africa (Kuman 1994; Brain 1993); dating of these and other archaeological contexts at these sites is not as straightforward as in the East African Rift Valley, but such artefacts are probably between 2.0 and 1.7 million years old (Klein 1989; Kuman 1994). Somewhat younger Acheulean occurrences are also known at both sites (Klein 1989), as well as elsewhere in Gauteng, notably the Vaal River gravels discussed above and the Wonderboompoort area of Pretoria (qv; Mason 1962). Middle and Later Stone Age archaeology in the province has, however, remained comparatively unexplored. Though Lyn Wadley's (1987) recent project on the Later Stone Age of the Magaliesberg Range between Johannesburg and Pretoria included field surveys within what is now Gauteng, with the exception of two small shelters with terminal Later Stone Age late Holocene occupation (Fort Troje and Kloofendal Shelter), all her excavated sites fall within the boundaries of the North West Province (qv).

Despite the significance of archaeological sites in Gauteng for the development of archaeology in southern Africa, very few artefacts from the province occur in the British Museum collections (**Fig. 16**). Those from Meyerton and Vereeniging, however, come from the river gravels along the Vaal River which at one time formed the basis for much of the chronology for the Stone Age in the sub-continent. The Sturge Collection, ex Leith, from Pretoria is also of interest as it includes several eoliths and recalls Leith's (1898) involvement in the 'eolith controversy' at the end of the 19th century.

GAUTENG (TRANSVAAL), NO FURTHER PROVENANCE

Christy Collection, ex Anderson, +7908

A group of 3 hornfels unmodified artefacts, all of them rolled and patinated, collected between 1880 and 1881. Though provenanced only to the former 'Transvaal' province, they have the same accession number as a Middle Stone Age knife found near Pretoria and for this reason have been included in the Gauteng section of the Gazetteer.
3 unmodified flakes (in hornfels).

MEYERTON 28° 34'S, 28° 02'E

Collins and Smith (1919: 82) record that the British Army dug trenches on the road between Meyerton and Vereeniging (qv) after it took control of Pretoria in June 1900. Stone Age artefacts were found in fine gravel and sand from a depth of about 4 feet (1.2 m) below the surface while excavating a terrace some 40-60 feet (12-19 m) above the present level of the Vaal River. The four quartzite artefacts present in the British Museum collection from this locality form only some of the total found here by Collins (Collins & Smith 1919: 85).

Collins Collection, 1919.2-10.14-17

1 handaxe, 1 large irregular core, 2 unmodified flakes.

Fisher Collection 1929.4-9.2-9, 11-16, 18-32, 34-36, 38-43

This is a mixed collection of Early and Middle Stone Age origin that should total 43 artefacts, although only 38 could be

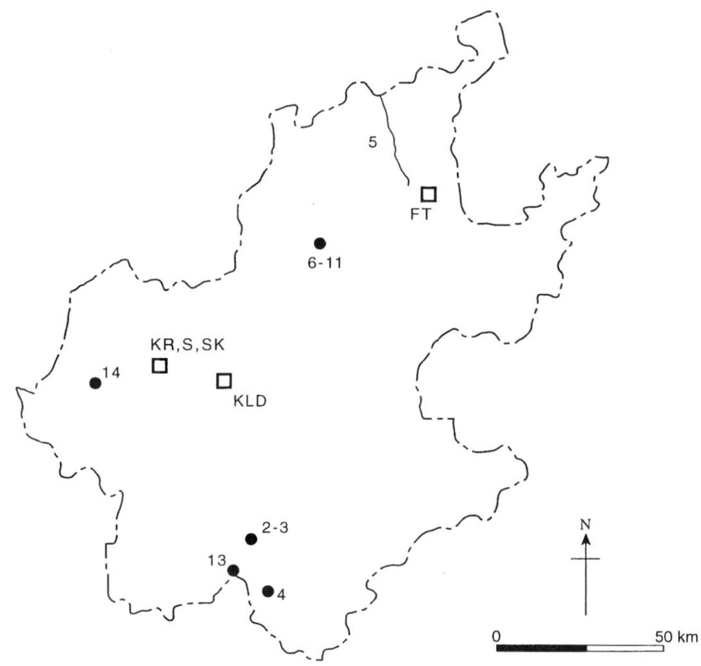

Site names

1 Gauteng (Transvaal), No Further Provenance - location unknown
2 Meyerton
3 Meyerton (Kookfontein Farm 56)
4 Panfontein Farm
5 Pienaarsrivier
6 Pretoria
7 Pretoria (Arcadia)
8 Pretoria (Camp Gravels)
9 Pretoria (Meintjeskop)
10 Pretoria (Muckleneuk)
11 Pretoria (Wonderboom)
12 Pretoria Environs - precise location unknown
13 Vereeniging
14 Vogelstruisfontein Farm

Site acronyms

FT Fort Troje
KLD Kloofendal
KR Kromdraai
S Sterkfontein
SK Swartkrans

Fig. 16. Location of archaeological sites in Gauteng and of Stone Age collections from there in the British Museum

located. While the handaxes and cleavers are of Early Stone Age origin, both sections come from flake-blades and the proximal section has a faceted platform. The possibility that a Later Stone Age component is also present is indicated by the fact that the single opaline scraper has adze-like lateral retouch, which is generally found on scrapers of early and/or middle Holocene age.

Table 28. The Fisher Collection from Meyerton

	Opaline	Hornfels	Quartzite	Dolerite	Sandstone	Total
Cleavers	-	-	-	1	2	3
Handaxes	1	-	5	6	2	14
Irregular cores	2	-	2	5	-	9
Pièces esquillées	1	-	-	-	-	1
Flakes	-	1	-	-	-	1
Proximal sections	-	-	1	-	-	1
Mesial sections	-	-	-	1	-	1
Scrapers	1	-	2	-	-	3
Points	3	-	2	-	-	5
Total	8	1	12	13	4	38

Additional material Department of Ethnography, British Museum (Appendix 1).Cambridge University Museum (Appendix 3).

MEYERTON (KOOKFONTEIN FARM 56) APPROXIMATELY 28° 34'S, 28° 02'E

Fisher Collection, P1983.11-2.1-3

Collected on Kookfontein Farm 56 on the banks of the Klip River in 1923-28, this collection comprises 3 artefacts.
1 Early Stone Age handaxe (in quartzite), 1 Middle Stone Age unifacial point with a faceted platform (in quartzite), 1 large scraper (in patinated dolerite).

PANFONTEIN FARM 26° 44'S, 28° 01'E

Collins found this artefact, described as a 'pointed ovate implement, perfect except for the extreme point and having an even cutting-edge all round' in the earth heap excavated from an aardvark burrow. Presumably speaking from an aesthetic point of view, he considered this his 'best find' from South Africa (Collins & Smith 1919: 86-87).

Collins Collection, 1919.2-10.13

1 handaxe (in lava).

PIENAARS RIVIER FROM 25° 39'S, 28° 32'E TO 25° 10'S, 28° 09'E

The Pienaars river originates in Gauteng north of Pretoria and then flows through the extreme south of the Northern Province before entering the North West Province near Swartbooistad. Without more specific provenance information, the site is included in this section of the Gazetteer on the assumption that the Smith Collection from it derives from Gauteng.

Smith Collection, 1902.8-14.1

A single patinated Early Stone Age artefact.

1 handaxe (in hornfels).

PRETORIA 25° 44'S, 28° 12'E

The British Museum has a number of specimens acquired for the Sturge and Christy Collections from Sir George Leith and described in greater detail in his paper in the *Journal of the Royal Anthropological Institute* (Leith 1898). Markings on some of these artefacts allow them to be provenanced to specific localities within Pretoria, though some can only be more generally located in, or close to, the city. Many are eoliths, i.e. crudely chipped flakes once thought to have been among the oldest artefacts, but now recognised to be the result of the action of natural agencies.

Christy Collection, ex Leith, 99, 525-528

These four 'artefacts' come from 'the high gravels above Pretoria', although they are not more specifically provenanced.
1 notched flake (in quartzite), 3 eoliths (in ironstone).

Sturge Collection, ex Leith

A group of six artefacts comprising two of Early Stone Age origin, a culturally undiagnostic, but fresh-looking flake and 3 eoliths.
2 handaxes (in quartzite), 1 unmodified flake (in quartzite), 3 eoliths (in ironstone).

Based on the similarity in the style of lettering used to mark them and on the presence of 'P' (for Pretoria) in combination with other letters (presumably denoting more specific findspots) a further four artefacts also form part of the Leith Collection acquired by Sturge from Pretoria. However, it has not so far proved possible to identify the localities from which they come with any more precision. They comprise:
2 unmodified flakes (in dolerite, 1 extremely rolled, the other in much fresher condition, both marked B. F. P.), 2 eoliths (in ironstone, both marked 'X. P').

Additional material Cambridge University Museum (Pretoria, Appies River; Pretoria, Sunnyside), Manchester Museum, The Natural History Museum, Pitt Rivers Museum (Appendix 3).

PRETORIA (ARCADIA) 25° 45'S, 28° 12'E

Two artefacts in patinated dolerite, of which the cleaver at least is of Early Stone Age origin.

Sturge Collection, ex Leith, unnumbered

1 cleaver, 1 unmodified flake.

PRETORIA (CAMP GRAVELS) 25° 44'S, 28° 12'E

Sturge Collection, ex Leith

All marked 'Camp P', these six artefacts come from gravels within the area of the then military camp at Pretoria. They are all very heavily rolled and should probably be considered to be eoliths.
2 irregular cores (in ironstone), 3 unmodified flakes (3 in ironstone, 1 in sandstone).

PRETORIA (MEINTJESKOP) 25° 44'S, 28° 13'E

Sturge Collection, ex Leith

2 eoliths (in ironstone).

PRETORIA (MUCKLENEUK) 25° 45'S, 28° 12'E

Sturge Collection, ex Leith

4 eoliths (2 in dolerite, 2 in sandstone).

PRETORIA (WONDERBOOM) 25° 41'S, 28° 12'E

Located in a *nek* or constricted valley a few kilometres to the north of Pretoria city centre, Wonderboom has been more recently explored by Mason (1962), who excavated a hill rubble deposit here in the 1950s. He attributed the finds to the so-called 'Later Acheulean', but Sampson (1974: 121) cautions that this is a purely typological argument and that there is no independent basis on which to date the site. The single artefact from this site in the British Museum collections is in a much fresher condition than any other of the Leith material from Pretoria.

Sturge Collection, ex Leith

1 unmodified flake (in quartzite)

PRETORIA ENVIRONS WEST OF 25° 44'S, 28° 12'E

Christy Collection, ex Anderson, +7908

A single Middle Stone Age retouched artefact marked 'on open plain w(est of ?) Pretoria', having the same accession number as 3 unmodified hornfels flakes provenanced solely to the 'Transvaal'.
1 bilaterally retouched knife (in hornfels).

VEREENIGING 26° 40'S, 27° 56'E

Lying on the Vaal River on the boundary between the present day Free State and Gauteng provinces, Vereeniging has a succession of gravel terraces above the Vaal itself. The 45 ft (15 m) terrace served as the typesite for the earliest stage of the Acheulean Industry in South Africa as this was defined in the middle of the 20th century (Clark 1959: 44). It is now recognised that such definitions were made on the basis of selected samples from the surface of sites and that the so-called 'gravels' are themselves often derived hill washes that offer no suitable chronological controls for the artefacts found within them (Sampson 1974: 114).

Braunholtz Collection, (Ethno) 1930.1-24

Five rolled artefacts. The faceting on the platform of one of the dolerite flakes may suggest a Middle Stone Age affiliation for them all.
1 irregular core (in quartzite), 4 unmodified flakes (3 in dolerite, 1 in quartzite).

Collins Collection, 1919.2-10.2-6

Collins collected material from Vereeniging as the result of his involvement in military entrenchment construction in the Vereeniging-Meyerton area of the Vaal River Valley in mid-1900 (Collins & Smith 1919: 82). As in the case of those from Meyerton, it is clear that the five artefacts in the British Museum collections form only a fraction of those found (Collins & Smith 1919: 82-85). They are all in a slightly rolled condition and are marked 'Vg-V-T', presumably for 'Vereeniging-Vaal River-Transvaal'. The two bifaces suggest the presence of an Early Stone Age component, while the knife is of Middle Stone Age origin; the two remaining artefacts are culturally undiagnostic.
1 handaxe (in quartzite), 1 biface (in hornfels), 2 irregular cores (1 in hornfels, 1 in quartzite), 1 unilaterally retouched knife (in quartzite).

Additional material Cambridge University Museum, Institute of Archaeology, The Natural History Museum, Pitt Rivers Museum (Vereeniging, Taaibosch Spruit, Appendix 3).

VOGELSTRUISFONTEIN FARM 26° 10'S, 27° 34'E

These seven artefacts collected in March 1890 and donated to the British Museum on March 29th of that year are marked as coming from the 'top of Witwatersrand'. A farm Vogelstruisfontein has been located in this general area just southwest of the modern town of Brandvlei and due west of the city of Randfontein. Directions given in the Christy Slip Catalogue which locate Vogelstruisfontein as being 'about 50 miles (80 km) west of Johannesburg and 50 miles (80 km) north of Potchefstroom, i.e. on the Witwatersrand', would place it in the area of Mathopestad, substantially too far west, and are clearly inaccurate.

Christy Collection, ex Rothwell, +4677-+4683

All seven Early Stone Age artefacts are in dolerite, unless otherwise stated.
1 cleaver, 3 handaxes (1 in quartzite), 1 spheroid (in quartzite), 2 unmodified flakes (1 in hornfels).

2.4 South Africa: KwaZulu-Natal

Although, as this Gazetteer indicates, the collection of archaeological artefacts has an antiquity in KwaZulu-Natal as old, if not older, than virtually anywhere else in South Africa (e.g. Sanderson 1878), it was only around 1970 that the province began to see the development and execution of sustained programmes of field survey and excavation. Before then and since, much of the survey work that has been done has concentrated on the recording of the province's outstandingly rich rock art heritage, largely in the Drakensberg Mountains. Here the work of Patricia Vinnicombe (1976) and, in the more localized setting of Ndedema Gorge, Harald Pager (1971) is particularly noteworthy, with Aron Mazel (1981) having undertaken a comprehensive survey of the rock art of the northern part of the Escarpment. Except for the University of the Witwatersrand's excavations in the Cathedral Peak area of the northern Drakensberg in the 1930s (Stein 1933; Wells 1933), small *ad hoc* projects characterized other forms of archaeological survey and excavation in KwaZulu-Natal before the late 1960s. Such work includes that of Bazley (1905) in Alfred County (qv), King & Chubb (1932) in the Thukela Basin, Farnden (1965, 1966, 1969) in the foothills of the Drakensberg and Schoute-Vanneck and Walsh (1959, 1960, 1961) along the coast. Van Riet Lowe's (1935) paper on the so-called 'Smithfield N' culture marked an early recognition in southern African archaeology of the role of activity variation in assemblage variability. Cable (1984: 59-74) provides a fuller discussion of these and other projects and Davies (1951) an earlier synthesis emphasizing the Early and Middle Stone Ages.

The first real attempt at a region-wide project with clearly defined aims and theoretical orientation was undertaken at the beginning of the 1970s by Pat Carter. Though most of his excavations were carried out at sites in the southeastern highlands of Lesotho, he proposed a hypothetical reconstruction of Later Stone Age landscape exploitation in the southern part of KwaZulu-Natal (Carter 1970). His excavations at Good Hope Shelter were later written up by Charles Cable (Cable *et al.* 1980), who carried out further field survey and excavation in southern KwaZulu-Natal to test Carter's (1970) model (Cable 1984). Neither Umbeli Belli nor Borcher's Shelter, however, have sequences extending back beyond *c.* 3000 BP (Cable 1984) and the early/middle Holocene and Pleistocene archaeological records of southern KwaZulu-Natal remain virtually unknown. In the central part of the province's lowland belt excavation has also been limited. Davies (1975) excavated at Shongweni on the Mlazi River, but this site has a confused stratigraphy, though with excellent organic preservation in its upper levels. More important is Kaplan's (1990) excavation of Umhlatuzana Shelter between Durban and Pietermaritzburg which revealed a complex stratigraphic sequence that includes a series of Middle and Later Stone Age occurrences, including a Howieson's Poort assemblage at its base and others that have been identified as transitional between MSA and LSA technologies. Unfortunately, Umhlatuzana too has stratigraphic problems, with part of the deposit apparently having slipped vertically against the rest, it is not clear whether this is responsible for such anomalies as the otherwise unique association of unifacially retouched points with a bladelet-rich Robberg assemblage (Kaplan 1990).

The two most comprehensive excavation programmes of Stone Age sites in KwaZulu-Natal remain to be described. In the far north of the province, and lying almost on its frontier with Swaziland, Border Cave is a site of international importance because its long Middle Stone Age sequence has produced the remains of four anatomically modern *Homo sapiens* individuals (Rightmire 1979), previously estimated to date to 70-100,000 BP (Grün *et al.* 1990; Miller *et al.* 1993), but more recently suggested to be intrusive from much later deposits (Sillen & Morris 1996). First investigated in the 1940s (H. Cooke *et al.* 1945), the site has been extensively excavated by Peter Beaumont (1978) in two campaigns, but full details of these excavations remain unpublished, except for several important studies of late Quaternary environmental change (e.g. Klein 1977; D.M. Avery 1982a). Furthermore, whatever the exact status accorded the stone artefact assemblage from its ± 38,000 BP levels (*cf.* Mitchell 1988; Wadley 1993), the presence in them of ostrich eggshell beads, bored stones and worked bone is some of the earliest evidence for the manufacture of such items anywhere in the world (Beaumont *et al.* 1978).

The Thukela River and its tributaries occupy the central third of KwaZulu-Natal, extending from the Drakensberg Escarpment to the Indian Ocean coast. Aron Mazel, previously of the Natal Museum, has directed a programme of Later Stone Age research in the upper and middle parts of the Thukela Basin since the beginning of the 1980s and has excavated at over 20 sites. The published version of his doctoral thesis (Mazel 1989) provides a synthesis of the first decade of this project, offers fuller references to individual site reports and explores the application of historical materialist models to the writing of the history of Holocene hunter-gatherer communities in the Basin. In particular, Mazel has sought to identify what he terms 'social regions', the material expressions of changing patterns of alliance networks between forager bands, while also investigating Later Stone Age gender relations and the developing relationship between indigenous foragers and Iron Age agropastoralists over the last 2000 years. Though other interpretations of these data have also been advanced (e.g. Wadley 1989; Barham 1992; *cf.* Mazel 1992b), Mazel's more recent excavations have led him largely to confirm, albeit with some refinements, his general model (Mazel 1993). Prominent among the sites that he has excavated, many of which have well preserved plant, as well as faunal, remains, are Collingham Shelter (Mazel 1992c) and Maqonqo Shelter (Mazel 1994). The high quality of organic preservation at the first of these, and the richness of the material culture at the second, offer some idea of what further research in KwaZulu-Natal may yield.

The British Museum Stone Age collections from KwaZulu-Natal (Fig. 17) reflect perhaps more than those from the remainder of South Africa's provinces the influences of a single political event, in this case the Anglo-Zulu War of 1879. As a result of the interest of two particular collectors (Colonel J. H. Bowker and Major

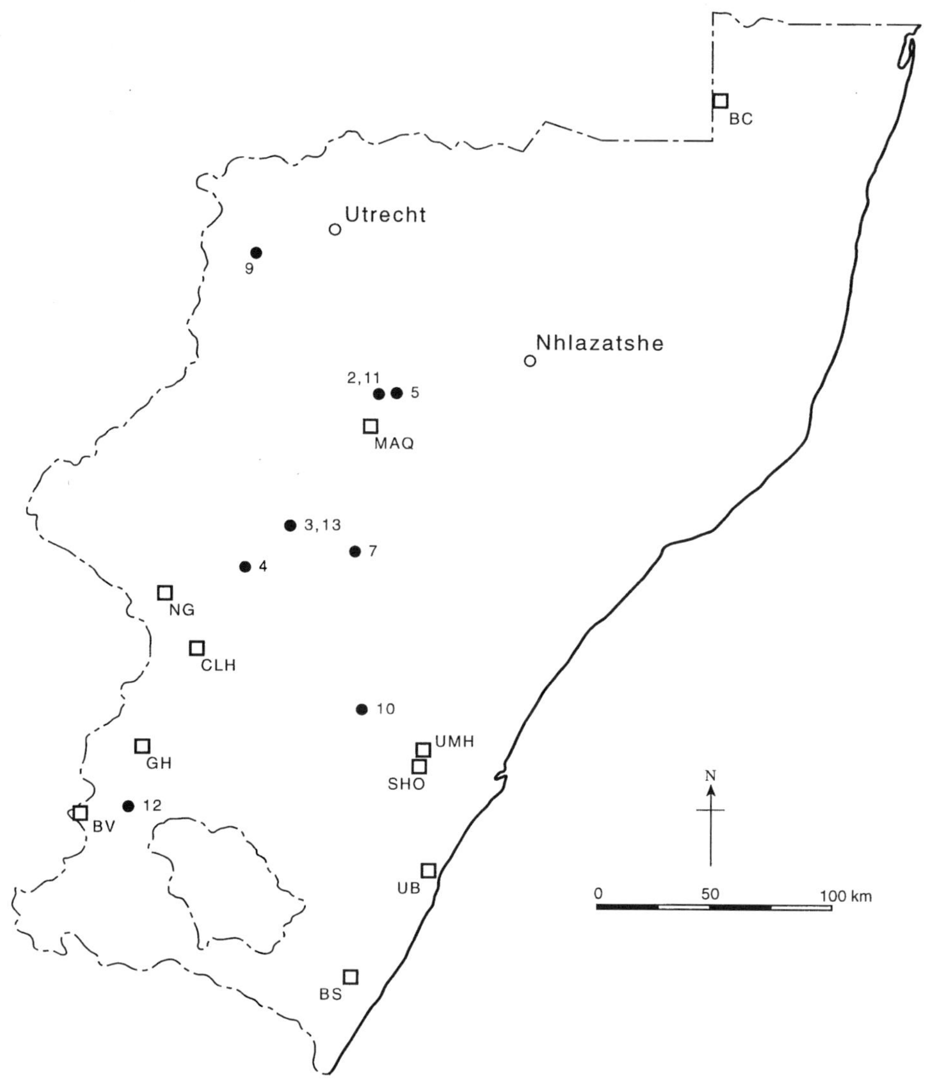

Site names

1 Alfred County Cave- location unknown
2 Buffalo River
3 Bushman's River (near Weenen)
4 Estcourt
5 Isandhlwana
6 Kaffirland (sic), No Further Provenance - location unknown
7 Muden
8 Natal, No Further Provenance - location unknown
9 Newcastle
10 Pietermaritzburg
11 Rorke's Drift
12 The Curragh
13 Weenen
14 Zululand, between Utrecht and Nhlazatshe - precise location unknown

Site acronyms

BC	Border Cave
BS	Borchers Shelter
BV	Belleview
CLH	Collingham
GH	Good Hope
MAQ	Maqonqo
NG	Ndedema Gorge
SHO	Shongweni
UB	Umbeli Belli
UMH	Umhlatuzana

Fig. 17. Location of archaeological sites in KwaZulu-Natal and of Stone Age collections from there in the British Museum

Feilden) the British Museum acquired artefacts from two of the War's major battlefields - Rorke's Drift and Isandhlwana - as well as collections from other parts of the province. However, by far the most important component of the KwaZulu-Natal part of the collections is the Christy Collection, ex Bazley, per Read, from Alfred County Cave. Excavated near the beginning of the 20th Century, all material from this site was lost until the present project located over 200 artefacts in the British Museum. They confirm the potential significance of this rock-shelter for understanding the prehistory of southern Africa by demonstrating the presence of at least two Middle and two Later Stone Age industries at it. It is to be hoped that the site will be relocated in the future so that further work can be undertaken at it.

ALFRED COUNTY CAVE APPROXIMATELY 30° 45'S, 30° 00'E, EXACT LOCATION UNKNOWN

Christy Collection, ex Read, ex Bazley, unnumbered

This represents the collection made by W. Bazley from his excavation of a large rock-shelter somewhere in the then Alfred County (modern magisterial districts of Harding and Port Shepstone) of southern KwaZulu-Natal, possibly after his retirement in January 1904 (V. Ward, pers. comm.). It was donated to Charles Hercules Read, who then presented it to the British Museum in 1905. One of the first excavations of an archaeological site within the province, its exact location is unfortunately not recorded in the only published report. A search by the KwaZulu-Natal branch of the South African Archaeological Society in 1998 failed to locate the site, though a large rock-shelter with paintings was rediscovered near Nyanisweni. This second site has been extensively excavated, but it is unclear if this was excavation carried out by Bazley, or some other worker (Ward 1998). The size of the site as recorded by Bazley would suggest that he could not have excavated the whole of it. His account, as well as the indications of its cultural stratigraphy provided by the British Museum collection, indicate that, if it could be relocated, further work would probably prove highly informative, especially given the complete absence of any comparably deep site in southern KwaZulu-Natal (*cf.* Cable 1984).

The shelter is described by Bazley (1905) as being 120 feet (37 m) across by 20 feet (6 m) deep. His description of its stratigraphy is sketchy, but, converting all measurements to the metric system and citing Bazley (1905: 10-11), indicates the presence of the following layers:

an uppermost stratum 'of soft soil' approximately 1 m deep;
a harder or more compact soil, containing layers of ashes and wood charcoal, with burnt and human bones' of about 1.2 m depth;
a lot of loose stones' of between 0.35 and 0.45 m thickness that he assumed to be of human rather than natural origin and that covered the 'whole extent of the cave floor;
a good hard firm soil up to 0.9 m thick in which the presence of stone artefacts was noted;
an extensive roof fall of up to 0.6 m thickness;
a very hard soil extending down between and below the roof fall which contained numerous stone artefacts and the remains of three human skeletons. This layer had an average thickness of 1.5 m.

Bazley's description of his excavations ends at this point, without making it clear if he had reached bedrock. The total depth of his excavation appears to have been something in the order of 5.6 m.

Industries definitely represented in the British Museum collection from this site include the Howiesons Poort (from the presence of four large segments) and the post-classic Wilton (the numerous small scrapers and rarer adzes and spokeshaves) (Figs. 18 and 19). The presence of at least one other MSA assemblage may be indicated by the rolled condition of some of the MSA artefacts, while the presence of several naturally-backed knives raises the possibility of an

Table 29. The Christy, ex Read, ex Bazley, Collection from Alfred County Cave

	Opaline	Hornfels	Quartz	Silicified limestone	Siltstone/ mudstone	Tuff	Other	Total
Irregular cores	4	1	2	21	-	-	1	29
Disc cores	-	-	-	2	-	-	-	2
Bladelet cores	1	-	-	1	-	-	-	2
Crested blades	-	-	-	3	-	-	-	3
Flakes	2	9	1	13	4	1	4	34
MSA flake-blades	5	-	2	11	2	2	-	22
Mesial sections (flake-blades)	-	-	-	1	-	-	-	1
Distal sections (flake-blades)	-	-	-	3	-	-	-	3
Utilised flakes	1	-	-	2	1	-	2	6
Edge-ground flakes	-	-	-	-	-	-	1	1
Heavy edge-flaked piece	-	1	-	-	-	-	-	1
Bored stones	-	-	-	-	-	-	1	1
Scrapers	71	2	-	4	2	-	-	80
Adzes	3	2	1	-	-	1	1	7
Spokeshaves	1	1	-	-	-	-	-	2
Awls	-	-	-	-	1	-	-	1
Backed flakes	1	1	-	-	-	-	-	2
Naturally backed knives	-	4	-	-	1	-	-	5
Howieson's Poort segments	-	-	-	4	-	-	-	4
MSA points	-	-	-	1	1	-	2	4
MSA retouched flake-blades	-	-	-	4	-	-	-	4
Total	89	21	4	70	12	3	12	214

Four pieces of unworked stone and two pieces of ground red ochre are also present.

Oakhurst or even late Robberg assemblage. Unfortunately, the collection is lacking in any stratigraphic provenance and it is not possible to assign any of the artefacts present to the layers that Bazley (1905) describes. Further detailed inference is probably unwarranted given the obviously highly selected nature of the collection, which consists almost entirely of cores and formally retouched tools. Raw materials comprise both hornfels and opalines, the latter certainly derived from rivers draining the Drakensberg Escarpment, as well as what may be a silicified form of limestone. The latter is rather variable in grain and a few pieces closely resemble the fine-grained nature of an opaline, suggesting perhaps that some of it has been baked. Raw materials of minor importance include vein quartz, tuff, siltstone/mudstone, baked siltstone/mudstone, dolerite and baked sandstone.

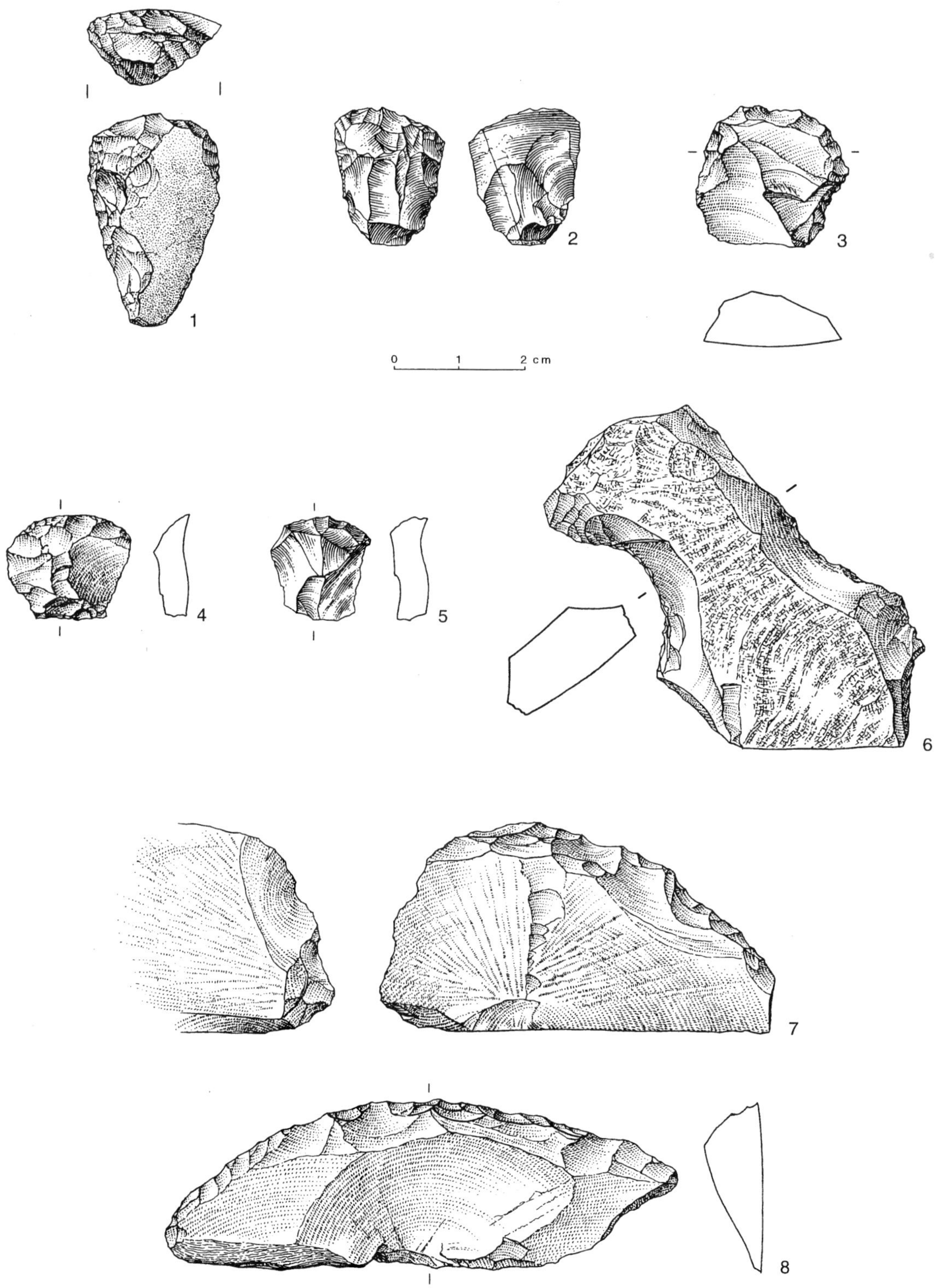

Fig. 18. Later Stone Age Artefacts from the Bazley Collection from Alfred County Cave.

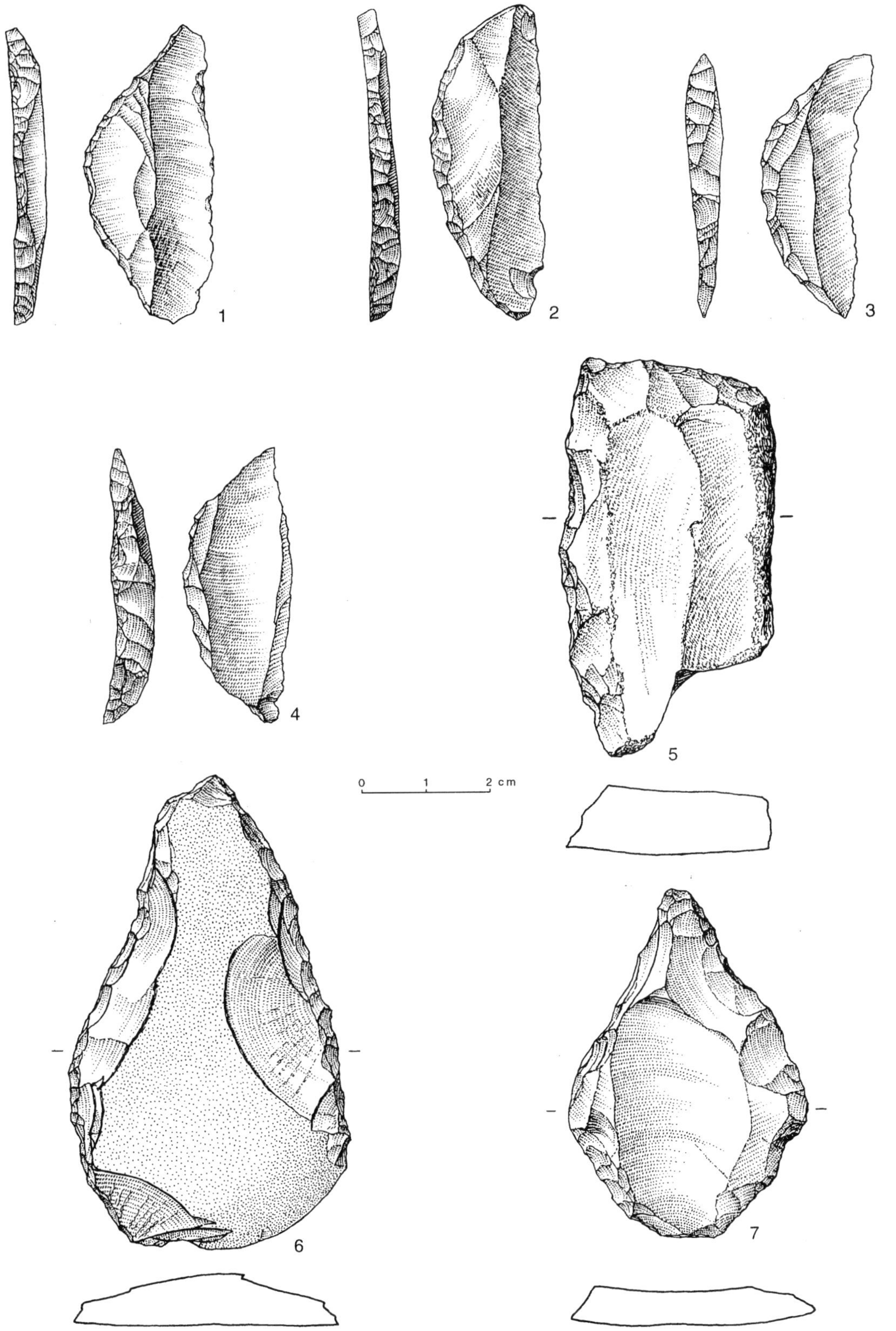

Fig. 19. Later Stone Age Artefacts from the Bazley Collection from Alfred County Cave.

BUFFALO RIVER PROBABLY ABOUT 28° 22'S, 30° 33'E

The Buffalo River flows past Rorke's Drift (qv), scene of one of the first battles of the Anglo-Zulu War of 1879. Feilden served in the British army in South Africa shortly afterward in 1881 and collected this culturally undiagnostic artefact then. It forms part of a much larger collection from the Buffalo River valley that he exhibited to the Royal Anthropological Institute at its meeting of May 22nd, 1883 (Feilden 1883: 165-168).

Christy Collection, ex Feilden, +7841
1 scraper (in hornfels and in slightly rolled condition).

Additional material Cambridge University Museum (Appendix 3).

BUSHMAN'S RIVER (NEAR WEENEN) 28° 51'S, 30° 06'E

Goodwin and Van Riet Lowe (1929: 103) report the discovery by H. P. Thomasset of a 'rich' Middle Stone Age site along the banks of the Bushman River near Weenen in 1928 and the dispatch of 'a considerable number of implements' to the collections of the University of Cape Town. They commented on the similarities they noted with Middle Stone Age material found by Lebzelter elsewhere in the KwaZulu-Natal Midlands and assigned the Weenen artefacts to their Glen Grey variation of the MSA. This was subsequently found to be an erroneous designation as the original assemblage from the Glen Grey Falls type-site is stratigraphically mixed (Clark 1959: 163-164).

Thomasset Collection, (Ethno) 1924.10-25.1-33
A total of 33 artefacts all of them Middle Stone Age in origin, with the exception of the spokeshave, which is probably of later Holocene date. Patination on the hornfels artefacts is highly variable: some are virtually unpatinated and others completely covered by a light reddish-brown patina. A group of four flakes and one flake-blade is distinctive in that they are rolled and have a much heavier reddish patina.

Table 30. The Thomasset Collection from Bushman's River

	Opaline	Hornfels	Dolerite	Tuff	Total
Crested blades	-	1	-	-	1
Flakes	-	14	1	-	16
Flake-blades	-	5	-	-	5
Mesial sections	-	1	1	-	2
Distal sections	-	3	-	-	3
Scrapers	-	1	-	-	1
Spokeshaves	1	-	-	1	1
Points	-	2	-	-	2
Knives - unilateral	-	2		-	2
Total	1	29	2	1	33

Thomasset and Walsh Collection, (Ethno) 1924.10-11.1-11 and 18
A group of 11 hornfels Middle Stone Age artefacts and 3 unworked pieces of stone. The degree of retouch on the points is highly variable: some are steeply retouched along the entirety of both lateral margins, others have retouch present only at the distal extremity, while one is an unifacial point.
2 unmodified flake-blades, 1 unmodified flake, 8 points.

Additional material Department of Ethnography, British Museum (Appendix 1). Cambridge University Museum (Appendix 3).

ESTCOURT 29° 00'S, 29° 55'E

Estcourt was an important British military base in the middle of what is now KwaZulu-Natal in the mid-19th century and these four, probably Middle Stone Age hornfels artefacts were collected there in February 1881. Feilden (1883: 168) locates them specifically to a point about 200 metres below a bridge on the right bank of the Bushman River.

Christy Collection, ex Feilden, +7843-+7846
1 unmodified flake (with a faceted platform), 1 unmodified flake (much more heavily patinated than the other artefacts), 2 unmodified flake-blades.

Additional material Liverpool Museum, Pitt Rivers Museum (Appendix 3).

ISANDHLWANA (ISANDULANA) 28° 32'S, 30° 40'E

Isandhlwana (fought on January 20th, 1879) was the site of the first major battle of the Anglo-Zulu War and one of the worst British military disasters of the 19th century; virtually all the troops left at the base camp of Lord Chelmsford's invasion force - totalling over 1300 - were killed (D.R. Morris 1990). British forces remained in the area after the conclusion of the War and Middle Stone Age artefacts were collected here by Major Feilden and at Rorke's Drift (qv) nearby by Colonel J. H. Bowker in 1880-81. The label on one of this pair of artefacts (+7837) more specifically places the date of collection in the field as August 1881 and Feilden (1883: 168) records the exact provenance as at about the centre of the former British camp.

Christy Collection, ex Feilden, +7836 - +783

A group of two hornfels Middle Stone Age artefacts, both of which are in a rolled and heavily patinated condition.
1 unmodified flake (with a faceted platform), 1 unmodified flake-blade (of which the tip and bulb are both broken off).

Additional material Cambridge University Museum (Appendix 3).

KAFFIRLAND [*sic*], NO FURTHER PROVENCE

The word 'Kaffir' (for most of the 20th century a racist term of abuse for Black South Africans) was employed in the 19th century principally to refer to the IsiXhosa-speaking communities of the Eastern Cape, although it was also used more widely with reference to other Nguni-speaking peoples. Since Sir Bartle Frere contributed other material from KwaZulu-Natal to the British Museum, it seems likely that these artefacts too were obtained from that province, probably from the area close to or north of the Thukela River. In the mid-19th century this river marked the frontier between the British colony of Natal and the Zulu kingdom, the invasion of which Sir Bartle orchestrated in January 1879. The date of November 20th 1878 on one of the artefacts supports this hypothesis for their origin as Frere had been in Natal for some two months by this time (Laband 1997).

Frere Collection, 1910.10-5.89-90

Donated as part of a much larger ethnographic collection, this material comprises two Middle Stone Age hornfels artefacts, the proximal ends of which are missing in both cases. The flake has a now partially illegible label on its ventral surface, on which only the date 20.11.78 can still be read. This may be the date on which the artefact was found or acquired by Sir Bartle.
1 unmodified flake (in hornfels), 1 unmodified flake-blade (in hornfels).

MUDEN 28° 59'S,30° 23'E

D. M. Cookson is known to have collected extensively in dongas (erosion gullies) in the Muden area. In addition to the material held by the British Museum, B. Malan (1956) published an account of an engraved Middle Stone Age flake from this locality. Farnden (1965, 1968) subsequently collected both Middle and Later Stone Age artefacts from several sites near Muden.

Cookson Collection, (Ethno) 1955.Af 22 3-6, 8-10, 12, 14-17, 19

This is a small, but mixed, group of 13 artefacts found in eroded dongas at depths of up to 20 feet (6 m) and within 6 miles (10 km) of Muden. Though accessioned in the mid-1950s, a note made by Braunholtz later included in the British Museum register comments that they had been sent to the Museum in 1931/32 and offered for sale. Cookson wrote saying that he intended to come to Britain to discuss the matter, but nothing more was heard of him. The artefacts formally became part of the British Museum collections in 1955 under regulations governing unclaimed property.

A virtually unpatinated hornfels spokeshave is most likely of fairly recent Later Stone Age (second half of the Holocene) origin, whereas two hornfels scrapers, both again unpatinated, are also of LSA origin, though possibly earlier than the spokeshave. The remaining 10 artefacts are attributable to the Middle Stone Age and all are in hornfels unless otherwise stated.
1 irregular core, 2 unmodified flakes (both with faceted platforms), 5 points (1 in baked sandstone has a faceted platform), 2 partly bifacial points.

Additional material Department of Ethnography, British Museum (Appendix 1).

Newall Collection, ex Cookson, (Ethno) 1954.Af 22 2-6

A group of five Middle Stone Age hornfels artefacts, all with faceted platforms except for one of the flakes. The British Museum register notes that Cookson had collected them 'on the surface in eroded areas up to 2 feet deep', which suggests they may have come from the same locality, and perhaps at the same time, as the Cookson collection from Muden just described.
2 unmodified flakes, 3 retouched points.

Additional material Department of Ethnography, British Museum (Appendix 1). The Natural History Museum (Appendix 3).

NATAL, NO FURTHER PROVENANCE FROM 27° 45'S, 29° 56'E TO 28° 22'S, 30° 33'E

Although these three groups of artefacts are all considered here under the rubric 'Natal, no further provenance', Feilden's (1883) publication on the material that he collected in South Africa does, in fact, strongly suggest that they come from along his line of march between Newcastle and Rorke's Drift. This is reflected in the co-ordinates given here. During this march he 'took advantage of every opportunity that arose for leaving the line of march and examining the 'dongas' and denuded surfaces that lay contiguous to this route' (Feilden 1883: 165).

Christy Collection, ex Feilden, +7847 - +7857, +7859 - +7866

Seven of this group of 75 artefacts are marked with one of two dates (8.viii.81 and 18.vi.81), presumably indicating the dates in 1881 on which they were collected. The group as a whole is clearly almost entirely Middle Stone Age in affiliation, based on the presence of several flake-blades and the large number of retouched points and knives. However, the opaline scraper and one of those in hornfels with adze-like lateral retouch (elsewhere generally seen as an early or middle Holocene feature; J. Deacon 1984b) are both of Later Stone Age origin. The artefacts display considerable variation in their condition, from fresh to quite rolled, suggesting they are not all of the same age and/or that they have not all had the same depositional history. This would be consistent with the two different dates noted above.

Table 31. The Christy Collection, ex Feilden, from Natal, no further provenance

	Opaline	Hornfels	Quartz	Quartzite	Tuff	Siltstone/ mudstone	Dolerite	Sandstone	Total
Irregular cores	1	1	-	-	-	-	1	-	3
Flakes	2	13	2	1	-	-	-	4	22
Flake-blades	-	5	1	-	-	-	-	-	6
Proximal sections (flake-blades)	-	1	-	-	-	-	-	-	1
Utilised flakes	-	-	-	-	1	-	-	-	1
Scrapers	1	4	-	-	-	-	-	-	5
Knives - unilateral	-	11	-	-	1	-	-	1	13
Points	-	16	1	-	1	1	-	3	22
Unifacial points	-	2	-	-	-	-	-	-	2
Total	4	53	4	1	3	1	1	8	75

Two further stone artefacts (+7858 and +7867) are described in the Christy Slip Catalogue as follows:
'+7858 - 1 flake of a greenish, ochreous stone trimmed to form a tongue-shaped implement [*sic*], measuring 56 mm by 38 mm; +7867 - 1 unmodified flake made from bright green quartz [*sic*].'

Christy Collection, ex Feilden, unnumbered

A group of 26 artefacts and 18 unworked pieces of stone. Where it is possible to suggest an affiliation most of the artefacts are of Middle Stone Age origin and were stored with Christy material acquired from Feilden. That they have a similar origin is also suggested by the use on some of them of the same system of dating (and the correspondence of two of the dates themselves). However, the bulk of these artefacts are unmarked.

The four dated artefacts are:

1 hornfels flake and a hornfels flake-blade from which the tip is broken off - 18.vi.81

1 hornfels retouched point - 8.viii.81

1 hornfels flake - 1.v.81

The unmarked artefacts show great variation in their physical condition from fresh to quite rolled and the hornfels artefacts are variably patinated (from not at all to quite thickly), again suggesting a varied age and/or depositional history. The single scraper has adze-like lateral retouch and is almost certainly a Later Stone Age piece.

Table 32. Unmarked artefacts in the Christy, ex Feilden, Collection from Natal

	Opaline	Hornfels	Quartz	Quartzite	Sandstone	Total
Core-reduced pieces	-	1	-	-	-	1
Flakes	1	9	1	1	1	13
Flake-blades	-	3	-	-	-	3
Scrapers	1	-	-	-	-	1
Knives - unilateral	-	2	-	-	-	2
Points	-	1	-	-	1	2
Total	2	16	1	1	2	22

Additional material Ashmolean Museum, Liverpool Museum, The Natural History Museum, Pitt Rivers Museum (Appendix 3).

NEWCASTLE 27° 45'S, 29° 56'E

Feilden (1883: 163-164) records that the bulk of his collections were made while quartered in the Newcastle area of northwestern KwaZulu-Natal. He exhibited five of them (described as 'two spear-heads, two arrow-heads' and what was obviously a bored stone) to the Royal Anthropological Institute, but only one is present in the collections of the British Museum.

Christy Collection, ex Feilden, +7842

This is a single Middle Stone Age artefact with a faceted platform.
1 unmodified flake (in dolerite).

Additional material Cambridge University Museum (Appendix 3).

PIETERMARITZBURG 29° 38'S, 30° 28'E

Pietermaritzburg was known as a source of stone artefacts from at least the time of the first publication on the archaeology of KwaZulu-Natal (Sanderson 1878). Feilden (1883: 169) collected from several localities and records finding artefacts close to or on the surface to the south, east and west of the city, as well as in the gravels of the Msunduze River, which flows through it. Subsequently artefacts were collected here by several other amateur archaeologists.

Christy Collection, ex Feilden

Four probably Middle Stone Age artefacts, three of them dated 1882, 26.3.1882 and 1.4.1882, presumably indicating the dates on which they were collected. One of the two patinated hornfels flakes and the single example made in siltstone/mudstone have faceted platforms.
4 unmodified flakes (3 in hornfels, 1 in siltstone/mudstone).

Rev. R. L. White Collection, (Ethno) 1935.10-23.4, 5, 7

A group of three Middle and Later Stone Age artefacts collected by the Rev. White before his death in 1932.

1 Middle Stone Age bilaterally retouched knife (in hornfels, with a faceted platform), 1 Later Stone Age (probably 4000 BP) spokeshave (in hornfels), 1 culturally undiagnostic unmodified flake (in siltstone/mudstone).

Additional material Department of Ethnography, British Museum (Appendix 1).Cambridge University Museum (Pietermaritzburg, Greytown Road; Pietermaritzburg, Msunduze River), Pitt Rivers Museum (Appendix 3).

RORKE'S DRIFT 28° 22'S, 30° 33

Rorke's Drift was a Swedish mission station taken over and used as a supply base by the British Army because of its strategic location as a crossing point on the Buffalo River (which formed the border between Zululand and the British colony of Natal) during the Anglo-Zulu War of 1879. Following the disastrous defeat suffered by the British at Isandhlwana (qv), Rorke's Drift was successfully defended against a Zulu attack later the same day (January 22nd, 1879; D.R. Morris 1990). The mission remained in military hands until October 1879 when troops finally moved into a purpose-built fort (Fort Melvill) nearby (Webley 1993). Excavations undertaken at Rorke's Drift to investigate further the course of events here in 1879 produced a number of mostly hornfels Middle Stone Age artefacts from basal red gravels beneath the historical occupation horizons (Webley 1993: 32-33).

Colonel J. H. Bowker, from whom the British Museum obtained its Rorke's Drift material by donation in August 1880, was a member of the expedition to the site of the death of the Prince Imperial, heir to the Bonaparte throne of France, who had been killed earlier in the War. In an account published in the *Natal Witness* on April 17th, 1880 he refers to the presence of prehistoric artefacts 'in the dongas and hollows near Rorke's Drift and Isandhlwana', some of which were found while excavating the foundations of the Queen's Cross Memorial (Gooch 1881: 175).

Christy Collection, ex Bowker, +7539, +7580

With two exceptions, this assemblage of 42 artefacts appears to be entirely of Middle Stone Age origin. However, the hornfels artefacts are variably patinated and rolled, suggesting that they may not all have had the same depositional history and/or that they are not all of the same age, while one of the quartz flakes and the opaline flake are both in fresh condition and thus possibly more recent than the remaining artefacts listed in Table 34. The two clearly non-MSA artefacts are a rolled dolerite handaxe, of Early Stone Age origin, and a single spokeshave that is in much fresher condition than any of the other hornfels artefacts and probably belongs to a Later Stone Age industry dating to the second half of the Holocene.

Table 33. The Christy Collection, ex Bowker, from Rorke's Drift

	Opaline	Hornfels	Quartz	Sandstone	Dolerite	Total
Handaxes (ESA)	-	-	-	-	1	1
Irregular cores	-	2	-	-	-	2
Flakes	1	9	2	2	-	14
Flake-blades	-	6	-	1	-	7
Proximal sections (flake-blades)	-	3	-	-	-	3
Mesial sections (flake-blades)	-	1	1	-	-	2
Distal sections (flake-blades)	-	1	-	-	-	1
Utilised flake-blades	-	1	-	-	-	1
Scrapers	-	1	-	-	-	1
Spokeshaves (LSA)	-	1	-	-	-	1
Knives - unilateral	-	1	-	-	-	1
Knives - bilateral	-	1	-	-	-	1
Points	-	4	-	1	-	5
Bifacial points	-	2	-	-	-	2
Total	1	33	3	4	1	42

THE CURRAGH 29° 58'S, 29° 22'E

Christy Collection, ex Frames, 99496-507, 510-524

This is a group of 25 artefacts and 4 unworked pieces of stone excavated by M. E. Frames in 1899 from The Curragh cave in the foothills of the Drakensberg Mountains of East Griqualand. Frames (1899), in his report on this, the first recorded excavation of an archaeological site in KwaZulu-Natal, also mentions the presence of several rock-paintings, including one of an elephant, and the shelter was recorded by Vinnicombe (1976) as a painted site in the second half of the 20th century. The artefacts were donated to the British Museum on November 30th, 1899, having previously been exhibited at a meeting of the Anthropological Institute of Great Britain and Ireland.

This assemblage, though obviously selected (and the surviving artefacts are fewer in number than those mentioned by Frames (1899: 253-257)), is clearly of Later Stone Age origin. The number of formal tools is too small to suggest a more specific cultural affiliation with any degree of conviction, but the large number of adzes suggests that a later Holocene age is most likely, although the naturally backed knife and the three large sidescrapers may indicate that a terminal Pleistocene/early Holocene (*cf.* Oakhurst Complex) component is also present. One of the adzes is backed and another has been made on a reused Middle Stone Age flake-blade. Several of the adzes and flakes, including this one, are rolled.

Table 34. The Christy Collection, ex Frames, from The Curragh

	Opaline	Hornfels	Total
Bladelet cores (bipolar)	1	-	1
Core-reduced pieces	1	-	1
Flakes	1	7	8
Utilised flakes	-	1	1
Scrapers	2	2	4
Adzes	2	6	8
Spokeshaves	-	1	1
Naturally backed knives	-	1	1
Total	7	18	25

WEENEN (TOWNLANDS) 28° 51'S, 30° 06'E

Thomasset Collection, 1938.10-7.1-24, 26-42

A collection of 41 hornfels Later Stone Age artefacts, all but two of them spokeshaves or adzes. Three of the adzes have a light grey patina and may thus be older than the others. The entire collection is probably of Holocene age, the predominance of adzes and spokeshaves strongly suggesting a date of 4000 BP.
1 patinated unmodified flake, 1 scraper, 20 adzes, 19 spokeshaves.

Additional material Cambridge University Museum, The Natural History Museum (Appendix 3).

ZULULAND, NO FURTHER PROVENCE FROM 27° 40, 30° 10'E TO 28° 12'S, 31° 11E

Feilden (1883: 168) records that two of his military colleagues, Colonel Curtis and Captain Pennefather of the Inniskilling Dragoons, gathered a total of 12 artefacts along the line of their march from near Utrecht to 'the Inlazatche mountain', modern Nhlazatshe just north of the White Mfolozi River and to the northwest of Ulundi. At the time of Curtis and Pennefather's march Nhlazatshe was the headquarters of Melmoth Osborn, the second British Resident in Zululand (Laband 1997). Pennefather himself remained in Zululand until at least 1888, taking part in further military operations there at that time with the Inniskilling Dragoons (Laband 1997).

Christy Collection, ex Feilden, ex Curtis and Pennefather, +7838 - +7840

A group of ten artefacts two of which - a sandstone flake and a hornfels point - are marked 'Sept. 1881 H.W.F.', which may be the date on which they were collected. All the artefacts are in hornfels unless otherwise stated. The formal tools and the faceting of the platform on the quartz flake suggest that the entire collection may be of Middle Stone Age origin.
4 unmodified flakes (including 1 each in vein quartz, opaline and sandstone), 1 crested blade (in sandstone), 1 flake-blade (of which the tip is broken off), 1 point, 1 unilaterally retouched knife.

2.5 South Africa: Mpumalanga

Like the Northern Province, Mpumalanga has seen far more intensive investigation of the Iron Age component of its archaeological record than of its Stone Age past (summarized by Evers 1981; Meyer 1986). Two rock-shelters, both with long Stone Age sequences, have, however, been excavated on opposite sides of the Blyde River. Bushman Rock Shelter was excavated by Louw (1967) and then by a team from the University of Pretoria. Superimposed on a series of Middle Stone Age levels, over 2 m of deposit spans the last 12,000 years, although discrepancies between radiocarbon dates on bone and charcoal from the immediately underlying layers remain unresolved (Plug 1978, 1981). The bulk of the Later Stone Age sequence appears to be of terminal Pleistocene/early Holocene age, may belong to the Oakhurst Complex (Plug 1981) and is associated with a rich worked bone assemblage (Plug 1982); Wadley's (1987) reanalysis of artefacts from Layers 15-18 indicates that a short-lived (?) Robberg occupation preceded this. A few kilometres to the southeast Beaumont (1981) carried out test-excavations at Heuningneskrans rock-shelter in 1968. Though not comprehensively published, the Heuningneskrans sequence may have a basal age of *c.* 32,000 BP and contains both Oakhurst-like and Robberg-like assemblages (Beaumont 1981). Re-examination of part of them suggests that a Robberg-like bladelet-rich occurrence may be restricted to the period *c.* 12-24,000 BP (Mitchell 1988: 122-129); as with the dating discrepancies present in the nearby Bushman Rock Shelter sequence, there is clearly a need, if at all possible, to undertake further excavations in order to resolve such problems. Klein's (1984b) analysis of the Heuningneskrans fauna, which indicates relatively little difference between Pleistocene and recent environments, does, however, provide some ecological basis for the view that LSA cultural trajectories in the Mpumalanga lowveld may have been rather different from those in parts of South Africa where such environments contrast more markedly.

The last two decades have seen relatively little Stone Age research in Mpumalanga. Binneman & Niekerk (1986) have examined cleavers and débitage from several Early Stone Age sites in the Barberton area and have shown that they were reused relatively recently, perhaps by Iron Age communities, in processing and dressing hides. Wadley (1987) excavated at Hope Hill shelter near Leslie, which was occupied during the middle Holocene (Wadley & Turner 1987). Most recently, Korsman & Plug (1994) have published the results of excavations carried out in the 1950s by H. Sentker at two rock-shelters near Badplaas, both of which have evidence of a basal mid-Holocene occupation underlying more extensive late Holocene levels with evidence of contact with Iron Age farmers. Beyond this, archaeological research in the Chrissiesmeer area, where an increasingly marginalized and assimilated Bushman community survived into the 20th century (Potgieter 1955), has yet to be commenced.

Reflecting the comparatively limited extent of Stone Age research in Mpumalanga, this province has by far the fewest artefacts or collections of any part of South Africa in the British Museum (**Fig. 20**). The presence of Early, Middle and Later Stone Age artefacts from the two localities represented does, however, suggest that much more remains to be discovered in Mpumalanga about all aspects of southern Africa's prehistory.

BARBERTON 25° 42'S, 31° 01'E

The town of Barberton was founded in 1884 after a local gold rush precipitated by the discovery of the Pioneer Reef the previous year. The resulting boom was short-lived and over-capitalization of the relatively small mines in the area and the discovery of gold on the Witwatersrand resulted in it coming to an end soon after 1888 (Reader's Digest 1994b: 262-64). It seems likely that the artefacts in the Ward Collection from this area were found in the course of gold prospecting, though there is no definite evidence of this.

Ward Collection, 1934.10-18.1-19, 21

Twenty artefacts, mostly in fresh condition and consisting of a mixture of seven Middle Stone Age and six Later Stone Age implements, as well as six artefacts that are culturally undiagnostic.

Undiagnostic elements:

1 irregular core (in a red metamorphic rock), 2 irregular cores (in hornfels), 2 unmodified flakes (in quartz), 1 unmodified flake (in opaline);

MSA elements: 2 disc cores (in hornfels), 4 unmodified flake-blades (all of them with faceted platforms, 3 in hornfels and 1 in opaline)), 1 retouched point (in hornfels);

LSA elements: 5 scrapers (4 in hornfels, 1 in opalin

The small size and form of the opaline scraper indicates that it is of Wilton or post-classic Wilton affiliation. The larger hornfels scrapers, two of which are sidestruck, may belong to the Oakhurst Complex. One of them is made on part of a MSA flake-blade attesting to the reuse of older MSA artefacts by later people.

Additional material Department of Ethnography, British Museum (Appendix 1).

STEYNSDORP 26° 01'S, 31° 05'E

Located less than 30 km south of Barberton, Steynsdorp also developed in the mid 1880s after gold was found in the nearby Mlondozi stream. Recognised formally as a town by the then South African Republic in 1887, it had a population of 3000 at its height, but was soon deserted as miners moved away to the more lucrative goldfields of the Witwatersrand

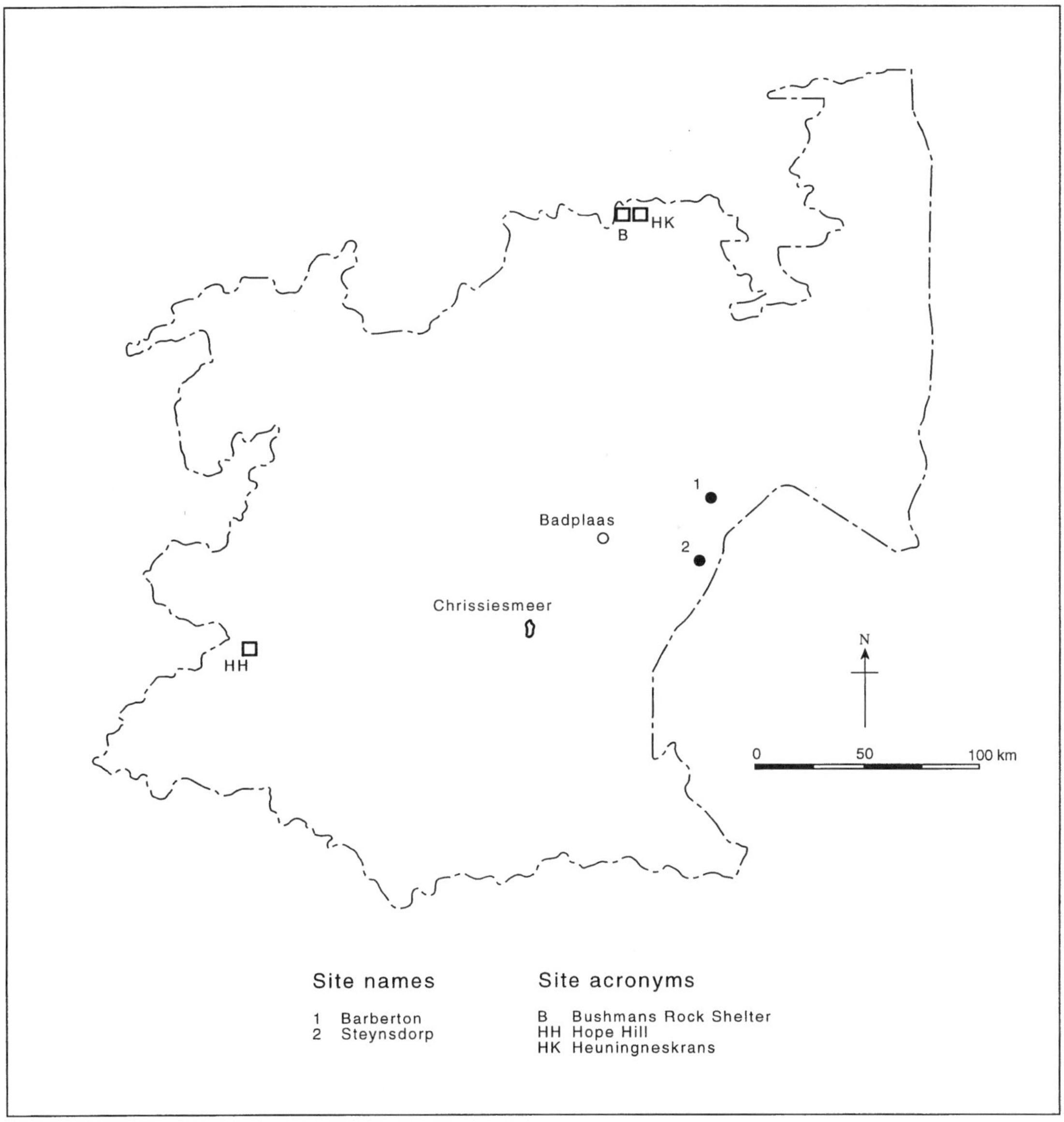

Fig. 20. Location of archaeological sites in Mpumalanga and of Stone Age collections from there in the British Museum

(Reader's Digest 1994b: 223). The two Early Stone Age artefacts from here in the British Museum collections were both probably obtained in the course of geological survey work; Trevor was a senior civil servant in the South African Mines Department whose published work on archaeology examined evidence for Iron Age mining in South Africa and Zimbabwe (Trevor 1930); he also contributed a series of bored stones from the Northern Province to the collections of the British Museum's Ethnography Department.

Trevor Collection, (Ethno) 1920.2-7.6
1 Early Stone Age cleaver (in lava).

F. White Collection, 1922.6-6.27
1 dolerite pebble worked bifacially at one end. This artefact is in fresh condition, but not, by itself, chronologically diagnostic.

2.6 South Africa: North West Province

While much of the North West Province has witnessed comparatively little Stone Age archaeological research, two areas on its periphery are particularly important, in addition to the one-time significance for understanding southern African prehistory of the stratigraphic sequence of the Vaal River gravels (Clark 1959). Finds from localities such as Christiana and Sheppard's Island (qqv) in the British Museum collections result from this early work. On the southwestern edge of the province Taung (qv) achieved archaeological prominence because of Raymond Dart's recognition of the hominid status of the *Australopithecus africanus* infant found here in mining operations in 1924 (Dart 1925; Sampson 1974: 19-21). Though no further australopithecine remains have been found at Taung, other limestone caves in the vicinity have come to be important archaeological sites. Following initial exploration of some of them by a University of California expedition in the 1940s (Peabody 1954), Holocene Later Stone Age occupations have been excavated at Little Witkrans (Humphreys & Thackeray 1983), Powerhouse Cave (Humphreys 1978) and several neighbouring shelters (Beaumont & Morris 1990: 166-168).

The second principal area in which Stone Age research in the North West Province has been conducted lies at the other end of the province, close to Johannesburg. Here, building on earlier investigations of Holocene Later Stone Age sites such as Kruger Cave (Mason 1988), Lyn Wadley (1987) initiated an extensive programme of excavation and survey focused on the Later Stone Age prehistory of the Magaliesberg Range in the early 1980s, concentrating on the excavation of two rock-shelters: Jubilee Shelter and Cave James (Wadley 1987); other important sites investigated included the open-air Oakhurst Complex quarries of Xanadu, Serpent Quarry and Silkaatsnek (Wadley 1988). Jubilee Shelter is the most extensively excavated of these sites and has yielded a rich sequence of artefact, faunal and palaeobotanical assemblages extending back in excess of 30, 000 BP. While it and Cave James provided a firm cultural-stratigraphic outline and palaeoenvironmental record for the terminal Pleistocene and Holocene of the area, including the first clear demonstration of a middle Holocene human presence in the former Transvaal (Wadley 1986), their significance lies also in the fact that they formed the basis for one of the first historical materialist interpretations of the southern African Later Stone Age. Wadley's (1987) synthesis of her research in the Magaliesberg involved deducing the material implications for the archaeological record of a model of seasonal aggregation and dispersal derived from Bushman ethnography and assessing the Cave James and Jubilee Shelter artefact and faunal assemblages in relation to this model (*cf.* Walker 1995: 213-218 for a critique). Though the study of rock art was not a major part of this project, important rock engravings also exist in the province (Mason 1962: 340-370); those at Doornspruit just south of the Magaliesberg Range have contributed to the inclusion of rock engravings within the development of the ethnographically-informed paradigm for rock art research loosely called the 'trance hypothesis' (Dowson 1988).

As is the case for the Free State on the opposite side of the Vaal River, many of the artefacts in the British Museum collections from the North West Province **(Fig. 21)** were collected by H. Braunholtz during his 1929 visit to South Africa for the meeting there of the British Association for the Advancement of Science. Christiana, an important source of Early Stone Age artefacts in the gravel terraces of the Vaal River, is the best known of the sites in the North West Province represented in the Braunholtz Collection. Also of interest among the Early and Middle Stone Age artefacts from this province is the Van Riet Lowe Collection from Sheppard Island, the stratigraphy at which was used by Goodwin and Van Riet Lowe (1929) to date assemblages from these early periods of southern African prehistory. Early and Middle Stone Age artefacts from Taung, type-site of the genus *Australopithecus*, in the Armstrong, Favell and Jones Collections also form part of the British Museum holdings from the North West Province.

BECHUANA PROVINCE APPROXIMATELY CENTRED ON 27° 00'S, 24° 00'E

White Collection, unnumbered

A small assemblage of 45 artefacts stated to come from 'north of the Vaal and Harts Rivers', i.e. within the former colony of British Bechuanaland that is now part of the Northern Cape and North West Provinces. A variety of materials is present, but the assemblage has no features specifically diagnostic of any Middle or Later Stone Age industry. Three Whites contributed to the British Museum southern African Stone Age collections and there is no documentation to indicate which one was responsible for the donation of this particular assemblage. Two of them, F. White and, more extensively, Major-General H. G. White, contributed collections from Griqualand West, now within the Northern Cape Province, and one or other of them was therefore probably also the donor of this collection.

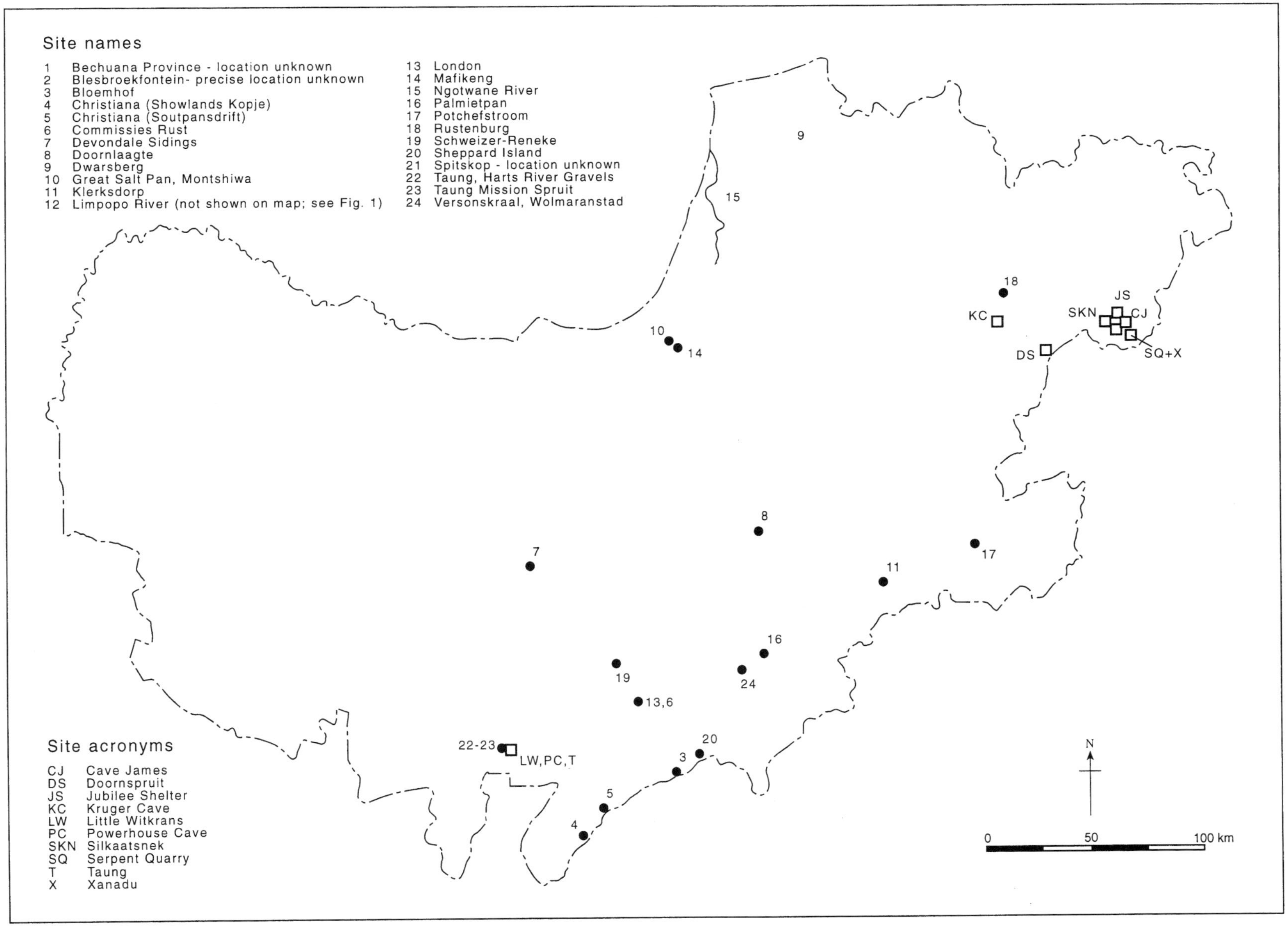

Fig. 21. Location of archaeological sites in the North West Province and of Stone Age collections from there in the British Museum

Table 35. The White Collection from Bechuana Province, North West Province

	Opaline	Hornfels	Silcrete	Quartz	Quartzite	Ironstone	Total
Irregular cores	-	-	-	1	-	-	1
Core-reduced pieces	-	-	-	1	-	-	1
Flakes	9	12	4	4	6	1	36
Utilised flakes	1	-	-	2	-	-	3
Scrapers	-	1	-	1	-	-	2
Miscellaneous retouched pieces	-	-	-	2	-	-	2
Total	10	13	4	11	6	1	45

BLESBROEKFONTEIN APPROXIMATELY 27° 30', 25° 36'E

Fuller Collection, ex Braunholtz, (Ethno) 1930.2-5.5-6

Two Early Stone Age artefacts from an unidentified locality within the Bloemhof Magisterial District found at a depth of 4 feet (1.2 m) below the surface.
2 handaxes (in dolerite).

BLOEMHOF 27° 30'S, 25° 36'E

Braunholtz Collection, (Ethno) 1930.1-24

A small assemblage of nine artefacts with Early Stone Age affinities from the Bloemhof Townland factory site, near the Vaal River. Except for one of the chopper-like pebble tools, which is in vein quartz, all these artefacts are made in dolerite.
1 handaxe, 2 bifacially worked chopper-like pebble tools, 1 biface, 1 irregular core, 4 unmodified flakes.

CHRISTIANA (SHOWLANDS KOPJE) 27° 57'S, 25° 08'E

Braunholtz Collection, (Ethno) 1930.1-24

This material comprises a total of 109 artefacts from all three major sub-divisions of southern African prehistory. The Early Stone Age artefacts, stated to derive from the 50-80 feet (15-24 m) terrace of the Vaal River, consist of 67 artefacts all made in dolerite:
7 cleavers, 9 handaxes, 2 heavily rolled bifaces, 2 spheroids, 18 irregular cores, 2 radial cores, 1 trimming flake, 24 unmodified flakes, 1 utilised flake, 1 scraper.
The probably Middle Stone Age component, in which some artefacts are lightly rolled, consists of 42 artefacts, among them two small points with faceted platforms, superficially resembling those from a terminal MSA excavated context at Sibebe Shelter, Swaziland (Price-Williams 1981); the likely LSA component totals 49 artefacts.

Table 36. The probable Middle Stone Age component of the Braunholtz Collection from Christiana (Showlands Kopje)

	Opaline	Hornfels	Quartzite	Dolerite	Tuff	Other	Total
Irregular cores	-	-	2	2	-	1	5
Flakes	-	3	2	4	1	2	12
Flake-blades	-	2	2	2	-	-	6
Proximal sections (flake-blades)	-	-	1	2	-	-	3
Scrapers	1	1	-	1	-	2	5
Points	1	-	2	-	1	-	4
Knives - unilateral	-	1	5	1	-	-	7
Total	2	7	14	12	2	5	42

Table 37. The probable Later Stone Age component of the Braunholtz Collection from Christiana (Showlands Kopje)

	Opaline	Hornfels	Quartz	Quartzite	Dolerite	Siltstone/ mudstone	Total
Irregular cores	3	-	-	2	1	-	6
Blade cores	-	-	-	1	-	-	1
Flat bladelet cores	1	-	-	-	-	-	1
Flakes	5	1	3	4	-	-	13
Bladelets	-	1	-	-	-	-	1
Scrapers	7	1	2	9	-	3	22
Adzes	2	-	-	-	-	-	2
Retouched bladelets	-	1	-	-	-	-	1
Miscellaneous retouched pieces	1	1	-	-	-	-	2
Total	19	5	5	16	1	3	49

Additional material Cambridge University Museum (Christiana, Diamond Workings), The Natural History Museum (Christiana, Townlands; Christiana, Dramant's Farm) (Appendix 3).

CHRISTIANA (SOUTPANSDRIFT) 27° 58'S, 25° 08'E

Though Soutpansdrift (formerly Zoutpansdrift) lies on the Free State of the Vaal River, the provenance of these two artefacts to 'Christiana (Soutpansdrift)' suggests that they were found just across the Vaal and to the immediate south of the town of Christiana itself, i.e. within the North West Province of modern South Africa.

Seton-Karr Collection, unnumbered

Two dolerite artefacts, of which the cleaver is of Early Stone Age origin.
1 cleaver, 1 miscellaneously retouched piece.

COMMISSIES RUST 27° 22'S, 25° 26'E

Fuller Collection, ex Braunholtz, (Ethno) 1930.2-5.13

A single Middle Stone Age artefact from a farm of this name in the northern part of the Bloemhof District north of Wolmaranstad (qv; D. Morris, pers. comm.).
1 point (in hornfels).

DEVONDALE SIDINGS 26° 46'S, 24° 54'E

Devondale Sidings was identified by Collins & Smith (1919: 91) as a prolific area for finding stone artefacts two miles (3 km) from the railway line connecting Mafikeng and Vryburg. In addition to what he describes as 'neolithic' (presumably Later Stone Age) flakes, four Early Stone Age artefacts were found in hollows along a dry stream bed.

Collins Collection, 1919.2-10.19

1 handaxe (in dolerite and in a heavily rolled condition).

Additional material Cambridge University Museum (Appendix 3).

DOORNLAAGTE 26° 38'S, 26° 07'E

This site is identified by Collins & Smith (1919: 88) as a farm located some 64 km northwest of Klerksdorp and on the watershed of the Schoonspruit, Harts and Vaal Rivers. Two such farms were located in the *Reader's Digest Atlas of Southern Africa* and the latitude and longitude given are those for a point midway between them. Seven artefacts were found on the surface along the northern slope of a stream, some of them rolled. Two made in dolerite belong to the British Museum collections.

Collins Collection, 1919.2-10.11-12

1 handaxe, 1 steeply retouched large flake. The latter has probably been reused as the retouch is noticeably fresher than the patina that covers the remainder of the artefact.

Additional material Cambridge University Museum (Appendix 3).

DWARSBERG FROM ABOUT 25° 00'S, 26° 00'E TO ABOUT 25° 00'S, 26° 45'E

The Dwarsberge are a roughly east/west trending mountain range lying within South Africa and to the southeast of the Botswanan capital of Gaborone. Dwarsberg itself (24° 57'S, 26° 40'E) is a small settlement toward the eastern end of the range. This is one of several localities from which A.A. Anderson (1887a) collected artefacts in the 1860s and 1870s. As was his normal practice, Anderson wrote additional details on this Middle Stone Age artefact itself, in this case that it was found in a kloof (side-valley) of the mountain in 1877.

Christy Collection, ex Anderson, +7904

1 unmodified flake (in patinated hornfels, with a faceted platform and in rolled condition).

GREAT SALT PAN, MONTSHIWA (*MONTSIVA*) APPROXIMATELY 25° 52'S, 25° 39'E

According to the Christy Slip Catalogue this probably Middle Stone Age artefact was found 'on surface of Great Salt Pan, Montsiva (Lotlakana) British Bechuanaland' in 1865; the modern spellings of these localities are Montshiwa and Lotlhakane respectively and Montshiwa itself is now part of the modern city of Mmabatho, the capital of the North West Province.

Christy Collection, ex Anderson, +7898

1 unmodified flake (in patinated dolerite).

KLERKSDORP 26° 45'S, 27° 11'E

Major Collins collected from several localities on the farms Beentjeskraal, Kaffirskraal and Elandsheuwel along the Schoonspruit stream north of the town of Klerksdorp (Collins & Smith 1919). In addition to 'neoliths' (i.e. Middle or Later Stone Age artefacts) found on the surface, the following four artefacts were among several Early Stone Age artefacts discovered in gravel terraces 10-13 m above the then level of the Schoonspruit.

Collins Collection, 1919.2-10.7-10

2 patinated hornfels handaxes (1 in patinated hornfels, 1 in opaline), 1 unfinished handaxe (in dolerite), 1 scraper (in dolerite).

Additional material Cambridge University Museum (Klerksdorp, Elandsheuwel; Klerksdorp, Kaffirskraal; Klerksdorp, Schoonspruit) (Appendix 3).

LIMPOPO RIVER , FROM APPROXIMATELY 23° 40'S, 27° 00'E TO 22° 20'S, 31° 30'E

Although Andrew Anderson travelled extensively throughout southern Africa from the 1860s to the early 1880s and often recorded in detail the provenances of the artefacts that he collected, in this instance he provided only the most minimal information. It is therefore not possible to say where exactly along the Limpopo River these two artefacts were found, other than that this was probably somewhere along the border between present-day South Africa and Botswana. The flake-blade is of Middle Stone Age origin, but the broken flake is culturally undiagnostic.

Christy Collection, ex Anderson, +7907

1 unmodified flake (in sandstone and in a heavily rolled condition), 1 unmodified flake-blade (in opaline).

LONDON 27° 22'S, 25° 26'

Fuller Collection, ex Braunholtz, (Ethno) 1930.2-5.7 and 11

Two Early and/or Middle Stone Age artefacts, part of a group of 13 artefacts purchased from Fuller in 1930, the others also having originally been collected by Braunholtz from sites in the North West and Northern Cape Provinces.
1 handaxe (in dolerite); 1 disc core (in hornfels).

MAFIKENG (*MAFEKING*) 25° 48'S, 25° 30'E

Heanley Collection, 1937.7-13.1

A single Early Stone Age artefact found at the railway station in Mafikeng on February 11th 1936.
1 handaxe (in banded ironstone).

Additional material Cambridge University Museum, Pitt Rivers Museum (Appendix 3).

NGOTWANE (*NOTUANE*) RIVER BETWEEN APPROXIMATELY 25° 19'S, 25° 54'E AND 23° 45'S, 26° 58'E

Christy Collection, ex Anderson, +7906

A group of 12 Middle Stone Age artefacts. Though the Notwane/Ngotwane River now flows largely through eastern Botswana, A.A. Anderson (1888: 123) indicates that these artefacts were almost certainly collected along one of its tributaries in the North West Province of South Africa. Eight of them were found in a 'mountain sluit' in 1878:

5 unmodified flakes (4 in hornfels, 1 each in opaline and tuff), 1 unmodified flake-blade (in opaline), 1 scraper (in hornfels), 1 bilaterally retouched knife (in tuff).

Four other hornfels artefacts have slightly different provenances:

1 heavily rolled point collected from the Notuane River in 1868;

1 heavily rolled unmodified flake from the River in 1877;

2 large utilised flake-blades from a 'mountain sluit' in 1877.

PALMIETPAN PRECISE LOCATION UNKNOWN, POSSIBLY 27° 02'S, 26° 10'E

Collins & Smith (1919: 89) state only that this site is in the 'Western Transvaal'. However, as it follows two pages in which they describe artefacts from the Klerksdorp area it seems likely that it is located near here and thus within the present day North West Province. A Palmietfontein lies southwest of Klerksdorp about two-thirds of the way between there and Wolmaransstad and could be the locality in question. In their description of the finds from the site they refer only to what is probably a handaxe and three flakes and do not mention the single, culturally undiagnostic artefact in the British Museum collection.

Collins Collection, 1919.2-10.18

1 irregular core (in quartzite).

POTCHEFSTROOM 26° 44'S, 27° 06'E

Swan Collection, 1938.5-2

A single chronologically and culturally undiagnostic artefact.

1 unmodified flake (in opaline).

RUSTENBURG 25° 34'S, 27° 10'E

Christy Collection, ex Feilden, ex Ayres, +7835

Although Feilden (1883: 163) collected mostly in what is now KwaZulu-Natal he obtained a group of five artefacts from a Mr Thomas Ayres of Potchefstroom (qv), who had collected them near Rustenburg. Only one of these is now present in the British Museum collections; like the artefacts that Feilden collected in KwaZulu-Natal, it was donated to the Museum on October 5th 1883.

1 handaxe (in dolerite).

Additional material Cambridge University Museum (Appendix 3).

SCHWEIZER-RENEKE (*SCHWENER-RENEKE*) 27° 10'S, 25° 20'E

Although this Early Stone Age artefact is labelled 'Schwener-Reneke', this is almost certainly a mistranscription of 'Schweizer-Reneke', a town only 25 km further northwest along the R34 road from London (qv), where Braunholtz collected two further artefacts.

Fuller Collection, ex Braunholtz, (Ethno) 1930.2-5.8

1 bifacially worked implement (in dolerite). This artefact is peculiar in having a hollow base and cannot be readily classified as either a handaxe or a cleaver.

SHEPPARD ISLAND 27° 40'S, 2 45'E

Sheppard Island lies in a bend of the Vaal River about 16 km upstream of the town of Bloemhof, but is only an island when the Vaal is in flood and runs through both its present channel and a former one to the north. Van Riet Lowe investigated the site following the discovery of fossil mammoth bones here in the 1920s (Dart 1927) and provides a full description of its stratigraphy (Goodwin & Van Riet Lowe 1929: 235-243). Stone artefacts are present throughout what he referred to as the C and D gravels, as well as in the overlying surface deposits. The D gravels contain rolled and unrolled Acheulean artefacts, with 'rolled and unrolled remains of Fauresmith type' in the C gravels (Goodwin & Van Riet Lowe 1929: 240); Later Stone Age artefacts, originally attributed to the 'Smithfield B' occur at the surface.

Van Riet Lowe Collection, 1930.1-15.1-72

This is a mixed group of 73 Early and Middle Stone Age artefacts. Many are, as might be expected from their location, in a more-or-less rolled condition. No stratigraphic information exists for the collection and it is therefore not possible to say whether it comes from the D gravels in which Goodwin & Van Riet Lowe reported the presence of Acheulean artefacts, or from the C gravels in which a Fauresmith assemblage was present (Goodwin & Van Riet Lowe 1929: 235-243).

Table 38. The Van Riet Lowe Collection from Sheppards Island

	Opaline	Hornfels	Dolerite	Sandstone	Total
Cleavers	-	-	9	1	10
Handaxes	-	1	17	1	19
Spheroids	-	-	1	2	3
Irregular cores	1	-	3	-	4
Flakes	3	4	8	-	15
Flake-blades	-	2	7	-	9
Proximal sections (flake-blades)	-	2	-	-	2
Utilised flakes	1	-	-	-	1
Scrapers	-	-	1	-	1
Knives - unilateral	-	1	-	-	1
Knives - bilateral	-	-	2	-	2
Points	-	-	6	-	6
Total	5	10	54	4	73

Additional material Department of Ethnography, British Museum (Appendix 1).

SPITSKOP POSSIBLY IN THE GENERAL AREA OF 25°40'S, 26° 00'E

Christy Collection, ex Anderson, +7893

A single patinated artefact 'found on top of Spitskop, Kalahari Desert, 1866'. A.A. Anderson (1888: 124) mentions a 'Spitzkop' near Dwarsberg (qv) and it is likely, given that several other findspots of his are in the same general area, that this is the one meant, although he also comments on the many hills called Spitskops because of their pointed and rounded form.

1 unmodified flake (in hornfels and in rolled condition).

TAUNG *(TAUNGS)*, HARTS RIVER GRAVELS APPROXIMATELY 27° 37'S, 24° 37'E

Taung's principal claim to fame is as the home for the type specimen of the genus *Australopithecus*, the so-called Taung child (*A. africanus*), found here during lime-quarrying operations in 1924 and first published by Dart (1925). The *A. africanus* type-site lies close to the village of Norlim, headquarters of the Northern Lime Company, some 11 km southeast of Taung itself, at one time the administrative headquarters of a 'native reserve' and location of a mission station. The Armstrong and Favell collections from this locality derive from close to a stream near this mission, while the Jones material comes from the gravels of the Harts River slightly to the west of the settlement.

Although no further hominid remains have been found at Taung, systematic excavations have produced a Plio-Pleistocene fauna that most likely dates to about 2.4-2.3 million years ago (Beaumont & Morris 1990: 155). Several other important archaeological and palaeontological sites occur close to the type-site just east of the Ghaap Escarpment. These include Equus Cave (which has produced a few teeth of Upper Pleistocene age belonging to anatomically modern humans; Grine & Klein 1985), the mid- and late Holocene Later Stone Age site of Little Witkrans (Humphreys 1979) and Witkrans Cave (which produced a small Middle Stone Age assemblage; Beaumont & Morris 1990: 155).

Jones Collection, 1919.10-10.1-21

A group of 21 artefacts, the diagnostic elements of which are both Early Stone Age (cleavers and handaxes) and Middle Stone Age (retouched knives, scrapers made on flakes with faceted platforms) in origin. The cleavers, handaxes and irregular cores are notably more rolled than the other artefacts, which may indicate that the group is a mixed assemblage of differing ages.

Table 39. The Jones Collection from Taung

	Hornfels	Quartzite	Dolerite	Baked sandstone	Metamorphic rock - unidentified	Total
Handaxes	1	1	3	-	-	5
Cleavers	1	2	1	1	2	7
Irregular cores	3	-	-	-	-	3
Levallois cores	1	-	-	-	-	1
Scrapers	3	-	-	-	-	3
Knives - unilateral	1	-	-	-	-	1
Knives - bilateral	-	1	-	-	-	1
Total	10	4	4	1	2	21

Additional material Cambridge University Museum, Institute of Archaeology, Pitt Rivers Museum (Appendix 3).

TAUNG (*TAUNGS*) MISSION SPRUIT 27° 37'S, 24° 37'E

Armstrong Collection, 1959.7-12

A group of 46 artefacts, mostly made in dolerite, that appears to include Early, Middle and Later Stone Age elements. All the artefacts are rolled, some of them quite heavily. The unfinished bored stone is the only obvious Later Stone Age artefact, while the formal tools are of Middle Stone Age origin and the bifaces belong to the Early Stone Age.

Table 40. The Armstrong Collection from Taung Mission Spruit

	Opaline	Hornfels	Quartzite	Dolerite	Siltstone/ mudstone	Total
Cleavers	-	-	-	2	-	2
Handaxes	-	2	-	6	-	8
Irregular cores	-	-	-	3	-	3
Flakes	-	6	-	5	-	11
Flake-blades	-	1	-	2	-	3
Bored stone	-	-	-	1	-	1
Scrapers	-	-	1	5	-	6
Knives - unilateral	1	2	-	1	-	4
Knives - bilateral	1	2	-	2	-	5
Points	1	1	-	1	1	4
Total	3	14	1	28	1	47

Favell Collection, 1936.5-8.21-23

Three quartzite Early Stone Age artefacts in a rolled condition.
1 cleaver, 2 handaxes.

Additional material ? Liverpool Museum (Taungs River) (Appendix 3).

VERSONKRAAL, WOLMARANSSTAD APPROXIMATELY 27° 12'S, 26° 0'E

Fuller Collection, ex Braunholtz, (Ethno) 1930.2-5.10

A single dolerite handaxe forming part of a group of five artefacts (Fuller Collection, ex Braunholtz, (Ethno) 1930 2-5 9-13) originally collected by Braunholtz and offered to the Museum 'with other objects, by Captain A. W. F. Fuller for £ 17'. The other artefacts come from London (qv) and from sites in the general area of Barkly West and/or Kimberley in the Northern Cape Province. This particular specimen was found at a depth of 5 feet 6 inches (1.65 m) below the surface.
1 handaxe (in dolerite).

2.7 South Africa: Northern Cape Province

The size of South Africa's largest province makes any brief synthesis of the history of its Stone Age archaeological research even more difficult than those of the other eight. The Northern Cape Province is, however, well served by several major publications, though both Humphreys & Thackeray (1983) and Beaumont & Morris (1990) emphasize the area to the north of the Gariep and Vaal Rivers. Here sustained archaeological research got off to an early start in the context of Early and Middle Stone Age occurrences found during diamond-mining operations along the Vaal River; key sites include Canteen Kopje, Nooitgedacht and Pniel (qqv). Observation of the stratigraphic positions of these occurrences was important in early 20th-century attempts to construct a relative dating sequence for the Lower, Middle and early Upper Pleistocene parts of the South African Stone Age sequence (Clark 1959: 43). Though now largely discarded (Partridge & Brink 1967), several of these sites have more recently been investigated by Beaumont in order to clarify their content and associations (Beaumont & Morris 1990: 4-16). Beaumont has also excavated important Upper Pleistocene deposits at Kathu, southwest of Kuruman (Beaumont & Morris 1990: 75-100), but arguably the single most significant Stone Age site to have been excavated in this part of the Northern Cape is Wonderwerk. First excavated in the 1940s (B. Malan & Wells 1943), Wonderwerk's long and complex sequence, which extends from the Acheulean to the late Holocene, has been clarified by the much more extensive and controlled excavations carried out there by Anne Thackeray (Humphreys & Thackeray 1983) and Beaumont (Beaumont & Morris 1990: 101-134). Though not yet fully published, these excavations have shown that the site has one of the most comprehensive Stone Age sequences in southern Africa, including the discovery of engraved stones dating to the early Holocene (Thackeray *et al.* 1981). Moving beyond Wonderwerk, Later Stone Age research in the northern part of the Northern Cape has also included excavation of prehistoric specularite mines at Blinkklipkop (Thackeray *et al.* 1983), several rock-shelters along the southern edge of the Ghaap Escarpment (Humphreys & Thackeray 1983) and the stone-walled settlements of Khoisan pastoralists in the lower Riet River Valley (Humphreys 1972a).

Though Garth Sampson's work along the Gariep River in advance of construction of the Gariep Dam concentrated in what is now the Eastern Cape Province, he did excavate at Blydefontein Shelter (Sampson 1972) and also carried out work around the P. K. Le Roux Dam further downstream. Blydefontein, which provided stratigraphic confirmation for much of Sampson's (1970, 1972) Later Stone Age sequence, has since been re-investigated by Bousman (1991) in a combined archaeological and palaeoecological study. Sampson's more recent field survey in this area has concentrated in the Seacow River Valley, a little to the north and west. Beginning with one of the most comprehensive field survey projects to have been undertaken in Africa (Sampson 1985), the Seacow Valley research has attempted the investigation and delineation of forager social boundaries through the analysis of the motifs used to decorate Smithfield ceramics (Sampson 1988), also explored relations between pastoralists and foragers (e.g. Sampson 1984, Sampson *et al.* 1989) and is now concentrating on the effects of European colonial settlement of the area on indigenous hunter-gatherers (e.g. Sampson 1994, 1995); associated projects have included more detailed studies of Smithfield ceramic technology (e.g. Bollong 1996) and Acheulean and Middle Stone Age settlement systems (Wallsmith 1990).

At the time of the initial European settlement of South Africa the Northern Cape had a strong pastoralist presence and Andy Smith (1995) has recently edited a volume considering the relations between pastoralists, foragers, Iron Age farmers and the advancing colonial frontier along the Gariep River. Further to the west, Lita Webley (1984, 1990) has carried out an ethnoarchaeological study among surviving Nama pastoralists and also excavated a series of sites that demonstrate the presence of a herding economy in the Richtersveld/Namaqualand area from around 2000 BP (Webley 1992). With these exceptions and survey work by Beaumont (1986) in Bushmanland and by Smith & Ripp (1978) in the Doorn/Tanqua Karoo area, the remaining western third of the Northern Cape remains little known archaeologically. Except for sporadic work, such as that by Jansen (1926) around Victoria West and the more recent rescue excavations of Lloyd Evans et al. (1983) near Sutherland, the same is true of the southern part of the Karoo.

Rock art, particularly the recording of rock-engravings such as those at particularly rich sites like Driekopseiland (Beaumont & Morris 1990: 22-31), forms an important and longstanding part of the archaeological record and the history of archaeological research here, as elsewhere in southern Africa (e.g. Wilman 1933; Fock 1979). The Northern Cape's significance in this field has been boosted since the early 1980s because it was the Kenhardt/Prieska area of the province that was the homeland of the /Xam Bushmen interviewed by Wilhelm Bleek and Lucy Lloyd in the late 19th century (Deacon 1986). Their records provide an unparalleled insight into the way of life and beliefs of a South African Bushman community and form much of the ethnographic basis for current understanding of southern African rock art (Lewis-Williams & Dowson 1989), and indeed of the Later Stone Age as a whole. Janette Deacon, in particular, has carried out archaeological work in the area from which Bleek and Lloyd's informants came, identifying many of the features of the landscape of which they spoke, interviewing surviving /Xam descendants and excavating at some Contact period sites in the area (J. Deacon 1988, 1994, 1996). Investigation of the associations between rock-engravings and other components of the archaeological record in the Northern Cape remains an ongoing research priority (e.g. Beaumont & Vogel 1989; D. Morris & Beaumont 1994).

In terms of both numbers of artefacts (almost 1000) and number of distinct sites from which those artefacts come, the Northern Cape Province is one of the best represented parts of South Africa in the British Museum collections (**Fig. 22**). In large part this reflects the discovery of diamonds here in the middle of the 19th century, but

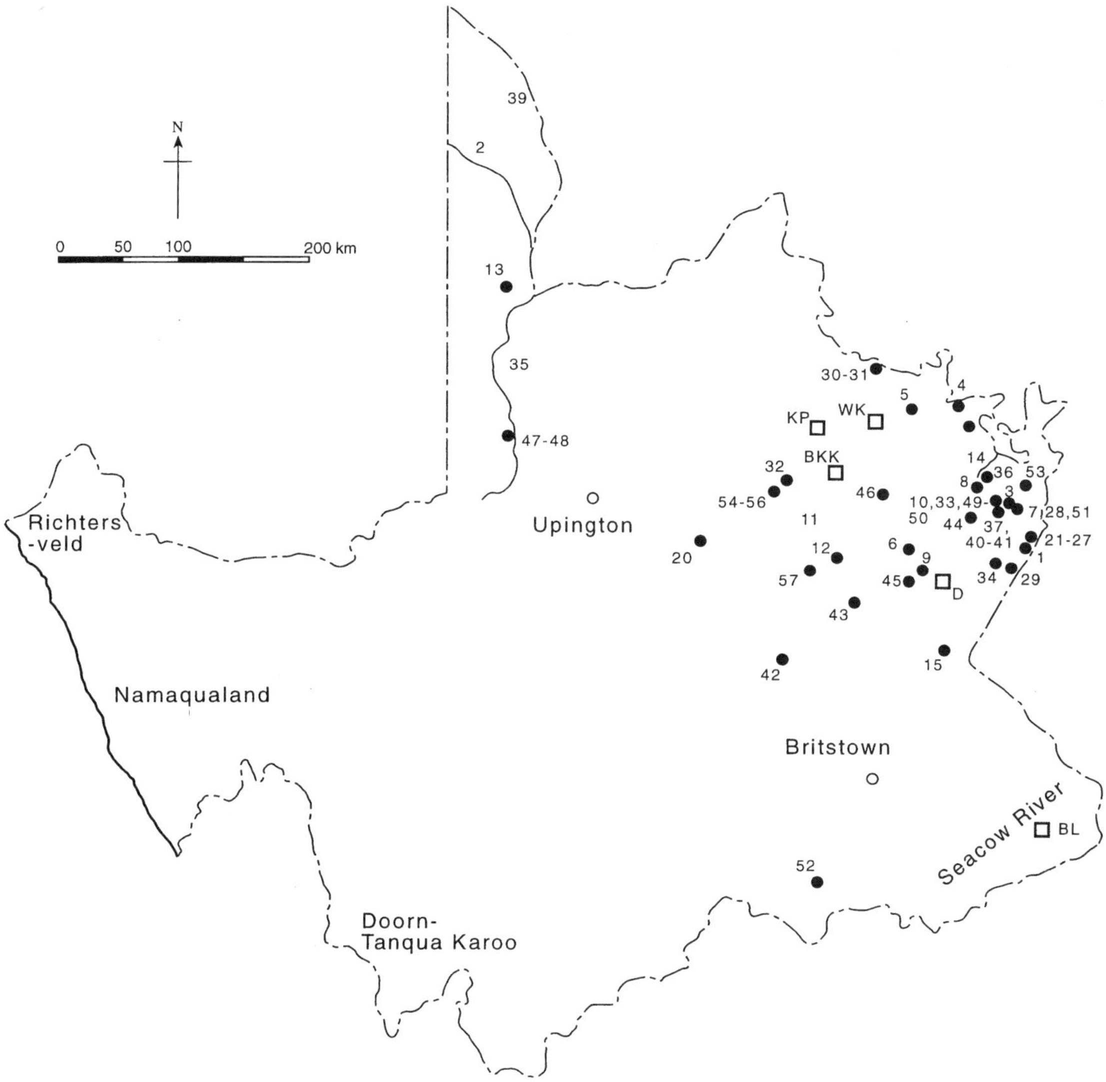

Site names

1 Alexandersfontein
2 Auob River
3 Barkly West - approximate location of provenances
4 Blesmanspoort
5 Blikfontein
6 Campbell
7 Canteen Kopje
8 Chue Pan
9 Douglas
10 Gong-Gong/Waldecks Plant
11 Griqualand West
12 Griquatown
13 Hakskeenpan
14 Harts River
15 Hopetown Bridge
16 Hosluit - location unknown (near Prieska)
17 Kalahari, No Further Provenance - location unknown
18 Kalahari Desert, No Further Provenance - location unknown
19 Karrieput - location unknown (west of Britstown)
20 Kheis
21 Kimberley
22 Kimberley (Belts)
23 Kimberley (Boskop Road)
24 Kimberley (Bultfontein Mine)
25 Kimberley (Du Toits Pan)
26 Kimberley (Golf Links)
27 Kimberley Sluits
28 Klip Drift
29 Koodoosberg Drift
30 Kuruman
31 Kuruman (Cotton End)
32 Langeberg
33 Last Hope
34 Modder River
35 Molopo River
36 Newlands
37 Nooitgedacht
38 Northern Cape 'Near Prieska and Upington'
39 Nossob River
40 Pniel
41 Pniel Mission Station
42 Prieska
43 Read's Drift
44 Rooipoort
45 Sivonel
46 Silver Streams
47 Swartmodder
48 Swartmodder ? (Kalahara)
49 Sydney
50 Sydney Estate
51 Vaal River
52 Victoria West
53 Windsorton
54 Witsands
55 Witsands Site I
56 Witsands Site II
57 Witwater

Site acronyms

BKK Blinkklipkop
BL Blydefontein
D Driekopseiland
KP Kathu Pan
WK Wonderwerk

Fig. 22. Location of archaeological sites in the Northern Cape Province and of Stone Age collections from there in the British Museum

also the collecting activities of two particular individuals, Andrew Anderson and James Swan (qqv; Appendix 4). As well as a range of Middle and Later Stone Age artefacts from sites around Alexandersfontein Pan, an important source of palaeoenvironmental data for the Quaternary of the region (Butzer 1984), the Museum collections include artefacts from several key sites along the terraces of the Vaal River. Represented here, for example, are Canteen Kopje and Pniel, both of which have long stratigraphic sequences emphasizing Early and Middle Stone Age occurrences. Kimberley, the centre for the diamond industry, is also well represented, not only in the Christy, ex Anderson, and Swan Collections, but also in those of Armstrong, Braunholtz, Fuller, ex Braunholtz, Routley, Sturge and Wilman. Artefacts collected by Andrew Anderson and now forming part of the Christy Collection attest to Middle and Later Stone Age occupation of some of the most arid parts of southern Africa (e.g. Auob River, Hakskeenpan, Nossob River, Swartmodder). The Jansen Collection is also of interest since it comprises many of the Victoria West prepared cores that F. J. Jansen first drew to archaeological attention from his collecting activities around Victoria West (Smith 1919; Jansen 1926).

ALEXANDERSFONTEIN 28° 50'S, 24° 45'E

Alexandersfontein Pan lies a few kilometres south of Kimberley and mostly within the Northern Cape Province, although its eastern end crosses into the Free State. The palaeoenvironmental potential of the pan has been extensively investigated, notably by Butzer (1984), who notes the presence of several rich archaeological occurrences around it. The palaeolacustrine deposits around the pan document several major changes in lake level, most impressively a high stand in the late Pleistocene that suggests rainfall may have been as much as 670-860 mm p.a. (compared to about 400 mm p.a. today) between 16 100 and 13 600 BP (Butzer 1984: 41).

Goodwin & Van Riet Lowe (1929: 140) note that Swan and Power collected extensively at Alexandersfontein for the McGregor Museum of Kimberley, finding both Later Stone Age ('Smithfield') material in a relatively unpatinated condition and much older, patinated Middle Stone Age artefacts which were used in the mid-20th century to designate a further 'variation' of the MSA (*cf.* Clark 1959: 163). A mixture of Middle and Later Stone Age artefacts, the latter including Oakhurst, Smithfield and Wilton material, is apparent in the British Museum holdings from this locality. Almost all the artefacts are in hornfels, though a few are made in opaline. In general terms, the degree of patination of the hornfels artefacts is proportional to their gross age, but patination is variably developed within artefacts of the same industrial tradition.

Armstrong Collection, 1959.7-12

Two of these three Later Stone Age scrapers are lightly patinated, with one being both side- and end-retouched; both are probably post-classic Wilton or Smithfield in affiliation. The third scraper is more heavily patinated, larger and may belong to the Oakhurst Complex.
3 scrapers (in hornfels).

Braunholtz Collection, (Ethno) 1930.1-24

A mixed collection of 93 Middle and Later Stone Age artefacts, almost entirely in hornfels. The reamer and lower grindstone fragment are definite Later Stone Age elements, while the flake-blades and retouched points are clearly of Middle Stone Age affiliation; other artefacts cannot be so readily attributed. The variation present in the degree to which the hornfels artefacts are patinated also suggests that not all are of the same age.

A card in one of the boxes of this collection states that seven of the artefacts are marked in ink and come from the Kimberley Museum. On inspection, only three such artefacts were found, one of them a large unpatinated hornfels scraper marked 'Modder M.R. R' and the two others lightly patinated large hornfels scrapers both marked 'Alexandersfontein'.

Table 41. The Braunholtz Collection from Alexandersfontein

	Opaline	Hornfels	Total
Irregular cores	-	4	4
Disc cores	-	3	3
Core-reduced pieces	1	-	1
Flakes	-	17	17
Flake-blades	-	14	14
Mesial sections (flake-blades)	2	-	2

Table 41 cont. The Braunholtz Collection from Alexandersfontein

	Opaline	Hornfels	Total
Utilised flakes	-	1	1
Reamers	-	1	1
Lower grindstone fragment	-	1	
Scrapers	1	35	36
Points	-	4	4
Retouched flakes	-	1	1
Retouched flake-blades	-	8	8
Total	4	89	93

Jones Collection, (Ethno) 1928.10-15.24, 37

Two virtually unpatinated Later Stone Age scrapers probably of Wilton Complex and/or Smithfield Industry origin.
2 scrapers (in hornfels).

Swan Collection, 1938.5-2.61-69

Nine scrapers, all in fresh condition, but probably of different ages. An opaline duckbill scraper and a hornfels frontal scraper (*sensu* Sampson 1972) both probably belong to the Oakhurst Complex. Two further scrapers in hornfels are also classically Oakhurst; one is D-shaped and the other also sidestruck. Of the remainder, a hornfels scraper and three opaline examples belong to the Wilton Complex and an opaline endscraper probably belongs within the Smithfield Industry.

In addition to these stone artefacts, 42 engraved fragments of ostrich eggshell are present. The engraved decoration takes the form of multiple horizontal grooves, sometimes combined with horizontally infilled diagonal bands. In some cases the area between the horizontal grooves themselves is also infilled with vertical grooves so as to produce a hatched pattern. These engraved fragments are almost certainly derived from one or more broken ostrich eggshell containers.
9 scrapers (5 in hornfels, 4 in opaline), 42 engraved fragments ostrich eggshell.

Wilman Collection, (Ethno) 1930.1-20.14-17

Four hornfels artefacts, of which one is a patinated blade - probably of Middle Stone Age origin - later reused as an adze along both its lateral edges. The remaining three artefacts are all more lightly patinated large hornfels scrapers, clearly of the Oakhurst Complex. By comparison with other material in the British Museum collections, the markings on the artefacts suggest that these four artefacts were originally part of the collections of the McGregor Museum, Kimberley, of which Wilman was the first Director.
3 scrapers (in hornfels), 1 adze (in hornfels).

Additional material Department of Ethnography, British Museum (Appendix 1).Cambridge University Museum, The Natural History Museum, Pitt Rivers Museum (Appendix 3).

AUOB (*OOP*) RIVER FROM 24° 00'S, 18° 10'E TO 26° 55'S, 20° 41'E

The Auob River rises in central Namibia and flows in a southeasterly direction and then through South Africa before joining with the Nossob River (qv) to form part of the border between the Northern Cape Province and Botswana. Since the remainder of the Christy +7893 artefacts can, where this is possible, be specifically provenanced to places within modern South Africa, this artefact is included in the Northern Cape part of the Gazetteer, although it is recognised that it may have been collected inside what is now Namibia.

Christy Collection, ex Anderson, +7893

A single Middle Stone Age artefact.
1 unmodified flake (in patinated hornfels, with a faceted platform, found in 1864).

BARKLY WEST APPROXIMATELY 28° 32'S, 23° 30'E

The magisterial district of Barkly West includes several of the original diamond digging areas along Vaal River, localities in which stone artefacts have been found since the late 19th century. All those parts of the British Museum collections provenanced to 'Barkly West' are thus likely to come from the terraces of the Vaal River - even where this is not specifically stated - rather than from elsewhere in the magisterial district.

Armstrong Collection, 1959.7-12

1 lightly patinated hornfels flake, probably Later Stone Age to judge from its minimal patination, but this is no more than a guess; the artefact itself is not diagnostic.

Christy Collection, ex Anderson, +7910

This artefact forms part of a much larger collection made by Andrew Anderson (1887b: 161) in and around Kimberley between 1870 and 1882.

1 patinated Middle Stone Age bilaterally retouched knife made in dolerite collected in 1874 from a diamond claim '30 ft below sur(face) in (an) old riverbed'.

Jones Collection, 1928.10-15.10-11

2 Early Stone Age cleavers (in dolerite).

Unknown Collection

1 Later Stone Age scraper (in opaline) found in the Vaal River gravels near Barkly West according to the accompanying card.

Additional material Department of Ethnography, British Museum (Appendix 1).Hunterian Museum, Pitt Rivers Museum (Appendix 3).

BLESMANSPOORT 27° 44'S, 24° 11'E

This artefact is said to come from Blesmanspoort near Reivilo, now in the North West Province. James Swan did a lot of collecting in the Boetsap area further south and the Hol river can be followed from there north to the town of Blesmanspos, due south of Reivilo and just within the boundary of the Northern Cape Province. The plateau nature of the terrain here means that there is little scope for finding a 'poort', i.e. a pass between mountains, making it likely that Blesmanspos is, in fact, the same place as what Swan termed Blesmanspoort (D. Morris, pers. comm.).

Swan Collection, 1938.5-2.60

1 scraper (in opaline) with adze-like lateral retouch, probably belonging to the Oakhurst, or possibly the Wilton Complex.

BLIKFONTEIN *(BLIKFONTEIN)* 27° 49'S, 23° 55'E

Swan Collection, 1938.5-2.17

1 bifacial Middle Stone Age point (in hornfels).

CAMPBELL 28° 48'S, 23° 43E

Christy Collection, ex Anderson, +7910

Andrew Anderson collected widely in the Northern Cape in the middle of the 19th century and this artefact was found on top of a limestone ridge near Campbell in 1873, site of a mission station built by the London Missionary Society at an originally Griqua settlement. Though not by itself culturally diagnostic, the condition of the artefact suggests that it is most likely to be of Middle Stone Age origin.

1 heavily rolled and patinated flake (in dolerite) with a plain platform.

CANTEEN KOPJE 28° 33'S, 24° 32'E

A prominent *kopje* (steeply rising hill) on the banks of the Vaal River just to the southeast of the town of Barkly West (qv), Canteen Kopje was the site of South Africa's first alluvial diamond diggings. Diamond exploitation continued here until the late 1920s and the site was proclaimed a National Monument in 1948 (Beaumont & Morris 1990: 14). It lies immediately opposite the mission station (and prehistoric site) of Pniel (qv). As described by Beaumont & Morris (1990), Canteen Kopje has been the scene of considerable archaeological and geological interest. Sporadic Later Stone Age artefacts occur on the surface of the uppermost stratum, with rare Middle Stone Age ones within this. The underlying stratum 2 consists of up to 11 m of mostly angular andesite clasts within which three Acheulean occurrences have been found, the top two containing Victoria West prepared cores, although they lack true blades (Beaumont & Morris 1990: 14-15). Reflecting the Abbé Breuil's comment that 'not only are there enough specimens to fill a museum to overflowing, but to build them of it also' (Clark 1959: 127), a small number of these artefacts occur in the British Museum collections.

Braunholtz Collection, (Ethno) 1930.1-24

This group of 48 dolerite Early and Middle Stone Age artefacts was found in the 60 feet river terrace at Canteen Kopje.

3 cleavers, 5 handaxes, 9 irregular cores, 15 Levallois cores, 1 Victoria West core, 13 unmodified flakes, 2 unmodified flake-blades.

L. J. Spencer Collection, ex Braunholtz, (Ethno) 1930.3-8.1

Braunholtz collected this Early Stone Age artefact on July 21st 1929 from the left gravel terrace in the diamond washings at Canteen Kopje.

1 handaxe (in dolerite).

Van Riet Lowe Collection, 1930.1-15.73-74
The original artefacts from which these two casts were made are stated in an accompanying label to be in the collections of the University of the Witwatersrand and to have come from 'an ancient alluvial terrace of the Vaal River at Canteen Kopje, Barkly West'.
2 plaster casts of Victoria West cores.

Additional material Cambridge University Museum, The Natural History Museum, Pitt Rivers Museum (Appendix 3).

CHUE PAN TO THE NORTH OF 28° 25'S, 24° 19'E

Although not precisely located, A.A. Anderson's (1888: 58) description of what he refers to as 'Great Chue Pan' makes it clear that it lay within a two day journey north of the Vaal River in the general vicinity of the modern town of Delportshoop, the co-ordinates of which are those given here.

Christy Collection, ex Anderson, +7914
A single Middle Stone Age artefact found on the open flats above Chue Pan in 1869.
1 unmodified flake-blade (in hornfels).

DOUGLAS 29° 03'S, 23° 46'E

Originally founded as a mission in 1848, Douglas developed into a small town after 1867 when a group led by Francis Orpen obtained the agreement to this of the Griqua chief Nicholas Waterboer. Immediately to the east of the town is the major rock engraving site of Driekopseiland (Wilman 1933).

Wilman Collection, ex Orpen, (Ethno) 1930.1-20.13
A single Middle Stone Age unmodified artefact.
1 unmodified flake (in hornfels).

Additional material Pitt Rivers Museum (Appendix 3).

GONG-GONG/WALDECKS PLANT *(GONGGONG/WALDECK'S POINT)* APPROXIMATELY 28° 29'S, 24° 25'E

Fuller Collection, ex Braunholtz, (Ethno) 1930.2-5.2
These two localities, both in the general area of Barkly West (qv), are no more than 2.5 km apart, hence presumably their combination in designating the provenance of this Early Stone Age artefact which derives from 'deep diggings' in the Vaal River's gravels.
1 handaxe (in dolerite).

Additional material Pitt Rivers Museum (Appendix 3).

GRIQUALAND WEST APPROXIMATELY CENTRED ON 28° 30'S, 23° 20'E

Christy Collection, ex Colonel H. G. White, +6819
This is a group of 23 artefacts, in a diverse range of raw materials, stated to come (from more than one locality perhaps ?) from 'Bechuanaland and Griqualand West, principally north of the Vaal River and Harts River.' The two retouched points are clearly Middle Stone Age pieces; one of them, as well as the opaline flake-blade and three of the hornfels flakes have faceted platforms. The truncated flake recalls similar artefacts with abrupt, straight or (as in this case) oblique distal truncation found in the ± 20 000 BP layer at Sehonghong rock- shelter in the Lesotho highlands (Mitchell 1994b), but is of a type otherwise known almost entirely from MSA contexts in southern Africa (*cf.* Volman 1984)

Table 42. The Christy Collection, ex Colonel H. G. White, from Griqualand West.

	Opaline	Chert	Hornfels	Quartz	Quartzite	Banded ironstone	Total
Irregular cores	1	-	-	-	-	-	1
Pièces esquillées	1	-	-	-	-	-	1
Flakes	3	-	8	1	-	1	13
Flake-blades	1	-	-	-	-	-	1
Utilised flakes	-	-	1	-	-	-	1
Utilised flake-blades	-	-	1	-	-	-	1
Scrapers	-	1	-	-	-	-	1
Points	-	-	2	-	-	-	2
Truncated flakes	-	1	-	-	-	-	1
Retouched flakes	-	-	-	-	1	-	1
Total	6	2	12	1	1	1	23

F. White Collection, 1922.6-6.24

This is a single Early Stone Age artefact in a slightly rolled condition.
1 handaxe (in patinated dolerite).

Additional material Cambridge University Museum, Pitt Rivers Museum (Appendix 3).

GRIQUATOWN 28° 50'S, 23° 15'E

Christy Collection, ex Anderson, +909

A single Middle Stone Age artefact found 'in valley at Griquatown 1872'.
1 mesial section of an unmodified flake-blade (in hornfels).

F. White Collection, ex Dunn, 1922.6-6.25

E. J. Dunn, with whose name this remarkably fresh-looking artefact is marked, collected widely in the late 19th century in the Northern Cape and elsewhere in the South African interior. This is the only southern African Stone Age artefact from his collections in the British Museum; the bulk of them were left to the Pitt Rivers Museum, Oxford (Appendix 3).
1 Early Stone Age cleaver (in banded ironstone).

Additional material Pitt Rivers Museum (Appendix 3).

HAKSKEENPAN *(HOGSKIN VLEI)* CENTRED ON 26° 50'S, 20° 12'E

Christy Collection, ex Anderson, +7893

A single artefact, culturally undiagnostic, previously curated with the remainder of Christy +7893 under 'Kalahari Desert' (qv).
1 unmodified flake (in lightly patinated hornfels, found in 1865).

HARTS RIVER APPROXIMATELY 27° 45'S, 24° 45'E

Christy Collection, ex Anderson, +7910

These three artefacts were collected over a period of ten years and are all of Middle Stone Age origin. They are:

1 bilaterally retouched, broken hornfels knife, of which the tip and butt of the flake-blade are broken off found 'on surface by salt pan Harts River 1864.' This artefact is rolled and patinated;
1 retouched and now patinated dolerite point with a faceted platform found 'on bank of salt pan Harts River 1868'; and
1 unmodified and almost completely unpatinated hornfels flake with a faceted platform 'found on bed of Harts River, Griqualand West, 1874'.

HOPETOWN BRIDGE 29° 36'S, 24° 06'E

Hopetown was where the first alluvial diamond in South Africa was discovered in 1866, an event which, after confirmation of its identity by Dr W. A. Atherstone (Appendix 4), sparked the Kimberley diamond rush and was thus indirectly responsible for the acquisition of much of the British Museum stone artefact collections from the Northern Cape Province. However, the material held by the Museum from Hopetown Bridge itself results from the much later collecting activities of James Swan (Appendix 4).

Swan Collection, 1938.5-2.28-48

This is a group of 34 Later Stone Age artefacts. A banded ironstone scraper with adze-like lateral retouch may be of early Holocene age, but the other scrapers all clearly belong to the Wilton Industry. All the artefacts are in opaline unless otherwise stated.
1 irregular core, 1 bladelet core, 3 core-rejuvenation flakes, 4 unmodified flakes, 5 unmodified bladelets, 1 proximal section of an unmodified bladelet, 18 scrapers (1 in banded ironstone, 1 in chert), 1 segment (in chert).

In addition to these flaked stone artefacts, this collection includes several pieces of jewellery:
1 sub-spherical stone bead, 8 worked fragments of ostrich eggshell, 1 unfinished, though pierced, ostrich eggshell bead blank.

HOSLUIT APPROXIMATELY 29° 40'S, 22° 38'E

Seton-Karr Collection, ex Du Toit, unnumbered

Originally collected by the geologist A. L. Du Toit in 1908, this artefact is probably of Middle Stone Age origin to judge from its large size and thick red-brown patina. Hosluit has not been located further, other than that is recorded as being 'near Prieska'.
1 scraper (in dolerite).

KALAHARI - NO FURTHER PROVENANCE

The Kalahari Desert extends across parts of Namibia, Botswana and South Africa, but, in the absence of further information, it seems more economical to assume that this Early Stone Age artefact was collected closer to the area under British control during Sir Bartle Frere's Governorship of the Cape Colony (1877-80). This would argue for an origin in the Northern Cape Province or North West Province of South Africa.

Frere Collection, (Ethno) 1928.11-6.6
1 handaxe (in quartzite).

KALAHARI *(KALAHARA)* DESERT, NO FURTHER PROVENCE

Christy Collection, ex Anderson, +7893
A collection of 17 artefacts, each individually labelled with some further information as to the year and locality in which it was found. In most cases the locality is designated only as 'Kalahara', which is insufficient to determine whether the artefacts were found in what is now Botswana or in what is now South Africa. However, where more specific information is given it is always a locality within present-day South Africa's Northern Cape Province that is meant. It therefore seems likely that this entire collection comes from this area. The variability in the dates at which these artefacts were found attests to the long time over which A.A. Anderson (1887a) pursued his archaeological interests, as well as the intensity with which he did so. The more specifically provenanced artefacts are separately catalogued under Auob River, Hakskeenpan, Nossob River and Witsands (qqv).
Three artefacts are marked with the localities from which they were collected, but these placenames have not been identified:

1 unmodified flake in patinated hornfels found in an old river bed at Kala (not identified) in 1864. As with a fragment of a Later Stone Age dolerite bored stone labelled 'from top of Mt. Kala', it seems likely that 'Kala' here is no more than an abbreviation of the word 'Kalahari';
1 unmodified hornfels flake found on the surface in the Inassem (?) Hills in 1866.

The remaining 14 artefacts come from completely unspecified places within the 'Kalahara'. At least nine, and probably several more, are of Middle Stone Age origin. With their dates of collection they are:

2 Middle Stone Age unmodified flakes (in dolerite, both with faceted platforms and found in 1871);
2 unmodified flakes (in patinated hornfels, picked up 'on a limestone ridge 1873');
2 unmodified Middle Stone Age flake-blades (in patinated hornfels, one with its tip broken off, both found in 1866);
1 Middle Stone Age unmodified flake-blade (in patinated dolerite, found in 1872);
1 Middle Stone Age utilised flake-blade (in hornfels, found in 1872);
1 scraper (in hornfels, made on a faceted flake, found in 1866);
1 probably Later Stone Age scraper (in lightly patinated hornfels, found in 1870);
1 scraper (in patinated dolerite, no date given);
1 bilaterally retouched Middle Stone Age knife (in opaline, found in 1865);
1 Middle Stone Age point (in patinated dolerite and in rolled condition, found in 1869);
1 Middle Stone Age bifacial point (in quartzite, found in 1872).

KARRIEPUT 30° 29'S, 23° 04'E

Passmore Edwards Museum Collection, ex Fox, ex Du Toit, P1995.4-1.227
Found, according to the markings on it, by the geologist A. L. Du Toit in 1908 on the farm of this name (now Kareeput) to the west of Britstown, this lightly patinated artefact is clearly of Later Stone Age origin and may belong to the Oakhurst Complex, though a more recent age and affiliation cannot be excluded.
1 scraper (in hornfels).

KHEIS 28° 50'S, 22° 04'E

Christy Collection, ex Anderson, +7911
The first of these two flakes was found 'in bed of Orange River at Kheis' and is of Middle Stone Age origin with a faceted platform and a grey patina. The other, found 'in bed of Orange River below Kheis' has a plain platform and a red-brown patina; it is also less heavily rolled and, by itself, adiagnostic. Both artefacts were found in 1872.
2 unmodified flakes (in hornfels).

Additional material Pitt Rivers Museum (Appendix 3).

KIMBERLEY 28° 44'S, 24° 45'E

While the first diamond rush in the Northern Cape centred on Hopetown (in 1867) and the second (in 1870) on the Vaal River gravels at Barkly West, the third, and most extensive, was prompted by their discovery at Du Toits Pan in 1871 (Reader's Digest 1994b). Located approximately half-way between the Modder and the Vaal Rivers, Kimberley grew from the digger's camp that resulted from this discovery, rapidly becoming the largest settlement in the Northern Cape. The diamonds discovered here not only provided the basis for the fortunes of several industrial magnates of the late 19th century - notably Cecil Rhodes - but also helped fix the attention of South African antiquarians and archaeologists on the possibilities offered by both the diamond diggings and the alluvial terraces of the Vaal for finding Stone Age artefacts. Stow (1905: 24), for example, discovered 'finely formed chipped implements made of lydite' (i.e. of hornfels) on the edge of the Roodepan pan north of Kimberley in 1874 and records the presence of ostrich eggshell beads at depths of up to 2 m in diamond-diggings at Du Toits Pan (Stow 1905: 23).

Armstrong Collection, 1959.7-12

With the exception of single examples of Middle Stone Age points and unilaterally retouched knives (both made in hornfels), this collection of 19 artefacts seems to be entirely of Later Stone Age affiliation, the size and morphology of the scrapers suggesting that an attribution to the Oakhurst Complex is likely. The LSA part of the collection comprises 17 artefacts, all in hornfels except where otherwise stated.

2 irregular cores (including 1 in opaline), 1 crested blade, 5 unmodified flakes (including 1 in opaline), 1 utilised flake (in opaline), 6 scrapers (including 1 in opaline and 1 in quartzite), 2 adzes.

Braunholtz Collection, (Ethno) 1930.1-24

Three hornfels artefacts representative of the three main stages of the southern African Stone Age. The handaxe is of Early Stone Age origin, the point of Middle Stone Age origin and the scraper most probably of Later Stone Age affiliation.

1 handaxe (patinated), 1 point, 1 scraper (lightly patinated scraper).

Christy Collection, ex Anderson, +7871

This group of 15 artefacts comes from 'blue ground 250 ft below surface diamond fields' and was at least partly collected in Feburary 1883.

10 unmodified flakes (9 in hornfels, 1 in opaline), 1 scraper (in hornfels), 3 Middle Stone Age points (1 each in hornfels, opaline and chert), 1 bilaterally retouched Middle Stone Age knife with a faceted platform (in dolerite).

Christy Collection, ex Anderson, +7872

Christy +7872 refers to material from several different provenances, with only a few artefacts coming from Kimberley itself. Others are catalogued here under Kimberley (Du Toits Pan), Klip Drift and Vaal River (qqv).

Six artefacts specified as coming from Kimberly (*sic*) derive from depths of between 50 and 170 ft and at least in part from well-digging. A.A. Anderson (1887b: 164-165) notes the importance of well-digging as a source for finding stone artefacts

1 rolled hornfels Middle Stone Age point, found in 1872;

1 dolerite flake with faceted platform of Middle Stone Age origin, collected in 1881;

1 very rolled hornfels Middle Stone Age point, found on October 11th 1882;

1 lightly patinated and fresh hornfels adze made on a Middle Stone Age flake-blade, collected in 1882;

1 rolled unmodified hornfels flake-blade marked '27 ft we dig a well';

1 faceted butt of a further unmodified Middle Stone Age hornfels flake-blade.

Fuller Collection, ex Braunholtz, (Ethno) 1930.2-5.9 and 12

Two Early Stone Age artefacts provenanced only to 'K' in the British Museum accession register, but most likely from Kimberley, or close to it.

1 cleaver, 1 handaxe (both in dolerite).

Sturge Collection

This single Early Stone Age artefact is marked in red with the letter 'K', presumably for 'Kimberley'.

1 handaxe (in hornfels).

Swan Collection, 1922.11-6.1-5

A small group of five artefacts, of which the handaxe belongs to the Early Stone Age and three, perhaps all four of the remainder, to the Later Stone Age.

1 handaxe (in dolerite), 1 core-rejuvenation flake (in opaline), 3 scrapers (in opaline).

Swan Collection, 1930.6-11.1-24

With the exception of two Middle Stone Age points, both in patinated hornfels, this group of 45 artefacts seems to be entirely Later Stone Age in origin. The LSA artefacts, some of which are marked with the letters 'E' or 'MR' (presumably Modder River), total 43 and are all in opaline except where otherwise indicated.

1 unmodified bladelet, 1 proximal section of an unmodified bladelet, 1 milled-edge pebble, 37 scrapers (19 in opaline, 18 in hornfels), 1 segment, 2 backed flakes.

The hornfels scrapers show a varying degree of patination which may indicate that not all are of the same age. It is otherwise difficult to be sure which subdivision of the Later Stone Age is present: the majority of the opaline scrapers are of the small, thumbnail type characteristic of the Wilton Industry, but one has adze-like lateral retouch, a form more commonly found in the early or middle Holocene.

Swan Collection, 1930.10-14.6-7, 10-19

A mixed group of five stone artefacts and 13 worked pieces of ostrich eggshell. The handaxe is of Early Stone Age origin, the scrapers and ostrich eggshell from a Later Stone Age context. One of the scrapers, which, from its size and D-shape probably comes from an Oakhurst-like assemblage of terminal Pleistocene/early Holocene age, is marked 'A'.
1 small handaxe (in an unidentified metamorphic rock), 4 scrapers (2 in patinated hornfels, 1 unpatinated and in fresh condition).
7 blanks for ostrich eggshell bead production, 4 unfinished ostrich eggshell beads, 2 polished circular ostrich eggshell discs.

Swan Collection, 1931.7-7.1-9

This is a group of 25 artefacts and one unworked piece of stone representing the Early, Middle and Later Stone Ages of southern African prehistory.
Early Stone Age component: 4 handaxes (in patinated hornfels).
Middle Stone Age component: 2 unmodified flakes (in patinated hornfels, both with faceted platforms), 1 unifacially retouched point (in chert).
Later Stone Age component, the segments of which suggest an affiliation to the Wilton Industry. All are in opaline:
1 unmodified bladelet, 1 proximal section from an unmodified bladelet, 8 segments, 5 backed bladelets, 2 backed flakes, 1 backed fragment.

Swan Collection, 1938.5-2 remaining artefacts

This collection of 302 artefacts clearly belongs to a recent (i.e. classic Wilton or post-classic Wilton) expression of the Later Stone Age to judge from the predominance of small, thumbnail scrapers and backed microliths among it. The higher numbers of backed bladelets than segments may, if not due to collecting bias, suggest that a post-classic Wilton affiliation is most likely as segments are generally most common in mid-Holocene, classic Wilton Industry contexts. This would also fit with the overall morphology of the scrapers, almost all of which (save eight with adze-like lateral retouch) are of thumbnail type.

Table 43. The Swan Collection 1938 5-2 from Kimberley.

	Opaline	Chert	Hornfels	Quartz	Tuff	Total
Crested blades	3	-	-	-	-	3
Flakes	28	1	-	3	-	32
Blades	3	-	-	-	-	3
Bladelets	48	-	-	2	-	50
Proximal sections (bladelets)	48	1	-	6	-	55
Mesial sections (bladelets)	-	-	1	-	-	1
Distal sections (bladelets)	3	-	-	-	-	3
Utilised bladelets	2	-	-	-	-	2
Scrapers	103	1	3	-	1	108
Borers	-	-	-	1	-	1
Segments	9	1	-	1	-	11
Backed bladelets	17	-	-	-	-	17
Backed points	2	-	-	-	-	2
Backed flakes	3	-	-	-	-	3
Broken backed pieces	9	-	-	-	-	9
Retouched bladelets	1	-	-	-	-	1
Awls	-	1	-	-	-	1
Total	279	5	4	13	1	302

Wilman Collection, (Ethno) 1930.1-20.1

As Director of the Kimberley-based McGregor Museum Maria Wilman carried out extensive archaeological fieldwork in the Northern Cape Province, particularly in the study of rock-engravings (Wilman 1933; J. Deacon 1987). However, her contribution to the British Museum collections from Kimberley itself is limited to a single Early Stone Age artefact.
1 handaxe (in patinated hornfels).

Additional material Department of Ethnography, British Museum (Appendix One).Cambridge University Museum (Kimberley; Kimberley; Alexanders Pan; Kimberley, Diamond Fields; Kimberley (Halfway House), Liverpool Museum, Pitt Rivers Museum (Appendix 3).

KIMBERLEY (BELTS) APPROXIMATELY 28° 44'S, 24° 45'E

Swan Collection, 1930.6-11.1

A single Middle Stone Age artefact with a faceted platform. The term 'Belts' is unexplained.
1 scraper (in patinated hornfels scraper, marked 'Kim Belts').

KIMBERLEY (BOSKOP ROAD) APPROXIMATELY 28° 44'S, 24° 45'E

Swan Collection, 1938.5-2.6

A single Early Stone Age artefact found 10 feet (3 m) down in a quarry hole.
1 handaxe (in dolerite, now completely covered with an orange patina).

KIMBERLEY (BULTFONTEIN MINE) 28° 46'S, 24° 47'E

Swan Collection, 1930.10-14.9

This single, patinated Early Stone Age artefact is marked 'K Bult Ftns', indicating that it comes from the Bultfontein mine, one of two major diamond mines on the south side of Kimberley.
1 handaxe (in hornfels, broken).

KIMBERLEY (DU TOITS PAN) 28° 46'S, 24° 48'E

Christy Collection, ex Anderson, +7872

A.A. Anderson (1887b: 165-166) records that in sorting diamantiferous blue ground for diamonds at this, one of two major diamond mines on the south side of Kimberley city centre, in 'the early part of 1883' he and his co-diggers 'found many of these arrowheads'. Of the more than 15 artefacts he mentions as having found, three Middle Stone Age artefacts are in the British Museum collections:
1 bilaterally retouched knife (in hornfels, found 140 ft (43 m) below the surface on September 15th 1882);
1 utilised flake (in hornfels, with a faceted platform found in 1882 at a depth of 290 ft (89 m) in 'blue ground');
1 unmodified flake-blade (in dolerite, found in 1882 at a depth of 290 ft (89 m) in 'blue ground').

Additional material Department of Ethnography, British Museum (Appendix 1).Pitt Rivers Museum (Appendix 3).

KIMBERLEY (GOLF LINKS) APPROXIMATELY 28° 44'S, 24° 45'E

Routley Collection, per Swan, 1938.5-1.1

A single Middle Stone Age hornfels artefact with a faceted platform, covered all over with an orange-brown patina.
1 point (in hornfels).

Swan Collection, 1930.10-14.8

A single Middle Stone Age artefact.
1 point (in patinated hornfels, marked 'Kim Golf Links').

Swan Collection, 1938.5-2.7

A single Early Stone Age artefact. The accompanying label warns potential golfers that such artefacts are 'liable to occur in bunkers in red soil, but near bottom of soil layer overlying dolerite'!
1 handaxe (in dolerite, completely covered with an orange-brown patina).

Additional material Pitt Rivers Museum (Appendix 3).

KIMBERLEY SLUITS APPROXIMATELY 28° 42'S, 24° 59'E

The term 'sluits' refers to diamond diggings in general and no more specific provenance to a particular locality within Kimberley is possible. Six Early Stone Age artefacts in the Swan Collection come from here.

Swan Collection, 1930.10-14.4

1 handaxe (in patinated hornfels, marked 'Kim Sluits').

Swan Collection, 1938.5-2.1-5

A group of five Early Stone Age hornfels artefacts in a rolled condition.
5 handaxes (in hornfels).

Additional material Pitt Rivers Museum (Appendix 3).

KLIP DRIFT 28° 32'S, 23° 30'E

The 'Klip Drift' referred to on these artefacts is the ford across the Vaal River at which the town of Barkly West (qv) developed (A.A. Anderson 1887b: 161).

Christy Collection, ex Anderson, +7869

A single brown-coloured, undecorated body sherd lacking in any visible grass or grit temper. Undiagnostic, but dating to within the last 2000 years, it is not clear if this sherd come from the same site as Christy +7868, which is more loosely provenanced to the Vaal River (qv).
1 undecorated sherd (found 'on gravel Diamond claim 20 ft (i.e. 6 m) below s(urface) 1872 Klip Drift').

Christy Collection, ex Anderson, +7872

Two Middle Stone Age hornfels artefacts, both with more precise details of their provenance marked in ink on them. A.A. Anderson (1887b: 161-164) provides a graphic description of the circumstances in which he recovered these and other artefacts from the gravels of the Vaal River.
1 bilaterally retouched knife (found 45 ft deep in the old river bed on a diamond claim in 1870);
1 point ('f(oun)d in my claim 20 ft below surface (in) 1873').

KOODOOSBERG DRIFT 28° 57'S, 24° 24'E

Swan Collection, 1938.5-2.24-25

This group comprises two ostrich eggshell bead necklaces. One has 434 beads and the other 1186 beads. The beads were not measured, but have an estimated average diameter of between 3 and 4 mm. Though undated, they are clearly of Later Stone Age origin and are probably recent in origin.
2 necklaces of ostrich eggshell beads.

KURUMAN 27° 08'S, 23° 20'E

Kuruman was founded as a mission station of the London Missionary Society in 1824 and became the principal mission among the Tswana-speaking people of the Northern Cape and North West Provinces, as well as a major centre for missionary activity and exploration further north (Beaumont & Morris 1990: 143-147). It is therefore not surprising that Anderson should have frequently visited it on his travels.

Christy Collection, ex Anderson, +7899

A group of four Middle Stone Age artefacts collected in 1869-1870 at or near Kuruman:

- 1 large patinated hornfels flake-blade, lightly trimmed towards its tip, found on 'limestone flats near Kuruman 1869';
- 1 thickly patinated hornfels flake-blade found 'at the post of Kuruman 1869';
- 1 patinated dolerite flake-blade 'found at Hangvlei above Kuruman 1870';
- 1 thickly patinated hornfels MSA point with faceted platform found 'on the veldt [*sic*] near Kuruman 1870'.

KURUMAN (COTTON END) 27° 08'S, 23° 20'E

Swan Collection, 1938.5-2.14-16

Three artefacts, of which the opaline scraper most probably belongs to an early to middle Holocene expression (Oakhurst Complex or Wilton Industry) of the Later Stone Age.
1 unmodified bladelet (in opaline), 1 scraper (in opaline, with adze-like lateral retouch along both sides), 1 broken scraper (in quartz crystal).

LANGEBERG CENTRED ON 28° 30'S, 22° 35'E

The Langeberg Mountains run almost due north-south for a distance of over 150 km north of the Gariep River and west of the town of Postmasburg. As reported by Stow in 1873 Bushman people were still living here in the second half of the 19th century (Beaumont & Morris 1990: 62) when Andrew Anderson collected stone artefacts over a period of at least 11 years. Witsand (qv) lies at the southern end of the Langeberge.

Christy Collection, ex Anderson, +7914

Six artefacts (all of which are patinated and more- or-less heavily rolled). The last three are clearly of Middle Stone Age origin, although the first three are not by themselves culturally diagnostic. A bored stone found 'on the summit of one of the lofty ranges of Langberg Mountain' in April 1864 (A.A. Anderson 1887b: 159-160) is, however, not among them.

- 1 unmodified hornfels flake found 'on top of Langeberg above Cowries 1869';
- 1 utilised hornfels flake found 'on top of Langeberg';
- 1 utilised hornfels flake found 'on top of Langeberg above veldt sand 1873';
- 1 utilised hornfels flake-blade found 'on top of Langeberg mts 6400 ft (i.e. 1969 m) above sea Nov 1869';
- 1 bilaterally retouched dolerite point made on a flake-blade found 'in a kloof Langeberg with other loose stones 1876';
- 1 unmodified dolerite flake-blade found 'in kloof Langeberg 1865'.

LAST HOPE 28° 30'S, 24° 28'E

Fuller Collection, ex Braunholtz (Ethno) 1930.2-5.3-4

Two Early Stone Age artefacts from deep diggings in the Vaal River gravels at this locality just west of Barkly West (qv). 2 unifacially worked handaxe-like implements (in chert).

MODDER RIVER 29° 01'S, 24° 38'E

The Modder River rises in the central Free State and flows into the Vaal River south-southwest of Kimberley close to the small town of the same name. Although the term 'Modder River' is therefore not a geographically precise one, this artefact was originally curated with the remainder of the 1930 10-14 part of the Swan Collection, which is provenanced to Kimberley. For this reason the co-ordinates given here are those of the town of Modderrivier and it is included in the Northern Cape part of the Gazetteer.

Swan Collection, 1930.10-14.5

1 point (in dolerite, marked Modder River).

Additional material Pitt Rivers Museum (Kimberley, Modder River, Appendix 3).

MOLOPO (*MOLAPO*) RIVER FROM 25° 37'S, 25° 45'E TO 26° 53'S, 20° 42'E

Rising north of Mafikeng, the Molopo River forms the boundary between South Africa's Northern Cape Province and the Republic of Botswana before joining the Nossob River and draining (though now often intermittently because of drought) into the Gariep River. Stone Age artefacts were collected here by Andrew Anderson over a period of 13 years in the third quarter of the 19th century. Because several of the artefacts collected by Anderson and provenanced to 'Kalahari Desert' and 'Swartmodder' (qqv) come from the Gordonia area of the Northern Cape Province, which lies due south of the Molopo River, it seems likely that these six artefacts also come from within the Northern Cape.

Christy Collection, ex Anderson, +7896

Six artefacts, all more-or-less rolled and all probably Middle Stone Age in origin. Detailed descriptions and provenances based on information written on to the artefacts are as follows:

1 dolerite flake with faceted platform found 'on surface Molapo 1864';
1 truncated flake in hornfels found 'on gravel in Molapo River 1867';
1 utilised hornfels flake 'found in old river bed on Molapo 1867';
1 hornfels flake-blade found 'on bank of Molapo River, Bechuanaland 1869';
1 broken hornfels bilaterally retouched knife found 'on open plain south of Molapo River 1869';
1 opaline flake 'thrown out of wolf (*cf.* hyena or aardwolf) hole in veldt on Molapo River 1877'.

NEWLANDS 28° 19'S, 24° 23'E

Although Newlands is a not uncommon place-name in South Africa, with examples occurring in the suburbs of both Cape Town and Durban, the fact that this Middle Stone Age artefact forms part of the collection obtained from Maria Wilman, first Director of the McGregor Museum, Kimberley, suggests that it has an origin in the Northern Cape. Newlands is, in fact, the name of a small settlement on the lower reaches of the Harts River to the north west of Barkly West (qv).

Wilman Collection, (Ethno) 1930.1-20.10

1 opaline point, retouched along both lateral margins and with a faceted platform.

Additional material Pitt Rivers Museum (Appendix 3).

NOOITGEDACHT 28° 37'S, 24° 27'E

Nooitgedacht lies some 20 km north west of Kimberley (qv) and 16 km from Canteen Kopje (qv) in an area where older deposits that include stone artefacts are discontinuously covered by up to 3 m of sand. The assemblage reported from the site by Beaumont & Morris (1990: 4) is said to include 'refined prepared cores, coarse blades, convergent points and rare (mainly) small handaxes' made almost exclusively in chert and quartzite, indicating that the Fauresmith is not simply a variant of the Acheulean that resulted from the use of hornfels.

Braunholtz Collection, (Ethno) 1930.1-24

A group of six artefacts, all of them in quartzite except for a single flake, belonging to the Fauresmith Industry.
1 cleaver, 1 handaxe, 1 irregular core, 1 unmodified flake (in sandstone), 1 proximal section of an unmodified flake-blade with a faceted platform, 1 scraper

Swan Collection, 1938.5-2.13

A single large naturally backed sidescraper made in dolerite reminiscent of the naturally backed knives most commonly

found in Later Stone Age assemblages of terminal Pleistocene/early Holocene age (Parkington 1984).
1 scraper (*cf.* naturally backed knife - in dolerite).

Additional material The Natural History Museum, Pitt Rivers Museum (Appendix 3).

NORTHERN CAPE 'NEAR PRIESKA AND UPINGTON' APPROXIMATELY 29° 30'S, 21° 30'E

Newberry Collection, (Ethno) 1913.196-204

A group of nine chert artefacts of which at least the formal component is of Middle Stone Age origin.
4 unmodified flakes, 2 notched flakes, 2 bilaterally retouched knives (one with a faceted platform), 1 retouched point.

NOSSOB *(NOSOP)* RIVER FROM 21 57'S, 17 36'E TO 26 55'S, 20 41'E

The Nossob River rises in central Namibia and flows in a southeasterly direction before leaving Namibia to form the border between Botswana and South Africa. Having merged with the Auob River (qv) it then flows into the Molopo River (qv). Since some of the remaining Christy +7893 artefacts can be specifically provenanced to places within modern South Africa, this artefact is included in the Northern Cape part of the Gazetteer, although it is recognised that it may have been collected inside what is now Namibia; François Balsan's Panhard-Capricorn expedition located 24 archaeological sites in the river terraces of the Botswanan part of the river (Tobias 1967). A.A. Anderson (1887b: 158) refers to the discovery along the Nossob of 'many perfect and beautifully worked spear-heads of yellow flint' in 1859, apparently the first time that his 'attention was called to this subject'. It is possible that the specimen held by the British Museum was among the artefacts he found at this time, making him one of the earliest collectors of prehistoric stone artefacts anywhere in the sub-continent (D. Morris 1997).

Christy Collection, ex Anderson, +7893

A single culturally undiagnostic artefact found on the banks of the Nossob River.
1 unmodified flake (in sandstone).

PNIEL 28° 37'S, 24°35'E

The farm Pniel lies 22 km north west of Kimberley on the banks of the Vaal River and was the scene of extensive diamond digging activity in the late 19th and early 20th centuries. The main site (Pniel 6) abuts a low andesite hill immediately downslope of the mission station founded here in 1845 by the Berlin Missionary Society. Stone artefacts were recognised here by Stow (1905: 23) and A.A. Anderson (1887b: 161) in the 1870s and the archaeological deposits were later described by Van Hoepen (1926, 1927), Burkitt (1928) and Goodwin & Van Riet Lowe (1929), though they have since largely been destroyed by diamond digging operations. Peter Beaumont has undertaken more recent work in the hope of dating the sequence of lithic assemblages present (Beaumont & Morris 1990: 7-13). An early Middle Stone Age assemblage is present in the colluvial stratum 3 and is characterised by narrow blades and rare retouched points and scrapers; this assemblage probably dates to oxygen isotope stage 6 (127-190, 000 BP; Beaumont & Morris 1990: 11). The much more ancient stratum 4 contains Acheulean artefacts comparable to material from the nearby Pniel 1 site which is dated on faunal grounds to about 0.5 million years ago (Beaumont & Morris 1990: 11). Faunal material is present in both strata, though not yet recovered from *in situ* contexts.

Braunholtz Collection, (Ethno) 1930.1-24

A group of 39 artefacts, all in either dolerite or hornfels, showing a mixture of 'classic' Early and Middle Stone Age characteristics that reflects the presence of both traditions at the Pniel sites. One unworked piece of stone is also present. All the artefacts are patinated and more-or-less heavily rolled.

Table 44. The Braunholtz Collection from Pniel.

	Hornfels	Dolerite	Total
Cleavers	-	2	2
Handaxes	-	13	13
Irregular cores	1	1	2
Flakes	-	10	10
Flake-blades	7	-	7
Utilised flakes	1	-	1
Hammerstones	-	1	1
Scrapers	-	1	1
Knives - unilateral	1	-	1
Points	1	-	1
Total	11	28	39

Van Alphen Collection, (Ethno) 1929.3-6.1-2
Two Early Stone Age handaxes, both in hornfels and covered by a greyish-white patina.

Wilman Collection, (Ethno) 1930.1-20.2-9, 11
A group of nine artefacts, all in hornfels. A very rolled and patinated hornfels handaxe is marked 'Pniel below M.S.' (= Mission Station), but the others, all of which are rolled, are unmarked and patinated.
1 handaxe, 1 unmodified flake, 5 unmodified flake-blades (4 of which have faceted platforms), 1 point.

Additional material Department of Ethnography, British Museum (Appendix 1). Cambridge University Museum, Institute of Archaeology, Pitt Rivers Museum (Appendix 3).

PNIEL (MISSION STATION) 28° 37'S, 24° 35'E

Swan Collection, 1930.10-14.1-3
Two patinated hornfels artefacts of Middle Stone Age origin described as coming 'from Vaal River gravels' and one unworked piece of stone.
1 flake-blade (with a faceted platform), 1 unilaterally retouched knife.

Swan Collection, 1938.5-2.12
This single Early Stone Age artefact is marked 'Pniel B.W.'.
1 handaxe (in dolerite).

PRIESKA 29° 40'S, 22° 38'E

Swan Collection, 1938.5-2.11
This Later Stone Age artefact has a total of six U-shaped grooves across its surface, which vary in length and depth. The U-shaped cross-section of these grooves suggests that they were not used to sharpen bone points, while the absence of any indication of heating suggests that the artefact was not used to straighten arrows. Only one of the grooves seems long and deep enough to have been used in finishing off ostrich eggshell beads, but the convex profile at its base is against this interpretation. A function in applying poison to arrows is thus likely (Clark 1959: 225-226).
1 grooved stone (in sandstone).

Additional material Department of Ethnography, British Museum (Appendix 1). Cambridge University Museum, Pitt Rivers Museum (Appendix 3).

READ'S DRIFT 29° 13'S, 23° 21'E

Swan Collection, 1938.5-2.27
Occasionally unworked pieces of stone were collected and donated to the British Museum as part of larger assemblages. This single object from the banks of the Gariep River is an example of such a mistake made by one of the most prolific antiquarian collectors to have worked in the Northern Cape Province.
1 unworked piece of stone.

Additional material Pitt Rivers Museum (Appendix 3).

ROOIPOORT 28° 38'S, 24° 17'E

In the British Museum register for 1938 Rooipoort is glossed as 'De Beers shooting-box', clearly a reference to the well known De Beers game farm some 45 km north-west of Kimberley. While some of the artefacts are described as coming from the surface, others were found while digging for water on the property. Rooipoort is home to a spectacular complex of rock engravings, known as Klipfontein (Fock 1979), now thought, from a combination of geomorphological and cation ratio dating, to be between 1200 and 10,000 years old (Butzer *et al.* 1979; Whitley & Annegarn 1994).

Swan Collection, 1938.5-2.8-10, 58-59
A small chronologically mixed group of five artefacts. The cleaver is an Early Stone Age element, while the partly unifacial point is of Middle Stone Age origin. Later Stone Age elements are the bored stone, the thumbnail scraper (probably of Wilton Industry affiliation) and the grooved stone. Unlike the example from Prieska (qv), this artefact has a U-shaped cross-section to its groove, suggesting that it was probably used in finishing the manufacture of ostrich eggshell beads (Clark 1959).
1 cleaver (in a greenish metamorphic rock), 1 unifacial point (in opaline), 1 scraper (in quartz), 1 bored stone (broken, in dolerite), 1 grooved stone (in dolerite).

Additional material Cambridge University Museum, Pitt Rivers Museum (Appendix 3).

SILVER STREAMS 28° 21'S, 23° 35'E

This Middle Stone Age artefact is said to have come from near Kimberley. Quite what is meant by this is unclear since Silver Streams is the name of a locality on the southeastern edge of the Asbestos Mountains south of Daniëlskuil, an area in which Swan is likely to have been active as a collector. Kimberley is some 60 km to the southeast.

Swan Collection, 1938.5-2.49

1 mesial section of a bifacial point (in hornfels).

SIVONEL (*SIFFONELS*) 28° 49'S, 24° 00'E

Christy Collection, ex Anderson, +7910

A single Middle Stone Age artefact found on the banks of the Vaal River in 1872 at this location, which is named after a Tswana chief (hence the genitive form of the name in Anderson's handwriting on the artefact; D. Morris, pers. comm.).
1 proximal section from an unmodified flake-blade (in hornfels).

SWARTMODDER 28° 01'S, 20° 33'E

Christy Collection, ex Anderson, +7897

A single culturally undiagnostic rolled flake with a reddish patina found in the bed of the Molopo (formerly Hygap) River in 1871.
1 unmodified flake (in hornfels).

Additional material Department of Ethnography, British Museum (Appendix 1).

SWARTMODDER ? (*KALAHARA*) 28° 01'S, 20° 33'E

Christy Collection, ex Anderson, +7878 - +7887, +7890 - +7891,

An accompanying note in the Christy Slip Catalogue refers to these artefacts, erroneously, as 'small flint borers supposed to be for perforating the shell of the ostrich egg for making beads and rounding them into shape, as these shells with holes in them are found all over the Kalahari Desert mixed up in the sands, and where these borers are also found'. This description almost exactly parallels A.A. Anderson's (1888: 204-205) reference to 'several flint borers, many of them in a finished state, for making holes in the shell of the ostrich-egg to form beads' that he found in sand dunes on the left bank of the Molopo River at Swartmodder. It also seems very likely that the so-called 'borers' for making ostrich eggshell beads illustrated by Stow (1905:) from Swartmodder are, if not the very same artefacts, then probably from the same collection. Consequently, this collection, previously curated as coming simply from the Kalahari, is here catalogued under Swartmodder (?). It comprises a group of 37 Later Stone Age microlithic artefacts, the majority of them unmodified bladelets, along with several fragments of ostrich eggshell and ostrich eggshell beads.
2 unworked pieces of ostrich eggshell, 2 worked pieces of ostrich eggshell, 29 ostrich eggshell beads.

Table 45. The Christy Collection ex Anderson, from Swartmodder ? (Kalahara)

	Opaline	Hornfels	Silcrete	Total
Crested blades	4	-	1	5
Flakes	1	-	-	1
Blades	2	-	-	2
Bladelets	17	-	1	18
Proximal sections (bladelets)	6	1	-	7
Mesial sections (bladelets)	1	-	-	1
Utilised flakes	-	-	1	1
Ventrally utilised bladelets	1	-	-	1
Ventrally retouched bladelets	1	-	-	1
Total	33	1	3	37

SYDNEY 28° 27'S, 24° 20'E

The labels attached to these artefacts and to those from Sydney Estate (qv) from near Kimberley are similar to those used for the material in the Sturge Collection, also acquired from an unknown collector, from an otherwise unknown site called Mitria Cave in the Drakensberg Foothills (qv).

Sturge Collection, ex Unknown Collector

A group of 15 artefacts, all but one of which are probably of Middle Stone Age origin, recovered from a depth of about 1000 feet (300 m) below the surface in boulder clay. The only Later Stone Age component is the broken bored stone. The

14 probably MSA artefacts are all heavily rolled and variably patinated. All are in hornfels unless otherwise stated.
12 unmodified flakes, 1 unmodified flake-blade, 1 bilaterally retouched knife, 1 bored stone (broken, in dolerite).

A further group of six artefacts, all of which again are likely to be of Middle Stone Age origin, were found on the surface. All are in hornfels unless otherwise stated.
4 unmodified flakes (1 in opaline has a faceted platform), 2 unmodified flake-blades.

SYDNEY ESTATE 28° 27'S, 24° 20'E

Sturge Collection, ex Unknown Collector

A group of five Middle Stone Age artefacts all marked in red ink from a locality stated to be 3 miles (5 km) from the Vaal River near Kimberley. The artefacts, which are in a rolled and variably patinated condition, were recovered 250 feet (75 m) above the river in boulders and gravels below 12 feet (3.6 m) of sand. Goodwin & Van Riet Lowe (1929: 142) refer to a MSA point from this site forming part of the collections of the Port Elizabeth Museum (P.E.M. 718).
2 unmodified flakes (1 in dolerite, 1 in quartzite), 1 unmodified flake-blade (in dolerite), 1 proximal section of an unmodified flake-blade (in hornfels, with a faceted platform), 1 unilaterally retouched knife (in hornfels, with a faceted platform).

VAAL RIVER APPROXIMATELY 28° 32'S, 23° 30'E

As is already clear from discussion of material more specifically provenanced to Canteen Kopje, Nooitgedacht, Pniel (qqv) and other sites, the terraces of the Vaal River have been a major source of Stone Age artefacts since the discovery of alluvial diamonds in the Northern Cape at the end of the 1860s. Through the middle of the 20th century, and until Partridge & Brink's (1967) re-examination of the gravel and sand sequences along the River with the concomitant rejection of the so- called 'pluvial hypothesis', they also formed the basis for the relative, and absolute, dating of much of southern African prehistory (see Clark 1959: 43-45).

Christy Collection, ex Anderson, +7868

A single brown-coloured, undecorated body sherd lacking in any visible grass or grit temper. Undiagnostic, but dating to within the last 2000 years, it is not clear if this sherd come from the same site as Christy +7869, which is more precisely provenanced to Klip Drift (qv).
1 undecorated sherd (found '36 ft (i.e. 11 m) below sur(face) in gravel D(iamond) claim Vaal R(iver))'.

Christy Collection, ex Anderson, +7872

Seven artefacts, each marked with further information as to the depth at which it was recovered and, in some cases, the date of its finding. Some, possibly all, are of Middle Stone Age origin.
1 opaline crested blade found 10 ft (3 m) below the surface;
1 unmodified hornfels flake found at a depth of 22 ft (7 m);
1 extremely rolled unmodified hornfels flake found at the bottom of a diamond claim at a depth of 37 ft (11 m) in 1871;
1 fresh unmodified hornfels flake found in 1872 at a depth of 42 ft (13 m) on bedrock at the bottom of the 'Old Vaal River';
1 faceted butt of an utilised Middle Stone Age hornfels flake-blade found at a depth of 74 ft (22 m) in the old river bed;
1 hornfels Middle Stone Age point with a faceted platform found in 1872 in gravels 20 ft (6 m) below the surface in the old Vaal River;
1 bilaterally retouched Middle Stone Age knife bearing more recent adze retouch on one edge and made in opaline, found at a depth of 37 ft (11 m) on a diamond digger's claim in 1873.

Van Alphen Collection, (Ethno) 1930.1-14.2-11, 14-17, 19-27, 29-51, 54-55

A group of 39 Early Stone Age artefacts, the majority of them in dolerite which shows a variable degree of patination. Some are marked in ink with labels that suggest more precise provenances, viz: PNIEL (in dark ink); BW (= Barkly West) in pale ink; WIND(sorton) in black ink. The artefacts are variably rolled and comprise:

Table 46. The Van Alphen Collection from the Vaal River.

	Hornfels	Quartzite	Dolerite	Total
Cleavers	-	-	10	10
Handaxes	3	1	17	21
Other bifaces	1	-	-	1
Irregular cores	-	-	3	3
Radial cores	-	1	-	1
Flakes	-	-	1	1
Scrapers	-	-	2	2
Total	4	2	33	39

Additional material Department of Ethnography, British Museum (Appendix 1).Cambridge University Museum, Royal Museum of Scotland, Pitt Rivers Museum (Appendix 3).

VICTORIA WEST 31° 37'S, 23° 05'E

Victoria West is the centre for the magisterial district of the same name of which F.J. Jansen was *landdros* (magistrate) in the early 20th century. Jansen sent some of his finds to the British Museum in 1918 and these were published by Smith (1919), who suggested parallels between the two kinds of prepared cores that came to be termed Victoria West I and Victoria West II and Middle Palaeolithic cores from Egypt, Britain and France. Jansen's (1926) own account of his finds gave more detailed descriptions of their morphology and provenances and formed the basis for the recognition of a 'Victoria West culture' as a late component of the Early Stone Age (Goodwin 1935). The term 'Victoria West core' is still used for the first (*hoenderbek* or hen's beak) variant recognised by Jansen (1926), Victoria West II cores being now referred to simply as Levallois cores. The 'culture' that they defined has since been jettisoned for being imprecisely defined on the basis of material not found in primary context (Sampson 1974), but the presence of these prepared core forms in Acheulean contexts continues to provide an element of technological continuity between Early and Middle Stone Age stone-working traditions (Inskeep 1978: 53).

Jansen Collection, 1918.2-2.1-48

A group of 48 artefacts, all made in dolerite and all quite heavily rolled and patinated.
1 cleaver, 14 handaxes, 1 irregular core, 2 disc cores, 4 radial cores, 25 Victoria West cores, 1 unmodified flake.

Additional material Ashmolean Museum (Victoria West, Princess Fontein)Cambridge University Museum (Victoria West; Victoria West, Moonlight Hill), Pitt Rivers Museum (Appendix 3).

WINDSORTON 28° 20'S, 24° 50'E

Windsorton is yet another locality along the Vaal River that experienced a diamond rush in the second half of the 19th century and, subsequently, also produced prehistoric stone artefacts.

Christy Collection, ex J. A. Lee Doux, (Ethno) 1912.136-144

A group of nine Early Stone Age artefacts all in rolled condition, derived from a terrace gravel below a 6-12 ft (2-4 m) thick stratum of red brick earth on the banks of the Vaal River. Lee Doux (1914: 49) records that he found these artefacts when sieving the gravel while digging for diamonds and that he kept only 'a few of the best specimens of different types' (**Fig. 23**).
9 handaxes (7 in dolerite, 1 in quartzite, 1 in an unidentified metamorphic rock).

Van Alphen Collection, (Ethno) 1929.3-6.3

A single patinated artefact of Early Stone Age origin.
1 handaxe (in dolerite).

Additional material Cambridge University Museum, Institute of Archaeology (Windsorton, The Homestead; Windsorton, Riverview Estates; Windsorton Road Station), Liverpool Museum, The Natural History Museum (Windsorton, Riverview Estates; Windsorton, Newman's Point site, Riverview Estates, Pitt Rivers Museum (Appendix 3).

WITSANDS 28° 35'S, 22° 30'E

Witsands, on the western side of the Langeberg Mountains, was still inhabited by Bushmen in 1872 when visited by George Stow and Francis Orpen on a tour of inspection for the Cape Colony Government (Beaumont & Morris 1990: 62). As well as being a contemporary tourist attraction for the high white sand dunes that rise from the surrounding flat red Kalahari sands, Witsand is a centre of localised biological endemism and a secure source of water in a highly arid environment, making it a 'natural focus for human activity in the past' (Beaumont & Morris 1990: 62). Fock (1961) documented several Middle and Later Stone Age sites in the vicinity in 1959. More recent work has identified both Classic Wilton occurrences - dominated by segments, other backed pieces and scrapers - and Ceramic Wilton occurrences in which formal tools are rare, but thin-walled, grit-tempered pottery is present. The former are undated, but the latter have produced radiocarbon dates on ostrich eggshell of 360 BP (Beaumont & Morris 1990: 62-64).

Christy Collection, ex Anderson, +7893

This single artefact has been re-used since the formation of the patina on its surface, but is culturally undiagnostic. The spelling 'Vitsands' on the artefact itself is obviously Anderson's partly phonetic version of this Afrikaans placename.
1 utilised hornfels flake (in patinated hornfels, found in 1873).

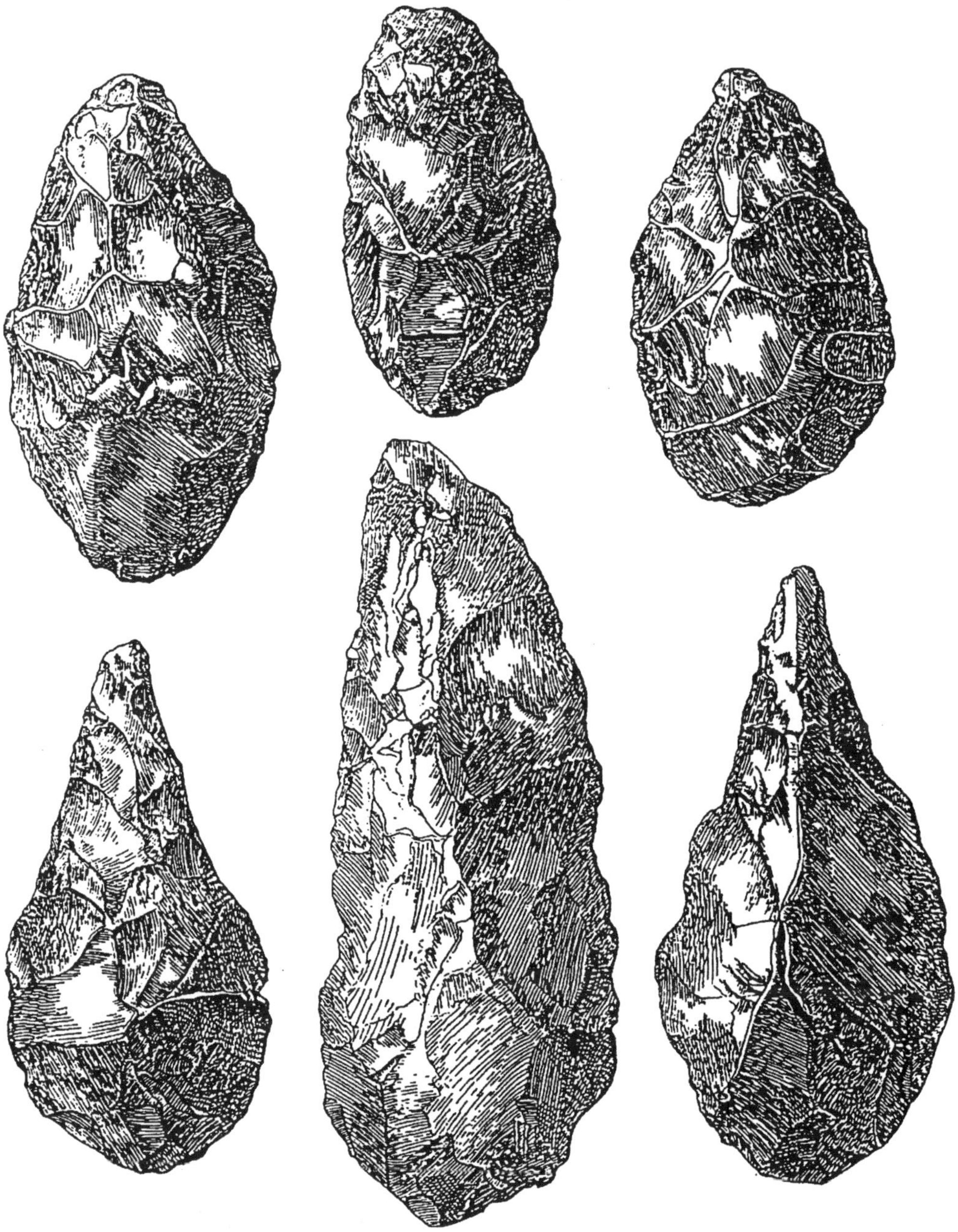

Fig. 23. Early Stone Age artefacts from the Lee Doux Collection from Windsorton,Northern Cape Province (after Lee Doux 1914:Plate D). All are handaxes (in dolerite).

WITSANDS SITE I APPROXIMATELY 28° 35'S, 22° 30'E

One of two unidentified sites at which Swan collected within the general Witsands area.

Swan Collection, 1938.5-2.51-56c

A small group of ten Later Stone Age artefacts for which a Classic Wilton affiliation is indicated by the morphology and size of the scrapers. All are in opaline unless otherwise stated.

2 upper grindstones, one of which is marked 'A' (to designate the findspot ?; both in quartzite), 6 scrapers (3 of them in chert), 1 backed scraper, 1 segment.

Additional material Pitt Rivers Museum (Appendix 3).

WITSANDS SITE II APPROXIMATELY 28° 35'S, 22° 30'E

The second of two unidentified sites at which Swan collected within the general Witsands area. The British Museum register for 1938 records that these artefacts were found at the bottom of an eroded stream channel within the dunes.

Swan Collection, 1938.5-2.18-22

A group of five Middle Stone Age points.

2 retouched points (1 in chert and 1 in baked sandstone), 3 unifacial points (1 in sandstone, 1 in chert and 1 in opaline).

Additional material Pitt Rivers Museum (Appendix 3).

WITWATER (*WITT WATER*) 28° 59'S, 23° 00'E

Christy Collection, ex Anderson, +7898

A culturally undiagnostic artefact found 'on surface close to Witt Water below Griqua Town 1872'.
1 unmodified flake (in quartzite).

2.8 South Africa: Northern Province

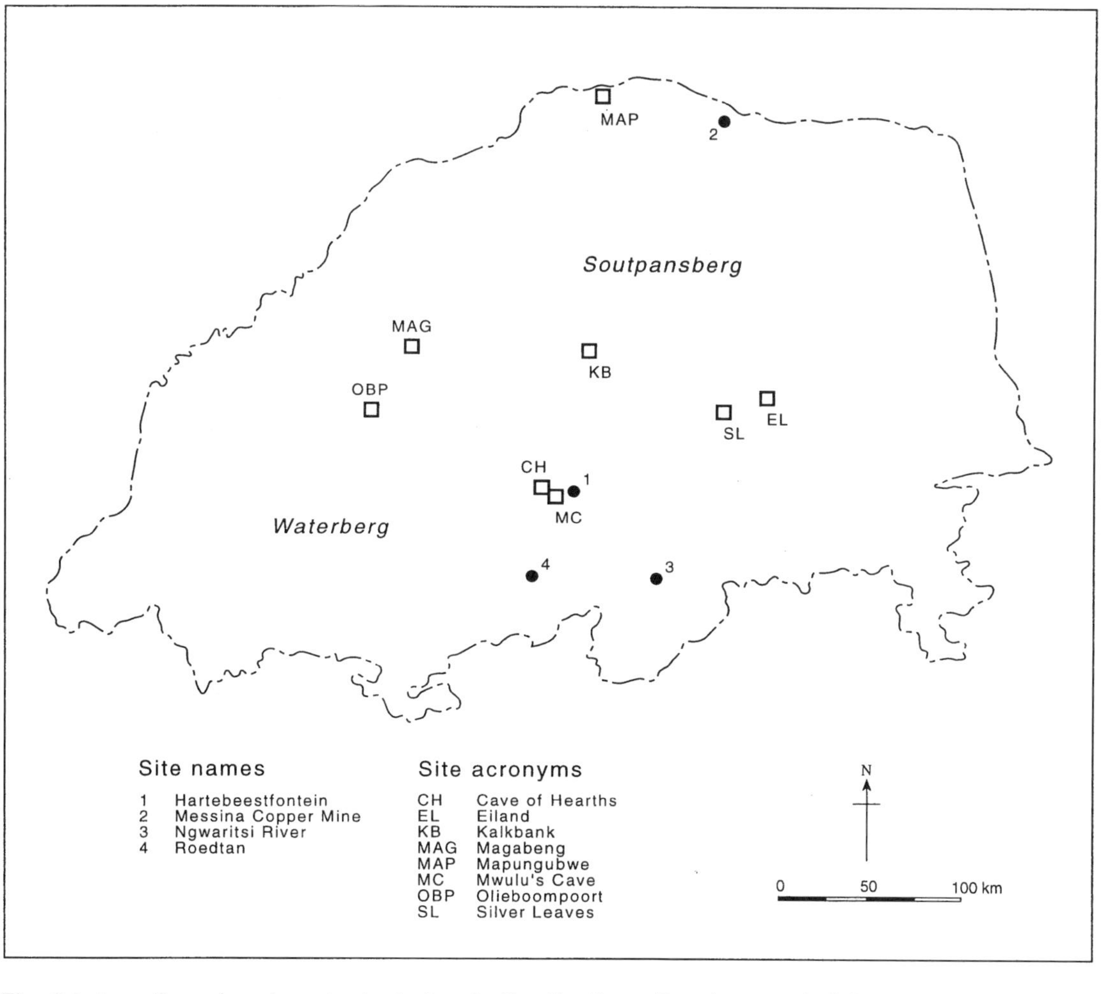

Fig. 24. Location of archaeological sites in the Northern Province and of Stone Age collections from there in the British Museum

2.8 South Africa: Northern Province

With the exception of the important australopithecine-yielding fossil locality of Makapansgat and the nearby site of Cave of Hearths, with its long Acheulean and Middle Stone Age sequence (Van Riet Lowe 1954; Mason 1962; Taylor 1988), recently reinvestigated by a team led by Tony Sinclair and Patrick Quinney of the University of Liverpool, relatively little Stone Age archaeology has been undertaken in South Africa's Northern Province. Research has, instead, focused on the region's rich Iron Age archaeological remains, notably the site of Mapungubwe in the Shashi-Limpopo Basin - arguably the capital of the first state-level society to emerge in southern Africa - (Voigt 1983, 1987), as well as the antecedents of the Venda (Loubser 1988), northern Ndebele (Loubser 1994) and others (e.g. S. Hall 1981). Important work has also been carried out on the archaeology of earlier Iron Age farming communities (e.g. at Eiland (Evers 1975) and Silver Leaves (Klapwijk & Huffman 1996)); relations between them and aboriginal hunter-gatherer groups are a subject of ongoing research (S. Hall, pers. comm.). Nevertheless, some other Stone Age sites have been excavated, with Kalkbank (Mason 1962) and Mwulu's Cave (Mason 1957) both producing important Middle Stone Age sequences. Later Stone Age sites appear, on present evidence, to be few. Mason (1962) excavated at Olieboompoort and Magabeng, both of which have occupations dating to approximately within the second millennium AD, though Olieboompoort also has evidence of MSA occupation. Assemblages from these and other sites within the region have been attributed to the 'Smithfield B' in the past (Mason 1962; Sampson 1974: 388-391), but their antecedents and relationships remain unknown. On present evidence they represent the earliest definite LSA occupation of the Northern Province, though it is possible that Oakhurst occurrences are present at Cave of Hearths and two other nearby sites (Mason 1962; Sampson 1974: 271). The extent to which this picture may change with further fieldwork remains to be seen, but Hanisch (1981: 3) comments that Stone Age assemblages are 'common' in the open air and 'frequently found' in rock-shelters in the general area of the Soutpansberg Mountains. Many of these shelters are painted (e.g. Eastwood *et al.* 1995), and some are still venerated as part of the rain-making rites of indigenous communities (Loubser & Dowson 1988). A further concentration of rock paintings occurs in the Waterberg Range where van der Ryst (1996) has shown that Later Stone Age settlement appears to have been linked (perhaps through exchange and tributary networks) to the local establishment of Iron Age farming villages in the second millennium AD.

As is the case with Mpumalanga, relatively little Stone Age work has been undertaken in the Northern Province, except for what has been carried out in and around the Makapansgat area. Correspondingly, the British Museum has relatively few artefacts from the province (**Fig. 24 previous page**), the majority of them collected by the Dutch mining engineer C. Frylinck from near Roedtan.

HARTEBEESTFONTEIN 24° 08'S, 29° 16'E

On the original label accompanying this single culturally undiagnostic artefact (from the Star Butchery, Potgietersrus !) its provenance is given in Afrikaans as 'Hartebeestfontein, Distrik Pietersburg, 5 myl suid van Eersteling 1932' (Hartebeestfontein, Pietersburg District, 5 miles south of Eersteling, 1932). Eersteling itself was the site of the first gold discovery in the former Transvaal and is now a ghost town. Makapansgat, with its numerous fossils of *Australopithecus africanus*, and the important Acheulean/Middle Stone Age site of the Cave of Hearths are only a few kilometres away (Mason 1962; Taylor 1988).

Frylinck Collection, 1934.1-16.1

1 large unmodified flake (in quartzite).

MESSINA COPPER MINE APPROXIMATELY 29° 51'S, 30° 02'E

Messina was an important area for Iron Age copper production and communities living in this area may have become heavily dependent on the specialized production and exchange of copper and bronze artefacts (Van Warmelo 1940; Maggs 1984: 357). The artefact in the British Museum collections was found in No. 8 shaft of a mine on the property of the Northern Transvaal (Messina) Copper Exploration Co. Ltd.

Liepner Collection, 1928.10-13.1

A massive cobble with polished upper and lower surfaces, identified on the accompanying label as 'hammerstone/rubber ? Later Stone Age ?' Given the artefact's apparent provenance, it seems possible, however, that it may have been used in the crushing or further processing of copper ore. If so, it would be of Iron Age rather than Stone Age origin.
1 polished cobble (in dolerite).

NGWARITSI *(MARITSE)* RIVER APPROXIMATELY 24° 43'S, 29° 46'E

This material is provenanced to the right bank of the Maritse (now Ngwaritsi) River approximately 5 miles (8 km) north of Fort Weber. Fort Weber (or Weeber) was one of two forts built by the South African Republic in 1878 during its war against the BaPedi people, its function being to deny them access to the rich grazing lands west of the Leolu Mountains, while simultaneously serving as a base for further military operations (Delius 1983: 208-209).

Wansborough Collection, (Ethno) 1932.10-21.1-68a

This material is Middle Stone Age in origin and consists of a total of 61 artefacts in a wide variety of materials. Eight unworked pieces of stone are also present. The variable physical condition of the artefacts from heavily rolled to fresh and, in the case of those made out of hornfels, from heavily patinated to completely unpatinated, is not inconsistent with the possibility that the collection is a mixture of artefacts of varying ages, but nothing unequivocally diagnostic of the Later Stone Age is present.

Table 47. The Wanborough Collection from Ngwaritsi (*Maritse*) River.

	Opaline	Hornfels	Quartz	Tuff	Other	Total
Irregular cores	2	2	1	-	3	8
Flakes	1	16	4	2	15	38
Proximal sections (flake-blades)	-	4	-	-	1	5
Utilised flakes	-	4	-	1	1	6
Lower grindstones	-	-	-	-	1	1
Scrapers	1	1	-	-	-	2
Knives - bilateral	1	-	-	-	-	1
Total	5	27	5	3	21	61

ROEDTAN 24° 36'S, 29° 05'E

In 1932 when the quartzite flake from Hartebeestfontein recorded above was sent to him, Frylinck was living in Roedtan, a small settlement on the Springbok Flats east of the town of Naboomspruit, centre of a major tin and platinum mining area.

Frylinck Collection, 1934.1-16.2-100

A Middle Stone Age assemblage of 96 artefacts. Though a majority are made in dolerite, other materials are also present. Three further artefacts could not be located during the present project.

Table 48. The Frylinck Collection from Roedtan.

	Opaline	Chert	Hornfels	Quartzite	Dolerite	Baked siltstone/ mudstone	Sandstone	Total
Chunks	-	-	-	-	1	-	-	1
Core rejuvenation flakes	-	-	-	1	-	-	-	1
Pièces esquillées	-	-	-	-	1	-	-	1
Flakes	7	3	2	9	6	5	2	34
Proximal sections (flake-blades)	-	-	-	-	-	1	-	1
Mesial sections (flake-blades)	-	-	-	-	-	1	-	1
Utilised flakes	-	1	-	-	4	-	-	5
Notched flakes	-	-	-	-	1	-	-	1
Scrapers	-	-	-	1	1	-	-	2
Knives - unilateral	-	1	1	3	1	-	-	6
Knives - bilateral	1	-	-	1	9	1	-	12
Points	3	-	4	3	17	3	-	30
Miscellaneous retouched pieces	1	-	-	-	-	-	-	1
Total	12	5	7	18	41	11	2	96

2.9 South Africa: Western Cape Province

Though the earliest collecting of stone artefacts in southern Africa appears to have been undertaken in what is now the Eastern Cape Province, the Cape Flats, the flat, sand-covered area that links the Cape Peninsula to the African mainland, were equally, if not more important, in the initial stages of antiquarian research in the late 19th century (J. Deacon 1990a). Though he was not alone, the collection here of both Middle and Later Stone Age artefacts by Sir Langham Dale (Appendix 4) was significant in establishing the relevance of southern Africa within the rapidly evolving discipline of Palaeolithic archaeology; many of these artefacts were sent to London for exhibition, entered the collections of the British Museum and are catalogued below. Because of their proximity to Cape Town, the Cape Peninsula, Cape Flats and immediately adjacent Boland (centred around Stellenbosch and Paarl - qqv), saw the greatest initial concentration of work: Leith's (1898) excavations at Cape St. Blaize near Mossel Bay (qv) stand out as an exception to this rule, but Péringuey's (1911) demonstration of the presence of *in situ* Acheulean artefacts in river gravels at Stellenbosch (qv) was of more long-lasting importance as it provided definitive confirmation of the presence in southern Africa of an equivalent to the then better known Lower Palaeolithic of Europe.

Excavations at several sites in the Western Cape played an important part in the evolution of Goodwin and Van Riet Lowe's (1929) taxonomy of the southern African Stone Age. Skildegat Cave (qv) on the Cape Peninsula, for example, was the only stratified site available to them for defining their MSA Stillbay Industry (J. Deacon 1979), while Goodwin & Malan (1935) re-excavated Cape St. Blaize. Excavations at Glentyre (Fagan 1960) and, more importantly, Oakhurst shelters (Goodwin 1938; Schrire 1962) provided the basis for defining the Later Stone Age sequence in the southern Cape, including a demonstration of the stratigraphic relations between 'Wilton' and 'Smithfield' industries. Further inland, Montagu Cave (Goodwin 1929) is one of the few rock-shelters in southern Africa to have a stratified sequence of Early Stone Age deposits; Keller (1973) subsequently re-excavated the site, showing that a Howieson's Poort assemblage is also present.

The coastal area between Knysna and the mouth of the Storms River is especially rich in rock-shelters and shell-middens and has been a focus of archaeological investigation since the work of Bain (1880) in the 19th century. Unfortunately, many of these sites were, in Goodwin's (1946a: 111) phrase 'attacked' rather than carefully excavated: though Kingston (1900) and FitzSimons (1926) may be partly excused given the date at which they worked, the same can scarcely be said of the excavation or interpretation of the massive shell-midden accumulations at Matjes River Rock Shelter (Louw 1960) where a sequence of at least 11 m of deposit spans the last 12 000 years (J. Deacon 1979). Far more detailed, systematic and productive have been the excavations carried out at Nelson Bay Cave on the Robberg Peninsula. Following initial testing of the site by Ray Inskeep (1972), Richard Klein (1972) investigated the Pleistocene and early Holocene parts of the sequence, while Inskeep concentrated on excavation of the later Holocene levels. Volman (1981) used the Middle Stone Age artefact assemblages from Klein's excavations as the focal point for his reassessment of the MSA of the southern Cape as a whole, while Janette Deacon's analysis of the LSA artefacts from the same excavations was central to her synthesis of the LSA of the same region (J. Deacon 1978, 1984a). Inskeep's (1987) own work at the site provides a benchmark for studies of later Holocene cultural change in the southern Cape and gives some indication of the potential of what Goodwin (1946a: 115-116) was moved to describe as 'the capital of certain phases of Later Stone Age culture'.

Further to the west, coastal fish-traps are particularly common along the Cape Agulhas and Bredasdorp coasts and have been studied by both Goodwin (1946b) and G. Avery (1975). Important individual sites along the coastal strip from False Bay to Mossel Bay include Die Kelders (Schweitzer 1979) and Byneskranskop (Schweitzer & Wilson 1982), the former with both a long Middle Stone Age sequence and some of the oldest evidence for pottery in the Western Cape, the latter with an extensive series of terminal Pleistocene/Holocene Later Stone Age occupations. Die Kelders has recently been re-excavated with a focus on recovering further remains of early modern humans and investigating their subsistence ecology (Grine *et al.* 1991), while Chris Henshilwood (1996) has initiated a research programme on the Middle and Later Stone Age sequence at Blombos cave near Stillbay, another site with excellent preservation of Upper Pleistocene fauna, including indications of fishing and bone point manufacture by MSA hominids (Henshilwood & Sealy 1997).

The location in the Western Cape of two of the three University Departments of Archaeology in South Africa has greatly facilitated research in the province over the last 20-30 years. A brief review cannot do more than give an overview of their work, but three long-standing research programmes stand out. In the late 1970s Hilary Deacon (1995) directed the excavation of Boomplaas A, a cave in the Cango Valley near Oudtshoorn. His principal focus, in a model study of its kind, was on the inter-disciplinary investigation of the late Quaternary palaeoenvironmental history of the southern Cape, as well as the subsistence ecology of Middle and Later Stone Age hunter-gatherers (H. J. Deacon & Brooker 1976; H. J. Deacon *et al.* 1984). Related projects included excavations at the site of Buffelskloof (Opperman 1978), definition of the southern Cape LSA sequence and the relations between technological and environmental change (J. Deacon 1984b) and a survey of the potential of the Cango Caves (J. Deacon 1979). Work at Boomplaas itself initiated *inter alia* the archaeological study of charcoals (H. J. Deacon *et al.* 1983) and micromammals (D.M. Avery 1982b) in southern Africa.

On the Atlantic coast of the Western Cape, John Parkington and his colleagues and students have studied the relations between past foragers and the landscapes within which they lived via a combination of excavation, field survey and the analysis of the region's rock art (Parkington & Hall 1987). Elands Bay Cave provides the focal point for understanding much of the area's cultural-stratigraphic sequence (Parkington 1992), particularly the way in which people's perception of its 'place' within the landscape shifted as a result of changes in the region's ecology across the Pleistocene/Holocene boundary (e.g. Parkington 1988). A more recent focus has been Dunefield Midden, an open air late Holocene campsite preserving virtually undisturbed the material remains of a shortlived visit by hunter-gatherers some 600 years ago (Parkington *et al.* 1992). While several other sites have also been excavated in the same general area, notably Diepkloof (Parkington & Poggenpoel 1987) and Mike Taylor's Midden (Jerardino & Yates 1997), other research has emphasized the study of rock art inland of the coast and in the Cedarberg Mountains, including the development of a stylistic sequence that can be combined with excavated evidence and the results of field survey (e.g. Manhire 1987) to begin writing a history of social change in the area (Yates *et al.* 1994). Recent excavations at Steenbokfontein Cave (Jerardino & Yates 1996) show also that the rock painting tradition in this part of southern Africa is at least 3500 years old and that, contrary to previous belief, the Atlantic coast was not abandoned during the mid-Holocene dry phase.

For most of the last 2000 years hunter-gatherers shared the Western Cape landscape with pastoralists and the relations between the two, as well as the nature of pastoralist societies themselves, have been the subject of a further research programme. Central to the understanding of prehistoric pastoralism in the region is Andy Smith's (1992) excavation of Kasteelberg on the Vredenburg Peninsula, which shows how pastoralists integrated exploitation of marine resources into their economy, as well as demonstrating that cattle were a secondary introduction to the area. Excavation and survey elsewhere on the Peninsula have provided a basis for the recognition of what are claimed to be distinctive herder and forager signatures in the archaeological record (Smith *et al.* 1991), part of an argument for the long-term survival side-by-side of two socially and economically distinct populations. The contrary view, based on an alternative interpretation of the historical record for the Western Cape and the excavation of the early Dutch colonial outpost of Oudepost 1 (Schrire & Deacon 1989) is that of a socio-economic continuum embracing both herders and people temporarily without livestock. Debate continues between the two positions, just as it does on the extent to which foragers may, or may not, have practised a seasonal pattern of mobility between coast and interior (e.g. Sealy & Van der Merwe 1988). The two debates interface in Jerardino's (1996) recent argument that the development of a system of delayed returns and increasing coastal sedentism between 3000 and 2000 BP was, in part, disrupted by the arrival of stock-owning groups, an arrival coped with through a series of different responses, including assimilation, avoidance and conflict.

The early development of Stone Age archaeology in the Western Cape Province and the ease with which those working in Cape Town could keep in touch with developments in Britain in the latter half of the 19th century make this province one of the most important contributors to the British Museum collections from South Africa (**Fig. 25**). In addition to a small number of artefacts in the Braunholtz Collection from the important Middle Stone Age site of Skildegat Cave (*cf.* also the Hardy and Van Heerden Collections from Fish Hoek), the main significance of the British Museum collections from the Western Cape Province lies in two areas. First, there is a series of assemblages in the Christy Collection provenanced to the Cape Flats. Collected in the main by C. J. Busk, Sir Langham Dale and E. L. Layard, these are among the earliest Middle and Later Stone Age artefacts to have been systematically collected in South Africa. Several of them, in fact, were exhibited at the Norwich Congress of Prehistory in 1868 and later published in its proceedings (Busk 1869), while others were illustrated by Gooch (1881) in the first general synthesis of the South African Stone Age. The Sturge Collection also includes many artefacts collected definitely or possibly by Dale from the Cape Flats. The second area in which the British Museum collection from the Western Cape Province is important is the Early Stone Age. ESA handaxes, cleavers and cores are common around both Paarl and Stellenbosch and are represented in the Braunholtz, Brown, De Villiers, Elliott, Kenyon, Read, Van Heerden and F. White Collections. A single artefact in the Seton-Karr, ex Péringuey, Collection comes, in fact, from Bosman's Crossing at Stellenbosch, the type-site for the Acheulean in southern Africa. Finally, we can note the historical importance of the Sturge Collection, ex Leith, from Mossel Bay, which consists of artefacts recovered there between 1887 and 1889 in excavations that demonstrated a human origin for prehistoric shell-middens within coastal caves. Further along the coast to the west the Christy Collection, ex Evans, ex Thurburn, consists of Middle and Later Stone Age artefacts from probably two localities at Port Beaufort near Cape Infanta that also figured prominently in Gooch's (1881) synthesis of the southern African Stone Age.

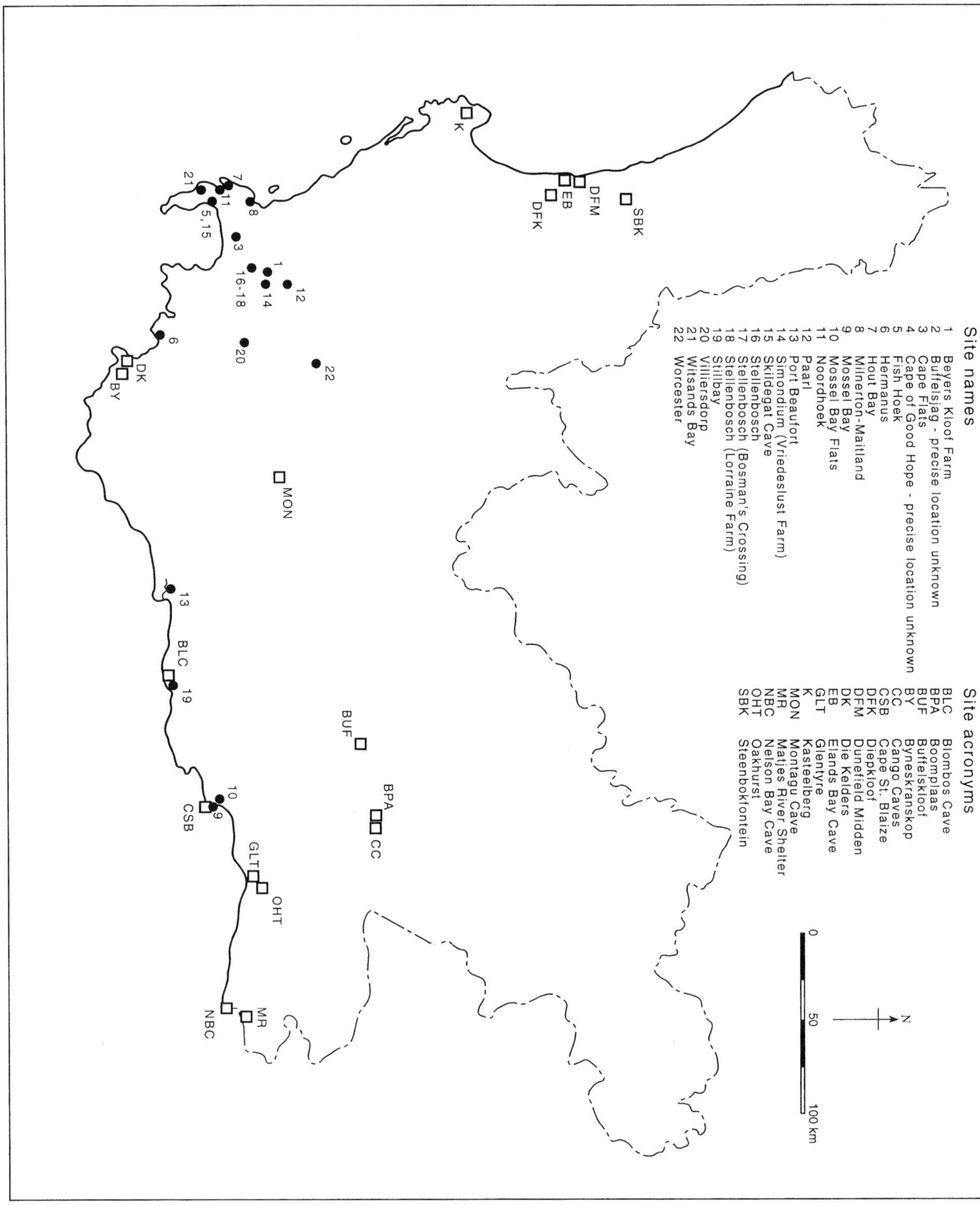

Fig. 25. Location of archaeological sites in the Western Cape Province and of Stone Age collections from there in the British Museum

BEYERS KLOOF FARM 33° 50'S, 18° 53'E

The British Museum register for 1921 remarks that these artefacts were 'all from the veldt [*sic*] between Stellenbosch and Paarl, Cape colony [*sic*], mostly from the ploughed lands of Beyers Kloof Farm'. This farm, on the northeastern side of Stellenbosch, was purchased in the early 1930s by the Baron von Steirnhelm and renamed Lievland after his eastern European homeland; it is now a well-known wine estate (Kench *et al.* 1983). Early Stone Age artefacts, like this group of six, are common as surface finds in the Paarl/Stellenbosch area (qqv; Clark (1959: 129)).

Brown Collection, 1921.7-11.1-6

6 handaxes (in quartzite).

Additional material Pitt Rivers Museum (Appendix 3).

BUFFELSJAG APPROXIMATELY 33 45'S, 18 59'E

Buffelsjag, like Beyerskloof, is a farm close to the town of Paarl (qv) from which the British Museum has other material catalogued below.

Van Heerden Collection, (Ethno) 1930.10-8.44-61, 118-119

Nineteen Early Stone Age artefacts, all in quartzite except for one of the cleavers, which is in sandstone. One unworked piece of stone is also present.
14 handaxes, 5 cleavers, 2 irregular cores.

CAPE FLATS CENTRED ON 34° 00'S, 18° 45'E

Several different collections come from the Cape Flats area immediately east of Cape Town, including some of the first archaeological assemblages to be collected and described from South Africa. The first reference to Stone Age finds from this area is Gregory's (1868) report of his discovery of 'spear-heads, knives and arrowheads with a bored stone' (Goodwin 1935: 295), but the oldest material in the British Museum collections is that acquired from George Busk (1869) and originally collected by his brother, C.J. Busk, and Langham Dale (Appendix 4). Some of these artefacts were published in the Proceedings of the International Congress of Prehistory held in Norwich in 1868. Others were published by Sir John Lubbock (1869, 1870a, 1870b) in a series of papers that helped ensure his becoming the first President of the newly combined Anthropological and Ethnological Society of London (Goodwin 1935: 295). Subsequently, Layard (1870) exhibited further artefacts from the Cape Flats to the Society, while Dale (1871), acting again through George Busk, presented a series of largely MSA artefacts to the Society's successor, the Anthropological Institute of Great Britain and Ireland.

The Stone Age archaeology of the Cape Flats comprises two main elements. First, is a series of Middle Stone Age assemblages recovered from extensive open air artefact scatters that Goodwin & Van Riet Lowe (1929) attributed to their Stillbay Industry. The second consists of recent Later Stone Age assemblages that are sometimes associated with pottery and otherwise best represented by a range of ground stone artefacts.

Christy Collection, ex C.J. Busk, +7779-+7782, +7785, +7787-+7792, +7794

A group of 11 Middle Stone Age artefacts labelled 'Aug 1869' and donated at that time to the British Museum. All are in silcrete except where otherwise indicated.
2 unmodified flakes (1 in quartz), 1 unmodified flake-blade (with its butt broken off), 1 unilaterally retouched knife, 1 proximal section of a bilaterally retouched knife or point, 5 retouched points (2 in quartz), 1 bifacial point.

Christy Collection, ex C.J. Busk, +7783, +7784, +7786, +7793, +7796, +7799

A group of six artefacts (**Fig. 26**), mostly of Middle Stone Age origin illustrated in the Proceedings of the 1868 Norwich Congress of Prehistory (Busk 1869). They were donated to the British Museum in August 1869 and are:

Christy No.	Artefact	Raw material	Period	Figure No. in Congress Proceedings (Busk 1869)
+7783	Retouched point	Silcrete	MSA	Fig. 2
+7784	Unifacial point	Silcrete	MSA	Fig. 1
+7786	Unmodified flake (with faceted platform)	Silcrete	MSA	Fig. 4
+7793	Unmodified flake-blade	Silcrete	MSA	Fig. 7
+7796	Pestle	Quartzite	LSA	Fig. 11
+7799	Upper grindstone	Quartzite	LSA	Fig. 12

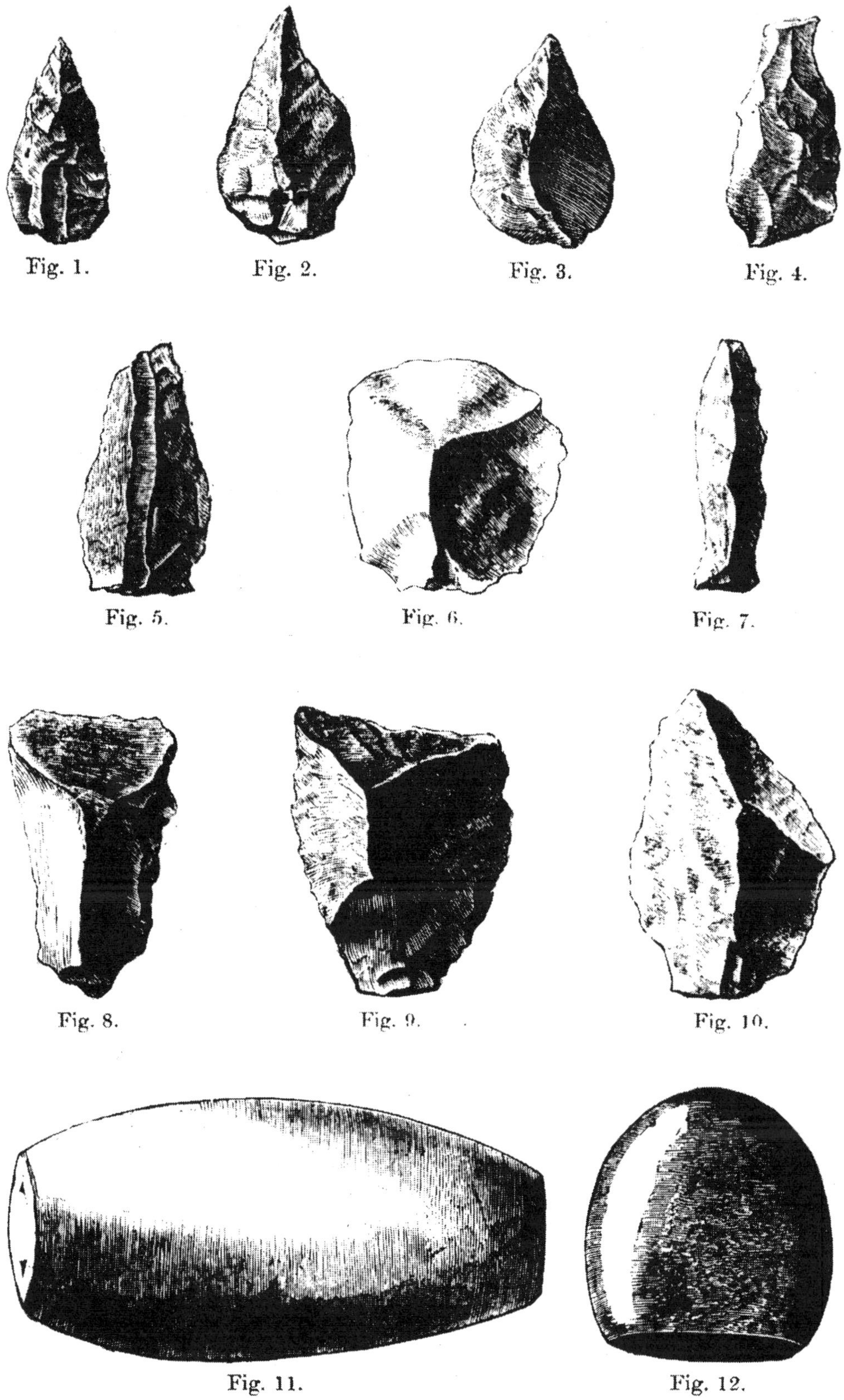

Fig. 26. Middle and Later Stone Age artefacts from the Christy ex Busk and Christy ex Dale Collection from Cape Flats, Western Cape Province (after Busk 1869:facing p.70).

Christy Collection, ex C.J. Busk, +7795 - +7804

A group of seven Later Stone Age stone artefacts and one potsherd. This is of Khoi type and from the body of a pot. It is black in colour and has a grit temper. Decoration consists of a series of irregular banded channel-like impressions that run roughly horizontally across the sherd. The lithic component is entirely made of quartzite except where otherwise indicated. The bored stone is almost certainly that mentioned by George Busk (1869) in his paper on some of the finds sent to by him by his brother and by Dale; this was the first paper on southern African archaeology published in Britain. Gooch (1881: 143) seems to refer to the two unworked quartzite pebbles in a discussion of pestles from the Cape Flats. All the artefacts form part of those donated to the British Museum in August 1869.

1 irregular core, 1 bored stone (broken, in dolerite), 1 pestle, 2 upper grindstones, 2 polished, but unworked pebbles.

Christy Collection, ex C.J. Busk

A group of 37 Middle Stone Age artefacts, all in silcrete except where otherwise stated. Eight of the silcrete flakes and all those in quartzite have faceted platforms.

3 radial cores, 20 unmodified flakes (including 1 in opaline and 5 in quartzite), 8 unmodified flake-blades (including 1 in quartzite), 1 scraper, 4 points, 1 unifacially retouched point.

Christy Collection, ex Dale, +7648 - +7652

A group of five Later Stone Age quartzite artefacts, all exhibited at the 1868 Norwich Congress of Prehistory and donated, like Christy +7653 - +7697, on June 4th 1872.

3 upper grindstones, 1 deeply hollowed lower grindstone, 1 pestle (?) that is highly polished, roughly cylindrical in shape and tapers towards one end.

Christy Collection, ex Dale, +7653 - +7683

A group of 30 Middle Stone Age artefacts, one of which (+7669, a chert (= silcrete ?) unmodified flake) could not be located during the examination of the British Museum collections. It is worth noting that +7653 is a tanged example of a bifacially retouched silcrete point, while four of the silcrete flakes and all of the flake-blades present have faceted platforms. All the artefacts are in silcrete except where otherwise stated.

1 irregular core, 2 radial cores, 8 unmodified flakes (including 2 in quartzite), 3 unmodified flake-blades (including 1 in opaline), 2 unmodified flake-blade proximal sections, 1 unmodified flake-blade mesial section (in quartzite), 2 unilaterally retouched knives, 4 points, 3 unifacially retouched points, 4 bifacially retouched points.

Christy Collection, ex Dale, +7684 - +7693, +7695, +7697

This material consists of both Middle and Later Stone Age artefacts. Of the nine MSA artefacts the knife, both flake-blades and all four silcrete flakes have faceted platforms.

1 irregular core (in silcrete), 5 unmodified flakes (1 in quartz, 4 in silcrete), 1 unmodified flake-blade (in quartzite), 1 unmodified flake-blade proximal section (in silcrete), 1 unilaterally retouched knife (in silcrete).

The Later Stone Age artefacts are seven fragments of coarse, quartz-tempered black pottery, one of which has a projecting boss pierced in a straight line to serve as a handle. Two further sherds (+7694 and +7696) are described in the Christy Slip Catalogue as follows:

+7694 - 1 fragment of coarse pottery containing quartz grains, with a red exterior and black interior;

+7696 - 1 fragment of coarse black pottery containing quartz grains measuring 50 mm by 50 mm.

Christy Collection, ex Dale, +7754 - +7760 and +7762 - +7765

A group of 11, mostly Middle Stone Age, artefacts exhibited at the Norwich Congress of Prehistory in 1868 (**Fig. 26**), some of which were described and illustrated in its Proceedings (Busk 1869). The collection was donated to the British Museum in August 1869 like Christy +7761.

Christy No.	Artefact	Raw material	Period	Figure No. in Congress Proceedings Busk (1869)
+7754	Sinker	Shale	LSA	p. 72
+7755	Retouched point	Silcrete	MSA	Fig. 3
+7756	Retouched point	Silcrete	MSA	Not illustrated
+7757	Retouched point	Silcrete	MSA	Not illustrated
+7758	Retouched point	Silcrete	MSA	Not illustrated
+7759	Scraper	Silcrete	MSA	Fig. 9
+7760	Unilaterally retouched knife	Quartzite	MSA	Fig. 8
+7762	Unmodified flake (with faceted platform)	Quartzite	MSA	Fig. 10
+7763	Unmodified flake(with faceted platform)	Quartzite	MSA	Fig. 6
+7764	Unmodified flake-blade (with faceted platform)	Silcrete	MSA	Fig. 5
+7765	Body sherd (broken, undecorated black, with coarse quartz temper)	-	LSA	Not illustrated

Christy Collection, ex Dale, +7761

A group of eight Middle Stone Age quartzite artefacts labelled 'L. Dale Aug. 1869', five of which have faceted platforms.
7 unmodified flakes, 1 utilised flake.

Christy Collection, ex Layard, +7766 - +7777

This group of artefacts forms part of those exhibited by Layard (1870) to the Ethnological Society in London in 1868. Like Christy +7778, it was donated to the British Museum on September 23rd of that year. It comprises 12 Middle Stone Age artefacts, all of them made in silcrete, unless otherwise stated.
1 unmodified flake, 1 utilised flake-blade, 1 scraper, 7 unifacial points (1 in quartzite), 2 bifacial points.

A single undecorated black potsherd with many quartz gritty inclusions may, from his account (Layard 1870: xcix), come from a collection made by T.H. Bowker (Appendix 4) in the Albany District of the Eastern Cape Province, rather than from the Cape Flats.

Christy Collection, ex Layard, +7778

A group of 17 Middle Stone Age artefacts, mostly in silcrete. As with Christy +7766 - +7777, these artefacts form part of those exhibited by Layard (1870) to the Ethnological Society in London in 1868. All are in silcrete except where otherwise stated.
10 unmodified flakes (including 1 each in quartzite and shale), 2 unmodified flake-blades (including 1 in quartzite), 1 unmodified flake-blade proximal section, 1 scraper, 1 bilaterally retouched knife (in quartzite), 2 points.

Christy Collection, ex Unknown Collector, +7723 - +7751

A group of 29 Middle Stone Age artefacts, of which all but two of the silcrete flakes and one of those in quartzite have faceted platforms. All the artefacts are in silcrete except where otherwise stated. It is possible that these form part of a series of artefacts presented to the British Museum in 1865 by E.L. Layard from a locality near Cape Town.
1 radial core, 9 unmodified flakes (including 1 in quartzite), 1 unmodified flake-blade, 7 points (including 1 in quartzite), 4 unifacial points, 6 bifacial points.

Christy Collection, ex Unknown Collector, +7814 - +7818

Five utilised artefacts described as coming 'probably from the Cape Flats', all of them marked 'F'. If found together all are probably of Later Stone Age origin since grindstones are only rarely found in MSA contexts. The combination upper grindstone/hammerstone in particular is referred to by Gooch (1881: 142, note 2) in his pioneering synthesis of South African archaeology.
1 anvil, 1 lower grindstone and 2 upper grindstones (all in quartzite) and 1 combination upper grindstone/hammerstone (in dolerite).

The Geological Museum Collection, ex South African Museum, P1989.3-1.95

A single artefact, probably of Later Stone Age origin and from a similar context (i.e. coastal shell midden sites) to other LSA material from the Cape Flats in the British Museum.
1 upper grindstone (in quartzite).

Hillier Collection, ex Atherstone, 1887.4-6.1-3

Three Middle Stone Age silcrete points.
2 partly unifacial points, 1 partly bifacial point.

Passmore Edwards Museum Collection, ex Fox, P1995.4-1.226

The butt of this single Middle Stone Age bilaterally retouched artefact is now missing.
1 point (in silcrete).

Sturge Collection, ex Dale, 963-968

A group of six Middle Stone Age artefacts illustrated in Smith's (1931) Catalogue of the Sturge Collection (**Fig. 27**). Each individual piece is numbered and figured as follows:

A (963)	1 unifacial quartzite point with a faceted platform
B (964)	1 unifacial silcrete point with a plain platform
C (965)	1 silcrete flake with a faceted platform
D (966)	1 silcrete flake with a faceted platform
E (967)	1 silcrete flake with a faceted platform
F (968)	1 midsection of a bifacial silcrete point

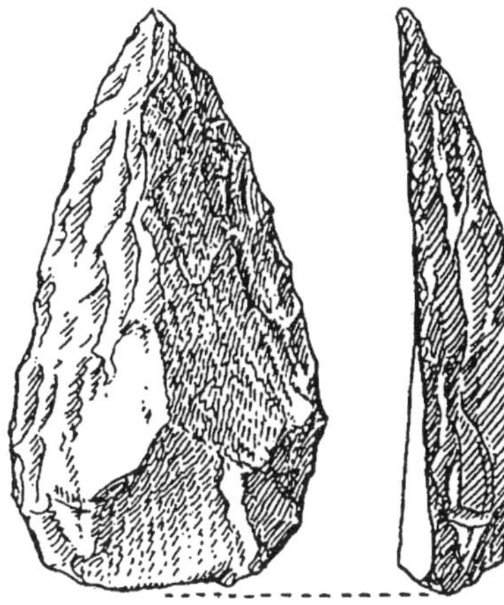

963. 'Point', front and side, Cape Flats. ($\frac{1}{1}$)

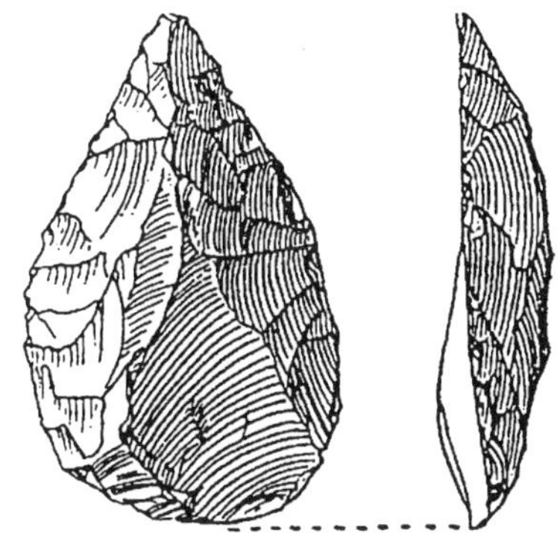

964. 'Point', front and side, Cape Flats. ($\frac{1}{1}$)

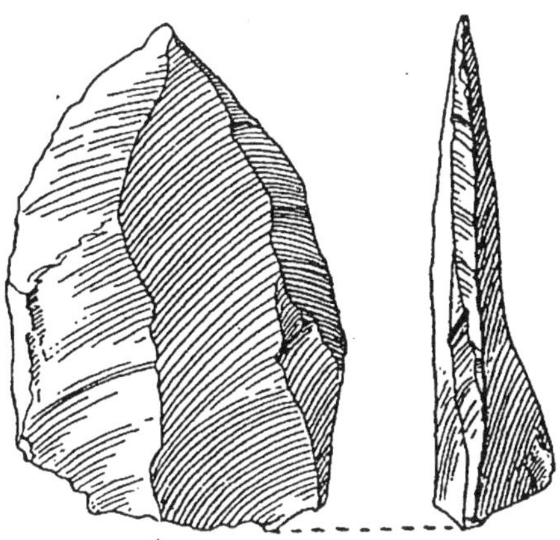

965. 'Point', front and side, Cape Flats. ($\frac{1}{1}$)

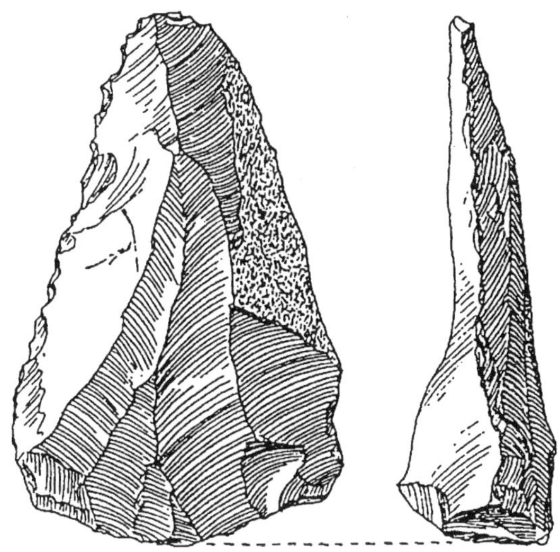

966. Flake, front and side, Cape Flats. ($\frac{1}{1}$)

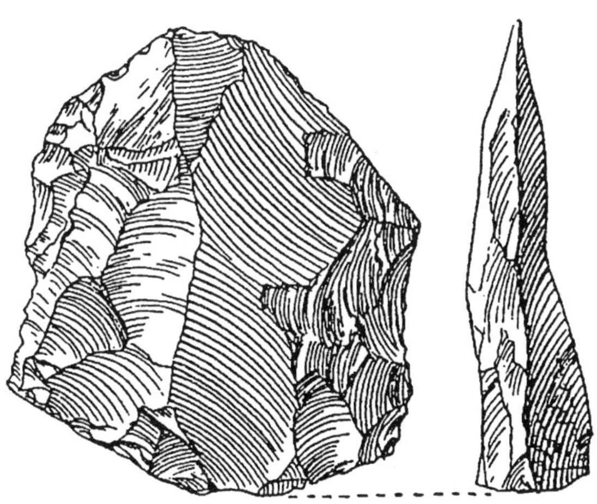

967. Flake-implement, front and side, Cape Flats. ($\frac{1}{1}$)

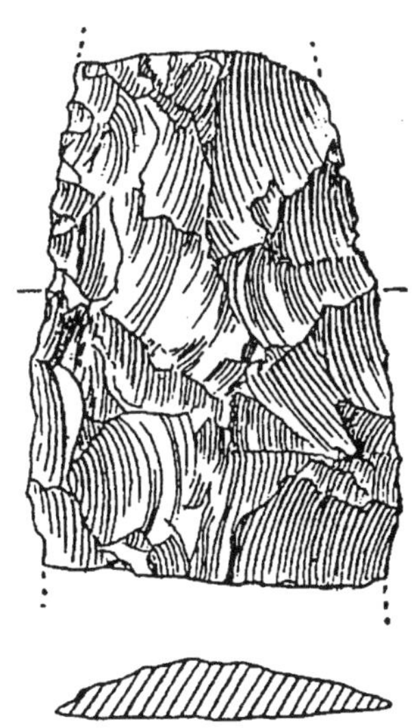

968. Blade, with section, Cape Flats. ($\frac{1}{1}$)

Fig. 27. Middle Stone Age artefacts from the Sturge ex Dale Collection from Cape Flats, Western Cape Province (after Smith 1931).

Sturge Collection, ex Dale

A group of 23 artefacts, all but three of them Middle Stone Age in origin. The MSA artefacts are all in silcrete except where otherwise stated. All but one of the flakes have faceted platforms. One unworked piece of stone is also present.
1 radial core, 5 unmodified flakes (3 in quartzite), 1 proximal section of an unmodified flake-blade, 1 bilaterally retouched knife fragment, 10 retouched points, 1 unifacial point, 1 midsection of a bifacial point.
The Later Stone Age artefacts comprise:
1 bladelet core (in silcrete), 1 upper grindstone (in quartzite), 1 coarse, quartz-tempered, black undecorated potsherd.

Sturge Collection, ex Dale

A group of seven Middle Stone Age artefacts, all in silcrete and all with faceted platforms.
4 unmodified flakes, 3 retouched points.

Sturge Collection, ex Unknown Collector, possibly Dale

A collection of 200 Middle Stone Age artefacts and 3 unworked pieces of stone. Where platforms survive and can be identified, 65 % of flakes and 81 % of flake-blades and their proximal sections have faceted platforms.

Table 49. The Sturge Collection, ex Unknown Collector, possibly Dale, from the Cape Flats.

	Silcrete	Quartzite	Sandstone	Total
Flakes	122	22	2	146
Flake-blades	8	2	-	10
Proximal sections (flake-blades)	16	-	-	16
Mesial sections (flake-blades)	2	-	-	2
Distal sections (flake-blades)	4	-	-	4
Utilised flakes	1	-	-	1
Knives - unilateral	4	-	-	4
Knives - bilateral	7	-	-	7
Points	9	-	-	9
Bifacial points	1	-	-	1
Total	174	24	2	200

Additional material Department of Ethnography, British Museum (Appendix 1).Cambridge University Museum (Cape Flats; Cape Flats, Elsies River; Cape Flats, Kaapman's Camp; Cape Flats, Muizenberg Shell Mounds), Liverpool Museum, The Natural History Museum, Pitt Rivers Museum, Sheffield City Museum (Appendix 3).

CAPE OF GOOD HOPE NO PRECISE LOCATION AVAILABLE

Almost certainly the term 'Cape of Good Hope' used as a provenance for these 20 artefacts and two casts refers not to the Cape itself, situated at the southernmost tip of the Cape Peninsula at 34° 21'S, 18° 30'E, but to the Cape Colony in general, since this was the official designation of both the British colony and the later (1910-1994) South African province. Some of these artefacts may come from the Cape Flats. Equally, however, Layard (1870: xcix) explicitly refers to the presence of artefacts collected by T.H. Bowker (Appendix 4) in the Albany District of the Eastern Cape Province among the artefacts that he exhibited to the Ethnological Society in 1868; Christy +7778 may thus also come from the Eastern, rather than the Western, Cape Province.

Christy Collection, ex Layard, +7778

This single silcrete artefact marked 'Cap de Bonne Esperance, Presd by E.L. Layard Esq. 23.9.68'.
1 unmodified flake (with a faceted platform).

Christy Collection, ex Spence, +7753

A group of 7 sandstone artefacts, all probably of Middle Stone Age origin, presented to the British Museum in 1868.
5 unmodified flakes, 2 unmodified flake-blades (one of which has lost its proximal section).

The Geological Museum Collection, ex Whitaker, P1989.3-1.96-100

Five silcrete artefacts, all of them probably Middle Stone Age in origin. Both the point and the flake-blade butt have faceted platforms.
1 unmodified flake, 1 proximal section, 1 mesial section, 1 distal section, 1 point.

Sturge Collection, ex Unknown Collector
A group of seven artefacts, of which at least the point, and perhaps also all the flakes, are of Middle Stone Age origin.
6 unmodified flakes (2 in quartzite, 2 in sandstone, 2 in silcrete), 1 point (in silcrete).

Sturge Collection, ex Dale?
A group of six extensively rolled silcrete artefacts, of which at least the points - and perhaps also all the flakes - have a Middle Stone Age origin.
4 unmodified flakes, 2 points.

Sturge Collection, ex Unknown Collector, unregistered casts
A pair of casts, respectively of Early and Middle Stone Age artefacts. The original pieces are in the South African Museum, Cape Town.
1 handaxe, 1 unmodified flake (both casts).

Additional material Derby Museum, Liverpool Museum, Manchester Museum, The Natural History Museum, Pitt Rivers Museum (Appendix Three).

FISH HOEK 34° 08'S, 18° 26'E
Goodwin & Van Riet Lowe (1929: 123) describe the collection by Colonel Hardy over a number of years of artefacts from a site in the Fish Hoek Valley at the base of the hill on which Skildegat (Peers) Cave (qv) is situated. They attributed both this material, which probably includes the artefacts from Fish Hoek in the British Museum collections, and MSA artefacts that he collected from Noordhoek (qv) to their Still Bay Industry. They make specific reference to the presence of large numbers of lunates or crescents (what is here termed a 'large segment') in both the Hardy collection from Fish Hoek and in a collection made from a site near Fish Hoek in the 19th century by Sir Langham Dale (Goodwin & Van Riet Lowe 1929: 125). This is consistent with the presence of a Howieson's Poort assemblage in the excavated sequence from Peers Cave (Volman 1981).

Hardy Collection, 1930.10-8.11-14
A group of four Middle Stone Age quartzite artefacts, of which both the point and the flake have faceted platforms. All four artefacts are marked 'F', presumably for Fish Hoek.
1 unmodified flake, 1 point, 2 large segments.

Van Heerden Collection, (Ethno) 1930.10-8.27-30
Four Middle Stone Age silcrete artefacts, of which both the flake and the flake-blade have faceted platforms.
1 bladelet core-rejuvenation flake, 1 crested blade, 1 unmodified flake, 1 unmodified flake-blade.

Additional material Department of Ethnography, British Museum (Appendix 1).Cambridge University Museum, Institute of Archaeology, Pitt Rivers Museum (Appendix 3).

HERMANUS 34° 15'S, 19° 10'E
Van Heerden Collection, (Ethno) 1930.10-8.31-39
In addition to eight silcrete stone artefacts belonging to the Wilton Industry, this group includes a single, small fragment of undecorated ostrich eggshell.
1 unmodified flake, 4 backed scrapers, 1 thumbnail scraper, 1 backed flake, 1 segment.

Additional material Department of Ethnography, British Museum (Appendix 1).Cambridge University Museum (Appendix 3).

HOUT BAY 34° 03'S, 18° 21'E
Rudner & Rudner (1956) grouped surface collections from Later Stone Age open air shell-midden sites on the Cape Peninsula into a 'Sandy Bay Industry' typified by high frequencies of unmodified quartzite flakes, a low frequency of formal tools and pottery. Hout Bay is one of the localities where such assemblages have been found (Sampson 1974: 411).

Armstrong Collection 1959.7-12
A group of seven artefacts and four pieces of ochre, two yellow and two red. The store artefacts are all probably of Middle Stone Age origin, and the quartz and silcrete flakes both have faceted platforms.
3 irregular cores (in quartzite). 3 unodified flakes (1 each in vein quartz, quartzite and silcrete), 1 scraper (in vein quartz).

Christy Collection, ex Thurburn, +7600
1 thin-walled undecorated sherd with a grit temper and modern breaks.

Additional material Department of Ethnography, British Museum (Appendix 1).

MILNERTON-MAITLAND 33° 54'S, 18° 30'E

Sir Langham Dale collected extensively in the Milnerton-Maitland area of Cape Town from 1866 onward (Goodwin & Van Riet Lowe 1929: 119-120), not least for the practical reason that this was close to his own home. The greater part of his collection was presented to the South African Museum, although it is likely that at least some of the Dale Collection from the Cape Flats (qv) derives from this locality. Subsequently, Colonel Hardy carried out further extensive collecting activity at a Middle Stone Age site between Milnerton and Maitland that, according to Goodwin & Van Riet Lowe (1929: 124), may have been a continuation of Dale's site and which they classified as belonging to their Still Bay Industry. The Braunholtz collection from Milnerton-Maitland almost certainly derives from the area in which Hardy was working in the 1920s.

Braunholtz Collection, (Ethno) 1930.1-24

A collection of 132 Middle Stone Age artefacts, dominated, like others from the Cape Flats, by silcrete. The majority of the flakes and flake-blades in the assemblage have faceted platforms.

Table 50. The Braunholtz Collection from Milnerton-Maitland.

	Silcrete	Quartz	Quartzite	Sandstone	Total
Irregular cores	1	-	-	-	1
Radial cores	1	-	4	-	5
Flakes	59	2	14	1	76
Flake-blades	1	-	-	-	1
Proximal sections (flake-blades)	16	-	-	-	16
Mesial sections (flake-blades)	18	-	1	-	19
Distal sections (flake-blades)	2	-	-	-	2
Utilised flakes	1	-	1	-	2
Utilised flake-blades	1	-	-	-	1
Scrapers	2	-	1	-	3
Knives - unilateral	3	-	-	-	3
Points	3	-	-	-	3
Total	108	2	21	1	132

Additional material Pitt Rivers Museum (Appendix 3).

MOSSEL BAY 34° 12'S, 22° 10'E

The Cape St. Blaize Cave at Mossel Bay is a site of considerable significance in the development of southern African archaeology. Barrow (1801: 67), who visited the site at the end of the 18th century, mistakenly referred to the presence here of 'many thousands of living shellfish scattered on the surface of a heap of shells'. Though Lichtenstein (1928-30: 219) correctly inferred that they were the food refuse of aboriginal people, the debate was renewed in the second half of the 19th century between Dr Atherstone (1871), who took Lichtenstein's part, and the unknown author 'F' (1871), who argued that they were a natural beach formation. The first excavations at the site, however, were undertaken only between 1887 and 1889 by Leith (1898), who was able to show that the shell middens were of human origin and provided the first description of the Middle and Later Stone Age sequence at the site. Part of this highly selected material was curated in the National Museum, Bloemfontein, and formed the basis for Van Hoepen's (1932) definition of a 'Mossel Bay culture', subsequently placed on a firmer footing as a result of re-excavation of remnants of the same deposit within the cave (Goodwin & Malan 1935). The latter were able to show that their 'Mossel Bay Industry' was an overwhelmingly quartzite-dominated industry characterised by triangular flakes and flake-blades made from prepared cores, but with little if any retouched tools; it is now probably to be attributed to Volman's (1981) MSA 2.

Sturge Collection, ex Leith, 958

A group of 26 artefacts, all of which, except for a single quartzite Early Stone Age handaxe, are of Middle Stone Age origin. The sole silcrete artefact (an unmodified flake) is also unique, and unexplained, in being marked 'G Cave'. The majority of both the flakes (71 %) and flake-blades (60 %) have faceted platforms. Unless otherwise indicated, all the artefacts are made in quartzite.

1 handaxe, 14 unmodified flakes (1 in silcrete), 6 unmodified flake-blades, 2 proximal sections of unmodified flake-blades, 1 mesial section of an unmodified flake-blade mesial section, 1 utilised flake-blade, 1 point.

Additional material Bristol Museum, Hunterian Museum, Liverpool Museum, Cambridge University Museum (Mossel Bay; Mossel Bay, St. Blaize Promontory), The Natural History Museum, Pitt Rivers Museum, Sheffield City Museum, (Appendix 3).

MOSSEL BAY FLATS 34° 10'S, 22° 09'E

In addition to excavating at Cape St. Blaize Cave and in other rock-shelters on the southern Cape coast, Leith also investigated open air sites on the 'hills and on the sandy flats behind Cape St. Blaize' (Leith 1898: 266). These produced further Middle Stone Age assemblages and it is likely that all of the British Museum material from the Mossel Bay Flats derives from his fieldwork.

Sturge Collection, ex Leith ?

A group of 8 Middle Stone Age quartzite artefacts all with faceted platforms. Each is either marked in black ink or labelled, the handwriting and labelling being similar to that employed on artefacts collected by Leith (1898) around Pretoria and subsequently acquired for the Sturge Collection. The artefacts are:

White label 'A'	1 unmodified flake-blade
White label 'AA'	1 unmodified flake-blade with its tip missing
White label 'AA'	1 bilaterally retouched knife
Marked in ink 'AC'	1 utilised flake
Marked in ink 'F'	1 unmodified flake
Marked in ink 'GG'	1 utilised flake-blade with its tip missing
Green label 'H'	1 unmodified flake
Green label 'H'	1 unmodified flake

Sturge Collection, ex Leith ?

A group of 41 Middle Stone Age artefacts, all made in quartzite except where otherwise indicated. Twelve of the flakes (11 in quartzite, 1 in silcrete) and the two utilised flake-blades have faceted platforms.
20 unmodified flakes (1 in hornfels, 1 in silcrete), 13 unmodified flake-blades, 2 proximal sections of unmodified flake-blades, 2 utilised flakes, 2 utilised flake-blades, 2 unilaterally retouched knives.

Additional material Sheffield City Museum (Appendix 3).

NOORDHOEK (*NORDHOOK*) 34° 06'S, 18° 22'E

Goodwin & Van Riet Lowe (1929: 124) record that Colonel Hardy collected Middle Stone Age artefacts from close to the surface at Noordhoek, at the opposite end of the Fish Hoek Valley to Fish Hoek (qv). Closer to the modern coast they also report the presence of a number of LSA shell-midden sites with pottery and it is undoubtedly from this kind of context that the Noordhoek material in the British Museum derives.

Hardy Collection, 1930.10-8.1-10

A group of ten Later Stone Age (Wilton or post- classic Wilton) backed formal tools, all made in silcrete.
6 backed scrapers, 1 segment, 3 backed bladelets.

Additional material Department of Ethnography, British Museum (Appendix 1).Cambridge University Museum, Pitt Rivers Museum (Appendix Three).

Passmore Edwards Museum Collection, ex Fox, P1995.4-1.228-229

Two artefacts, both made in silcrete.
1 core-reduced piece, 1 backed flake.

PAARL 33° 45'S, 18° 59'E

Specific details of the provenance of these artefacts are lacking and they may have been collected anywhere in the general neighbourhood of the town of Paarl, from the vicinity of which the British Museum also has material more exactly provenanced to the farms of Beyerskloof and Buffelsjag (qqv). Paarl lies approximately 25 km north-northeast of Stellenbosch (qv), which is much better known as a source of Early Stone Age artefacts, but these are widely distributed in this general area (Clark 1959: 129).

De Villiers Collection, (Ethno) 1930.10-9.1-2

A group of two Early Stone Age artefacts, both made in quartzite.
2 handaxes.

Kenyon Collection, (Ethno) 1930.4-19.1-8

Eight quartzite artefacts, of which the handaxes belong to the Early Stone Age, the irregular core is culturally adiagnostic and the grindstones are almost certainly of Later Stone Age origin.
5 handaxes, 1 irregular core, 2 lower grindstones

Van Heerden Collection, (Ethno) 1930.10-8.72-100, 144-148
A group of 61 Early Stone Age artefacts, all made in quartzite and accompanied by the casts of a further handaxe and cleaver. One unworked piece of stone is also present. The stone artefacts are all in quartzite unless otherwise stated.
12 cleavers (1 in sandstone), 38 handaxes (19 in sandstone), 7 irregular cores (1 in sandstone), 3 disc cores, 1 unmodified flake.

Additional material Department of Ethnography, British Museum (Appendix 1).The Natural History Museum, Pitt Rivers Museum (Appendix 3).

PORT BEAUFORT 34° 24'S, 20° 50'E
This collection of material from sand dunes at Port Beaufort close to Cape Infanta on South Africa's south coast was made in 1871 by Capt H. Thurburn and presented to the British Museum by Sir J. Evans in 1873. Both Middle and Later Stone Age artefacts are present, though it is possible that the exclusively Middle Stone Age character of the unnumbered artefacts may indicate that they come from a slightly different locality within the Port Beaufort area.

This collection is briefly discussed by Gooch (1881: 146; 150; 152) in his synthesis of South African Stone Age archaeology, although he mistakenly attributes it to Fort Beaufort in the Eastern Cape Province. He mentions the presence of 'several pieces of bone, which have been polished by sand drift...found with pottery and flakes on sand hills'. He goes on to state that 'there are also two pieces of the walls of a skull, an ankle-bone, a broken piece of a tibia, which appears to have been burnt, and a further piece of bone which however I do not think is human' (Gooch 1881: 152). These human remains (if that is what they were) are not present in the British Museum collections from this site. The only organic remains associated with the artefacts are five small pieces of bone (one of them probably a jaw fragment of an unidentified animal) and three unworked fragments of ostrich eggshell.

Christy Collection, ex Evans, ex Thurburn, +7581, +7587-+7588, +7590, +7592-+7595, +7805-+7808, +7810+7812
This is a culturally mixed assemblage with both Middle and Later Stone Age elements present. The stone artefacts total 40.

Table 51. The Christy Collection, ex Evans, ex Thurburn, from Port Beaufort (i)

	Opaline	Silcrete	Quartz	Quartzite	Total
Irregular cores	-	1	1	-	2
Core rejuvenation flakes	-	1	-	-	1
Flakes	1	7	1	21	30
Upper grindstones	-	-	-	2	2
Bored stone (broken)	-	-	-	1	1
Adzes	-	1	-	-	1
Knives - unilateral	-	-	-	1	1
MSA points	-	2	-	-	2
Total	1	12	2	25	40

Twenty-two sherds of pottery are also present and two groups of sherds can be identified. The larger is comparatively thin and poorly fired, buff to black in colour, with a variable degree of grit tempering. All 18 sherds in this group (of 15 body sherds and 3 rim sherds) are undecorated, except for the presence of light burnishing on three of them; one of the rims is flat and the two others everted. The smaller group of four sherds is better fired, much thicker and exhibits relatively little use of grit as a temper. The one rim sherd has a distinctly everted rim, while the three body sherds all have two lugs each; one of these body sherds shows some light burnishing or polishing as a result of use around one of the lugs, but no decoration is otherwise present on any of them. This second group of sherds is referred to by Gooch (1881: 150), who compares it to similarly lugged sherds from the Cape Flats. Both groups of sherds fall within the Cape coastal ware defined by Rudner (1968).

Christy Collection, ex Evans, ex Thurburn, unnumbered
This is a group of 20 artefacts all unmarked and thus possibly from a different locality in the Port Beaufort area. This argument may be supported by their uniquely Middle Stone Age character. Two of the silcrete flakes, one of those in quartzite, two of the retouched points and both of the knives have faceted platforms.

Table 52. The Christy Collection, ex Evans, ex Thurburn, from Port Beaufort (ii).

	Hornfels	Silcrete	Quartzite	Total
Flakes	1	6	4	11
Proximal sections	-	1	-	1
Mesial sections	-	1	-	1
Distal sections	-	2	-	2
Knives - unilateral	-	1	-	1
Knives- bilateral	-	-	1	1
Points	-	3	-	3
Total	1	14	5	20

Additional material Department of Ethnography, British Museum (Appendix 1). Pitt Rivers Museum (Appendix 3).

SIMONDIUM *(VRIEDESLUST FARM)* 33° 50'S, 18° 57'E
Simondium is only a few kilometres to the north of the Stellenbosch localities reviewed by Seddon (1967) and like them has produced Early Stone Age artefacts, ten of which, all made in sandstone, are in the British Museum collections.

Elliott Collection, (Ethno) 1906.1-2
2 cleavers.

Read Collection, ex Elliott, (Ethno) 1906.3-9
7 handaxes.

F. White Collection, ex Elliott, 1922.6-6.23
1 handaxe.

SKILDEGAT CAVE 34° 07'S, 18° 25'E
This site is a cave (also known as Peers Cave) on the southern face of the hill that divides the Fish Hoek-Noordhoek Valley on the Cape Peninsula. Initial excavations were undertaken in 1925 by Goodwin (1929), with more extensive work carried out thereafter by V. and B. Peers (1927, 1928, 1929) and K. Jolly (1947, 1948). Below a recent Holocene occupation rich in organics and associated with several burials, several layers with Middle Stone Age assemblages were found, though, as Volman (1981) shows, the stratigraphic conclusions drawn by Peers and Jolly are mutually contradictory and the cultural designations they employed were vague and ill-defined. Anthony's (1967, 1972) more recent excavations yielded more securely provenanced assemblages which Volman (1981: 173) considers come from 'closely related successive stages within an early MSA industrial tradition, quite possibly dating to oxygen isotope stage 6'.

Braunholtz Collection, (Ethno) 1930.1-24
A small group of five quartzite artefacts from the lowest stratum in the Peers' excavation of the site, belonging to the MSA 1 stage of Volman (1981).
1 cleaver, 2 irregular cores, 2 unmodified flakes

Additional material The Natural History Museum (Appendix 3).

STELLENBOSCH 34° 00'S, 18° 55'E
As Seddon (1967) makes clear, Early Stone Age artefacts are distributed at well over 20 localities within the Stellenbosch area, some of them lying on the surface, others found during excavations, often of gravel deposits. In two cases, Lorraine Farm and Bosman's Crossing, more exact information is available as to the provenance of the material in the British Museum collections.

Braunholtz Collection, (Ethno) 1930.1-24
Sixteen quartzite artefacts, all probably of Early Stone Age origin.
1 handaxe, 1 cleaver, 1 other bifacially worked implement, 4 irregular cores, 1 disc core, 8 unmodified flakes.

Van Heerden Collection, (Ethno) 1930.10-8.40-43
Four quartzite Early Stone Age artefacts.
1 cleaver, 1 handaxe, 2 handaxe roughouts.

Additional material Cambridge University Museum (Stellenbosch; Stellenbosch, Eerste River), Institute of Archaeology, The Natural History Museum (Stellenbosch, Smit's Brickfield), Pitt Rivers Museum, Royal Museum of Scotland (Appendix 3).

STELLENBOSCH (BOSMAN'S CROSSING) 34° 00'S, 18° 55'E
Bosman's Crossing, now a proclaimed National Monument, is the type-site of the Acheulean in southern Africa. It lies almost next to the bridge by which the road entering Stellenbosch from Cape Town crosses the Eerste River. Artefacts have been found here on the surface and on both sides of the railway line and at least one *in situ* horizon is present (Seddon 1967). The single Early Stone Age artefact from the typesite in the British Museum is marked with the name 'L. Peringuey', who first excavated here in the early 20th century (Péringuey 1911).

Seton-Karr Collection, ex Péringuey, unnumbered
1 handaxe (in heavily patinated quartzite and in rolled condition).

Additional material Bristol Museum, Cambridge University Museum, Liverpool Museum, The Natural History Museum, Pitt Rivers Museum (Appendix 3).

STELLENBOSCH (LORRAINE FARM) 34° 00'S, 18° 56'E
Goodwin & Van Riet Lowe (1929) and Seddon (1967) both refer to Early Stone Age artefacts from this farm being found all along the range of foothills from about 130 m to 400 m below the crest of Botmaskop peak to the east of Stellenbosch town centre.

Braunholtz Collection, (Ethno) 1930.1-24
Twelve artefacts, all probably of Early Stone Age origin and all of quartzite.
1 cleaver, 4 handaxes, 5 irregular cores, 1 Levallois core, 1 unmodified flake.

STILLBAY 34° 22'S, 21° 24'E
During the 1920s and 1930s overgrazing and subsequent erosion in the area of Stillbay exposed old land surfaces on which artefacts of Early, Middle and Later Stone Age origin were uncovered. As a result of the collecting activities of Heese (1933) and others these sites came to the attention of archaeologists and Goodwin and his coworkers chose the name 'Stillbay' for MSA assemblages featuring unifacial and bifacial points and denticulates (Goodwin & Van Riet Lowe 1929); this 'industry', for which properly stratified material was only ever available from the site of Skildegat Cave (qv), is now largely subsumed within the MSA 2 of Volman's (1981, 1984) typology.

Seton-Karr Collection, unnumbered
1 handaxe (in sandstone).

Additional material Cambridge University Museum, Pitt Rivers Museum (Appendix 3).

VILLIERSDORP 34° 0'S, 19° 18'E,
Van Heerden Collection, (Ethno) 1930.1-16.1, 3-8, 12
Eight Early Stone Age quartzite artefacts from a locality to the east of Stellenbosch (qv).
4 handaxes, 2 irregular cores, 2 unmodified flakes.

Additional material Department of Ethnography, British Museum (Appendix 1). Cambridge University Museum, Pitt Rivers Museum (Appendix Three).

WITSANDS BAY ? 34° 11'S, 18° 21'E
This group of artefacts was previously curated with the Swan collection from two sites (I and II) from Witsands in the Langeberg Mountains of the Northern Cape Province. However, it is quite distinct from them and was accompanied by a label marked 'Witsands Bay', a locality on the western side of the Cape Peninsula. As it is therefore possible that it comes from there, it is included in the Western Cape part of the Gazetteer. Middle Stone Age artefacts occur at several other localities on the Peninsula and Drennan (1931) excavated a recent LSA occurrence associated with Cape coastal ware and a rich assemblage of worked bone from a nearby rock-shelter.

Unknown Collection, unnumbered
A group of five Middle Stone Age points, of which all but the opaline example have faceted platforms. One is unifacially retouched, the remaining four bilaterally retouched.
4 points (2 in chert, 1 in hornfels, 1 in opaline), 1 unifacial point (in chert).
The British Museum register for 1938 records that a marble [*sic*] hammerstone from this same locality forms part of the Swan Collection (1938 5-2 26).

WORCESTER 33° 40'S, 19° 28'E

Van Alphen Collection, (Ethno) 1930.4-22.1-6

A group of six quartzite artefacts from the gravels of the Hex River. The bifaces have an Early Stone Age origin, the faceted platform of the utilised flake with a faceted platform suggests that it comes from a Middle Stone Age context and the remaining artefacts are not culturally diagnostic.

1 cleaver, 2 handaxes, 1 irregular core, 1 unmodified flake, 1utilised flake.

2.10 South Africa: No Further Provenance

AMANTIA

The location of this site is unknown. It may well be the name of a farm, perhaps in the Northern Cape or the North West Province, given that Maria Wilman spent most of her career as Director of the McGregor Museum in Kimberley. Although 'Amantia' is clearly what is written on the artefact, it is worth noting that a small settlement known as Amalia lies between Schweizer-Reneke and Taung in the North West Province and that the Newlands (qv, Northern Cape Province) from which the Museum has another artefact collected by Wilman lies not far south of Taung (*Reader's Digest* 1994a). The possibility that 'Amalia' may have been transformed (perhaps through a transcription error ?) into 'Amantia' is enhanced by the fact that Wilman is known to have looked at rock engravings in the Amalia area (D. Morris, pers. comm.).

Wilman Collection, (Ethno) 1930.1-20.12

1 Middle Stone Age flake-blade in slightly patinated hornfels with a faceted platform and slight trimming along its sides.

BLOEMFONTEIN MUSEUM

A group of 31 artefacts from the collections of the Bloemfontein Museum with no further information as to their original provenance, though perhaps part of the collections made by H. Braunholtz during his visit to southern Africa in 1929 as part of the meeting there of the British Association for the Advancement of Science. The single knife is a Middle Stone Age element, the handaxes of Early Stone Age origin. All the artefacts are made of dolerite except where otherwise indicated. Three additional pieces are of unworked stone.

Bloemfontein Museum Collection

1 spheroid, 4 handaxes, 3 irregular cores, 19 unmodified flakes, 2 unmodified flake-blades, 1 utilised flake (in opaline), 1 bilaterally retouched knife.

'DRAKENSBERG FOOTHILLS, MITRIA (?) CAVE'

The location of this site is unknown. A label accompanying the artefacts provenances them to a 'Cave, Drakensberg foothills, 3 feet below surface (A), NE Transvaal'. This would suggest a location in what is now either the Northern Province or Mpumalanga, with the adjective 'northeast' suggesting the former may be the most likely. It is not clear if 'A' refers to the site name or to the unknown collector of these artefacts having carried out excavations at more than one site. The labels attached to the artefacts are the similar to those used for the Sydney and Sydney Estate (qqv) material in the Sturge Collection from the Northern Cape Province.

Sturge Collection, ex Unknown Collector

2 hornfels flakes (1 with a faceted platform), 1 unworked pebble.

GARIEP (*ORANGE*) RIVER

Christy Collection, ex Atherstone, S. Afr. 10

It is not possible to establish with accuracy the province from which this artefact derives. Dr Atherstone was involved in the identification of the first diamonds from the Kimberley area in the 1860s and it may thus come from the Northern Cape Province or Free State. However, he worked mostly in the Eastern Cape Province and the remainder of the material in the British Museum's collections donated by him comes from there; the Gariep River forms the boundary between the Free State and the Eastern Cape Province.

1 highly polished and rolled unmodified hornfels flake labelled 'S Afr 10, Dr Atherstone, 19.5.76, Bed of Orange River'.

Additional material Cambridge University Museum (Appendix 3).

LEEUWFONTEIN

The concentration of the remaining Armstrong and Jones material from South Africa in the Northern Cape Province and Free State indicates that this site is probably also located in this general area. The 11 Later Stone Age artefacts are all scrapers. Attribution to a particular industry is difficult, but the adze-like lateral retouch on two of those in the Jones Collection suggests that at least these two artefacts may belong to the Oakhurst Complex.

Armstrong Collection, 1959.7-12

8 scrapers, (1 in chert, 1 in dolerite, 6 in hornfels). The dolerite example may be made on a fragment of a bored stone.

Jones Collection, (Ethno) 1928.10-15.18, 21, 25

3 scrapers (in lightly patinated hornfels).

SOUTH AFRICA: NO FURTHER PROVENANCE

In none of the following cases are any details of provenance available.

Christy Collection, ex Atherstone, S. Afr. 19-26

A group of eight rolled hornfels artefacts four of which have faceted platforms. This, and the fact that all are in the same physical condition, suggests that they may all be of Middle Stone Age origin. Atherstone spent most of his working life in the Eastern Cape Province and it is from there that all of the specifically provenanced material in the British Museum's collections that can be traced to him derives. Though there is no definite evidence to support the idea, it is thus likely that these eight artefacts also have an Eastern Cape origin.
8 unmodified flakes (in hornfels).

Christy Collection, ex Atherstone, S. Afr. 27-30

Four pieces of pottery donated on May 13th 1876. They are described in the Christy Slip Catalogue as follows:

- S. Afr. 27 - 1 red piece of pottery, 119 mm;
- S. Afr. 28 - 2 fragments dark pottery, 131 mm;
- S. Afr. 29 - light brown pottery;
- S. Afr. 30 - about 25 grey and red pottery fragments. One was ornamented with what appear from the illustration to be at least two parallel rows of small vertical impressions.

The Geological Museum, ex Goldsmid, Collection P1989.3-1.110

This artefact is of high quality tabular flint rather than very fine-grained silcrete, in which case it cannot be of southern African origin. Instead, it is very probably Egyptian in origin, although Goldsmid and The Geological Museum may have thought that it was from South Africa. (A. Roberts, pers. comm.).
1 silcrete or flint irregular core.

Swan Collection, 1931.7-7?

This bifacial implement was found boxed with part of the Swan Collection from Kimberley (1931 7-7 1-9, qv), but does not seem likely to be of southern African origin. Its raw material, which may be meteoric rock, suggests an origin in North Africa (J. Cook, pers. comm.).
1 biface (in ? meteoric rock, J. Cook, pers. comm.).

Additional material Department of Ethnography, British Museum (Appendix 1). Birmingham Museum, Cambridge University Museum, Liverpool Museum, Manchester Museum, The Natural History Museum, Pitt Rivers Museum, Royal Museum of Scotland (Appendix 3)

Unknown Collector

A single unmodified quartzite artefact marked with the letters 'SWAZ', possibly, but not certainly for Swaziland. As it is not clear to what they refer the artefact is included here, rather than in the Swaziland portion of the Gazetteer. If from Swaziland, it may be one of the artefacts collected there by George Leith (R. Jones 1898: 25).
1 unmodified flake (in quartzite).

WONTIMETIA

The location of this site (which may be no more than a farm name) is unknown. The artefact is labelled 'S', but whether this denotes the original collector or a South African locality, such as Stellenbosch, is unknown.

Seton-Karr Collection

1 patinated hornfels radial core, most likely of Middle Stone Age origin.

3. Angola

Angola is, in many ways, perhaps the archaeologically least researched country to appear in this Gazetteer (**Fig. 28**). Extensive early work on Stone Age sites was carried out in the northeast of the country, in large part under the auspices of local diamond mining companies (Janmart 1948; Leakey 1949; Clark 1963, 1966). It is from this area that the few artefacts from Angola in the British Museum collections derive. The coast and interior to the south of Luanda were also briefly studied by Breuil & De Almeida (1962), where numerous Middle Stone Age sites were found (Clark 1966; Gibson & Yellen 1978), but most of the interior remains largely unexplored from an archaeological standpoint. J. Rudner (1976) was able briefly to survey the south-west coast for open air Later Stone Age shell middens and added several further rock art sites to the few then known, while describing a series of recent stone tombs to the south-east of Luanda. Further archaeological research has been extremely limited by the continuous warfare that afflicted the country during its struggle for independence and the civil war of 1975-94 that followed. Recently, however, Gutierrez (1996a, 1996b) has been able to continue work on Angolan rock art and to excavate Early Stone Age sites in the southwest of the country.

MOUNT MAVOIO, UIGE REGION APPROXIMATELY 06° 01'S, 15° 22'E

J. C. F. Hall Collection, 1950.2-5.1-9

A group of nine artefacts that most likely belong to the Lupemban Industry of the Central African Middle Stone Age. Core axes and lanceolate points, which may be either unifacially or bifacially worked, are characteristic features of these assemblages, more than 80 of which were identified by Clark (1963) in northeastern Angola. However, though broadly homogenous from a typological point of view, none come from undisturbed primary contexts (Sampson 1974: 227). The artefacts in the J. C. F. Hall Collection exemplify this as they were collected on the gravels of a tributary of the Congo River at an altitude of about 1000 metres above sea level some 20 km south of Maquelo do Zambo.

8 bifacial core-axes (2 in opaline, 1 in quartzite, 3 in silicified mudstone, 2 in vein quartz), 1 lanceolate point (in vein quartz).

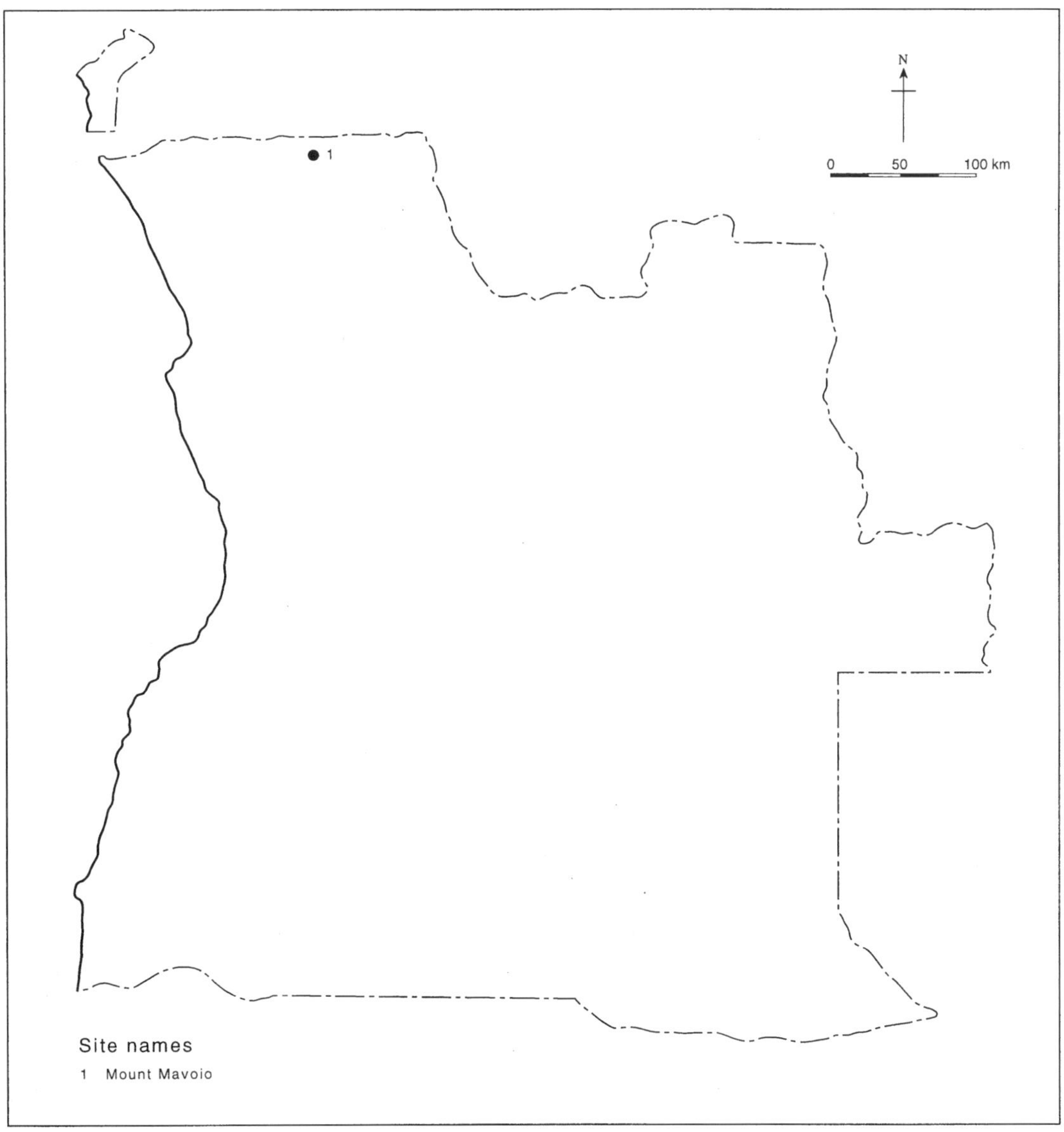

Fig. 28. Location of Stone Age sites from Angola in the British Museum

4. Botswana

Although as this Gazetteer makes plain, stone artefacts were occasionally collected in what is now Botswana as far back as the middle of the 19th century, more systematic Stone Age archaeological research was relatively slow in developing, no doubt for much the same reasons as in Lesotho and Swaziland: the absence of local museums or institutions of higher education, an undeveloped economy and, in this case, a large, scarcely populated terrain. However, Wayland (1954) records the dispatch to the South African Archaeological Survey in the 1930s of 60 cases of stone artefacts collected in the Tati River area and the collection by Neville Jones (qv, Appendix 4) of Early Stone Age artefacts in the gravels of the Botletli River near Maun; Vernay & Lang collected Early, Middle and Later Stone Age artefacts in the Ghanzi District at about the same time (Van Riet Lowe 1935), thereby offering the first clear evidence for long-term prehistoric occupation of the Kalahari. But only with Wayland's appointment to the then Bechuanaland Protectorate's Geological Survey did more extensive work begin, including F. Malan's (1950) investigation of a LSA site at /ai/ai in northwestern Botswana and C. Cooke & Paterson's (1960a, 1960b) collection of stone artefacts in the vicinity of Lake Ngami and the Makgadikgadi Pans (qqv). The University of New Mexico Kalahari Project has subsequently carried out largescale multiperiod surveys of the Makgadikgadi Pans area (Ebert and Hitchcock 1978).

In the north-west of the country, and following pioneering work summarized by I. Rudner (1965), Yellen (1971) worked in Ngamiland and excavated at Drotsky's Cave in the Kwihabe Hills in 1969, identifying a LSA sequence extending back into the terminal Pleistocene (Yellen *et al.* 1987). A much longer series of excavations has been carried out at ǂGi, an open air site, 55 km away and just east of the Botswanan-Namibian border. LSA assemblages are superimposed here on MSA occurences with a transitional assemblage also present (Brooks & Yellen 1977; Helgren & Brooks 1983). More recently, Larry Robbins has initiated a research project in the Tsodilo Hills (Robbins & Campbell 1989; Robbins *et al.* 1994) and carried out further work at Drotsky's Cave (Robbins *et al.* 1996). An Early Stone Age site with fauna has also recently been identified at Ngxaishini Pan, with other Acheulean occurrences identified along the Boteti and Kohiye Rivers (Robbins & Murphy 1994).

Botswana is, next to South Africa and Zimbabwe, the source of the largest number of Stone Age collections from southern Africa in the British Museum (**Fig. 29**). They provide a broad overview of the range of artefact assemblages present within the country, but no one collection can be singled out as being of particular importance. Unifacial points in the Gordon Collection from Ingwe River Farm 103 and from Tati, both in the North-East District of the country, may, however, be significant in indicating a terminal Middle Stone Age occupation of this area (*cf.* Price-Williams 1981).

BOATLANAME (*BARTLANARME*), KWENENG DISTRICT 23° 36'S, 25° 49'E

Andrew Anderson (1888: 159) passed through what he called Bartlanarme, a permanent water source between Molepolole (qv) and Shoshong (qv) in 1867, shooting several giraffe close by. He also collected this single rolled and patinated Middle Stone Age artefact.

Christy Collection, ex Anderson, +7894
1 unmodified flake (in hornfels).

BOTSWANA (*BECHUANALAND*) - NO FURTHER PROVENANCE

Christy Collection, ex Anderson, +7900
Since Andrew Anderson (1888) travelled extensively through what is now the eastern part of Botswana and the North West Province of South Africa in the 1860s and 1870s, it is not possible to be certain where this pair of rolled and patinated Middle Stone Age artefacts was acquired. That they form part of the same Christy Collection group as another hornfels Middle Stone Age artefact found at Boatlaname (qv) may suggest that they were found in the same general area, which would imply a locality in what is now Botswana, rather than in modern South Africa. On the other hand, 'Bechuanaland' was also used at this time to refer to areas now part of the Northern Cape and North West Provinces of South Africa and artefacts in the Christy ex Anderson Collection that come unequivocally from modern Botswana are all labelled with more definite provenances. The first of these artefacts, however, is labelled, rather endearingly, only to the effect that it was 'turned up by a mole on veldt in Bechuanaland, 1877'. The second was found 'on veldt Bechuanaland 1867'.
1 unmodified flake (in hornfels), 1 proximal section of an unmodified flake-blade (in hornfels).

Additional material Department of Ethnography, British Museum (Appendix 1).

Armstrong Collection, 1959.7-12
This artefact has no detailed provenance, but is of Early Stone Age origin.
1 bifacially worked implement (in vein quartz).

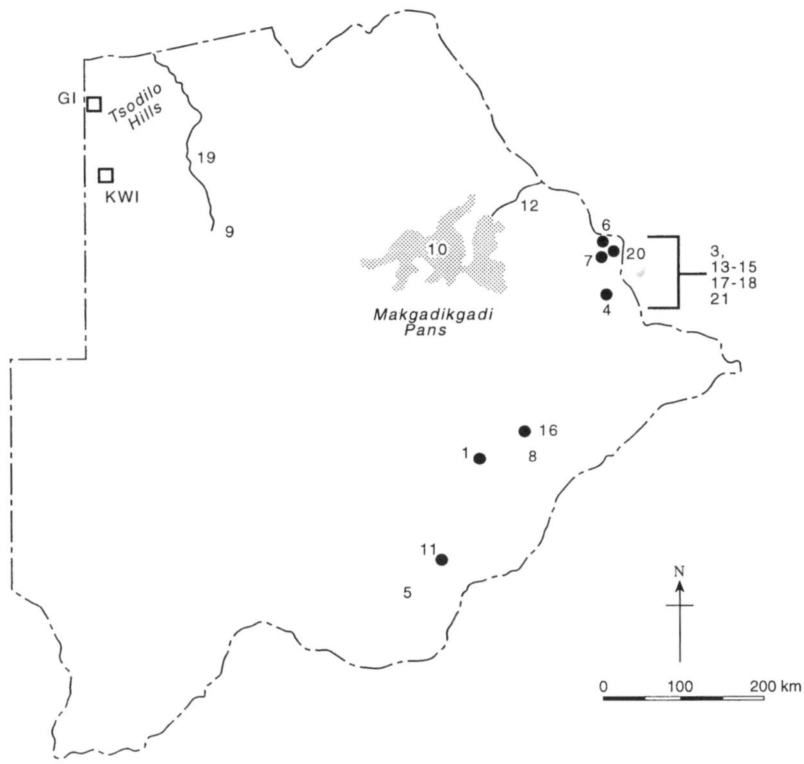

Site names

1 Boatlaname
2 Botswana, No Further Provenance - location unknown
3 Bulataga - precise location unknown
4 Francistown Kopje
5 Gaseitisive's Country
6 Gungwe Kopje
7 Ingwe River Farm 103
8 Khama's Country
9 Lake Ngami
10 Makgadikgadi Pans
11 Molepolole
12 Nata River
13 Ramatlabama - precise location unknown
14 Sekonje River - precise location unknown
15 Senyowe Drift - precise location unknown
16 Shoshong
17 Tati Goldfields - precise location unknown
18 Tati River - precise location unknown
19 Tonga River
20 Tshesebe
21 Vukwe Drift - precise location unknown

Site acronyms

GI ≠Gi
KWI Drotsky's Cave (Kwihabe)

Fig. 29. Location of archaeological sites in Botswana and of Stone Age collections from there in the British Museum

BULATAGA, NORTH-EAST DISTRICT AROUND 20° 25'S, 27° 20'E TO 21° 34'S, 28° 00'E, PRECISE LOCATION UNKNOWN

Gordon Collection, (Ethno) 1934.7-26.114-116

This is the first of several localities from Botswana from which H. S. Gordon collected artefacts. Most are provenanced only to a general location within the drainage area of the Tati River (qv), but some can be more precisely provenanced. The three artefacts from Bulataga are all partly rolled and of Middle Stone Age origin. Both the points are made in a tuff-like material and have faceted platforms.

1 scraper (in quartzite), 1 bifacial point (in tuff), 1 retouched flake with sufficient marginal retouch to suggest that it too was originally part of a point.

FRANCISTOWN KOPJE, NORTH-EAST DISTRICT 21° 06'S, 27° 32'E

This is a single Middle Stone Age artefact with a faceted platform.

Gordon Collection, (Ethno) 1930.7-26.117

1 point (in quartzite).

GASEITSIVE'S COUNTRY, SOUTHERN DISTRICT ? APPROXIMATELY 25° 00'S, 25° 20'E

A.A. Anderson (1888: 118-131) travelled through the area ruled by the BaNgwaketse chief Gaseitisive in 1867, visiting his capital at Kanye. He found this single, probably Middle Stone Age flake, which is in a rolled and partially patinated condition, 'on (the) open plain' according to the label written on the artefact itself, but elsewhere records finding stone artefacts in local river gravels (A.A. Anderson 1887b: 159).

Christy Collection, ex Anderson, +7913
1 utilised flake (in hornfels).

GUNGWE KOPJE, NORTH-EAST DISTRICT 20° 29'S, 27° 22'E
This is a single Middle Stone Age artefact in an extremely rolled condition that retains some of its original cortex.

Gordon Collection, (Ethno) 1934.7-26.124
1 point (in chert).

INGWE RIVER FARM103, NORTH-EAST DISTRICT 20° 47'S, 27° 23'E
Gordon Collection, (Ethno) 1934.7-26.28, 94-106
Fourteen artefacts, of which all but the probably Later Stone Age scraper are of Middle Stone Age origin. One piece of unworked stone is also present. The unifacial points from this site, like others from the Tati River (qv), recall those illustrated by Price-Williams (1981) from the terminal Middle Stone Age assemblage at Sibebe Shelter, Swaziland. Both the knives, as well as the flake-blade butt, the opaline point and one of the opaline flakes have faceted platforms.
The following artefacts are in fresh condition:
    1 unmodified flake-blade (in dolerite), 1 scraper (in chert), 2 unilaterally retouched knives (in quartz), 1 bilaterally retouched knife (in quartz).
The following artefacts are rolled:
    3 unmodified flake-blades (1 in chert, 2 in opaline), 1 unmodified flake-blade (in opaline), 1 unmodified flake-blade proximal section (in quartz), 1 scraper (in opaline), 3 unifacially retouched points (1 in opaline, 2 in quartz).

KHAMA'S COUNTRY, CENTRAL DISTRICT CENTRED ON 23° 01'S, 26° 30'E
Khama III was Chief of the BaNgwato people in the mid-19th century and had his capital at Shoshong when visited by A.A. Anderson (1888). Although further details are lacking, it is possible that these artefacts were found close to those which Anderson recorded as coming from Ba-Mangwato or Monquato (qv Shoshong).

Christy Collection, ex Anderson, +7903
Three artefacts, all very heavily rolled and probably of Middle Stone Age origin. The first two were found on the 'veldt' in 1867, the third in a 'water sluit'.
2 unmodified flakes (1 in hornfels, 1 in tuff), 1 unmodified flake-blade (in dolerite).

LAKE NGAMI, NGAMILAND DISTRICT 20 35'S, 22 35'E
Lake Ngami is almost as far north in Botswana as Andrew Anderson appears to have reached on his travels and this single Middle Stone Age artefact was found on a hill to the south of the lake. It is both patinated and in a rolled condition. C.Cooke & Paterson (1960a) report an extensive MSA surface scatter on the south-western edge of the lake.

Christy Collection, ex Anderson, +7893
1 unilaterally retouched knife (in dolerite).

MAKGADIKGADI (*MAKANIKANI*) SALT PANS, CENTRAL DISTRICT CENTRED ON 20 45'S, 26 20'E
The Magkadikgadi salt pans are a major topographic feature of north-central Botswana and were occupied by water at various times during the Pleistocene. C. Cooke & Paterson (1960b) report the presence of 'vast numbers of stone artefacts' all along the eastern side of the pan, those which they describe and illustrate being of Middle Stone Age origin.

Gordon Collection, (Ethno) 1930.7-26.125-129
A group of five Middle Stone Age artefacts of which the flake-blade and the unmodified siltstone/mudstone and chert flakes have faceted platforms. The latter has been reused at a more recent date than its manufacture and bears adze-like retouch on one edge. This reuse of Middle Stone Age flakes to make adzes is a well-documented practice in several recent Later Stone Age assemblages (e.g. Kaplan 1987).
3 unmodified flakes (1 in chert, 1 in quartzite, 1 in siltstone/mudstone), 1 utilised flake (in siltstone/mudstone), 1 utilised blade (in hornfels).

MOLEPOLOLE, KWENENG DISTRICT 24° 28'S, 25° 28'E
Christy Collection, ex Anderson, +7895
Two hornfels artefacts found on a 'mount' (not necessarily the same one ?) in the 'country' of Chief Sechele of the BaKwena people. The flake was found close to the 'station', i.e. the mission located at his capital. Both artefacts are in a rolled condition and the flake-blade is of Middle Stone Age origin.
1 unmodified flake (found in 1877), 1 utilised flake-blade from which the tip has been lost (found in 1867).

NATA RIVER, CENTRAL DISTRICT FROM 19° 45'S, 26° 32'E TO 20° 19'S, 26° 06'E

The Nata River rises in Matabeleland south of Hwange National Park and flows in a generally south-westerly direction to enter the Sowa Pan, one of the Makgadikgadi Pans (qv), although for most of its existence it thus runs within Zimbabwe (where it is known as the Manzamnyama River). Gordon collected from along it within Botswana, not far north of the general area of the Tati River from where most of the remainder of the British Museum's Gordon collection derives. Bond & Summers (1954) subsequently published a report of a Middle Stone Age open air site on the Nata River.

Gordon Collection, (Ethno) 1930.7-26.130-162

A group of 33 Middle Stone Age artefacts, with most of the flakes having faceted platforms.

Table 53. The Gordon Collection from Nata River.

	Opaline	Chert	Hornfels	Quartzite	Metamorphic rock	Total
Handaxes	-	-	-	-	1	1
Crested blades	1	-	-	-	-	1
Flakes	9	1	1	1	4	16
Flake-blades	-	-	-	-	1	1
Bladelets	1	-	-	-	-	1
Utilised flakes	1	1	-	-	-	2
Scrapers	1	-	-	-	3	4
Scraper-knives	-	-	-	-	1	1
Unifacial points	4	-	-	-	1	5
Tanged points	1	-	-	-	-	1
Total	18	2	1	1	11	33

RAMATLABAMA (*RAMAQUABANA*) RIVER, NORTH-EAST DISTRICT FROM 20° 31'S, 27° 44'E TO 21 34'S, 28 00'E

Gordon Collection, (Ethno) 1930.7-26.163-164

Two Early Stone Age artefacts in an unidentified metamorphic rock from a locality within the general Tati River area from which Gordon contributed much other material to the British Museum's collections.

1 cleaver, 1 handaxe (both in an unidentified metamorphic rock).

SEKONJE RIVER, NORTH-EAST DISTRICT APPROXIMATELY 21° 18'S, 27° 41' E

Gordon Collection, (Ethno) 1930.7-26.120

The label on this single Middle Stone Age artefact is now almost illegible, but states it to be a 'Bushman stone from riverbed at Sekonje... Tati'. It is in a rolled condition.

1 unmodified flake-blade (in hornfels, with a faceted platform).

SENYOWE DRIFT, NORTH-EAST DISTRICT BETWEEN 20° 28'S, 27° 22'E AND 20 56'S, 27 20'E

Gordon Collection, (Ethno) 1930.7-26.123

A single Later Stone Age (?) adze made on a reused Middle Stone Age artefact that has a faceted platform marked '16'. It has the same registration number as the two artefacts from Vukwe Drift (qv), which is also in the Tati area and is located somewhere along the Vukwe River.

1 adze (in opaline, made on a reused MSA flake).

SHOSHONG (*BAMANGWATO, MONQUATO*), CENTRAL DISTRICT 23° 01'S, 26° 30'E

Andrew Anderson (1888) appears to have used both Bamangwato and Monquato as aliases for Shoshong, the principal town of the BaNgwato chief Khama III, elsewhere employing the term 'Khama's Country' to refer to the general area inhabited by the BaNgwato people. This suggests that these three artefacts were found at or close to Shoshong itself. All three are unmodified flakes, +7905 at least being of Middle Stone Age given its faceted platform.

Christy Collection, ex Anderson, +7902

2 unmodified flakes (1 in hornfels, 1 in opaline, found respectively in 1867 and 1877).

Christy Collection, ex Anderson, +7905

1 unmodified flake (in patinated hornfels with a faceted platform, found in a local riverbed in 1877).

TATI GOLDFIELDS, NORTH-EAST DISTRICT CENTRED AROUND 21 18'S, 27 41' E

The Tati River area was the scene of considerable Iron Age gold-mining activity and reports of these mines by the German geologist Karl Mauch sparked off a gold rush here after 1866. Though the workings did not match the expectations of the early pioneers, gold continued to be extracted until the Monarch Mine closed down in 1964 (Bulpin 1986: 786). Finds collected by H. S. Gordon and provenanced more specifically to Bulataga, Gungwe Kopje, Ingwe River Farm 103, Ramatlabama, Sekonje River, Senyowe Drift, Tshesebe and Vukwe Drift (qqv) all come from the general Tati River area. The Nata River and Francistown Kopje (qqv), from both of which Gordon also collected stone artefacts, lie respectively to the north and at the southern end of the Tati goldfields. Though none seem to have reached the British Museum collections, Layard (1870: xcix) reports that he exhibited artefacts from 'near the Tatin [*sic*] Goldfields' to a meeting of the Ethnological Society in London in 1868.

Christy Collection, ex Anderson, +7902

Two Middle Stone Age points in rolled condition. The quartzite point has its tip and butt missing, while the hornfels example is marked in ink to the effect that it was found 'with gravel on surface Matabele 1878'. The latter description raises the possibility, but does not unequivocally demonstrate, that the artefact may have come from within what is now Zimbabwe, rather than from within modern Botswana.
2 points (1 in hornfels, 1 in quartzite).

TATI RIVER, NORTH-EAST DISTRICT FROM 20° 25'S, 27° 20'E TO 21° 34'S, 28° 00'E

Christy Collection, ex Anderson, +7901

A single, probably Middle Stone Age artefact in rolled and patinated condition. It shares the same Christy Slip Catalogue number as three artefacts from western Zimbabwe (qv Matabeleland, no further provenance; Mpakwe River) and may possibly have also come from within that country's borders.
1 unmodified flake (in hornfels, found on the surface in 1867).

Gordon Collection, (Ethno) 1930.7-26.1-27, 29-32, 35-87, 89-93, 107-111, 113, 165

This is the largest single collection made by Gordon, but is less specifically provenanced than the others. With the exception of the two adzes, which may be of Later Stone Age origin, the entire assemblage of 96 artefacts is probably of Middle Stone Age affiliation, as indicated by the presence of several flake-blades, unifacial points and knives; the majority of the flakes also have faceted platforms. All the artefacts are in opaline except where otherwise stated.
1 cleaver (in granite), 1 chunk, 54 unmodified flakes (including 1 in hornfels), 5 irregular cores, 1 disc core, 2 flat bladelet cores, 1 crested blade, 5 unmodified flake-blades, 3 unmodified bladelets, 1 unmodified flake-blade mesial section, 5 utilised flakes, 4 scrapers, 2 adzes, 1 unilaterally retouched knife, 6 unifacially retouched points (including 1 in quartzite), 4 miscellaneously retouched pieces.

TONGA RIVER, NGAMILAND DISTRICT FROM APPROXIMATELY 18° 04'S, 21° 28'E TO APPROXIMATELY 20° 25'S, 24° 45'E (AFTER ANDERSON 1888: 188)

A.A. Anderson's (1888: 310) account of his travels in southern Africa makes it plain that the 'Tonga River' is that part of the Kavango River that flows southeast from what is now the Angolan/Namibian border across the Caprivi Strip and thence into the Okavango Delta and Lake Ngami.

Christy Collection, ex Anderson, +7888, +7893

A group of two Middle Stone Age hornfels artefacts. The point is both patinated and in rolled condition.
1 bilaterally retouched knife (found on the river's banks in 1878), 1 point (found in the river's bed in 1876).

TSHESEBE (*TSESSEBE*), NORTH-EAST DISTRICT 20° 46'S, 27° 26'E

Gordon Collection, (Ethno) 1930.7-26.118-119

Two Middle Stone Age opaline artefacts, both of which have faceted platforms. The flake is marked 'On veld 4 miles SW of Tsesebe', while the small size of the unifacial point recalls those found in the Tati River and at Ingwe River Farm 103 (qqv).
1 unmodified flake, 1 unifacial point.

VUKWE DRIFT, NORTH-EAST DISTRICT BETWEEN 20° 28'S, 27° 22'E AND 20° 56'S, 27° 20'E

Gordon Collection, (Ethno) 1930.7-26.121-122

The precise river crossing meant by the term 'drift' in this provenance designation is unknown and the latitude and longitude given are for the full length of the Vukwe River. The collection consists of two opaline artefacts with the same accession number as the adze from Senyowe Drift (qv), which is within the general Tati River area. The spokeshave, which is in rolled condition, is marked '13' and is of Later Stone Age origin. The faceted platform of the flake indicates that it is very probably of Middle Stone Age manufacture.
1 unmodified flake, 1 spokeshave.

5. Lesotho

Because of its largely mountainous terrain and the absence until shortly before independence of any higher education institutions or a national museum, relatively little archaeological work had been carried out in Lesotho prior to the late 1960s (**Fig. 30**). Apart from the limited collecting activities of South African based archaeologists and local amateurs, this emphasized the recording of some of the hundreds of rock art sites found here. Rock art research has remained an important focus for archaeological work within Lesotho over the last three decades (Vinnicombe 1976; Smits 1983), but several major excavation and field survey projects have also been undertaken during this time. In addition to work carried out in advance of construction activities related to the Southern Perimeter Road (Parkington *et al.* 1987) and the Lesotho Highlands Water Project (Lewis-Williams & Thorp 1990; Mitchell & Parkington 1990; Kaplan 1992, 1995, 1996), this has included the survey of the Senqunyane Valley reported by Bousman (1988). However, most fieldwork has concentrated on field-survey and the excavation of rock-shelters with extensive Middle and/or Later Stone Age deposits in the Sehlabathebe Basin and along the Senqu River in the southeastern highlands (Carter 1978; Carter *et al.* 1988; Mitchell 1993, 1994a, 1996a, 1996b, 1996c, 1996d) and in the Phuthiatsana Basin on the opposite side of the country (Mitchell 1994b). Mitchell (1992) provides a review of Lesotho archaeology up until the beginning of the 1990s, with a recent development the excavation of a multi-phase open-air Later Stone Age site on the banks of the Senqu River (Mitchell & Charles 1996).

Lesotho is represented in the British Museum by a group of three Middle Stone Age artefacts, all in hornfels, acquired for the Christy Collection from Dr Exton, founder of the National Museum at Bloemfontein. It is possible that they form part of the material reported to have been collected (excavated ?) by Colonel T. H. Bowker around this time from Lesotho rock-shelters and sent by him to the United Kingdom (Goodwin 1946a: 18).

LESOTHO (*BASUTOLAND*), NO FURTHER PROVENANCE

Christy Collection, ex Exton, +7719, +7720

1 unmodified flake-blade, 1 retouched point (with a faceted platform).

Christy Collection, ex Exton

1 unmodified flake-blade.

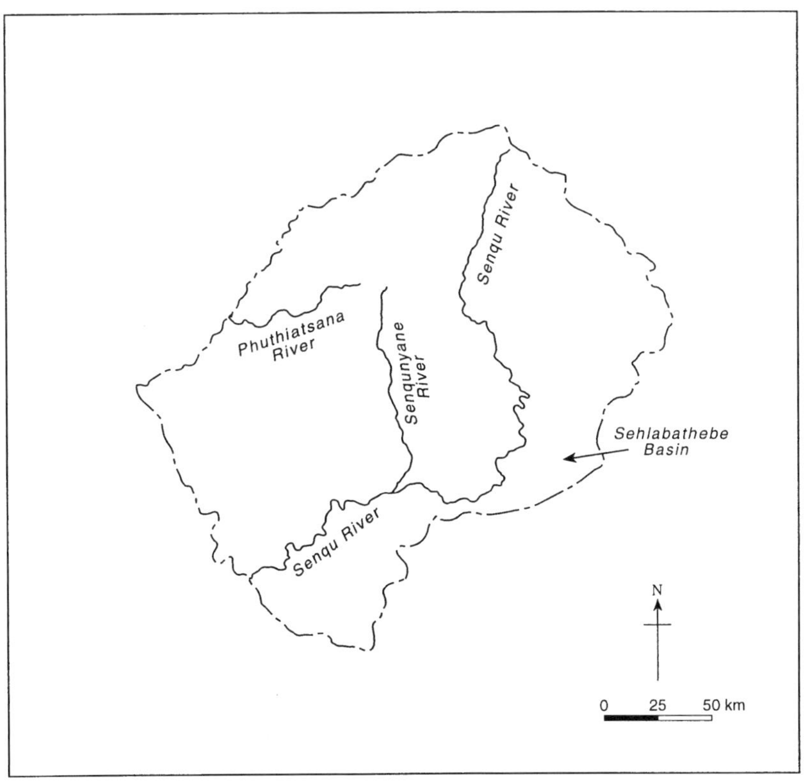

Fig. 30. Lesotho showing the location of key geographical features mentioned in the text

6. Mozambique

Morais (1984) and Sinclair *et al.* (1993) provide thorough overviews of the history and development of Mozambican archaeology. Although the then Bishop of Mozambique reported the existence of rock-paintings to the Academia Real das Ciências of Lisbon as early as 1721, not until well into the 20th century did any sustained interest in the country's prehistory develop. As with Angola, this can in part be attributed to the slow consolidation of colonial control (Morais 1984: 113) and only after the Salazar régime established the Anthropological Mission of Mozambique in 1936 did archaeological research begin to take off. In addition to the discovery of almost 70 Stone Age sites by the Mission's own staff (e.g. Dias 1947) and investigations of Quaternary stratigraphy (Barradas 1961) and rock art (Castro 1956), brief surveys were undertaken by visiting scholars from outside Mozambique (e.g. Van Riet Lowe 1943; Breuil 1944; Derricourt 1975). Nevertheless, until independence in 1975 archaeological research remained extremely limited in scale. Since then, not only has archaeology been taught at Eduardo Mondlane University, Maputo, but several extensive programmes of survey and excavation have been carried out, largely with Swedish funding (Sinclair *et al.* 1993). Though these research projects have emphasized the Iron Age, Stone Age sites have also been investigated, among them the first excavation of a rock-shelter in the southern half of the country (at Caimane, Morais 1988) and excavations at several painted sites in Namapula Province in the north. Analysis of lithic assemblages from the latter series of excavations shows no obvious similarities to the successive industrial complexes recognised in South Africa and adjacent areas (Adamowicz 1987). Meneses (1988) has recently reassessed all existing Stone Age museum collections and initiated a new programme of field research concentrating on the Early Stone Age (Meneses 1996).

Mozambique is represented in the British Museum southern African Stone Age collections by artefacts from only two localities (**Fig. 31**). Little can, unfortunately, be said about them, although the Wayland Collection is of some historical interest as it is one of the first archaeological collections made by this collector. Wayland subsequently went on to have a considerable influence on the development of Stone Age archaeology in both Uganda and Botswana (Appendix 4).

DERRE, ZAMBEZIA PROVINCE 16 57'S, 36 08'E

This is a single culturally undiagnostic artefact, the fresh condition of which might suggest that it is relatively recent (Later Stone Age ?) in date.

Warren Collection, unnumbered

1 unmodified flake (in opaline).

MONAPO RIVER ALLUVIAL TERRACES, ILHA PROVINCE APPROXIMATELY 15 00'S, 40 23'E

Wayland Collection, (Ethno) 1912.12-16.1-16

Wayland (1915) worked in Mozambique before the First World War and in the course of his geological surveys there in 1911 collected this group of 20 artefacts (**Fig. 32**), all but one of which is in a rolled condition; all save one come from the 'surface of the present alluvium' or the river's terraces (Wayland 1915: 98). The single flake-blade is of Middle Stone Age origin, but the other artefacts are culturally undiagnostic, although the hornfels core is in fresh condition and therefore perhaps of a different age, or from a slightly different locality, than the other pieces.

1 irregular core (in hornfels), 1 *pièce esquillée* (in opaline), 17 unmodified flakes (13 in opaline, 4 in sandstone), 1 unmodified flake-blade (in opaline).

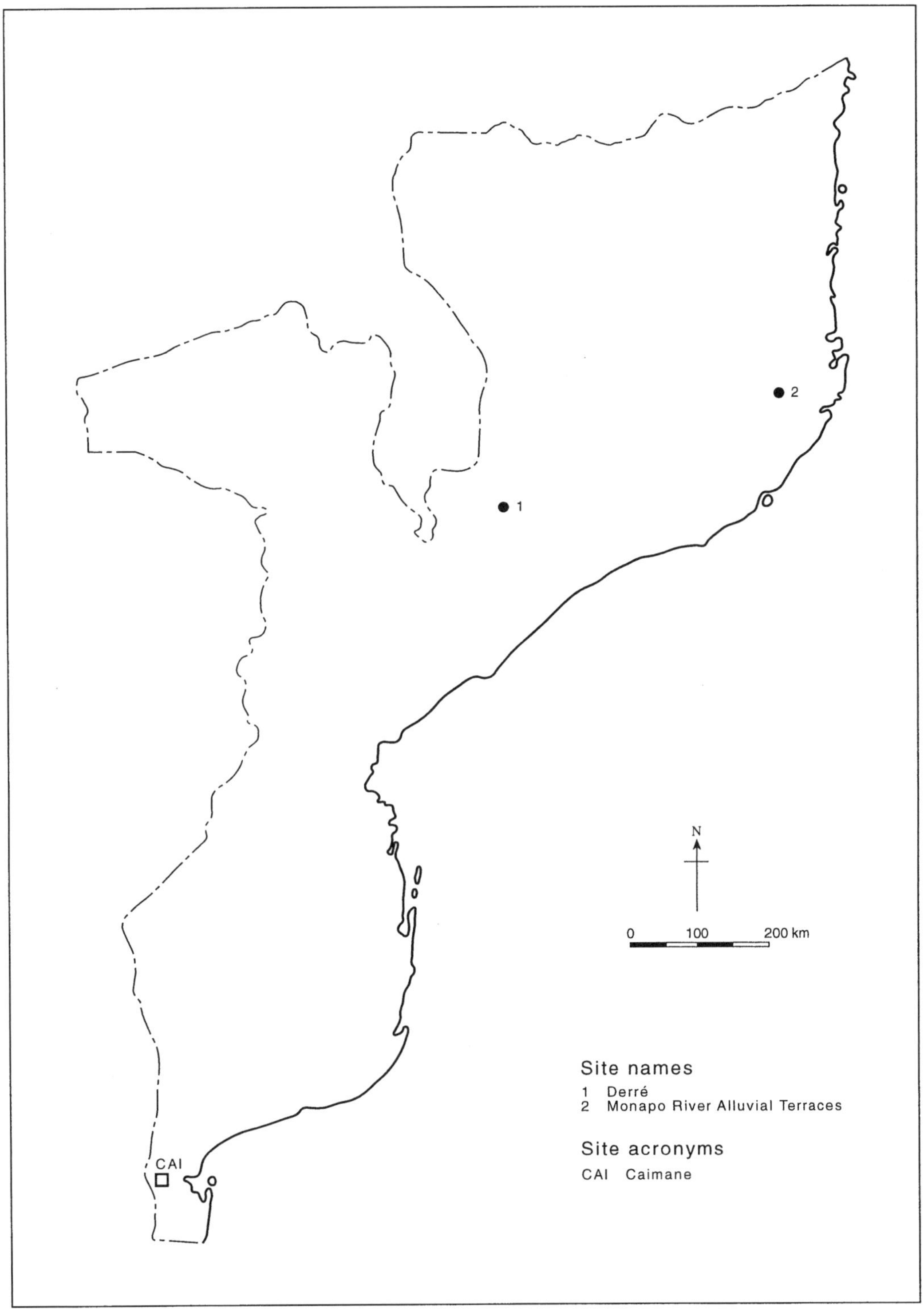

Fig. 31. Location of archaeological sites in Mozambique and of Stone Age collections from there in the British Museum

Fig. 32. Artefacts from the Wayland Collection from Monapo River alluvial terraces, Mozambique (after Wayland 1915: PLate H). All those shown are unmodified opaline and sandstone flakes, except for 13, which is an irregular core (in hornfels).

7. Namibia

Archaeological interest in Namibia's past began to take shape in the early part of the 20th century, with an initial concentration on the Central Namib Desert because of the discovery there of several important rock art sites (Kinahan 1991: 6). Early research was primarily antiquarian (e.g. Breuil 1948), but more systematic investigations began in the second half of the 20th century (e.g. J. Rudner 1957; Viereck 1967). Among these the work of Rona MacCalman was particularly important, not only in investigating Middle Stone Age sites in the Windhoek area (MacCalman 1962, 1963), but also in making one of the few firsthand observations of stone tool production and use in southern Africa (MacCalman & Grobbelaar 1965). Subsequently, wide-ranging surveys have also been undertaken in other parts of the country, notably those of Scherz & Scherz (1974) and Wendt (1972). Wendt's project is particularly significant since not only did it cover a large area, but in Apollo 11 Cave it also initiated excavation at one of the key long-term sites for Middle and Later Stone Age prehistory in the sub-continent, one spectacular consequence of which was the discovery of the oldest (± 27 000 BP) rock art in Africa (Wendt 1976). Within the Central Namib itself more recent studies have focused on rock art (e.g. Pager 1989), late Pleistocene and Holocene adaptations (e.g. Sandelowsky 1977; Wadley 1979; Shackley 1985) and the origins and development of pastoralism (Sandelowsky *et al.* 1979; Kinahan 1991; Smith & Jacobson 1995; Kinahan 1996). Earlier cultural-stratigraphic concepts have also been re-evaluated (e.g. Jacobson 1976). The history of Namibian archaeology is much more fully considered and reassessed by Kinahan (1994).

All of the British Museum Stone Age collections from Namibia (**Fig. 33**) were acquired for the Christy Collection from Andrew Anderson (1888), who travelled through parts of the country in the 1860s and 1870s. Reflecting the poorer state of contemporary knowledge of this part of southern Africa, his provenance information for these artefacts is regrettably less specific than for the artefacts he collected in either Botswana or South Africa. Though he does not make reference to collecting stone artefacts, A.A. Anderson (1888: 279-280) does mention stone burial cairns, abandoned stone huts and the collection of mineralogical specimens while travelling between Great Namaqualand and Damaraland.

CUBANGO RIVER FROM 17° 13'S, 18° 37'E TO 17° 55'S, 20° 34'E

Christy Collection, ex Anderson, +7875

This single patinated hornfels artefact is culturally undiagnostic. It is marked in ink to the effect that it was 'found south of the Cubango River SCA 1872'. The Cubango River rises in southeastern Angola before flowing east to form part of the border between Angola and Namibia. However, the reference in the Christy Collection Slip Catalogue to the Cubango River as '? Damaraland' (a part of Namibia) suggests that it may have been found on the Namibian side of the river. Anderson does not seem to have spent much, if any time, in Angola itself, while the letters 'SCA' almost certainly stand for 'South Central Africa', a designation that he employs elsewhere specifically with reference to 'Damaraland' and 'Ovampoland' (A.A. Anderson 1888: 242-255).
1 unmodified flake (in hornfels).

DAMARALAND CENTRED AROUND 20° 30'S, 14° 30'E

Christy Collection, ex Anderson, +7876

Two Middle Stone Age artefacts in rolled condition found on the surface.
1 proximal section of an unmodified flake-blade, 1 distal section of a point.

FISH RIVER (*GREAT FISH RIVER*) FROM 23° 19'S, 16° 28'E TO 28° 04'S, 17° 08'E

Christy Collection, ex Anderson, +7877

Two Middle Stone Age artefacts, one of them patinated, found in the bed of the Fish River.
2 points (in hornfels).

OWAMBO (*OVAMPOLAND*) CENTRED AROUND 17° 00'S, 16° 00'E

A.A. Anderson (1888) uses the term 'Ovampoland' quite broadly for the region between the Cunene River, 'Damaraland' and the Kalahari Desert. Assuming that he correctly measured the altitude at which one of these two finds was made, it is possible to provenance at least this artefact to one of two areas of high elevation in modern Kaokoland or to the highlands between Tsumeb and Grootfontein.

Christy Collection, ex Anderson, +7873, +7874

Two Later Stone Age artefacts. The scraper was found on the 'high veldt of Ovampoland' in 1870, while the bored stone was found 'on top of a mount 7100 ft (i.e. 2185 m) above sea level' in 1865.
1 bored stone (in soapstone), 1 scraper (in patinated hornfels).

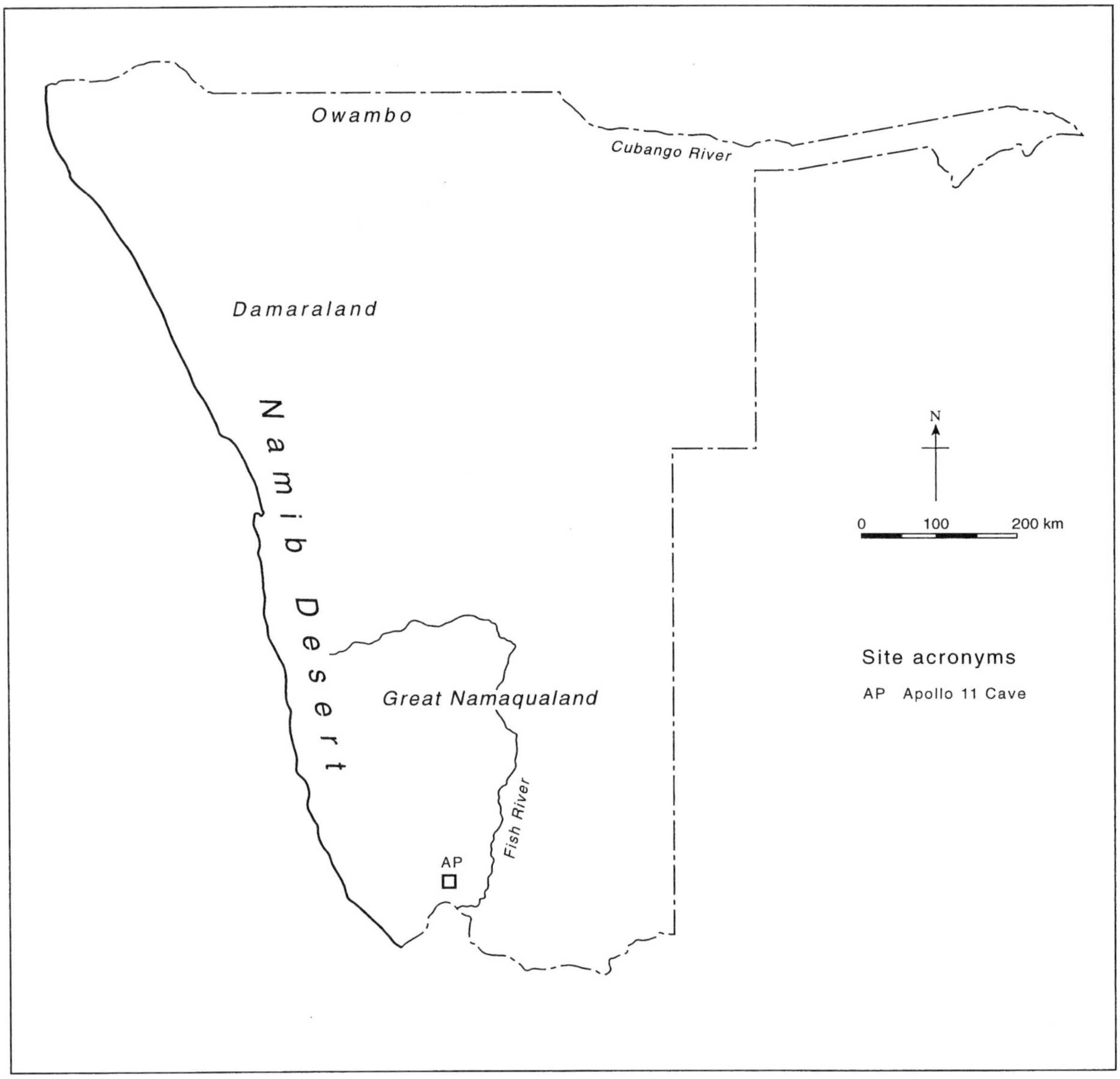

Fig. 33. Location of archaeological sites in Namibia and of the areas there from which the Stone Age collections in the British Museum derive

8. Swaziland

Although R. Jones (1898) described a series of Early and Middle Stone Age artefacts found by Sidney Ryan in the gravels of the Mbabane River and exhibited them to a meeting of the Anthropological Institute of Great Britain and Ireland, the three artefacts in the British Museum collections do not appear to have formed part of this material. His paper and his reference in it (R. Jones 1898: 52) to other artefacts collected in Swaziland by George Leith (qv, Appendix 4), do, however, attest to the early date at which archaeological exploration began in this country (**Fig. 34**). After sporadic collecting of further Early (Johnson 1907, 1908) and Middle Stone Age (e.g. B. Malan 1950) artefacts, more systematic research initially concentrated on the recording of rock art, with limited excavations undertaken at some painted sites (Masson 1961). The first sustained programme of archaeological research in Swaziland, however, emphasized sites in iron ore mines in the Ngwenya area (Dart & Beaumont 1968) and elsewhere. A much more extended project was initiated by David Price-Williams and others in the late 1970s (Price-Williams 1980). Excavation at Sibebe Shelter produced the first well-defined stratigraphic succession of Middle and Later Stone Age assemblages in the country (Price-Williams 1981) and was complemented by study of the archaeology and geomorphology of colluvium-filled dongas, many of which yielded MSA assemblages (Price-Williams & Watson 1982). Further excavations focused on Siphiso Shelter (Barham 1989), one of the first sites in southern Africa at which charcoals were systematically studied as a source of palaoeenvironmental data (Prior & Price-Williams 1985). Though this project produced the first major synthesis of Swaziland prehistory (Barham 1990), it has regrettably not yet been followed up.

MBABANE RIVER, MBABANE DISTRICT APPROXIMATELY CENTRED ON 26° 30'S, 31° 00'E

Wigram Collection, 1897.9-10.1-3

Three artefacts collected from the surface along the Mbabane River, a tributary of the Little Usuthu River, in 1897. The first is of Early Stone Age origin, while the other two are of Middle Stone Age origin.

1 cleaver (in hornfels), 1 unmodified flake (in hornfels, with a faceted platform), 1 mesial section of an unmodified flake-blade (in dolerite).

Additional material Pitt Rivers Museum (Appendix 3).

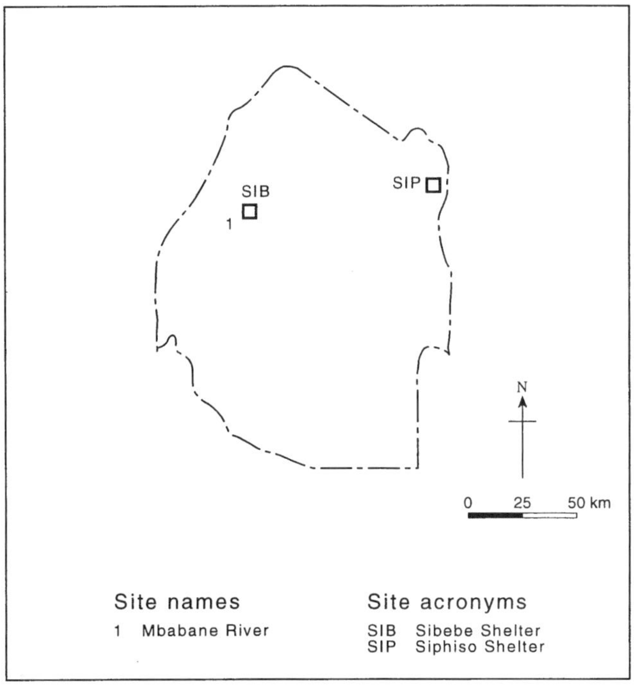

Fig. 34. Location of archaeological sites in Swaziland and of Stone Age collections from there in the British Museum

9. Zimbabwe

As in several other parts of southern Africa, Stone Age archaeological research in Zimbabwe began with geologists, surveyors and others recognising stone artefacts in the course of their professional work (Walker 1995: 17). Eyles (1902), Mennell (1904, 1908) and White (1905) collected stone artefacts and excavated at some of the many rock-shelters in the Matopo Hills in the southwest of the country, and were followed by other workers who emphasized Early Stone Age artefacts from river gravels (e.g. Lamplugh 1905a, 1905b; N. Jones 1938). However, it was Arnold & Jones' (1919) excavation of Bambata Cave (qv), also in the Matopos, that provided the first indications of a local cultural-stratigraphic sequence. Partly on the basis of his observations here, Neville Jones (1926) proposed the first periodization of Zimbabwean prehistory, anticipating the scheme developed a few years later by Goodwin & Van Riet Lowe (1929) for the whole of southern Africa. Encouraged by these early excavations, two major projects were conducted in 1929 in advance, and on behalf, of the second southern African meeting of the British Association for the Advancement of Science: Gertrude Caton-Thompson (1931) carried out further excavations at the key Iron Age site of Great Zimbabwe, while Albert Armstrong (1931) re-excavated Bambata. N. Jones (1930, 1933) later undertook further work in the Matabeleland area and the prominence of the Matopos as the reference point for Zimbabwean prehistory was reinforced by the location in Bulawayo of both the National Museum and the Southern Rhodesian Monuments Commission (Walker 1995: 18).

From the 1950s Stone Age research was for some two decades largely the province of Cran Cooke, who excavated the important open air Middle Stone Age site at Khami (qv; C. Cooke 1957) and several shelters in the Matopos (C. Cooke 1963; C. Cooke & Robinson 1954). He was able to produce a more detailed Stone Age sequence (C. Cooke 1975, 1984), although Walker (1995: 19) points out that some key occurrences were inadequately published or excavated. Despite the difficulties of conducting fieldwork during the Liberation War of the 1970s, Nick Walker (1980) was able to excavate at several rock-shelters in the Matopos, notably Nswatugi (qv), Pomongwe, Bambata (qv) and The Cave of Bees. In addition to developing a synthetic model of LSA land-use and settlement-subsistence strategies in the region over the past 12 000 years (Walker 1995), his research has also helped to define the introduction of domestic small stock and pottery into southern Africa (Walker 1983), obtained some indications of the antiquity of the local rock art tradition (Walker 1987) and clarified Cooke's observations on the Middle Stone Age sequence in Zimbabwe (Walker 1980, 1990).

Though the Matopos have witnessed more concentrated Stone Age research than other parts of Zimbabwe, important excavations were undertaken in Mashonaland as early as the 1920s, notably by Gardner (1928) at Gokomere (qv) and by C. Cooke (1971, 1978, 1979) at Zombepata, Redcliff and Diana's Vow respectively. Robinson (1954) excavated several sites in the Inyanga (qv) area of the eastern highlands, while Walker & Wadley (1984) reported an early microlithic LSA assemblage from Duncombe Farm. Since independence in 1980 the main focus of Zimbabwean archaeology has been the study of the Iron Age (e.g. Pikirayi 1993; Pwiti 1996). The limited Stone Age research that has been carried out includes a survey of sites in Hwange National Park (Klimowicz & Haynes 1996), analysis of the spatial organization of sites in Mashonaland (Bollong 1986), an overview of the local MSA (Larsson 1996) and, most significantly, an extensive programme of rock art studies marked by two major syntheses and several further papers (Garlake 1987, 1995).

Zimbabwe is represented in the British Museum southern African Stone Age collections by well over 4000 individual artefacts, the majority of them from the important site of Bambata Cave in the Matopo Hills of Matabeleland South (**Fig. 35**). These artefacts form part of the Armstrong Collection and Manchester Museum, ex Armstrong, Collection, and come from the excavations carried out at this site in 1929 by Armstrong (1931) on behalf of the British Association for the Advancement of Science. In addition to holding most of the artefacts recovered from Bambata, which has given its name to both a Middle Stone Age industry and to a pottery tradition associated with some of the earliest pastoralists in southern Africa, the British Museum also retains the tracings made during excavation of the paintings on the cave walls. Nswatugi Cave, another key site for understanding the prehistory of the Matopos (Walker 1995) is represented in the Armstrong and Favell, ex Bulawayo Museum, Collections. The much smaller Armstrong Collection from Gumali and the F. White Collections from Matopos Caves 1 and 2 are also of particular importance since most of the other artefacts from these sites cannot now be traced in Zimbabwe itself (Walker 1995). The British Museum collections from Zimbabwe also include artefacts from several other sites that have been of importance in the development of Stone Age archaeology in Zimbabwe. Among those originally excavated by Father Gardner are Driefontein (King Collection, ex Gardner), Gokomere Cave (Armstrong Collection, ex Gardner, and Favell Collection, ex Armstrong, ex Gardner). The Early Stone Age collections from Gweru Kopje (Armstrong, Bulawayo Museum and Favell Collections) come from one of the earliest sites to have been excavated with a view to obtaining stratigraphic information for this earliest phase of Zimbabwean prehistory. Hope Fountain, type-site of N. Jones's (1929) Hope Fountain Industry is also well represented in the Armstrong, Braunholtz, Favell and Jones Collections.

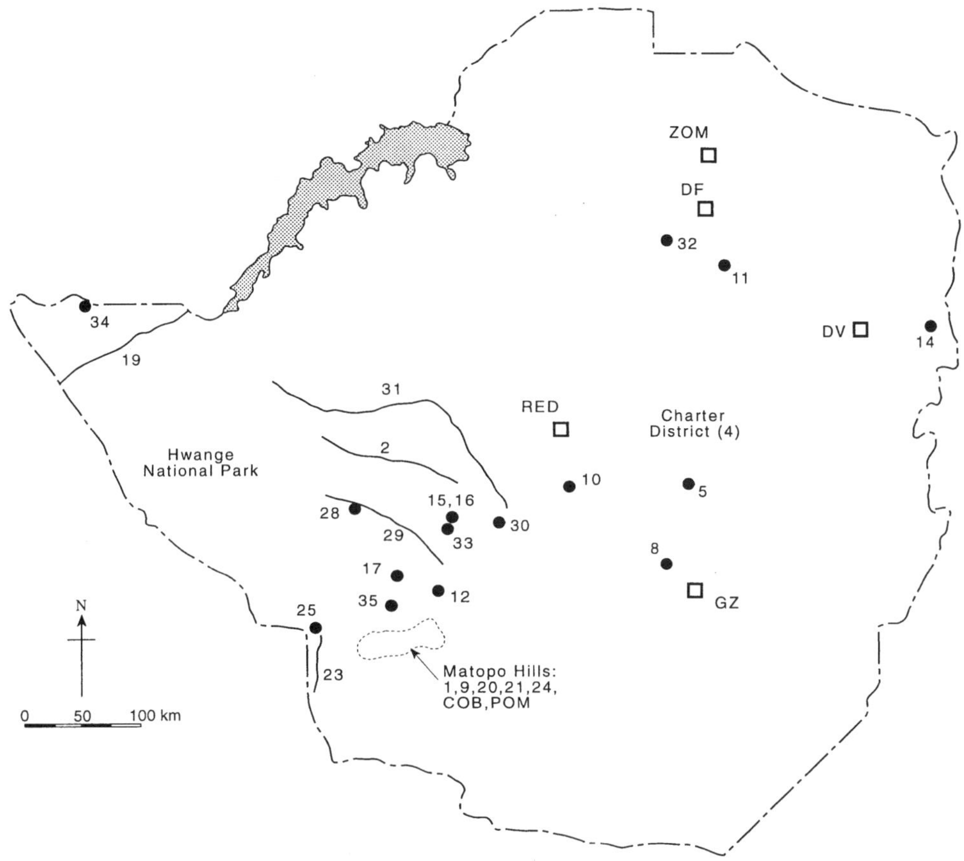

Site names

1 Bambata Cave
2 Bubi River
3 Carmarlo Drift - precise location unknown
4 Charter District
5 Driefontein
6 Ematjeni - precise location unknown
7 Embusini - precise location unknown
8 Gokomere Cave
9 Gumali Cave
10 Gweru Kopje
11 Harare
12 Hope Fountain
13 Imbusini Brook - precise location unknown
14 Inyanga
15 Inyati
16 Inyati (Huckle's Farm) - precise location unknown
17 Khami
18 Matabeleland, No Further Provenance - location unknown
19 Matetsi Valley
20 Matopos Cave 1
21 Matopos Cave 2
22 Mauchini Brook - precise location unknown
23 Mpakwe River
24 Nswatugi Cave
25 Plumtree
26 Pommeru (Grave site) - location unknown
27 Powola Brook - precise location unknown
28 Sawmills
29 Sawmills River
30 Shangani
31 Shangani River
32 Trelawney
33 Turk Mine
34 Victoria Falls
35 Westacre Farm
36 Zimbabwe, No Further Provenance - location unknown

Site acronyms

COB Cave of Bees
DF Duncombe Farm
DV Diana's Vow
GZ Great Zimbabwe
POM Pomongwe
RED Redcliff
ZOM Zombepata

Fig. 35. Location of archaeological sites in Zimbabwe and of Stone Age collections from there in the British Museum

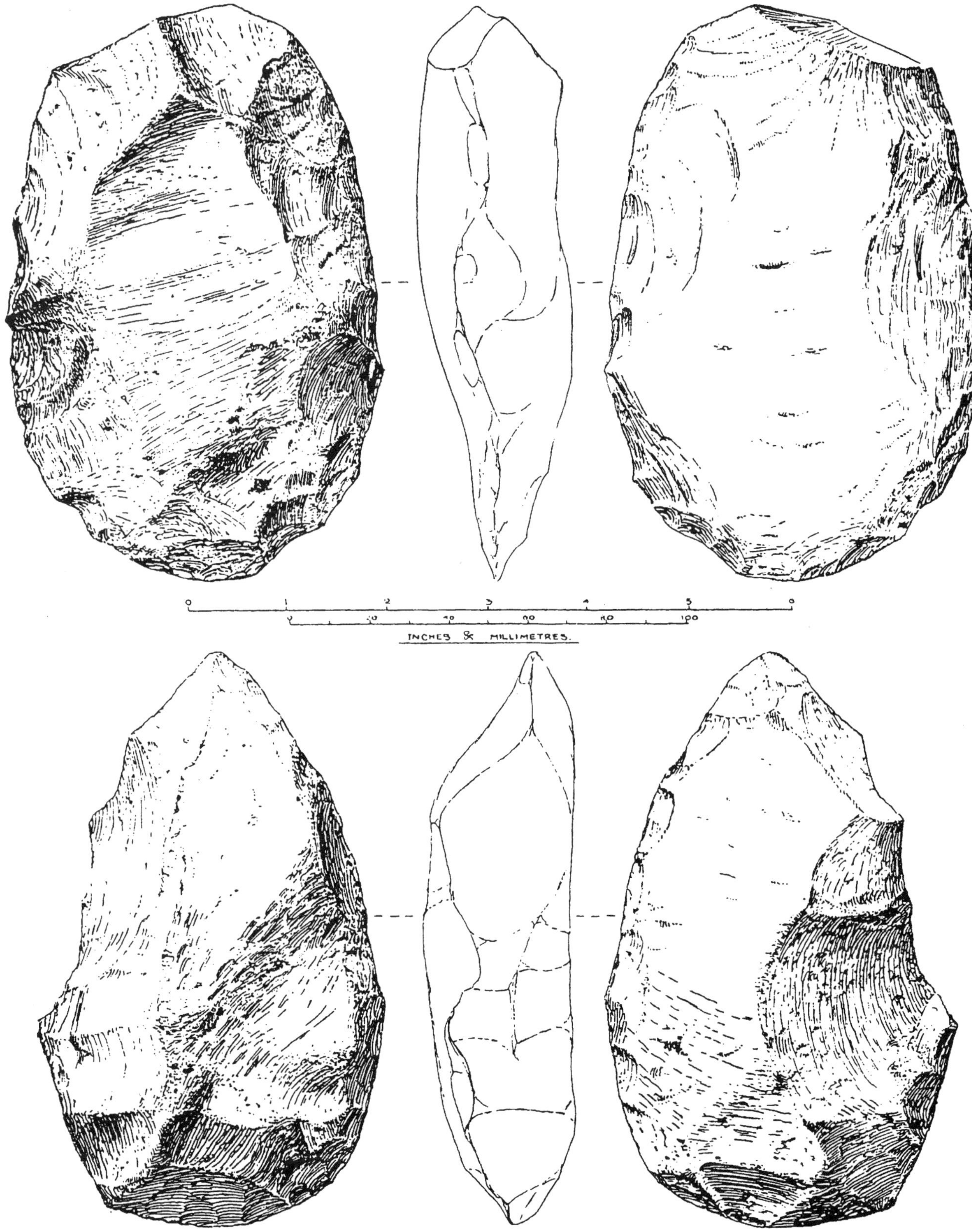

Fig. 36. Early Stone Age artefacts from the Armstronge Collection from Bambata Cave, Zimbabwe (after Armstronge 1931: Fig.14).Handaxes.

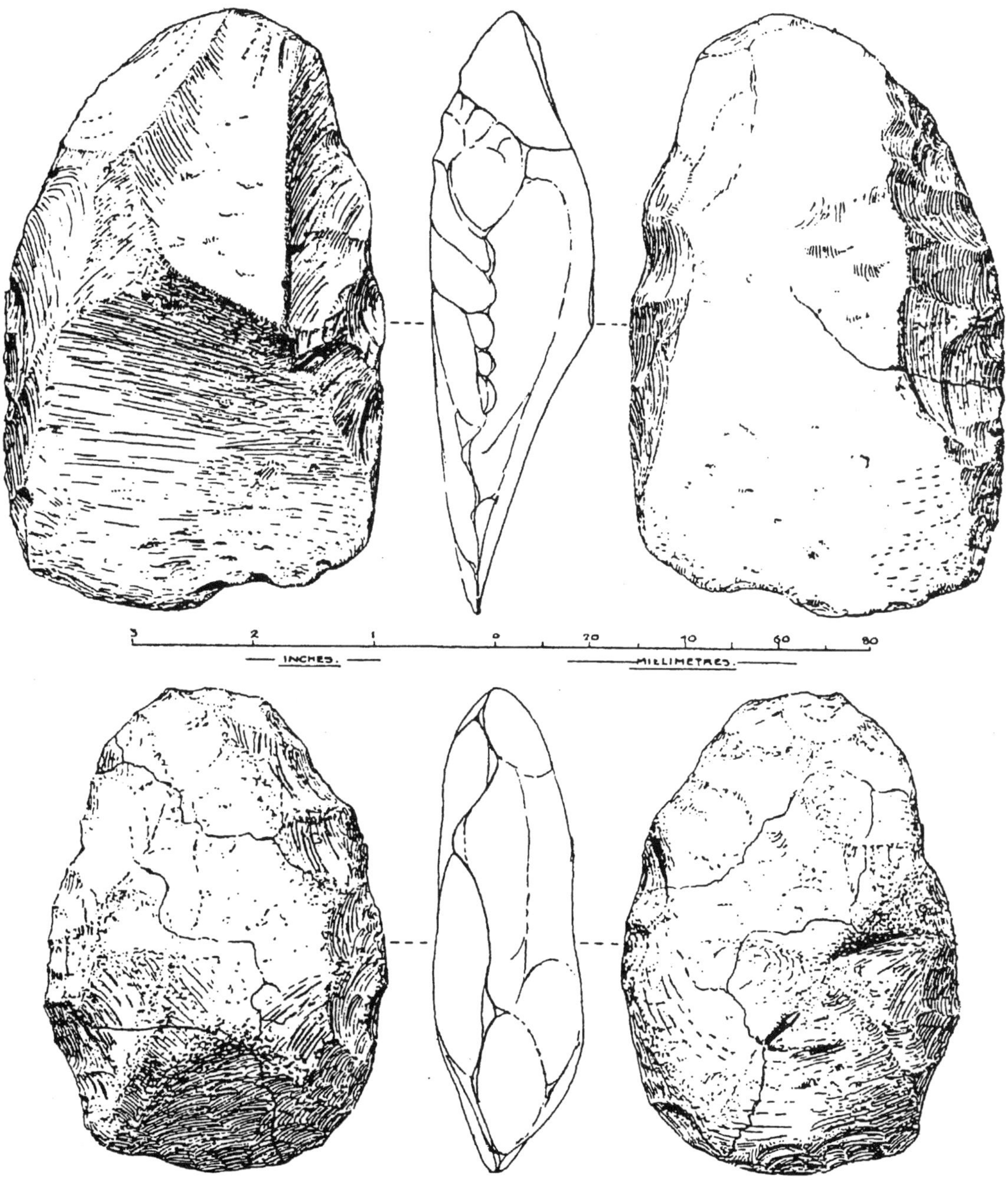

Fig. 37. Early Stone Age artefacts from the Armstronge Collection from Bambata Cave, Zimbabwe (after Armstronge 1915: Fig.15).Cleaver and biface.

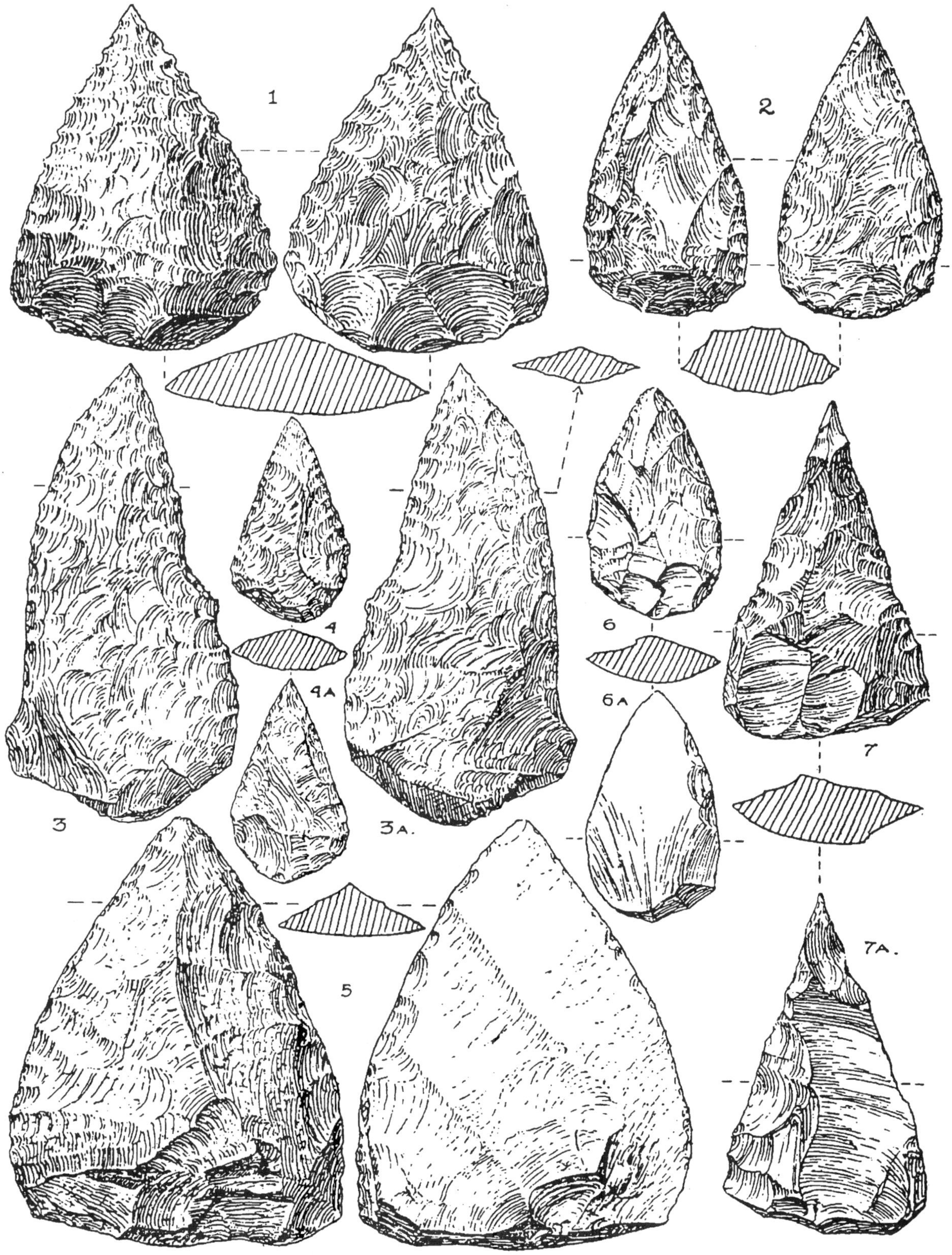

Fig. 38. Middle Stone Age artefacts from the Armstrong Collection from Bambata Cave, Zimbabwe (after Armstrong 1931: Fig 11). Bifacial and unifacial points.

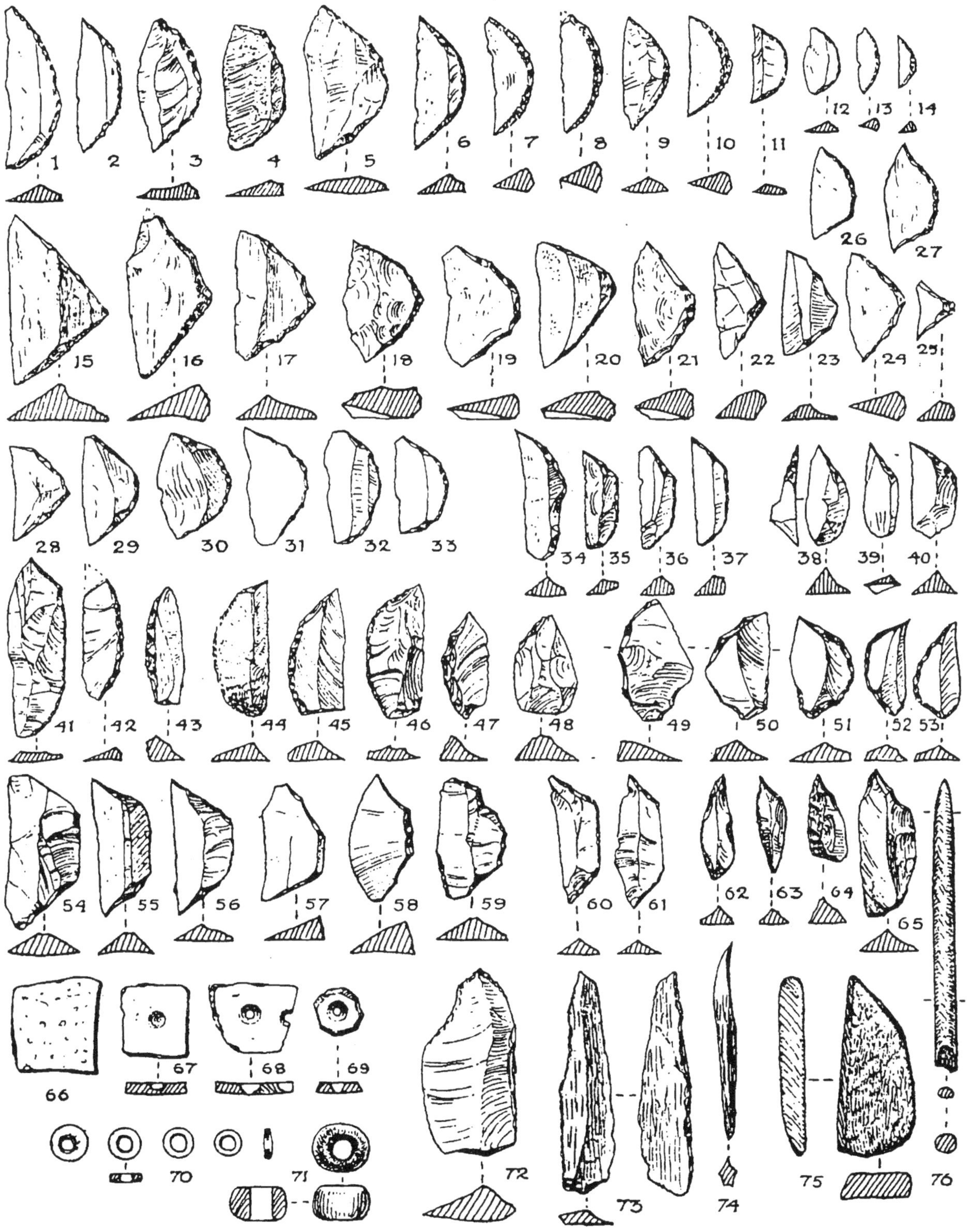

Fig. 39. Late Stone Age artefacts from the Armstrong Collection from Bambata Cave, Zimbabwe (after Armstrong 1931: Fig 8).Backed microliths, bores, ostrich eggshell beads and blanks, blades,ochre pencil,bone pin.

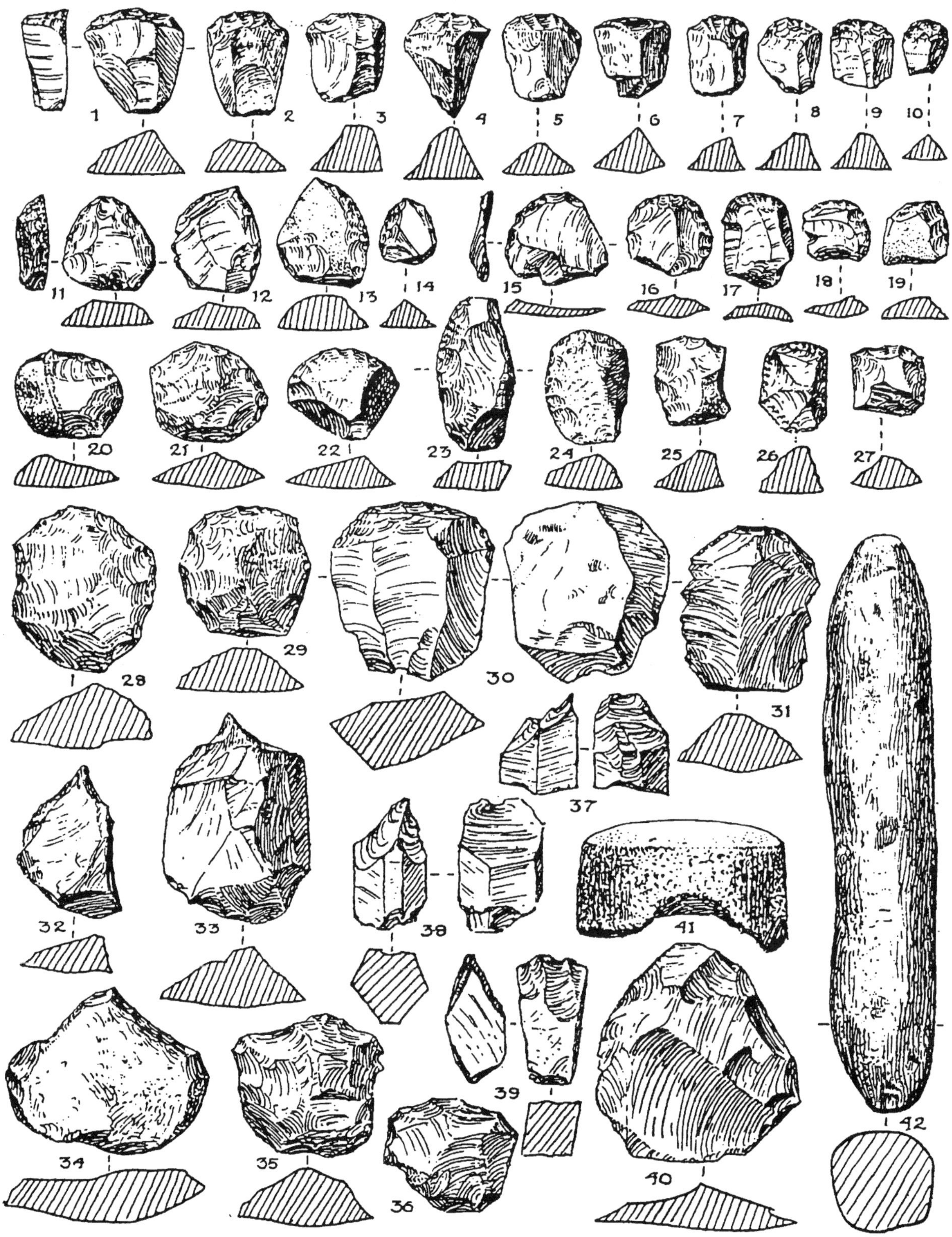

Fig. 40. Late Stone Age artefacts from the Armstrong Collection from Bambata Cave, Zimbabwe (after Armstrong 1931: Fig 9).Scrapers,awls,adzes,piéces esquillées(?),pestle,hammerstone(?).

BAMBATA CAVE, MATABELELAND SOUTH PROVINCE 20° 30'S, 28° 25'E

Bambata Cave is located on a prominent hill in the Matopo Hills of southwestern Zimbabwe (Walker 1995: 152). It forms a perfectly shaped hollow with a floor area of 120 square metres and has a deep deposit, first excavated by Arnold & Jones (1919). The Rhodesian Scientific Expedition of 1929 carried out further excavations at the site, directed by Albert Armstrong (1931). Since then, smaller scale excavations have been undertaken by N. Jones (1940) and by Walker (1980, 1983, 1995).

The site has impressive paintings on its walls. These were traced by Armstrong (1931) and these tracings, done in colour, form part of the British Museum collection from the site. The paintings have subsequently been described by Cooke (1959), Garlake (1987) and Walker (in press b). They include a thickset equid, possibly a representation of the now extinct Cape horse (*Equus capensis*), which would imply that at least some of the images may be as much as 10 000 years old. Other large, faint figures may be of Iron Age origin and are probably associated with rain-making rituals by recent farming groups (Walker 1995).

The assemblages excavated by Armstrong (1931) were distributed to a number of museums, including the British Museum. Through a process of exchange, largely with Manchester Museum, almost all the material from them known to be in Britain has now been concentrated in the British Museum. Its quantity precluded analysis during preparation of this Gazetteer, though it has been examined recently by Walker (1995: 152). Armstrong (1931) distinguished between a Lower and an Upper Cave Earth, together totalling 6 m in depth and containing Middle and Early Stone Age artefacts (**Figs. 36 - 38**). Disconformably overlying this sequence was up to a metre of grey ash containing Later Stone Age artefacts (**Figs. 39 - 40**), which Walker (1995: 154) has since been able to subdivide into five units. Both he and N. Jones (1940) also identified a further carbonaceous unit between this grey ash deposit and the Upper Cave Earth. Radiocarbon dates from the site are few, but indicate that much of the grey ash deposit is of late-middle Holocene age (Walker 1995: 73; 155).

Bambata is best known for two reasons: first, its long Middle Stone Age sequence (reviewed in Sampson 1974: 193-196), second, the presence of a distinctive pottery tradition now also identified elsewhere in the eastern part of southern Africa (Walker 1983). Though the MSA assemblages are undated, they are clearly of considerable antiquity. Initial but brief Later Stone Age occupation of the site by makers of Nswatugi assemblages was probably around 9000 BP. The more recent pre-ceramic LSA occupation, featuring much higher numbers of backed microliths and artefacts of worked bone and ostrich eggshell, belongs to the Amadzimba Industry (Walker 1995: 73).

Bambata Cave is also important for having one of the earliest dates for domestic livestock (almost certainly sheep) south of the Zambezi. The associated ceramics are thin, highly decorated and have affinities with Early Iron Age pottery (Huffman 1994). Generally known as Bambata Ware after the site, this pottery has been found in northern Botswana (Huffman 1994), elsewhere in Zimbabwe (Mupira 1994) and as far south as Gauteng (Wadley 1987). Its precise age, associations and significance remain matters of current research, but it seems likely to be linked to the southward spread of both pastoralism and pottery into southwestern and southeastern southern Africa around the beginning of the Common Era.

Armstrong Collection, 1959.7-12.1-1755

This collection is estimated to total some 3000 artefacts, but these have not been examined or counted in detail for the present study.

Manchester Museum Collection, ex Armstrong, P1987.4-2.1-3

This collection totals 141 artefacts. However, like the main Armstrong Collection from Bambata, they were not examined or counted in detail in the preparation of this Catalogue.

Additional material Department of Ethnography, British Museum (Appendix 1). Cambridge University Museum, Institute of Archaeology, Manchester Museum, Liverpool Museum, Pitt Rivers Museum, Sheffield City Museum (Appendix 3).

BUBI (*RUBIE*) RIVER, MATABELELAND SOUTH PROVINCE FROM 19° 34'S, 28° 54'E TO 18 59'S, 27 51'E

Christy Collection, ex Anderson, +7914

Culturally undiagnostic, the extensive edge damage on this lightly patinated flake is remarkably fresh-looking and thus not the result of use.

1 unmodified flake (in hornfels, found in the river bed in 1879).

Additional material ? Liverpool Museum (Appendix 3).

CARMARLO DRIFT, MATABELELAND SOUTH PROVINCE APPROXIMATELY 20° 34'S, 28° 19'E

Not precisely located, despite the directions for his marches that A.A. Anderson (1888: 333-341) gives, this ford was located 'on the topmost ridge of the watershed of the Mopolo at an elevation of 4360 feet (1340 m) above sea-level' (A.A. Anderson 1888: 333) at least 12 miles (19 km) west of the Matabele capital at KwaBulawayo.

Christy Collection, ex Anderson, +7913

Two culturally undiagnostic flakes found in 1877.
2 unmodified flakes (1 in hornfels, 1 in opaline).

CHARTER DISTRICT, NO FURTHER PROVENANCE, MIDLANDS PROVINCE

W. H. Kenny collected stone artefacts in the 'Bembesi and Charter Districts' over a period of eight years between 1904 and 1912, presenting them to the Bulawayo Museum; Mennell's (1904) report on 'Some stone implements in the Rhodesia museum' was largely inspired by his collection. Regrettably, Kenny did not provide any further details on the exact locations at which these artefacts were collected (N. Jones 1949: 10), although the Charter District was centred around the town of Enkeldoorn (modern Chivhu). MacGregor (1921) was the first of several collectors to find comparable Early Stone Age artefacts at sites in the Bembesi Valley, many of which are now recognised as part of the Sangoan Complex (Sampson 1974: 107).

Bulawayo Museum Collection, ex W. H. Kenny, 1921.7-28.2-3

Two artefacts of Early Stone Age origin, both marked 'W. H. Kenney'.
2 handaxes (1 in chert, 1 in vein quartz).

The Geological Museum Collection, ex W. H. Kenny, P1989.3-1.111-121

A group of 11 artefacts of Early Stone Age origin.
2 cleavers (1 in quartzite, 1 in vein quartz), 6 handaxes (2 in chert, 1 in granite, 1 in hornfels, 1 in microgranite, 1 in vein quartz), 1 large irregular core (in siltstone), 2 disc cores (1 in chert, 1 in hornfels).

DRIEFONTEIN MASVINGO PROVINCE APPROXIMATELY 19° 29'S, 30° 54'E

Gardner (*in litt.* 22.1.1931) reports that he had discovered stone artefacts on the surface of the escarpment on the western side of the farm Driefontein near Felixburg, one of the Jesuit missions at which he worked. However, the accession date of the King collection makes it clear that Gardner had sent examples of his finds to his fellow Jesuit several years before both this and the latter's visit to Zimbabwe in 1931/32.

King Collection, ex Gardner, (Ethno) 1926.5-7.1-85

A mixed assemblage of 82 Early and Middle Stone Age artefacts, the former represented by handaxes and cleavers, the latter probably by flakes with faceted platforms, though many individual artefacts cannot be considered diagnostic. Two pieces of unworked stone are also present.

Table 54. The King Collection, ex Gardner, from Driefontein.

	Opaline	Chert	Hornfels	Silcrete	Vein quartz	Ironstone	Total
Handaxes	-	1	-	-	-	19	20
Cleavers	-	-	-	-	-	4	4
Other bifaces	-	-	-	-	-	2	2
Chunks	-	-	-	-	1	1	2
Irregular cores	-	5	-	-	1	9	15
Disc cores	-	2	1	-	-	-	3
Levallois cores	-	4	-	-	-	-	4
Flakes	4	8	-	2	3	9	26
Utilised flakes	1	-	-	-	-	-	1
Scrapers	-	2	-	-	-	3	5
Total	5	22	1	2	5	47	82

This collection also includes two mollusc shells and several fragments of mollusc shell which it has not been possible to identify.

Additional material Department of Ethnography, British Museum (Appendix 1).Cambridge University Museum (Appendix 3).

EMATJENI RIVER, MATABELELAND SOUTH PROVINCE

This river flows within the Matopo Hills outside Bulawayo.

Jones Collection, (Ethno) 1928.10-15.12-13

Two Early Stone Age artefacts, both made in hornfels and in a rolled condition.
1 cleaver, 1 handaxe.

Additional material Cambridge University Museum (Appendix 3).

EMBUSINI, MATABELELAND SOUTH PROVINCE

Jones Collection, (Ethno) 1928.10-15.5-9

A group of five Early Stone Age artefacts from a locality within the Matopo Hills outside Bulawayo. Handaxes and cleavers from here are illustrated by N. Jones (1949: Figs. 18 and 19), who refers to them coming from 'gravel lying beneath a black alluvium' in streams draining the edge of the Kalahari (N. Jones 1949: 42).
1 cleaver (in chert), 4 handaxes (1 in dolerite, 2 in granite, 1 in hornfels).

Additional material Cambridge University Museum (Embusini River) (Appendix 3).

GOKOMERE CAVE MASVINGO PROVINCE 20° 02'S, 30° 49'E

Gokomere Cave, a painted shelter close to Masvingo, was completely excavated by Gardner (1928), who found a thin Middle Stone Age occurrence underlying a more substantial Later Stone Age deposit.

Armstrong Collection, ex Gardner, 1959.7-12

A large collection of 162 stone artefacts, mostly of scrapers and backed microliths comparable to those found in the Nswatugi and Amadzimba Industries of the Later Stone Age of the Matopo Hills (*cf.* Walker 1995). The single dolerite flake-blade and the five flakes with faceted platforms are of Middle Stone Age origin. Although it is possible that they may have been acquired by scavenging (for recycling ?) of an older site, the underlying Middle Stone Age assemblage is another possible source of these artefacts.

Table 55. The Armstrong Collection, ex Gardner, from Gokomere Cave.

	Opaline	Vein quartz	Crystal quartz	Hornfels	Chert	Dolerite	Other	Total
Chunks	-	2	1	1	-	-	-	4
Irregular cores	5	5	3	1	-	-	-	14
Bladelet cores	-	-	2	-	-	-	-	2
Flat bladelet cores	-	-	1	-	-	-	-	1
Disc cores	1	-	-	-	-	-	-	1
Core-reduced pieces	1	2	1	-	-	-	-	4
Core rejuvenation flakes	1	1	-	-	-	-	-	2
Flakes	21	26	27	-	1	4	2	81
Flake-blades	-	-	-	-	-	1	-	1
Bladelets	-	1	5	1	-	-	-	7
Proximal sections	1	-	-	-	-	-	-	1
Utilised flakes	-	-	-	-	-	-	1	1
Scrapers	7	17	12	-	-	-	-	36
Retouched bladelets	-	-	-	1	-	-	-	1
Backed flakes	-	1	-	-	-	-	-	1
Backed bladelets	-	-	-	2	-	-	-	2
Miscellaneous retouched pieces	1	-	-	2	-	-	-	3
Total	38	55	52	8	1	5	3	162

NB. The category 'Other' in this Table includes granite, quartzite and sandstone.
Two potsherds are of Iron Age origin. The first is a rim sherd with a carination and everted lip. The rim is burnished and there is an 8 mm wide band of hatched incised decoration at the neck immediately above the carination. The second sherd has an everted, flat rim and a body that is completely burnished. Irregular vertical stab marks are closely spaced together on the neck and are set between two parallel horizontal grooves. Both sherds are grit-tempered and black to dark grey in colour, but the second sherd has a coarser fabric than the first.
Also present in this collection are:

6 unworked quartz crystals, 2 pieces of yellow ochre, 3 pieces of red ochre (2 of them ground).

Organic finds are:

1 distal tibia fragment of an unidentified wild bovid, 3 teeth from unidentified wild bovids, several undecorated fragments of ostrich eggshell, and several ostrich eggshell beads.

Favell Collection, ex Armstrong, ex Gardner, 1936.5-8.79-96

A small group of 40 artefacts and 1 unworked piece of stone that derives from the same Later Stone Age microlithic industrial tradition as that represented in the Armstrong Collection from this site. Almost all the artefacts are scrapers and backed microliths made in quartz.

Table 56. The Favell Collection, ex Armstrong, ex Gardner, from Gokomere Cave.

	Opaline	Hornfels	Vein quartz	Crystal quartz	Total
Flakes	-	-	-	4	4
Bladelet mesial sections	-	-	-	1	1
Scrapers	1	-	15	1	17
Backed flakes	-	-	-	1	1
Backed bladelets	-	1	1	-	2
Segments	1	-	7	7	15
Total	2	1	23	14	40

Additional material Department of Ethnography, British Museum (Appendix 1).Cambridge University Museum, Pitt Rivers Museum (Appendix 3).

GUMALI (*GUMANI, IKOMENE*), MATABELELAND SOUTH PROVINCE 20 31'S, 28 27'E

This is a wide rock-shelter with a few surviving paintings under a huge boulder a few kilometres from Bambata (qv). Armstrong (1931) excavated here in order to check the correlation of rock-paintings and cultural material in the archaeological deposits that he had inferred at Bambata. He describes two layers, an upper 6 inches (15 cm) associated with a 'Wilton' assemblage and a further 6 inches (15 cm) of underlying deposit associated with a 'Middle Bambata' occupation. The two were separated by a sterile gravel and the remaining deposit was also sterile to bedrock. Walker (1995: 188) comments that 'the excavated material is no longer available', but that three large convex scrapers survive in Zimbabwean museum collections.

It is clear from Armstrong's (1931) paper reporting the activities of the 1929 Rhodesian Archaeological Expedition that, beyond working at Bambata, only three further rock-shelters were test-excavated: Nswatugi Cave (qv), Gumani Cave and the Cave of the Trumpeteer. The latter only produced evidence of Iron Age occupation, whereas at Gumani two distinct layers were found as described above. The fact that the material in the British Museum's Armstrong Collection provenanced to Ikomene is sub-divided stratigraphically in precisely the manner described for Gumani Cave in Armstrong's (1931) paper and that this represents a microlithic Later Stone Age component ('Wilton') overlying a mixed Later and Middle Stone Age one ('Middle Bambata') suggests that Ikomene and Gumani are one and the same site.

Armstrong Collection, 1959.7-12

A limited amount of stratigraphic information is available from this site and the material in the British Museum can be divided into three components as follows.

Surface finds

An iron pin, four blue glass beads and two potsherds. Both the sherds are rimsherds, black in colour and burnished. One of the rims is much more strongly everted than the other and this sherd is also steeply carinated. This material is clearly of recent Iron Age origin.

From the 0-6 in (0-15 cm) level of the deposit

This assemblage numbers 103 artefacts and belongs to the mid-/late Holocene microlithic tradition of the Later Stone Age represented in the Matopo Hills by the Nswatugi and Amadzimba Industries (Walker 1995). The artefacts are mostly in opaline and quartz.

Table 57. Artefacts in the Armstrong Collection from the upper 6 inches (15 cm) of the deposit at Gumali (*Gumani, Ikomene*) Cave.

	Opaline	Hornfels	Vein quartz	Crystal quartz	Total
Irregular cores	-	-	1	1	2
Bladelet cores	-	-	1	-	1
Flat bladelet cores	-	-	1	-	1
Core-reduced pieces	-	-	2	1	3
Flakes	26	2	19	16	63
Bladelets	-	-	3	1	4
Proximal sections (blades)	3	-	2	-	5

Table 57 cont. Artefacts in the Armstrong Collection from the upper 6 inches (15 cm) of the deposit at Gumali (*Gumani, Ikomene*) Cave.

Mesial sections (blades)	1	-	1	-	2
Scrapers	13	-	1	-	14
Backed flakes	2	-	-	-	2
Backed bladelets	2	-	1	-	3
Backed points	1	-	-	-	1
Segments	-	-	1	-	1
Miscellaneous retouched pieces	1	-	-	-	1
Total	49	2	33	19	103

Also present are the following:
6 unworked quartz crystals, 1 piece of yellow ochre, 2 two pieces of undecorated and unworked ostrich eggshell (1 burnt), 1 lower premolar or molar milktooth of an equid, 1 perforated phalange and 1 unidentifiable fragment of bone

From the 6-12 in (15-30 cm) level of the deposit
This seems to be a mixed Later and Middle Stone Age assemblage numbering 60 artefacts. The only clearly MSA artefacts are the single flake-blade butt, two flakes with faceted platforms and the unilaterally retouched knife. The scrapers, on the other hand, do not show any clear differences in size or morphology from those in the overlying horizon just described.

Table 58. Artefacts in the Armstrong Collection from the 6-12" (15-30 cm) level at Gumali (*Gumani, Ikomene*) Cave.

	Opaline	Hornfels	Vein quartz	Crystal quartz	Quartzite	Dolerite	Total
Chunks	-	-	-	1	-	-	1
Irregular cores	-	-	2	1	-	-	3
Bladelet cores	2	-	-	-	-	-	2
Core-reduced pieces	3	-	3	4	-	-	10
Flakes	12	6	9	5	2	1	35
Proximal sections (bladelets)	1	-	-	-	-	-	1
Proximal sections (flake-blades)	1	-	-	-	-	-	1
Notched flakes	1	-	-	-	-	1	2
Scrapers	3	-	1	-	-	-	4
Unilateral knives	-	-	1	-	-	-	1
Total	23	6	16	11	2	2	60

Also present are: 2 unworked quartz crystals, 1 fragment of burnt, undecorated and unworked ostrich eggshell.

Additional material ? Igumana Rock Shelter, Cambridge University Museum (Appendix 3).

GWERU (*GWELO*) KOPJE, MIDLANDS PROVINCE 19° 28'S, 29° 40'E
The kopje at Gweru is a well-known landmark on the western side of the city and was extensively quarried for road metal in the early 20th century; N. Jones (1949: 68) comments that the 'town...is paved with stone implements'. Long known as a site at which these artefacts could be collected, Gardner and Stapleton (1934) excavated here in 1932 to try and resolve their relative age, but concluded that degree of weathering was an unreliable criterion. However, their excavation, conducted at the base of the kopje, suggested that handaxes were concentrated towards its bottom and that flakes tended to become smaller with time. Cooke (1968) subsequently carried out a further excavation at the site, showing that an older Acheulean occurrence underlay a more recent Sangoan one, but the finds from this site have since been lost (Sampson 1974: 138).

Armstrong Collection, 1960.11-4.1-9
A group of 14 banded ironstone artefacts, most likely all of Early Stone Age origin. The handwriting on all of the Armstrong Collection artefacts from this site is the same as that on the artefacts in the Favell Collection from Gweru Kopje. Two of the flakes are labelled 'base', one flake and one of the cores 'middle' and a fourth flake 'top', presumably reflecting their location on the kopje. One unworked piece of stone is also present.
1 cleaver, 1 handaxe, 1 further bifacially worked implement, 3 irregular cores, 6 unmodified flakes, 2 retouched flakes.

Bulawayo Museum Collection, ex W. H. Kenny, 1921.7-28.4-7

Four artefacts, of which at least the point and probably also the unmodified flake are of Middle Stone Age origin; both have faceted platforms.
1 core-reduced piece (in chert), 1 unmodified flake (in chert), 1 scraper (in quartzite), 1 point (in chert).

Favell Collection, 1936.5-8.41-42

Two artefacts in banded ironstone, of which the flake is marked in ink 'Gwelo Kopje 1929 (top)'; the handwriting is the same as on the artefacts in the Armstrong Collection from this site. Neither artefact is culturally diagnostic.
1 irregular core, 1 utilised flake.

Additional material Cambridge University Museum (Appendix 3).

HARARE (*SALISBURY*), MASHONALAND EAST PROVINCE 17° 50'S, 31° 02'E

Armstrong Collection, 1959.7-12

Three quartzite artefacts probably all of Middle Stone Age origin.
1 irregular core, 1 unmodified flake, 1 point

Additional material Pitt Rivers Museum (Salisbury; Salisbury, Emerald Hill) (Appendix 3).

HOPE FOUNTAIN, MATABELELAND SOUTH PROVINCE 20° 14'S, 28° 40'E

This is the type-site for the 'Hope Fountain Industry' recognised here by Neville Jones (1929, 1930), who came to work as a missionary at the mission station here in 1912. Great numbers of artefacts occur both on the surface and immediately below it, mostly made in a very hard chert. N. Jones (1930) stressed that handaxes were found here together with so-called rostro-carinate implements and a wide variety of points and scrapers, but his argument that this should be recognised as a separate 'culture' won little support (Clark 1959: 128); it is now subsumed within the Sangoan Complex. The material from this site in the British Museum does include a few bifaces, but, perhaps reflecting a selectivity in collection, emphasizes the Middle Stone Age features of the Sangoan: flake-blades and formally retouched tools are of MSA character.

Armstrong Collection, 1959.7-12

A group of 133 artefacts and 17 unworked pieces of stone. The artefacts are all in rolled condition and mostly in chert. The handwriting on the artefacts is in the same hand as on those in the Favell and Jones Collections from this site. Like them, this collection has strong Middle Stone Age features, although two handaxes are also present. Although several formal tool classes were distinguished, the overall lack of standardization of retouch and morphology makes it difficult to be sure whether some artefacts should have been classified in one class or another.

Table 59. The Armstrong Collection from Hope Fountain.

	Chert	Hornfels	Siltstone/ mudstone	Banded ironstone	Total
Handaxes	1	-	-	1	2
Chunks	-	1	-	-	1
Irregular cores	8	3	-	-	11
Core rejuvenation flakes	2	-	-	-	2
Crested blades	1	-	-	-	1
Flakes	11	-	2	-	13
Utilised flakes	2	-	-	-	2
Utilised flake-blades	1	-	-	-	1
Notched flakes	10	1	-	-	11
Scrapers	2	1	-	1	4
Adzes	8	-	-	-	8
Backed flakes	7	-	-	-	7
Knives - unilateral	8	1	-	-	9
Knives - bilateral	16	1	-	-	17
Points	34	1	-	-	35
Miscellaneous retouched pieces	9	-	-	-	9
Total	120	9	2	2	133

Braunholtz Collection, (Ethno) 1930.1-24

A group of 12 artefacts and two unworked pieces of stone, all in rolled condition. All the flakes have faceted platforms. Along with the presence of a bilaterally retouched knife, this suggests that this collection is of Middle Stone Age origin.
2 irregular cores (in chert), 2 unmodified flakes (1 each in chert and hornfels), 1 notched flake (in chert), 4 scrapers (3 in chert, 1 in hornfels), 2 points (1 each in chert and hornfels), 1 bilaterally retouched knife (in chert).

Favell Collection, 1936.5-8.24-40 + additional

A group of 36 artefacts all in rolled condition. The handwriting on the artefacts is in the same hand as on those in the Armstrong and Jones Collections from this site. The formal tools are all typical of the Middle Stone Age, although the handaxe illustrates once again the 'transitional' features of the assemblages from Hope Fountain. All the artefacts are in chert unless otherwise stated.
1 handaxe, 4 irregular cores, 1 core rejuvenation flake (in hornfels), 1 unmodified flake, 5 scrapers, (including 2 in hornfels), 15 points (including 1 in hornfels), 3 unilaterally retouched knives, 5 bilaterally retouched knives, 1 miscellaneously retouched piece.

Jones Collection, (Ethno) 1930.1-13.1-13

A small group of 14 artefacts distinguishable from the remainder of the Hope Fountain material in either the Jones or the other collections from this site because they are both rolled *and* patinated. The handwriting on them is in the same hand as on those in the Armstrong and Favell Collections from this site.
1 handaxe (in chert), 1 cleaver (in chert), 3 irregular cores (in chert), 3 unmodified flakes (2 in chert, 1 in hornfels), 3 scrapers (1 each in banded ironstone, chert and hornfels), 2 unilaterally retouched knives (1 each in chert and hornfels), 1 bilaterally retouched knife (in chert).

Jones Collection, (Ethno) 1930.1-13.14-104

A group of 85 artefacts, all of Middle Stone Age origin to judge from the range of formal tools present. The handwriting on the artefacts is in the same hand as on those in the Armstrong and Favell Collections from this site.

Table 60. Middle Stone Age artefacts in the Jones Collection from Hope Fountain.

	Chert	Hornfels	Siltstone/ mudstone	Sandstone	Total
Irregular cores	15	3	-	-	18
Flakes	3	-	1	-	4
Flake-blades	-	-	1	-	1
Notched flakes	3	-	3	-	6
Scrapers	22	3	2	1	28
Backed flakes	5	-	-	-	5
Knives - unilateral	3	-	-	-	3
Knives - bilateral	10	1	-	-	11
Points	7	1	1	-	9
Total	68	8	8	1	85

Jones Collection, 1930.10-10.1-19

A group of 9 artefacts in rolled condition. The formal tools are all of Middle Stone Age origin, although the handaxe again indicates that the Hope Fountain material is transitional between Early and Middle Stone Age lithic technologies. All are in chert except where otherwise stated.
1 cleaver, 6 irregular cores, 1 unmodified flake (in hornfels), 2 notched flakes, 4 backed flakes, 1 unilaterally retouched knife, 4 points (including 1 in silcrete).

Additional material Department of Ethnography, British Museum (Appendix 1).Cambridge University Museum, Institute of Archaeology, Pitt Rivers Museum (Appendix 3).

IMBUSINI BROOK MATABELELAND SOUTH PROVINCE

This is a single Early Stone Age artefact in rolled condition. The artefact is marked in the same handwriting (W1.3/180) as that used on the artefacts in the Braunholtz Collection from Mauchini Brook and Powola Brook (qqv). Like them, it is located on the edge of the Bembezi Valley, the gravels of which are a well-known source of Early and Middle Stone Age occurrences (N. Jones 1938).

Braunholtz Collection, (Ethno) 1930.1-24
1 handaxe (in hornfels).

Additional material Liverpool Museum (Appendix 3).

INYANGA MANICALAND PROVINCE 18° 12'S, 32° 40'E
Following his earlier collection of Sangoan-like artefacts from the Inyanga Downs (N. Jones 1949), Keith Robinson (1958) carried out a series of excavations in the general area of Inyanga, the Later Stone Age microlithic occurrences from which formed a major part of the 'Pfupian Industry' designated by C. Cooke *et al.* (1966). This remains poorly defined and largely undated, with little Stone Age research having been conduced in the Inyanga highlands in recent years (Walker 1995: 19-20).

Armstrong Collection, 1959.7-12
A group of 38 Later Stone Age artefacts in opaline and quartz and five unworked pieces of stone. The microlithic nature of the artefacts and the presence of segments and a small scraper suggests a similarity to the Nswatugi Industry of the Matopo Hills (Walker 1995).

Table 61. The Armstrong Collection from Inyanga.

	Opaline	Vein quartz	Crystal quartz	Total
Chunks	-	1	-	1
Irregular cores	-	-	1	1
Flat bladelet cores	1	-	-	1
Core-reduced pieces	-	1	2	3
Core rejuvenation flakes	-	-	1	1
Flakes	9	2	15	26
Scrapers	-	1	-	1
Segments	-	2	-	2
Miscellaneous retouched pieces	1	-	1	2
Total	11	7	20	38

3 buff-coloured, undecorated and grit-tempered Iron Age bodysherds are also present.

INYATI MATABELELAND NORTH PROVINCE 19° 40'S, 28° 50'E
Inyati lies within the general area of the Bembezi Valley where Kenny (Appendix 4) collected in the early 20th century and where N. Jones (1938) worked subsequently. The 'Bembezi Industry' defined on the basis of these collections has since been shown to form part of the Sangoan Complex (Sampson 1974: 107).

Armstrong Collection, 1960.11-4.10-18 +additional
A group of 18 artefacts, the diagnostic elements of which are all Early Stone Age in origin. The handwriting on the artefacts is in the same hand as on that in the Favell Collection from this site.
8 cleavers (6 in quartzite, 2 in granite), 4 handaxes (in quartzite), 2 irregular cores (1 in hornfels, 1 in quartzite), 3 unmodified flakes (1 each in chert, granite, hornfels), 1 scraper (in quartzite).

Favell Collection, 1936.5-8.43
One Early Stone Age artefact. The handwriting on this artefact is in the same hand as on those in the Armstrong Collection from this site.
1 cleaver (in quartzite).

Jones Collection, (Ethno) 1928.10-15.1-2
Two Early Stone Age artefacts.
2 cleavers (in quartzite).

Additional material Cambridge University Museum, ? Manchester Museum (Appendix 3).

INYATI (HUCKLE'S FARM), MATABELELAND NORTH PROVINCE APPROXIMATELY 19° 40'S, 28° 50'E
A farm within the Inyati area, this material has previously been curated with that provenanced simply to Inyati (qv).

Jones Collection, (Ethno) 1928.10-15.3-4
Two Early Stone Age artefacts.
2 handaxes (in dolerite).

KHAMI, MATABELELAND SOUTH PROVINCE 20° 10'S, 28° 23'E
Khami is, next to Great Zimbabwe itself, perhaps the most impressive of all the Later Iron Age stone-walled sites of the Zimbabwe Tradition and was the capital of the Torwa kingdom from about AD 1450 until its destruction by fire about 1640 (Beach (1980). It was while visiting these ruins in 1900 that White (1900: 14) noticed the presence of stone artefacts 'on the surface and amongst ash deposits', probably, he thought, derived from the soil used to construct platforms behind the walls. Subsequent investigation confirmed the presence of a rich Middle Stone Age artefact scatter, which N. Jones & Summers (1949) attributed to the so-called 'Stillbay' and 'Magosian' Industries. A Later Stone Age assemblage related to the Nswatugi Industry of the Matopo Hills is also present, as well as a Sangoan (Charaman) assemblage in which handaxes and picks are typical (C. Cooke 1957).

Matley Collection, per Edwards, 1935.10-14.15
A single artefact in fresh condition, by itself culturally adiagnostic.
1 unmodified bladelet (in opaline).

F. White Collection, 1922.6-6.17-22
Six artefacts, all in fresh condition, some (and possibly all) of which are Middle Stone Age in origin, given the presence of the disc core and the fact that one each of the opaline and hornfels flakes has a faceted platform.
1 disc core (in opaline), 4 unmodified flakes (2 in hornfels, 2 in opaline), 1 proximal section of an unmodified flake-blade (in vein quartz).

Additional material Cambridge University Museum, Institute of Archaeology, Liverpool Museum, Pitt Rivers Museum (Appendix 3).

MATABELELAND, NO FURTHER PROVENANCE
Andrew Anderson (1888) visited King Lobengula of the Matabele more than once and travelled extensively through the areas that he controlled. Two of the other artefacts catalogued as Christy Collection +7901 come from locations to the west of Lobengula's capital at KwaBulawayo, close to the present day Botswanan/Zimbabwean border. It is thus possible that these two artefacts also come from the same general area.

Christy Collection, ex Anderson, +7901
Two rolled Middle Stone Age artefacts, both of them patinated and in rolled condition. all probably of Middle Stone Age origin.
2 unmodified flake-blades (in hornfels, found in gravels in 1877 and 1878).

MATETSI VALLEY, MATABELELAND NORTH PROVINCE APPROXIMATELY 18° 16'S, 25° 56'E
The Matetsi River flows in a generally northeasterly or easterly direction across the north-western corner of Zimbabwe to feed into the Zambezi just west of the beginning of Lake Kariba. This particular artefact was found close to the town of Matetsi itself, allowing a more precise latitude and longitude to be given for it. Lamplugh visited this area of Zimbabwe as part of the 1905 visit to southern Africa of the British Association for the Advancement of Science and was one of the first individuals to publish on the archaeology, geography and geology of the Victoria Falls (Lamplugh 1905a, 1905b).

G. W. Lamplugh Collection, 1906.5-19.6
A single, heavily rolled artefact that is culturally undiagnostic.
1 unmodified flake (in opaline).

MATOPOS CAVE 1, MATABELELAND SOUTH PROVINCE POSSIBLY 20° 30'S, 28° 30'E
White (1905) excavated at a painted site now known as World's View Shelter in one of the first archaeological excavations to take place in Zimbabwe. Around the same time Eyles (1902), Mennell (1908) and others also found stone artefacts at other sites in the Matopo Hills. The British Museum collections are clearly marked as coming from two different sites, only one of which can be the World's View Shelter excavated by White (1905). The other, whether excavated by White or by someone else, must be located elsewhere in the Matopo Hills. Walker (1995: 188) notes that most of the material from White's excavations has been lost, but from the little remaining in Zimbabwean museum collections he suggests that a large scraper tentatively indicates early-mid Holocene occupation; what were probably a Stone Age and an Iron Age burial were also found.

Additional material Department of Ethnography, British Museum (Appendix 1).

F. White Collection, (Ethno) 1922.6-5.8-25

A small group of 17 unmodified probably Later Stone Age artefacts (though two of the flakes have faceted platforms suggestive of a Middle Stone Age affiliation), including two pieces of red ochre.

Table 62. The F. White Collection from Matopos Cave 1.

	Opaline	Hornfels	Vein quartz	Crystal quartz	Total
Chunks	1	1	-	1	2
Irregular cores	1	1	-	1	2
Bladelet cores	1	-	-	-	1
Flakes	2	5	2	3	12
Total	5	7	2	3	17

MATOPOS CAVE 2, MATABELELAND SOUTH PROVINCE POSSIBLY 20° 30'S, 28° 30'E

This is the second of two sites in the Matopo Hills from which the British Museum has material donated by F. White. The same comments apply here as in the case of Matopos Cave 1 (qv).

F. White Collection, (Ethno) 1922.6-5.26-57

A group of 29 artefacts of probably Later Stone Age origin that also includes one unworked quartz crystal, one piece of red ochre and two unworked pieces of stone.

Table 63. The F. White Collection from Matopos Cave 2.

	Opaline	Hornfels	Vein quartz	Crystal quartz	Total
Core-reduced pieces	1	-	-	-	1
Flakes	9	10	4	1	24
Blades	1	-	-	-	1
Proximal sections (bladelets)	-	1	-	-	1
Scrapers	2	-	-	-	2
Total	13	11	4	1	29

MAUCHINI BROOK, MATABELELAND SOUTH PROVINCE

Braunholtz Collection, (Ethno) 1930.1-24

A single lightly patinated artefact with a faceted platform of probable Middle Stone Age origin. The artefact is marked in the same handwriting as that used on the artefacts in the Braunholtz Collection from Imbusini Brook and Powola Brook (qqv). Like them it is located on the edge of the Bembezi Valley the gravels of which are a well-known source of Early and Middle Stone Age occurrences (N. Jones 1938).

1 unmodified flake (in hornfels).

MPAKWE RIVER (*IMPAKWE*), MATABELELAND SOUTH PROVINCE FROM 20° 35'S, 27° 50'E TO 21° 13'S, 27° 50'E

The Mpakwe River is a small, south-flowing tributary of the Ramatlabama River (qv), which forms part of the border between Botswana and Zimbabwe. A.A. Anderson (1888: 332-333; 336) records crossing it en route between Tati (qv) and the Matabele capital of KwaBulawayo.

Christy Collection, ex Anderson, +7901

This is a single, probably Middle Stone Age artefact in a patinated and rolled condition that shares the same accession number as two others from western Zimbabwe (qv Matabeleland, no further provenance) and one from the Tati River (qv) in eastern Botswana.

1 unmodified flake (in hornfels, found in gravels in 1877).

NSWATUGI CAVE, MATABELELAND SOUTH PROVINCE 20° 32'S, 28° 29'E

Walker's (1995) more recent excavations at this shelter in the Matopo Hills have confirmed and refined the broad outlines of the site's stratigraphy recorded by N. Jones (1933) when it was first excavated; the shelter's well preserved paintings, dominated by three polychrome giraffes, are described by N. Jones (1933), C. Cooke (1959) and Garlake (1987). The bulk of the Later Stone Age part of the sequence dates to between 9700 and 6000 BP and is associated with a series of assemblages rich in backed microliths, small, convex scrapers, worked bone and ostrich eggshell beads, collectively assigned to the Nswatugi Industry. Below these a terminal Pleistocene occupation of the Pomongwe Industry rests unconformably on a deep series of Middle Stone Age deposits. Some chronological changes are apparent within this, but they are not well understood; the presence of several large segments suggests that at least the upper part of the sequence has affinities with the Howieson's Poort (Walker 1980).

Armstrong Collection, 1959.7-12

A group of five Later Stone Age artefacts which, if genuinely associated with each other, probably come from the Nswatugi Industry occupation of the site. All are in quartz unless otherwise stated.
2 unmodified flakes, 1 mesial section of an unmodified bladelet, 1 segment, 1 scraper (in opaline). An unworked quartz crystal is also present.

Favell Collection, ex Bulawayo Museum, 1936.5-8.61-78 + unnumbered

A group of 33 artefacts, most of them in quartz. The majority are clearly of Later Stone Age origin and probably derive from the Nswatugi Industry occupation of the site. However, three obviously Middle Stone Age elements are also present.

Table 64. The Favell Collection, ex Bulawayo Museum, from Nswatugi Cave.

	Opaline	Chert	Vein quartz	Crystal quartz	Total
Irregular cores	-	-	2	-	2
Flakes	-	1	1	1	3
MSA flake (faceted platform)	-	1	-	-	1
Scrapers	7	-	2	-	9
Backed scrapers	1	-	-	-	1
Backed bladelets	-	-	4	1	5
Backed points	1	-	2	-	3
Segments	2	-	2	3	7
MSA knife - unilateral	-	-	1	-	1
MSA point (faceted platform)	-	-	1	-	1
Total	11	2	15	5	33

Additional material Department of Ethnography, British Museum (Appendix 1).Cambridge University Museum (Appendix 3).

PLUMTREE MATABELELAND SOUTH PROVINCE 20° 27'S, 27° 55'E

N. Jones (1949: fig. 18) illustrates a handaxe from here and refers in passing to such Early Stone Age arfefacts being common in 'gravel lying beneath a black alluvium' in the beds of streams draining the edge of the Kalahari (N. Jones 1949: 42). The artefacts in the British Museum collections from Plumtree are, however, probably all of much more recent age.

Armstrong Collection, 1959.7-12

Four artefacts, none of which are clearly culturally diagnostic, and one unworked piece of stone.
1 irregular core (in vein quartz), 2 unmodified flakes (in vein quartz), 1 combination upper grindstone/hammerstone (in granite).

R. L. Cranswick Collection, 1934.10-12.1-12

A group of 12 opaline artefacts that may be either Middle and/or Later Stone Age in origin found during dam construction in gravel on the grounds of the Plumtree School Farm. All the artefacts are in fresh condition.
8 unmodified flakes, 1 proximal section of an unmodified bladelet, 1 scraper, 1 segment, 1 miscellaneously retouched piece.

F. White Collection, 1922.6-6.26

A single, slightly rolled artefact that is culturally adiagnostic.
1 unmodified flake (in opaline).

POMMERU (GRAVE SITE) PRECISE LOCATION UNKNOWN

Armstrong Collection, 1959.7-12

A single flaked pebble that is culturally adiagnostic.
1 chopping tool (? in chert).

POWOLA BROOK, MATABELELAND SOUTH PROVINCE

Braunholtz Collection, ex Bulawayo Museum, (Ethno) 1930.1-24

A single Early Stone Age artefact marked (W1.3/130) in the same handwriting as that used on the artefacts in the Braunholtz Collection from Imbusini Brook and Mauchini Brook (qqv). Like them, it is located on the edge of the Bembezi Valley, the gravels of which are a well-known source of Early and Middle Stone Age occurrences (N. Jones 1938).
1 handaxe (in hornfels).

SAWMILLS, MATABELELAND NORTH PROVINCE 19° 34'S, 28° 02'E

Stone artefacts from Sawmills in the valley of the Umguza River were recognised by Arnold as early as 1918 and subsequently published by N. Jones (1924). Details of the site's stratigraphy were later revised (N. Jones 1944). Archaeological material is present in a series of gravel terraces separated from each other by sterile sands and alluvial deposits. The oldest is an Acheulean occurrence, with classically Middle Stone Age, as well as more microlithic, material present higher up. N. Jones (1924) defined a 'Sawmills Industry' in these upper terraces that was later correlated with the 'Magosian' and seen as a Zimbabwean expression of the so-called Second Intermediate, i.e. an industry transitional chronologically and technologically between the Middle and Later Stone Ages (e.g. Clark 1959: 180). It is clear that Jones' collections here were neither complete, nor from a primary context. Nevertheless, Sampson (1974: 238) retained the term 'Umguzan' for reasons of historical precedence to refer to what were still thought in the 1970s to be mid-Upper Pleistocene occurrences transitional between MSA and LSA technologies. Referred to by others as 'Tshangulan' (e.g. Cooke 1984), several such assemblages from excavated sites have since been shown to be stratigraphically mixed (Walker 1990), a possibility that cannot be excluded in the case of Sawmills itself.

Favell Collection, ex Armstrong, 1936.5-8.44-60 + unnumbered

A group of 22 artefacts, the majority in opaline. Three of the flakes have faceted platforms, suggesting that they are of Middle Stone Age origin, but the remainder are not by themselves culturally diagnostic.
2 chunks (in opaline), 8 irregular cores (6 in opaline, 2 in quartzite), 1 *pièce esquillée* (in opaline), 9 unmodified flakes (4 in opaline, 3 in quartzite, 2 in hornfels), 2 scrapers (in opaline), 1 unworked quartz crystal.

Hobley Collection, 1947.7-2.91-95 + unnumbered

A group of 13 Middle Stone Age artefacts all of which are rolled. This collection is specifically provenanced to the highest terrace of the Umguza River.
5 unmodified flakes (3 in dolerite, 2 in quartzite), 1 unmodified flake-blade (in chert), 1 unmodified flake-blade proximal section (in dolerite), 4 scrapers (3 in dolerite, 1 in quartzite), 2 points (in dolerite).

Jones Collection, (Ethno) 1928.10-15.15-16

Two rolled dolerite artefacts of which at least the cleaver is of Early Stone Age origin.
1 cleaver, 1 scraper.

Additional material Cambridge University Museum, Institute of Archaeology, (Appendix 3).

SAWMILLS RIVER MATABELELAND NORTH PROVINCE FROM 20° 04'S, 28° 42'E TO 19° 30'S, 27° 47'E

Although a Sawmills River is not marked on the map, this is certainly a reference to the Umguza River, which rises east of Bulawayo and flows through Sawmills before joining the Gwayi River. The co-ordinates given for this locality reflect this. The collection is likely to come from close to Sawmills itself (qv).

Bulawayo Museum Collection, 1921.7-28.10-19

A group of ten Middle Stone Age artefacts, marked (W1.3/87) in the same handwriting as several other artefacts in the Bulawayo Museum Collection from Zimbabwe (e.g. Mauchini Brook, Powola Brook, qqv). The presence of a single large segment doubtless accounts for this group having been previously described in Museum records as 'Magosian' and suggests that it may possibly have associations with the Howieson's Poort Industry.
1 *pièce esquillée* (in chert), 6 unmodified flakes (4 in opaline, 1 in chert, 1 in hornfels), 1 unmodified flake-blade (in quartzite), 1 utilised flake (in hornfels), 1 segment (in opaline).

SHANGANI MATABELELAND SOUTH PROVINCE 19° 47'S, 29° 21'E

Bulawayo Museum Collection, ex W. H. Kenny, 1921.7-28.1

A single Early Stone Age artefact marked 'Shangani, Gwelo District, W. H. Kenney'.
1 handaxe (in vein quartz).

SHANGANI RIVER, MIDLANDS OR MATABELELAND NORTH PROVINCES FROM 19 28'S, 29 40'E TO 18 30'S, 27 11'E

Read Collection, (Ethno) 1913.6-18.1-3

Three Early Stone Age artefacts, the tip of one of them being missing. The artefact is provenanced no more precisely than to somewhere between Gweru and the Zambezi River. The Shangani River is the next major river to the east of the Bembezi Valley, the gravels of which are a well-known source of Early and Middle Stone Age occurrences (N. Jones 1938).
3 handaxes (in vein quartz).

TRELAWNEY, MASHONALAND NORTH PROVINCE 17° 32'S, 30° 26'E

Bird Collection, 1932.10-11.1-2

Two slightly rolled silcrete or silicified chert artefacts of Middle Stone Age origin.
1 irregular core, 1 bilaterally retouched knife (made on a flake-blade with a faceted platform).

TURK MINE, MATABELELAND NORTH PROVINCE 19° 42'S, 28° 47'E

A former gold-mine to the northeast of Bulawayo, this site lies in the Bembezi Valley where N. Jones (1938) identified numerous artefact-bearing localities, on the basis of which he recognised a Bembesi Industry as a locally transitional 'culture' between the Early and Middle Stone Ages; this material is now included within the Sangoan Complex (Sampson 1974; Volman 1984). An accompanying labels states that the artefact was found in a local 'spruit' or streambed.

Jones Collection, 1928.10-15.14

1 handaxe (in dolerite).

VICTORIA FALLS, MATABELELAND NORTH PROVINCE 17° 59'S, 25° 57'E

Stone artefacts were found in the area of the Victoria Falls at the beginning of the 20th century (N. Jones 1949: 10) and received the attention of several of those attending the 1905 meeting in southern Africa of the British Association for the Advancement of Science; Balfour (1906), Feilden (1905) and Lamplugh (1905a, 1905b) were among those who published accounts of artefacts found here in gravel deposits both above and below the Falls. More detailed investigations were undertaken by Cooke & Clark (1939) when engineering work exposed a long section of stratified deposits and Clark (1950) later produced a detailed cultural-stratigraphic sequence for the area based on the associations of particular assemblages with stages in the gradual recession of the Falls up the Zambezi, although not all the details of this can now be maintained (Sampson 1974: 114).

Bulawayo Museum Collection, 1921.7-28.8-9

Two very heavily rolled artefacts, both in chert. The adze is most likely to be of Later Stone Age origin, while the faceted platform of the flake suggests that it is probably of Middle Stone Age origin.
1 unmodified flake, 1 adze.

Additional material Department of Ethnography, British Museum (Appendix 1).Cambridge University Museum, Institute of Archaeology, Liverpool Museum, Pitt Rivers Museum (Appendix 3).

WEST ACRE FARM, MATABELELAND SOUTH PROVINCE 20° 19'S, 28° 21'E

Armstrong Collection, 1959.7-12

A single, rolled artefact of Early Stone Age origin.
1 cleaver (in dolerite).

ZIMBABWE (*RHODESIA*), NO FURTHER PROVENANCE

Armstrong Collection, 1959.7-12

Four opaline artefacts of Later Stone Age origin without any further provenance,
1 core tablet, 1 unmodified flake, 2 scrapers.

Braunholtz Collection, ex Bulawayo Museum, (Ethno) 1930.1-24

A rolled Early Stone Age artefact marked W1.3/183. Two other artefacts in the Bulawayo Museum Collection (from Mauchini and Powola Brooks, qqv) have similar markings, suggesting that this handaxe may have been acquired from the Bulawayo Museum and was perhaps obtained from a site close to these localities.
1 handaxe (in granite).

Additional material Cambridge University Museum, Liverpool Museum, Pitt Rivers Museum, Sheffield City Museum (Appendix 3).

Appendix I. Southern African Stone Age Collections in the Department of Ethnography of The British Museum

Introduction

This Appendix is organized following the same broad geographical divisions as used in the Gazetteer, that is to say first by country and then, within South Africa, by province. Old spellings are given in brackets and italics after the modern place-name and where a site can be located within a modern province in Mozambique or Zimbabwe this follows the placename. As these collections were not examined, only brief details of their contents are included, taken from the print-out of the department's registers provided by Julie Hudson of the British Museum's Department of Ethnography, to whom I am grateful. For those who wish to follow the activities of a particular collector a list of collectors with names of sites from which they collected follows at the end of the Appendix.

BOTSWANA, NO FURTHER PROVENANCE

1 bored stone (Later Stone Age, made of steatite ?). Christy Collection Af,3262

MOZAMBIQUE

Massengana (Manica Province). Stone artefact (1, 'arrowhead'). F. D. Bernhard Collection Af1939.12-4

SOUTH AFRICA

i) Eastern Cape Provenance

British Kaffraria. Bead (1, in agate, Later Stone Age ?). Lady Frere Collection Af1928.11-6.9.a-ac

Burgersdorp. Stone artefacts (40 scrapers and 1 bored stone, Later Stone Age). F. A. Saw Collection Af1902.1-3.44, 47

Burgersdorp Cave. Red ochre (sample). F. A. Saw Collection Af1902-46

Burgersdorp Cave. Ostrich eggshell (2 fragments). F. A. Saw Collection Af1902-48.a-b

Bushman's River. Pottery (9 sherds, Later Stone Age). Atherstone Collection Af1979.1-28.70.ag-at

Bushman's River. Stone artefacts (4). Ward Collection Af1979.1-13.51-54

Carnarvondale Farm. Stone artefacts (24). Ward Collection Af1931.3-7.8, 18, 20, 32-35, 40-49h These artefacts include:
1 backed scraper 48
1 borer 47
1 point 18
9 scrapers 8, 20, 33, 35, 41-42, 45-46
1 segment 32

Great Fish River (mouth). Stone artefacts (14, including 1 bored stone, Later Stone Age). Bays Collection Af1911.12-12.1- 14

Great Fish River (mouth). Pottery (8 sherds). Bays Collection Af1911.12-12.15-22

Halseton. Bored stone (1, Later Stone Age). Bays Collection Af1923.4-14.38

Halseton. Pottery (9 sherds, Later Stone Age). Bays Collection Af1923.4-14.40, 42-46, 48-50

Middledrift. Stone artefacts (3, including 2 bored stones, Later Stone Age). Wilson Bros. Collection Af1926.14-12.46, 122

Middledrift. Ostrich eggshell beads (3, Later Stone Age). Wilson Bros. Collection Af1926.14-12.132.a-c

Queenstown. Stone artefact (1). F. A. Saw Collection Af1902-45

Swartruggens (*Zwaart Ruggens*). Stone artefact (1, described as a 'spear whetstone'). M. C. Hobson Collection Af,SA.31

ii) Free State

Avalon. Stone artefacts (3, including 2 scrapers, Later Stone Age). Braunholtz Collection Af1979.1-28.60.a-cj and dz-ey

De Kiel Oost. Stone artefacts (4, including 1 bored stone, Later Stone Age). Braunholtz Collection Af1979.1-28.71.a-d

De Kiel Oost. Pottery (4 sherds, affiliation unknown). Braunholtz Collection Af1979.1-28.71.e-h

Fauresmith. Stone artefacts (1). Braunholtz (?) Collection ex Leviseur (?) Af1979.1-28.63.a-af

Heilbron. Grindstone (1, Later Stone Age ?). A. Lomax Collection Af1930.7-10.1

Heilbron. Spherical stones (3, 1 each made in granite, quartz and sandstone). Rousseau Collection Af1930.1-8.1-3

Koffiefontein. Stone artefacts (1). Braunholtz Collection Af1979.1-28.60.ck-dy, 62.a-an

Koffiefontein. Stone artefacts (6, including 1 grindstone and 2 scrapers, Later Stone Age). Fowler Collection Af1930.1-17.1-6

Schaapplaats Cave. Scraper (1, Later Stone Age). Braunholtz Collection Af1979.1-28.67.a

Sesfontein. Stone artefacts (4, including 2 scrapers). Braunholtz Collection Af1979.1-28.67.a-ah

Smithfield. Stone artefact (1). Hobley Collection Af1947.16-2.88

Vegkop, Heilbron. Pottery (4 sherds). Braunholtz Collection Af1979.1-28.68.a-d

Ventershoek. Scrapers (22, Later Stone Age). Braunholtz Collection Af1979.1-28.69.a-v

Wepener. Stone artefact (1). Braunholtz Collection Af1979.1-28.85.a-ba

iii) Gauteng

Meyerton. Stone artefacts (6, including 3 handaxes, 1 hammerstone, 1 point and 1 scraper, Early Stone Age). Fisher Collection Af1929.4-9.1, 10, 17, 23, 33, 37

iv) Kwazulu-Natal

Bushman's River, Weenen. Stone artefacts (6, Middle Stone Age points). Thomasset & Walsh Collection Af1924.10-11.12-17

Bushman's River, Weenen. Stone artefacts (2 points, Middle Stone Age ?; 1 in quartzite and 1 in opaline). Thomasset Collection Af1924.10-25.34-35

Muden. Stone artefacts (6, Middle Stone Age, 1 knife, 3 points and 2 scrapers). Cookson Collection Af1955.2-2.1-2, 7, 11, 13, 18

Muden. Stone artefacts (2, Middle Stone Age, 1 point and 1 scraper). Newall Collection ex Cookson Af1954.2-2.1 and 7

Pietermaritzburg (New Park). Bored stone (1, Later Stone Age). P. Sutherland Collection Af1979.1-28.29

Pietermaritzburg. Stone artefacts (4). Rev. R. L. White Collection Af1935.10-23.1-3, 6

Tongaat. Stone artefacts (6). J.F. Schofield Collection Af1937.2-8.1-6

v) Mpumalanga

Barberton (Kaap Valley). Bored stone (1, Later Stone Age). Trevor Collection Af1920.2 7.1

vi) North West Province

Sheppard Island. Stone artefacts (10). Braunholtz (?) Collection ex Van Riet Lowe (?) Af1979.1-28.64.a-k

vii) Northern Cape Province

Alexandersfontein. Stone artefacts (3). Braunholtz Collection Af1979.1-28.61.a-at

Alexandersfontein. Ostrich eggshell fragments (1). Braunholtz Collection Af1979.1-28.61.au

Barkly West. Stone artefacts (18). Braunholtz (?) Collection Af1979.1-28.65.a-r

Boetsap. Stone artefacts (17). Swan Collection Af1934.7-7.101-107, 110-117, 133. These artefacts include:
8 borers (Later Stone Age) 110-117
8 segments (Later Stone Age) 101-107

Bushmanland. Grindstones (2, Later Stone Age ?). H.A.P. Littledale Collection Af1951.3-1.4 and 5

Kimberley. Stone artefacts (24 microliths, Later Stone Age). Hobley Collection Af1947.1-6.309-332

Kimberley. Stone artefacts (117). Swan Collection Af1934.7-7.1-100, 108-109, 118-132 These artefacts include:
1 backed scraper (Later Stone Age) 94
1 handaxe (Early Stone Age) 1
72 scrapers (Later Stone Age) 2-57, 68-82, 109
28 segments (Later Stone Age) 58-67, 83-93, 95-100, 108

Kimberley. Ostrich eggshell bead (Later Stone Age). Swan Collection Af1930.6-11.1

Kimberley (Du Toits Pan). Microliths (4, Later Stone Age). R. Jones Collection Af1979.1-31.21.a-d

Koranna Kolk. Stone artefacts (4, including 1 broken hammerstone). H.A.P. Littledale Collection Af1951.3-1.6-9

Loogkolk. Upper grindstone (1, Later Stone Age ?). H.A.P. Littledale Collection Af1951.3-1.3

Pniel. Stone artefacts (11, including 1 Early Stone Age handaxe and 2 Later Stone Age bored stones). Braunholtz Collection Af1979.1-28.74-2884

Prieska. Ostrich eggshell and glass beads (Later Stone Age). Swan Collection Af1934.7-7.134

Swartmodder (*Zwartmodder*). Grindstones (2, Later Stone Age). H.A.P. Littledale Collection Af1951.3-1.1-2

Vaal River. Bored stone (1, Later Stone Age). Swan Collection Af1930.6-11.2

Vaal River. Stone artefacts (8, including 5 Early Stone Age handaxes and 3 Later Stone Age bored stones) Van Alphen Collection Af1930.1-14.1, 12-13, 21, 28, 51-53 provenanced to Barkly West and/or Pniel and/or Windsorton.

Vaal River. Handaxe (1, Early Stone Age). Unknown Collector Af1979.1-28.28

viii) Northern Province

Northern Transvaal, no further provenance. Bored stones (2, Later Stone Age, 1 made of soapstone). Colonel D. Reitz Collection Af1927-53 and 54

ix) Western Cape Province

Cape Flats. Stone artefact (1). H.D. Bellew Collection Af1924-130

Cape Flats. Pottery (3 sherds). H.D. Bellew Collection Af1924-131-133

Cape Flats. Pottery (4 sherds, Later Stone Age). Dale Collection Af,+7694 and +7696.a-c

Cape Flats. Stone artefacts (171). Hardy Collection Af1930.1-10.140-291, 294, 300-317. This collection includes the following artefacts, all of which are probably Later Stone Age in origin except where indicated:
36 backed scrapers 205-240, 242
34 borers 249-250, 254-278, 284-289, 311
4 cores 163-164, 184, 304
8 'core scrapers' 167-174
1 disc 302
3 flakes 281-283
25 Middle Stone Age points 140-157, 160, 279-280, 290-291, 300, 314
34 segments 185-204, 241, 243-248, 251-253, 307-310, 318
17 scrapers 161, 175-183, 303, 306, 312-313, 315-316, 317

Cape Flats. Ostrich eggshell fragments (6). Hardy Collection Af1930.1-10.292a-f

Cape Flats. Ostrich eggshell beads (28). Hardy Collection Af1930.1-10.293

Cape Flats. Pottery (1 sherd). Thurburn Collection Af1979.1-28.66.c

Cape Town. Stone artefact (1). Hardy Collection Af1930.1-10.136

Cape Town. Pottery (4 sherds). Hardy Collection Af1930.1-10.137-139

Fish Hoek. Stone artefacts (8, at least 3 of which are Middle Stone Age points and/or knives). Hardy Collection Af1930.1-10.2, 4-5, 7-9, 13, 15, 23, 29, 42, 61-75, 77-83, 121-125, 129-130, 133-135. These artefacts include:
5 backed scrapers (Wilton Industry, Later Stone Age) 79-83
11 blades/points (Middle Stone Age ?) 2, 4-5, 7-9, 13, 15, 23, 29, 42
2 borers (Later Stone Age) 129-130
1 'knife' (Middle Stone Age ?) 75
17 segments (Later Stone Age ?) 61-74, 77-78

Hermanus. Stone artefacts (16 scrapers). Hardy Collection Af1930.1-10.294-299

Hout Bay. Pottery (1 sherd, Later Stone Age). Thurburn Collection Af,+7600

Noordhoek. Stone artefacts (82) Hardy Collection Af1930.1-10.1, 3, 6, 10-12, 14, 16-18, 20-22, 24-28, 30-60, 76, 101-132. These artefacts include:
28 backed scrapers
(Later Stone Age, Wilton Industry) 30, 84-109, 111
31 blades/points (Middle Stone Age ?) 1, 3, 6, 10-12, 14, 16,18, 20-22, 24-28, 39-52, 76
2 borers (Later Stone Age) 131-132
7 core scrapers 31-35, 37-38
3 flakes 36, 53, 12
1 hammerstone 60
7 scrapers 54-59, 128
10 segments (Later Stone Age, Wilton Industry) 110, 112-120

Paarl. Handaxes (2, Early Stone Age). Braunholtz Collection (ex Van Heerden ?) Af1979.1-28.62.ao-be

Port Beaufort. Pottery (5 sherds, Later Stone Age). Evans Collection Af,+7809, 7811, 7813a-b

Port Beaufort. Stone artefacts (2, including 1 Middle Stone Age ? point). Thurburn Collection Af1979.1-28.66.b and Af,+7589

Port Beaufort. Pottery (5 sherds, Later Stone Age). Thurburn Collection Af,+7582 - +7586

Port Beaufort. Bone (4 fragments). Thurburn Collection Af,+7596 - +7598 and Af1979.1-28.66.d

Port Beaufort. Bovid teeth (2 fragments). Thurburn Collection Af1979.1-28.66.a

Port Beaufort. Ostrich eggshell (3 fragments). Thurburn Collection Af,+7599a-f

Swellendam. Bored stone (1, Later Stone Age) and stone disc (1, Later Stone Age). Van Heerden Collection Af1930.1-16.9-10

Villiersdorp. Handaxe (1, Early Stone Age). Van Heerden Collection Af1930.1-16.2

x) South Africa: No Further Provenance

W. White Cooper Collection Af1937.1-4.1-15: 14 scrapers, 1 bored stone (Later Stone Age)

J. Currey Collection Af,4665: 1 bored stone (1, Later Stone Age)

Franks Collection, ex Evans, Af,9614: 1 painted slab showing a quadruped (Later Stone Age) from De Wet's Cave, further provenance unknown

Frere Collection Af1910.10-5.86: 1 bored stone (1, Later Stone Age)
F. Galton Collection, ex Frere, Af,+.2089: Pigment sample
M.C. Hobson Collection Af,SA.10028.a-ak and AF,SA.62: Crystal and 1 grindstone (Later Stone Age)
Powles Collection collected by F. Ellenberger A,.6132: 1 bored stone (1, Later Stone Age)
J. Shaw Collection Af,SA.11: 1 bored stone (1, Later Stone Age)
G. W. Stow Collection Af,SA.72: 1 spherical stone ball
Swan Collection Af1930.6-11.3-11c: 1 borer, 2 segments, 14 scrapers, 4 stone ring fragments (all Later Stone Age)
Van Heerden Collection Af1930.1-16.11: ostrich eggshell beads provenanced to Villiersdorp (Western Cape) or De Kiel Oost (Free State)
Unknown collectors:
3 grindstones (Later Stone Age ?). Unknown Collector Af,SA.28-30
3 grindstones (Later Stone Age ?). Unknown Collector Af,SA.38-40
1 grooved stone (Later Stone Age). Unknown Collector Af1979.1-28.55
9 stone artefacts. Unknown Collector Af1979.1-28.47,52, 54, 56. 47 is described as a 'spear-head made of quartzite' suggesting it is a Middle Stone Age point and 49 - 51, 54 and 56 as 'arrowheads'.
1 painted slab showing several human figures (Later Stone Age) from Dellet's Cave (further provenance unknown). Unknown Collector Af1979.1-2 27.31
1 painted slab showing an antelope (Later Stone Age). Unknown Collector AF1979.1-26.52

SOUTH AFRICA/ ZIMBABWE, NO FURTHER PROVENANCE

Braunholtz Collection Af1979.1-28.86.a-29.31
47 stone artefacts, including:
2 handaxes (Early Stone Age). Braunholtz Collection Af1979.1-28.87-88
4 cores. Braunholtz Collection Af1979.1-29.31;
16 scrapers. Braunholtz Collection Af1979.1-28.89-29.00, 29.14-29.16, 29.25
2 borers. Braunholtz Collection Af1979.1-29.26-27

SOUTHERN AFRICA: NO FURTHER PROVENANCE

Braunholtz Collection Af1979.1-28.73.a-b
1 handaxe and 1 cleaver (Early Stone Age)
R. Fairbridge Collection Af1979.1-28.32
1 bored stone (Later Stone Age).
Lady Frere Collection Af1928.11-6.1, 3-5, 8, 12 and 13 including:
4 bored stones (Later Stone Age) all provenanced to the 'Kalahari';
1 pestle
1 scraper
D.K. Oldman Collection Af1949.46.606-607
1 bored stone (Later Stone Age).
T. Shaw Collection Af1979.1-28.31
1 bored stone (Later Stone Age).
Unknown collector Af1979.1-28.30
1 bored stone (Later Stone Age).
Unknown collector Af1979.1-13.36.a-e
5 conjoining parts of a single painted slab (Later Stone Age).

ZIMBABWE

Bambata Cave (Matabeleland South Province). Stone artefacts (1 'point'). Unknown Collector Af1979.1-13.41
Bambata Cave (Matabeleland South Province). Pigment sample. Unknown Collector Af1979.1-13.42
Driefontein (Masvingo Province). Stone artefacts (1). King Collection ex Gardner Af1926.5-7.65
Garezi River, Inyanga (Manicaland Province). Stone artefacts (2, 'arrowheads'). F. D. Bernhard Collection Af1939.1-2.2-3
Gatooma Road Cave, Harare (Mashonaland South Province). Stone artefacts (7). Goodall Collection Af1935.11-9.12-18. These artefacts include:
1 grindstone 12
3 scrapers 13-14, 16
Gokomere Cave (Masvingo Province). Stone artefacts (54, Later Stone Age). Gardner Collection Af1930.1-11.1-55. These artefacts include:
2 borers 42-43
1 point 24
12 scrapers 44-55
40 segments 1-23, 25-41
Gokomere Cave (Masvingo Province). Arrow foreshaft (with 5 points), made of wood, chalcedony and quartz and part of an arrow shaft made of cane and cord. Unknown Collector Af1979.1-29.72.a-b
Hope Fountain (Matabeleland South Province). Stone artefacts (6, Early Stone Age). Jones Collection Af1930.1-13.6 , 8, 15. These artefacts include:
1 core 47
3 handaxes 6, 8, 15
1 scraper 81
Makumbi Mission Cave (Mashonaland South Province). Stone artefacts (5). Goodall Collection Af1935.11-9.21-35h. These artefacts include:
1 bracelet fragment 32
pigment 34a-35h
5 scrapers 25-29
Marondera (*Marandellas*) **Rock Shelter (Mashonaland South Province).** Stone artefacts (19, Later Stone Age). K.R. Robinson Collection Af1935.4-15.1-19. These artefacts include:
1 blade 16
1 borer 17
6 scrapers 1-6
8 segments 8-15
Matopo Hills Cave (Matabeleland South Province). Stone artefacts (2). F. White Collection Af1922.6-4.58.a-b
Matopo Hills Cave (Matabeleland South Province). Ostrich eggshell fragments (4). F. White Collection Af1922.6-4.59.a-d
Mutare (*Umtali,* **Manicaland Province).** Stone artefacts (4 undiagnostic quartz flakes). Randall-MacIver Collection Af1905.12- 15.200-203
Nswatugi Cave (Matabeleland South Province). Stone artefacts (2 scrapers and 5 'points', Later Stone Age, Nswatugi or Amadzimba Industries). G. Rigg Collection Af1950.1-9.17-23
Siantete's Kraal, Lukienigube River (?). Pottery (1 sherd). Unknown Collector Af1979.1-28.53
Siantete's Kraal, Lukienigube River (?). Stone artefacts (1 porcelain scraper, Later Stone Age/Iron Age). Unknown Collector Af1979.1-28.53
Victoria Falls (Matabeleland North Province). Stone artefacts (16). G. Rigg Collection Af1950.1-9.1-16 These artefacts include:
3 cores 1-2, 5
1 point 13
4 scrapers 3-4, 6-7

List of Collectors, Dept. of Ethnography, Southern Africa
Biographical details of collectors who are enboldened here are given in Appendix 4.

Collector	Provenance
W. Atherstone	Bushman's River (Eastern Cape)
J. B. Bays	Great Fish River (mouth), Halseton (both Eastern Cape)
H. D. Bellew	Cape Flats (Western Cape)
F. D. Bernhard	Massengana (Mozambique), Garezi River
H. Braunholtz	Avalon, De Kiel Oost, Fauresmith, Koffiefontein, Schaapplaats Cave, Sesfontein, Vegkop, Ventershoek, Wepener (all Free State) Alexandersfontein, Barkly West, Pniel (all Northern Cape) Sheppard Island (North West Province) Paarl (Western Cape) South Africa/Zimbabwe, no further provenance Southern Africa, no further provenance
H. Christy	Botswana, no further provenance
H. Cookson	Muden (KwaZulu-Natal)
W. White Cooper	South Africa, no further provenance
J. Currey	South Africa, no further provenance
L. Dale	Cape Flats (Western Cape)
J. Evans	Port Beaufort (Western Cape), De Wet's Cave (South Africa, no further provenance)
R. Fairbridge	Southern Africa, no further provenance
B. B. Fisher	Meyerton(Gauteng)
Fowler	Koffiefontein (Free State)
A. Franks	De Wet's Cave (South Africa, no further provenance)
B. Frere	South Africa, no further provenance
Lady Frere	British Kaffraria (Eastern Cape), Southern Africa, no further provenance
F. Galton	South Africa, no further provenance
T. Gardner	Driefontein, Gokomere Cave (both Zimbabwe)
Goodall	Gatooma Road Cave, Makumbi Mission Cave (both Zimbabwe)
W. Hardy	Cape Flats, Cape Town, Fish Hoek, Hermanus, Noordhoek (all Western Cape)
F. Hobley	Smithfield (Free State)Kimberley (Northern Cape)
M. C. Hobson	Swartruggens (Eastern Cape), South Africa, no further provenance
N. Jones	Hope Fountain (Zimbabwe)
R. Jones	Kimberley (Du Toits Pan, Northern Cape)
E. King	Driefontein (Zimbabwe)
M. Leviseur	Fauresmith (Free State)
H. A. P. Littledale	Bushmanland, Koranna Kolk, Loogkolk, Swartmodder, (all Northern Cape)
A. Lomax	Heilbron (Free State)
R. Newall	Muden (KwaZulu-Natal)
D. K. Oldman	Southern Africa, no further provenance
D. Randall-MacIver	Mutare (Zimbabwe)
D. Reitz	Northern Transvaal, no further provenance (Northern Province)
G. Rigg	Nswatugi Cave, Victoria Falls (both Zimbabwe)
K. R. Robinson	Marondera Rock Shelter (Zimbabwe)
A. Rousseau	Heilbron (Free State)
F. A. Saw	Burgersdorp, Burgersdorp Cave, Queenstown (all Easter Cape)
J. Schofield	Tongaat (KwaZulu-Natal)
J. Shaw	South Africa, no further provenance
T. Shaw	Southern Africa, no further provenance
P. Sutherland	Pietermaritzburg (New Park, KwaZulu-Natal)
J. Swan	Boetsap, Kimberley, Prieska, Vaal River (all Northern Cape), South Africa, no further provenance
H. Thomasset	Bushman's River (KwaZulu-Natal)
H. Thurburn	Cape Flats, Hout Bay, Port Beaufort (all Western Cape)
J. Van Alphen	Vaal River (Northern Cape)
P. Van Heerden	Paarl, Swellendam, Villiersdorp (all Western Cape), South Africa, no further provenance
C. Van Riet Lowe	Sheppard Island (North West Province)
T. Walsh	Bushman's River (KwaZulu-Natal)
P. Ward	Carnarvondale Farm (Eastern Cape)
F. White	Matopo Hills Cave (Zimbabwe)
R. White	Pietermaritzburg (KwaZulu-Natal)
K. & R. Wilson	Middledrift (Eastern Cape)

Appendix 2. Other African Stone Age Archaeological Collections in The British Museum

Karen Perkins

Introduction

This appendix is organised on geographical lines using the political boundaries of African states as they existed on January 1st 1999. Within each country provenances are listed alphabetically with the name of the department, province or region in which they are located following immediately afterwards in parantheses. The second column gives the name of the collection and the third the registration or catalogue number. For those who wish to follow the activities of a particular collector a list of collectors with names of sites from which they collected follows at the end of the Appendix. As noted in the introduction, this does not include Egyptian material, while all items listed as coming from the Musée d'Histoire Naturelle, Paris, are casts.

AFRICA		
No further provenance	Institute of Archaeology	P.1989.1-4
	Reygasse	1934 12-6 1-9
ALGERIA		
Ain Babouche (Setif)	Lull	1947.10-1.252-292 + rem. x 163
Ain Hanech	Institute of Archaeology	P1989.1-4
	Musée d'Histoire Naturelle Paris	1967.4-6.58-61 casts
Ain Taya	Institute of Archaeology	P1989.1-4
Algiers (Alger)	Avebury	1916.6-5.32
	Sturge	Cat. No. 951
Bel Abbès	Sturge	Cat. No. 949
Bir el-Ater	Institute of Archaeology	P1989.1-4
El Araich (Jijel)	Lull	1947.10-1.1-28 + rem.x 267
El-Kala	Christy, ex Lukis	9208a
El Ma-El-Abiod (Tebessa)	Reygasse	1933.10-10.3, 5, 9-26
	Musée d'Histoire Naturelle Paris	1967.4-6.63 casts
Erg Tihodaine (Tamanrasset)	Musée d'Histoire Naturelle Paris	1967.4-6.27, 62 casts
Féringres	Sturge	Cat. No. 952-953, 955-957
Foughala (Biskra)	Lull	1947.10-1.29-67 + rem. x 153
Grotte des Grand Roche	Christy, ex Franks	Algeria 5-6
	Christy, ex Lukis	9207, 9209
Kerem	Institute of Archaeology	P1989.1-4
Koudiat Bou Gherara	Institute of Archaeology	P1989.1-4
Lac Karar	Institute of Archaeology	P1989.1-4
Laghouat	Christy, ex Flower	Cat. No. 3
Lichana (Biskra)	Lull	1947.10-1.68-96 + rem. x 249
Oran-Est	Sturge	Cat. No. 954
Oued Belcibis (Biskra)	Lull	1947.10-1.462-474 + rem. x 268
Oued Djouf El Djemel (Constantine)	Vaufrey	1936.10-12.1-25 + rem. x 16
Oued Falaous (Biskra)	Lull	1947.10-1.97-130 + rem. x 188
Oued M'lili (Biskra)	Lull	1947.10-1.293-338 + rem. x 140
Oued Ouzen (Biskra)	Lull	1947.10-1.131-199 + rem. x 215
Ougarla (Ougarla)	Avebury	1916.6-5.125-141
	Sturge	Cat. p. 113 (x 3)
	Trechmann	P1964.12-6.1503-1507
Oulmache (Biskra)	Lull	1947.10-1.396-461 + rem. x 135
Palikao	Sturge	Cat. No. 950
Rassouta (Biskra)	Lull	1947.10-1.475-491 + rem. x 90
Sidi Okba (Biskra)	Lull	1947.10-1.339-395 + rem. x 398
S'Baikia (Tebessa)	Institute of Archaeology	P1989.1-4
	Reygasse	1925.10-21.9-39
	Reygasse	1933.10-10.2, 6-8
S'Mair	Reygasse	1933.10-10.1, 4
Tabelbalat	Institute of Archaeology	P1989.1-4
Tabel Belat	Seligman	1926.2-11.1-6
Tachanghit (Bechar)	Musée d'Histoire Naturelle Paris	1967.4-6.17-19 casts
Teneit El Had (Bechar)	Wellcome	P1982.10-4.4501-4502
Ternifine (Mascara)	Musée d'Histoire Naturelle Paris	1967.4-6.45-57, 62a casts
	Sturge	Cat. p. 113 (x 1)
Texenna (Jijel)	Lull	1947.10 1.200 251 + rem. 247

Timassinin (Ougarla)	Fromholtz	1914.7-25.1-172 + unreg. rem. x 52
	Reygasse	1933.10-10.27-61 + unreg. rem. 15
Tlemcen	Wellcome	P1982.10-4 unreg.
Tolga (Biskra)	Lull	1947.10-1.1-491 + rem.
Touibia (Tebessa)	Reygasse	1925.10-21.1-8
No further provenance	Christy, ex Franks	Cat. No. 5399 + Algeria 4
	Institute of Archaeology	P1989.1-4
	Morell	ML188-1193
	Sturge	Cat. p. 113 (x 43)
	Sturge, ex Cartailhac	Cat. p. 113 (x 35)
	Wellcome	P.1982.10-4 unreg.
CAMEROON		
Babanki Tungau (Bamenda)	Newton	1937.10-18.12, 16-19
Bamenda Station (Bamenda)	Newton	1937.10-18.11, 13, 20-23
Kawngli (Bamenda)	Newton	1937.10-18.10
Lip (Bamenda)	Newton	1937.10-18.14-15
Mbem (Bamenda)	Newton	1937.10-18.9
No further provenance (Bamenda)	Newton	1913.10-18.24-31
CONGO (Kinshasa: formerly Zaire)		
Katenda (Katanga)	Tollefsen	1920.10-7.1-40
Lukando	Williams	1940.4-3.1
Makuta	Williams	1940.4-3.7
Matadi (Bas-Zaire)	Burrows (Christy)	1901.6-8.1-13
Mongo (Equateur)	Williams	1940.4-3.6
M'Bio (Kasai Occidental)	Williams	1940.4-3.9
Natumba	Williams	1940.4-3.8
Vila	Williams	1940.4-3.5
No further provenance	Institute of Archaeology	P1989.1-4
	Williams	1940.4-3.2-4, 10-62 + rem. x 75
	Unknown	rem. x 14
ETHIOPIA		
Daghabur (Harar)	Curle	1937.3-12.1-15 + rem. x 25
Danakil Depression (Welo/Tigray)	White	1922.4-3.1
No further provenance	White	1922.4-3.2
GHANA		
Abehenasi-Hohoe (Volta)	Junner	1936.11-7.5
Abomposu (Ashanti)	Wild	1938.2-11.65-69
Accra (Capital)	Clifford	Ethno. 1914 202-211
	Cremer	1937.11-24.1-30
	Cremer	1938.2-12.1-23
	Popham	1914.6-9.1-16
	Popham	1914.7-23.1-11
Akwatia	Wild	Unreg. x 1
Ashanti Province (Ashanti)	Wild	1937.10-15.19-24
Manso	Junner	1935.12-11.155
Axim	Junner	Unreg. x 101
Batabe	Junner	1935.12-11.132-133
Bombiri (Northern)	Wild	1933.10-28.1-4
Garkwa	Junner	1935.12-11.159
Guduri	Geological Survey, Gold Coast	1935.12-11.159a
Kele Nachi Kete Krachi (Volta)	Wild	1937.10-15.16-17
Koue-Tachi (Volta)	Junner	1936.11-7.6-7
Kintampo-Weila	Junner	1935.12-11.157-158
Mo River	Junner	1936.11-7.8
Nambiri (Northern)	Junner	1936.11-7.9
Navaro (Northern)	Cardinall	1924.4-7.8-10, 12-13, 15-16
Nsuta (Western)	Wild	1931.10-17.17
Obuasi (Ashanti)	McAlpine-Wood	Unreg. x 1
Obuasi (Ashanti)	Wild	1937.10-15.18-25
Takoradi (Western)	Geological Survey, Gold Coast	1935.12-11.156
Togoland, no further provenance (Volta)	Junner	1936.11-7.8
No further provenance	Dalrymple	Ethno. Cat. 1914-16
	Geological Museum Transfer	P1989.3-1.86-94
	Junner	Unreg. x 59
KENYA		
Agula	Armstrong	1959.7-12.rem(x10)
Aringo	Owen	1938.6-1.80

Site	Source	Registration
Asembo	Armstrong	1959.7-12.rem(x39)
Bunyore	Armstrong	1959.7-12.rem(x1)
Butere	Armstrong	1959.7-12.rem(x2)
Cartwright's Site	Institute of Archaeology	P1989.1-4
Chania Falls (Central)	East African Expedition	1925.4-10.42
Chianda	Owen	1938.6-1.85
Elmenteita	Hobley	1947.7-2.1-3
Endeph Drift	Institute of Archaeology	P1989.1-4
Engira	Armstrong	1959.7-12.rem(x1)
Gabe	Armstrong	1959.7-12.rem(x1)
Gamble's Cave (Rift Valley)	Braunholtz	1930.1-24.rem(x14)
	Hobley	1947.7-2.13-58 + rem. x 42
	Institute of Archaeology	P1989.1-4
	Leakey	1931.5-6.4-32
	Leakey (for East African Expedition)	1931.2-9.38-131, 144-201 +unreg. x 299
	Oakley (Coryndon Museum)	1947.10-6.43-58
	Unknown (Leakey ?)	Unreg. x 1
Gilgil Lake Beds	Institute of Archaeology	P1989.1-4
Holo	Armstrong	1959.7-12.rem(x7)
Ilsemya	Owen	Unreg. x 1
Kabete	East African Expedition	1925.4-10.41
	Leakey	1923.5-10.1-20, 22
	Leakey	1924.2-2.1-9
Kachuku (Nyanza)	The Natural History Museum	1926.1-4.1-4, 6-10, 13-15
Kadawa	Armstrong	1959.7-12.rem(x7)
Kagola	Armstrong	1959.7-12.rem(x3)
Kahuraya	Institute of Archaeology	P1989.1-4
Kamenya	Armstrong	1959.7-12.rem(x28)
Kapuorya	Armstrong	1959.7-12.rem(x9)
Karateng	Armstrong	1959.7-12.rem(x31)
Kariandusi (Central)	Institute of Archaeology	P.1989.1-4
	Leakey	1931.2-9.1-15
	Oakley (Coryndon Museum)	1947.10-6.14-20
Karungu (Nyanza)	The Natural History Museum	1926.1-4.1-16
Kasagam	Armstrong	1959.7-12.rem(x19)
Katuda	Oakley (Coryndon Museum)	1947.10-6.2-4
Katunda	Institute of Archaeology	P.1989.1-4
Kavirondo (Nyanza)	Hull	1933.11-8.1, 6-16, 21-38
Kavirondo District (Nyanza)	Owen	1930.1-21.1-20
Kedong	Institute of Archaeology	P.1989.1-4
Kiambu	Hobley	1919-19 to 1919-51
Kikuyu Station (Central)	Hobley	1913.10-6.1-12
	Hobley	1947.7-2.84-90 + rem. x 8
Kimplop Plateau	Institute of Archaeology	P.1989.1-4
Kisami (Nyanza)	Hull	1933.11-8.17-20
	Owen	1930.1-21.17-20
Kisiani River (Nyanza)	Hull	1933.11-8.2-5
	Owen	1930.1-21.2-3
Kisu	Owen	1930.1-21.4-5
Kisumu (Nyanza)	Owen	1938.6-1.65-73 + rem. x 7
Kombewa (Nyanza)	Owen	1938.6-1.1-23 + rem. x 41
Koobi Fora	Museum of Kenya, Nairobi	Unreg. x 12 casts
	Wheeler, ex The Natural History Museum	P.O.A.196 1-3 casts
Kwoyo	Armstrong	1959.7-12.rem(x52)
Kyambu	Leakey	1923.5-10.21
Lake Naivasha (Rift Valley)	Unknown	Unreg. x 8
Lake Turkana	Hobley ?	Unreg. x 13
Lela	Armstrong	1959.7-12.rem(x18)
Lewa	Institute of Archaeology	P.1989.1-4
	Robertson, ex Leakey	1936.2-3.1-8 + rem. x 6
Long's Drift (Central)	Hobley	1947.7-2.64-83
	Leakey	1931.5-6.33-45
Luanda	Armstrong	Unreg. x 1
Malewa Gorge (Rift Valley)	Museum of Kenya, Nairobi	Unreg. x 10 casts
Malewa River Valley (Rift Valley)	Hobley	1947.7-2.59-63
	Leakey	1931.2-9.24-37, 132-143, 202-214
	Oakley	1947.10-6.59
Marera	Armstrong	1959.7-12.rem(x2)
Masere	Armstrong	1959.7-12.rem(x37)
Mbeje (Nyanza)	Owen	1938.6-1.82
Mombasa	Armstrong	1959.7-12.rem(x1)

Mount Kenya	Institute of Archaeology	P.1989.1-4
Muguruk (Nyanza)	Institute of Archaeology	P.1989.1-4
	Oakley (Coryndon Museum)	1947.10-6.34-35
Muhwaya-Ramba	Institute of Archaeology	P.1989.1-4
Mut Ng'iya	Institute of Archaeology	P.1989.1-4
Nairobi	Harrison	1909-32 to 37
	Hobley	1913.10-6.10
Naivasha	Institute of Archaeology	P.1989.1-4
Naivasha Railway Shelter (Rift Valley)	Oakley (Coryndon Museum)	1947.10-6.61
Nakuru, Burial Site (Rift Valley)	Leakey	1931.5-6.49-70 + unreg. x 29
Nakuru, Lion Hill Cave (Rift Valley)	Oakley (Coryndon Museum)	1947.10-6.60
Nanyuki (Central)	Institute of Archaeology	P.1989.1-4
	Leakey	1931.2-9.16-23
	Oakley (Coryndon Museum)	1947.10-6.27-33
Nawasha	Institute of Archaeology	P.1989.1-4
Ng'ira (Nyanza)	Owen	1938.6-1.83
	Owen	1939.5-15.1-2
Ng'iya District	Institute of Archaeology	P.1989.1-4
	Owen	1930.1-21.11-16
Nira (Nyanza)	The Natural History Museum	1926.1-4.5, 11-12
Njoro (Rift Valley)	Hobley	1947.7-2.4-12 + rem. x 84
	Institute of Archaeology	P.1989.1-4
	Platt	1936.10-8.1-24 + rem. x 48
	Sturge	p. 113 (x 10)
Nyandwat Hill (Nyanza)	Owen	1938.6-1.74-76 + rem. x 3
Nyarota (Nyanza)	The Natural History Museum	1926.1-4.16
Ol Kalau	Institute of Archaeology	P.1989.1-4
Olorgesailie	Institute of Archaeology	P.1989.1-4
	Oakley (Coryndon Museum)	1947.10-6.21-26
	Museum of Kenya, Nairobi	Unreg. x 5 casts
Osweyo River (Nyanza)	Owen	1939.5-15.3
Oumahdi (Nyanza)	Oakley (Coryndon Museum)	1947.10-6.1
Pala (Nyanza)	Owen	1938.6-1.84
Rabuoi Kane	Armstrong	1959.7-12.rem(x11)
	Hull	1933.11-8.1-34
Rift Valley, no further provenance	Gregory	1930.12-9.1-7
Rongai Valley (Central)	Kensett Styles	1922.7-4.1
Seme	Armstrong	1959.7-12.rem(x12)
Sidke Kane	Armstrong	1959.7-12.rem(x1)
South Maragoli	Armstrong	1959.7-12.rem(x3)
Stable's Drift (Rift Valley)	Hobley	1947.7-2.117-118
	Leakey	1931.5-6.1-3
Uranga	Armstrong	1959.7-12.rem(x2)
	Owen	1930.1-21.6-10
Usengi Hill (Nyanza)	Owen	1938.6-1.24-64 + rem. x 77
Uhmahdi (Nyanza)	Owen	1938.6-1.81 + rem. x 1
Waulala	Institute of Archaeology	P.1989.1-4
Western Kenya	Armstrong	Unreg. x 449
Yala Alego	Coryndon Museum	1947.10-6.4
	Institute of Archaeology	P.1989.1-4
	Owen	1930.1-21.1
	Owen	1938.6-1.77-78
No further provenance	Armstrong	Unreg. x 66
	Leakey	1931.5-6.47-48
	Museum of Kenya, Nairobi	Unreg. x 33 casts
	Seton-Karr	Unreg. x 17
	Unknown	Unreg. x 25
LIBYA		
Ain Hofra (Cyrenaica)	Jowett	1950.4-3.1-5
Benghazi (Cyrenaica)	Jowett	1950.4-3.6
Cyrenaica Region (Cyrenaica)	McBurney & Watson	Unreg. x 1120
Darnah	McBurney & Watson	Unreg. x 2
Driana	McBurney & Watson	Unreg. x 1
Fued	McBurney & Watson	Unreg. x 1
Gharyan (Tripolitania)	English	1948.4-1.1-13
Haua Fteah (Cyrenaica)	McBurney	Unreg. x 135
	Sieveking	Unreg. x 1
Libyan Desert	Shaw W. Kennedy	1935.11-9.155-164 + rem. x 11
Ras Aamer	McBurney & Watson	Unreg. x 2
Tripoli (Tripolitania)	Unknown	Unreg. x 15

Tukrah Pass	McBurney & Watson	Unreg. x 3
Zlitan	Dauncey	1962.11-7.1-18
No further provenance	Institute of Archaeology	P.1989.1-4
MALI		
Jineiart	Capitan	1912.7-10.11
MAURITANIA		
Sahara, no further provenance	Dangelzer	1910.12-6.1-26
No further provenance (Cap Blanc ?)	Unknown	Unreg. x 1
MOROCCO		
El Hank	Institute of Archaeology	P.1989.1-4
Grotte des Ours	Musée d'Histoire Naturelle Paris	1967.4-6.23 casts
Grotte des Pigeons, Taforalt	Institute of Archaeology	P1989.1-4
Oued Arjet	Institute of Archaeology	P.1989.1-4
Sidi Abderrahman	Institute of Archaeology	P.1989.1-4
	Musée d'Histoire Naturelle Paris	1967.4-6.12-16, 20-22, 24-26, 28-37 casts
Sidi Abderrahman S.T.I.C. Quarry,	Musée d'Histoire Naturelle Paris	1967.4-6.1-11 casts
Souk el Arba du Rharb	Musée d'Histoire Naturelle Paris	1967.4-6.39-40, 44 casts
Tangier, Mackay Radio Station	Institute of Archaeology	P1989.1-4
Tardiguet	Musée d'Histoire Naturelle Paris	1967.4-6.38, 41-43 casts
No further provenance	Calvert	1863.1-5.1
NIGER		
Bilma	Pinaud	1947.2-3 rem. x 18
Kawar Oasis (Agadez)	Pinaud	1947.2-3.1-95
Termit (Zinder)	Pinaud	1947.2-3.96-143 + rem. x 4
NIGERIA		
Bauchi Plateau (Bauchi)	Falconer	1926.3-8.2-5, 7, 9-13
	Week	1924.10-13.1-9
Benin City	Lacaille	Unreg. x 1
Cross River	Chinnock ?	Unreg. x 1
Delimi River (Bauchi)	Williams	1925.5-14.2
	Williams	1927.5-11.1-17, 19-29, 31-32, 34-35 + unreg. x 25
Itu (Calabar)	Jeffreys	1926.3-12.2-7
Jos (Plateau)	D'Arcy Leaver	1926.2-12.1-7
	Langslow-Cock	1914.6-17.81-82, 85-90
	Williams	1926.4-5.2-10
Lagos Bay	Sturge	p. 113 (x 2)
Langjuyu	Chinnock	Unreg. x 9
M'Bar area (Kaduna)	United Africa Company Ltd.	1930.10-16.1
North-central Nigeria, no further provenance	Langslow-Cock	1914.6-17.70-72
Northern Nigeria, no further provenance	Wellcome	P1982.10-4.4560
Obubra (Imo)	Wellcome	P1982.10-4.4531-4559
Rafin Sainyi (Bauchi)	Williams	1925.5-14.1
Randa (Plateau)	Hepburn	1935.10-28.1
Ropp Rock Shelter	Soper & Eyo	Unreg. x 323
South Rop (Majapota) Camp (Plateau)	Terrell	1926.4-6.1-4
No further provenance	Temple	1913.10-13.103
	Unknown	Unreg. x 3
SOMALIA		
Berbera	Sturge ex Seton Karr	Cat. No. 937-941, 944-948 + x349
	Warren	Unreg. x 2
Derbiga Arad (Woqooyi)	Curle	1937.3-12.16
Hormo (Sanaag)	Collenette	1951.11-4.1-13 + rem. x 40
Marodiyeh	Passmore Edwards Museum	P1995.4-1.207
	Warren	Unreg. x 1
No further provenance	Buscall-Fox	1919.10-4.9
	Christy	Cat. No. 96-665 to 96-736
	Franks	95-1059 to 1134
	Lacaille	Unreg. x 1
	Trechmann	1964.12-6.1493-1500
	Warren	Unreg. x 13
	Wellcome	P1982.10-4.4561-4581
SUDAN		
Jebelein	Unknown	Unreg. x 14
Khartoum	Sturge	p. 115 (x 10)

Libyan Desert	Shaw W. Kennedy	1935.11-9.49-70, 131-154 + rem. x 263
Selima Oasis	Shaw	1935.11-9.202-212 + rem. x 18
Wadi Halfa	Archer	1886.11-16.1-46
Wadi Hamrah	Shaw	1935.11-9.201 + rem. x 29
No further provenance	Seton-Karr	Unreg. x 2
TANZANIA		
Kilwa (Mtwara)	Smith	1886.6-25.1
Kiwahi River	Leakey	Unreg. x 7
Lake Manyara (Arusha)	Oakley (Coryndon Museum)	1947.10-6.13, 36-42
Musoma (Mara)	Owen	1938.6-1.79
Olduvai Gorge (Arusha)	Leakey	1932.4-5.1-4; 1934.12-14.1-96
	Leakey	1937.2-8.1
	Oakley (Coryndon Museum)	1947.10-6.5-12
Tendaguru (Lindi)	Leakey	1925.4-10.1-40
TUNISIA		
Beni Barka	Institute of Archaeology	P.1989.1-4
Bir Dufan	Institute of Archaeology	P.1989.1-4
El Ayaïcha & Kasserine (Kasserine)	Statham	1934.7-13.51-75 + rem. x 19
El Maïa	Institute of Archaeology	P.1989.1-4
El Mekta (Gafsa)	Institute of Archaeology	P.1989.1-4
	Wellcome	P1982.10-4.4582
Fewasa Road, Gafsa (Gafsa)	Institute of Archaeology	P.1989.1-4
Gafsa (Gafsa)	Institute of Archaeology	P.1989.1-4
	Wellcome	P1982.10-4.4583
Jbel Aidudi	Christy	6875
Jbel Aziz	Christy	6877-6878
Jbel Haguet Ammor	Christy	6873
Jbel Kidna	Christy	6874
Limaguess	Institute of Archaeology	P.1989.1-4
Matmata	Institute of Archaeology	P.1989.1-4
Oued Djeneien (Kasserine)	Berry	1926.12-11.1-11
Redeyef (Gafsa)	Wellcome	P1982.10-4.4584-4625
Sbeitla	Institute of Archaeology	P.1989.1-4
Sidi Mansour	Institute of Archaeology	P.1989.1-4
Sidi Zin	Institute of Archaeology	P.1989.1-4
Tozeur (Gafsa)	Theobald	1927.5-14.1-11, 13-34
No further provenance	Christy	6861-6872, 6876
UGANDA		
Bugungu (Bugosa)	Institute of Archaeology	P.1989.1-4
	O'Brien	1936.11-10.61-78, 126-150 + rem. x 172
Bulo	Armstrong	Rem. x 49
Gayaza Hills (Southern Buganda)	O'Brien	1936.11-10.88-89
Jinja-Bugembe (Bugosa)	O'Brien	1936.11-10.56-60 + rem. x 7
	O'Brien	1937.10-8.17-18
Kafu River (Western)	Institute of Archaeology	P.1989.1-4
	O'Brien	1936.11-10.4-40 + rem. x 63
	O'Brien	1937.10-8.1-5
	Wayland	1940.4-6.1-15 + rem. x 7
Kafu & Kagera Rivers (Western & Southern)	Wayland	1940.4-6 + rem. x 4
Kagera River (Southern)	Institute of Archaeology	P.1989.1-4
	O'Brien	1936.11-10.41-48 + rem. x 6
Kagera Valley	O'Brien	1937.10-8.6-10, 14-16
Kagera River	Wayland	1940.4-6.19-38 + rem. x 17
	Wayland	1956.10-5 + rem. x 16
Kalebe Masaka (Southern Buganda)	Wayland	1940.4-6.54
Kalema (Southern Buganda)	Wayland	1923.3-5.10
Katale Hill (Southern Buganda)	Wayland	1923.3-5.6
Kibangya (Western)	Wayland	1940.4-6.16-18 + rem. x 2
Kigarama (Southern Buganda)	Wayland	1923.3-5.3, 7
Kigezi (Kigezi)	O'Brien	1936.11-10.90-92
Lukili Hill (Southern Buganda)	Wayland	1923.3-5.11
Luwala	Armstrong	rem. x 1
Mbarara Road (Southern)	Wayland	1940.4-6 + rem. x 1
Msozi Hill	Wayland	1923.3-5.1, 2, 4-5, 9, 12
Muzizi River (Western)	O'Brien	1936.11-10.49-55 + rem. x 9
Nakarah (Southern)	Wayland	1956.10-5.51
Nsongezi (Southern Buganda)	O'Brien	1936.11-10.1-3, 93-102, 169-180 + rem. x 494

	O'Brien	1937.10-8.11-13 + rem. x 12
	Wayland	1940.4-6.39-50, 52-53, 55-85, 88-151 + rem. x 2
	Wayland	1956.10-5.39-50, 52-61,89-113 + rem. x 63
Orichinga Valley (Southern Buganda)	O'Brien	1936.11-10.103-125 + rem. x 120
	O'Brien	1937.10-8.19-60
	Wayland	1940.4-6 + rem. x 9
Sango Hills (Southern Buganda)	Institute of Archaeology	P.1989.1-4
	O'Brien	1936.11-10.79-82, 84-87 + rem. x 4
Simba (Southern Buganda)	Wayland	1923.3-5.8
Soloman's Gulley, Orichinga Valley (Southern Buganda)	Wayland	1956.10-5.1-38, 62-88, 114-121 + rem. x 50
Walasi Hills	Institute of Archaeology	P.1989.1-4
	O'Brien	1936 11-10.151-168 + rem. x 292
No further provenance	Wayland	1940.4-6.152-158 + unreg. x 12
WEST AFRICA		
No further provenance	Christy	6856-6859
ZAMBIA		
Batoka Valley	Lamplugh	1910.12-28.4-5
Bilisau Village (Central/Eastern)	Lancaster	1938.11-5.19-27 + rem. x 2
Cheni Hills	Unknown	Unreg.
Chingongono Hills (Northern)	Lancaster	1938.5-6.1-7 + rem. x 7
Giese's Drift (Southern)	Lamplugh	1906.5-19.24
Kabwe	Codrington	1910.3-7.1-6
	Read	1913.6-18.4-5, 7, 9-13
Kaka Village (Northern)	Lancaster	1938.11-5.1-6
Kalambo Falls	Rhodes-Livingstone Museum	1964.6-3.1-313
Kapende River	Lamplugh	1910.12-28.8-10
Kapini Kasanga Hill (Northern)	Lancaster	1938.5-6 + rem. x 5
Kapundi (Southern)	Lamplugh	1906.5-19.5, 7, 19, 22
Kavingelo Hills (Northern)	Lancaster	1938.5-6.12-16 + rem. x 2
Kavingelo River (Northern)	Lancaster	1938.5-6.17-48 + rem. x 189
Kayamati Hills (Northern)	Lancaster	1939.10-8.1-9 + rem. x 11
Lilundi River	Lancaster	1938.5-6 + rem. x 6
Livingstone (Southern)	Lamplugh	1906.5-19.28
Livingstone Railway Station (Southern)	Allport	1928.10-16.1
Lukashi & Luangwa Rivers (Northern)	Lancaster	1938.11-5.1-31 + rem.
Lundi River (Northern)	Lancaster	1938.5-6.78-94 + rem. x 274
Madzi-Wa-Fipa (Northern)	Lancaster	1939.10-8.10-19 + rem. x 4
Malungwe Village (Central/Eastern)	Lancaster	1938.11-5.17-18
Mamba Camp (Southern)	Lamplugh	1906.5-19.12, 25
	Lamplugh	1910.12-28.12
Manga Village (Northern)	Lancaster	1938.5-6 + rem. x 3
Maramba River	Lamplugh	1910.12-28.7
Milvila Hill (Northern)	Lancaster	1938.5-6 + rem. x 6
Mulindwa Village (Northern)	Lancaster	1938.5-6.95-97 + rem. x 11
Mulopwe Village (Northern)	Lancaster	1939.10-8.20-42 + rem. x 19
Mulowelela (Northern)	Lancaster	1938.11-5.28-29
Mututumusha (Northern)	Lancaster	1938.11-5.7-16
Mviatama (Northern)	Lancaster	1939.10-8.43
Mwila (Northern)	Lancaster	1938.5-6.8-11 + rem. x 6
Nawombwe Rise (Northern)	Lancaster	1938.5-6.49-77 + rem. x 151
Ndebvu (Northern)	Lancaster	1938.11-5.31
Pompi Valley (Northern)	Lancaster	1938.11-5.30
Songwi (Southern)	Lamplugh	1906.5-19.8-10
Victoria Falls (Southern)	Armstrong	rem. x 296
	Braunholtz	1930.1-24 + rem. x 18
	Braunholtz	1947.7-2 + rem. x 32
	Braunholtz	rem. x 224
	Lamplugh	1906.5-19.2-4, 11, 13-18, 20-21, 23, 26-27
	Lamplugh	1910.12-28.1-12
	Matley	1935.10-14.1-14 + rem. x 21
	Read	1913.6-18.15-16, 18
	White	1922.6-6.1-16
	Wildon	rem. x 7
Zambezi River	Lamplugh	1910.12-28.1-3, 6

List of Collectors, North, West and East Africa
Biographical details of collectors who appear here enboldened are given in Appendix 4.

Allport	Zambia (Livingstone Railway Station)
Archer	Sudan (Wadi Halfa)
Armstrong	Kenya (Agula, Asembo, Bunyore, Butere, Engira, Gabe, Holo, Kadawa, Kagola, Kamenya, Kapuorya, Karateng, Kasagam, Kwoyo, Lela, Loanda, Malewa Gorge, Marera, Masere, Mombasa, Rabuoi Kane, Seme, Sidhe Kane, South Maragoli, Uranga, West Kenya, No further provenance) Uganda (Bulo, Uwala) Zambia (Victoria Falls)
Avebury	Algeria (Algiers, Ougarla)
Berry	Tunisia (Oued Djeneien)
Braunholtz	Kenya (Gamble's Cave) Zambia (Victoria Falls)
Burrows	Democratic Republic of Congo (Matadi)
Buscall-Fox	Somalia (No further provenance)
Calvert	Morocco (No further provenance)
Capitan	Mali (Jineiart)
Cardinall	Ghana (Navaro)
Cartailhac	Algeria (No further provenance)
Chinnock	Nigeria (Cross River ?, Langjuyu)
Christy	Algeria (El Kala, Grotte des Grand Roche, Laghouat, No further provenance) Democratic Republic of Congo (Matadi) Somalia (No further provenance) Tunisia (Jbel Aidudi, Jbel Aziz, Jbel Haguet Ammor, Jbel Kidna, No further provenance) West Africa (No further provenance)
Clifford	Ghana (Accra)
Codrington	Zambia (Kabwe)
Collenette	Somalia (Hormo)
Coryndon Museum, Nairobi	Kenya (Yala Alego)
Cremer	Ghana (Accra)
Curle	Ethiopia (Daghabur) Somalia (Derbiga Arad)
D'Arcy Leaver	Nigeria (Jos)
Dalrymple	Ghana (No further provenance)
Dangelzer	Mauritania (Sahara)
Dauncey	Libya (Zlitan)
East African Expedition	Kenya (Chania Falls, Gamble's Cave)
English	Libya (Gharyan)
Falconer	Nigeria (Bauchi Plateau)
Flower	Algeria (Laghouat)
Franks	Algeria (Grotte des Grand Roche, No further provenance) Somalia (No further provenance)
Fromholtz	Algcria (Timassinin)
Geological Museum	Ghana (No further provenance)
Geological Survey, Gold Coast	Ghana (Ayetta, Guduri, Takoradi)
Gregory	Kenya (Rift Valley)
Harrison	Kenya (Nairobi)
Hepburn	Nigeria (Randa)
Hobley	Kenya (Elmenteita, Gamble's Cave, Kiambu, Kikuyu, Kikuyu Station, Lake Turkana, Long's Drift, Malewa River Valley, Nairobi, Njoro, Stable's Drift)
Hull	Kenya (Kavirondo, Kisami, Kisiani River, Rabuoi Kane)
Institute of Archaeology	Africa (No further provenance) Algeria (Ain Hanech, Ain Taya, Bir el ater, Kerem, Koudiat Bou Gherard, Lac Karar, S'baikia, Tabelbala, No further provenance) Democratic Republic of Congo (No further provenance) Kenya (Cartwright's Site, Endeph Drift, Gamble's Cave, Gilgil Lake Beds, Kahuraya, Kariandusi, Katunda, Kedong, Kimplop Plateau, Lewa, Mount Kenya, Muguruk, Muhwaya-Ramba, Mut Ng'iya, Naivasha, Nanyuki, Nawasha, Ng'iya Distrcit, Njoro, Ol Kalau, Olorgesailie, Waulala, Yala Alego, No further provenance) Libya (No further provenance) Morocco (Grotte des Pigeons, Tangier) Tunisia (Beni Barka, Bir Dufan, Gafsa, El Ma•a, El Mekta, Fewana Road, Limaguess, Matmata, Sbeitla, Sidi Mansour, Sidi Zin) Uganda (Bugungu, Kafu River, Kagera, Sango Hills, Walasi Hills)
Jeffreys	Nigeria (Itu)
Jowett	Libya (Ain Hofra, Benghazi)
Junner	Ghana (Abehenasi-Hohoe, Axim, Batabe, Garkwa, Kintampo-Weila, Koue-Tachi, Manso, Mo River, Nambiri, Togoland, No further provenance)

Kensett-Styles	Kenya (Rongai Valley)
Lacaille	Nigeria (Benin City) Somalia (No further provenance)
Lamplugh	Zambia (Batoka valley, Giese's Drift, Kapende River, Kapundi, Livingstone, Mamba Camp, Maramba River, Songwi, Victoria Falls, Zambezi River)
Lancaster	Zambia (Bilisau Village, Chingongono Hills, Kaka Village, Kapini, Kasanga Hill, Kavingelo Hills, Kavingelo River, Kayamati Hills, Lilundi River, Lukashi & Luangwa Rivers, Lundi River, Madzi-Wa-Fipa, Malungwe Village, Manga Village, Milvila Hill, Mulindwa Village, Mulopwe Village, Mulowelela, Mututumusha, Mviatama, Mwila, Nawome Rise, Ndebvu, Pompi Valley)
Langslow-Cook	Nigeria (Jos, North-central Nigeria)
Leakey	Kenya (Gamble's Cave, Kabete, Kariandusi, Kyambu, Lewa, Long's Drift, Malewa River valley, Nakuru Burial Site, Nanyuki, Stable's Drift, Olorgesailie, No further provenance) Tanzania (Kiwahi River, Olduvai Gorge, Tendaguru)
Lukis	Algeria (Grotte des Grand Roche)
Lull	Algeria (Ain Babouche, El Araich, Foughala, Lichana, Oued Belcibis, Oued Falaous, Oued M'lili, Oulmache, Rassouta, Sidi Okba, Texenna, Tolga)
McAlpine-Wood	Ghana (Obuasi)
McBurney	Libya (Haua Fteah)
McBurney & Watson	Libya (Cyrenaica, Darnah, Driana, Fued, Ras Aamer, Tripoli, Tukrah Pass)
Matley	Zambia (Victoria Falls)
Morell	Algeria (No further provenance)
Musée d'Histoire Naturelle Paris	Algeria (Ain Hanech, El Ma-El-Abiod, Erg Tihodaine, Tachanghit, Ternifine) Morocco (Grotte des Ours, Sidi Abderraham, Souk el Arba du Rharb, S.T.I.C. Quarry, Tardiguet)
Museum of Kenya, Nairobi	Kenya (Koobi Fora, Malewa Gorge, Olorgesailie, No further provenance)
The Natural History Museum	Kenya (Kachuku, Karungu, Nyarota)
Newton	Cameroon (Babanki Tungau, Bamneda Province, Bamenda Station, Kawngli, Lip, Mbem)
O'Brien	Uganda (Bugungu, Gayaza Hills, Jinja-Bugembe, Kagera River, Kigezi, Muzizi River, Nsongezi, Orichinga Valley, Sango Hills, Walasi Hills)
Oakley	Kenya (Malewa River Valley)
Oakley (Coryndon Museum)	Kenya (Gamble's Cave, Kariandusi, Katuda, Musuruk, Naivasha Railway Shelter, Nanyuki, Oumahdi) Tanzania (Lake Manyara, Olduvai Gorge)
Owen	Kenya (Aringo, Chianda, Ilsemya, Kavirondo District, Kisami, Kisiani River, Kisu, Kisumu, Kombewa, Mbeje, Ng'ira, Ng'iya District, Nyandwat Hill, Pala, Uranga, Usengi Hill, Uumahdi, Yala Alego); Tanzania (Musoma)
Passmore Edwards Museum	Somalia (No further provenance)
Pinaud	Niger (Bilma, Kawar Oasis, Termit)
Platt	Kenya (Njoro)
Popham	Ghana (Accra)
Read	Zambia (Kabwe, Victoria Falls)
Reygasse	Algeria (El Ma-El-Abiod, S'Baikia, S'Mair. Timassinin, Touibia)
Rhodes-Livingstone Museum	Zambia (Kalambo Falls)
Robertson	Kenya (Lewa)
Seligman	Algeria (Tabel Balat)
Seton-Karr	Kenya (No further provenance) Sudan (No further provenance)
Shaw	Sudan (Libyan Desert, Selima Oasis, Wadi Hamrah)
Shaw W. Kennedy	Libya (Libyan Desert) Sudan (Libyan Desert)
Smith	Tanzania (Kilwa)
Soper & Eyo	Nigeria (Rep Rock Shelter)
Statham	Tunisia (El Ayaïcha & Kasserine)
Sturge	Algeria (Algiers, Bel Abbès, Fningres, Ougarla, Oran-Est, Palikao, Ternifine, No further provenance) Kenya (Njoro) Nigeria (Lagos Bay) Somalia (Berbera) Sudan (Khartoum)
Temple	Nigeria (No further provenance)
Terrell	Nigeria (South Rop)
Theobald	Tunisia (Tozeur)
Tollefsen	Democratic Republic of Congo (Katenda)
Trechmann	Algeria (Ougarla) Somalia (No further provenance)
United Africa Company Ltd.	Nigeria (M'Bar)
Vaufrey	Algeria (Oued Djouf El Djemel)
Warren	Somalia (Berbera, Marodiyeh, No further provenance)

Wayland	Uganda (Kafu River, Kafu & Kagera Rivers, Kagera River, Kalebe Masaka, Kalema, Katale Hill, Kibangya, Kigarama, Lukili Hill, Mbarara Road, Msozi Hill, Nakarah, Nsongezi, Orichinga Valley, Simba, Soloman's Gulley, no further provenance)
Week	Nigeria (Bauchi Plateau)
Wellcome	Algeria (Teneit El Had, Tlemcen, No further provenance) Nigeria (Northern Nigeria, Obubra) Somalia (No further provenance) Tunisia (El Mekta, Gafsa, Redeyef)
Wheeler	Kenya (Koobi Fora)
White	Ethiopia (Danakil Depression, No further provenance)
F. White	Zambia (Victoria Falls)
Wild	Ghana (Akwatia, Ashanti Province, Bombiri, Kele Nachi, Nsuta, Obuasi)
Wildon	Zambia (Victoria Falls)
Williams	Nigeria (Delimi River, Jos, Rafin Sainyi) Democratic republic of Congo (Lukando, Makuta, Mongo, M'Bio, Natumba, Vila, No further provenance).

Appendix 3. Stone Age Archaeological Collections from Southern Africa in other Museums in the United Kingdom

Alison Roberts

Introduction

This Appendix lists briefly the southern Stone Age collections held by other museums in the United Kingdom. It is arranged alphabetically by country and, within South Africa, by province following the same order as the Gazetteer, though Angola, Botswana and Mozambique are all unrepresented. Within each country or province collections are listed alphabetically according to institution and then by site. Information on the names of the collections is as supplied by the host institution. Site names have been modernized where necessary, with the original spelling placed in italics within parentheses. A summary list of donors is included, which indicates the museum(s) in which their collection is located and if they are also represented in the PEE collections which are the subject of this Catalogue. The Appendix was completed in 1996, and since then the transfer to PEE of all of the collections listed here as belonging to the Institute of Archaeology has been completed (P.1989.1-4).

SOUTH AFRICA

i) Eastern Cape Provence

University Museum of Archaeology and Ethnography, University of Cambridge, Downing Street, Cambridge, CB2 3DZ

Aliwal North	Prof. A. Radcliffe-brown Collection (1923.1435)
Burgersdorp	Mrs W.K. Foster Collection, ex. J.C. Rickard, site 3 (1903.876,99,94a,95a,128 Z 35748)
	A.F. Griffith Collection, ex J.C. Rickard (1918.93.51-56)
Burgersdorp, Red House	Mrs W.K. Foster Collection, ex J.C. Rickard (or Redhouse, near Burgersdorp ?) (1903.127; Z 35776)
Bushman's River	M.C. Burkitt Collection, 1920s (1961.31)
Cradock	Dr W.M. Tapp Collection, ex H.H. Cottell (1925.2.a9)
Dordrecht	M.C. Burkitt, 1920s Collection (1927.2090)
Dordrecht, Bowers Drift	M.C. Burkitt, 1920s Collection (1927.2098)
Dordrecht, Clark's Siding Cave	M.C. Burkitt, 1920s Collection (1927.2092; 1961.27)
Dordrecht, Shelter with Elephant Painting	M.C. Burkitt, 1920s Collection (1927.2088-89)
Dordrecht, Victory Farm	M.C. Burkitt, 1920s Collection (1927.2091; 1955.300)
Dordrecht Kloof Rock Shelter	M.C. Burkitt 1920s, Collection (1927.2086-87; 1961.26)
East London	Mrs W.K. Foster Collection, ex J.C. Rickard (1903.45,47,56-58,87a-89a,91a, 104,110,112, 114-5,117-120,131a-135a,139-142; Z 27296)
	Mrs W.K. Foster Collection, ex J.C. Rickard, Site 1 (1903.48,50,55,59,97,99, Z 27289,35741-3)
	A.F. Griffith Collection, ex J.C. Rickard (1918.93.4,18,35,37-50,78; Z 36052)
	J.C. Rickard Collection (Z 35830)
	F. White Collection (1902.274.271)
East London, Nahoon River Mouth	Mrs W.K. Foster Collection, ex J.C. Rickard (1903.117)
East London, west of Fort Glamorgan	Mrs W.K. Foster Collection, ex J.C. Rickard, Site 1b (1903.81,90a)
East London, near Fort Grey	Mrs W.K. Foster Collection, ex J.C. Rickard (1903.118)
Grahamstown, Glencraig Farm	M.C. Burkitt Collection, 1920s (1927.2016)
Halseton	Unknown Collector (1924.672)
Hanover	Unknown Collector (Z 36086)
Herschel District	J. Millard (or Milland) Collection (132.581-4)
Herschel, Stevenson's Farm Shelter	J. Milland (or Millard) Collection (1932.576-9,585-6; Z 36061)
Howieson's Poort	M.C. Burkitt Collection, 1920s (1927.2108-9; 1955.304)
I'kwaku River	Mrs W.K. Foster Collection, ex J.C. Rickard (1903.92a)
King Williams Town	M.C.Burkitt Collection, 1920s (1927.2100)
Middledrift	M.C. Burkitt Collection, 1920s (1927.2101-5; 1 (976.331,580,583)
Middledrift, Cildarra Road	M.C. Burkitt Collection, 1927 (1961.24c)
Middledrift, Euphorbia Kloof	M.C. Burkitt Collection, 1920s (1927.2103; 1976.326)
Middledrift, Fort Lex	M.C. Burkitt Collection, 1920s (1976.335)
Middledrift, Wilson's Farm	M.C. Burkitt Collection, 1920s (1927.2104-5)
Molteno	M.C. Burkitt Collection, 1920s (1927.2081-2; 1955.290,297; 1976.603)
Molteno, Kilgobbin Farm	M.C. Burkitt Collection, 1920s (1927.2083-4)
Port Elizabeth	M.C. Burkitt Collection, 1920s (1927.2110)
	Mrs W.K. Foster Collection, ex J.C. Rickard (1903.119a; Z 35792-3)
	A.F. Griffith Collection, ex J.C. Rickard, 1881 (1918.93.82,84,87,91-2,94,105)
Port Elizabeth, Algoa Bay	Mrs W.K. Foster Collection, ex J.C. Rickard, Site 36c (1903.72-4; Z 27275,27279
	A.F. Griffith Collection, ex J.C. Rickard 1881, Site 36c (1918.93.81)
	J.C. Rickard Collection, Site 36c (Z 27275)

Port Elizabeth, First Reservoir	Mrs W.K. Foster Collection, ex J.C. Rickard, Site 36b (1903.70,85; Z 27278)
	J.C. Rickard Collection, Site 36b (Z 27274)
Port Elizabeth, Second Reservoir	Mrs W.K. Foster Collection, ex J.C. Rickard (1903.121)
	J.C. Rickard Collection (Z 27276)
Port Elizabeth, Kitchen Midden	Mrs W.K. Foster Collection, ex J.C. Rickard, Site 38 (1903.44d; Z 27294,35797-8, 36047-8)
Port Elizabeth, Raised Beach	Mrs W.K. Foster Collection, ex J.C. Rickard, Site 36h (Z 35796)
Port Elizabeth, Richmond Hill	Mrs W.K. Foster Collection, ex J.C. Rickard, Site 36a (1903.68-9,84; Z 27290)
	A.F. Griffith Collection, ex J.C. Rickard, Site 36a (1918.93.77)
	J.C. Rickard Collection, Site 36a (Z 27273,36046)
Port Elizabeth, Sharks River	Mrs W.K. Foster Collection, ex J.C. Rickard, Site 36f (1903.52-3,123a,135,145-6; Z 35794)
Queenstown	M.C. Burkitt Collection 1920s (1927.2093; 1955.303)
	Mrs W.K. Foster Collection, ex J.C. Rickard (1903.60,80,86,125)
Queenstown, Ella's Farm	M.C. Burkitt Collection, 1920s (1955.508)
Queenstown, Glengrey Falls	M.C. Burkitt Collection, 1920s (1927.2097; 1976.342)
Queenstown, Newey's Farm	M.C. Burkitt Collection, 1920s (1927.2099)
Schildekranz Rock Shelter	M.C. Burkitt Collection, 1920s (1927.2096)
Stormberg, Bushman's Hoek	Mrs W.K. Foster Collection, ex J.C. Rickard, Site 11 (1903.87,93a,126; Z 35777)
Uitenhage District	A.F. Griffith Collection, ex J.C. Rickard (1918.93.102-4)
Whittlesea	M.C. Burkitt Collection, 1920s (1927.2095)
Wilton Rock Shelter	M.C. Burkitt Collection, 1920s (1927.2107)
Windvogelberg	Mrs W.K. Foster Collection, ex J.C. Rickard, Site 4 (1903.79,125; Z 27340, 35745)
Yardley, Sterkstroom	M.C. Burkitt Collection, 1920s (1955.294)

Liverpool Museum, William Brown Street, Liverpool, L300A

Alexandria	Miss Hobley Collection, per British Museum (47.31.321-3260
King Williams Town	Transfer from Norwich Museum, ex G.H. Thistleton Dyer, 1940 (56.28.956-8)

The Manchester Museum, University of Manchester, Oxford Road, Manchester M13 9PL

Burgersdorp	D.M.S. Watson Collection (1913: O.2656)
Burgersdorp, Bushman Cave	D.M.S. Watson Collection (1913: O.1691)
Graaf Reinet	Mr Foster Collection (1906: O.1367)
Port Elizabeth, Bank of Zak River	J.J. Cleverly Collection, 1885 (1920: O.2853-54)

The Natural History Museum, Cromwell Road, London SW7 5BD

Algoa Bay	Unknown Collector (E.1073)
East London	G.L. Griesbach, 1883 (E.168)
Grahamstown	Lady Prestwich, 1896 (E.3194-6)
Karreedouw	Presented by East London Museum, ex Dr Leppé (1953: E.2321-22)
Tharfield	A.G. Bain Collection, ex T.H. Bowker, 1860 (E.1034-42)
Wodehouse, Bushman Cave	Mrs Bradshaw, ex Mrs A.A.L. Bowie, 1891 (1946: E.1074-76)

Ashmolean Museum, University of Oxford, Beaumont Street, Oxford, OX1 2PH

Grahamstown	Sir J. Evans Collection, ex Sir C. Lyell, ex A.G. Bain, 1865 (1927.6599.a-d)
Molteno (Cape of Good Hope)	Sir J. Evans Collection, 1876 (1958.569-70)
Port Elizabeth	Sir J. Evans Collection, ex J.C. Rickard, 1880 (1928.265.a-h)
'Cape East District'	Wellcome Collection, ex Lovett Collection (1982.997)

Pitt Rivers Museum, University of Oxford, Parks Road, Oxford, OX2 6PN

Albert District	J.T. Hewitt Collection, ex Dr D. Kannemeyer (1928)
	Dr Schönland Collection (1910)
Algoa Bay	C.G. Bliss Collection (1926)
Carnavondale, Bushman's River	Miss P. Ward Collection (1934)
Carnavondale, Van Riet Lowe's Site	Miss P. Ward Collection (1935)
Carnavondale, Woodbury Site	Miss P. Ward Collection (1936)
Carnavondale Farm	Miss P. Ward Collection (1935)
East London	H. Balfour Collection (1910)
	Sir J. Evans Collection, ex J.C. Rickard, 1880 (1928)
	J.A. Swan Collection (1937)
Grahamstown	Sir J. Evans Collection, ex Sir C. Lyell, ex A.G. Bain, 1865 (1928)
	Transfer from Ipswich Museum
Groot River, near coast (Sea Caves)	Dr H.D.R. Kingston Collection (1900)
Howieson's Poort	J.T. Hewitt Collection, 1922 (1928)
	Donated by the Trustees of the Albany Museum, Grahamstown (1923)
Middledrift	J.T. Hewitt Collection, 1922 (1928)
Nahoon (*Nahun*) River	H. Balfour Collection (1910)
	J.A. Swan Collection (1937)
Port Alfred	Donated by the Trustees of the Albany Museum, Grahamstown (1923)

Port Elizabeth	H. Balfour Collection (1910)
	C.G. Bliss Collection (1927)
	Sir J. Evans Collection, ex J.C. Rickard, 1880 (1928)
	F.W. Fitzsimons Collection (1910)
	Prof. C.G. Seligman Collection (1940.12.680)
Queenstown	Anthropological Institute Collection, ex J. Sanderson (1900)
Stormberg	Prof. W. Boyd Dawkins Collection (1897)
Tsitsikamma (*Tzizikama*) Forest Cave	J.T. Butters Collection (1910)
Uitenhage	Sir J. Evans Collection (1928)
	Prof. C.G. Seligman Collection (1940.12.679)
Walmer	F.W. Fitzsimmons Collection (1910)
Wilton Rock Shelter	Donated by the Trustees of the Albany Museum, Grahamstown (1923, 1926)

Royal Museum of Scotland, Chambers Street, Edinburgh EH1 1IF

Mount Ayliff District	Unknown Collector (A.1920.534-39,790)

Sheffield City Museum and Art Gallery, Weston Park, Sheffield S10 2TP

Burgersdorp, open veld	G. Leith Collection, 1896 (Unnumbered)
Kowie River Shell Mounds	G. Leith Collection, 1896 (Unnumbered)
Stormberg, Cave Shelters	G. Leith Collection, 1896 (Unnumbered)

ii) Free State

Birmingham Museum and Art Gallery, Chamberlain Square, Birmingham B3 3DH

Bloemfontein, Kaffir Sp (Ruit ?)	Mr C.B.C. Braine Collection, ex T. Holmes (1948a11.6)

University Museum of Archaeology and Ethnography, University of Cambridge, Downing Street, Cambridge Cb2 3dz

Avalon	M.C. Burkitt Collection, 1920s (127.2064)
Bethulie	Mrs W.K. Foster Collection, ex J.C. Rickard, Site 19 (1903.49)
	A.F. Griffith Collection, ex J.C. Rickard (1918.189)
Bloemfontein	M.C. Burkitt Collection, 1920s (1976.341)
Bloemfontein, Samaria Road	M.C. Burkitt Collection, 1920s (1961.25)
Boshof	Mrs W. K. Foster Collection, ex J.C. Rickard, Site 35 (1903.82,117a,118a, Z 35752)
Brakfontein (*Brackfontein*)	M.C. Burkitt Collection, 1920s (1927.2070-71; 1961.30; 1976.340)
Commissiefontein (*Commetze Fontein*)	A.F. Griffith Collection, ex J.C. Rickard, 1882 (1918.93.59)
De Kiel Oost	M.C. Burkitt Collection, 1920s (1927.2073-4; 1961.28; 1976.604)
Fauresmith	M.C. Burkitt Collection, 1920s (1927.2067-9
	Mrs W.K. Foster Collection, ex J.C. Rickard, Site 23 (1903.61)
Fauresmith, north of	Mrs W.K. Foster Collection, ex J.C. Rickard, Site 24 (1903.105,133,178; Z 35746)
Fauresmith, 25 miles north of	Mrs W.K. Foster Collection, ex J.C. Rickard, Site 26 (1903.101,106)
Fauresmith, 12 miles south of	Mrs W.K. Foster Collection, ex J.C. Rickard (1903.100)
Fauresmith, between Bethulie and	Mrs W.K. Foster Collection, ex J.C. Rickard (1903.98a,99a,132)
Fauresmith, Brakfontein Farm	M.C. Burkitt Collection, 1920s (1976.340.5)
Fauresmith, Prospect Farm	M.C. Burkitt Collection, 1920s (1927.2066; 1955.298)
Harrismith	Col H.W. Fielden Collection, 1900 (Z 36077)
	Dr P. Van Heerden Collection (Z 36103)
	Unknown Collector (Z 36073)
Hermann's Cave Kopje	M.C. Burkitt Collection (1976.610)
Karee Kloof	A.E.P. Collins Collection (Z 36088)
Klein Philippolis	M.C. Burkitt Collection, 1920s (1927.2062; 1955.299)
Koffiefontein	Miss M. Wilman Collection (1927.2080)
Koffiefontein, Afvallingskop	M.C. Burkitt Collection, 1920s (1927.2072)
Kranskraal (*Krantz Kraal*)	? A.E.P. Collins Collection (Z 36059)
Kroonstad	Unknown Collector (Z 36072)
Maselspoort	Dr P. Van Heerden Collection (Z 36104)
Modder Bridge	Unknown Collector (Z 36068)
Paardeberg (*Paardsberg*)	M.C. Burkitt Collection, 1920s (1927.2077; 1961.29; 1976.585)
Petrus	M.C. Burkitt Collection, 1920s (1927.2078)
Process Bridge	M.C. Burkitt Collection, 1920s (1927.2067)
Riet River	Mrs W.K. Foster Collection, ex J.C. Rickard, Site 25 (1903.44b,54)
Riet-Modder River Junction	M.C. Burkitt Collection, 1920s (1927.2075)
	Mrs W.K. Foster Collection, ex J.C. Rickard, Site 30 (1903.64-5,76,104,107-12, 1341-44, Z 27288, 35773)
	A.F. Griffith Collection, ex J.C. Rickard (1918.93.62-6)
	J.C. Rickard Collection, Site 31 (Z 35832)
Riversdale	Unknown Collector (Z 36074)
Sand River	Unknown Collector (Z 36070)
Smithfield	Dr W.M. Tapp Collection, ex Dr D. Kannemeyer (1925.2.a3-4)
Spytfontein	Unknown Collector (Z 36062)
Tollkop Rock Shelter	M.C. Burkitt Collection, 1920s (1927.2055)

Wet River	Unknown Collector (Z 36071)

Institute of Archaeology, University College, University of London, 31-34 Gordon Square, London WC1h 0PY

Brakfontein	C. Van Riet Lowe Collection

Liverpool Museum, William Brown Street, Liverpool L3 00A

Bultfontein Floors	Miss Hobley Collection, per British Museum (47.31.327)
Modder River Valley	Miss Hobley Collection, per British Museum (47.31.314-17,319-20)

The Natural History Museum, Cromwell Road, London SW7 5BD

Brakfontein	J. Dekenah Collection (E.2283-88)
	Dr K.P. Oakley Collection (1953: E.2265; E.2325; E.2490-2)
Cornelia, Schoonspruit	Dr K.P. Oakley Collection (1953: E.2271, 2332)
Florisbad	Dr K.P. Oakley Collection (1953: E.2219-20) Presented by the National Museum, Bloemfontein, ex Drs A.C. Hoffman, T.F. Dreyer and A.J.D. Meiring (E.2226-31)
	Presented by the National Museum, Bloemfontein, ex Dr T.F. Dreyer (E.2232-42)
Rose Cottage Cave, Ladybrand	Dr K.P. Oakley Collection (1953: E.2273)
Vlakkraal (Prinsloo's Farm)	Dr K.P. Oakley Collection (1953: E.2221-25)

Pitt Rivers Museum, University of Oxford, Parks Road, Oxford, OX2 6PN

Bethulie	F.W. Fitzsimons Collection (1910)
Bloemfontein	Sir J. Evans Collection, ex J.C. Rickard, 1880 (1928)
Boshof District	Mr M.D.W. Jeffreys Collection (1949.7.30-41)
De Kiel Oost	H.J. Braunholtz Collection (1932)
Franshoek Farm, Ficksburg	Mrs G. Brunton Collection (1927)
Koffiefontein	Miss M. Wilman Collection (1930)

iii) Gauteng

Birmingham Museum and Art Gallery, Chamberlain Square, Birmingham B3 3DH

Groenfontein	Mr C.B.C. Baine Collection (1948a11.12,28)

University Museum of Archaeology and Ethnography, University of Cambridge, Downing Street, Cambridge CB2 3DS

Meyerton	A.E.P. Collins Collection (Z 36092)
Pretoria, Apies (*Appies*) River	Col. H.W. Fielden Collection, 1900 (1904.636)
Pretoria, Sunnyside	M.C. Burkitt Collection, ex Underwood (Z 30757)
Vereeniging	A.E.P. Collins Collection (Z 36094-5)
Vlakfontein, Witwatersrand	Unknown Collector (Z 36076)

Institute of Archaeology, University College, University of London, 31-34 Gordon Square, London WC1H0PY

Vereeniging	Archaeological Survey of South Africa Collection

The Manchester Museum, University of Manchester, Oxford Road, Manchester M13 9PL

Pretoria	G. Leith and W. Boyd Dawkins Collection (1894: O.189-208)
	E.J. Mellor Collection (1903: O.1092)

The Natural History Museum, Cromwell Road, London SW7 5BD

Henley-on-klip	Dr K.P. Oakley Collection (1953: E.2645-48, 2650, 2655)
Pretoria	Presented by the Scottish National Museum, Ex. P.W. Laidlaw Collection (1956: E.4641)
Sterkfontein, Bolt's Farm	Dr K.P. Oakley Collection (1953: E.3093-98)
Suikerbosrand, Van Der Elst's Donga	Dr K.P. Oakley Collection (1953: E.2636-44,2652-54)
Vereeniging	Dr K.P. Oakley Collection (1953: E.2396-2400) Presented by the Archaeological Survey of South Africa (E.2660-65)

Pitt Rivers Museum, University of Oxford, Parks Road, Oxford, OX2 6PN

Pretoria	Prof. W. Boyd Dawkins Collection (1897)
Vereeniging, Taaibosch Spruit	J.P. Johnson Collection (1907)

iv) KwaZulu-Natal

University Museum of Archaeology and Ethnography, University of Cambridge, Downing Street, Cambridge CB2 3DZ

Buffalo River	Rev. F.A. Fuggle Collection (1951.998)
Dumisa	R.U. Sayce Collection, 1925 (1928.729)
Durban	R.U. Sayce Collection (1928.730)
Inogane	Unknown Collector (Z 14992)
Isandhlwana	Unknown Collector (Z 36087)
Ladysmith	Col. H.W. Fielden Collection (Z 36084)
	Unknown Collector (Z 36085)
Newcastle	Col. H.W. Fielden Collection (Z 35827,36082)
Nqutu (*Nquthu*), St. Augustine's	Rev. F.A. Fuggle Collection (1951.999-1000)

Pietermaritzburg, Greytown Road	Col. H.W. Fielden Collection (Z 35846)
Pietermaritzburg, Msinduze (Umzimduzi) River	Col. H.W. Fielden Collection (Z 36083)
Van Reenen	M.C. Burkitt Collection 1920s (1927.2111)
Weenen	R.U. Sayce Collection (1928.733)
Weenen (*Weenan*), Bushman's River	T. Welsh Collection, 1924 (Z 36102)
No further provenance	M.C. Burkitt Collection 1920s (1955.309)
	E.C. Chubb Collection (1923.1434)
	Col. H.W. Fielden Collection (Z 35847-8)
	A.F. Griffith Collection, ex J.C. Rickard (1918.93.90)
	Unknown Collector (Z 36080-1)

Liverpool Museum, William Brown Street, Liverpool L3 00A

Estcourt	Transfer from Norwich Museum, ex Col. H.W. Fielden, 1905 (56.28.88-107)
Estcourt, Bushman's River	Transfer from Norwich Museum, ex Col. H.W. Fielden, 1905 (56.28.108-112)
Feniscoolco [*sic*], Durban	Transfer from Norwich Museum, ex Col. H.W. Fielden, 1905 (56.28.152)
Ladysmith	Transfer from Norwich Museum, ex Col. H.W. Fielden, 1905 (56.28.116)
No further provenance	Transfer from Norwich Museum, ex Col. H.W. Fielden, 1905 (56.28.126)

The Manchester Museum, University of Manchester, Oxford Road, Manchester M13 9pPL

Drakensberg Mountains, Cave in	M.S. Evans Collection, 1894 (1920: O.2846-52)

The Natural History Museum, Cromwell Road, London SW7 5BD

Bulwer	Dr R.F. Lawrence Collection (1953: E.2537)
Mjongosi	Dr R.F. Lawrence Collection (E.2538-39)
Muden	H. Cookson Collection (1955: E.3273)
Muden, Salisbury Plain Farm	H. Cookson Collection (1955: E.3274)
Umtavuna	Presented by the Department of Geology, University of Natal (1953: E.2635)
Weenen	Dr R.F. Lawrence Collection (1953: E.2536)
No further provenance	Prof. T.R. Jones Collection (E.504)

Ashmolean Museum, University of Oxford, Beaumont Street, Oxford OX1 2PH

Buffalo River	Exchange with Natal Museum, 1950 (1968.1962)
Izotsha (*Izotcha*)	Exchange with Natal Museum, 1950 (1968.1957)
Mgababa (*Umgababa*) River	Exchange with Natal Museum, 1950 (1968.1956)
Mlonjani (*Molonjeni*) Mountain	Exchange with Natal Museum, 1950 (1968.1964)
Nagle Dam, Msunduze River	Exchange with Natal Museum, 1950 (1968.1968-75)
Nqutu	Exchange with Natal Museum, 1950 (1968.1963)
Pietermaritzburg	Exchange with Natal Museum, 1950 (1968.1938-54)
Pomeroy	Exchange with Natal Museum, 1950 (1968.1959-61)
Rietvlei	Exchange with Natal Museum, 1950 (1968.1965-66)
Southport	Exchange with Natal Museum, 1950 (1968.1955)
Staalberg	Exchange with Natal Museum, 1950 (1968.1958)
Thornville	Exchange with Natal Museum, 1950 (1968.1967)

Pitt Rivers Museum, University of Oxford, Parks Road, Oxford OX2 6PN

Avoca	Anthropological Institute Collection, ex J. Sanderson (1900)
Durban	Sir J. Evans Collection, ex J. Sanderson, 1878 (1928)
Durban, Umbilo	Anthropological Institute Collection, ex J. Sanderson (1900)
Estcourt	Anthropological Institute Collection, ex J. Sanderson (1900)
Hillary	J.A. Swan Collection (1953.8.1-2)
Karridene	C.G. Bliss Collection (1927)
Kelso	J.A. Swan Collection (1946.12.63-64)
Mgababa (*Umgababa*) Lagoon	J.A. Swan Collection (1952.7.1)
Mooiriver	C.G. Bliss Collection (1926)
Nottingham Road	Anthropological Institute Collection, ex J. Sanderson (1900)
Pietermaritzburg	C.G. Bliss Collection, 1925 (1926; 1927) (includes material given more specific provenances within Pietermaritzburg, viz: Alexandra Road West; Burger Street Gaol; Claridge; College Road; Golf Course; King Edward Avenue; New Sports Ground; Pentrieb; Pietermaritzburg College; Race Course; Scotsville; Slang Spruit)
	Sir J. Evans Collection, ex L. Evans, ex E. Crompton, 1905 (1928)
Richmond	Anthropological Institute Collection, ex J. Sanderson (1900)
Talana	C.G. Bliss Collection (1927)
Umzinto River	Rev. J.R. Ward Collection (1902)
No further provenance	Sir J. Evans Collection, ex Col. J.H. Bowker, 1880 (1928)
	Anthropological Institute Collection, ex J. Sanderson (1900)

v) Mpumalanga

Birmingham Museum and Art Gallery, Chamberlain Square, Birmingham B3 3DH

Hamelfontein, near Davel Station	Mr C.B.C. Braine Collection (1948a11.5)

University Museum of Archaeology and Ethnography, University of Cambridge, Downing Street, Cambridge, CB2 3DZ

Hectorspruit	L.E. Brown Collection (Z 38589)

Liverpool Museum, William Brown Street, Liverpool L3 00A

Lydenburg District	Transfer from Norwich Museum, ex Lt. Col. Pennefather Evans, 1937 (56.28.995-6)

Pitt Rivers Museum, University of Oxford, Parks Road, Oxford OX2 6PN

Sabi Game Reserve	H. Balfour Collection (1929)

vi) North West Province

University Museum of Archaeology and Ethnography, University of Cambridge, Downing Street, Cambridge, CB2 3DZ

Christiana, Diamond Workings	M.C. Burkitt Collection, 1920s (1927.2041)
Devondale Sidings	A.E.P. Collins Collection (Z 36089)
Doornleegte	A.E.P. Collins Collection (Z 36093)
Klerksdorp, Elandsheuwel	A.E.P. Collins Collection (Z 36091)
Klerksdorp, Kaffirskraal	A.E.P. Collins Collection (Z 36067)
Klerksdorp, Schoonspruit	A.E.P. Collins Collection (Z 36066)
Mafikeng	M.C. Burkitt Collection, 1920s (1927.2043)
	M.H. Giffen Collection (1932.77)
Palmietfontein	? A.E.P. Collins Collection (Z 36069)
Rustenburg	Col. H.W. Fielden Collection (1890.63)
Taung	M.C. Burkitt Collection, 1920s (1927.2044)

Institute of Archaeology, University College, University of London, 31-34 Gordon Square, London WC1H0PY

Taung	Dr E.C. Curwen Collection (Lp 574)

Liverpool Museum, William Brown Street, Liverpool L3 00A

Taung River	Miss Hobley Collection, per British Museum (47.31.337-8)

The Natural History Museum, Cromwell Road, London SW7 5BD

Christiana, Dramant Farm	Dr K.P. Oakley Collection (1953: E.2320)
Christiana Townlands	Dr K.P. Oakley Collection (1953: E.2365, 2391-5, 2408-9)

Pitt Rivers Museum, University of Oxford, Parks Road, Oxford OX2 6PN

Mafikeng (*Mafeking*)	H. Balfour Collection (1905)
Taung	Rev. E.N. Jones Collection, 1919 (1920)
Tiger Kloof	Rev. E.N. Jones Collection, 1919 (1920)
Vryburg, Glencairn	Donated by the Macgregor Museum, Kimberley (1925)
No further provenance	H. Balfour Collection (1905)
	Purchased from Rev. E.N. Jones, 1920.
	Donated by the Macgregor Museum, Kimberley (1925)

vii) Northern Province

University Museum of Archaeology and Ethnography, University of Cambridge, Downing Street, Cambridge, CB2 3DZ

Potgietersrus, Uitloop Farm	Dr B. Malan Collection (1957.108)
Springbok Flats	J.F. Eloff Collection (1961.223)

Institute of Archaeology, University College, University of London, 31-34 Gordon Square, London WC1H0PY

Nylstroom	C. Van Riet Lowe Collection

The Natural History Museum, Cromwell Road, London SW7 5BD

Cave of Hearths, Makapan Valley	Dr K.P. Oakley Collection (1953: E.2353-58)
Potgietersrus	Dr K.P. Oakley Collection (1953: E.2482)
Rainbow Cave, Makapan Valley	Dr K.P. Oakley Collection (1953: E.2340-50)
Tuinplaas, Springbok Flats	Dr K.P. Oakley and Mrs P. Raephaely Collection (1955: 3277-85)

viii) Northern Cape Province

University Museum of Archaeology and Ethnography, University of Cambridge, Downing Street, Cambridge, CB2 3DZ

Alexandersfontein	M.C. Burkitt Collection, 1920s (1976.586)
Bultfontein Diamond Fields	Mrs W.K. Foster Collection, ex J.C. Rickard, Site 33 (1903.67,145-6)
Canteen Kopje	M.C. Burkitt Collection, 1920s (1976.337)
	Miss Scholfield Collection (1930.37)
Griqualand	Miss M. Wilman Collection (1927.1536)
Hopetown	Unknown Collector (Z 36060,36063)
Kimberley	Mrs W.K. Foster Collection, ex J.C. Rickard(1903.63,95-6,116a,121-3,128a-130a, 145, Z 27337)
	Dr W.M. Tapp Collection (1925.2.a6-7)
	Miss M. Wilman Collection (1927.2137)
Kimberley, Alexanderspan	M.C. Burkitt Collection, 1920s (1927.2040; 1955.299)
Kimberley Diamond Fields	Mrs W.K. Foster Collection, ex J.C. Rickard (1903.44c; Z 35744)
	A.F. Griffith Collection, ex J.C. Rickard (1918.93.71-76,96)
Kimberley, Halfway House	M.C. Burkitt Collection, 1920s (1927.2037)

	Miss Scholfield Collection (1930.38)
Pandamfontein	Mrs W.K. Foster Collection, ex J.C. Rickard, Site 32 (1903.66,113,114a-115a; Z 27295,35791)
	A.F. Griffith Collection, ex J.C. Rickard, Site 32 (1918.93.67-8,70)
Pniel	M.C. Burkitt Collection, 1920s (1927.2038-9; 1955.293,296; 1976.329,333,582)
	Mrs W.K. Foster Collection, ex J.C. Rickard, Site 34 (1903.92)
Prieska	J.M. Bain Collection (Z 38550)
Riverton	M.C. Burkitt Collection, 1920s (1955.306)
	Miss M. Wilman Collection (1927.2141)
Ronaldsvlei	Miss M. Wilman Collection (1927.2138)
Rooipoort (*Rouipoort*), Witpan	Miss M. Wilman Collection (1927.1534b,2139)
Vaal River	F. White Collection (1902.274-5)
Victoria West	M.C. Burkitt Collection, 1920s, ex F. Jansen (1927.2034)
	M. C. Burkitt Collection, 1920s (1955.302)
	Dr W.M. Tapp Collection (1925.2.a8)
Victoria West, Moonlight Hill	M.C. Burkitt Collection, 1920s (1927.2035)
Vosburg	M.C. Burkitt Collection, 1920s (1927.2036; 1976.581)
Windsorton	M.C. Burkitt Collection, 1920s (1976.334)
	Miss M. Wilman Collection (1927.1533)

Hunterian Museum and Art Gallery, University of Glasgow, University Avenue, Glasgow G12 8QQ

Barkly West	J.A. Blair Collection (A.1984.49-51)

Institute of Archaeology, University College, University of London, 31-34 Gordon Square, London WC1H 0PY

Augrabies Falls	C. Van Riet Lowe Collection
Gemsbok Plain	Unknown Collector, 1968
Klipkraal, near Upington	Unknown Collector, 1966
Pietersburg	Archaeological Survey of South Africa Collection
Pniel	Archaeological Survey of South Africa Collection
Windsorton, the Homestead	Archaeological Survey of South Africa Collection
Windsorton, Riverview Estates	Archaeological Survey of South Africa Collection
Windsorton, Station	Archaeological Survey of South Africa Collection

Liverpool Museum, William Brown Street, Liverpool L3 0OA

Elandsfontein, Griqualand West	Miss Hobley Collection, per British Museum (47.31.328)
Kimberley	Miss Hobley Collection, per British Museum (47.31.329-31)
Riverton	Miss Hobley Collection, per British Museum (47.31.332-3)
Windsorton	Miss Hobley Collection, per British Museum (47.31.339-42)

The Natural History Museum, Cromwell Road, London SW7 5BD

Alexandersfontein	Dr K.P. Oakley Collection (1953: E.2326, 2496-8, 2500-15)
Canteen Kopje	Dr K.P. Oakley Collection (1953: E.2266-8; 2312-8; 4612-22)
Harrisdale	Dr K.P. Oakley Collection (1953: E.2324,2333-4, 2337-9,2359,2379-84)
Holsdam	Dr K.P. Oakley Collection (1953: E.2327)
Koffie Kopje Diamond Diggings	Prof. W.J. Gordon Collection (1950: E.1435-56)
Nooitgedacht	Dr K.P. Oakley Collection (1953: E.2272)
Steinkopf	Presented by the Scottish National Museum, ex P.W. Laidlaw Collection, 1913 (1956: E.4642)
Windsorton, Riverview Estates	Dr K.P. Oakley Collection (1953: E.2299)
	Mr Larsen Collection (1953: E.2297-8)
Windsorton, Newman's Point Site	Dr K.P. Oakley Collection (1953: E.2465, 2516-34)
	Mr Larsen Collection (1953: E.2297-8)

Ashmolean Museum, University of Oxford, Beaumont Street, Oxford, OX1 2PH

Princessfontein, Victoria West	Sir J. Evans Collection, ex E.J. Dunn, 1873 (1928.262)

Pitt Rivers Museum, University of Oxford, Parks Road, Oxford OX2 6PN

Alexandersfontein	H. Balfour Collection, 1929 (1930)
	J.A. Swan Collection (1927; 1928; 1929; 1935; 1937; 1945.6.129; 1946.3.7; 1946.4.87,90,97; 1947.2.486,490-1;1947.4.9-12,16-9; 1947.6.27-8; 1947.11.7-8; 1952.1.10; 1953.2.21-78; 1954.2.136; 1954.6.79-81
	Miss M. Wilman Collection (1930)
	Donated by the Macgregor Museum, Kimberley (1925)
Alexandersfontein, Romald's (Ronald's ?) Vlei	J.A. Swan Collection (1946.1.2-3; 1947.4.13-5)
Barkly West	Mr M.D.W. Jeffreys Collection (1949.7.28-9)
	J.A. Swan Collection (1937; 1946.1.1; 1946.6.96)
	Miss M. Wilman Collection (1930)
	Donated by the Macgregor Museum, Kimberley (1925)
Barkly West, Holsdam	J.A. Swan Collection (1945.8.3-4)
Boetsap	J.A. Swan Collection (1945.3.18; 1946.4.86; 1947.2.493; 1952.1.8; 1953.2.79-81; 1954.1.5-8)

Boetsap, Hol River Falls	J.A. Swan Collection (1946.4.86,88-9; 1948.2.124; 1952.1.11; 1952.5.93; 1954.6.82-5; 1954.7.12)
Borrel's Kop	J.A. Swan Collection (1946.6.91; 1947.11.16)
Britstown	Prof. C.G. Seligman Collection (1940.12.686)
	J.A. Swan Collection (1952.12.14)
Canteen Kopje	H. Balfour Collection, 1929 (1930)
	Mr M.D.W. Jeffreys Collection (1949.7.42-53)
	J.A. Swan Collection (1928)
	J.G. Van Alphen Collection (1929)
	Donated by the Macgregor Museum, Kimberley (1925)
Delportshoop (*Delports Hoop*)	J.A. Swan Collection (1946.6.92-4,101; 1948.1.107-9; 1952.1.3; 1952.2.85; 1953.4.1-3)
Douglas	Dr R. Broom Collection (1930)
	J.A. Swan Collection (1954.2.129-31, 134-5)
Dunmurray	J.A. Swan Collection (1946.6.121)
Gong-gong	J.A. Swan Collection (1928)
Griqualand West	Miss M. Wilman Collection (1929)
	Donated by the Macgregor Museum, Kimberley (1925)
Griquatown	E.J. Dunn Collection (1936)
	J.A. Swan Collection, 1933 (1937)
Grootfontein, Danielsküil	J.A. Swan Collection (1937)
Hamburg	J.A. Swan Collection (1927)
Kamfersdam	J.A. Swan Collection (1946.3.2)
Kheis (Keis)	J.A. Swan Collection (1937)
Kenilworth	J.A. Swan Collection (1927)
Kimberley	Anthropological Institute Collection, ex J. Sanderson (1900)
	J.A. Swan Collection (1914; 1926; 1927; 1928; 1929; 1937; 1946.1.5; 1947.11.6)
	Donated by the Macgregor Museum, Kimberley (1925)
Kimberley, Bissets	J.A. Swan Collection (1929)
Kimberley, Boshof Road	J.A. Swan Collection (1947.11.5)
Kimberley, De Beers Diamond Mines	J.A. Swan Collection (1945.3.15-7; 1954.7.10)
Kimberley, De Beers Shooting Estate (= Rooipoort ?)	J.A. Swan Collection (1926)
Kimberley, Diamond Fields	Sir J. Evans Collection, ex J.C. Rickard, 1880 (1928)
Kimberley, Dutoitspan	Sir J. Evans Collection, ex J.C. Rickard, 1880 (1928)
	J.A. Swan Collection (1927)
Kimberley, Golf Links	J.A. Swan Collection (1937; 1946.3.1; 1954.1.1-3)
Kimberley, Halkett Road	J.A. Swan Collection (1945.6.13)
Kimberley, Homestead	J.A. Swan Collection (1927; 1928; 1929; 1937; 1945.6.130; 1946.1.4; 1946.3.2,4-6; 1946.6.95; 1947.11.4; 1952.5.89-91)
Kimberley, Mosesberg Diggings	J.A. Swan Collection (1927)
Kimberley, Mud River	J.A. Swan Collection (1927)
Kimberley, Otto's Kopje	J.A. Swan Collection (1953.4.4)
Kimberley, Samaria Road	J.A. Swan Collection (1947.11.6)
Kimberley, Schmidt's Drift Road	J.A. Swan Collection (1947.2.487)
Kimberley, Sluits	J.A. Swan Collection (1927; 1928; 1929; 1937)
Kimberley, Vaal River	J.A. Swan Collection (1923; 1927; 1928; 1936; 1937)
Kimberley, West End	J.A. Swan Collection (1947.2.488; 1947.6.29; 1947.11.9-10)
Klipheuwel Farm Cave, Frasersburg	J.G. Van Alphen Collection (1931)
Klipdam, Vaal River	Donated by the Macgregor Museum, Kimberley (1925)
Knockbarragh	J.A. Swan Collection (1947.4.4-8; 1948.2.125; 1948.3.4; 1952.1.9; 1954.1.4)
Koegas	J.A. Swan Collection (1937; 1952.12.17-8)
Lilykstad Farm, Orange River	J.A. Swan Collection (1937)
Longlands	Dr M.D.W. Jeffreys Collection (1949.7.54-73)
	J.A. Swan Collection (1948.2.1)
	Miss M. Wilman Collection (1930)
Matsap	J.A. Swan Collection (1937)
Mayeng Native Reservation	J.A. Swan Collection (1948.2.123)
Modder River	J.A. Swan Collection (1927; 1928; 1929)
Niekerkshoop (*Niekerk's Hope*)	J.A. Swan Collection (1952.12.20-3)
Newlands, Vaal River	Donated by the Macgregor Museum, Kimberley (1925)
Nooitgedacht	H. Balfour Collection (1910; 1930)
	J.A. Swan Collection (1928)
Pniel	H. Balfour Collection (1929)
	J.A. Swan Collection (1936; 1952.2.83-4; 1954.1.9; 1954.7.14)
Prieska	J.A. Swan Collection (1927)
Read's Drift, Orange River	J.A. Swan Collection (1937)
Ricket's Road Drift, Harts (*Hartz*) River	J.A. Swan Collection (1948.1.97-102; 1954.7.11)
Riverton	Prof. W. Sollas Collection (1905)
	J.A. Swan Collection (1929; 1935; 1948.1.103-6; 1948.2.118-21)
	Donated by the Macgregor Museum, Kimberley (1925)

Rondeskop	J.A. Swan Collection (1947.2.492)
Rondeskop, Mamutla Native Reserve	J.A. Swan Collection (1947.2.489; 1952.5.92,95)
Rooipoort	J.A. Swan Collection (1927; 1952.12.15-6)
Shalin Native Reserve, near Boetsap	J.A. Swan Collection (1952.5.94; 1954.7.13)
Spytfontein	J.A. Swan Collection (1947.11.11-5)
Vaal River	H. Balfour Collection (1910)
	J.A. Swan Collection (1937; 1948.2.127)
	Doanted by the Macgregor Museum, Kimberley (1925)
Vaal-Harts Dam	J.A. Swan Collection (1947.6.26)
Victoria West	Sir J. Evans Collection, ex E.J. Dunn, 1873 (1928)
Warrenton	J.A. Swan Collection (1927)
Windsorton	J.G. Van Alphen Collection (1929)
	Donated by the Macgregor Museum, Kimberley (1925)
Witsands, Langeberg	J.A. Swan Collection (1937; 1952.12.19)
No Further Provenance	J.A. Swan Collection (1914; 1927)

Royal Museum of Scotland, Chambers Street, Edinburgh EH1 1JF

Vaal River	Unknown Collector (A.1928.238-46)

ix) Western Cape Province

Bristol Museums and Art Gallery, Queen's Road, Bristol BS8 1RL

Brak River	Mr G. Leith Collection (C. 1898: E.244)
Coast Caves (? Mossel Bay)	Mr G. Leith Collection (C. 1898: E.247-9)
Mossel Bay	Mr G. Leith Collection (C. 1898: E.246)
Stellenbosch, Bosman's Siding	Prof. Reynolds Collection (1922: E.3838-41)
Thorne	Mr G. Leith Collection (C. 1898: E.245)

University Museum of Archaeology and Ethnography, University of Cambridge, Downing Street, Cambridge, CB2 3DZ

Beaufort West	R.S. Newall Collection, 1920s (1976.32-3)
Beaufort West, Bushmans Kop	Dr W.M. Tapp Collection (1925.2.a5)
Blouberg (*Blauwberg*)	M.H. Giffen Collection (1928.1001)
Blouberg Shell Mounds	Col. H.W. Fielden Collection (1904.622.10,19,22, 638,644,652-3,657; Z 21530-1, 35831,35833-7, 36050-1)
Bot River	M.C. Burkitt Collection, 1920s (1927.2132)
Buffels Bay	M.H. Giffen Collection (1928.1003)
	F. White Collection (1902)
Caledon, Stanford	Dr W.M. Tapp Collection, ex L. Péringuey (1925.2.a2)
Cape Flats	M.C. Burkitt Collection, 1920s (1976.601)
	Col. H.W. Fielden Collection, 1900 (1904.2.9,622,637,645-7,649-50; Z 35825-6, 36079)
Cape Flats, Elsies River	M.C. Burkitt Collection, 1920s (1976.596-600)
	M.C. Burkitt Collection, 1920s, ex Col. W.H. Hardy (1927.2128)
Cape Flats, Kaapmans Camp	Col. H.W. Fielden Collection, 1900 (Z 35824)
Cape Flats, Muizenberg Shell Mounds	Col. H.W. Fielden Collection, 1900 (1904.622.17)
'Cape Peninsula'	M.C. Burkitt Collection, 1920s, ex Col. W.H. Hardy (1927.2124)
Coopers Siding	M.C. Burkitt Collection, 1920s (1927.2114)
Fish Hoek	A.L. Armstrong Collection, 1928 (1959.463)
	M.C. Burkitt Collection, 1920s (1927.2125)
	M.H. Giffen Collection (1928.1000)
	Unknown Collector (Z 35839)
Gordon's Bay Kitchen Midden	M.H. Giffen Collection (1928.998)
	Miss M. Wilman Collection (1927.1532)
Hermanus	M.C. Burkitt Collection, 1920s (2131)
Knysna	Col. H.W. Fielden Collection, 1900 (1904.641)
Mossel Bay	M.C. Burkitt Collection, 1920s (1927.2112; 1955.295; 1976.328,33
	Miss M. Wilman Collection (1927.1531; Z 35838)
	Unknown Collector (Z 35842)
Mossel Bay, St. Blaize Promontory	M.C. Burkitt Collection, 1920s (1927.2113)
Noordhoek	M.C. Burkitt Collection, 1920s (1927.2126-7)
	Mrs W.K. Foster Collection, ex J.C. Rickard (1903.126)
	M.H. Giffen Collection (1928.999)
Riversdale, Cave of the Hands	M.C. Burkitt Collection, 1920s (1927.2115-6; 1976.607)
Rondebosch	Col. H.W. Fielden Collection (Z 21532,53817-22)
Simonstown	M.C. Burkitt Collection, 1920s (1955.307)
	M.H. Giffen Collection (1928.1002)
	Dr W.M. Tapp Collection, ex L. Péringuey (1925.2.a1)
Stellenbosch	M.C. Burkitt Collection, 1920s (1927.2129; 1955.290)
	Col. H.W. Fielden Collection, 1900 (1904.625,673; Z 36078)
	L. Péringuey Collection (1905.448,450,457)
	Unknown Collector (Z 35840-1)

Stellenbosch, Bosman's Siding	Col. H.W. Fielden Collection, 1900 (1904.622,710-2; Z 35801,35814-5)
Stellenbsoch, Eerste River	Col. H.W. Fielden Collection, 1900 (1904.628,640,671-2,676,687,692-4,699, 701,709; Z 35816)
Still Bay	M.C. Burkitt Collection, 1920s (1927.2117-23; 1955.305; 1976.330)
	M.C. Burkitt Collection, 1920s, ex Hesse (1927.2117a)
Table Mountain	Col. H.W. Fielden Collection (Z 35828)
	Unknown Collector (Z 35843)
Villiersdorp	M.C. Burkitt Collection, 1920s (1955.291; 1976.332)
Wellington	M.C. Burkitt Collection, 1920s (1927.2130)

Hunterian Museum and Art Gallery, University of Glasgow, University Avenue, Glasgow G12 8QQ.

Mossel Bay	H.G. Thorpe Collection, 1893 (A.71-72)

Institute of Archaeology, University College, University of London, 31-34 Gordon Square, London WC1H 0PY

Fish Hoek	Unknown Collector
Hangklip	Unknown Collector
Klipfonteinrand	Unknown Collector, 1966
Melkbosstrand	Unknown Collector, 1960s
Stellenbosch	C. Van Riet Lowe Collection
Stillbay	Unknown Collector
Stompiesfontein	Unknown Collector

Liverpool Museum, William Brown Street, Liverpool L3 00A

Blouberg (*Blueberg*) Flats	Transfer from Norwich Museum, ex Col. H.W. Fielden, 1914 (56.28.148-51,153-4, 997)
Blouberg Flats Kitchen Midden	Transfer from Norwich Museum, ex Col. H.W. Fielden, 1914 (56.28.156-61,167, 174-5)
Cape Flats	Transfer from Norwich Museum, ex Lord Avebury, per Sir H. Read, 1886 (56.28.959-60,962-8,972,974-5
Eerste River Valley	Transfer from Norwich Museum, ex Col. H.W. Fielden, 11914 (56.28.117-8,123, 125)
Mossel Bay	Miss Hobley Collection, per British Museum 47.31.335-6)
Mossel Bay, Coast Caves	Unknown Collector (47.17.422-3)
Stellenbosch, Bosman's Siding	Transfer from Norwich Museum, ex Col. H.W. Fielden, 1905 (56.28.62-85)

The Natural History Museum, Cromwell Road, London SW7 5BD

Cape Flats	Exchange with Archaeological Survey of South Africa, ex Col. W.H. Hardy (E.3275)
Elandsfontein	Dr K.P. Oakley Collection (1953: E.2243-49)
	Presented by the University of Cape Town, ex Mr K. Johy (1953: E.2252-64)
Gordon's Bay, Shell Midden	Dr K.P. Oakley Collection (1953: E.2564-5)
Hangklip	Dr K.P. Oakley Collection (1953: E.2541-46)
Klein Drakenstein	Presented by the Scottish National Museum, ex P.W. Laidlaw Collection, 1913 (1956: E.4636-37)
Matjes River Rock Shelter	Presented by the National Museum, Bloemfontein, ex Drs T.F. Dreyer, A.C. Hoffman and A.J.D. Meiring (1953: E.2300-11)
Montagu, Brakfontein Valley Floor	Dr K.P. Oakley Collection (1953: E.2547)
Montagu Cave	Dr K.P. Oakley Collection (1953: E.2548-63)
Mossel Bay	Presented by the South African Museum, Cape Town (1953: E.2323)
Oakhurst Rock Shelter, George	Presented by the University of Cape Town (1953: E.2296)
Paarl	Presented by the Scottish National Museum, ex P.W. Laidlaw Collection, 1912 (1956: E.4630-35)
Skildegat Cave, Fish Hoek	Dr K.P. Oakley Collection (1953: E.2351)
	Presented by the University of Cape Town (1953: E.2269)
Somerset West	Presented by the Scottish National Museum, ex P.W. Laidlaw Collection, 1913 (1956: E.4639-40)
Steenberg	I. Strachan Collection (1954: E.2679)
Stellenbosch, Bosman's Crossing	F.E. Hiley Collection (1949: E.1372)
Stellenbosch, Smits' Brickfield	Dr K.P. Oakley Collection (1953: E.2483-85)
Wellington	Dr K.P. Oakley Collection (1953: E.2486-88,2493-94)

Ashmolean Museum, University of Oxford, Beaumont Street, Oxford, OX1 2PH

Rondebosch, Cape of Good Hope	Sir J. Evans Collection, ex F.P. Barlow, 1887 (1928.263)

Pitt Rivers Museum, University of Oxford, Parks Road, Oxford, OX2 6PN

Beyerskloof (*Beyer's Kloof*)	Prof. H.T. Brown Collection (1913)
Cape Flats	Anthropological Institute Collection, ex J. Sanderson, ex Sir L. Dale (1900)
	Sir J. Evans Collection, ex Sir L. Dale (1928)
	Sir J. Evans Collection, ex Capt. H. Thurburn (1928)
	A.H.J. Goodwin Collection (1929)
	Col. W.H. Hardy Collection (1929)

	Prof. C.G. Seligman Collection (1940.12.685)
	Transfer from Oxford University Museum, ex C. Bell, 1875
	Transfer from Oxford University Museum, ex Sir L. Dale, 1875
	Transfer from Oxford University Museum, ex J.W. Flower, ex Sir L. Dale, 1872
Cape Point Caves	Transfer from Oxford University Museum, ex G. Gulliver
Cape Town, Table Mountain	Original Pitt-Rivers Collection, ex Sir L. Dale
Eerste River Valley	H. Balfour Collection (1929)
	Sir J. Evans Collection, ex Col. H.W. Fielden, 1905
Fish Hoek	Col. W.H. Hardy Collection (1929)
Maitland	H. Balfour Collection (1929)
Mossel Bay	Prof. W. Boyd Dawkins Collection (1897)
	Sir J. Evans Collection, ex Capt. H. Thurburn, 1873 (1928)
	Donated by the Macgregor Museum, Kimberley (1925)
	Transfer from Ipswich Museum
Noordhoek	Col. W.H. Hardy Collection (1929)
Paarl	L. Péringuey Collection (1899; 1905)
Port Beaufort	Sir J. Evans Collection, ex Mrs T. Herolf, 1872 (1928)
	Sir J. Evans Collection, ex Capt. H. Thurburn, 1873 (1928)
Port Nolloth	E.J. Dunn Collection (1936)
Stellenbosch	H. Balfour Collection (1905)
	A.C. Bell Collection, ex A.M. Bell, ex A.J. Herbertson, 1905 (1920)
	L. Péringuey Collection (1899; 1905)
Stellenbosch, Bosman's Siding	Sir J. Evans Collection (1928)
Stillbay	E.J. Dunn Collection (1940.10.2)
Swellendam	Dr P. Van Heerden Collection (1929)
Villiersdorp	H. Balfour Collection (1929)
	Dr P. Van Heerden Collection (1929)
Wellington	Miss F.M. Snell Collection (1924)

Royal Albert Memorial Museum, Queen Street, Exeter EX4 3RX

Georgeheim, Mossel Bay District	Unknown Collector
Simonsvlei, Factory Site	Unknown Collector

Royal Museum of Scotland, Chambers Street, Edinburgh EH1 1JF

Darling District	Unknown Collector (A.1928.247-51)
Stellenbosch	Unknown Collector

Sheffield City Museum and Art Gallery, Weston Park, Sheffield S10 2TP

Cape Flats	Sheffield Literary and Philosophical Society Collection, 1875 (X.1969.242/3)
Mossel Bay, Coast Caves	G. Leith Collection, 1896 (Unnumbered)
Mossel Bay Flats	G. Leith Collection, 1896 (Unnumbered)

c) South Africa - Uncertain Provenance

Birmingham Museum and Art Gallery, Chamberlain Square, Birmingham B3 3DH

Hirloop, Northern Transvaal	Mr C.B.C. Braine Collection (1948a11.10) [Probably Northern Province]
Honingkloof, Northern Transvaal	Mr C.B.C. Braine Collection (1948a11.23) [Probably Northern Province]
Polteisrust, Chatwin's Farm, Northern Transvaal	Mr C.B.C. Braine Collection (1948a11.3) [Probably Northern Province]
South Africa, no further provenance	Mr C.B.C. Braine Collection (1948a11.1-2,4,7-9,11,13-22,24-27,29-33)

University Museum of Archaeology and Ethnography, University of Cambridge, Downing Street, Cambridge, CB2 3DZ

Alex Fort	Miss M. Wilman Collection (1927.1537)
Barberspan, Transvaal	? A.E.P. Collins Collection (Z 36075)
Elandsfontein	Unknown Collector (Z 35844)
Fort Savage	Unknown Collector (Z 14855)
Groote River, J. Albub's Farm, Cape Province	Mrs W.K. Foster Collection, ex J.C. Rickard, Site 50b (1903.94)
Groote River, Nash's, Cape Provinc	Mrs W.K. Foster Collection, ex J.C. Rickard, Site Xlc (1903.44e; Z 35799-800, 36049)
Klippies Pan	Miss M. Wilman Collection (1930.172; 1931.172)
Kromme Port, Vilgoen's [*sic*] Farm	Mrs W.K. Foster Collection, ex J.C. Rickard, Site 50 (1903.125a)
Mange River, 7 miles south of Modder River	Mrs W.K. Foster Collection, ex J.C. Rickard (1903.88.1)
[Free State or Northern Cape Province]	M.C. Burkitt Collection, 1920s (1927.2076; 1976.587-94)
	A.E.P. Collins Collection (Z 36064-5]
	Mrs W.K. Foster Collection, ex J.C. Rickard, Site 28 (1903.102)
	Mrs W.K. Foster Collection, ex J.C. Rickard, Site29 (1903.62,91,103; Z 35775)
	A.F. Griffith Collection, ex J.C. Rickard (1918.93.60)
Modder River, 12 miles south of	Mrs W.K. Foster Collection, ex J.C. Rickard (Z 35774)
Orange River, north bank	Mrs W.K. Foster Collection, ex J.C. Rickard, Site 18 (1903.90,145; Z 35749-50)
Orange River, 7 miles south of	Mrs W.K. Foster Collection, ex J.C. Rickard, Site 15 (1903.129-30; Z 35751)
Orange River, 20 miles south of Renmark	Mrs W.K. Foster Collection, ex J.C. Rickard (1903.96a)
	M.C. Burkitt Collection, 1920s (1976.578)

Rockwood, Eliott's Farm	M.C. Burkitt Collection, 1920s (1927.2094)
Rooikop (*Rooe Kop*)	M.C. Burkitt Collection, 1920s (1976.802)
Silverdale	Miss M. Wilman Collection (1927.1535)
Tigerskloof	M.C. Burkitt Collection, 1920s (1927.2045)
'Transvaal'	Dr Brincker Collection (Z 35853)
Vingerfontein	Unknown Collector (Z 36167)
Wildebeeste Kraal, Transvaal	A.E.P. Collins Collection (Z 36090)
Zuur Kop	Ipswich Museum Loan (1960.301)
South Africa, no further provenance	M.C. Burkitt Collection, 1920s (1976.595)
	Col. H.W. Fielden Collection, 1900 (1904.648,659; Z 35823,35849)
	Mrs W.K. Foster Collection, ex J.C. Rickard (1903.41-44,46,75; Z 36138,36169-70)
	A.F. Griffith Collection, ex J.C. Rickard (1918.93.5-6,10-13,19-20,32-33,36,57-58,74,79-80,83,85-86,97-100,107
	J.C. Rickard Collection (Z 27277,35802-13)
	Dr W.M. Tapp Collection (1925.2)
	Unknown Collector (Z 36090,36165,35850-52,35857)

Derby Museum and Art Gallery, The Strand, Derby DA1 1BS

Cape of Good Hope [Possibly East London, Eastern Cape Province]	Lord Avebury Collection, per British Museum (1916-696/43-52)

Institute of Archaeology, University College, University of London, 31-34 Gordon Square, London WC1H 0PY

Kleingroenfontein (Bushman Rock Shelter)	Unknown Collector
Strydfontein Cave 2	C. Van Riet Lowe Collection

Liverpool Museum, William Brown Street, Liverpool L3 00A

Bushman Cave, Cape Province	Unknown Collector (47.17.421)
Cape of Good Hope [Possibly Cape Flats, Western Cape Province]	Transfer from Norwich Museum, ex Lord Avebury, per Sir H. Read, 1886 (56.28.969-71,973,976-86,988-94)
Modder River Valley [Free State or Northern Cape Province]	Transfer from Norwich Museum, ex Col. H.W. Fielden, 1914 (56.28.119-22,124)
Zait Pan	Miss Hobley Collection, per British Museum (47.31.334)
South Africa, no further provenance	Mr Beaseley Collection (54.161.184a-c)
	Mr H. Cookson Collection (55.127.1-9)
	Mr J. Lee Hunt Collection (1933: Unnumbered)
[Possibly Cape Flats, Western Cape Province]	Transfer from Norwich Museum, ex Lord Avebury, per Sir H. Read, 1886 (56.28.961,987)
[Free State or Northern Cape Province]	Transfer from Norwich Museum, ex Col. H.W. Fielden, 1914 (56.28.128)

The Manchester Museum, University of Manchester, Oxford Road, Manchester M13 9PL

Cape Colony	P.C. Johnson Collection (1905: O.1385)
Cape of Good Hope	Layard Collection (1899: O.524-5)
Transvaal	Mrs K.K. Atkinson Collection (1913: O.1690)
South Africa, no further provenance	Lord Avebury Collection, per British Museum (1916: O.2628)
[possibly East London, Eastern Cape Province]	Hadfield Collection (Unnumbered)

The Natural History Museum, Cromwell Road, London SW7 5BD

Cape of Good Hope, 300 Foot Beach	Dr K.P. Oakley Collection (1953: E.2328,2352, 2489)
Cape of Good Hope, Windsorton Road	Dr K.P. Oakley Collection (1953: E.2495,2499)
'Cape Province'	L.E. Townnoe Collection (E.1031)
	Unknown Collector (E.1044-46,1072)
Fanspoort	Miss D.E. Warren Collection (E.3569)
Rooiwal	Dr K.P. Oakley Collection (1953: E.2466-72)
Salusbury Donga, Transvaal	Dr K.P. Oakley Collection (1953: E.2473-81)
South Africa, no further provenance	Exchange with the National Museum, Bloemfontein (1953: E.2048-2115)
	Presented by the Scottish National Museum, ex P.W. Laidlaw Collection, 1912 (1956: E.4638)

Ashmolean Museum, University of Oxford, Beaumont Street, Oxford, OX1 2PH

South Africa, no further provenance	Unknown Collector (1988.1)

Pitt Rivers Museum, University of Oxford, Parks Road, Oxford OX2 6PN

Cape of Good Hope	Sir J. Evans Collection, ex Dr H.D.R. Kingston (1928)
	Sir J. Evans Collection, ex W. Whitaker, 1866 (1928)
	Dr H.D.R. Kingston Collection (1900)
	Original Pitt-Rivers Collection, ex Sir L. Dale (1888)
Orange River Scheme Area [Free State or Eastern Cape Province]	Dr C.G. Sampson Collection (1970)
Zuur Kop	Transfer from Ipswich Museum

South Africa, no further provenance	Anthropological Institute Collection, ex J. Sanderson (1900)
	E. Armour Collection (1913)
	E.J. Dunn Collection (1940.10.1-4,22,26)
	Sir J. Evans Collection, ex J.C. Rickard, 1880 (1928)
[Very probably Western Cape Province]	Sir J. Evans Collection, ex Capt. H. Thurburn (1928)
[Possibly Northern Cape Province]	J.A. Swan Collection (1928)

Royal Museum of Scotland, Chambers Street, Edinburgh EH1 1JF

South Africa, no further provenance	Unknown Collector (A.1956.1138)

LESOTHO

University Museum of Archaeology and Ethnography, University of Cambridge, Downing Street, Cambridge, CB2 3DZ

Ha Soloja Rock Shelter	Permanent Loan from the Government of Lesotho (1991.134)
Maseru	R.U. Sayce Collection (1928.731)
Melikane Rock Shelter	Permanent Loan from the Government of Lesotho (1991.136)
Moshebi's Rock Shelter	Permanent Loan from the Government of Lesotho (1991.133)
Sehonghong Rock Shelter	Permanent Loan from the Government of Lesotho (1991.135)

NAMIBIA

University Museum of Archaeology and Ethnography, University of Cambridge, Downing Street, Cambridge, CB2 3DZ

Sambio	Exchange with the Windhoek State Museum (1962.14-18)
Namibia, no further provenance	R.U. Sayce Collection, 1925 (1928.732)

Institute of Archaeology, University College, University of London, 31-34 Gordon Square, London WC1H0PY

Grootfontein District	C. Van Riet Lowe Collection
Harinchas, Mariental District	C. Van Riet Lowe Collection

The Natural History Museum, Cromwell Road, London SW7 5BD

Karib	Prof. W.J. Gordon Collection (1950: E.1437-38)
Runtu	Presented by the University of Cape Town, ex Dr W.H.G Kusche (1953: E.2289-95)

SWAZILAND

Birmingham Museum and Art Gallery, Chamberlain Square, Birmingham B3 3DH

Swaziland, no further provenance	Unknown Collector (1914a39)

University Museum of Archaeology and Ethnography, University of Cambridge, Downing Street, Cambridge, CB2 3DZ

Mbabane	M.C. Burkitt Collection, 1920s (1961.23)
	Miss C.O. Evereitt Collection (1925.741)
Swaziland, no further provenance	Unknown Collector (1925.742)

The Manchester Museum, University of Manchester, Oxford Road, Manchester M13 9PL

Swaziland, no further provenance	E.J. Mellor Collection (1903: O.1091)

Pitt Rivers Museum, University of Oxford, Parks Road, Oxford OX2 6PN

Mbabane (*Embabaan*) Valley	Sir J. Evans Collection, ex J.B. Taylor, 1895 (1928.261a-h)

Scunthorpe Museum and Art Gallery, Oswald Road, Scunthorpe DN15 7BD

Swaziland, no further provenance	Seton-Lloyd Collection, C. 1920s-1930s

ZIMBABWE

University Museum of Archaeology and Ethnography, University of Cambridge, Downing Street, Cambridge, CB2 3DZ

Bambata Cave	M.C. Burkitt Collection, 1920s (1955.267)
Bembesi River	M.C. Burkitt Collection, 1920s (1955.273)
Bembesi Valley	Ipswich Museum Loan (1960.302)
Bulawayo	Dr F.R.C. Reed Collection (1924.1325)
	F. White Collection (1902.274; Z 36057)
Bulawayo, Lola	M.C. Burkitt Collection, 1920s (1976.614)
Chelmer, near Bulawayo	M.C. Burkitt Collection, 1920s (1955.268; 1976.584)
Domboshawa Cave	M.C. Burkitt Collection, 1920s (1927.2055)
Driefontein	Rev. Fr. T. Gardner Collection, 1925 (Z 36098)
Ematjeni River	M.C. Burkitt Collection, 1920s (1927.2049)
Embusini River	M.C. Burkitt Collection, 1920s (1927.2145; 1961.33)
Felixburg, Railway Station	M.C. Burkitt Collection, 1920s (1927.2059)
Gokomere Cave	Rev. Fr. T. Gardner Collection (1931.200)
Gweru	Sir John Myres Collection, ex Rev. Fr T. Gardner, 1929 (1946.10.54
Hope Fountain	M.C. Burkitt Collection, 1929 (1961.32)
	Rev. N. Jones Collection (Z 36099)

Igumana (= Gumani ?) Rock Shelter	Dr A.C. Haddon Collection, ex E. Haddon (1929.98)
Inyati	M.C. Burkitt Collection, 1920s (1927.2050; 1955:288; 1976.327,336)
	M.C. Burkitt Collection, 1920s, ex N. Davies (1955.275)
Iram, Allendale Farm	M.C. Burkitt Collection, 1920s (1927)
Khami	M.C. Burkitt Collection, 1920s, ex C.K. Cooke (1955.272)
	C.K. Cooke Collection (1957.41-51)
Khami Ruins	Col. H.W. Fielden Collection, 1905 (1905.430)
Mawanga Hills Rock Shelter	M.C. Burkitt Collection, 1920s (1927.2058)
Nswatugi Cave	Dr A.C. Haddon Collection, ex E. Haddon (1929.96)
Pomongwe Cave	Dr A.C. Haddon Collection, ex E. Haddon (1929.97)
Sawmills	A.L. Armstrong Collection (1959.460-2)
	M.C. Burkitt Collection, 1920s (1927.2046-7; 1955:274)
Sebakwe River	F. White Collection, 1902 (Z 36056,36058)
Victoria Falls	M.C. Burkitt Collection, 1920s (1976.338,421,577)
World's View (Bushman Cave), Matopo Hills	M.C. Burkitt Collection, 1920s (1927.2062)
Zimbabwe, no further provenance	M.C. Burkitt Collection, 1920s (1927.2048)

Institute of Archaeology, University College, University of London, 31-34 Gordon Square, London WC1H0PY

Bambata Cave	Unknown Collector
Bembesi River	Unknown Collector
Hope Fountain	ex Bulawayo Museum (Lp 1003-09)
	ex Ipswich Museum, ex Rev. N. Jones (R. 1930-101)
	Unknown Collector (Mc39; Lp 1043-55)
Hunyani River	ex Bulawayo Museum (Lp 942-51)
Khami	Unknown Collector
Lochard	ex Bulawayo Museum (Lp 877,882,886-7)
Madilungiwa Rock Shelter	Unknown Collector
Sawmills	ex Bulawayo Museum (Lp 919-25,927-30,932,940,952-4,958-60)
Victoria Falls	ex Bulawayo Museum (Lp 909-18)

Liverpool Museum, William Brown Street, Liverpool L3 00A

Bambata Cave	Miss Hobley Collection, per British Museum (47.31.343-47)
Bubi (*Buli*) District	Miss Hobley Collection, per British Museum (47.31.306)
Imbusini Spruit	Miss Hobley Collection, per British Museum, ex G. Arnold (47.31.307-10)
Khami	Transfer from Norwich Museum, ex Col. H.W. Fielden, 1914 (56.28.129 41,143, 147,820)
Matopos, Bushman Rock Terrace	Transfer from Norwich Museum, ex Col. H.W. Fielden,1914 (56.28.178-206)
Panola Spruit (North of Bija)	Miss Hobley Collection, per British Museum (47.31.311)
Victoria Falls	Transfer from Norwich Museum, 1936 (56.28.998)
Zimbabwe, no further provenance	Miss Hobley Collection, per British Museum (47.31.312-3)

The Manchester Museum, University of Manchester, Oxford Road, Manchester M13 9PL

Bambata Cave	A.L. Armstrong Collection (Unnumbered)
Imjati (= Inyati ?)	W.N.G. Davies Collection, per Prof. Fleure (1931: O.4499)

Pitt Rivers Museum, University of Oxford, Parks Road, Oxford, OX2 6PN

Bambata Cave	Exchange with the National Museum of Southern Rhodesia, Bulawayo (1948.5.18-20,22-25)
Belingwe, Germania	J.C. Mance Collection (1922)
Bembesi River	Exchange with the National Museum of Southern Rhodesia, Bulawayo (1948.5.17; 6.7-9)
Bembesi Station	Exchange with the National Museum of Southern Rhodesia, Bulawayo (1948.5.10,12-16)
Bulawayo	H. Balfour Collection (1905; 1906)
	Rev. Fr. T. Gardner Collection (1910)
Bulawayo, Criterion Mine	J.C. Mance Collection (1922)
Chikupu Cave, Chinamora	Mrs A. Mozley Collection (1942.12.55)
Craighleigh Farm Rock Shelter	Exchange with the National Museum of Southern Rhodesia, Bulawayo (1948.5.40-54)
Dhlo Dhlo Ruins	H. Balfour Collection (1915)
Embusini	Miss F.M. Snell Collection, 1923 (1984)
	Exchange with the National Museum of Southern Rhodesia, Bulawayo (1948.5.8-11)
Fillabusi, Blue Reef	J.C. Mance Collection (1922)
Gokomere Cave	Sir John Myres Collection, ex Rev. Fr T. Gardner, 1929 (1946.10.54)
Great Zimbabwe	Capt E.M. Andrews Collection (1905)
	H. Balfour Collection (1906)
Gwanda, Nautch Girl	J.C. Mance Collection (1922)
Harare (*Salisbury*)	Mrs A. Mozley Collection (1942.12.56-60)
[includes material given more specific provenances within Harare, viz: Acumbe Cave; Elladale Farm; Glen-Norah Farm]	
Harare (*Salisbury*), Emerald Hill	Rev. Fr. T. Gardner Collection (1910)

Hope Fountain	H. Balfour Collection, 1929 (1929)
	Rev. N. Jones Collection(1929)
	Exchange with the National Museum of Southern Rhodesia, Bulawayo (1948.5.2-7)
Khami	H. Balfour Collection (1906)
	Exchange with the National Museum of Southern Rhodesia, Bulawayo (1948.5.26-39)
Lydiate	Exchange with the National Museum of Southern Rhodesia, Bulawayo (1948.5.1)
Morven, Bembesi District	J.C. Mance Collection (1922)
Rusape, Fishervale Farm	Mrs A. Mozley Collection (1942.12.59)
Sabi River, 6 miles east of	Capt. E.M. Andrews Collection (1906)
Selukwe District	F. White Collection (1910)
Shamva, Lion's Head Kopje	C.P. May Collection, 1930 (1958.5.3)
Umtali Ruins	H. Balfour Collection (1906)
Victoria Falls	H. Balfour Collection (1907; 1917)
	H. Balfour Collection, 1905 (1906; 1939)
	D.W. Jeffreys Collection (1954.7.9)
	Lamplugh Collection, 1905 (1906)
	J.A. Swan Collection (1947.6.30-33)
	F. White Collection (1910)
	A.E.V. Zealley Collection, 1911 (1912)
Webster Ruin	Capt E.M. Andrews Collection (1907)
Zambezi River	Miss Rhodes Collection, ex Col. F. Rhodes, 1905 (1906)
Zimbabwe, no further provenance	H. Balfour Collection (1905)
	H.H. Coghlan Collection, ex R. Summers(1956.12.39)
	J.C. Mance Collection, 1899 (1922)
	Transferred from the Ashmolean Museum, Oxford, ex Sir A. Evans, 1941 (1951.1.4)
	Purchased from the Ashmolean Museum, Oxford (1949.6.b1)

Sheffield City Museum and Art Gallery, Weston Park, Sheffield S10 2TP

Bambata Cave	A.L. Armstrong Collection (Unnumbered)
Zimbabwe, no further provenance	A.L. Armstrong Collection (Unnumbered)

Alphabetical list of Collectors of Stone Age Material Housed in British Museums

Bold type indicates biographical details in Appendix 4

Andrews, Capt. E.M. (Pitt Rivers)
Armour, E. (Pitt Rivers)
Armstrong, A.L. (Cambridge, Manchester, Sheffield)
Arnold, G. (Liverpool)
Atkinson, Mrs K.K. (Manchester)
Avebury, Lord (Derby, Liverpool, Manchester)
Bain, A.G. (Ashmolean, Natural History, Pitt Rivers)
Bain, J.M. (Cambridge)
Balfour, H. (Pitt Rivers)
Barlow, F.P. (Ashmolean)
Beaseley, Mr (Liverpool)
Bell, A.C. (Pitt Rivers)
Blair, J.A. (Huntarian)
Bliss, C.G. (Pitt Rivers)
Bowie, Mrs A.A.L. (Natural History)
Bowker, T.H. (N, Pitt Rivers)
Bradshaw, Mrs (Natural History)
Braine, Mr C.B.C. (Birmingham)
Braunholtz, H.J. (Pitt Rivers)
Brinkner, Dr (Cambridge)
Broom, Dr. R. (Pitt Rivers)
Brown, Prof. H.T. (Pitt Rivers)
Brown, L.E. (Cambridge)
Brunton, Mrs G. (Pitt Rivers)
Burkitt, M.C. (Cambridge)
Butters, J.T (Pitt Rivers)
Chubb, E.C. (Cambridge)
Cleverly, J.J. (Manchester)
Coghlan, H.H. (Pitt Rivers)
Collins, A.E.P. (Cambridge)
Cooke, C.K. (Cambridge)
Cookson, H. (Liverpool, Natural History)
Crompton, E. (Pitt Rivers)
Dale, Sir L. (Pitt Rivers)
Davies, W.N.G. (Manchester)
Dawkins, Prof. W. Boyd (Manchester, Pitt Rivers)
Dekenah, J. (Natural History)
Dreyer, Dr. T.F. (Natural History)
Dunn, E.J. (Ashmolean, Pitt Rivers)
Dyer, G.H. Thistleton (Liverpool)
Eloff, J.F. (Cambridge)
Evans, Sir J. (Ashmolean, Pitt Rivers)
Evans, M.S. (Manchester)
Evans, Lt. Col. Pennefather (Liverpool)
Evereitt, Miss C.O. (Cambridge)
Fielden, Col. H.W. (Cambridge, Liverpool, Pitt Rivers)
Fitzsimmons, F.W. (Pitt Rivers)
Flower, J.W. (Pitt Rivers)
Foster, Mr (Manchester)
Foster, Mrs W.K. (Cambridge)
Fuggle, Rev. F.A. (Cambridge)
Gardner, Rev. Fr. T. (Cambridge, Pitt Rivers)
Giffen, M.H. (Cambridge)
Goodwin, A.H.J. (Pitt Rivers)
Gordon, Prof. W.J. (Natural History)
Griesback, G.L. (Natural History)
Griffith, A.F. (Cambridge)
Gulliver, G (Pitt Rivers)
Hadfield (Manchester)
Hardy, Col. W.E. (Natural History, Pitt Rivers)
Herolf, Mrs T. (Pitt Rivers)
Herbertson, A.J. (Pitt Rivers)
Hewitt, J.T. (Pitt Rivers)
Hiley, F.E. (Natural History)

Hobley, Miss (Liverpool)
Hoffman, Dr. A.C. (Natural History)
Holmes, T. (Birmingham)
Hunt, Mr J. Lee (Liverpool)
Jeffreys, Mr M.D.W. (Pitt Rivers)
Johnson, J.P. (Pitt Rivers)
Johnson, P.C. (Manchester)
Johy, Mr K. (Natural History)
Jones, Rev. N. (Cambridge, Pitt Rivers)
Jones, Prof. T.R. (Natural History)
Kannemeyer, Dr. D. (Cambridge, Pitt Rivers)
Kingston, Dr. H.D.R. (Pitt Rivers)
Kusche, Dr. W.H.G. (Natural History)
Laidlaw, P.W. (Natural History)
Lamplugh (Pitt Rivers)
Larsen, Mr. (Natural History)
Lawrence, Dr. R.F. (Natural History)
Layard (Manchester)
Leith, G. (Bristol, Manchester, Sheffield)
Léppe, Dr (Natural History)
Lovett (Ashmolean)
Lyell, Sir C. (Ashmolean, Pitt Rivers)
Malan, Dr. B. (Cambridge)
Mance, J.C. (Pitt Rivers)
May, C.P. (Pitt Rivers)
Meiring, A.J.D. (Natural History)
Mellor, E.J. (Manchester)
Milard (Milland), J. (Cambridge)
Mozley, Mrs A (Pitt Rivers)
Myers, Sir J. (Cambridge)
Newall, R.S. (Cambridge)
Oakley, Dr. K.P. (Natural History)
Péringuey, L. (Cambridge, Pitt Rivers)
Pitt-Rivers, General (Pitt Rivers)
Prestwich, Sir J. (Natural History)
Radcliffe-Brown, Prof. A. (Cambridge)
Raephaely, Mrs P. (Natural History)
Reed, Dr. F.R.C. (Cambridge)
Reynolds, Prof. (Bristol)
Rhodes, Col. F. (Pitt Rivers)
Rickard, J.C. (Ashmolean, Cambridge, Pitt Rivers)
Sampson, Dr. C.G. (Pitt Rivers)
Sanderson, J. (Pitt Rivers)
Sayce, R.U. (Cambridge)
Scholfield, Miss (Cambridge)
Schönland, Dr S. (Pitt Rivers)
Seligman, Prof. C.G. (Pitt Rivers)
Seton-Lloyd (Scunthorpe)
Snell, Miss F.M. (Pitt Rivers)
Sollas, Prof. W. (Pitt Rivers)
Strachan, I. (Natural History)
Summers, R. (Pitt Rivers)
Swan, J.A. (Pitt Rivers)
Tapp, Dr. W.M. (Cambridge)
Taylor, J.B. (Pitt Rivers)
Thorpe, H.G. (Huntarian)
Thurburn, Capt. H. (Pitt Rivers)
Townnoe, L.E. (Natural History)
Underwood, (Cambridge)
Van Alphen, J.G. (Pitt Rivers)
Van Heerden, Dr P. (Cambridge, Pitt Rivers)
Ward, Miss P. (Pitt Rivers)
Ward, Rev. J.R. (Pitt Rivers)
Warren, Miss D.E. (Natural History)
Watson, D.M.S. (Manchester)
Welsh, T. (Cambridge)
Whitaker, W. (Pitt Rivers)
White, F. (Cambridge, Pitt Rivers)
Wilman, Miss M. (Cambridge, Pitt Rivers)
Zealley, A.E.V. (Pitt Rivers)

List of Contributing Institutions

Birmingham Museum and Art Gallery, Chamberlain Square, Birmingham B3 3DH. Information provided by Mr P. Watson, Acting Keeper, Dept of Archaeology and Ethnography.

Bristol Museums and Art Gallery, Queen's Road, Bristol BS8 1RL. Information provided by Ms S. Giles, Curator of Ethnography and Foreign Archaeology.

University Museum of Archaeology and Ethnography University of Cambridge, Downing Street, Cambridge CB2 3DZ. Information provided by Dr R. Boast, Assistant Curator (Archaeology).

Derby Museum and Art Gallery, The Strand, Derby DE1 1BS. Information provided by Mr R. Langley, Documentation Officer.

Hunterian Museum and Art Gallery, University of Glasgow, University Avenue, Glasgow G12 8QQ. Information provided by Dr L. Keppie, Senior Curator/Reader in Roman Archaeology.

Institute of Archaeology, University College, University of London, 31-34 Gordon Square, London WC1H 0PY. (Collections currently housed at the British Museum, pending possible transfer of material). Information provided by Ms A. Roberts, formerly Assistant Curator, Quaternary Section, Dept of Prehistoric and Romano-British Antiquities, the British Museum.

Liverpool Museum, William Brown Street, Liverpool L3 00A. Information provided by Ms H.L. Stumpe, Curator of Oceanic, North American and Arctic Ethnology.

The Manchester Museum, Oxford Road, Manchester M13 9PL. Information provided by Dr A.J.N.W. Prag, Keeper of Archaeology.

The Natural History Museum, Cromwell Road, London SW7 5BD. Information provided by Mr R. Kruszynski, Curator, Human Origins Group.

Ashmolean Museum, University of Oxford, Beaumont Street, Oxford OX1 2PH. Information provided by Ms A. Roberts, Collections Manager, Dept of Antiquities.

Pitt Rivers Museum, University of Oxford, Parks Road, Oxford OX2 6PN. Information provided by Dr P.J. Mitchell, Curator of African Archaeology/Lecturer in African Prehistory.

Royal Albert Memorial Museum, Queen Street, Exeter EX4 3RX. Information provided by Dr J. Allan, Curator of Antiquities.

Royal Museum of Scotland, Chambers Street, Edinburgh EH1 1JF. Information provided by Ms B. Crozier, Curator: Africa, Americas and the Pacific.

Scunthorpe Museum and Art Gallery, Oswald Road, Scunthorpe DN15 7BD. Information provided by Mr K. Leahy, Keeper of Archaeology.

Sheffield City Museum and Art Gallery, Weston Park, Sheffield S10 2TP. Information provided by Mr J. Parsons, Keeper of Archaeology and Ethnography.

Appendix 4. Individual Collectors Represented in The British Museum Southern African Stone Age Collections

Dr Alan Cohen

Introduction

This Appendix gives biographical information on those individuals who contributed to the British Museum's Department of Prehistory and Early Europe (PEE) collections of Stone Age artefacts from southern Africa. All contributing collectors are listed alphabetically with dates of birth and death where known, followed by the provenances from which they collected material; provenances are spelt following the format used in the Gazetteer (Chapter 5) and can be located within it using the Concordance at its beginning. Further biographical information follows, emphasizing the southern African and/or archaeological connections of the individuals concerned. Where appropriate, key references are given from which further information can be obtained.

To check if a particular individual also contributed to the southern African Stone Age collections of the British Museum's Department of Ethnography reference should be made to the list of collectors at the end of Appendix 1. Similar lists for collectors of other African material held by PEE, and for collectors of Southern African material held at other museums in Britain are included in Appendices 2 and 3 respectively.

Anderson, Andrew A. before 1845 - after 1896

Sites: Auob River; Barkly West; Boatlaname; Boshof; Botswana, no further provenance; Bubi River; Campbell; Carmarlo Drift; Chue Pan; Cubango River; Damaraland; Dwarsberg; Freevast; Gaseitisive's Country; Great Fish River; Griquatown; Great Salt Pan (Montshiwa); Hakskeenpan; Harts River; Kalahari Desert; Khama's Country; Kheis; Kimberley; Kimberley (Du Toits Pan); Klip Drift; Kuruman; Lake Ngami; Langeberg; Limpopo River; Matabeleland; Molapo River; Molepolole; Mpakwe River; Ngotwane River; Nossob River; Owambo; Shoshong; Sivonel; Spitskop; Steenbokpan (Steinbok Farm); Steenbokpan (Steinbok Pan); Swartmodder; Swartmodder ?; Tati Goldfields; Tati River; Tonga River; Transvaal, no further provenance; Vaal River; Witwater.

Born in Scotland, Anderson emigrated to South Africa and from 1860 travelled extensively in the interior of the sub-continent, including Namibia, Botswana and western Zimbabwe, where he visited King Lobengula of the Matabele in 1878. The following year he fought in the Zulu War and was then briefly in Pretoria, living in England between 1884 and 1888; it was during this period (October 20th 1885) that his collections were purchased for the Christy Collection. He left South Africa in 1890 to retire to Britain.

Little else is known of him, beyond what he published in two accounts of his travels (A.A. Anderson 1887a, 1887b). Both include references to the collection of stone artefacts from across the northern half of the sub-continent, as well as observations on ruined stone-walled enclosures of Iron Age date. Collecting stone artefacts as early as 1859, he was among the first to do so anywhere in southern Africa (D. Morris 1997). The Royal Geographical Society published his map of South Africa *c.* 1885. A collection of his water-colours is housed in the Africana Museum in Johannesburg (Kennedy 1963) with smaller collections in the Libraries of the South African Parliament, Cape Town, and the Royal Commonwealth Society, London. Some, such as those of Kora encampments on the farm Rooipoort (qv) in the Northern Cape Province, are of considerable ethnohistoric importance (D. Morris 1995).

Additional information *Dictionary of South African Biography* 3: 22.

Armstrong, Albert L. 1878-1958

Sites: Alexandersfontein; Bambata Cave; Barkly West; De Kiel Oost; Fish Hoek; Gokomere Cave; Gumali Cave; Gweru Kopje; Harare; Hope Fountain; Inyanga; Inyati; Jacobsdal; Kimberley; Leeuwfontein; Nswatugi Cave; Paardeberg; Petrus; Plumtree; Pommeru; Pommeru (Grave Site); Pommeru; Sawmills; Taung; Westacre Farm; Zimbabwe, no further provenance.

Born in England, Armstrong first worked as an art teacher and then as a surveyor and valuer. He became interested in archaeology while serving in Egypt during the First World War. He took a leading part in the excavation of a Neolithic flint mine at Grimes Graves, Norfolk, in 1920-24 and also excavated Upper Palaeolithic cave sites at Creswell Crags, Derbyshire. He directed the Rhodesian Archaeological Expedition of 1929, which formed part of the activities associated with the visit to southern Africa of the British Association for the Advancement of Science, publishing the results of his excavations at Bambata Cave two years later (Armstrong 1931). A second report on the Expedition's results was published in 1936 (Armstrong *et al.* 1936). Fellow of the Society of Antiquaries.

Additional information Obitury in *Transactions of the Hunter Archaeological Society,* vol. 8 (1963).

Atherstone, Hon. William G. 1814-1898

Sites: Bushman's River (Eastern Cape); Cape Flats; East London; Keiskamma River; Kleinemonde; Orange River.

Born in England, Atherstone's family were among the 1820 English settlers in the Eastern Cape Province. Having studied widely in Europe, he returned to South Africa to practise as a doctor, including a spell as a military surgeon in the Frontier Wars. In addition to pioneering the use of anaesthetics in the Cape Colony, he had extensive interests in botany and geology, founding the Grahamstown Botanical Gardens and the Scientific and Literary Society, the eventual ancestor of the Albany Museum. Among other claims to fame, he was the person to identify as such the first diamond found in South Africa, became a member of the Cape Colony's House of Assembly in 1881 and was Honorary President of the South African Association for the Advancement of Science at its first meeting in 1896. Linked by marriage with **T. H. Bowker** and **J. H. Bowker,** he was also associated with Dr D. Kannemeyer (1890), author of an important early work on southern African stone artefacts, and **A.G. Bain**. Fellow of the Geological Society.

Additional information *Dictionary of South African Biography* 1: 25-27.

Avebury, Lord (Lubbock, Sir John) 1834-1913

Sites: Buffalo River; East London

Lubbock inherited a bank from his father at the age of 14 and gave up a formal education in order to become involved in its management. He served on several financial commissions before entering the House of Commons as Member of Parliament for Maidstone in 1874. He sat as Member of Parliament for the University of London after 1880, having been elected as its Vice-Chancellor in 1872. He was a close friend of Charles Darwin and Sir Augustus Franks and son-in-law of General Pitt-Rivers, as well as an important figure in the development of archaeology and anthropology in his own right, serving as President of the Society of Antiquaries of London and of the Anthropological Institute. His chief work *Pre-Historical Times* (Lubbock 1865) ran through several editions until 1913 and was the major English language introductory text to prehistoric archaeology of its time. In it he coined the terms Palaeolithic and Neolithic. Raised to the Peerage in 1900, he was responsible for the introduction of bank holidays and Britain's first antiquities protection legislation (the 1882 Ancient Monuments Act). He published several papers on stone implements from Africa (1869, 1870a, 1870b, 1871).

Additional information *Dictionary of National Biography of the Twentieth Century, 1912-1921*, pp. 345-347; Hutchinson (1914).

Ayres, Thomas
Sites: Rustenburg

Feilden (1883: 163) records that he acquired a group of five artefacts from a Mr Thomas Ayres of Potchefstroom who had collected them near Rustenburg. Only one of these artefacts is now in the British Museum collections and the whereabouts of the others are unknown. No further information has been obtained as to the identity of Mr Ayres, though **A.A. Anderson**'s (1887b:160) reference to seeing 'very good stone implements in the possession of a medical gentleman' when he visited Potchefstroom in 1865 might be connected.

Bain, Andrew G. 1797-1864
Sites: Kleinemonde.

Born in Scotland, Bain arrived in South Africa in 1816 and explored parts of the Northern Cape Province and Botswana in 1825-26 and Pondoland (now in the Eastern Cape Province) in 1829 (Bain 1949). He served in the Colonial forces during the Sixth Frontier War of 1834-35 and in 1837 was attached to the Royal Engineers as a supervisor for the construction of military roads. He subsequently oversaw the construction of several important roads that tied the Cape Colony together, including that between Ceres and Wellington which passes through Bainskloof, named after him. Generally recognised as the father of South African geology, he compiled the first geological map of the country and was the first to discover the fossil remains of mammal-like reptiles in the rocks of the Karoo System. Associated with **Sir C. Lyell** and friend of **W.G. Atherstone**. Fellow of the Geological Society.

Additional information Hockly (1966); *Dictionary of South African Biography* 1: 35-38.

Bays, Dr. J. Bruce
Sites: Halseton.

Bays qualified in medicine in London in 1887 and remained on the British Medical Register until 1957, when he was living in East London, Eastern Cape Province. He is known to have met Miles Burkitt during the latter's visit to South Africa in 1927.

Bazley, William d. 1908
Sites: Alfred County Cave.

Vinnicombe (1976: 112) records that Bazley first farmed, unsuccessfully, in the Richmond area of KwaZulu-Natal and later moved to the coast. There he worked as a surveyor and engineer in the construction of the harbour at Port Shepstone, quarried marble and built the road linking Port Shepstone to Harding (magisterial seat of Alfred County). He retired in January 1904 and died four years later. Correspondent of **Sir C.H. Read**.

Bird, P. C.
Sites: Trelawney.

The only information obtained about Mr Bird indicates that he was living in Essex at the time of his donation of the Trelawney artefacts to the British Museum and subsequently moved to the village of Assington, where he is buried.

Bowker, James H. Colonel 1822-1900
Sites: Rorke's Drift.

Born in England, Bowker's family were among the 1820 Settlers and were granted a farm at Tharfield in the then Albany District of the Cape Colony. Having fought in the Frontier Wars of 1846 and 1850-53, Bowker was appointed commandant of the Frontier Armed and Mounted Police left in occupation of Xhosa lands in the eastern part of what is now the Eastern Cape Province. He continued in this position until 1866, held several other Government appointments and then became High Commissioner of Basutoland on its annexation to the Cape Colony in 1868. As well as conducting excavations (sadly unrecorded as far as is known) in rock-shelters in Lesotho, Bowker was also an entomologist and botanist of some note and was in KwaZulu-Natal in 1879 during the Zulu War where he collected stone artefacts at Rorke's Drift. Associated with Sir C. Lyell. Brother of **T. H. Bowker**.

Additional information Gooch (1881); Hockly (1966).

Bowker, Thomas H. Commandant 1808-1885
Sites: probable source of the material donated by **Grey** from Tharfield.

Born in England, Bowker's family were among the 1820 Settlers and were granted a farm at Tharfield in the then Albany District of the Cape Colony. He served in the Colonial military forces in the Frontier Wars of the 1828 to 1853 period, was Resident Magistrate of the Kat River settlement in 1848 and was the founder of Queenstown, now an important town in the northern part of the Eastern Cape Province. Bowker represented Albany and later Queenstown in the Cape Colony's House of Assembly and served in Kimberley as Secretary to the Land Commission on the Diamond Fields in 1872. He was one of South Africa's first antiquarians, collecting stone artefacts from several localities in the Eastern Cape Province, some of which were later presented to the Rotunda Museum of Artillery in Woolwich (now at the Albany Museum, Grahamstown).

Additional information Goodwin (1955); Hewitt (1955); Hockly (1966).

Braunholtz, Hermann J. 1888-1963
Sites: Alexandersfontein; Avalon; Barkly West; Bloemhof; Brakfontein; Canteen Kopje; Cape Flats; Christiana (Showlands Kopje); De Kiel Oost; Fauresmith (Factory site); Fauresmith (Town Spruit site); Hope Fountain; Koffiefontein (Engravings Site); Koffiefontein (Sekretaris Kop); Lockshoek; Mauchini Brook; Milnerton-Maitland; Nooitgedacht; Pniel; Powola Brook; Skildegat Cave; Stellenbosch; Stellenbosch (Lorraine Farm); Ventershoek (Christol Cave); Ventershoek (Talus below Christol Cave); Ventershoek (west of Christol Cave); Vereeniging; Zimbabwe, no further provenance.

Born in England and educated at Cambridge, Braunholtz began work at the British Museum in 1913 and had a distinguished career there as an ethnographer, becoming Keeper of the Department of Oriental Antiquities and Ethnography in 1938, and then Keeper of the newly created Department of Ethnography from 1945-53. He also served three terms as President of the Royal Anthropological Institute (1926-35, 1937-39, 1941-43). Visited Southern Africa for the meeting of the British Association for the Advancement of Science n 1929.

Additional information *Who Was Who* 6: 130.

Brown, Horace L.
Sites: Beyers Kloof Farm.

The only information available about Mr Brown is that he was living in Kensington at the time of his donation of the Beyers Kloof Farm implements to the British Museum in 1921.

Busk, Charles J.
Sites: Cape Flats.

Mr Busk was a residant of Cape Town and associate of **Rev. L. Dale** and **George McKay**. Little is known about him, except by reference to his brother, the eminant surgeon and palaeontologist George Busk (1807-1886). At the 1868 International Congress of Prehistoric Archaeology at Norwich, George Busk exhibited stone implements sent from South Africa by his brother, Charles, and the **Rev. Langham Dale**. These implements were presented via George Busk to the Christy Collection at the British Museum in 1869.

Christy, Henry 1810-1865
Sites: Auob River; Boatlaname; Boshof; Botswana, no further provenance; Bubi River; Buffalo River; Bushmans River; Campbell; Cape Flats; Cape of Good Hope; Carmarlo Drift; Chue Pan; Cubango River; Damaraland; Dwarsberg; East London; East London, (British Kaffraria); Estcourt; Freevast; Gaseitisive's Country; Grahamstown; Great Fish River; Great Salt Pan; Griqualand West; Griquatown; Hakskeenpan; Harts River; Hout Bay; Isandhlwana; Kaffirland (*sic*); Kalahari Desert; Keiskamma River; Khama's Country; Kheis; Kimberley; Kimberley (Du Toits Pan); Kimberley (Sluits); Kleinemonde; Klip Drift; Kuruman; Lake Ngami; Langeberg; Lesotho, no further provenance; Limpopo River; Matabeleland, no further provenance; Molapo River; Molopolole; Natal, no further provenance; Newcastle; Ngotwane River; Nossob River; Orange River; Owambo; Pietermaritzburg; Port Beaufort; Pretoria; Prieska; Rustenburg; Rorke's Drift; Sivonel; South Africa, no further provenance; Spitskop; Steenbokpan (Steinbok Farm); Steenbokpan (Steinbok Pan); Swartmodder; Swartmodder ?; The Curragh; Tonga River; Transvaal, no further provenance; Vaal River; Vogelstruisfontein Farm; Witwater; Zululand, no further provenance.

Born in London, Christy took over and further developed his father's millinery company in Stockport and expanded his fortune by introducing Turkish towelling to Britain and by inheriting a joint stock bank. While travelling for business reasons he amassed a huge ethnographic collection and by 1863 was so interested in the problem of human antiquity and the possibility of human evolution that he financed the excavations of the eminent French palaeontologist Edouard Lartet. Several of these excavations were at caves in the Dordogne region of France, including several (such as Laugerie Haute, La Madeleine and Le Moustier) that became classic sites for the European Upper Palaeolithic (Lartet & Christy 1865-75). After Christy's death Sir Augustus Franks was responsible for adding to his collection and money left by Christy for this purpose permitted the acquisition of Stone Age material that might not otherwise have been acquired in competition with more glamorous material for Museum funding.

Additional information *Dictionary of National Biography*, pp. 295-296.

Collins, Colonel E. R. born 1870, died after 1935
Sites: Burgersdorp; Devondale Sidings; Doornlaagte; Klerksdorp; Meyerton; Palmietpan; Panfontein; Riversdale Farm; Vereeniging.

A major in the Second South African War of 1899-1902, Collins was a career Army officer who went on to fight in the First World War. Some of the finds made during his military service in South Africa were later donated to the British Museum and published (Collins & Smith 1919). His archaeological interests later saw him become (in 1919) a member of the Prehistoric Society of East Anglia.

Cookson, H.
Sites: Muden.

The only information available about Mr Cookson is that he was living in Natal at the time of the donation of the material from Muden in 1955. The donation was arranged with the assistance of the archaeologist Robert S. Newall (1884-1978), excavator of Stonehenge with Colonel Hawley and long-time supporter of Salisbury Museum.

Cranswick, Rev. Rupert L. 1894-1978
Sites: Plumtree.

An Anglican priest, Cranswick was ordained in 1924 and became Curate of the Church of St. John the Baptist in Bulawayo in 1926, before becoming Vicar of Plumtree and Chaplain of Plumtree School between 1930 and 1937. He subsequently served in a variety of localities within Zimbabwe, before retiring as Honorary Canon of Mashonaland from 1961 to 1967.

Additional information *Who Was Who* 7: 180.

Dale, Rev. Dr Sir Langham 1826-1894
Sites: Cape Flats; East London.

Graduating from Oxford in 1848, Dale was offered the Chair of Classics and English Literature at the South African College, Cape Town in the same year. He played a highly important role in the development of education in the Cape Colony, serving as Superintendant-General of Education from 1859 to 1881 and being instrumental in the passage of the 1865 Education Act, which made English the medium of instruction in state schools. He campaigned for the establishment of a university and became Vice-Chancellor when the South African College developed into the University of Cape Town in 1873; he was elected Chancellor in 1892. In addition to collecting stone artefacts, he also published on the South African Stone Age (Dale 1870a, 1870b, 1871). He presented material to the British Museum both directly and via **George Busk**.

Additional information *Dictionary of South African Biography* 1: 201-204; Goodwin (1928).

De Villiers, Roland
Sites: Paarl.

The only information available about Master De Villiers is that his objects from Paarl were donated to the British Museum in 1930 through David De Villiers of Keurfontein, North Paarl.

Du Toit, Alexander L. 1878-1948
Sites: Karrieput.

Educated in Cape Town, Du Toit graduated in mining engineering at the Royal Technical College, Glasgow and studied geology at the Royal College of Science, London, before being appointed lecturer in geology at both institutions in 1901. Returning to South Africa two years later he joined the Cape Colony's geological commission and surveyed much of the Karoo, Transkei and KwaZulu-Natal, establishing himself as an authority on both the geology and palaeontology of South Africa. Joining the Transvaal Geological Survey in 1912, he then became consulting geologist for De Beers in 1927, retiring to Cape Town in 1947. Author of numerous geological papers, he was successively President of the Geological Society of South Africa, the South African Association for the Advancement of Science and the South African Archaeological Society, as well as a Fellow of the Royal Society.

Additional information *Dictionary of South African Biography* 1: 266-268.

Dunn, Edward J. 1844-1937
Sites: Griquatown

Born in Britain, Dunn emigrated to Australia in 1849 and qualified there as a mining surveyor. He came to South Africa in 1871 as government geologist of the Cape Colony and played a role in the development of the Kimberley diamond mines and subsequently the goldfields of the Rand. Principally a collector of ethnographic material from southern Africa, Dunn also collected and wrote about stone artefacts, mostly in the Karoo and on the Cape Peninsula (Dunn 1880, 1908, 1931). Returning to Australia in 1886 he took most of his southern African collection with him, although much of this subsequently came into the possession of the Pitt Rivers Museum, Oxford. Fellow of the Geological Society, and recipient of the Murchison Medal in 1905.

Additional information *Dictionary of South African Biography* 2: 204-205.

Edwards, Wilfred N. Dr 1890-1956.
Sites: Khami.

Educated at Cambridge, Edwards was a palaeobotanist and historian of geology who worked at The Natural History Museum between 1913 and 1955, ending his career as Keeper of Geology. His wideranging researches on fossil plants spanned the globe from New Zealand to Greenland.

Additional information *Proceedings of the Geological Society of London* 1554: 142-144.

Elliott, Clarence 1881-1969
Sites: Simondium (Vriedeslust Farm)

British by birth, Elliott spent only three years in South Africa, working as a fruit farmer near Paarl from 1902 to 1905. He then returned to Britain, setting up the Six Hills Nursery in Stevenage, which became world famous for its alpine and rockery plants, many of which he collected in the course of numerous expeditions to the Mediterranean, South America and elsewhere. He sold several artefacts to the British Museum in 1906, although his name is incorrectly recorded in the Accession Register as 'Charles Elliott'. He sold the remainder of his collection to **Dr W. A. Sturge** in 1908.

Additional information *Who Was Who* 6: 346; Letters in Sturge archive.

Evans, John Sir 1823-1908
Sites: Port Beaufort.

A businessman and owner of a paper mill in Hemel Hempstead, Evans developed an interest in geology and fossil collecting at an early age. A close friend of Sir Augustus Franks, in 1858 he joined with Sir Joseph Prestwich to investigate the claims made by the French antiquarian Boucher de Perthes for the antiquity and contemporaneity of stone artefacts and the bones of extinct animal species at sites in the Somme gravels (Daniel 1975). Confirmation of these claims was instrumental in demonstrating that the origins of humanity lay in a period far beyond the traditional Bible-derived time-frame. Evans combined his geological and Palaeolithic interests with the study of Celtic coinage, stone tools, and late prehistoric metalwork, producing the standard texts of his time on these aspects of British archaeology (i.e. Evans 1864, 1872, 1881, 1898). Among other offices he held, he was President of the Numismatic Society of London (1872-1908), Vice-President of the Anthropological Society of Great Britain and Ireland (1897) and Treasurer of the Royal Society (1878-98), as well as a Trustee of the British Museum.

Additional information *Dictionary of National Biography Supplement*, pp. 634-637; Evans (1943).

Exton, Hugh Dr 1833-1903
Sites: Lesotho, no further provenance.

Born in England, Exton emigrated to the Cape Colony in 1861 and practised briefly as a doctor in Grahamstown before travelling in Botswana where he collected birds, later publishing on the anthropology and ornithology of the area in the *Cape Monthly Magazine*. He moved to Bloemfontein in 1870 and worked there as a doctor, also serving as Mayor between 1881 and 1883. He was instrumental in establishing the National Museum and was its Honorary Curator from 1877. He moved to Johannesburg in 1888, but served as a doctor on the British side during the Second South African War (1899-1902). He was the first President of the South African Geological Society and also a President of the South African Medical Society.

Additional information *Dictionary of South African Biography* 3: 282.

Favell, Dr Richard V. 1881-1936
Sites: Gokomere Cave; Gweru Kopje; Hope Fountain; Inyati; Nswatugi Cave; Sawmills; Taung.

English by birth, Favell was a doctor who retired to Cornwall in 1924 where he became a member of the County Council and served as High Sheriff in 1934. He was closely associated with **A. L. Armstrong**, working with him not only at Grimes Graves and in Derbyshire, but also on the Rhodesian Archaeological Expedition of 1929. They were elected at the same time (March 5th 1925) and on the nomination of the same individuals as Fellows of the Society of Antiquaries of London.

Additional information Obituary in *Proceedings of the Prehistoric Society* (1936) p. 261.

Feilden, Colonel Henry W. 1838-1921
Sites: Buffalo River; Estcourt; Isandhlwana; Natal, no further provenance; Newcastle; Pietermaritzburg; Rustenburg; Zululand, no further provenance.

A career soldier, Feilden saw service in the Indian Mutiny (1857-58), the Second Opium War (1860) and the American Civil War (on the Confederate side, 1862-65), before fighting in both the First and Second South African Wars (1881, 1900-02). The majority of his South African collections were made in 1881 (Feilden 1883), although collections (not in the British Museum) made from the Cape Flats were the result of his second South African posting as Paymaster of the Imperial Yeomanry in 1900-02. He subsequently travelled in both the Northern Cape Province and Zimbabwe, and was the first person to draw attention to the presence of stone artefacts in the gravels of the Zambezi River above and below Victoria Falls (Feilden 1905). The breadth of his interests are indicated by the fact that he served as a naturalist on the British Polar Expedition of 1875-76 and travelled widely in the Arctic, as well as by his observation that nineteenth-century Bushmen made use of abandoned sodawater bottles to make stone artefacts (Feilden 1883). In addition to the British Museum, he also donated archaeological material from Southern Africa to Norwich Museum (now at Liverpool Museum) and Cambridge A & E.

Additional information *Who Was Who* 2; Obituary in *Trans Norfolk & Norwich Naturalists Society* (1921) p. 220-21. Letters held by Liverpool Museum.

Fisher, B. B.
Sites: Meyerton.

Probably Mr Bernard Fisher, his association with Southern Africa is unknown.

Frames, Minett E. 1862-1923
Sites: The Curragh.

Born in Port Elizabeth, South Africa, Frames was a mining engineer who worked in South Africa and Kenya, before dying during a surveying expedition in Angola. He excavated The Curragh Cave in the Drakensberg Mountains of KwaZulu-Natal of which he published a brief account (Frames 1898). Associated with **G.W. Lamplugh**. Fellow of the Geological Society.

Additional information Obituary *Proc. Geol. Soc.* 83, (1927) p. lix.

Frere, Sir H. Bartle E. 1815-1884.
Sites: Kaffirland [*sic*]; Kalahari Desert.

A grandson of John Frere of early antiquarian fame (Daniel 1975), Frere entered the Indian Civil Service in 1834, becoming Governor of Bombay between 1862 and 1867 and Special Commissioner to East Africa in 1873 with a remit to negotiate the abolition of the slave trade with the Sultan of Zanzibar. He was appointed Governor of the Cape Colony and British High Commissioner in South Africa in 1877 by Disraeli's Conservative Government and was charged by the Colonial Office with the task of uniting the British colonies and the independent Boer republics within a British controlled federation. Partly to acquire Boer support for this idea, he provoked war with the Zulu in 1879, a war which began disastrously for the British with the destruction of a large part of Lord Chelmsford's army at Isandhlwana and the death of the Prince Imperial, heir to the exiled Bonaparte Dynasty of France. Though the Zulu were defeated in 1880, Frere was recalled to London the same year. As well as the evidence of the ethnographic and archaeological collections that he made and which were subsequently donated to the British Museum, his wider interests are demonstrated by his Presidency of the Asiatic Society in 1872 and the Geographical Society in 1873.

Additional information *Dictionary of National Biography* pp. 697-706. *Dictionary of South African Biography* 2: 243-246.

Frylinck, Carel P. M. 1896-?
Sites: Hartebeestfontein; Roedtan.

A mining engineer of Dutch ancestry working in the then northern Transvaal, Frylinck had studied in the Netherlands before returning to South Africa. He subsequently worked briefly in Indonesia (then the Dutch East Indies), before settling in Holland.

Fuller, Capt. A. W. F.
Sites: Barkly West; Bloemhof.

Very little is known about Captain Fuller, except that he was living in London SW2 at the time of the purchase of the material by the British Museum in 1930. The purchase included both archaeological and ethnographic material and is noted as having been 'collected by HJB' (perhaps **Hermann J. Braunholtz**). How Fuller obtained the material is unclear.

Gardner, Rev. Fr. Thomas I. 1866-1944
Sites: Driefontein; Gokomere Cave.

Born in England, Gardner was ordained as a priest of the Society of Jesus in 1899 and shortly thereafter (1902) was posted to Bulawayo to teach at St. George's School. He subsequently worked at several other missions in Zimbabwe, including that at Gokomere near Masvingo (formerly Fort Victoria). Having explored archaeological sites while training as a Jesuit in north Wales, he went on to carry out some of the earliest archaeological excavations in Zimbabwe. He was close friends with Father Philip Stapleton, another amateur archaeologist, who himself taught at St. George's College, Harare, between 1929 and 1938 and who had previously been based in Grahamstown, where he had collaborated with **John Hewitt** .

Additional information *Our Dead 1939-1945* (Society of Jesus) pp. 308-311.

Goldsmid, Albert E. W. Colonel 1846-1904
Sites: South Africa, no further provenance.

Goldsmid served on the British Army's General Staff, taking part in the Second South African War of 1899-1902 as Assistant Adjutant General of the Sixth Division. He fought at the Battle of Paardeberg in 1900.

Additional information *Who Was Who* 1: 281.

Gordon, Sir Home Seton 1845-1906
Sites: Bulataga; Francistown Kopje; Gungwe Kopje; Ingwe River Farm 103; Makgadikgadi Pans; Nata River; Ramatlabama; Sekonje River; Senyowe Drift; Tati River; Tshesebe; Vukwe Drift.

Gordon was trained at the Royal Military College, Sandhurst, and served briefly with the 44th East Essex Regiment of Foot, and later with the Royal Glamorgan Light Infantry Militia. He travelled extensively throughout the world, including Africa. His collection of material from the 'Tati Territory' (Botswana) was donated to the British Museum by his son (also H. S. Gordon) in 1934. A detailed contemporary plan of the Tati Territory showing location of farms and acreage of plots of land accompanied the donation (Ethno Doc 80).

Additional information *Who Was Who* 1

Grey, Sir George 1812-1898
Sites: Cape Flats; Tharfield.

Grey was one of the most distinguished British colonial administrators of the Nineteenth Century, being appointed Governor of South Australia in 1840 the year after he sold his army commission. He subsequently served as Governor of New Zealand (1846-53), Governor of the Cape Colony (1854-61) and once more as Governor of New Zealand (1861-68). After spending part of his retirement in Britain, he returned to New Zealand and became Prime Minister in 1877, an office he held for two years. He continued to serve in the New Zealand House of Representatives until 1893 when he finally returned to England. He published an article on stone tools in 1869.

Additional information *Dictionary of National Biography Suppl.* pp. 782-789; *Dictionary of South African Biography,* 1.

Hall, J. C. F.
Sites: Mavoio.

Hardy, Colonel W. E. 1866-1959
Sites: Fish Hoek; Noordhoek.

Born in Britain and qualifying as a doctor in 1888, Hardy was commissioned into the Royal Army Medical Corps in 1891 and served as a medical officer in the Second South African War (1899-1902) and subsequently served in India as Assistant Director of Medical Services at Peshawar (now in Pakistan). Retiring from the army, he settled in Cape Town in 1924 and spent part of his retirement pursuing his archaeological interests on the Cape Peninsula. He was both a founder member and the first President of the South African Archaeological Society (1945-46).

Additional information Goodwin 1926a; Malan 1939.

Heanley, T. W.
Sites: Mafikeng.

The only information available about Mr Heanley is that he was living near Liss in Hampshire at the time of the donation of the handaxe to the British Museum in 1937, and that he had been at the railway station at Mafeking on 11 Feb. 1936 when he found the implement.

Hewitt, Dr John 1880-1961
Sites: Cape Padrone.

Primarily a biologist with an international reputation in herpetology and entomology, Hewitt was born in England and worked as a teacher after leaving Cambridge. He was Curator of the Kuching Museum, Sarawak, between 1905 and 1909 and moved to South Africa in 1909 to work at the Transvaal Museum in Pretoria. The following year he was appointed Director of the Albany Museum in Grahamstown (Eastern Cape Province, South Africa), a position which he held until 1958. He pioneered systematic archaeological excavation in the Eastern Cape, working *inter alia* at both the type sites of the Wilton and the Howieson's Poort industries (Hewitt 1921; Hewitt & Stapleton 1927). He was President of the South African Archaeological Society from 1948 to 1949.

Additional information *Dictionary of South African Biography* 4: 232-233.

Hillier, Dr Alfred P. 1858-1911
Sites: Buffalo River Drift; Buffalo (River) Shell Mound; Cape Flats; East London.

Having first gone to South Africa from Britain to learn ostrich farming, Hillier graduated from the University of Cape Town in 1877 and then obtained medical training at Edinburgh University. After working as a doctor in Britain he returned to South Africa and worked as a surgeon in both East London (Eastern Cape Province) and Kimberley (Northern Cape Province). He was President of the South African Medical Congress in 1893 and a member of the Johannesburg-based Reform Committee in 1895-96 involved with the attempt by Cecil Rhodes and Dr Jameson to invade and take over the South African Republic. For his participation in the Jameson Raid of 1896 he was imprisoned in Pretoria, but returned to Britain on his release in 1897. Hillier (1898) published an account of his experiences of the Jameson Raid, including a reprint of an earlier work on 'The Antiquity of Man in South Africa' (1890). Elected Member of Parliament for Hitchin in 1910, he committed suicide the following year.

Additional information *Dictionary of South African Biography* 5: 346; *Who Was Who* 1897-1916.

Hobley, Charles W. 1867-1947
Sites: Sawmills.

A geologist who worked with the Imperial British East African Company in 1890 during the initial British acquisition of Kenya. He subsequently held several positions within the East African Civil Service and was a member of the East African Protectorate's Legislative Council from 1912 to 1920. After his retirement and return to Britain he served on the Councils of the Geological Society, the Royal Geographical Society and the Royal Anthropological Institute and was Vice President of the Geological Society in 1930. His collection was donated to the British Museum in 1947 by his daughter, Frances,

Additional information *Who Was Who*, 4.

Jansen, François J. 1869-1930
Sites: Victoria West.

Born at Graaf-Reinet, Jansen became Magistrate of the Victoria West District in what is now South Africa's Northern Cape Province and collected mainly in this area. His one published work (Jansen 1926) described the Victoria West technique in detail and he also collaborated with C. H. T. D. Heese and A. J. H. Goodwin in further investigations (Goodwin & Van Riet Lowe 1929).

Jones, Rev. Dr. Neville 1880-1954
Sites: Alexandersfontein; Bambata Cave; Barkly West; De Kiel Oost; Ematjeni River; Embushini; Hope Fountain; Inyati; Inyati (Huckle's Farm); Jacobsdal; Leeuwfontein; Petrus; Sawmills; Taung; Turk Mine.

Born in Britain, Jones was ordained in 1909 and was appointed a missionary at Hope Fountain near Bulawayo in 1912. His archaeological interests began to develop with his discovery of an important Early Stone Age site at the Mission the following year and he went on to play the leading role in the early development of Stone Age archaeology in Zimbabwe. He discovered and then excavated at Bambata Cave in 1919 (Arnold & Jones 1919) and returned there in 1929 in collaboration with A. L. Armstrong and at the invitation of the University of Cape Town and the British Association for the Advancement of Science. He was the first archaeologist to identify the Middle Stone Age in Zimbabwe, but also worked in South Africa, excavating at the key Iron Age site of Mapungubwe in 1933 (Fouché 1937). In 1936 he was appointed Keeper of Prehistory of the National Museum of Southern Rhodesia and his collections formed the initial basis of its archaeological exhibits. He was also largely responsible for the creation of the Southern Rhodesian Monuments Commission, as well as author of the first overall surveys of Zimbabwean prehistory (N. Jones 1926, 1949). He served as President of the South African Archaeological Society 1953-54.

Additional information *South African Archaeological Bulletin* 9: 141; *Man* January 1955, pp. 5-6.

Kenny, W. H.
Sites: Charter District; Gweru Kopje; Shangani.

A prospector active in what is now Zimbabwe at the end of the nineteenth/beginning of the twentieth centuries (N. Jones 1949: 10). His material came to the British Museum by transfer from both Bulawayo Museum (1921) and the Geological Museum (1989).

Kenyon, Dame Kathleen M. 1906-1978
Sites: Paarl.

Educated at Oxford, Kenyon assisted Gertrude Caton-Thompson (1931) in her 1929 excavations at Great Zimbabwe conducted on behalf of the British Association for the Advancement of Science. She subsequently worked as secretary of the Institute of Archaeology in London (1935-48) and was its acting Director from 1942 to 1946. She lectured in Palestinian archaeology at the University of London from 1948 to 1962 and was director of the British School of Archaeology at Jerusalem between 1951 and 1966, with major programmes of research at Jericho and Jerusalem to her credit (1960, 1967). Following her retirement from London, she became Principal of St. Hugh's College, Oxford in 1962 until 1973. While there she was instrumental in securing funding for a Research Fellowship in Archaeology, which provided the financial basis on which the College decided in 1994 to create a Tutorial Fellowship in Archaeology linked with Oxford University's Lecturership in African Prehistory (one of the few teaching positions designated for African archaeology within the United Kingdom).

Additional information *Who Was Who* 7: 431.

Kettlewell, Rev. Percy W. H. 1868-1950
Sites: Alicedale; Kasouga River; Sugar Loaf Hill; Wilton Large Rock Shelter.

Educated at Oxford, Kettlewell was ordained an Anglican priest in 1896. He became Headmaster of St. Andrews College, a leading private school in Grahamstown (Eastern Cape Province) in 1909, a position he held for 24 years. Following his retirement from the College, he became Vicar of Bucksland, Aylesbury, in England (1934-44) and Canon Emeritus of Grahamstown Cathedral (1945-50). He organised a transfer of material from the Albany Museum to the British Museum in 1922.

Additional information *Who Was Who* 4: 636; *Dictionary of South African Biography*, 5.

King, Rev. Fr. Edward 1874-1936
Sites: Driefontein.

Born in England, King was ordained as a priest of the Society of Jesus in 1908 and taught at Hodder School until 1921. He then spent 15 years as the editor of *the Zambezi Mission Record* and the *Missionary Magazine* and three years as editor of the *Jesuit Directory*. He played an important part in missionary conferences in the late 1920s and was Chairman of the Joint Committee for Foreign Missions in 1930. He toured Zimbabwe between October 1931 and October 1932 and presumably met **Father Gardner** at that time. A letter from Gardner dated 22nd January 1931 (Ethnographic document 20) records that Gardner had sent two cases of stone implements found at Felixburg to Rome for exhibition at the Vatican and it is possible that this is the source of the material that King donated to the British Museum.

Additional information Obituary in Society of Jesus *Letters and Notes* 51 (1936).

Lamplugh, G. W. 1859-1926
Sites: Matetsi Valley.

A business man and amateur geologist until the age of 33, Lamplugh turned professional in 1892, joining the Geological Survey of Great Britain. He rose to become its Assistant Director between 1914 and 1920 and was also President of the Geological Society from 1918 until 1920. His main research was on glaciology, but he also investigated the geology and archaeology of the Victoria Falls area during the visit to southern Africa of the British Association for the Advancement of Science in 1905 (Lamplugh 1905a, 1905b).

Additional information Penny, L.F. 1964; 'Early Discoverers XXIV: George William Lamplugh 1859-1926', *Journal of Glaciology*.

Layard, Edgar L. 1824-1900
Sites: Cape Flats; Cape of Good Hope.

Layard followed his father's footsteps into the Ceylon Civil Service and was called to the bar there in 1846. He moved to the Cape Colony in 1855 as Private Secretary to Sir George Grey, its then Governor, and later moved with him to New Zealand. He returned to the Cape in 1862 as Arbitrator for cases brought under treaties regulating the suppression of the slave trade and became a judge in 1867 before being transferred to the Consular Service. There he was both the first British administrator of Fiji and later Consul in New Caledonia (1876-90). While in Cape Town he founded and became the first curator of the precursor of the South African Museum, publishing accounts of its mammalian and ornithological collections, as well as writing on archaeology (Layard 1870). He was a friend of **T. H. Bowker** and brother to Sir Henry Austin Layard, who pioneered the study of Assyrian archaeology (Daniel 1975).

Additional information *Who Was Who* 1: 417; *Dictionary of South African Biography* 1: 467-468.

Lee Doux, James A.
Sites: Windsorton.

Author of a paper reporting on his finds in the Vaal gravels (Lee Doux 1914), no further biographical information on this individual has come to light.

Leith, Dr George 1852-1903
Sites: Mossel Bay; Mossel Bay Flats; Pretoria; Pretoria (Arcadia); Pretoria (Camp Gravels); Pretoria (Meintjeskop); Pretoria (Muckleneuk); Pretoria (Wonderboom).

Born in Scotland, Leith came to South Africa in 1879 as a teacher, but subsequently established himself as a farmer and then as a lawyer (B. Leith 1964). He was introduced to archaeology by Kannemeyer (1890) and was prompted by him to excavate at Cape St. Blaize Cave, Mossel Bay to vindicate **Dr Atherstone**'s views that shell-rich deposits there were of human origin. He subsequently excavated shell middens in rock-shelters at East London and then moved to Pretoria where he settled as an attorney in 1889. As well as collecting stone artefacts and eoliths there, he was also a member of the committee that founded the Pretoria Museum in 1897, and the Transvaal correspondent of *The Scotsman* during and after the Second South African War of 1899-1902. He gave some artefacts to the Royal Anthropological Institute in 1898, others were donated to the British Museum, or were acquired later as part of the **Sturge** Collection (see Chapter 3, pp. 25-26). Professor Rupert Jones noted that Leith had also collected stone tools from Swaziland (1898).

Leviseur, Max 1884-1959
Sites: De Puts.

Son of a prominent German-born businessman who settled in Bloemfontein and was instrumental in establishing the National Museum in Bloemfontein, Leviseur served in the 2nd Imperial Light Hussars during the First World War. He trained and worked as a civil engineer and later moved to Germiston, near Johannesburg. In addition to collecting stone artefacts from De Puts Farm, he was the first person to report their presence at Fauresmith (qv). His collection was donated to the British Museum by his father, Moritz Leviseur, in 1919.

Additional information Goodwin & Van Riet Lowe 1929.

Liepner, Nicholas
Sites: Messina Copper Mine.

Lyell, Sir Charles 1797-1875
Sites: Grahamstown; Kleinemonde.

Educated at Oxford, Lyell was introduced to geology by William Buckland, Dean of Christ Church, but was called to the bar in 1825. He retired from the law two years later to pursue geology full-time, becoming President of the Geological Society in 1835. Without doubt one of the leading scientists of his time, he received public recognition through a Knighthood in 1848 and conferment of a Baronetcy in 1864. His *Principles of Geology* (Lyell 1830-33) demonstrated the overwhelming strength of evidence in support of a uniformitarian, rather than a catastrophic, paradigm of geological history. An early convert to Darwin's theory of evolution by natural selection, he summarized archaeological evidence for human antiquity in *The Antiquity of Man* (Lyell 1864).

Additional information *Dictionary of National Biography*, pp. 319-324.

McKay, George R.
Sites: East London; East London *(British Kaffraria)*.

McKay published two accounts of his fieldwork in the East London area (McKay 1896, 1897; Hillier 1898), but no specifically biographical information on him has thus far come to light. He was, however, one of the earliest collectors of stone artefacts and excavators of Stone Age sites in southern Africa (Binneman 1990).

The geologist Henry W. Piers, Curator of the South African Museum in Cape Town during the 1890s, was instrumental in arranging for the donation of some of McKay's material to the Geological Museum in 1867. That material was subsequently transferred to the British Museum in 1989 and includes a hand-drawn and coloured map of the area which McKay investigated (Fig. 13, p. 62).

Matley, Dr Charles A. 1866-1947
Sites: Khami.

Having completed a B.Sc. in geology at the University of London, Matley entered the Civil Service, retiring from the Indian Finance Department in 1920. Throughout his career he maintained his geological interests and was Lecturer in Geology at the Birmingham and Midland Institute between 1898 and 1902. Although his principal research was conducted in Gwynedd, north Wales, he travelled extensively after his retirement and between 1932 and 1933 led an expedition to India to search for dinosaur fossils. His material from Khami was donated to the British Museum via Dr W. N. Edwards, later Keeper of Geology at the Brtish Museum (Natural History).

Additional information *Quarterly Journal of the Geological Society of London* 104: lviii-lix; *Who Was Who* 4: 775.

Newall, Robert S. 1884-1978
Sites: Muden.

Born in England, Newall's first archaeological activities were undertaken as a teenager at Camp Hill, South Newton. He became interested in ethnography during a world tour in 1909 and after the First World War devoted himself primarily to the archaeology of Wiltshire. He excavated at Stonehenge with Colonel Hawley between 1919 and 1926 (Newall 1929a, 1929b, 1956) and rediscovered and excavated the Aubrey holes at the site. He had a long association with Salisbury Museum, becoming a Trustee in 1937 and Vice-President in 1971. He assisted **H. Cookson** to donate his collection.

Orpen, Francis H. S. 1824-1893
Sites: Douglas ?

Born in Ireland, Orpen emigrated to south Africa for health reasons in 1844. Training as a surveyor, he was appointed in 1852 to assist in land surveys of the Orange River Sovereignty. After its abandonment by Britain in 1854 and the establishment of the Orange Free State republic, he settled on the farm Sinclair near Douglas and developed the surrounding area for settlement in 1867, becoming Magistrate and Civil Commissioner. After the discovery of diamonds he promoted British annexation of Griqualand West and became the territory's Magistrate and Surveyor-General in 1871, surveying the boundary line with the Free State that left the diamond diggings under British control. He later served as member of the House of Assembly for Barkly West (1881-83) and was a Fellow of both the Royal Astronomical Society and the Royal Geographical Society.

Maria Wilman recorded only that she obtained from 'Orpen' the material from Douglas which she donated in 1930. While the name 'Orpen' could refer to any member of the family, it is most likely that the original collector was Francis Orpen given the date of the donation and geographic location of the findspot.

Although Francis is the most likely donor of the Douglas material, his brother Joseph (1828-1923) also worked in South Africa where he developed ethnographic interests. Joseph was the British Government's official mediator with King Moshoeshoe I of the Basotho between 1862 and 1868, writing a history of the Basotho (Orpen 1857), and subsequently served as Magistrate of No Man's Land (East Griqualand) from 1873 to 1875. In the course of travelling through the Lesotho highlands in 1873 he visited several key archaeological sites and recorded unique information on the myths and legends of the Maluti Bushmen (Orpen 1874). He was the Cape Colony's Agent in Basutoland between 1881 and 1883 before Lesotho reverted to Imperial control, represented three different Eastern Cape seats in the Colonial House of Assembly and in 1896 moved to Zimbabwe where he was Surveyor-General of Rhodesia until his retirement in 1903.

Additional information *Dictionary of South African Biography* 1: 602-603; *Dictionary of South African Biography* 3: 666-667.

Passmore Edwards Museum
Sites: Burgersdorp; Cape Flats; Karrieput.

Péringuey, Louis A. 1855-1924
Sites: Stellenbosch (Bosman's Crossing).

Born in Bordeaux, France, Péringuey fought in the Franco-Prussian War of 1870-71 and then took a Master's degree in Science, collecting plant and animal specimens for French museums in Senegal, Gambia and Madagascar. He emigrated to South Africa in 1879 to teach French at the South African College, Cape Town and joined the staff of the South African Museum in 1884. After ten years as Assistant Director, he became Director of the Museum in 1906, a position that he held until his death. He simultaneously served briefly as Inspector of Vineyards (from 1885) and Colonial Viticulturalist (from 1889), returning to France to research phylloxera, which severely attacked the Cape's vineyards at this time. His archaeological interests developed from about 1890, possibly from contacts with Kannemeyer (1890) and he located *in situ* Acheulean artefacts at Stellenbosch (qv) in 1899. His *The Stone Ages in South Africa* (Péringuey 1911) was one of the first synthetic treatments of southern African prehistory.

Additional information *Dictionary of South African Biography* 2: 537-539.

Piers, Henry W.
Sites: East London.

A geologist who served as Curator of the South African Museum in Cape Town in the early 1890s, Piers published brief accounts of the geology and archaeology of the Cape Peninsula (Piers 1871, 1873). Correspondence in the British Museum dating to June 18th 1867 shows that Piers was instrumental in arranging for the transfer to British institutions of some of the finds made by **McKay** in the East London area.

Read, Sir Charles H. 1857-1929
Sites: Shangani River; Simondium (Vriedeslust Farm).

Read was put in charge of the Christy Collection in 1874, having previously worked as secretary to R. Smith at what later became the Victoria and Albert Museum. He was appointed Assistant Keeper in the Department of British and Medieval Antiquities at the British Museum in 1880 and succeeded Sir Augustus Franks as Keeper in 1896. He took an important part in expanding the ethnographic collections of the Museum, as well as in publicizing them by writing several guides and catalogues, among them *Antiques from Benin* (1899). He also founded the first Friends of the British Museum and served as President of several learned societies: Section H of the British Association for the Advancement of Science (1899); the Royal Anthropological Institute (1899-1901 and 1917-19); and the Society of Antiquaries of London (1908-14 and 1919-24).

Additional information *Dictionary of National Biography of the Twentieth Century, 1922-1930*, pp. 712-713.

Robertson, (Robinson) W. D.
Sites: Burgersdorp.

Rothwell, P.
Sites: Vogelstruisfontein Farm.

Correspondence in the PEE archives shows Rothwell to have been present in London in 1890 when he was introduced to Sir Augustus Franks, at that time Keeper of the Department of British and Medieval Antiquities. In 1893 and 1894 when back in Johannesburg he wrote to Franks several times reporting his discovery of several stone artefacts, including balls of quartz, which **George Leith** had compared to examples known from Scotland.

Routley, S. H.
Sites: Kimberley (Golf Links).

Mr Routley gives his address as The Diamond Corporation Ltd, London EC1 at the time of the donation in 1938. The donation was made in person by **James Swan** at the same time that he donated material himself. The artefact is from one of Swan's surface sites.

Seton-Karr, Captain Heywood W. 1859-1938
Sites: Christiana (Soutpansdrift); Hosluit; Soutpansdrift; Stellenbosch (Bosman's Crossing); Stillbay.

After a university education at Oxford and Florence, Seton-Karr served in the British Army in Egypt and went on to travel and explore in Africa, India and the Arctic. He collected prehistoric artefacts in many of the areas that he visited, among them Somalia, Egypt and India, as well as South Africa, publishing accounts of his adventures in a series of books and papers. It is probable that his South African material came to the British Museum as part of the **Sturge** Collection.

Additional information *Who Was Who* 3: 1218.

Smith, Major Frederick 1858-1933
Sites: Pienaarsrivier.

Born in England, Smith joined the British Army as a medical student and served in the ranks in both the Zulu War of 1879 and the First South African War of 1880-81. He completed his medical training in Dublin in 1889 and was commissioned as a Captain in the Royal Army Medical Corps in 1890, subsequently serving on both the North West Frontier of the Indian Empire and in Sierra Leone. He was on active service in the Second South African War of 1899-1902 and later commanded field hospitals during the First World War.

Additional information *British Medical Journal* August 26th 1933.

Spence, Charles
Sites: Cape of Good Hope.

Nothing is known of Charles Spence except that he donated material found at the Cape of Good Hope to the Christy Collection in 1868.

Spencer, Dr Leonard J. 1870-1959
Sites: Canteen Kopje.

Born in England, Spencer graduated from Cambridge and joined the Mineralogy Department of the British Museum of Natural History in 1894, eventually serving as the Keeper of Mineralogy between 1927 and his retirement in 1935. He was a Fellow of both the Geological Society and the Royal Society and served as President of the Mineralogical Society of Great Britain from 1936 until 1939. He attended the meeting in South Africa in 1929 of the British Association for the Advancement of Science.

Sturge, Dr. William A. 1850-1919
Sites: Cape Flats; Cape of Good Hope; Drakensberg Foothills; Grahamstown; Mossel Bay; Mossel Bay Flats; Pretoria; Pretoria (Arcadia); Pretoria (Camp Gravels); Pretoria (Meintjeskop); Pretoria (Muckleneuk); Pretoria (Wonderboom).

Having studied medicine in Bristol, London and Paris, Sturge was appointed as a physician at the Royal Free Hospital in 1877, but moved to Nice in 1881 because of his wife's deteriorating health. A man of considerable leisure, Sturge collected Greek and Etruscan art, as well as prehistoric stone artefacts. Following his return to Britain in 1907 his home in Suffolk became a centre of his Palaeolithic and Neolithic research, and he was the first President of the Prehistoric Society of East Anglia. His private collection of over 100 000 artefacts was bequeathed to the British Museum. His collection contained material from South Africa collected by several people including **Elliott, Leith** and **Seton-Kerr**. Correspondance preserved (PEE) shows that some material was purchased and others obtained by exchange.

Additional information *Who Was Who* 2: 1012; R. Smith 1937.

Swan, James A. 1867-1954
Sites: Alexandersfontein; Blesmanspos; Blikfontein; Hopetown Bridge; Kimberley; Kimberley (Bultfontein); Kimberley (Boshof Road); Kimberley (Golf Links); Kimberley (Sluits); Koodoosberg Drift; Kuruman (Cotton End); Langeberg; Nooitgedacht; Pniel; Potchefstroom; Prieska; Read's Drift; Rooipoort; Silver Streams; South Africa, no further provenance; Vaal River; Witsands I; Witsands II.

Born in Scotland, Swan emigrated to South Africa in 1888 and for much of his life was employed by De Beers in Kimberley. After his retirement in 1931 he spent much of his time collecting prehistoric artefacts, mostly in the Northern Cape Province and along the South Coast of KwaZulu-Natal with a particular concentration on the Later Stone Age. Dying in a thunderstorm while collecting artefacts on the open veld at the age of 87, he bequeathed investments to the University of Oxford that form the basis of the Swan Fund, which has been, and continues to be, a major support for Stone Age archaeological research in southern Africa.

Additional information *South African Archaeol. Bull.* 9 (1954) 11; 10 (1955) 29.

Thomasset, Hans P. 1862-1949
Sites: Bushmans River (KwaZulu-Natal); Weenen.

Though a godson of Hans Christian Anderson, the Danish author, Thomasset was born in England and emigrated to South Africa before 1895. An engineer, he quarried lime at Sterkfontein for several years after 1895, discovering the fossil-bearing breccias that were subsequently made famous by the presence in them of the remains of *Australopithecus africanus*. As well as having an interest in archaeology and palaeontology, he was also an amateur malacologist and retired to farm at Weenen in Kwazulu-Natal.

Additional information Goodwin & Van Riet Lowe (1929).

Thurburn, Capt. Henry 1826-1897
Sites: Hout Bay; Port Beaufort.

Born in Egypt, Thurburn was educated in Britain and joined the East India Company as a military officer in 1842. He saw active service there, leaving in 1859 because of ill-health and retiring from the army in 1861 to live in Scotland.

Additional information McKannand (1967).

Trechmann, Charles T. 1885-1964
Sites: Coega; Zwartkops River.

A British-born chemist and invertebrate palaeontologist, Trechmann also had interests in archaeology and was a member of the Prehistoric Society from 1935. Following the sale of his family business he travelled widely making important contributions to the study of the geology of New Zealand and the Caribbean in particular.

Additional information Fleming & Westoll (1964).

Trevor, Major Tudor G. 1865-1954
Sites: Steynsdorp.

Born in Wales, and a graduate of the Royal School of Mines, Trevor worked briefly in Spain before emigrating to South Africa in 1887. He worked in various mining operations in the then South African Republic and travelled extensively in southern Africa. At the outbreak of the Second South African War he joined the British forces and served as an intelligence officer both then and later during the First World War in Namibia and East Africa. He was Inspector of Mines, Pretoria (with responsibility for the whole of the Transvaal outside the Rand) between 1901 and 1925 and Secretary of Mines and Works in Northern Rhodesia (now Zambia) between 1925 and 1928, when he retired to Britain. During this last post, he was responsible for sending the Kalomo cranium to Prof. Raymond Dart in Johannesburg.

Additional information *Dictionary of South African Biography* 5: 780-781.

Tribe, Rev. Father Reginald 1881-1945
Sites: Modderpoort.

Born in England, Tribe qualified as a doctor and worked as such before entering the priesthood in 1912. He served as a Captain in the Royal Army Medical Corps in the First World War and became Director of the Society of the Sacred Mission in 1925, a position he occupied until his death. During this time he visited South Africa eight times between 1926 and 1937. Although there is little to suggest that he personally had an interest in archaeology, the Society had two priories at Modderpoort. It seems likely that it was one of the incumbents of these missions who actually collected the artefacts that Tribe donated to the British Museum (P. Hughes, *in litt.* 5/8 1996). PEE archives preserve a sketch map of the find-area

Additional information *Society of the Sacred Mission News* May 1995.

Van Alphen, J. G. 1875-1944
Sites: Pniel; Vaal River; Windsorton; Worcester.

Following an initial appointment as a Dutch interpreter in the District Court at Grahamstown, Van Alphen served as Magistrate in several districts of the then Cape Colony/Cape Province between 1901 and 1935, Worcester among them. With a life-long interest in South African prehistory, he was involved with the discovery of the Canteen Kopje skull and collected stone artefacts from several localities, publishing two brief articles on the subject (Van Alphen 1930).

Additional information *Diamond Fields Advertiser*, 21/10/1944.

Van Heerden, Dr. Petronella A. 1887-1975
Sites: Bloemfontein; Brakfontein; Buffelsjag; Fishhoek; Harrismith; Hermanus; Paarl; Stellenbosch; Villiersdorp.

Born in the Free State, Van Heerden studied at Stellenbosch and then in Amsterdam, becoming the first Afrikaner woman to qualify as a doctor. She returned to South Africa in 1916 and worked in Bloemfontein and Harrismith before reading for a doctorate in gynaecology at Amsterdam, a thesis she completed in 1923. She settled in Cape Town in 1924 and, as well as practising as a gynaecologist, played an active part in the struggle for women's suffrage and in the National Party. Her contacts with the British Association for the Advancement of Science led to her visiting **Caton-Thompson**'s (1931) excavations at Great Zimbabwe in 1929 and she subsequently worked on Dorothy Garrod's excavations at Wadi el-Mughara on Mount Carmel, Israel, in 1931. Retiring to a farm in Harrismith in 1942, she travelled extensively through the Free State with the Abbé Breuil on his visit to South Africa in 1949.

Additional information *Dictionary of South African Biography* 5: 812-813.

Van Riet Lowe, Prof. Clarence 1894-1954
Sites: Canteen Kopje; Sheppards Island.

Born in South Africa and educated in Bloemfontein and Cape Town, Van Riet Lowe saw military service in the First World War and became interested in archaeology while collecting handaxes in Egypt. He went on to study engineering at the University of Cape Town and from 1923 worked in the Free State, combining his career with the location and collection of archaeological materials. Much of this experience was pooled with that of A. J. H. Goodwin to produce *Stone Age Cultures of South Africa* (Goodwin & Van Riet Lowe 1929). Having served as President of Section E of the South African Association for the Advancement of Science in 1931, he was appointed the first Director of the Bureau of Archaeology (later the Archaeological Survey) in 1934. He simultaneously held a Chair in Archaeology at the University of the Witwatersrand in Johannesburg, served as Secretary of the National Monuments Commission and was President of the South African Archaeological Society in 1952.

Author of numerous papers, among his other principal contributions were his work with **Wayland** on the prehistory and Pleistocene geology of Uganda (Wayland & Van Riet Lowe 1952), the identification of the Smithfield Culture (Goodwin & Van Riet Lowe 1929) and the archaeological survey of the Little Caledon and Vaal River Valleys (Van Riet Lowe 1937, 1952b, 1956). His material was transferred from the Institute of Archaeology, London, to the British Museum in 1989.

Additional information *South African Archaeological Bulletin* 11: 82-83; B. Malan (1962).

Walsh, T.
Sites: Bushman's River.

Joint donor of artefacts collected by **H. P. Thomasset** at Weenen, KwaZulu-Natal, there is a remote possibility that he was the latter's illegally adopted son, who is mentioned, but never named, in extant correspondence in the British Museum's archives (Ethno).

Wansborough, Ivon S. d. 1951
Sites: Ngwaritsi River.

English by birth, Wansborough was a school teacher who later emigrated to South Africa.

Ward, Penelope F. A.
Sites: Barberton; Carnarvondale Farm; Carnarvondale (Bushy Park site); Carnarvondale (Hillary site); Carnarvondale (Van Riet Lowe site); Carnarvondale (Woodbury site).

Warren, S. Hazzledine
Sites: Derré.

Well-known British archaeologist and geologist who donated his massive archaeological collection to the British Museum in 1958. How he acquired this single artefact from Mozambique is unknown.

Wayland, Edward J. 1888-1966.
Sites: Monapo River.

British by birth, Wayland studied as an architect and only later as a geologist, collecting his first stone artefacts in Cheddar Gorge, England, in 1901. Before the First World War he had worked for mining companies in Egypt, Mozambique (Wayland 1915) and Sri Lanka. Sent to Uganda to prospect for minerals useful for Britain's war effort, he remained there as Director of the Geological Survey for 20 years, though he briefly studied archaeology at Cambridge during this period. After further military service in the Second World War, he was sent to Botswana in 1943 and became Director of the Bechuanaland Geological Survey. In addition to the few artefacts from Mozambique included in the present Catalogue, Wayland located numerous archaeological sites in East Africa, excavating some of them, notably Nsongezi (Wayland & Van Riet Lowe 1952), and also wrote on Botswanan prehistory (Wayland 1954).

Additional information *Proceedings of the Geological Society of London* 1642: 231-232; *Who Was Who* 6: 1178.

Whitaker, William 1836-1925
Sites: Cape of Good Hope.

A British geologist who spent most of his career (1857-96) working in the Geological Survey of England and was also President of the Geology Society (1898-1900) and of the Geologists' Association (1901-02; 1920-21). His work was almost exclusively concentrated in the south-east of England.

Additional information *Who Was Who* 2: 1115.

White, Franklin 1850-1928
Sites: Bechuana Province (?); Griqualand West; Griquatown; Khami; Matopos Cave 1; Matopos Cave 2; Plumtree; Simondium; Steynsdorp.

Born in England, White worked as a mining engineer in Colombia before emigrating to South Africa in 1889 to assume the management of a number of gold mines in the then South African Republic. A member of the Institute of Mining and Metallurgy, he published papers on aspects of gold mining and travelled in South Africa as well as Australia before settling in Zimbabwe. He was the first person to report the presence there of prehistoric stone artefacts (at Khami, qv) and the first to excavate a Stone Age site in Zimbabwe (White 1905). He subsequently also worked at the early homind site of Broken Hill Cave in Zambia, from which he collected faunal remains (J. D. Clark, pers. comm.).

Additional information *South African Who's Who* 1908.

White, Maj-Gen. Henry G. 1835-1906
Sites: Bechuana Province (?); Griqualand West.

With a long military career behind him in the Crimean War, the Indian Mutiny and the British occupation of Cyprus in 1878, White commanded the 1st Battalion The Royal Scots in the 1884 expedition that annexed the area south of the Molopo River to Britain's South African territories as the Colony of British Bechuanaland. White retired from the army in 1886.

Additional information *Who Was Who* 1: 757.

White, Very Rev. Ralph L. d. 1954
Sites: Pietermaritzburg.

Educated at Oxford, White was ordained in 1896 and served as a chaplain to British forces in South Africa between 1901 and 1903. He went on to hold a variety of ecclesiastical appointments that culminated in his being Dean and Vicar of St. Saviours Parish, Pietermaritzburg between 1929 and 1934. He subsequently returned to Britain where he also worked as a priest.

Additional information *Crockford's Clerical Directory 1953-54.*

Wigram, Eliza R. 1838-1899
Sites: Mbabane River.

Museum records refer to this lady having expressed an interest in donating ethnographic specimens from Zululand in 1895, two years before a similar request relating to the Wigram Collection from Mbabane River was made by her sister **Miss H. Wigram** (1829-1908) of Bransfield, Godstone, Surrey. Though no further details are available, it is possible that the two ladies had travelled and/or lived in southeastern southern Africa. Several of their cousins served in the British Army during the Second South African War of 1899-1902, but the connection (if any) between this and the Mbabane River material remains unclear.

Additional information Wigram (1913).

Wilman, Maria 1867-1957
Sites: Alexandersfontein; Amantia; Douglas; Kimberley; Newlands; Pniel.

Born in Cape Town, Wilman read Natural Sciences at Cambridge and on her return to South Africa was employed in the Geological Survey at Cape Town. Having returned to Cambridge to study botany, she then worked with **L. Péringuey** (qv) in Cape Town before helping to found the McGregor Museum in Kimberley in 1908. She was its first Director and held this position until her retirement in 1946. She carried out research in botany and geology, as well as archaeology, travelling into the Kalahari with Dorothea Bleek in 1910-11 to study the Naron Bushmen (Bleek 1928) and recording rock paintings in Lesotho around the same time (Wilman 1911). Rock art was one of her major interests and she produced the first systematic study of rock-engravings in the Northern Cape Province (Wilman 1933).

Additional information J. Deacon (1987); *South African Archaeol. Bull.* 48 (1957), 152.

Wilson, K. G. & Wilson, R. W.
Sites: Middledrift.

Little is known about these two brothers except that they were living at Middledrift at the time of the donation in 1926. A letter from them dated 1/12/25 is contained in the PEE 'Paeolithic-Neolithic Scrapbook'.

Bibliography

Note: Archives relating to the collections are found in the following departments at the British Museum: Prehistoric and Early Europe; Medieval and Modern Europe; and Ethnography.

Abrahams, G. 1989. A review of the South African cultural heritage legislation. In: H. Cleere (ed.) *Archaeological Heritage Management in the Modern World*, pp. 207-220. London: Unwin Hyman.

Adamowicz, L. 1987. Projecto 'CIPRIANA' 1981-1985. *Trabalhos de Arqueologia e Antropologia* 3: 47-114.

Anderson, A. A. 1887a. *Twenty-Five Years in a Waggon in the Gold Regions of Africa*. London: Chapman & Hall (2nd edn 1888)

Anderson, A. A. 1887b. *Terra: On a Hitherto Unsuspected Second Axial Rotation of Our Earth*. London: Reeves & Turner.

Anderson, J. 1878. Notes in connection with stone implements from Natal. *Journal of the Anthropological Institute* 8: 1878-1879.

Anthony, B. 1967. Excavations at Peers Cave, Fish Hoek, South Africa. *Palaeoecology of Africa* 2: 58-59.

Anthony, B. 1972. The Stillbay question. In: H. J. Hugot (ed.) *Actes du Cinquieme Congrès Panafricain de Préhistoire*, pp. 80-82. Chambéry: Les Imprimeries Réunies de Chambéry.

Armstrong, A. L. 1929. Rhodesian cave expedition, 1929. *Prehistoric Society of East Anglia* 5: 144.

Armstrong, A. L. 1931. Rhodesian archaeological expedition, 1929. Excavations in Bambata Cave, etc. *Journal of the Royal Anthopological Institute* 61: 239-276.

Armstrong, A. L. & Jones, N. 1936. The antiquity of man in Rhodesia as demonstrated by the stone implements of the ancient Zambezi gravels, south of Victoria Falls. With notes on the geology of the area by H. B. Maufe. *Journal of the Royal Anthropological Institute* 66: 379-392.

Arnold, G. & Jones, N. 1919. Notes on the Bushman Cave at Bambata, Matopos. *Proceedings of the Rhodesian Association for the Advancement of Science* 17: 5-19.

Atherstone, Dr. 1871. Letter on Cape St. Blaize Cave, Mossel Bay. *Cape Monthly Magazine* 3: 125.

Avery, D. M. 1982a. The micromammalian fauna from Border Cave, Kwazulu, South Africa. *Journal of Archaeological Science* 9: 187-204.

Avery, D. M. 1982b. Micromammals as palaeoenvironmental indicators and an interpretation of the late Quaternary in the southern Cape Province, South Africa. *Annals of the South African Museum* 85: 183-374.

Avery, G. 1975. Discussion on the age and use of tidal fish-traps (*viswyers*). *South African Archaeological Bulletin* 30: 105-113.

Bain, A. G. 1949. *Journals of Andrew Geddes Bain*, M. H. Lister (ed). Cape Town: Van Riebeeck Society.

Bain, T. 1880. Bone caves at Knysna. *Cape Monthly Magazine* 2: 255-256.

Balfour, H. 1906. Notes upon an implement of palaeolithic type from the Victoria Falls, Zambezi. *Journal of the Royal Anthropological Institute* 36: 170-171.

Balfour, H. 1910. Archaeological and ethnological research. *The Times (South African Supplement)* 5 Nov. 1910.

Barber, M. E. 1872. In the Claims. *Cape Monthly Magazine* 4: 39-45.

Barham, L. S. 1989. A preliminary report on the Later Stone Age artefacts from Siphiso Shelter in Swaziland. *South African Archaeological Bulletin* 44: 33-43.

Barham, L. S. 1990. *The Later Stone Age of Swaziland*. Unpublished PhD Thesis, University of Pennsylvania.

Barham, L. S. 1992. Let's walk before we run: an appraisal of historical materialist approaches to the Later Stone Age. *South African Archaeological Bulletin* 47: 44-51.

Barham, L. S. 1995. The Mumbwa Caves project, Zambia, 1993-1994. *Nyame Akuma* 43: 66-72.

Barradas, L. 1961. Chronologia do Quaternario do sul de Moçambique. *Boletim do Instituto de Investigação Científica de Moçambique* 2: 374-388.

Barrow, J. 1801. *An Account of Travels into the Interior of Africa in the Years 1797 and 1798*. London: Cadell & Davies.

Bazley, W. 1905. Exploration of a Bushman cave in Alfred County, Natal. *Man* 5: 10-11.

Beach, D. 1980. *The Shona and Zimbabwe 900-1850*. Gweru: Mambo Press.

Beaumont, P. B. 1978. *Border Cave*. Unpublished MA Thesis, University of Cape Town.

Beaumont, P. B. 1981. The Heuningneskrans Shelter. In: E. Voigt (ed.)*Guide to Archaeological Sites in the Northern and Eastern Transvaal*, pp. 133-145. Pretoria: Southern African Association of Archaeologists.

Beaumont, P. B. 1986. Where did all the young men go during O-18 stage 2 ? *Palaeoecology of Africa* 17: 79-86.

Beaumont, P. B., De Villiers, H. & Vogel, J. C. 1978. Modern man in sub-Saharan Africa prior to 49,000 years BP: a review and evaluation with particular reference to Border Cave. *South African Journal of Science* 74: 409-419.

Beaumont, P. B. & Morris, D. 1990. *Guide to Archaeological Sites in the Northern Cape*. Kimberley: McGregor Museum.

Beaumont, P. B., Smith, A. B. & Vogel, J. C. 1995. Before the Einiqua: the archaeology of the Frontier Zone. In: A. B. Smith (ed.) *Einiqualand: Studies of the Orange River Frontier*, pp. 236-264. Cape Town: University of Cape Town Press.

Beaumont, P. B. & Vogel, J. C. 1972. On a new radiocarbon chronology for Africa south of the Equator. Part 1. *African Studies* 31: 66-89.

Beaumont, P. B. & Vogel, J. C. 1989. Patterns in the age and context of rock art in the northern Cape. *South African Archaeological Bulletin* 44: 73-81.

Binford, L. R. 1984. *Faunal Remains from Klasies River Mouth*. New York: Academic Press.

Binneman, J. N. F. 1982. *Mikrogebruikstekene op Steenwerktuie: Eksperimentele Waarmnemings en 'n Studie van Werktuie afkomstig van Boomplaasgrot*. (Micro-use Traces on Stone Tools: Experimental Observations and a Study of Artefacts from Boomplaas Cave). Unpublished MA Thesis, University of Stellenbosch.

Binneman, J. N. F. 1985. Research along the south-eastern Cape coast. In: S. L. Hall & J. N. F. Binneman (eds) *Guide to Archaeological Sites in the Eastern and North-eastern Cape*, pp. 117-134. Grahamstown: Southern African Association of Archaeologists.

Binneman, J. N. F. 1990. History of archaeology in Eastern Cape, Part 1: the spade brigade. *The Phoenix* 3 (1): 12-15.

Binneman, J. N. F. 1994a. The Holocene lithic industries at Klasies River Mouth Cave 5, South Africa: an example of group identity maintenance. Unpublished paper delivered at the Society of Africanist Archaeologists, Bloomington, April.

Binneman, J. N. F. 1994b. Notes on a digging stick from Augussie Shelter, eastern Cape. *Southern African Field Archaeology* 3: 112-113.

Binneman, J. N. F. 1996. *Symbolic Construction of Communities during the Holocene Later Stone Age in the South-eastern Cape*. Unpublished D. Phil. thesis, University of the Witwatersrand.

Binneman, J. N. F. 1997. Results from a test excavation at The Havens Cave, Cambria Valley, south-eastern Cape. *Southern African Field Archaeology* 6: 93-105.

Binneman, J. N. F. & Deacon, J. 1984. Experimental determination of use wear on stone adzes from Boomplaas Cave, South Africa. *Journal of Archaeological Science* 13: 219-228.

Binneman, J. N. F. & Van Niekerk, J. C. 1986. Polished stone implements from the Barberton District, eastern Transvaal. *South African Archaeological Bulletin* 41: 87-89.

Bishop, W. W. & Clark, J. D. 1967. *Background to Human Evolution in Africa.* Chicago: University of Chicago Press.

Bleek, D. F. 1928. *The Naron: A Bushman Tribe of the Central Kalahari.* Cambridge: Cambridge University Press.

Bollong, C. A. 1986. Work in progress: Stone Age research at Ruchera cave, Mutoko District, Zimbabwe. *Cookeia* 1: 49-61.

Bollong, C. A. 1996. *Later Stone Age Ceramic Chronology and Production in Central South Africa.* Unpublished PhD Thesis, Southern Methodist University.

Bollong, C. A. & Sampson, C. G. 1996. Later Stone Age ceramic stratigraphy and direct dates on pottery: a comparison. *Southern African Field Archaeology* 5: 3-16.

Bond, G. & Summers, R. F. H. 1954. A Late Stillbay hunting-camp site on the Nata River, Bechuanaland Protectorate. *South African Archaeological Bulletin* 9: 35.

Bousman, C. B. 1988. Prehistoric settlement in the Senqunyane Valley, Lesotho. *South African Archaeological Bulletin* 43: 33-37.

Bousman, C. B. 1991. *Holocene Palaeoecology and Later Stone Age Hunter-Gatherer Adaptations in the South African Interior Plateau.* Unpublished PhD Thesis, Southern Methodist University.

Bowker, J. H. 1872. Note on perforated stones. *Cape Monthly Magazine* 25: 55-57.

Bowker, J. H. 1884. Other days in South Africa. *Transactions of the South African Philosophical Society* 3 (2): 68-73.

Brain, C. K. 1981. *The Hunters or the Hunted ?* Chicago: University of Chicago Press.

Brain, C. K. 1988. New information from the Swartkrans cave of relevance to "robust" australopithecines. In: F. E. Grine (ed.) *The Evolutionary History of the Robust Australopithecines*, pp. 311-316. New York: Aldine.

Brain, C. K. 1993. *Swartkrans: A Cave's Chronicle of Early Man.* Pretoria: Transvaal Museum.

Breuil, H. 1930. Premières impressions de voyage sur la préhistoire sud-africaine. *L'Anthropologie* 40: 209-223.

Breuil, H. 1931. *L'Afrique Préhistorique.* Paris: Cahiers d'Art.

Breuil, H. 1944. Il parte das primeiras impressões duma viagem de estudos arqueológicos no sul de Moçambique. *Moçambique Documentário Trimestral* 40: 39-48.

Breuil, H. 1948. The White Lady of the Brandberg, South West Africa, her companions and her guards. *South African Archaeological Bulletin* 3: 2-11.

Breuil, H. & De Almeida, A. 1962. Sur les gravures et les peintures rupestres du désert de Moçamedes (Angola). *Actes du IVe Congrès Panafricain de Préhistoire, Annales du Musée Royal de l'Afrique Centrale* 40: 451-456.

Brink, J. S. 1987. The archaeozoology of Florisbad, Orange Free State. *Memoirs van die Nasionale Museum, Bloemfontein* 24: 1-151.

Brink, J. S., Henderson, Z. L. & Rossouw, L. 1996. Guide to the Florisbad Quaternary Site. In J. S. Brink, J. Dreyer, Z. L. Henderson & S. Ouzman (eds) *Guide to Archaeological Sites in the Free State and Lesotho*, pp. 70-76. Bloemfontein: Southern African Association of Archaeologists.

Brink, J. S. & Lee Thorp, J. A. 1992. The feeding niche of an extinct springbok, *Antidorcas bondi* (Antilopini, Bovidae) and its palaeoenvironmental meaning. *South African Journal of Science* 88: 227-229.

Brooker, M. 1980. Rescue excavations at the Welbedacht Dam site. *Humanitas* 6: 35-42.

Brooks, A. S. & Yellen, J. E. 1977. Archaeological excavations at Gi: preliminary report on the first two field seasons. *Botswana Notes and Records* 9: 21-30.

Brown, A. 1870. Note to Dale's Stone implements in South Africa. *Cape Monthly Magazine* 1: 366-367.

Bulpin, T. V. 1986. *Discovering Southern Africa.* Muizenberg: Treasury of Travel.

Burkitt, M. C. 1928. *South Africa's Past in Stone and Paint.* Cambridge: Cambridge University Press.

Burrows, H. R. (ed.) 1951. *Archaeology and Natural Resources of Natal, Natal Regional Survey Volume I.* Oxford: Oxford University Press.

Busk, G. 1869. Stone antiquities found in Africa. *Transactions of the International Congress of Prehistoric Archaeology* (Third Session, London 1868).

Butzer, K. W. 1984. Archaeogeology and Quaternary environment in the interior of southern Africa. In: R. G. Klein (ed.) *Southern African Prehistory and Palaeoenvironments*, pp. 1-64. Rotterdam: A. Balkema.

Butzer, K. W., Fock, G. J., Scott, L. & Stuckenrath, R. 1979. Dating and context of rock engravings in southern Africa. *Science* 203: 1201-1214.

Cable, J. H. C. 1984. *The Late Stone Age of Southern Natal.* Oxford: British Archaeological Reports.

Cable, J. H. C., Scott, K. & Carter, P. L. 1980. Excavations at Good Hope Shelter, Underberg District, Natal. *Annals of the Natal Museum* 24: 1-34.

Carter, P. L. 1970. Late Stone Age exploitation patterns. *South African Archaeological Bulletin* 25: 55-58.

Carter, P. L. 1978. *The Prehistory of Eastern Lesotho.* Unpublished PhD Thesis, University of Cambridge.

Carter, P. L., Mitchell, P. J. & Vinnicombe, P. 1988. *Sehonghong: The Middle and Later Stone Age Industrial Sequence at a Lesotho Rock-Shelter.* Oxford: British Archaeological Reports.

Castro, S. 1956. *Pinturas Rupestres do Niassa.* Lourenço Marques (Maputo): Boletim da Sociedade de Estudos de Moçambique.

Caton-Thompson, G. 1931. *The Zimbabwe Culture: Ruins and Reactions.* Oxford: Clarendon Press.

Chubb, E. C., King, G. N. & Mogg, A. O. D. 1934. A new variation of Smithfield culture from a cave on the Pondoland coast. *Transactions of the Royal Society of South Africa* 22: 245-268.

Clark, J. D. 1950. *The Stone Age Cultures of Northern Rhodesia, with Particular Reference to the Cultural and Climatic Succession in the Upper Zambezi Valley and its Tributaries.* Cape Town: South African Archaeological Society.

Clark, J. D. 1958. Some stone age woodworking tools in southern Africa. *South African Archaeological Bulletin* 13: 144-152.

Clark, J. D. 1959. *The Prehistory of Southern Africa*. Penguin: Harmondsworth.

Clark, J. D. 1963. Prehistoric cultures of north-east Angola and their significance in tropical Africa. *Museo do Dundo Publicaçãoes Culturais* 62.

Clark, J. D. 1966. The distribution of prehistoric cultures in Angola. *Museu do Dundo Publicaçãoes Culturais* 73.

Collins, E. R. & Smith, R. A. 1919. Stone implements from South African gravels. *Journal of the Royal Anthropological Institute* 45: 79-91.

Cook, J. 1997. A curator's curator: Franks and the Stone Age collections. In: M. Caygill & J. Cherry (eds) *A. W. Franks: Nineteenth Century Collecting and the British Museum*, pp. 115-129. London: British Museum Press.

Cooke, C. K. 1957. The Waterworks site at Khami, Southern Rhodesia: Stone Age and Proto-historic. *Occasional Papers of the National Museum of Southern Rhodesia* 3: 1-60.

Cooke, C. K. 1959. Rock art of Matabeleland. In: R. Summers (ed.) *Rock Art of the Federation of Rhodesia and Nyasaland*, pp. 112-162. Glasgow: National Publications Trust.

Cooke, C. K. 1963. Report on excavations at Pomongwe and Tshangula Caves, Matopo Hills, Southern Rhodesia. *South African Archaeological Bulletin* 18: 73-151.

Cooke, C. K. 1966. Reappraisal of the industry hitherto named Proto-Stillbay. *Arnoldia* 2: 1-14.

Cooke, C. K. 1968. The Early Stone Age in Rhodesia. *Arnoldia* 3: 1-12.

Cooke, C. K. 1971. Excavations in Zombepata Cave, Sipolilo District, Mashonaland, Rhodesia. *South African Archaeological Bulletin* 26: 104- 126.

Cooke, C. K. 1975. The Rhodesian Stone Age succession. *Proceedings of the Sixth Pan-African Congress of Prehistory*, pp. 36-46. Addis Ababa: Pan-African Congress on Prehistory.

Cooke, C. K. 1978. The Redcliff Stone Age site, Rhodesia. *Occasional Papers of the National Museum of Rhodesia (A, Human Sciences)* 1: 45-73.

Cooke, C. K. 1979. Excavations at Diana's Vow Rock Shelter, Makoni District, Zimbabwe-Rhodesia. *Occasional Papers of the National Museum of Zimbabwe-Rhodesia (A, Human Sciences)* 4: 115-148.

Cooke, C. K. 1984. The industries of the Upper Pleistocene in Zimbabwe. *Zimbabwea* 1: 23-27.

Cooke, C. K. & Paterson, M. L. 1960a. A Middle Stone Age open site: Ngamiland, Bechuanaland Protectorate. *South African Archaeological Bulletin* 15: 36-39.

Cooke, C. K. & Paterson, M. L. 1960b. Stone Age sites: Lake Dow area, Bechuanaland. *South African Archaeological Bulletin* 15: 119-122.

Cooke, C. K. & Robinson, K. R. 1954. Excavations at Amadzimba Cave, located in the Matopo Hills, Southern Rhodesia. *Occasional Papers of the National Museum of Southern Rhodesia* 2: 699-728.

Cooke, C. K., Summers, R. & Robinson, K. R. 1966. Rhodesian prehistory re-examined: Part I, the Stone Age. *Arnoldia* 2: 1-7.

Cooke, H. B. S. & Clark, J. D. 1939. New fossil elephants from the Victoria Falls, Northern Rhodesia; and a preliminary note on the geology and archaeology of the deposit. *Transactions of the Royal Society of South Africa* 27: 287-320.

Cooke, H. B. S., Malan, B. D. & Wells, L. H. 1945. Fossil man in the Lebombo Mountains, South Africa: The "Border Cave," Ingwavuma district, Zululand. *Man* 45: 6-13.

Cooke, R., Warren, A. & Goudie, A. 1993. *Desert Geomorphology.* London: University College, London Press.

Coombes, A. 1994. *Reinventing Africa: Museums, Material Culture and Popular Imagination in Late Victorian and Edwardian England.* New Haven: Yale University Press.

Dale, L. (Delta) 1870a. Stone implements in South Africa. *Cape Monthly Magazine* 1: 236-239.

Dale, L. (Delta) 1870b. Stone implements in South Africa. *Cape Monthly Magazine* 1: 365-366.

Dale, L. 1871. On a collection of stone implements and pottery from the Cape of Good Hope. *Journal of the Anthropological Institute* 1. 163- 185.

Daniel, G. 1975. *One Hundred and Fifty Years of Archaeology.* London: Duckworth.

Dart, R. A. 1925. *Australopithecus africanus*: the man-ape of South Africa. *Nature* 115: 195-199.

Dart, R. A. 1927. Mammoth and man in the Transvaal. *Nature* 120: 41.

Dart, R. A. 1957. The osteodontokeratic culture of *Australopithecus prometheus*. *Transvaal Museum Memoirs* 10: 1-105.

Dart, R. A. & Beaumont, P. B. 1968. Ratification and retrocession of earlier Swaziland iron ore mining radiocarbon dates. *South African Journal of Science* 64: 241-246.

Darwin, C. *On the Origin of Species by Means of Natural Selection, or the Preservation of Favoured Races in the Struggle of Life*, London: Murray 1859.

Davenport, T. R. H. 1978. *South Africa: A Modern History.* Cambridge: Cambridge University Press.

Davies, O. 1951. Archaeology of Natal. *Natal Regional Survey* 1: 1-29.

Davies, O. 1975. Excavations at Shongweni South Cave: the oldest evidence to date for cultigens in southern Africa. *Annals of the Natal Museum* 22: 627-662.

De Vos, A. 1975. *Africa, the Devastated Continent ?* The Hague: W. Junk.

Deacon, H. J. 1972. A review of the Post-Pleistocene in South Africa. *South African Archaeological Society Goodwin Series* 1: 26-45.

Deacon, H. J. 1970. The Acheulian occupation at Amanzi Springs, Uitenhage District, Cape Province. *Annals of the Cape Provincial Museums (Natural History)* 8: 89-189.

Deacon, H. J. 1975. Demography, subsistence and culture during the Acheulean in southern Africa. In: K. W. Butzer & G. Ll. Isaac (eds) *After the Australopithecines*, pp. 543-569. The Hague: Mouton.

Deacon, H. J. 1976. *Where Hunters Gathered: A Study of Holocene Stone Age People in the Eastern Cape.* Claremont: South African Archaeological Society Monograph Series 1: 1-232.

Deacon, H. J. 1989. Late Pleistocene palaeoecology and archaeology in the southern Cape, South Africa. In: P. A. Mellars & C. B. Stringer (eds) *The Human Revolution*, pp. 547-564. Edinburgh: Edinburgh University Press.

Deacon, H. J. 1993. Southern Africa and modern human origins. In: M. Aitkens, C. B. Stringer & P. A. Mellars (eds) *The Origin of Modern Humans and the Impact of Chronometric Dating*, pp. 104-117. Princeton: Princeton University Press.

Deacon, H. J. 1995. Two late Pleistocene-Holocene archaeological depositories from the southern Cape, South Africa. *South African Archaeological Bulletin* 50: 121-131.

Deacon, H. J. & Brooker, M. 1976. The Holocene and Upper Pleistocene sequence in the southern Cape. *Annals of the South African Museum* 71: 203-214.

Deacon, H. J. & Deacon, J. 1963. Scott's Cave: a Late Stone Age site in the Gamtoos Valley. *Annals of the Cape Provincial Museums (Natural History)* 3: 96-121.

Deacon, H. J. & Deacon, J. 1980. The hafting, function and distribution of small convex scrapers with an example from Boomplaas Cave. *South African Archaeological Bulletin* 35: 31-37.

Deacon, H. J., Deacon, J., Scholtz, A., Thackeray, J. F., Brink, J. S. & Vogel, J. C. 1984. Correlation of palaeoenvironmental data from the Late Pleistocene and Holocene deposits at Boomplaas Cave, southern Cape. In: J. C. Vogel (ed.) *Late Cainozoic Palaeoclimates of the Southern Hemisphere*, pp. 375-390. Rotterdam: A. Balkema.

Deacon, H. J. & Geleijnse, V. B. 1988. The stratigraphy and sedimentology of the main site sequence, Klasies River, South Africa. *South African Archaeological Bulletin* 43: 5-14.

Deacon, H. J., Scholtz, A. & Daitz, L. D. 1983. Fossil charcoals as a source of palaeoenvironmental information in the fynbos region. In: H. J. Deacon, Q. B. Hendey & J. J. N. Lamprechts (eds) *Fynbos Palaeoecology: A Preliminary Synthesis*, pp. 174-182. Pretoria: Council for Scientific and Industrial Research.

Deacon, H. J. & Thackeray, J. F. 1984. Late Quaternary environmental changes and implications from the archaeological record in southern Africa. In: J. C. Vogel (ed.) *Late Cainozoic Palaeoclimates of the Southern Hemisphere*, pp. 375-390. Rotterdam: A. A. Balkema.

Deacon, J. 1972. Wilton: an assessment after 50 years. *South African Archaeological Bulletin* 27: 10-45.

Deacon, J. 1974. Patterning in the radiocarbon dates for the Wilton/Smithfield complex in southern Africa. *South African Archaeological Bulletin* 29: 3-18.

Deacon, J. 1978. Changing patterns in the late Pleistocene/early Holocene prehistory of southern Africa, as seen from the Nelson Bay Cave stone artifact sequence. *Quaternary Research* 10: 84-111.

Deacon, J. 1979. *Guide to Archaeological Sites in the Southern Cape.* Stellenbosch: Southern African Association of Archaeologists.

Deacon, J. 1983. Editorial. *South African Archaeological Bulletin* 38: 49-50.

Deacon, J. 1984a. *The Later Stone Age of Southernmost Africa.* Oxford: British Archaeological Reports.

Deacon, J. 1984b. Later Stone Age people and their descendants in southern Africa. In: R. G. Klein (ed.) *Southern African Prehistory and Palaeoenvironments*, pp. 221-328. Rotterdam: A. A. Balkema.

Deacon, J. 1986. "My place is the Bitterputs": the home territory of Bleek and Lloyd's /Xam San informants. *African Studies* 45: 135-155.

Deacon, J. 1987. The remarkable Maria Wilman. *The Digging Stick* 4 (2): 1.

Deacon, J. 1988. The power of a place in understanding southern San rock engravings. *World Archaeology* 20: 129-140.

Deacon, J. 1990a. Weaving the fabric of Stone Age research in southern Africa. In: P. Robertshaw (ed.) *A History of African Archaeology*, pp. 39-58. London: Heinemann.

Deacon, J. 1990b. Changes in the archaeological record in South Africa at 18 000 BP. In: C. Gamble & O. Soffer (eds) *The World at 18 000 BP Volume 2 Low Latitudes*, pp. 170-188. London: Unwin Hyman.

Deacon, J. 1992. Editorial. *South African Archaeological Bulletin* 47: 73-74.

Deacon, J. 1994. Rock engravings and the folklore of Bleek & Lloyd's /Xam San informants. In: T. A. Dowson & J. D. Lewis-Williams (eds) *Contested Images: Diversity in Southern African Rock Art Research*, pp. 237-256. Johannesburg: Witwatersrand University Press.

Deacon, J. 1995. An unsolved mystery at the Howieson's Poort name site. *South African Archaeological Bulletin* 50: 110-120.

Deacon, J. 1996. A tale of two families: Wilhelm Bleek, Lucy Lloyd and the /Xam San of the Northern Cape. In: P. Skotnes (ed.) *Miscast: Negotiating the Presence of the Bushmen*, pp. 93-114. Cape Town: University of Cape Town Press.

Deacon, J. & Lancaster, N. 1988. *Late Quaternary Palaeoenvironments of Southern Africa*. Oxford: Clarendon Press.

Delius, P. 1983. *The Land Belongs to Us: The Pedi Polity, the Boers and the British in the Nineteenth Century Transvaal.* Johannesburg: Ravan Press.

Derricourt, R. 1975. Some coastal shell middens in southern Mozambique. *Azania* 7: 135-139.

Derricourt, R. M. 1977. *Prehistoric Man in the Ciskei and Transkei.* Cape Town: C. Struik.

Dias, M. e B. 1947. Relatório da campanha de reconhecimento geo-arqueológico, regioes de Umbelúzi e Changalane. Unpublished report.

Dowson, T. A. 1988. Engravings and the pan-San cognitive system: a preliminary case study from Doornspruit, Magaliesberg. In: T. M. Evers, T. N. Huffman & L. Wadley (eds), *Guide to Archaeological Sites in the Transvaal*, pp. 40-51. Johannesburg: Southern African Association of Archaeologists.

Drennan, M. R. 1931. A ground stone axe from a Cape rock shelter. *Transactions of the Royal Society of South Africa* 19: 45-48.

Dunn, E. J. 1880. Stone implements from South Africa. *Transactions of the South African Philosophical Society* 2 (1): 6-21.

Dunn, E. J. 1908. *Ethnological Collections etc. made by E. J. Dunn in South Africa, New Zealand, Australia.* Melbourne: Victoria Museum.

Dunn, E. J. 1931. *The Bushman.* London: Griffin and Co.

Eastwood, E., Fish, W. & Cnoops, C. 1995. Sheep paintings in the rock art of the Limpopo River Valley and Soutpansberg. *The Digging Stick* 12 (3): 1-2.

Ebert, J. I. & Hitchcock, R. K. 1978. Ancient Lake Makgadikgadi, Botswana: mapping, measurement and palaeoclimatic significance. *Palaeoecology of Africa* 10/11: 47-56.

Esterhuysen, A. B. 1996. *Palaeoenvironmental Reconstruction from Pleistocene to Present: An Analysis of Charcoal from Sites in the Eastern Free State and Lesotho.* Unpublished MA Thesis, University of the Witwatersrand.

Evans, Joan 1943. *Time and Chance. The Story of Arthur Evans and his Forebears*. London, Longmans, Green and Co.

Evans, John 1864. *Coins of the Ancient Britons,* London, J. Russell Smith.

Evans, John 1872 and 1898. *The Ancient Stone Implements, Weapons and Ornaments of Great Britainand Ireland.* London, Longmans, Green, Reader & Dyer.

Evans, J. 1881. *The Ancient Bronze Implements, Weapons and Ornaments of Great Britainand Ireland.* London, Longmans, Green & Co.

Evers, T. M. 1975. Recent Iron Age research in the eastern Transvaal, South Africa. *South African Archaeological Bulletin* 30: 71-83.

Evers, T. M. 1981. The Iron Age in eastern Transvaal, South Africa. In: E. A. Voigt (ed.) *Guide to Archaeological Sites in the Northern and Eastern Transvaal*, pp. 64-109. Pretoria: Southern African Association of Archaeologists.

Eyles, F. 1902. On a cave with Bushman paintings in the Matopos. *Transactions of the Rhodesian Scientific Association* 3: 65-69.

"F" 1871. Upheaval of the coast. *Cape Monthly Magazine* 3: 316-318.

Fagan, B. M. 1960. The Glentyre Shelter and Oakhurst re-examined. *South African Archaeological Bulletin* 15: 80-94.

Farnden, T. H. J. 1965. Notes on two Late Stone Age sites at Muden, Natal. *South African Archaeological Bulletin* 20: 19-23.

Farnden, T. H. J. 1966. Excavation of a Late Stone Age shelter at New Amalfi, East Griqualand. *South African Archaeological Bulletin* 21: 122- 124.

Farnden, T. H. G. 1968. Notes on Middle Stone Age sites in the Muden/Keates Drift areas of Natal. *South African Archaeological Bulletin* 23: 40-44.

Farnden, T. H. J. 1969. A Late Stone Age site in the Karkloof, Natal. *South African Archaeological Bulletin* 24: 147-149.

Feely, J. M. 1987. *The Early Farmers of Transkei, Southern Africa, Before AD 1870.* Oxford: British Archaeological Reports.

Feilden, H. W. 1883. Notes on stone implements from South Africa. *Journal of the Anthropological Institute* 13: 162-173.

Feilden, H. W. 1905. The Stone Age in the Zambezi valley and its relation in time. *Nature* 63: 77-78.

FitzSimons, F. W. 1926. Cliff dwellers of the Tsitsikamma: results of recent excavations. *South African Journal of Science* 23: 813-817.

Fleming, C. A. & Westoll, T. S. 1964. Charles Taylor Trechmann. *Proceedings of the Geological Society of London* 1628: 207-208.

Fock, G. J. 1961. Preliminary archaeological survey of the Witsand. *Annals of the Cape Provincial Museums (Natural History)* 1: 81-85.

Fock, G. J. 1979. *Felsbilder in Südafrika Teil 1: Die Gravierungen auf Klipfontein, Kaapprovinz.* Köln: Böhlau Verlag.

Frames, E. M. 1898. Stone implements found in a cave in Griqualand East, Cape Colony. *Journal of the Royal Anthropological Institute* 28: 251-257.

Frere, B. 1881. Relations between civilised and savage life. *Journal of the Anthropological Institute* 11: 313-352.

Gardner, T. 1906. Traces of the stone age around Bulawayo. *Zambezi Missionary Records* 3 (34): 149-155.

Gardner, T. 1907. Stone implements on Bulawayo commonage. *Proceedings of the Rhodesian Scientific Association* 7 (1): 17-24.

Gardner, T. 1928. Excavations in a Wilton industry at Gokomere, Fort Victoira, Southern Rhodesia. *Journal of the Royal Anthropological Institute* 58: 497-510.

Gardner, T. & Stapleton, P. 1934. Gwelo Kopje - Southern Rhodesia. *Proceedings of the Rhodesian Scientific Association* 33: 4-14.

Gardner, T., Wells, L. H. & Schofield, J. F. 1940. The recent archaeology of Gokomere, Southern Rhodesia. *Transactions of the Royal Society of South Africa* 28: 219-254.

Garlake, P. J. 1987. *The Painted Caves.* Harare: Modus.

Garlake, P. J. 1995. *The Hunter's Vision: The Prehistoric Art of Zimbabwe.* London: British Museum Press.

Gibson, G. D. & Yellen, J. E. 1978. A Middle Stone Age assemblage from the Munhino Mission, Huila Region, Angola. *South African Archaeological Bulletin* 33: 76-83.

Gill, E. L. 1926. Can archaeological work in South Africa be regulated ? *South African Journal of Science* 23: 810-812.

Gooch, W. D. 1881. Stone Age of South Africa. *Journal of the Anthropological Institute* 11: 124-182.

Goodwin, A. J. H. 1926a. The Hardy collection of stone implements. *South African Journal of Science* 23: 826-832.

Goodwin, A. J. H. 1926b. South African stone implement industries. *South African Journal of Science* 23: 784-788.

Goodwin, A. J. H. 1928. Sir Langham Dale's collection of stone implements. *South African Journal of Science* 25: 419-425.

Goodwin, A. J. H. 1929. The Montagu Cave: a full report of the investigation of the Montagu rock-shelter. *Annals of the South African Museum* 24: 1-16.

Goodwin, A. J. H. 1933. The Cape Flats complex. *South African Journal of Science* 30: 515-523.

Goodwin, A. J. H. 1935. A commentary upon South African prehistory up to the introduction of the new terminology. *Bantu Studies* 9: 293- 417.

Goodwin, A. J. H. 1938. Archaeology of the Oakhurst Shelter, George. *Transactions of the Royal Society of South Africa* 25: 229-324.

Goodwin, A. J. H. 1946a. *The Loom of Prehistory.* Cape Town: South African Archaeological Society.

Goodwin, A. J. H. 1946b. Prehistoric fishing methods in South Africa. *Antiquity* 20: 134-141.

Goodwin, A. J. H. 1947. The bored stones of South Africa. *Annals of the South African Museum* 37: 1-210.

Goodwin, A. J. H. 1955. Thomas Holden Bowker: our archaeological centenary. *South African Archaeological Bulletin* 10: 20.

Goodwin, A. J. H. 1958. Formative years of our prehistoric terminology. *South African Archaeological Bulletin* 13: 25-33.

Goodwin, A. J. H. & Malan, B. D. 1935. Archaeology of the Cape St. Blaize cave and raised beach. *Annals of the South African Museum* 24: 111-140.

Goodwin, A. J. H. & Van Riet Lowe, C. 1929. The Stone Age cultures of South Africa. *Annals of the South African Museum* 27: 1-289.

Government Gazette of the Republic of South Africa 1969. *National Monuments Act (No. 28 of 1969).* Pretoria: Government Printer.

Gregory, J. G. 1868. Stone implements from South Africa. *Geological Magazine* pp. 532-533.

Grey, G. Sir 1869. On quartzite implements from the Cape of Good Hope. *Journal of the Ethnological Society of London* 1: 39-43.

Grine, F. E. & Klein, R. G. 1985. Pleistocene and Holocene human remains from Equus Cave, South Africa. *Anthropology* 8: 55-98.

Grine, F. E., Klein, R. G. & Volman, T. P. 1991. Dating, archaeology and human fossils from the Middle Stone Age levels of Die Kelders, South Africa. *Journal of Human Evolution* 21: 363-395.

Grün, R., Beaumont, P. B. & Stringer, C. B. 1990. ESR dating evidence for early modern humans at Border Cave, South Africa. *Nature* 344: 537-539.

Gutierrez, M. 1996a. L'art pariétal de l'Angola: essai de chronologie et d'interprétation. In: G. Pwiti & R. Soper (eds) *Aspects of African Archaeology: Papers from the Tenth Congress of the Pan-African Association for Prehistory and Related Studies*, pp. 361-370. Harare: University of Zimbabwe Press.

Gutierrez, M. 1996b. Recherches récentes sur la bande cotière au Sud de Benguela (Angola). Unpublished paper delivered at the Society of Africanist Archaeologists, Poznán, September.

Guy, J. 1983. *The Heretic, the Life of John William Colenso 1814-1883.* Johannesburg: Ravan Press.

Haddon, A. C. 1905. Presidential address to Section H. *Report of the British Association for the Advancement of Science*, pp. 515-527.

Hall, M. 1987. *The Changing Past: Farmers, Kings and Traders in Southern Africa, 200 - 1860.* Cape Town: David Philip.

Hall, S. L. 1981. *Iron Age Sequence and Settlement in the Rooiberg, Thabazimbi Area.* Unpublished MA Thesis, University of the Witwatersrand.

Hall, S. L. 1990. *Hunter-Gatherer-Fishers of the Fish River Basin: A Contribution to the Holocene Prehistory of the Eastern Cape.* Unpublished DPhil Thesis, University of Stellenbosch.

Hall, S. L. & Binneman, J. N. F. 1987. Later Stone Age burial variation in the Cape: a social interpretation. *South African Archaeological Bulletin* 42: 140-152.

Hamy, E. T. 1899. Note sur une hache en quartzite du type de St. Acheul trouvée dans l'Etat Libre d'Orange. *Bulletin du Museum d'Histoire Naturelle* 6: 270-274.

Hanisch, H. 1958. A possible Sangoan site from East London. *South African Archaeological Bulletin* 13: 159-160.

Hanisch, E. O. M. 1981. The Northern Transvaal: environment and archaeology. In: E. A. Voigt (ed.), *Guide to Archaeological Sites in the Northern and Eastern Transvaal*, pp. 1-6. Pretoria: Southern African Association of Archaeologists.

Harding, J. R. 1951. Notes on some rock-paintings in the eastern Orange Free State. *South African Archaeological Bulletin* 6: 116-119.

Heese, C. H. T. D. 1933. The evolution of palaeolithic technique. *Annals of the University of Stellenbosch* 11 (B, 2): 1-63.

Helgren, D. M. & Brooks, A. S. 1983. Geoarchaeology at Gi, a Middle Stone Age and Later Stone Age site in the northwest Kalahari. *Journal of Archaeological Science* 10: 181-197.

Henderson, Z. L. 1992. The context of some Middle Stone Age hearths at Klasies River Shelter 1B: implications for understanding human behaviour. *Southern African Field Archaeology* 1: 14-26.

Henderson, Z. L. & Binneman, J. N. F. 1997. Changes in the significance of a site: the Klasies Cave complex in the Middle and Later Stone Ages. In: C. Bonsall & C. Tolan-Smith (eds) *The Human Use of Caves*, pp. 175-184. Oxford: British Archaeological Reports International Series 667.

Henshilwood, C. 1996. A revised chronology for pastoralism in southernmost Africa: new evidence of sheep at *c.* 2000 b.p. from Blombos Cave, South Africa. *Antiquity* 70: 945-949.

Henshilwood, C. & Sealy, J. 1997. Bone artefacts from the Middle Stone Age at Blombos Cave, southern Cape, South Africa. *Current Anthropology* 38: 890-895.

Hewitt, J. 1921. On several implements and ornaments from Strandloper sites in the eastern Province. *South African Journal of Science* 18: 454-467.

Hewitt, J. 1931. Artefacts from Melkhoutboom. *South African Journal of Science* 28: 540-548.

Hewitt, J. 1955. Further light on the Bowker implements. *South African Archaeological Bulletin* 10: 94-95.

Hewitt, J. & Stapleton, P. R. 1925. On some remarkable stone implements in the Albany Museum. *South African Journal of Natural History* 5: 23-38.

Hillier, A. P. 1898. *Raid and Reform, by a Pretoria Prisoner.* London: Macmillan.

Hockly, H. E. 1966. *The Story of the British Settlers of 1820 in South Africa.* Cape Town: Jutas.

Holub, E. 1880. The central South African tribes from the south coast to the Zambezi. *Journal of the Anthropological Insititute* 10: 2-20.

Horowitz, A., Sampson, C. G., Scott, L. & Vogel, J. C. 1978. Analysis of the Voigtspost site, O.F.S., South Africa. *South African Archaeological Bulletin* 33: 152-159.

Huffman, T. N. 1994. Toteng pottery and the origins of Bambata. *Southern African Field Archaeology* 3: 3-9.

Humphreys, A. J. B. 1972a. *The Type R Settlements in the Context of the Later Prehistory and Early History of the Riet River Valley.* Unpublished MA Thesis, University of Cape Town.

Humphreys, A. J. B. 1972b. Comments on aspects of raw material usage in the Later Stone Age of the Middle Orange River area. *South African Archaeological Society Goodwin Series* 1: 46-53.

Humphreys, A. J. B. 1978. The re-excavation of Powerhouse Cave and an assessment of Dr Frank Peabody's work on Holocene deposits in the Taung area. *Annals of the Cape Provincial Museums (Natural History)* 11: 217-244.

Humphreys, A. J. B. 1979. *The Holocene Sequence in the Northern Cape and its Position in the Prehistory of South Africa.* Unpublished PhD Thesis, University of Cape Town.

Humphreys, A. J. B. & Maggs, T. O'C. 1970. Further graves and cultural material from the banks of the Riet River. *South African Archaeological Bulletin* 25: 116-126.

Humphreys, A. J. B. & Thackeray, A. I. 1983. *Ghaap and Gariep: Later Stone Age Studies in the Northern Cape*. Claremont: South African Archaeological Society Monograph Series 2: 1-328.

Humphries, R., Rapoo, T. & Friedman, S. 1994. The shape of the country: negotiating regional government. In: S. Friedman & D. Atkinson (eds) *South African Review 7. The Small Miracle: South Africa's Negotiated Settlement*, pp. 148-181. Johannesburg: Ravan Press.

Hutchinson, H. G. 1914. *Life of Sir John Lubbock, Lord Avebury*. London.

Inskeep, R. R. 1967. The Late Stone Age in southern Africa. In: W. W. Bishop and J. D. Clark (eds) *Background to Evolution in Africa*, pp. 557- 582. Chicago: University of Chicago Press.

Inskeep, R. R. 1972. Nelson's Bay Cave, Robberg Peninsula, Plettenberg Bay. *Palaeoecology of Africa* 6: 247-249.

Inskeep, R. R. 1978. *The Peopling of Southern Africa.* Cape Town: David Philip.

Inskeep, R. R. 1987. *Nelson Bay Cave, Cape Province, South Africa: The Holocene Levels.* Oxford: British Archaeological Reports.

Isaac, G. Ll. 1989. *The Archaeology of Human Origins*. Cambridge: Cambridge University Press.

Jacobson, L. 1976. A critical review of the Damaraland Culture. *Cimbebasia (B)* 2: 203-208.

Janmart, J. 1948. La station préhistorique de Candala (District de la Lunda, Angola du Nord-Est). *Museu do Dundo Publicaçãoes Culturais* 2.

Jansen, F. J. 1926. A new type of stone implement from Victoria West. *South African Journal of Science* 23: 818-825.

Jerardino, A. 1996. *Changing Social Landscapes of the Western Cape Coast of Southern Africa over the Last 3500 Years.* Unpublished PhD Thesis, University of Cape Town.

Jerardino, A. & Yates, R. 1996. Preliminary results from excavations at Steenbokfontein Cave: implications for past and future research. *South African Archaeological Bulletin* 51: 7-16.

Jerardino, A. & Yates, R. 1997. Excavations at Mike Taylor's Midden: a summary report and implications for a re-characterisation of megamiddens. *South African Archaeological Bulletin* 52: 43-51.

Johnson, J. P. 1905. A summary of recent discoveries of stone implements in South Africa. *Addresses and Papers of the British Association for the Advancement of Science 1905* 3 (3): 308-318.

Johnson, J. P. 1907. *The Pre-historic Period in South Africa*. London: Longmans, Green & Co.

Johnson, J. P. 1908. *The Stone Implements of South Africa*. London (second edition).

Jolly, K. 1947. Preliminary note on new excavations at Skildergat, Fish Hoek. *South African Archaeological Bulletin* 2: 11-12.

Jolly, 1948. The development of the Cape Middle Stone Age in the Skildegat Cave, Fish Hoek. *South African Archaeological Bulletin* 3: 106- 107.

Jolly, P. A. 1986. A first generation descendant of the Transkei San. *South African Archaeological Bulletin* 41: 6-9.

Jolly, P. A. & Prins, F. E. 1994. M - a further assessment. *South African Archaeological Bulletin* 49: 16-23.

Jones, N. 1920. On the implement-bearing deposits of Taungs and Tiger Kloof in the Cape Province of South Africa. *Journal of the Royal Anthropological Institute* 50: 412-424.

Jones, N. 1924. On the palaeolithic deposits of Sawmills, Rhodesia. *Journal of the Royal Anthropological Institute* 54: 276-286.

Jones, N. 1926. *The Stone Age in Rhodesia.* Oxford: Oxford University Press.

Jones, N. 1929. Hitherto undescribed early stone age industry near Hope Fountain, Rhodesia. *South African Journal of Science* 26: 631-647.

Jones, N. 1930. On the occurrence of rostro-carinates at Hope Fountain, Rhodesia. *Journal of the Royal Anthropological Institute* 60: 73-80.

Jones, N. 1932. Further excavations at Gokomere, Southern Rhodesia. *Man* 32: 197.

Jones, N. 1933. Excavations at Nswatugi and Madiliyangwa and notes on new sites located and examined on the Matopo Hills, Southern Rhodesia. *Occasional Papers of the Rhodesian Museum* No. 2.

Jones, N. 1938. The Bembesi industry. *Occasional Papers of the National Museum, Southern Rhodesia* 1 (7): 7-31.

Jones, N. 1940. Bambata Cave: a reorientation. *Occasional Papers of the National Museum of Southern Rhodesia* 9: 11-28.

Jones, N. 1944. The climatic and cultural sequences at Sawmills, Southern Rhodesia. *Occasional Papers of the National Museum of Southern Rhodesia* 11: 39-46.

Jones, N. 1949. *The Prehistory of Southern Rhodesia.* Cambridge: Cambridge University Press.

Jones, P. R. 1980. Experimental butchery with modern stone tools and its relevance for Palaeolithic archaeology. *World Archaeology* 12: 153- 175.

Jones, R. 1898. Exhibition of stone implements from Swaziland. *Journal of the Royal Anthropological Institute* 28: 48-54.

Kannemeyer, D. R. 1890. Stone implements of the Bushmen. *Cape Illustrated Magazine* 1: 120-130.

Kaplan, J. 1987. Settlement and subsistence at Renbaan Cave. In: J. E. Parkington & M. Hall (eds) *Papers in the Prehistory of the Western Cape*, South Africa, pp. 350-376. Oxford: British Archaeological Reports.

Kaplan, J. 1990. The Umhlatuzana Rock Shelter sequence: 100 000 years of Stone Age history. *Natal Museum Journal of Humanities* 2: 1-94.

Kaplan, J. 1992. Archaeological Excavations at Liphofung Cave. Unpublished report submitted to the Lesotho Highlands Development Authority.

Kaplan, J. 1995. The Archaeology of the Muela Rockshelter. Unpublished report submitted to the Lesotho Highlands Development Authority.

Kaplan, J. 1996. Archaeological Excavations at Lithakong Shelter. Unpublished report submitted to the Lesotho Highlands Development Authority.

Keller, C. M. 1973. Montagu Cave in prehistory: a descriptive analysis. *Anthropological Records of the University of California* 28: 1-98.

Kench, J., Hands, P. & Hughes, D. 1983. *The Complete Book of South African Wine*. Cape Town: C. Struik.

Kennedy, R. F. 1963. Pictures by A. A. Anderson in the Africana Museum. *Africana Notes and News* 15: 340-344.

Kenyon, K. M. 1960. *Archaeology of the Holy Land*. New York: F. A. Praeger.

Kenyon, K. M. 1967. *Jerusalem: Excavating 3000 Years of History*. London: Thames and Hudson.

Kinahan, J. 1991. *Pastoral Nomads of the Central Namib Desert: The People History Forgot*. Windhoek: Namibia Archaeological Trust.

Kinahan, J. 1994. Theory, practice and criticism in the history of Namibian archaeology. In: P. Ucko (ed.) *World Perspective on Archaeological Theory: Diversity in Theory and Practice*, pp. 78-96. London: Routledge.

Kinahan, J. 1996. Alternative views on the acquisition of livestock by hunter-gatherers in southern Africa: a rejoinder to Smith, Yates & Jacobson. *South African Archaeological Bulletin* 51: 106-108.

King, G. B. & Chubb, E. C. 1932. Remarks on stone implements and strandloper middens of Natal and Zululand. Part II: Stone implements from a rock shelter in the Drakensberg. *South African Journal of Science* 29: 768-769.

Kingston, H. D. R. 1900. On some caves in the T'Ztitztikamma or Outeniqua district near Knysna, South Africa, and the objects found therein. *Journal of the Royal Anthropological Institute* 30: 45-49.

Klapwijk, M. & Huffman, T. N. 1996. Excavations at Silver Leaves: a final report. *South African Archaeological Bulletin* 51: 84-93.

Klatzow, S. 1994. Roosfontein: a contact site in the eastern Orange Free State. *South African Archaeological Bulletin* 49: 9-15.

Klein, R. G. 1972. Preliminary report on the July through September 1970 excavations at Nelson Bay Cave, Plettenberg Bay (Cape Province, South Africa). *Palaeoecology of Africa* 6: 177-208.

Klein, R. G. 1977. The mammalian fauna from the Middle and Later Stone Age (later Pleistocene) levels of Border Cave, Natal Province, South Africa. *South African Archaeological Bulletin* 32: 14-27.

Klein, R. G. 1984a. The large mammals of southern Africa: Late Pliocene to Recent. In: R. G. Klein (ed.) *Southern African Prehistory and Palaeoenvironments*, pp. 107-146. Rotterdam: A. Balkema.

Klein, R. G. 1984b. Later Stone Age faunal samples from Heuningneskrans Shelter (Transvaal) and Leopard's Hill Cave (Zambia). *South African Archaeological Bulletin* 39: 109-116.

Klein, R. G. 1989. *The Human Career.* Chicago: University of Chicago Press.

Klein, R. G. & Cruz-Uribe, K. 1996. Exploitation of large bovids and seals at Middle and Later Stone Age sites in South Africa. *Journal of Human Evolution* 31: 315-334.

Klimowicz, J. & Haynes, G. 1996. The Stone Age archaeology of Hwange National Park, Zimbabwe. In: G. Pwiti & R. Soper (eds) *Aspects of African Archaeology: Papers from the Tenth Congress of the Pan-African Association for Prehistory and Related Studies*, pp. 121-128. Harare: University of Zimbabwe Press.

Korsman, S. & Plug, I. 1994. Two Later Stone Age sites on the farm Honingklip in the eastern Transvaal. *South African Archaeological Bulletin* 49: 24-32.

Kuman, K. 1994. The archaeology of Sterkfontein - past and present. *Journal of Human Evolution* 27: 471-495.

Kuman, K. & Clarke, R. J. 1986. Florisbad - new investigations at a Middle Stone Age site in South Africa. *Geoarchaeology* 1: 103-125.

Laband, J. 1997. *The Rise and Fall of the Zulu Nation*. London: Arms and Armour.

Laidler, P. W. 1934. The archaeological sequence in the Transkei and Ciskei. *South African Journal of Science* 31: 535-546.

Laidler, P. W. 1935. Shell mound cultures. *South African Journal of Science* 32: 560-571.

Laidler, P. W. 1937. A Late Stone Age cave deposit in the Transkei. *South African Journal of Science* 33: 888-892.

Lamplugh, G. W. 1905a. Exhibition of stone implements from Zambezi. *Report of the British Association for the Advancement of Science 1905*, p. 531.

Lamplugh, G. W. 1905b. Report on an investigation of the Batoka Gorge and adjacent portions of the Zambezi River. *Report of the British Association for the Advancement of Science 1905*, pp. 292-301.

Lane, P. 1996. Archaeological survey and excavation in southeast Botswana, 1992. *Nyame Akuma* 45: 11-23.

Larsson, L. 1996. The Middle Stone Age of Zimbabwe: some aspects of former research and future aims. In: G. Pwiti & R. Soper (eds) *Aspects of African Archaeology: Papers from the Tenth Congress of the Pan-African Association for Prehistory and Related Studies*, pp. 201-206. Harare: University of Zimbabwe Press.

Lartet, E. & Christy, H. 1865-75. *Reliquiae Aquitanicae, being Contributions to the Archaeology and Palaeontology of Périgord and the Adjoining Provinces of Southern France.* London.

Layard, E. L. 1870. Note on the stone implements of South Africa. *Proceedings of the Ethnological Society of London* xcvii-c (Incorporated in the *Journal of the Anthroopological Institute* for 1871).

Le Doux, J. A. 1914. Stone implements from South Africa. *Man* 14: 49.

Leakey, L. S. B. 1949. Tentative study of the Pleistocene climatic changes and Stone-Age culture sequence in North-Eastern Angola. *Museu do Dundo Publicaçãoes Culturais* 4.

Leith, B. A. 1964. *A Chapter from the Life of George Leith.* Somerset West: Standard Press.

Leith, G. 1898. Caves, shell-mounds and stone implements of South Africa. *Journal of the Royal Anthropological Institute* 28: 258-274.

Leslie, M. 1989. The Holocene sequence from Uniondale rock shelter in the eastern Cape. *South African Archaeological Society Goodwin Series* 6: 17-32.

Lewis-Williams, J. D. 1986. The last testament of the southern San. *South African Archaeological Bulletin* 41: 10-11.

Lewis-Williams, J. D. 1993. Southern African archaeology in the 1990s. *South African Archaeological Bulletin* 48: 45-50.

Lewis-Williams, J. D. & Dowson, T. A. 1989. *Images of Power*. Johannesburg: Southern Book Publishers.

Lewis-Williams, J. D. & Thorp, C. A. 1989. Archaeology: Lesotho Highlands Water Project Environmental Study. Unpublished report submitted to the Lesotho Highlands Development Authority.

Lichtenstein, H. 1928-30. *Travels in Southern Africa*. Cape Town: Van Riebeeck Society.

Lloyd Evans, T., Thackeray, A. I. & Thackeray, J. F. 1985. Later Stone Age rescue archaeology in the Sutherland district. *South African Archaeological Bulletin* 40: 106-108.

Loubser, J. N. H. 1988. The ethnoarchaeology of Venda-speakers in South Africa. *Navorsinge van die Nasionale Museum, Bloemfontein* 7: 146- 464.

Loubser, J. N. H. 1994. Ndebele archaeology of the Pietersburg area. *Navorsinge van die Nasionale Museum, Bloemfontein* 10: 61-147.

Loubser, J. N. H. & Dowson, T. A. 1988. Tombo-la-Ndou: the Venda perception of San rock art. *South African Archaeological Bulletin* 42: 51- 54.

Loubser, J. N. H. & Lourens, G. 1994. Depictions of domestic ungulates and shields: hunter-gatherers and agropastoralists in the Caledon River Valley area. In: T. A. Dowson & J. D. Lewis-Williams (eds) *Contested Images: Diversity in Southern African Rock Art Research*, pp. 83-118. Johannesburg: University of the Witwatersrand Press.

Louw, A. W. 1967. Bushman Rock Shelter, Ohrigstad, Eastern Transvaal, a preliminary investigation. *South African Archaeological Bulletin* 24: 39-51.

Louw, J. T. 1960. Prehistory of the Matjes River Rock Shelter. *Memoirs van die Nasionale Museum, Bloemfontein* 1: 1- 143.

Lubbock, J. 1865. *Pre-historic Times, as Illustrated by Ancient Remains, and the Manners and Customs of Modern Savages.* London: Williams and Norgate.

Lubbock, J. 1869.On a collection of stone implements from the Cape of Good Hope. *Proceedings of the Anthropological and Ethnological Society of London* 1: 51.

Lubbock, J. 1870a. Notes on some implements from Africa and Syria. *Proceedings of the Ethnological Society of London 1870*, pp. xcii-xcvii.

Lubbock, J. 1870b. Remarks on stone implements from Western Africa. *Athenaeum* 2241: 467-468.

Lubbock, J. 1871. Exhibition of stone implements. *Proceedings of the Society of Antiquaries of London* 5: 167-225.

Lyell, C. 1830-33. *Principles of Geology.* London: John Murray.

Lyell, C. 1864. *The Geological Evidences of the Antiquity of Man, with Remarks on Theories of the Origin of Species by Variation.* London: John Murray

McBrearty, S. 1988. The Sangoan and Middle Stone Age sequence at the Muguruk site, western Kenya. *World Archaeology* 19: 388-420.

McKannand, A.1967. Captain Henry Thurburn (1826-1897) 42nd Madras Native Infantry. *Journal of the Society for Army Historical Research* 45: 24-30.

McKay, G. R. 1896. The antiquity of man in southern Africa. In: G. M. Theal (ed.), *Belangrijke Historiche Dokumenten* 2: 1-6.

McKay, G. R. 1897. Evidence on the antiquity of man in East London, Cape Colony, with a note on the castor oil plant. *Natural Science* 11: 334-336.

MacCalman, H. R. 1962. Gungams, an early Middle Stone Age site in the Windhoek district. *Cimbebasia* 3: 2-13.

MacCalman, H. R. 1963. The Middle Stone Age in South West Africa. Part II: The Neuhoff-Kowas Middle Stone Age, Windhoek district. *Cimbebasia* 7: 42-54.

MacCalman, H. R. 1965. Carbon-14 dates from South West Africa. *South African Archaeological Bulletin* 20: 80, 215.

MacCalman, H. R. & Grobbelaar, B. J. 1965. Preliminary report of two stone-working OvaTjimba groups in the northern Kaokoveld of South West Africa. *Cimbebasia* 13: 1-39.

Macfarlane, D. 1935. Evidence in support of a pre-Chellean culture from the East London clays. *South African Journal of Science* 32: 537-550.

Macfarlane, D. 1936. On the East London Levallois. *South African Journal of Science* 33: 893-903.

MacGregor, A. M. 1921. Note on older Palaeolithic implements from the Umguza and Bembesi Valleys. *South African Journal of Science* 17: 230-235.

Maclver, D. R. 1906. *Medieval Rhodesia.* London: Macmillan.

Maggs, T. O'C. 1984. The Iron Age south of the Zambezi. In: R. G. Klein (ed.) *Southern African Prehistory and Palaeoenvironments*, pp. 329- 360. Rotterdam: A. Balkema.

Malan, B. D. 1939. The Middle Stone Age of the Cape Peninsula, Part 1: The Hardy Collection. *Bureau of Archaeology, University of South Africa Archaeological Series* 3: 5-23.

Malan, B. D. 1946. The distribution and chronology of the Modderpoort culture. *South African Journal of Science* 42: 254-260.

Malan, B. D. 1950. The Middle Stone Age in the eastern Transvaal and Swaziland. *South African Journal of Science* 47: 146-150.

Malan, B. D. 1956. An engraved flake from Muden, Natal. *South African Archaeological Bulletin* 11: 63-65.

Malan, B. D. 1958. The final phase of the Middle Stone Age in South Africa. In: L. S. B. Leakey (ed.) *Proceeedings of the Pan-African Congress on Prehistory*, pp. 188-194. Oxford: Blackwells.

Malan, B. D. 1962. Biographical sketch of 'Peter' Van Riet Lowe. *South African Archaeological Bulletin* 17: 38-42.

Malan, B. D. & Wells, L. H. 1943. A further report on the Wonderwerk Cave, Kuruman. *South African Journal of Science* 40: 258-270.

Malan, F. 1950. A Wilton site at Kaikai, Bechuanaland Protectorate. *South African Archaeological Bulletin* 5: 140-142.

Manhire, A. H. 1987. *Later Stone Age Settlement Patterns in the Sandveld of the South-Western Cape Province, South Africa.* Oxford: British Archaeological Reports.

Mason, R. J. 1957. The Transvaal Middle Stone Age and statistical analysis. *South African Archaeological Bulletin* 12: 119-137.

Mason, R. 1962. *Prehistory of the Transvaal.* Johannesburg: University of the Witwatersrand Press.

Mason, R. J. 1988. *Kruger Cave.* Johannesburg: University of the Witwatersrand, Archaeological Research Unit Occasional Paper 17.

Masson, J. R. 1961. Rock paintings in Swaziland. *South African Archaeological Bulletin* 16: 130-135.

Mazel, A. D. 1981. *Up and Down the Little Berg. Archaeological Resource Management in the Natal Drakensberg.* Unpublished MA Thesis, University of Cape Town.

Mazel, A. D. 1989. People making history: the last ten thousand years of hunter-gatherer communities in the Thukela Basin. *Natal Museum Journal of Humanities* 1: 1-168.

Mazel, A. D. 1992a. Early pottery from the eastern part of southern Africa. *South African Archaeological Bulletin* 47: 3-7.

Mazel, A. D. 1992b. Gender and the hunter-gatherer archaeological record: a view from the Thukela Basin. *South African Archaeological Bulletin* 47: 122-126.

Mazel, A. D. 1992c. Collingham Shelter: the excavation of late Holocene deposits, Natal, South Africa. *Natal Museum Journal of Humanities* 4: 1-51.

Mazel, A. D. 1993. KwaThwaleyakhe Shelter: the excavation of mid and late Holocene deposits in the central Thukela Basin. *Natal Museum Journal of Humanities* 5: 1-36.

Mazel, A. D. 1994. Hunter-gatherer occupation of the eastern Biggarsberg: a view from Maqonqo Shelter. In: A. D. Mazel & T. O'C. Maggs (eds) *Southern African Association of*

Archaeologists Conference Excursion KwaZulu-Natal, pp. 16-22. Pietermaritzburg: Southern African Association of Archaeologists.

Mazel, A. D. & Parkington, J. E. 1981. Stone tools and resources: a case study from southern Africa. *World Archaeology* 13: 16-30.

Mellars, P. A. (ed.) 1991. *The Origins of Modern Humans*. Edinburgh: Edinburgh University Press.

Mellars, P. A. & Stringer, C. B. (eds) 1989. *The Human Revolution*. Edinburgh: Edinburgh University Press.

Meneses, P. 1988. Idade da Pedra em Mozambique. *Trabalhos de Arqueologia e Antropologia* 5: 3-56.

Meneses, P. 1996. Some aspects regarding the Acheulean in southern Mozambique. In: G. Pwiti & R. Soper (eds) *Aspects of African Archaeology: Papers from the Tenth Congress of the Pan-African Association for Prehistory and Related Studies*, pp. 129-138. Harare: University of Zimbabwe Press.

Mennell, F. P. 1904. *Some Stone Implements in the Rhodesia Museum: Annual Report of the Rhodesia Museum*. Bulawayo: Rhodesia Museum.

Mennell, F. P. 1908. Some aspects of the Matopos. Part 2. *Transactions of the Rhodesian Scientific Association* 7: 5-11.

Meyer, A. 1986. *'n Kultuurhistoriese Interpretasie van die Ystertydperk in die Nasionale Krugerwildtuin (A Cultural Historical Interpretation of the Iron Age in the Kruger National Park)*. Unpublished PhD Thesis, University of Pretoria.

Miller, G., H., Beaumont, P. B., Jull, A. J. T. & Johnson, B. 1993. Pleistocene geochronology and palaeothermometry from protein diagenesis in ostrich eggshells: implications for the evolution of modern humans. In: M. J. Aitken, C. B. Stringer & P. A. Mellars (eds) *The Origin of Modern Humans and the Impact of Chronometric Dating*, pp. 49-68. Princeton: Princeton University Press.

Mitchell, P. J. 1988. *The Early Microlithic Assemblages of Southern Africa*. Oxford: British Archaeological Reports.

Mitchell, P. J. 1992. Archaeology in Lesotho: a review of 120 years. *African Archaeological Review* 10: 3-34.

Mitchell, P. J. 1993. Late Pleistocene hunter-gatherers in Lesotho: report on fieldwork at Sehonghong Rockshelter, July to September 1992. *Nyame Akuma* 39: 43-49.

Mitchell, P. J. 1994a. Understanding the MSA/LSA transition: the pre-20 000 BP assemblages from Sehonghong Shelter, Lesotho. *Southern African Field Archaeology* 3: 15-25.

Mitchell, P. J. 1994b. The archaeology of the Phuthiatsana-ea-Thaba Bosiu Basin, Lesotho, southern Africa: changes in Later Stone Age regional demography. *Antiquity* 68: 83-96.

Mitchell, P. J. 1995. Revisiting the Robberg: new results and a revision of old ideas at Sehonghong Rockshelter, Lesotho. *South African Archaeological Bulletin* 50: 28-38.

Mitchell, P. J. 1996a. Filling the gap: the early and middle Holocene assemblages from new excavations at Sehonghong Rock-Shelter, Lesotho. *Southern African Field Archaeology* 4: 17-27.

Mitchell, P. J. 1996b. Sehonghong: the late Holocene assemblages with pottery. *South African Archaeological Bulletin* 51: 17-25.

Mitchell, P. J. 1996c. The late Quaternary landscape at Sehonghong in the Lesotho highlands, southern Africa. *Antiquity* 70: 623-638.

Mitchell, P. J. 1996d. The late Quaternary of the Lesotho highlands, southern Africa: preliminary results and future potential of ongoing research at Sehonghong Shelter. *Quaternary International* 33: 35-43.

Mitchell, P. J. 1997. Holocene Later Stone Age hunter-gatherers south of the Limpopo River, ca. 10,000-2000 B.P. *Journal of World Prehistory* 11: 359-424.

Mitchell, P. J. & Charles, R. 1996. Archaeological investigation of an open air hunter-gatherer site in the Lesotho highlands: preliminary report on the 1995 season at Likoaieng. *Nyame Akuma* 45: 40-49.

Mitchell, P. J. & Parkington, J. E. 1990. *The Archaeology of the Hololo Crossing Rock-shelter*. Cape Town: Archaeology Contracts Office, University of Cape Town.

Mitchell, P. J., Parkington, J. E. & Yates, R. 1994. The later Holocene archaeology of southern and western Lesotho. *South African Archaeological Bulletin* 49: 33-52.

Mitchell, P. J., Yates, R. & Parkington, J. E. 1996. At the transition: the archaeology of southern Africa at the Pleistocene/Holocene boundary. In: L. G. Straus, G. A. Frison, J. Erlandson & B. Eriksen (eds) *Humans at the End of the Ice Age: The Archaeology of the Pleistocene/Holocene Transition*, pp. 15-42. New York: Plenum Press.

Mitford-Barberton, I. & Mitford-Barberton, R. 1952. *The Bowkers of Tharfield*. Oxford: Oxford University Press.

Molyneux, A. J. C., White, F. *et al.* 1909. Further notes on Rhodesian stone implements. *Proceedings of the Rhodesian Scientific Association* 9: 8-14.

Moon, B. P. & Dardis, G. F. (eds) 1988. *The Geomorphology of Southern Africa*. Johannesburg: Southern Book Publishers.

Morais, J. 1984. Mozambican archaeology: past and present. *African Archaeological Review* 2: 113-128.

Morais, J. 1988. *The Early Farming Communities of Southern Mozambique*. Stockholm: Swedish Central Board of National Antiquities.

Morris, A. G. 1987. The reflection of the collector: San and Khoi skeletons in museum collections. *South African Archaeological Bulletin* 42: 12-22.

Morris, A. G. 1992. *A Master Catalogue: Holocene Human Skeletons from South Africa*. Johannesburg: Witwatersrand University Press.

Morris, A. G. 1996. Trophy skulls, museums and the San. In: P. Skotnes (ed.) *Miscast: Negotiating the Presence of the Bushmen*, pp. 67-80. Cape Town: University of Cape Town Press.

Morris, D. 1995. The Kora at Mamusa, pre-1870. *The Digging Stick* 12 (1): 1-2.

Morris, D. 1997. A description of stone artefacts and ostrich eggshell beads in the Kalahari in the year 1859 ? *The Digging Stick* 14 (2): 4-6.

Morris, D. & Beaumont, P. B. 1994. Portable rock engravings at Springbokoog and the archaeological contexts of rock art of the Upper Karoo. In: T. A. Dowson & J. D. Lewis-Williams (eds) *Contested Images: Diversity in Southern African Rock Art Research*, pp. 11-28. Johannesburg: Witwatersrand University Press.

Morris, D. R. 1990. *The Washing of the Spears*. London: Sphere.

Mupira, P. 1994. Another possible Bambata sherd from Nyanga, Zimbabwe. *Zimbabwean Prehistory* 21: 43-44.

Newall, R. S. 1929a. Stonehenge. *Antiquity* 3: 75-88.

Newall, R. S. 1929b. Stonehenge: the recent excavations. *Wiltshire Archaeology and Natural History Society Magazine* 44: 150.

Newall, R. S. 1956. Stonehenge: a review. *Antiquity* 30: 137-141.

Opperman, H. 1978. Excavations in the Buffelskloof rock shelter near Calitzdorp, southern Cape. *South African Archaeological Bulletin* 33: 18-38.

Opperman, M. 1987. *Later Stone Age Hunter-Gatherers of the Drakensberg Range and its Foothills*. Oxford: British Archaeological Reports.

Opperman, H. & Heydenrych, B. 1990. A 22 000 year-old Middle Stone Age camp site with plant food remains from the north-eastern Cape. *South African Archaeological Bulletin* 45: 93-99.

Opperman, H. 1996. Strathalan Cave B, north-eastern Cape Province, South Africa: evidence for human behaviour 29,000 - 26,000 years ago. *Quaternary International* 33: 45-54.

Orpen, J. M. 1857. *History of the Basutus of South Africa*. Cape Town: Argus.

Orpen, J. M. 1874. A glimpse into the mythology of the Maluti

Bushmen. *Cape Monthly Magazine* 9: 1-13.
Ouzman, S. 1995. The fish, the shaman and the peregrination. San rock paintings of mormyrid fish as social and religious metaphors. *Southern African Field Archaeology* 4: 3-17.
Ouzman, S. 1997. Hidden in the common gaze: collective and idiosyncratic rock paintings at Rose Cottage Cave, South Africa. *Navorsinge van die Nasionale Museum Bloemfontein* 13: 225-256.
Ouzman, S. & Wadley, L. 1997. A history in paint and stone from Rose Cottage Cave, South Africa. *Antiquity* 71: 386-404.
Pager, H. 1971. *Ndedema: A Documentation of the Rock Paintings of the Ndedema Gorge.* Graz: Akademische Druck.
Pager, H. 1989. *The Rock Paintings of the Upper Brandberg. Part 1: Amis Gorge.* Köln: Heinrich Barth Institute.
Pakenham, T. 1979. *The Boer War.* Johannesburg: Jonathan Ball.
Parkington, J. E. 1980. Time and place: some observations on spatial and temporal patterning in the Later Stone Age sequence in southern Africa. *South African Archaeological Bulletin* 35: 73-83.
Parkington, J. E. 1984. Changing views of the Later Stone Age of South Africa. *Advances in World Archaeology* 3: 89-142.
Parkington, J. E. 1988. The Pleistocene/Holocene transition in the western Cape, South Africa: observations from Verlorenvlei. In: J. Bower & D. Lubell (eds) *Prehistoric Cultures and Environments in the Late Quaternary of Africa*, pp. 197-205. Oxford: British Archaeological Reports
Parkington, J. E. 1989. Interpreting paintings without a commentary. *Antiquity* 63: 13-26.
Parkington, J. E. 1990. A view from the south: southern Africa before, during and after the Last Glacial Maximum. In: C. Gamble & O. Soffer (eds) *The World at 18 000 BP Vol. 2 Low Latitudes*, pp. 214-230. London: Unwin Hyman.
Parkington, J. E. 1991. A critique of the consensus view on the age of Howieson's Poort assemblages in South Africa. In: P. A. Mellars (ed.) *The Origins of Modern Humans*, pp. 34-55. Edinburgh: Edinburgh University Press.
Parkington, J. E. 1992. Making sense of sequence at the Elands Bay Cave, western Cape, South Africa. In: A. B. Smith & B. Mütti (eds) *Guide to Archaeological Sites in the South-western Cape*, pp. 6-12. Cape Town: Southern African Association of Archaeologists.
Parkington, J. E. 1993. The neglected alternative: historical narrative rather than cultural labelling. *South African Archaeological Bulletin* 48: 94-97.
Parkington, J. E. & Hall, M. (eds) 1987. *Papers in the Prehistory of the Western Cape, South Africa.* Oxford: British Archaeological Reports.
Parkington, J. E., Nilssen, P., Reeler, C. & Henshilwood, C. 1992. Making sense of space at Dunefield Midden campsite, western Cape, South Africa. *Southern African Field Archaeology* 1: 63-70.
Parkington, J. E. & Poggenpoel, C. A. 1987. Diepkloof Rock Shelter. In: J. E. Parkington & M. Hall (eds) *Papers in the Prehistory of the Western Cape, South Africa*, pp. 269-293. Oxford: British Archaeological Reports.
Parkington, J. E., Poggenpoel, C., Buchanan, W., Robey, T., Manhire, A. H. & Sealy, J. C. 1986. Holocene coastal settlement patterns in the western Cape. In: G. N. Bailey & J. E. Parkington (eds) *The Archaeology of Prehistoric Coastlines*, pp. 22-41. Cambridge: Cambridge University Press.
Parkington, J. E., Yates, R. & Poggenpoel, C. 1987. *Lesotho Rescue Archaeology 1982.* Cape Town: University of Cape Town.
Partridge, T. & Brink, A. B. A. 1967. Gravels and terraces of the Lower Vaal River Basin. *South African Geographical Journal* 49: 21-38.
Peabody, F. E. 1954. Travertines and cave deposits of the Kaap Escarpment of South Africa and the type locality of *Australopithecus africanus* Dart. *Bulletin of the Geological Society of America* 65: 671-706.
Peers, B. 1927. Excavation report of 1927 on Peers Cave. Unpublished manuscript, University of Cape Town Library.
Peers, B. 1928. Ancient Fish Hoek and man his home. Unpublished manuscript, University of Cape Town Library.
Peers, B. 1929. Preliminary report on the archaeology of the Fish-hoek-Noord-hoek Valley. Unpublished paper presented at the meeting of the British Association for the Advancement of Science, 1929, South Africa.
Péringuey, L. 1899. Stone implements from Paarl and Stellenbosch. *Transactions of the South African Philosophical Society* 11. Min. Proc. p. iv.
Péringuey, L. 1905. The stone age in South Africa. *Report of the British Association for the Advancement of Science 1905*, pp. 527-528.
Péringuey, L. 1911. The stone ages of South Africa. *Annals of the South African Museum* 8: 1-218.
Péringuey, L. & Corstophine, G. S. 1900. Stone implements from Bosman's Crossing. *South African Philosophical Society* 11, Min. Proc. p. xxiv. (*Nature* 62: 336).
Phillipson, D. W. & Phillipson, L. 1970. Patterns of edge-damage on the Late Stone Age industry from Chiwemupula, Zambia. *Zambia Museums Journal* 1: 40-75.
Piers, H. W. 1871. On the geology of the Cape Peninsula. *Cape Monthly Magazine* 3: 171-173.
Piers, H. W. 1873. Stone implements. *Cape Monthly Magazine* 7: 191-192.
Pikirayi, I. 1993. *The Archaeological Identity of the Mutapa State: Towards an Historical Archaeology of Northern Zimbabwe.* Uppsala: Societas Archaeologica Upsaliensis.
Plug, I. 1978. *Die Latere Steentydperk van die Boesmanrotskuiling in Oos-Transvaal. (The Later Stone Age of the Bushman Rock Shelter in the Eastern Transvaal).* Unpublished MA Thesis, University of Pretoria.
Plug, I. 1981. Some research results on the Late Pleistocene and Early Holocene deposits of the Bushman Rock Shelter, eastern Transvaal. *South African Archaeological Bulletin* 36: 14-21.
Plug, I. 1982. Bone tools and shell, bone and ostrich eggshell beads from Bushman Rock Shelter (BRS), eastern Transvaal. *South African Archaeological Bulletin* 37: 57-62.
Plug, I. & Engela, R. 1992. The macrofaunal remains from recent excavations at Rose Cottage Cave, Orange Free State. *South African Archaeological Bulletin* 47: 16-25.
Potgieter, E. F. 1955. *The Disappearing Bushmen of Lake Chrissie.* Pretoria: Van Schaik
Price-Williams, D. 1980. Archaeology in Swaziland. *South African Archaeological Bulletin* 35: 13-18.
Price-Williams, D. 1981. A preliminary report on recent excavations of Middle and Late Stone Age levels at Sibebe Shelter, north-west Swaziland. *South African Archaeological Bulletin* 36: 22-28.
Price-Williams, D. & Watson, A. 1982. New observations on the prehistory and palaeoclimate of the Late Pleistocene in southern Africa. *World Archaeology* 13: 372-381.
Prins, F. E. 1990. Southern Bushman descendants in the Transkei - rock art and rain-making. *South African Journal of Ethnology* 13: 110-116.
Prins, F. E. & Grainger, J. 1993. Early farming communities in northern Transkei: the evidence from Ntsitsana and adjacent areas. *Natal Museum Journal of Humanities* 5: 153-174.
Prior, J. & Price-Williams, D. 1985. An investigation of climatic change in the Holocene epoch using archaeological charcoal from Swaziland, southern Africa. *Journal of Archaeological Science* 12: 457-475.
Pwiti, G. 1996. Settlement and subsistence of prehistoric farming communities in the mid-Zambezi valley, northern Zimbabwe. *South African Archaeological Bulletin* 51: 3-6.
Rautenbach, G. B. 1967. A Late Stone Age shelter in the Clarens

District, Orange Free State. *South African Archaeological Bulletin* 21: 183-186.

Reader's Digest 1994a. *Reader's Digest Illustrated Atlas of Southern Africa*. Cape Town: The Reader's Digest Association South Africa.

Reader's Digest 1994b. *Reader's Digest Illustrated Guide to Southern Africa*. Cape Town: The Reader's Digest Association South Africa.

Rees, W. (ed.). 1958. *Colenso Letters from Natal*. Pietermaritzburg: Shuter and Shooter.

Reid, A., Lane, P., Segobye, A., Borjeson, L., Mathibidi, N. & Sekgarametso, P. 1997. Tswana architecture and responses to colonialism. *World Archaeology* 28: 370-392.

Rickard, J. C. 1881a. Notes on four series of palaeolithic implements from south Africa. *Cambridgeshire Antiquarian Society* 5: 57-66.

Rickard, J. C. 1881b. Notes on some Neolithic implements from South Africa. *Cambridgeshire Antiquarian Society* 5: 67-74.

Rightmire, G. P. 1979. Implications of the Border Cave skeletal remains for later Pleistocene human evolution. *Current Anthropology* 20: 23- 35.

Robbins, L. H. & Campbell, A. C. 1989. The Depression rock shelter, Tsodilo Hills. *Botswana Notes and Records* 20: 1-3.

Robbins, L. H. & Murphy, M. L. 1994. The Early Stone Age in the Kalahari. Unpublished paper delivered at the Society of Africanist Archaeologists, Bloomington, April.

Robbins, L. H., Murphy, M. L., Stevens, N. J., Brook, G. A., Ivester, A. H., Haberyan, K. A., Klein, R. G., Milo, R., Stewart, K. M., Matthiesen, D. G. & Winkler, A. J. 1996. Paleoenvironment and archaeology of Drotsky's Cave: western Kalahari Desert, Botswana. *Journal of Archaeological Science* 23: 7-22.

Robbins, L. H., Murphy, M. L., Stewart, K. M., Campbell, A. C. & Brook, G. A. 1994. Barbed bone points, paleoenvironment and antiquity of fish exploitation in the Kalahari Desert, Botswana. *Journal of Field Archaeology* 21: 257-264.

Robinson, K. R. 1958. Some Stone Age sites in Inyanga District. In: R. Summers (ed.) *Inyanga: Prehistoric Settlements in Southern Rhodesia*, pp. 270-309. Cambridge: Cambridge University Press.

Robertshaw, P. 1979. *Coastal Settlement, Freshwater Fishing and Pastoralism in the Later Prehistory of the Western Cape, South Africa*. Unpublished PhD Thesis, University of Cambridge.

Robertshaw, P. 1984. Excavations at Fairview Rock Shelter - a contribution to the prehistory of the Eastern Cape Province, South Africa. *Annals of the Cape Provincial Museums* 1: 55-92.

Rubidge, B. S. & Brink, J. S. 1985. Preliminary survey of the extent and nature of the Pleistocene sedimentary deposits at Florisbad. *Navorsinge van die Nasionale Museum, Bloemfontein* 5: 69-76.

Rudner, I. 1965. Archaeological report on the Tsodilo Hills, Bechuanaland. *South African Archaeological Bulletin* 20: 51-70.

Rudner, J. 1957. The Brandberg and its archaeological remains. *Journal of the South West African Scientific Society* 12: 7-44.

Rudner, J. 1976. An archaeological reconnaissance tour of Angola. *South African Archaeological Bulletin* 31: 99-111.

Rutherford, M. C. & Westfall, R. H. 1986. The biomes of southern Africa: an objective categorization. *Memoirs of the Botanical Survey of South Africa* 54: 1-98.

Sampson, C. G. 1970. The Smithfield Industrial Complex: further field results. *Memoirs of the National Museum, Bloemfontein* 5: 1-172.

Sampson, C. G. 1972. The Stone Age industries of the Orange River Scheme and South Africa. *Memoirs of the National Museum, Bloemfontein* 6: 1-288.

Sampson, C. G. 1974. *The Stone Age Archaeology of Southern Africa*. New York: Academic Press.

Sampson, C. G. 1984. A prehistoric pastoralist frontier in the Upper Zeekoe Valley, South Africa. In: M. Hall, G. Avery, D. M. Avery, M. L. Wilson & A. J. B. Humphreys (eds) *Frontiers: Southern African Archaeology Today*, pp. 96-110. Oxford: British Archaeological Reports.

Sampson, C. G. 1985. Atlas of Stone Age settlement in the central and upper Seacow Valley. *Memoirs van die Nasionale Museum, Bloemfontein* 20: 1-116.

Sampson, C. G. 1988. *Stylistic Boundaries among Mobile Hunter-Foragers*. Washington: Smithsonian Institution.

Sampson, C. G. 1994. Ostrich eggs and Bushman survival on the north-east frontier of the Cape Colony, South Africa. *Journal of Arid Environments* 26: 383-399.

Sampson, C. G. 1995. Acquisition of European livestock by the Seacow River Bushmen between AD 1770-1890. *Southern African Field Archaeology* 4: 30-36.

Sampson, C. G., Hart, T. J. G., Wallsmith, D. L. & Blagg, J. D. 1989. The ceramic sequence in the upper Seacow Valley: problems and implications. *South African Archaeological Bulletin* 44: 3-16.

Sampson, C. G. & Vogel, J. C. 1995. Radiocarbon chronology of Later Stone Age decorations in the upper Seacow River Valley. *Southern African Field Archaeology* 4: 84-94.

Sandelowsky, B. H. 1977. Mirabib - an archaeological study in the Namib. *Madoqua* 10: 221-283.

Sandelowsky, B. H., Van Rooyen, J. H. & Vogel, J. C. 1979. Early evidence for herders in the Namib. *South African Archaeological Bulletin* 34: 50-51.

Sanderson, J. 1878. Notes in connection with stone implements from Natal. *Journal of the Royal Anthropological Institute* 8: 15-21.

Scherz, E. R. & Scherz, A. 1974. *Afrikanische Felskunst: Malereien auf Felsen in Südwest-Afrika*. Köln: Dumont.

Schiffer, M. B. & Gumerman, G. J. 1977. *Conservation Archaeology: A Guide for Cultural Resource Management Studies*. New York: Academic Press.

Schoute-Vanneck, C. A. & Walsh, R. C. 1959. The shell middens of the Ingane river mouth, Natal South Coast. *South African Archaeological Bulletin* 14: 43-45.

Schoute-Vanneck, C. A. & Walsh, R. C. 1960. The Tongaat variant of the Wilton culture. *South African Archaeological Bulletin* 25: 29-35.

Schoute-Vanneck, C. A. & Walsh, R. C. 1961. The Umlaas variant of the Smithfield C culture. *South African Archaeological Bulletin* 16: 137- 143.

Schrire, C. 1962. Oakhurst: a re-examination and vindication. *South African Archaeological Bulletin* 17: 181-195.

Schrire, C. 1995. *Digging through Darkness: Chronicles of an Archaeologist*. London: University Press of Virginia.

Schrire, C. & Deacon, J. 1989. The indigenous artefacts from Oudepost 1, a colonial outpost of the VOC at Saldanha Bay, Cape. *South African Archaeological Bulletin* 44: 105-113.

Schweitzer, F. R. 1979. Excavations at Die Kelders, Cape Province, South Africa. *Annals of the South African Museum* 78: 101-233.

Schweitzer, F. R. & Wilson, M. L. 1982. Byneskranskop 1: a late Quaternary living site in the southern Cape Province, South Africa. *Annals of the South African Museum* 88: 1-203.

Sealy, J. C. & Van der Merwe, N. J. 1988. Social, spatial and chronological patterning in marine food use as determined by ^{13}C measurements of Holocene human skeletons from the southwestern Cape. *World Archaeology* 20: 87-102.

Sealy, J. C. and Yates, R. 1994. The chronology of the introduction of pastoralism to the Cape, South Africa. *Antiquity* 68: 58-67.

Seddon, D. 1967. Some Early Stone Age surface sites around Stellenbosch, S.W. Cape. *South African Archaeological Bulletin* 22: 57-59.

Shackley, M. L. 1985. *Palaeolithic Archaeology of the Central Namib Desert: A Preliminary Survey of Chronology, Typology and Site Location*. Cimbebasia Memoir 6.

Shillington, K. 1985. *The Colonisation of the Southern Tswana 1870-1900.* Johannesburg: Ravan Press.

Sinclair, P. J. J. 1989. Urban origins in eastern Africa: a regional cooperation project. *World Archaeological Bulletin* 3: 33-51.

Sinclair, P. J. J., Morais, J. M. F., Adamowicz, L. & Duarte, R. T. 1993. A perspective on archaeological research in Mozambique. In: T. Shaw, P. J. J. Sinclair, B. Andah & A, Okpoko (eds) *The Archaeology of Africa: Food, Metals and Towns*, pp. 409-431. London: Routledge.

Singer, R. and Wymer, J. 1982. *The Middle Stone Age at Klasies River Mouth in South Africa.* Chicago: University of Chicago Press.

Skotnes, P. (ed.) 1996. *Miscast: Negotiating the Presence of the Bushmen.* Cape Town: University of Cape Town Press.

Smith, A. B. 1992. Kasteelberg. In: A. B. Smith & B. Mütti (eds) *Guide to Archaeological Sites in the South-western Cape*, pp. 28-30. Cape Town: Southern African Association of Archaeologists.

Smith, A. B. (ed.) 1995. *Einiqualand: Studies of the Orange River Frontier.* Cape Town: University of Cape Town Press.

Smith, A. B. & Jacobson, L. 1995. Excavations at Geduld and the appearance of early domestic stock in Namibia. *South African Archaeological Bulletin* 50: 3-14.

Smith, A. B. & Ripp, M. R. 1978. An archaeological reconnaissance of the Doorn/Tanqua Karoo. *South African Archaeological Bulletin* 33: 118- 133.

Smith, A. B., Sadr, K., Gribble, J. & Yates, R. 1991. Excavations within the south-western Cape, South Africa, and the archaeological identity of prehistoric hunter-gatherers within the last 2000 years. *South African Archaeological Bulletin* 46: 71-91.

Smith, J. 1997. *Stable Isotope Analysis of Fauna and Soils from Sites in the Eastern Free State and Western Lesotho, Southern Africa: A Palaeoenvironmental Interpretation.* Unpublished MA Thesis, University of Cape Town.

Smith, R. A. 1919. Recent finds of the Stone Age in South Africa. *Man* 19: 100-106.

Smith, R. A. 1926. *Guide to the Antiquities of the Stone Age in the Department of British and Medieval Antiquities.* London, British Museum.

Smith, R. A. 1937. *The Sturge Collection: An Illustrated selection of Foreign Flints bequeathed in 1919 by William Allen Sturge.* London, British Mseum.

Smits, L. G. A. 1983. Rock paintings in Lesotho: site characteristics. *South African Archaeological Bulletin* 38: 62-76.

Smuts, J. C. 1932. Climate and man in Africa. *South African Journal of Science* 29: 98-131.

Solomon, A. 1995. *Rock Art Incorporated: An Archaeological and Interdisciplinary Study of Certain Human Figures in San Art.* Unpublished PhD Thesis, University of Cape Town.

Soper, R. 1994. Ancient fields and agricultural systems: new work on the Nyanga Terrace complex. *Nyame Akuma* 42: 18-20.

Stapleton, P. & Hewitt, J. 1927. Stone implements from a rock shelter at Howieson's Poort near Grahamstown. *South African Journal of Science* 24: 574-87.

Stein, H. B. 1933. Stone implements from the Cathkin Peak area. *Bantu Studies* 7: 161-182.

Stow, G. W. 1872. Vaal River diamond gravels. *Quarterly Journal of the Geological Society* 28: 3-21.

Stow, G. W. 1905. *Native Peoples of South Africa.* London: Sonneschein.

Stow, G. W. & Bleek, D. F. 1930. *Rock Paintings in South Africa.* London: Methuen.

Stow, G. W. & Jones, R. 1874. Notes upon the geology of Griqualand West. *Quarterly Journal of the Geological Society* 30: 581.

Stringer, C. B. & Gamble, C. S. 1993. *In Search of the Neanderthals.* London: Thames & Hudson.

Taylor, M. O. V. 1988. Cave of Hearths. In: T. M. Evers, T. N. Huffman & L. Wadley (eds), *Guide to Archaeological Sites in the Transvaal*, pp. 96-107. Johannesburg: Southern African Association of Archaeologists.

Thackeray, A. I. 1989. Changing fashions in the Middle Stone Age: the stone artefact sequence from Klasies River, South Africa. *African Archaeological Review* 7: 35-59.

Thackeray, A. I. 1991. The Middle Stone Age south of the Limpopo River. *Journal of World Prehistory* 6: 385-440.

Thackeray, A. I., Thackeray, J. F., Beaumont, P. B. & Vogel, J. C. 1981. Dated rock engravings from Wonderwerk Cave, South Africa. *Science* 214: 64-67.

Thackeray, A. I., Thackeray, J. F. & Beaumont, P. B. 1983. Excavations at the Blinklipkop specularite mine near Postmasburg, northern Cape. *South African Archaeological Bulletin* 38: 17-25.

Thorp, C. R. 1996. A preliminary report on evidence of interaction between hunter-gatherers and farmers along a hypothesised frontier in the eastern Free State. *South African Archaeological Bulletin* 51: 57-63.

Tobias, P. V. 1967. Foreword. In: A. J. Clement (ed.) *The Kalahari and its Lost City*. Johannesburg: Longmans.

Trevor, T. G. 1930. Some observations on the relics of pre-European culture in Rhodesia and South Africa. *Journal of the Royal Anthropological Institute* 60: 389-400.

Trigger, B. 1984. Alternative archaeologies: nationalist, colonialist, imperialist. *Man* 19: 355-370.

Trigger, B. 1989. *A History of Archaeological Thought.* Cambridge: Cambridge University Press.

Van Alphen, J. G. 1930. On South African stone implements. *Die Huisgenoot,* 28.3.1930, 13.12.1930.

Van Andel, T. J. 1989. Late Quaternary sea-level changes and archaeology. *Antiquity* 63: 733-745.

Van Hoepen, E. C. N. 1926. Die indeling en relatiewe ouderdom van Suid-Afrikaanse klipwerktuie. (The sub-division and relative age of South African stone tools). *South African Journal of Science* 23: 793-809.

Van Hoepen, E. C. N. 1928. Die Kononigse kultuur. I: Die Koningse industrie. (The Koning culture. I: The Koning industry). *Argeologiese Navorsinge van die Nasionale Museum, Bloemfontein* 1 (1): 1-11.

Van Hoepen, E. C. N. 1932. Die Koningse kultuur. II: Die verspreiding van die Koningse industrie. (The Koning culture. II: The distribution of the Koning industry). *Argeologiese Navorsinge van die Nasionale Museum, Bloemfontein* 1 (2): 13-15.

Van der Ryst, M. M. 1996. *The Later Stone Age Prehistory of the Waterberg, with Special Reference to Goergap Shelter.* Unpublished MA Thesis, University of the Witwatersrand.

Van Riet Lowe, C. 1929. The Smithfield Industry of the Orange Free State. *Annals of the South African Museum* 27: 151-234.

Van Riet Lowe, C. 1930. Fresh light on the prehistoric archaeology of South Africa. *Bantu Studies* 3: 385-394.

Van Riet Lowe, C. 1931. Early graves from the Riet River valley. *South African Journal of Science* 28: 430-434.

Van Riet Lowe, C. 1935. Scientific results of the Vernay-Lang Kalahari Expedition, March to September 1930: remains of the Stone Age. *Annals of the Transvaal Museum* 16: 495-496.

Van Riet Lowe, C. 1937. The archaeology of the Vaal River Basin. *Memoirs of the Geological Survey of South Africa* 35: 61-184.

Van Riet Lowe, C. 1936. The Smithfield N culture. *Transactions of the Royal Society of South Africa* 23: 367-372.

Van Riet Lowe, C. 1938. A projected regional survey of the prehistory of South Africa. *Bureau of Archaeology Series* 2: 3-18.

Van Riet Lowe, C. 1944. A contribution to the prehistory of Moçambique. *Moçambique Documentário Trimestral* 36: 1-5.

Van Riet Lowe, C. 1952a. The distribution of prehistoric rock engravings and paintings in South Africa. *Archaeological*

Series VII. Pretoria: Department of Education, Arts and Science.

Van Riet Lowe, C. 1952b. The Vaal River chronology: an up-to-date summary. *South African Archaeological Bulletin* 7: 135-149.

Van Riet Lowe, C. 1954. The Cave of Hearths. *South African Archaeological Bulletin* 33: 25-29.

Van Riet Lowe, C. 1956. The geology and archaeology of the Little Caledon River Valley: Part II. *Archaeological Memoir of the Geological Survey of South Africa* 47: 1-48.

Van Warmelo, N. J. 1940. The copper miners of Messina. *South African Department of Native Affairs Ethnology Publication* 8.

Viereck, A. 1967. The Damaraland Culture. *Journal of the South West African Scientific Society* 21: 13-31.

Vinnicombe, P. 1976. *People of the Eland.* Pietermaritzburg: University of Natal Press.

Voigt, E. A. 1983. *Mapungubwe: An Archaeozoological Interpretation of an Iron Age Community.* Pretoria: Transvaal Museum.

Volman, T. P. 1981. *The Middle Stone Age of the Southern Cape.* Unpublished PhD Thesis, University of Chicago.

Volman, T. P. 1984. Early prehistory of southern Africa. In: R. G. Klein (ed.) *Southern African Prehistory and Palaeoenvironments*, pp. 169-220. Rotterdam: A. Balkema.

Wadley, L. 1979. Big Elephant Shelter and its role in the Holocene prehistory of central South West Africa. *Cimbebasia (B)* 3: 1-76.

Wadley, L. 1986. Segments of time: a mid-Holocene Wilton site in the Transvaal. *South African Archaeological Bulletin* 41: 54-62.

Wadley, L. 1987. *Later Stone Age Hunters and Gatherers of the Southern Transvaal: Social and Ecological Interpretations.* Oxford: British Archaeological Reports.

Wadley, L. 1988. Stone Age sites in the Magaliesberg. In: T. M. Evers, T. N. Huffman & L. Wadley (eds), *Guide to Archaeological Sites in the Transvaal*, pp. 9-39. Johannesburg: Southern African Association of Archaeologists.

Wadley, L. 1989. Review article: gender relations in the Thukela Basin. *South African Archaeological Bulletin* 44: 122-126.

Wadley, L. 1991. Rose Cottage Cave: background and preliminary report on the recent excavations. *South African Archaeological Bulletin* 46: 125-130.

Wadley, L. 1992. Rose Cottage Cave: the Later Stone Age levels with European and Iron Age artefacts. *South African Archaeological Bulletin* 44: 8-12.

Wadley, L. 1993. The Pleistocene Later Stone Age south of the Limpopo River.*Journal of World Prehistory* 7: 243-296.

Wadley, L. 1996. Review of dated Stone Age sites recently excavated in the eastern Free State, South Africa. *South African Journal of Science* 91: 574-579.

Wadley, L. 1997. Rose Cottage Cave: archaeological work 1987 to 1997. South *African Journal of Science* 93: 439-444.

Wadley, L. & Binneman, J. N. F. 1994. Arrowheads or pen knives ? A microwear analysis of mid-Holocene stone segments from Jubilee Shelter, Transvaal. *South African Journal of Science* 91: 153-155.

Wadley, L. & Harper, P. 1989. Rose Cottage Cave revisited: Malan's Middle Stone Age collection. *South African Archaeological Bulletin* 44: 23-32.

Wadley, L. & Turner, A. 1988. Hope Hill Shelter: A Later Stone Age site in the southern Transvaal. *South African Journal of Science* 83: 98- 105.

Walker, N. J. 1980. Later Stone Age research in the Matopos. *South African Archaeological Bulletin* 35: 113-120.

Walker, N. J. 1983. The significance of an early date for pottery and sheep in Zimbabwe. *South African Archaeological Bulletin* 38: 88-92.

Walker, N. J. 1987. The dating of Zimbabwean rock art. *Australian Rock Art Research* 4: 137-149.

Walker, N. J. 1990. Zimbabwe at 18 000 BP. In: C. Gamble & O. Soffer (eds) *The World at 18 000 BP, Vol. 2 Low Latitudes*, pp. 206-213. London: Unwin Hyman.

Walker, N. J. 1995. *Late Pleistocene and Holocene Hunter-Gatherers of the Matopos: An Archaeological Study of Change and Continuity in Zimbabwe.* Uppsala: Societas Archaeologica Upsaliensis.

Walker, N. J. in press a. The Late Stone Age of Botswana. *Botswana Notes and Records.*

Walker, N. J. in press b. *The Painted Hills: Rock Art of the Matopos.* Gweru: Mambo Press.

Walker, N. J. & Wadley, L. 1984. Evidence for an early microlithic industry at Duncombe Farm in Mashonaland, Zimbabwe. *Cookeia* 1: 4-13.

Wallsmith. D. L. 1990. Driekoppen: a Middle Stone Age rockshelter. *Nyame Akuma* 33: 13-16.

Ward, V. 1998. Can you help ? Archaeological sites in Alfred County, KwaZulu-Natal. *The Digging Stick* 15(3): 11-12.

Wayland, E. J. 1915. Notes on the occurrence of stone implements in the province of Mozambique. *Man* 5: 97-101.

Wayland, E. J. 1954. Outlines of prehistory and Stone Age climatology in the Bechuanaland Protectorate. *Mémoires de l'Académie Royale des Sciences Coloniales* 25: 1-46.

Wayland, E. J. & Van Riet Lowe, C. 1952. The Pleistocene geology and prehistory of Uganda. *Geological Memoir of the Geological Survey of Uganda* 6: 1-113.

Webley, L. 1984. *Archaeology and Ethnoarchaeology in the Leliefontein Reserve and Surrounds.* Unpublished MA Thesis, University of Stellenbosch.

Webley, L. 1990. The use of stone 'scrapers' by semi-sedentary pastoralists in Namaqualand, South Africa. *South African Archaeological Bulletin* 45: 28-32.

Webley, L. 1992. *The History and Archaeology of Pastoralist and Hunter-Gatherer Settlement in the North-Western Cape.* Unpublished PhD Thesis, University of Cape Town.

Webley, L. 1993. Archaeological investigations at the battlefield of Rorke's Drift, northern Natal. *Southern African Field Archaeology* 2: 24-34.

Wellington, J. H. 1955. *Southern Africa: A Geographical Study. Volume 1 Physical Geography.* Cambridge: Cambridge University Press.

Wells, L. H. 1933. The archaeology of Cathkin Peak: introductory. *Bantu Studies* 7: 113-129.

Wendt, W. E. 1972. Preliminary report on an archaeological research programme in South West Africa. *Cimbebasia (B)* 2: 1-61.

Wendt, W. E. 1976. 'Art mobilier' from the Apollo 11 Cave, South-West Africa: Africa's oldest dated works of art. *South African Archaeological Bulletin* 31: 5-11.

White, F. 1900. On the Khami Ruins near Bulawayo. *Proceedings of the Rhodesian Scientific Association* 1: 14.

White, F. 1905. Notes on rock paintings and stone implements near World's View, Matopos. *Proceedings of the Rhodesian Scientific Association* 5: 7-10.

White, F. 1909. Notes on Rhodesian stone implements. *Proceedings of the Rhodesian Scientific Association* 9: 8-14.

Whitley, D. & Annegarn, H. J. 1994. Cation-ratio dating of rock engravings from Klipfontein, Northern Cape. In: T. A. Dowson & J. D. Lewis-Williams (eds), *Contested Images: Diversity in Southern African Rock Art Research*, pp. 189-197. Johannesburg: Witwatersrand University Press.

Whitten, D. G. A. & Brooks, J. R. V. 1972. *The Penguin Dictionary of Geology*. Harmondsworth: Penguin

Wigram, W. A. 1913. *Register of the Wigram Family 1743-1913.* Privately published.

Wilman, M. 1911. Notes on some Bushman paintings in the Thaba Bosigo District, Basutoland. *South African Journal of Science* 7: 417-421.

Wilman, M. 1933. *Rock-engravings of Griqualand West and Bechuanaland, South Africa.* Cambridge: Cambridge

University Press.
Woodhouse, B. 1996. *The Rock Art of the Golden Gate and Clarens Districts.* Rivonia: William Waterman Publications.
Yates, R., Manhire, A. & Parkington, J. E. 1994. Rock painting and history in the south-western Cape. In: Dowson, T. A. & Lewis-Williams, J. D. (eds) *Contested Images: Diversity in Southern African Rock Art Research*, pp. 29-60. Johannesburg: Witwatersrand University Press.
Yellen, J. E. 1971. Archaeological excavations in western Ngamiland. *Botswana Notes and Records* 3: 276.
Yellen, J. E., Brooks, A. S, Stuckenrath, R. & Welbourne, R. 1987. A terminal Pleistocene assemblage from Drotsky's Cave, western Ngamiland, Botswana. *Botswana Notes and Records* 19: 1-6.